Western North America

"Planning a trip with *50 Great Family Vacations* is like consulting with a knowledgeable, trustworthy friend. Whether she's recommending the best hotels, nature excursions, or restaurants; warning about possible disappointments; or listing an area's highlights—from festivals to all-night pharmacies—Stapen provides a reassuring and enthusiastic voice for families on the go."

—Christine Loomis, *Family Life* magazine

"This book is a tour de force, a compendium in which a family can window-shop among 50 carefully chosen family outings. Directions to attractions, food, shelter, and information are meticulous, and always attuned to the needs of the whole family. This is the book to start with when a family shops for a perfect vacation."

—Robert Scott Milne, *Travelwriter Marketletter*

Also by Candyce H. Stapen

50 Great Family Vacations: Eastern North America

50 GREAT FAMILY VACATIONS

Western North America

Candyce H. Stapen

A Voyager Book

The Globe Pequot Press

Old Saybrook, Connecticut

Library of Congress Cataloging-in-Publication Data
Stapen, Candyce H.
    50 great family vacations. Western North America / Candyce H. Stapen.
— 1st ed.
        p.   cm.
    "A Voyager book."
    Includes index.
    ISBN 1-56440-383-1
    1. West (U.S.)—Guidebooks. 2. Canada, Western—Guidebooks.
3. Alaska—Guidebooks. 4. Hawaii—Guidebooks. 5. Family recreation—
West (U.S.)—Guidebooks. 6. Family recreation—Canada, Western—
Guidebooks. 7. Family recreation—Alaska—Guidebooks. 8. Family
recreation—Hawaii—Guidebooks. I. Title. II. Title: Fifty great family
vacations. Western North America.
F590.3.S73 1994   94-7265
917.804'33—dc20   CIP

Manufactured in the United States of America
First Edition/Third Printing

To my favorite traveling companions
Alissa, Matt, and David

CONTENTS

THE PACIFIC NORTHWEST AND CALIFORNIA

ALASKA

HAWAII

CANADA

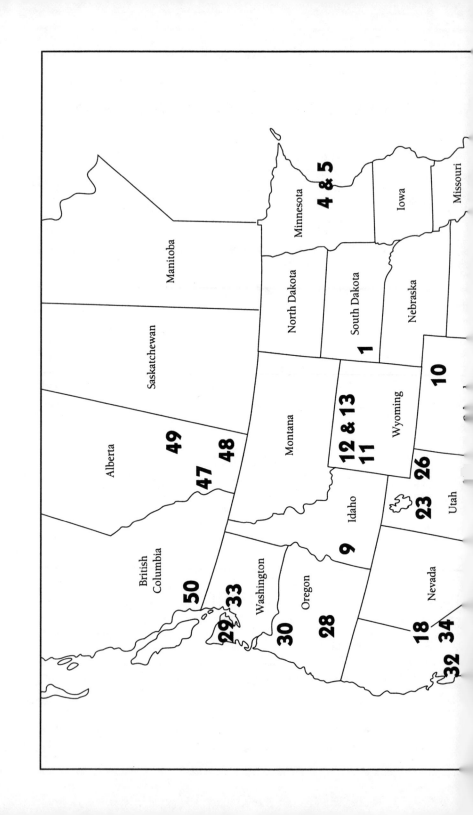

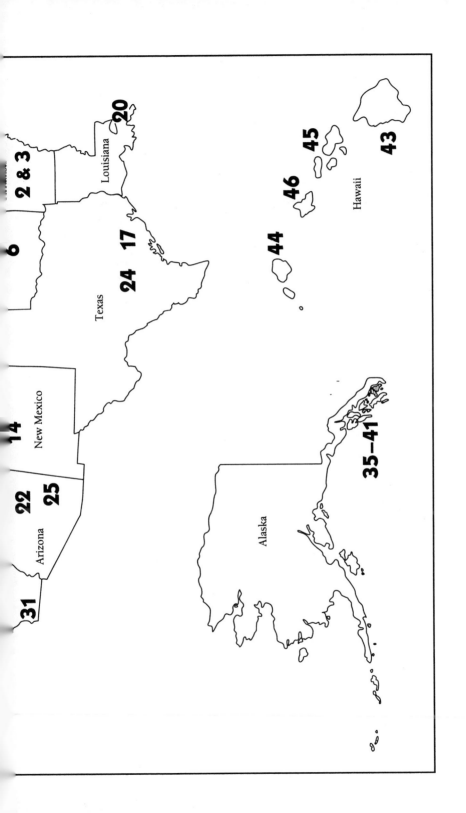

2 & 3

6

20

Louisiana

14

New Mexico

Texas

24 17

Arizona

22

25

31

Alaska

35–41

44

46

45

43

Hawaii

ACKNOWLEDGMENTS

I want to thank my editors, Mace Lewis and Mike Urban, for their patience and assistance, and my agent, Carol Mann, for her support. Special thanks goes to Carol Eannarino, whose fine writing contributed much to this book, and to Jayne Blanchard for her work on Minneapolis/St. Paul. I appreciate the help of my editorial assistants, Kerry Sheriden, Jennifer Consalvo, Francis Cratil, Karen Gould, and Linn Edwards.

As a family travel writer I want to acknowledge Dorothy Jordon, of Travel With Your Children, New York City, for her pioneering leadership in the field.

INTRODUCTION

There is a Chinese proverb that says the wise parent gives a child roots and wings. By traveling with your children you can bestow many gifts upon them: a strong sense of family bonds, memories that last a lifetime, and a joyful vision of the world.

Traveling with your children offers many bonuses for you and your family. These days no parent or child has an excessive amount of free time. Whether you work in the home or outside of it, your days are filled with meetings, deadlines, household errands, and carpool commitments. Your child most likely keeps equally busy with scouts, soccer, music lessons, computer clinics, basketball, and/or ballet. When your family stays home, your time together is likely to be limited to sharing quick dinners and overseeing homework. If there's a teen in your house, an age known for endless hours spent with friends, your encounters often shrink to swapping phone messages and car keys.

But take your child on the road with you, and both of you have plenty of time to talk and be together. Traveling together gives your family the luxury of becoming as expansive as the scenery. Over donuts in an airport lounge or dinner in a new hotel, you suddenly hear about that special science project or how it really felt to come in third in the swim meet. By sharing a drive along a country road or a visit to a city museum, your children get the space to view you as a person and not just as a parent.

Additionally, both you and your kids get new perspectives on life. Children who spend time in a different locale, whether it's a national forest or a city new to them, expand their awareness. For you as a parent, traveling with your kids brings the added bonus of enabling you to see again with a child's eye. When you show a six-year-old a reconstructed Polynesian village or share the stars in a Colorado mountain night sky with a thirteen-year-old, you feel the world twinkle with as much possibility as when you first encountered these sites long ago.

Part of this excitement is a result of the exuberance kids bring, and part is from the instant friendships kids establish. Street vendors save their best deals for pre-schoolers, and, even on a crowded rush hour bus, a child by your side turns a fellow commuter from a stranger into a friend. Before your stop comes, you'll often be advised of the best toy shop in town and directed to a local cafe with a kid-pleasing menu at prices guaranteed to put a smile on your face.

New perspectives also come from the activities you participate in with your children. Most of these activities you would probably pass up when shuttling solo. Whether it's finding all the dogs in the paintings at the Metropolitan Museum of Art, going for a sleigh ride at a ski resort, or trying cross-country skiing in a park, you always learn more when you take your kids.

Surprisingly, traveling with your kids can also be cost-effective and practical. By combining or by extending a work-related trip into a vacation, you save money since your company picks up a good part of your expenses. Because tag-along-tots on business trips are an increasing trend, several hotel chains have responded with a range of family-friendly amenities including children's programs, child-safe rooms, and milk and cookies at bedtime.

For all these reasons, traveling with your children presents many wonderful opportunities. It is a great adventure to be a parent, and it is made more wondrous when you travel with your children. You will not only take pleasure in each other's company, but you will return home with memories to savor for a lifetime.

FAMILY TRAVEL TIPS

Great family vacations require careful planning and the cooperation of all family members. Before you go you need to think about such essentials as how to keep sibling fights to a minimum and how to be prepared for medical emergencies. While en route you want to be sure to make road trips and plane rides fun, even with a toddler. You want to be certain that the room that is awaiting your family is safe and that your family makes the most of being together. When visiting relatives, you want to eliminate friction by following the house rules. These tips, gathered from a host of families, go a long way toward making your trips good ones.

General Rules

1. Meet the needs of the youngest family member. Your raft trip won't be fun if you're constantly worried about your three-year-old being bumped overboard by the whitewater the tour operator failed to mention or if your first-grader gets bored with the day's itinerary of art museums.
2. Underplan. Your city adventure will dissolve in tears—yours and your toddler's—if you've scheduled too many sites and not enough time for the serendipitous. If your child delights in playing with the robots at the science museum, linger there and skip the afternoon's proposed visit to the history center.
3. Go for the green spaces. Seek out an area's parks. Pack a picnic lunch and take time to throw a frisbee, play catch, or simply enjoy relaxing in the sun and people watching.
4. Enlist the cooperation of your kids by including them in the decision making. While family vacation voting is not quite a democracy, con-

sider your kids' needs. Is there a way to combine your teens' desire to be near "the action" with your spouse's request for seclusion? Perhaps book a self-contained resort on a quiet beach that also features a nightspot.

5. Understand your rhythms of the road. Some families like traveling at night so that the kids sleep in the car or on the plane. Others avoid traveling during the evening cranky hours and prefer to leave early in the morning.

6. Plan to spend time alone with each of your children as well as with your spouse. Take a walk, write in a journal together, play ball, share ice-cream in the snack shop, etc. Even the simplest of things done together create valuable family memories.

Don't Leave Home Without

1. *Emergency medical kit.* The first thing we always pack is the emergency medical kit, a bag I keep ready to go with all those things that suddenly become important at 3:00 A.M. This is no hour to be searching the streets for baby aspirin or Band-Aids. Make sure your kit includes items suitable for adults as well as children. Be sure to bring:
   - aspirin or an aspirin substitute
   - a thermometer
   - cough syrup
   - a decongestant
   - medication to relieve diarrhea
   - bandages and Band-Aids
   - gauze pads
   - antibiotic ointment
   - a motion-sickness remedy
   - sunscreen
   - insect repellant
   - ointments or spray to soothe sunburn, rashes, and poison ivy
   - something to soothe insect stings
   - any medications needed on a regular basis
   - tweezers and a sterile needle to remove splinters

   Keep this kit with you in your carry-on luggage or on the front seat of your car.

2. *Snack food.* As soon as we land somewhere or pull up to a museum for a visit, my eleven-year-old daughter wants food. Instead of arguing or wasting time and money on snacks, I carry granola bars with me. She munches on these reasonably nutritious snacks while we continue on schedule.

3. *Inflatable pillow and travel products.* Whether on the road or in a plane, these inflatable wonders help me and the kids sleep. For travel

pillows plus an excellent variety of light yet durable travel products including hair dryers, luggage straps, alarms, adaptor plugs for electrical outlets, and clothing organizers, call Magellan's (800–962–4943). TravelSmith (800–950–1600) carries these items as well as clothing, mostly for teens and adults.

4. *Travel toys.* Kids don't have to be bored en route to your destination. Pack books, coloring games, and quiet toys. Some kids love story tapes on their personal cassette players. For innovative, custom-tailored travel kits full of magic pencil games, puzzles, and crafts for children three and a half or older, call Sealed With A Kiss (800–888–SWAK). The packages cost about $30. Surprise your kids with this once you are on the road. They'll be happy and so will you.

5. *Travel Tapes.* Buy your kids their own portable cassette player with headphones. That way they can hear all their favorite songs and stories over and over again and you don't have to. Several companies feature audio cassette tapes (and even CDs) of well-known children's stories and songs as well as sing-along tapes and even fun-to-do-together audio games like *Carmen Sandiego* sleuthing mysteries. Browse the collections of Rabbit Ears (800–676–2272), Discovery Music (800–451–5175), and Zoom Express (212–274–0200).

Flying with Tots

1. Book early for the seat you like. Whether you prefer the aisle, window, or bulkhead for extra legroom, reserve your seat well in advance of your departure date.

2. Call the airlines at least forty-eight hours ahead to order meals that you know your kids will eat: children's dinners, hamburger platters, salads, etc.

3. Bring food on board that you know your kids like even if you've ordered a special meal. If your kids won't eat what's served at meal time, at least they won't be hungry if they munch on nutritious snacks.

4. Be sure to explain each step of the plane ride to little kids so that they will understand that the airplane's noises and shaking do not mean that a crash is imminent.

5. Stuff your carry-on with everything you might need (including medications, extra kids' clothes, diapers, baby food, formula, and bottles) to get you through a long flight and a delay of several hours . . . just in case.

6. Bring a child safety seat (a car seat) on board. Although presently the law allows children under two to fly free if they sit on a parent's lap, the Federal Aviation Administration and the Air Transport Association support legislation that would require all kids to be in child

safety seats. In order to get a seat on board, the seat must have a visible label stating approval for air travel, and you must purchase a ticket for that seat. Without a ticket, you are not guaranteed a place to put this child safety seat in case the plane is full.

7. With a toddler or young child, wrap little surprises to give as "presents" throughout the flight. These work wonderfully well to keep a wee one's interest.

8. Before boarding, let your kids work off energy by walking around the airport lounge. Never let your child nap just before take-off—save the sleepy moments for the plane.

9 If you're traveling with a lot of luggage, check it curbside before parking your car. This eliminates the awkward trip from long-term parking loaded down with kids, luggage, car seats, and strollers.

Road Rules

1. Use this time together to talk with your children. Tell them anecdotes about your childhood or create stories for the road together.

2. Put toys for each child in his or her own mesh bag. This way the toys are easily located and visible instead of being strewn all over the car.

3. Avoid long rides. Break the trip up by stopping every two or three hours for a snack or to find a restroom. This lets kids stretch their legs.

4. When driving for several days, plan to arrive at your destination each day by 4:00 or 5:00 P.M., so that the kids can enjoy a swim at the hotel/motel. This turns long hauls into easily realized goals that are fun.

At the Destination

1. When traveling with young children, do a safety check of the hotel room and the premises as soon as you arrive. Put matches, glasses, ashtrays, and small items out of reach. Note if stair and balcony railings are widely spaced or easily climbed by eager tots. Find out where the possible dangers are, and always keep track of your kids.

2. Schedule sightseeing for the morning, but plan to be back at the resort or hotel by early afternoon so that your child can enjoy the pool, the beach, miniature golf, or other kid-friendly facilities.

3. Plan to spend some time alone with each of your children every day. With pre-teens and teens, keep active by playing tennis or basketball, jogging, or doing something else to burn energy.

4. Establish an amount of money that your child can spend on souvenirs. Stick to this limit, but let your child decide what he or she wants to buy.

With Relatives

1. Find out the rules of your relatives' house before you arrive, and inform your kids of them. Let them know, for example, that food is allowed only in the kitchen or dining room so that they won't bring sandwiches into the guest bedroom or den.
2. Tell your relatives about your kids' eating preferences. Let the person doing the cooking know that fried chicken is fine, but that your kids won't touch liver even if it is prepared with the famous family recipe.
3. To lessen the extra work and expense for relatives and to help eliminate friction, bring along or offer to shop and pay for those special items that only your kids eat—a favorite brand of cereal, juice, frozen pizza, or microwave kids' meal.
4. Discuss meal hours. If you know, for example, that grandma and grandpa always dine at 7:00 P.M. but that your pre-schooler and first-grader can't wait that long, feed your kids earlier at their usual time, and enjoy an adult dinner with your relatives later.
5. Find something suitable for each generation that your kids and relatives will enjoy doing together. Look over old family albums, have teens tape record oral family histories, and have grade-schoolers take instant snapshots of the clan.
6. Find some way that your kids can help with the work of visiting. Even a nursery-school age child feels good about helping to clear a table or sweep the kitchen floor.

Tips for Choosing a Family Resort

1. Make sure the resort has suitable activities and facilities for the youngest member of your family.
2. Are there programs, sports, activities, or events that each family member, including teens, parents, and grandparents, can enjoy?
3. Be certain that the activities you want will be operating for the dates you've reserved. Not all programs run all the time.
4. Consider the resort's layout and safety. Must you drag a stroller up two flights of stairs to reach your room-with-a-view? If the balcony railings are easily scaled by your pre-schooler, request a ground floor patio room. Are there safe areas far from cars and crowds for playing ball or frisbee or bicycling? Are the recreational centers near enough so that an older child feels confident walking by himself?
5. Can you easily obtain the kinds of food your kids like? Does the dining room open early? Does the snack shop offer healthy food?
6. Find out if the hotel is on a beach, a quiet street, or a main thoroughfare. Does the resort have a baby pool, kids' programs, room service, and inexpensive restaurants? Know what type of room your package or rate quoted guarantees you—deluxe, standard, ocean or mountain view.

How to Assess a Kids' Program

1. Kids' groups should be divided into appropriate age groupings. When a five-year-old and a ten-year-old are in the same group, neither one has a good time.
2. Groups should not be too large. For preschoolers the ratio of care givers to kids should be about 1:4; for young school-age children that ratio can jump to 1:7. Preteens and teens may need fewer counselors, but they need good ones.
3. The program's supervisors should have experience in childhood recreation or education.
4. Most, if not all, staff should be trained in CPR (cardiopulmonary resuscitation), lifesaving, and emergency medical procedures.
5. Check the hours. A program that runs for just two hours in the morning doesn't give you enough time to play a round of golf. Some programs are so comprehensive that if your children signed up for all available hours, you'd never see them. Stay flexible. Register your children for activities they find appealing, but also block out time for your own parent/child adventures. Feel free, once you've informed the directors, to take your child in and out of the program.
6. Look for a designated children's center. This not only indicates the resort's commitment to the program but also serves as a gathering place. Hours and locations of activities should be posted, making it easy for you to pick up your child early or join the group later.
7. The children's center should be safe, attractive, well-lit, and easily accessible to the outdoors. Kids should be allowed to enjoy outdoor activities, not just indoor crafts and movies.
8. Good programs keep track of children. Parents should be asked to fill out a form stating who is allowed to pick up your child and whether an older child may leave unattended. Forms should also ask about allergies, food restrictions, room numbers, other important information (Matt won't nap without his stuffed teddy), and where parents are likely to be in case of emergencies.
9. Find out about swimming. Some programs take children in the water and others do not. If the program includes swimming or water play, be sure to tell the counselors about your child's ability. Ask whether a lifeguard is on duty and whether counselors know CPR. Then, no matter how many assurances you receive, find out the time of your child's group swims and observe to be certain that the level of supervision is adequate.
10. Programs that include sports are wonderful. Find out if the resort has an adequate supply of child-sized rental equipment or if you must bring your own gear. Ask if equipment rental costs are included in the fee.

Money-Saving Vacation Strategies

1. Consider renting a condominium. Condos give you more space for the money as well as the convenience and savings of dining in, especially for breakfast and snacks.
2. Play the seasons. During shoulder and low seasons, rates drop from 10 percent to 40 percent. At those times, a fantasy resort may be within your budget.
3. Book the right place for your daily needs. On days when you know that you will be arriving late and leaving early or out touring from dawn to dusk, book economical accommodations. On days when you plan to be around to enjoy the resort's elaborate pool, the plush rooms, and the great tennis, then book the expensive resort.
4. Investigate packages. A good travel agent should be able to recommend a reputable company that can offer airfare, lodging, and rental cars at significant savings over what you'd pay if you booked these yourself. A travel agent's services are free.
5. Be aware of cancellation policies and penalty fees. For big-ticket items that must be prepaid, such as package tours, consider buying trip cancellation insurance. This generally covers cancellations for medical emergencies but not for a whimsical change. Pin down details about any money-back guarantees.

Family Travel Planners

These specialists can help you assess your family's needs and find the vacation that's best for you.

- **Family Travel Times.** This monthly newsletter (ten issues per year) offers the latest information on hotels, resorts, city attractions, cruises, airlines, tours, and destinations. $55 for ten issues from Travel With Your Children, 45 West Eighteenth Street, Seventh-floor Tower, New York, NY 10011. For information call (212) 206–0688.
- **Rascals in Paradise.** Specializing in family and small-group tours to the Caribbean, Mexico, and the South Pacific, Rascals' tours usually include nannies for each family and an escort to organize activities for the kids. Call (800) U–RASCAL for more information.
- **Grandtravel.** This company offers a variety of trips for grandparents and grandchildren 7 through 17. Domestic trips include visits to New York, New England, and the Grand Canyon. Foreign destinations include safaris to Kenya. Call (800) 247–7651 for more information.
- **Grandvistas.** Grandparents can take their grandkids on a variety of trips including tours of Mount Rushmore, Custer State Park, and Yellowstone National Park. Call (800) 647–0800 for more information.
- **Families Welcome!** This agency offers travel packages for families in London, Paris, and New York. Soon the company will expand their

services to include Venice, Rome, and Florence. With their packages, you can choose to stay at a hotel or an apartment. Their "Welcome Kit" includes tips on sightseeing, restaurants, and museums. Call (800) 326–0724 for more information.

Cruising to Alaska and Hawaii: How to Save Money on the Seas

Cruising can be a memorable family vacation, and a good buy, but only if you choose the cruise ship that's right for you and for your family. Since several cruise lines offer passage to Alaska, don't just compare prices. Look for the services, itinerary, features, and programs—including children's programs—that meet your family's needs. American Hawaii Cruises offers the most Hawaiian islands. At times, other cruise lines make a stop or two in the islands. (See the chapters on Alaska and Hawaii for more advice.)

Remember to book your reservation as early as possible, up to a year in advance. Many cruise lines offer special advance booking rates and you may save up to several hundred dollars. You will also have your choice of cabins.

More Ways to Save Money

1. **Consider a less expensive line, and ship.** The flagships of the fleet cost more, but a voyage on the line's older sister ships can get you the same itinerary and service without the glitz, or the price tag, of a new luxury ship. Consider the amenities. Decide whether you want to pay for top-of-the-line luxuries—television in cabins, name entertainment, and gourmet meals. A dash less panache saves money.
2. **Check newspapers for regional specials.** Several lines cut cabin prices from specialized cities of departure.
3. **Find children's rates with airfare.** When kids fly and cruise for a week at one low price, parents gain a great bargain.
4. **Use single parent rates.** Find a line with a single parent rate that lets kids sail at the reduced children's rate instead of being bumped to the adult fare.
5. **Consider a repositioning cruise.** When available, these cruises take ships from summer to winter ports or vice versa. The savings can be as much as several hundred dollars less per person than traditional routes. But go only if you like sea days as these voyages usually come with few ports.

How to Pick a High-Volume Cruise Agency

Many large agencies offer savings for most ships, for most sailings, for most dates: The heavily demanded holiday sailings are usually the exceptions. A toll-free call connects you with an agent. But choosing an agency requires savvy. Look for an agency with membership in the National Association of Cruise Only Agencies (NACOA). These agents book only cruises, so these people know their ships. NACOA preview the ships, can describe their nuances, and often get the best discounts.

Determine if the agent listens to your needs, or if the agent just pushes you into his or her prebooked inventory. The agent should fit you to a cruise by discovering what vacations, ports, and places you like rather than trying to sell you on a company's package deal.

Find out with which cruise lines the agency does the most business. The agent may have better savings on these sailings.

Ask if the agent has been on board the ships he or she recommends.

Here is a list of high-volume cruise agencies.

- South Florida Cruises, Inc., 3561 Northwest Fifty-third Street, Ft. Lauderdale, Florida 33309; (800) 327–SHIP or (305) 739–SHIP.
- The Cruise Line, Inc., 4770 Biscayne Boulevard, Miami, Florida 33137; (800) 327–3021 or (800) 777–0707 in Florida.
- Personal Touch Cruise Consultants, 113 West Sunrise Highway, Freeport, New York 11520; (800) 477–4441 or (516) 378–8934.
- Cruise Holidays International, Inc., executive offices at 9089 Clairemont Mesa Boulevard, Suite 306, San Diego, California 92123. In the U.S., call (800) 477–5550.
- For more agencies, contact NACOA, P.O. Box 7209, Freeport, New York 11520; (516) 378–8006.

How to Find the Cruise That's Right for You

Don't book just by the numbers. You'll get your money's worth when you sail on the cruise that meets your needs, not just the one that comes in with the lowest fare. To find your dream cruise, consider these voyage realities.

Ports or Sea Days. Do you want to shop and explore five ports in seven days, or relax at sea for three days?

Intimate or Bustling Ships. Do you prefer the intimacy and educational focus of a small World Explorer Cruise, or do you want the bustle, children's programs, and activities of a 1,500-plus passenger ship.

Professional or Passenger Entertainment. Do you want name entertainment and elaborate evening shows, or does a sailing with lectures by experts on Alaskan wildlife seem more to your liking?

Day-long Kids' Activities or Intermittent Events. Do you children need a supervised activity program with day-long and evening events? These programs keep kids happy with pool and deck games, scavenger hunts, and movies.

Choose kids' programs carefully. Children's programs vary by cruise line, and within cruise lines by ships and sailings. Some programs operate on every sailing, and others operate only in summer and on Christmas and Easter. On some sailings, the cruise directors only offer sign-up volleyball, or horseshoes for kids at selected hours. These programs tend to appeal to older teens, but won't keep you elementary school kids supervised or busy while you snooze on deck. Make sure the program you want operates on your sailing, and for the ages of your kids.

Some programs continue in the evenings, thus keeping kids happy and allowing adults time in the cabarets and casinos. Some programs take kids on their very own shore tours to beaches and museums. Check to see if kids' programs operate in port. This allows you time to explore some port sites with your kids, but also to slip away for several hours of kid-free shopping, and kayaking.

For a complete guide to kids' programs, buy *Cruising With Children,* by Dorothy Jordon; it's available from Travel With Your Children, 45 West Eighteenth Street, Seventh-floor Tower, New York, New York 10011 (212–206–0688).

The prices and rates listed in this guidebook were confirmed at press time. We recommend, however, that you call establishments before traveling to obtain current information.

THE NORTHERN AND SOUTHERN PLAINS

1

THE BLACK HILLS, THE BADLANDS, AND MT. RUSHMORE
South Dakota

South Dakota's natural beauty and unusual geological features, plus its wild west history and Native American presence, combine to offer families, especially city dwellers, an interesting landscape for a family vacation.

The Sioux Nation, despite being driven from the Black Hills by U.S. troops in 1874 after the discovery of gold in the area, still maintain a sizable presence in South Dakota. More than 50,500 Native Americans, most of the Lakota, Dakota, and Nakota tribes of the Sioux Nation, live within the state's boundaries, both on and off reservations.

GETTING THERE

South Dakota has two major airports; the one in **Rapid City** provides better access to the Black Hills and Badlands areas. The other airport is in Sioux Falls. The **Rapid City Regional Airport** (605–394–4195), 9 miles southeast of town, is served by several carriers, including **Continental Express** (800–525–0280), **Delta** (800–221–1212), **Northwest** (800–225–2525), **United** and **United Express** (800–241–6522).

Among Rapid City's car rental companies are **Avis** (800–331–1212),

Hertz (800–654–3131), Budget (800–527–0700), National (800–227–7368), and Thrifty (800–367–2277).

Greyhound/Trailways routes run between Rapid City and Sioux Falls; (605) 336–0885. Amtrak does not provide any service to South Dakota. I–90 and I–29 are two of the major highways leading to Rapid City.

GETTING AROUND

With a lot of wide open spaces, South Dakota is best seen by car. For those who prefer not to drive, Gray Line of Rapid City (605–342–4461) offers tours of the Black Hills and the Badlands.

WHAT TO SEE AND DO

The Black Hills, approximately 50 miles wide and 120 miles long, have much to offer families, including four national park areas: Mount Rushmore National Memorial, Wind Cave National Park, Jewel Cave National Monument, and Devils Tower National Monument, which lies just west of South Dakota in Wyoming. East of the Black Hills lies another not-to-be-missed site, the Badlands National Park.

The Black Hills

The Black Hills National Forest, 10 miles west of Rapid City on U.S. 16, covers roughly 6,000 square miles. In 1874 when General George Custer led a military expedition through the Black Hills, the region was sacred Sioux land. The Sioux named the region *Paha Sapa,* or "Black Hills," a place to communicate with *Wakan Tanka,* the "Great Spirit." Despite this, much of the land was taken from the Sioux after gold was discovered here in 1874. Among the Black Hills highlights are the following.

The Mount Rushmore National Monument, P.O. Box 268, Keystone, South Dakota 57751 (605–574–2523), is about 25 miles southwest of Rapid City off U.S. 16A, and two miles southwest of Keystone. It's what first comes to mind when people think of South Dakota. The chiseled faces of George Washington, Thomas Jefferson, Abraham Lincoln, and Theodore Roosevelt, carved by Gutzon Borglum in monumental scale, gaze out at the land. Each head is about 60 feet long, twice the size of the Sphinx in Egypt, a scale that would have made each man 465 feet tall. Borglum began sculpting this massive project in 1927 at age sixty, and he died in 1941 before completing the carvings, which were to feature also the shoulders, chest, and waist of each president. For the most spectacular light, arrive at dawn.

The thirteen-minute film at the visitors center details the crafting of the monument, as do the photographs and tools on display.

Seventeen miles southwest of Mt. Rushmore, a fifth face takes shape in stone. Still being built is the **Crazy Horse Memorial** on U.S. 16-385; (605) 673–4681. When completed this tribute to the Sioux Warrior, will be the largest statue in the world at 563 feet high and 641 feet long. Lakota Chief Henry Standing Bear invited sculptor Korczak Ziolkowski to carve this monument because, wrote Standing Bear, "My fellow chiefs and I would like the white man to know the red man has great heroes, too." Ziolkowski began the project in 1947, and although he died in 1982, this monumental carving continues.

Ziolkowski, desiring not to depict a realistic image of this Sioux leader, but rather a rendering of the Sioux spirit, portrayed Crazy Horse astride a steed, his arm extended, responding to the goading question "Where are your lands now?" asked by a white man after the Battle of Little Big Horn when many Sioux were pushed onto reservations. The dramatic and dignified warrior points, answering "My lands are where my dead lie buried."

During the first weekend in June, families are allowed to explore the nearby Indian trails and to climb on the back of Crazy Horse. At other times, this memorial-in-progress offers an interesting look at the rare art of mountain carving.

The **Indian Museum of North America** features more than 20,000 artifacts of North American tribes. A special wing is devoted to the Lakota, a majority of whom live in the Dakotas.

The **Jewel Cave National Monument** (605–673–2288) is 59 miles southwest of Rapid City and 13 miles west of Custer on Highway 16. It features more than 80 miles of accessible passageways, making it the fourth largest cave in the world. Unusual calcite formations hang from the ceiling. Three tours, each covering about ½ mile, offer different views of the cave. While the Scenic Tour follows a paved lighted path, the Historic Tour, conducted by candlelight, traces the route of the earliest cave explorers, and the Spelunking Tour, more rigorous and recommended for ages sixteen and older, winds through undeveloped passages and caverns. Hiking boots are required. Whatever tour you choose, be sure to wear layers of warm clothing as the average cave temperature hovers at a chilly 47 degrees Fahrenheit.

Forty-two miles north of Rapid City is Deadwood, an 1876 gold rush boom town in the northern section of the national forest, on I-90 and U.S. Alt. 14; (605) 578–1876 or (800) 999–1876. Although the city is a designated National Historical Landmark with the facades of many buildings along Main Street sparkling with a turn-of-the-century flair, the town is not exactly as it was in the gold rush days. Now more than eighty gambling establishments lure tourists. While these might contribute to

Every member of the family will be awed by the epic faces of Mt. Rushmore. (Courtesy South Dakota Tourism)

the wild west spirit of this frontier village where Wild Bill Hickok was murdered, the gaming also lends a somewhat tawdry air which detracts from the family allure.

One mile from town the **Mount Moriah Cemetery**, known also as "Boot Hill," features the graves of such western legends as "Wild Bill" Hickok and Calamity Jane. If your kids crave wax museums, Deadwood's **Ghosts of Deadwood Gulch, Western Heritage Museum**, Old Towne Hall, Lee Street (605–578–3583), features eighteen scenes of pioneer days.

For some more gold rush days ambiance, take an underground tour of the once prosperous **Broken Boot Gold Mine**, on U.S. Alt. 14; (605) 578–9997. It brought up gold from 1878 until 1904. Or, explore the surface workings of one of the oldest and largest gold mines in the western hemisphere, the still-operating **Homestake Gold Mine**, in **Lead**, 3 miles from Deadwood, Main and Mill streets; (605) 584–3110. Children under four not permitted.

Nearby, **Lead Terry Peak** and **Deer Mountain** offer skiing in season.

Custer State Park
Adjacent to the Black Hills National Forest is **Custer State Park**, 42

miles southwest of Rapid City, on Highway 16A, HC 83 Box 70, Custer 57730; (605) 255-4515. Featuring 73,000 acres of rolling grasslands and pine forests, the park is home to about 1,500 head of buffalo, one of the nation's largest herds. Besides eyeing these formidable beasts, symbols of the West, you're likely to see deer, elk, pronghorn antelope, and bighorn sheep.

Among the park's highlights are three scenic drives. Along the 14-mile **Needles Highway Scenic Drive**, on Highway 87 from Legion Lake to the base of the highest mountain in the Black Hills, you thread through the towering granite pinnacles, popular with rock climbers. On the **Iron Mountain Road**, which spans alternate 16, for 17 miles from Custer State Park to Mount Rushmore, you drive through granite tunnels, past Black Hills overlooks, and through stands of spruce and pine. You're likely to see buffalo, coyotes, prairie dogs, wild burros (don't feed them even though they may beg at your car window), and elk, especially in the early morning or at dusk along the **Wildlife Loop Road**, which forms an 18-mile loop passing the Wildlife Station and the park's three resorts (see Where to Stay).

Pick up park information at the **Peter Norbeck Visitor Center**, 15 miles east of Custer on Highway 16A; (605) 255-4464. **Sylvan Lake**, 7 miles north of Custer on Routes 87 and 89, is known for its setting amid massive rock formations, and for its fishing, and **Legion Lake** has good fishing, swimming, and family-oriented budget cabins.

Wind Cave National Park

Wind Cave is the highlight of the 28,000 acres of grasslands of the **Wind Cave National Park**, 53 miles south of Rapid City, near Hot Springs and south of Custer State Park; (605-745-4600). It's a sure winner for kids fascinated by underground wonders. Said to be the world's eighth longest cave, this attraction offers more than 53 miles of mapped passages, with lots of boxwork ceiling formations. Remember warm clothing and good walking shoes. Above ground keep an eye out for the frequent buffalo, elk, pronghorn, and deer herds.

The Badlands National Park

The **Badlands**, 83 miles east of Rapid City (605-433-5361), exits 109, 110, and 131 off I-90, will intrigue your family. Designated by Congress as a National Monument in 1939, and upgraded to a National Park in 1978, the Badlands has dense deposits of fossils from the Oligocene Epoch, the Golden Age of Mammals, including giant turtles, three-toed horses, and saber-toothed tigers. Once a saltwater sea, later a marsh, the area is now a remnant of one of the world's great grasslands, with jutting peaks, twisting canyons, and vast prairies. The formations reveal amazing colors as erosion has exposed the formations' layers of purple, yellow, tan, gray, red, and orange. Some of the best colors can be seen at sunup and sundown.

Wind and the movements of ice and water created the wild assortment of pinnacles, cones, gorges, and other geologic oddities that caused the Sioux, or Lakota, to label the region *Mako Sica*, or "Land Bad." French trappers and traders referred to the area as *Mauvaises Terres a Traverser*—"Badlands to Travel Across." Soon after these trappers arrived came soldiers, miners, cattlemen, and homesteaders who struggled with each other and the Sioux for the land. As a result of the 1890 Wounded Knee Massacre, the Lakota were confined to reservations.

The park offers a variety of programs, including a Junior Ranger Program for ages five to twelve, which reward kids with a badge (parents pay a nominal fee) after they answer questions about the park and about ranger-led programs they attended.

Look for deer, buffalo, and pronghorn antelope, but don't settle for just driving through the Badlands. Spend some time on foot. Obtain information about the hiking trails from the **White River Visitor Center**, open Memorial Day through mid-September, Highway 27 in the Stronghold Unit, 20 miles south of the town of Scenic. Hiking information is also available year-round from the **Ben Reifel Visitor Center at Cedar Pass**, off Highway 240, on the park's eastern side. Kids like the Touch Room with its fossils, rocks, and plants.

It's a completely different experience to walk among the unusual knobs, pyramids, and points. Six developed trails cut through the Badlands. **The Fossil Exhibit Trail**, west of the visitor center on S.D. 240, south of Wall, is great for kids. This ¼-mile loop, which is wheelchair and stroller accessible, features replicas of area fossils. **The Cliff Shelf Nature Trail**, another ¼-mile loop just east of the visitor center on 240, passes through a juniper grove, and cattail marsh that attracts Badlands wildlife. While easy, a few steps make this not wheelchair accessible.

For teens, **the Castle Trail**, northeast of the visitor center on 240, above the Cliff Shelf Trail, offers a 5¼-mile one-way stretch through rolling grasslands and Badlands formations, or a 6-mile loop when combined with the **Medicine Root Trail**. As weather changes can be sudden in the Badlands, be sure to take proper clothing and provisions, including adequate food and water, when hiking any distance.

Special Tours

For a western adventure while in Custer, sign on with the **Dakota Badland Outfitters**, P.O. Box 85, Custer; for booking (206) 659–2255 or for general information (605) 673–5363. Born-and-raised Dakota cowboys guide you through the Black Hills wilderness and the Badlands on day or overnight trips. Ride horseback or, more suitable with young ones, sit in a mule-drawn ranch wagon as guides relate local history and

legend, and provide picnic lunches. For more adventure, book an overnight pack trip into the Badlands back country.
    Black Hills Balloons, P.O. Box 210, Custer 57730 (605–673–2520), floats you over such scenic spots as Mount Rushmore, Crazy Horse Monument, and herds of grazing buffalo. Check on minimum age and height requirements for children.

MORE ATTRACTIONS

In Rapid City the free **Story Book Island,** 1301 Sheridan Lake Road (605–342–6357), is a good place to let little ones romp on replicas of popular storybook characters, and cross a moat to enter a fairy-tale castle.
    At **Bear Country U.S.A.,** off U.S. 16, 8 miles south of Rapid City (605–343–2290), roll up your windows and surround yourself with grizzly bear, timber wolves, mountain lion, buffalo, moose, bighorn sheep, and black bear as you drive through this 220-acre natural Black Hills habitat. After the drive, take the kids to see the young animals in "Babyland," or go for pony rides.
    In season two ski areas not far from Deadwood offer downhill fun. **Terry Peak Ski Area,** P.O. Box 774, Lead 57754, 3 miles southwest of Lead, is open generally Thanksgiving through Easter. Call (605) 584–2165 or (605) 342–7609; twenty-four-hour ski conditions, (800) 456–0524. The 20 miles of trails make this facility relatively easy to manage. From Memorial Day through Labor Day, take the chairlift ride for the splendid Black Hills views. There's also **Deer Mountain,** southwest of Lead on Highway 85, P.O. Box 622, Deadwood 57732; (605) 584–3230 or (605) 578–2141. It features 25 miles of downhill trails, plus groomed cross-country trails, a ski school, and a kids' program.

Shopping
    In Rapid City, **Rushmore Mall** offers department stores and traditional mall shops. Stroll down **Main Street** and **St. Joseph's Street** for the specialty shops, including the **Sioux Trading Post,** 913 Mt. Rushmore Road, for authentic Plains arts and crafts.

Theater
    Call the **Rushmore Plaza Civic Center,** 444 Mt. Rushmore Road (800–247–1095), to find out about performances of the **Group Theater** (605–394–1787) and the **South Dakota Symphony Orchestra** (605–335–7933).

Sports
    The **Rushmore Plaza Civic Center,** 444 Mt. Rushmore Road

(800–247–1095) has times and schedules for the **Rapid City Thrillers** basketball team.

SPECIAL EVENTS

February: Dakota Winter Games, Lead.

June: Crazy Horse Memorial Open House, held the first weekend of June. The only time of year when the public can climb the memorial. Black Hills Bluegrass Festival, Rapid City. Fort Sisseton Historical Festival, Fort Sisseton.

July: Black Hills Heritage Festival, Rapid City, featuring barrel racing, and calf roping among the western skills.

At the Black Hills and Northern Plains Indian Powwow and Arts Market, Rapid City, celebrate Native American dancing and art.

The Black Hills Roundup, Belle Fourche, a top three-day rodeo.

Gold Discovery Days, Custer, features a pageant, a parade, and street fair.

Mammoth Days, Hot Springs, brings out Fred Flintstone–type characters for the prehistoric theme event. Eat a mammoth burger and enjoy the caveman contest.

August: Days of '76, Deadwood, features reenactments of the gold rush, plus a rodeo.

September: Crazy Horse Open House and Night Blast, Crazy Horse Memorial, lights up the night with an actual dynamite blast of the monument.

At the Deadwood Jam, Deadwood, bands play all day on Main Street.

October: At the Buffalo Round-up, Custer State Park, see a buffalo herd corralled by rangers and wranglers.

WHERE TO STAY

A good base is Rapid City, which has lots of lodging choices. The **Rapid City Hilton Inn**, 445 Mt. Rushmore (at Main Street), Rapid City (605–348–8300 or 800–446–3750), has moderately priced rooms, plus a pool with a water slide.

The **Holiday Inn-Rushmore Plaza**, 505 North Fifth Street, is another moderately priced lodging with a pool; (605) 348–4000 or (800) 465–4329. At the **Best Western Town and Country**, 2505 Mt. Rushmore Road, Rapid City (605–343–5383 or 800–528–1234), there are both indoor and outdoor pools. **The Quality Inn**, 2208 Mt. Rushmore Road, has two outdoor pools, and some suites with jacuzzis; (605) 342–3322 or

(800) 221–2222. The **Alex Johnson Hotel**, 523 Sixth Street, has a downtown location, a Native American and western decor, and often special family rates; (605) 342–1210 or (800) 888–2539.

Keystone and **Hill City** are close to Mt. Rushmore. In Keystone the **Powder House Lodge**, U.S. 16, Keystone (605–666–4646), offers cottages. In Hill City, the **High Country Ranch Bed and Breakfast**, HC 87, Box 9, Hill City (605–574–9003), provides some western flare with free half-hour horseback rides, and family rates.

Custer State Park offers four lodges as well as campgrounds. **Blue Bell Lodge and Resort**, Highway 87S, has rustic cabins with modern amenities, plus horseback rides and chuck wagon cookouts; (605) 255–4531 or (800) 658–3530. The **State Game Lodge Resort** (605–255–4541 or 800–658–3530), where President Calvin Coolidge summered in 1927, offers lodge rooms, motel units, and cabins, as well as a restaurant and grocery store. Nearby Grace Coolidge Creek is noted for its trout. The **Sylvan Lake Resort** (605–574–2561) overlooks—what else—Sylvan Lake. It's in the shadow of Harney Peak, the highest peak east of the Rockies. The resort has guest rooms, cabins, and a restaurant. **Legion Lake Resort**, Legion Lake (605–255–4521), offers twenty-five rustic cabins on the waterfront; it's a good spot for swimming, fishing, and paddleboating.

You can also camp at one of the seven campgrounds. Some sites are on a first-come basis while others may be reserved by calling (605) 255–4000.

The **American Presidents Cabins and Camp** is on Highway 16A, 1 mile east of Custer, P.O. Box 446, Custer 57730; (605) 673–3373. It has cabins, many but not all of which feature kitchens. The grounds have RV hookups and tent sites. Kids like the pool and the free miniature golf.

The Deadwood/Lead area offers several motels and hotels, including the **Best Western Golden Hills Resort**, 900 Miners Avenue, Lead 57754 (605–584–1800 or 800–528–1234); and the **Best Western Hickock House**, 137 Charles, Deadwood 57732 (605–578–1611 or 800–528–1234). There's also the **Bullock Hotel and Gambling Complex**, 633 Main Street, Deadwood 57732; (605) 578–1745 or (800) 336–1876. It puts you in the heart of downtown in an 1895 lodging; families with older teens may be more comfortable here than those with younger children because the hotel sports a casino. The **Historic Franklin Hotel**, 700 Main Street, Deadwood 57732 (605–578–2241 or 800–688–1876), has a range of rooms as well as on-premises slot machines, poker, and blackjack.

Shearer's Western Dakota Ranch Vacations, HCR1 Wall (605–279–2198), 10 miles from **Wall**, features horseback and wagon rides, chuck wagon suppers, and all the chores you want. Stay in the ranch home, log cabins, tepees, or in a sheepherder wagon.

WHERE TO EAT

Try the **Flying T Chuckwagon Suppers**, on U.S. 16, 6 miles south of Rapid City; (605) 342–1905. Sample a cowboy chuckwagon meal of barbecued beef, beans, baked potatoes, and biscuits served up in tin plates and cups. Live country and western music along with western decorations add to the atmosphere. Meals are moderately priced, and reservations are recommended.

Just a few miles outside of Rapid City, check out the **Chute Rooster**, U.S. 385 in Hill City; (605) 574–2122. Traditional western meals are served in this barn-turned-restaurant. In summer kick up your heels and join in the square dancing.

While visiting Mt. Rushmore a great place for lunch is the **Buffalo Room**, on S.D. 244 in Keystone; (605) 574–2515. This inexpensive cafeteria overlooks the memorial.

When you visit **Wall Drug Store**, 510 Main Street, Wall (605–279–2175), sample the cafeteria. Although the food is plain, the atmosphere and collection of western art is not. While you peruse the murals and memorabilia, munch on a buffalo burger, and linger over homemade pie. A cup of coffee is still only 5 cents.

In Custer State Park, check out the **Pheasant Dining Room**, U.S. 16A, Custer; (605) 255–4541. This **State Game Lodge** restaurant serves hearty fare and good homemade desserts at moderate prices.

In Deadwood, go with trusted allies. **BJ's Grinder King**, 902 Main Street (605–348–3166), serves the best pizza in town.

DAY TRIPS

A stop at **Wall Drug**, 510 Main Street (605–279–2175), just 8 miles north of the Badlands, is a must. This small 1930s family drugstore got its boost by offering free ice water to hot and weary drivers during the Great Depression. Today Wall Drug often serves 20,000 visitors each day. If you're wondering how a store in a town of 800 attracts so many visitors, you've never driven the highways of South Dakota where signs relentlessly beckon you to come on by. This is the place for kids to stretch their legs, climb on the outdoor covered wagon, and get a photo with a six-foot-tall rabbit. Inside they can search for souvenirs and admire the funky western decor.

Evans Plunge, in **Hot Springs**, just 9 miles south of Wind Cave, is a naturally heated, 87-degree mineral water spring. This indoor-outdoor swimming complex features three water slides and a spa. Also in Hot Springs, visit **the Mammoth Site**, on Highway 18; (605) 745–6017 or

(800) 325–6991. It boasts the world's largest concentration of Columbian and woolly mammoth bones discovered in their primary context.

For trout fishing go to **Spearfish,** 45 miles northwest of Rapid City on I–90; (605) 642–2626 or (800) 626–8013. Spearfish Creek and the area's lakes offer peaceful blue-ribbon trout fishing. A walk through the nearby canyon reveals waterfalls. The **Black Hills Passion Play** is another Spearfish event. Set on a stage 2 blocks long and peopled with 250 actors, this play recounts the last seven days of Christ's life.

Fort Sisseton, Roy Lake State Park (605–448–5701), about a seven-hour trek from Rapid City, is a thirteen-building frontier fort built in 1864, and open Memorial Day through Labor Day. During the first weekend in June's festival, watch infantry and cavalry drills.

FOR MORE INFORMATION

South Dakota Department of Tourism, 711 East Wells Avenue, Pierre, South Dakota 57501-3369; (605) 773–3301 or (800) 952–3625.

Black Hills, Badlands and Lakes Association, 900 Jackson Boulevard, Rapid City, South Dakota 57702; (605) 341–1462.

Deadwood/Lead Area Chamber of Commerce, 735 Main Street, Deadwood 57732; (605) 578–1876.

Wall Tourism Committee, Box 424, Wall, South Dakota 57790; (605) 279–2127.

Custer County Chamber of Commerce, 447 Crook Street, Custer 57730; (605) 673–2244 or (800) 992–9818.

Emergency Numbers

Ambulance, fire, police: 911

Hospital: **Rapid City Regional Hospital,** 353 Fairmont Boulevard; (605) 341–8222

Pharmacy: Although there are no twenty-four-hour pharmacies in Rapid City, **Albertsons,** 555 Omaha Street, is open weekdays 9:00 A.M. to 9:00 P.M., and Saturday 9:00 A.M. to 6:00 P.M.; (605) 343–8542.

Poison Control: in Rapid City (605) 341–3333, or throughout South Dakota (800) 232–2562

2 and 3
HOT SPRINGS NATIONAL PARK AND THE OZARKS
Arkansas

Hot Springs National Park, 50 miles southwest of Little Rock, is the only national park in the middle of a city. At the turn of the century, the park's geothermal springs, believed to have healing powers, attracted the wealthy from around the world. While it's still possible to enjoy a soak, the Hot Springs area woos families by offering a wide variety of attractions plus recreation in the park, at nearby lakes, and in the surrounding Ouachita Mountains.

GETTING THERE

The nearest airport to Hot Springs is the **Little Rock Regional Airport,** 2 miles east of downtown Little Rock on I–440; (501) 372–3430. **Hot Springs-Little Rock Airport Shuttle,** 217 Ward Street, offers regularly scheduled service by reservation from the airport to downtown Hot Springs. Call (501) 321–9911—Hot Springs; 376–4422—Little Rock; or (800) 643–1505. The drive takes one hour; kids under twelve are half price.

Amtrak's station is at Markham and Victory streets, Little Rock; (501) 372–6841 or (800) USA–RAIL. **Greyhound** provides bus service, 118 East Washington Street, North Little Rock; (501) 372–1861 or (800) 231–2222. By car, Hot Springs can be reached from the north and south by Scenic Route 7, from the east by U.S. 70, and from the east and west by U.S. 270.

GETTING AROUND

Most Hot Springs attractions are within walking distance of downtown. **Hot Springs Intracity Transit**, 429 Alcorn Street (501–321–2020), offers a trolley throughout the historic district and to the top of Hot Springs Mountain in the park. Buses operate hourly throughout the city.

WHAT TO SEE AND DO

National Park

As national parks go, **Hot Springs National Park's** 4,800 acres qualifies it as rather small, although the park offers miles of scenic drives and hiking trails. A total of forty-seven steaming springs (several uncapped so visitors can observe them) bubble about a million gallons daily at a constant temperature of 143 degrees F. Along with bathing and hydrotherapy, these odorless waters are used in drinking and geothermal heating.

The park's main attractions are Bathhouse Row, Hot Springs Mountain Tower, Grand Promenade, 10 miles of good mountain roads for scenic drives, and walking trails of varying degrees of difficulty.

You can enter the park, which has no admission fee, from several points. Begin your tour on **Central Avenue's Bathhouse Row** in the heart of the compact downtown. These vintage buildings line the east side of Central Avenue, while shops, restaurants, and attractions, many housed in historic buildings, line the west side. In the 1890s, twelve bathhouses operated, most of which were wooden frame Victorian buildings that soon were replaced because the hot water vapor rotted the timber. As a result, the bathhouses you see (dating from 1878 to 1923) are built of brick with iron, concrete, and marble.

A therapeutic and relaxing soak can still be had at several places, including **Buckstaff Bathhouse**, 509 Central Avenue (501–623–2308), but only **Hot Springs Health Spa**, 500 Reserve Street (501–321–9664 or 321–1997), has coed pools where children are allowed. Massages are also offered.

Fordyce Bathhouse on Bathhouse Row, 369 Central Avenue (501–623–1433), now houses the **Hot Springs National Park Visitors Center**, with historical exhibits and an audiovisual presentation on the springs' early years. Built in 1915, the Fordyce Bathhouse is the largest and most ornate structure on the row. Park rangers lead guided tours of the interior and of the grounds, including the nearby exposed springs.

Behind the Fordyce Bathhouse, steps lead up to the **Grand Promenade**, a ¼-mile walk along a hillside, offering wonderful photo opportunities. The Promenade overlooks cascading thermal springs that flow downhill. This is the start of a number of trails that wind up **Hot Spring**

Mountain, about a 2½-mile moderately strenuous hike. **Dead Chief Trail,** which starts at the Promenade, is one of the most popular. Other options: drive to the mountain top or board a motorized trolley from downtown. Once you arrive, take a glass elevator up to **The Mountain Tower** observation deck, 401 Hot Springs Mountain Drive (501–623–6035), for the spectacular views spanning 70 miles in every direction, revealing the surrounding Ouachita Mountains, sparkling lakes, and the busy downtown.

Attractions

The town of Hot Springs is a curious blend of the historic and the tacky. You'll find the usual kitschy resort tourist traps right across the street from gracious buildings that recall the grandeur of days gone by. Here are some of the more popular attractions in town.

Arkansas Alligator Farm and Petting Zoo, 847 Whittington Avenue (501–623–6172), houses more than one hundred Arkansas alligators of all shapes and sizes, plus mountain lions, monkeys, and huge turtles. The petting zoo comes with a llama, deer, ostriches, and pygmy goats. If you like your animals performing, stop by the **Educated Animal Zoo,** 380 Whittington Avenue (501–623–4311), which claims to feature the largest trained animal show in America, with both wild and domestic critters.

Mid-America Museum, 500 Mid-America Boulevard; (501) 767–3461 or (800) 632–0583—Arkansas. Kids take part in enjoyable, hands-on exhibits about energy, gravity, sound waves, and perception. Kids can also design a model of mountain ranges and rivers, create sparking electricity, and launch a hot-air balloon.

Tiny Town, 374 Whittington Avenue (501–624–4742), is a miniature city of hand-carved figurines, buildings, and landscapes. Teeny-tiny moving trains weave through little mountain ranges as animated scaled-down celebrities such as Marilyn Monroe and Clark Gable travel around town.

Josephine Tussaud Wax Museum, 250 Central Avenue; (501) 623–5836. Talk about variety: This place features lifelike wax figures that range from sixteenth-century explorer Hernando de Soto who, legend goes, discovered the spring, to a young Elvis to a recreation of the Last Supper.

National Park Aquarium, 209 Central Avenue; (501) 624–FISH. Here fish of Arkansas, such as large mouth bass, breams, and alligator gars, plus other colorful saltwater species swim in underwater scenes that recreate their natural habitats. Kids like to say "hi" to a ninety-pound snapping turtle.

Magic Springs Theme Park is at 1701 East Grand Avenue, on the eastern fringes of the National Park; (501) 624–5411. All summer, plus selected spring and fall weekends, intrepid older kids get their kicks on the 60 mph Arkansas Twister and on other wild rides. This theme park offers a children's area with appropriate rides for the younger set. Weekend

Visitors of all ages enjoy testing the hot springs. (Courtesy Hot Springs Convention and Visitors Bureau)

concerts and daily comedy and country music shows round out the fun.

Kids dig for their own precious quartz crystals at **Ron Coleman's Mining,** 14 miles north of downtown on Highway 7; (501) 984–5396. The shop features such already-discovered treasures as large and small quartz, agates, whetstones, and amethysts.

Stop at **Castleberry Riding Stables,** off Highway 7 at 537 Walnut Valley Road, 8 miles north of downtown; (501) 623–6609 or 624–7291. They offer hayrides and mountain excursions, plus horseback riding (age six and up can ride alone) and lessons, and campouts.

Green Spaces

Lake Hamilton. The pine-dotted shores of 18½-mile **Lake Hamilton** hug the southwest corner of Hot Springs. From downtown follow Central Avenue (Highway 7) south, 270 West, or 70 West. The latter route leads to the free swimming area, **Wheatley Park,** where you'll find a sandy beach, picnic tables, and playground, but no lifeguard. *Belle of Hot Springs,* 5100 Central Avenue (Highway 7 South), features evening and day cruises every day from February to November; (501) 525–4438. Limited reservations are also available for a tour of **Twentieth Century Gardens,** a forty-five-acre woodland garden accessible only by *The Belle* or its sister ship, *The Queen*. Wear comfortable shoes; lunch is available on the dock. **Taylor's Water Toys**, 4901 Central Avenue, Highway 7 South, at the Island Complex (501–525–4146), offers miniboats, five-person wave-cutters, ski boats and equipment, party barges, paddleboats, and parasail rides. For another lake ride, try a "duck tour." These are water excursions aboard refurbished W.W. II amphibious vehicles. Call **White and Yellow Ducks**, 406 Central Avenue (501–623–1111); or **National Park Duck Tours**, 418 Central Avenue (501–321–2911 or 800–682–7044).

Special Tours. Another favorite town tour is of sites related to President Bill Clinton, who spent his boyhood in Hot Springs. Obtain a pamphlet from the Convention and Visitors Bureau. Drive by such places as President Clinton's former residence, his grade school, the site of his senior prom, and his favorite weekend hangouts. **Outdoor Adventure Tours**, 300 Long Island Drive (501–525–4457 or 800–489–TOUR), offers guided van tours of Clinton's haunts as well as walking tours, mountain biking and canoeing excursions, and customized packages. See the sights on a mule-drawn trolley with **Hot Springs Mule Trolley**, 264 Central Avenue (501–624–2202); or **The Mule Line**, 308 Central Avenue (501–624–2202), right across the street from Bathhouse Row.

Theater, Music, and the Arts

On Central Avenue, between Canyon and Market streets, dozens of renovated Victorian and early twentieth-century buildings now serve as galleries and working studios. Walks the first Thursday and Friday of each month explore about twenty-five gallery/studios. While the galleries are open at other times, during these walks the gallery's hours are extended, and sometimes there are special presentations. At the **Children's Cultural Center**, 516 Central Avenue, Suite B (501–321–0222), which exhibits artwork by kids enrolled in their courses, "walk" days often feature special performances by kids.

The most popular forms of entertainment here are various comedy and music revues, many suitable for all ages.

Bath House Show, 701 Central Avenue; (501) 623–1415. This two-hour, humorous musical includes toe-tapping fifties and sixties songs. **Central Country Music Theater**, 1008 Central Avenue (501–624–2268), features live entertainment combining original country melodies and comedy done by eight animated life-size puppets. This recently renovated building is the oldest theater in Hot Springs. For more country tunes try the **Music Mountain Jamboree**, 2720 Albert Pike; (501) 767–3841. Here country and comedy sing out on most summer evenings, plus several nights a week in other seasons. To while away preshow moments, try the mini-Gator Golf (501–767–8601) located just outside the theater.

For a more serious tone, try **Mid-America Amphitheater**, Highway

270 West; (501) 623–9781. In season they hold outdoor showings of *The Witness,* a religious musical/drama. Every Friday and Saturday an actor portrays the apostle Peter who recounts the life of Jesus.

SPECIAL EVENTS

Contact the Hot Springs Convention and Visitors Bureau or the individual state parks for more information on the following events.

January: Eagles Et Cetera Weekend, DeGray Lake, honors the seasonal return of bald eagles.

March: Ouachita Indians Spring Fest/Pow Wow, with traditional dances, games, arts and crafts, and children's workshops.

April: Caddo River Spring Fest, Norman, with youth fishing derby, canoe races, and more; Easter festivities at DeGray Lake, Lake Catherine, Lake Ouachita state parks; Earth Day Weekend, DeGray Park, features environmental education, recycling demonstrations, and gardening tips; Wildflower Walks at various state parks.

May: Let the Summer Days Begin Memorial Day Weekend, Lake Catherine, with water balloon tosses, barge tours, canoe races, and nature trail hikes.

June: Brickfest in Malvern features a brick toss, baby contest, live entertainment, and "best-dressed brick" contest; Junior Naturalist Weekend at Lake Catherine offers wildlife programs for ages seven to fourteen; Miss Arkansas Pageant, Hot Springs; Father's Day Cruises, DeGray Lake.

July: Independence Day festivities include goofy contests, films, and owl prowls at Lake Catherine; watermelon-eating contests and live entertainment at Crater of Diamonds; hayrides, music, and movies at Queen Wilhelmina; Waterfest at Lake Ouachita; fireworks in Hot Springs.

August: Mountainfest, with live music and craft booths, Queen Wilhelmina.

September: Hot Spring County Fair and Rodeo, Malvern; Rod Run and Antique Car Show, Queen Wilhelmina.

October: Arkansas Oktoberfest, with German food, music, crafts, and more, Hot Springs; Fall Foliage Weekend, Lake Ouachita.

November: Healthfest, with races, including a kids' run, Mountain Bike Challenge, weight-lifting demonstrations, Hot Springs.

November–January: Holiday in the Park, with music, theater, tree lighting, craft shows, cookie sales, caroling, Gallery Walk and Christmas Parade, Hot Springs.

December: Hot Springs Jaycees Christmas Parade.

Shopping

Thirty stores offer brand name bargains at **Hot Springs Factory Out-**

let, Highway 7 South (Central Avenue just past Oaklawn); (501) 525–0888. You'll find Capezio, Book Warehouse, Fieldcrest Cannon, Geofrey Beene, and more. **Hot Springs Mall**, 4501 Central Avenue, Highway 7 South (501–525–3254), has four large department stores, including Sears and JC Penney, plus seventy specialty shops.

WHERE TO STAY

The Hot Springs area has a good variety of lodgings. The Convention and Visitors Bureau has a brochure describing discount packages.

Hotels: **Hill Wheatley Downtowner Hotel and Spa**, 135 Central Avenue (501–624–5521), has thermal baths and whirlpools, plus three-room suites, swimming pool, and restaurant. Another good choice is **Arlington Resort Hotel and Spa**, Central Avenue at Fountain Street, at the end of Bathhouse Row; (501) 623–7771 or (800) 643–1502. They offer 486 rooms and suites, three restaurants, in-house bathhouse, mountainside thermal water hot tub, country club privileges, game room, and twin cascading thermal pools on the lawn.

Motels: **Happy Hollow Motel**, 231 Fountain Street (501–321–2230), has refrigerators in all rooms, and some kitchenettes. **The Hot Springs Inn**, 1871 East Grand Avenue (501–624–4436), has fifty rooms, pool, and a nine-hole golf course. **Quality Inn**, 1125 East Grand Avenue (501–624–3321), has a game room, playground, and pool.

Bed-and-Breakfast Home & Inns

The **Vintage Comfort Bed-and-Breakfast Inn**, 303 Quapaw Avenue (501–623–3258), accepts children age six and older, and promises a friendly stay in an antiques-decorated Victorian inn. **Wildwood 1884**, 808 Park Avenue (501–624–4267), a restored 1884 Victorian mansion, is within walking distance of downtown.

Lake Hamilton. Try **Sunbay**, 4810 Central Avenue; (501) 525–4691 or (800) 468–0055. They offer luxury rooms with boat rentals, waterskiing, indoor/outdoor pools, tennis, health spa, playground, picnic tables, and outdoor grills. The **Holiday Inn Lake Hamilton**, P.O. Box 906, Lake Hamilton 71901 (501–525–1391 or 800–HOLIDAY), has a pond, playground, tennis court, and lake view. Children under nineteen sharing a room with parents stay for free. Another option is **Lake Hamilton Resort**, 2803 Albert Pike; (501) 767–5511. It has a private beach, lake views from each of its 104 all-suite accommodations, and features in-room refrigerators, indoor and outdoor pools, golfing privileges, private swimming beach, and marina with water sports and rentals. **Resorts Condominium Rentals**, 5380 Central, Hot Springs

(501–525–3500 or 800–643–1000), features furnished vacation homes all around the lake available by the night, the week, or the month. *DeGray Lake:* **DeGray Lake Resort** is on Route 3, off I–30 on Scenic Arkansas 7; (501) 865–2851 or (800) 737–8355. It includes a lodge with ninety-six rooms, with lake or wood views, plus a pool, full-service marina, and restaurant. Kitchenette-furnished cottages with a play area are located adjacent to the State Park at DeGray Lakeview Cottages; (501) 865–3389.

Campgrounds: Inside **Hot Springs National Park** is a rustic campground, **Gulpha Gorge**, 2 miles northeast of downtown. (Take Highway 70 east 1 mile until you come to a huge sign indicating the turn for the entrance.) There are forty-seven tent sites with concrete bases, but no electricity, showers, or water. From June through August, campfire talks at the Gulpha Gorge Amphitheater detail the history of the park. For information on the campground, call the Convention and Visitors Bureau at 800–SPA–CITY.

WHERE TO EAT

Try some of the places that Bill Clinton frequented in his youth, such as **Bailey's Dairy Treat** (formerly the Polar Bar), 510 Park Ave.; (501) 624–4085. Enjoy the ice cream and milkshake treats, or "have what he was having" and order a chili cheeseburger and Arkansas Grapette drink. The ribs, homemade tamales, and fresh coleslaw at **McClard's Barbecue**, 505 Albert Pike (501–624–9586), continue to be as popular as they were with Clinton and his boyhood buddies. For a hot breakfast, go to the **Pancake Shop**, 216 Central Avenue; (501) 624–9465. **Cafe New Orleans**, 210 Central Avenue, serves up southern-cooked Cajun breakfasts and seafood dinner delicacies; (501) 624–3200. **Mrs. Miller's Chicken and Steak House**, 4723 Central Avenue (501–525–8861), is family owned and features kid's meals, fried chicken, seafood, and steak. **The Arlington Hotel** (see Where to Stay) serves up an expansive seafood buffet every Friday night, and every Sunday features a brunch of smoked salmon, fresh fruit, and made-to-order omelettes.

DAY TRIPS

Arkansas has some truly outstanding state parks, most with interpretive programs. The following, in the **Ouachita foothills**, range from rustic retreats to full-size resorts to a park where you can actually dig for diamonds. All are within striking distance of Hot Springs. (While all of the parks are open year-round, programs and some park amenities are limited in the off-season.)

Lake Catherine State Park, 1200 Catherine Park Road (501–844–4176 or 800–264–2422), 10 miles southeast of Hot Springs, includes 2,180 acres of **Ouachita Mountain scenery**. There's also a playground, swimming area, and nature cabin with summer ranger-led interpretive programs for kids. The marina rents boats, life jackets, and fishing poles, and the park offers a **Party Barge Scenic Tour**. A grocery store/restaurant and laundry on premises add to the convenience. Seventeen cabins come with kitchens (some with fireplaces) and access to a boat dock. Nineteen of the seventy campsites may be reserved.

Lake Ouachita State Park, 5451 Mountain Pine Road; (501) 767–9366 or (800) 264–2441. About 15 miles west of the city is the state's largest man-made lake (48,000 acres with 975 miles of shoreline). It's considered one of two cleanest lakes in the U.S.A. At the eastern end, visit legendary Three Sisters' Springs, once believed to have healing power. Enjoy scuba diving, boating (rent fishing boats or party barges at the marina), fishing, swimming, and picnicking. The visitor center sports a store and snack bar. The park also has more than one hundred campsites and seven fully equipped cabins with kitchens. In summer, only twenty-eight of the campsites may be reserved ahead of time; cabins can be reserved year-round.

DeGray Lake Resort State Park, off I–30 on Scenic Arkansas 7, 21 miles south of Hot Springs; (501) 865–2801 or (800) 737–8355—lodge. This resort on the north shore of a 13,800-acre lake comes complete with an island lodge (accessible by a causeway) with luxurious rooms, outdoor pool, walking trails, tennis courts, eighteen-hole golf course, and a marina that rents everything from canoes and sailboats to party barges and houseboats, plus jet and water skis. There is always activity, from interpretive party barge tours, movies, and outdoor workshops to special events, including fall color hayrides and cruises. There are 113 campsites; call for reservations (see Where to Stay for off-park lodging).

Crater of Diamonds State Park, southeast of Murfreesboro on Arkansas 301, about an hour southwest of Hot Springs; (501) 285–3113. It contains a forty-acre field of what was once a gem-bearing volcanic area. Visitors can dig for diamonds (the park furnishes the tools) and bring home what they find in the field—the only diamond area in North America open to the public. As you dig and sift through eroded rubble, you might also find jasper, agate, and amethyst. The park weighs your find and certifies whether or not it's the real thing. To give you some encouragement: An average of more than 600 diamonds are found each year. The biggest: the 40.3-carat Uncle Sam diamond. The park, on 888 acres along the banks of the Little Missouri River, offers orientation programs. Sixty campsites are equipped with electricity, water, laundry facilities, and an on-site restaurant; limited reservations available.

Queen Wilhelmina State Park, west of Mena on Arkansas 88 (Tail-mena Scenic Drive), 90 miles west of Hot Springs; (501) 394–2863 or (800) 264–2477. High in the sky on **Rich Mountain**, the state's second highest peak at 2,700 feet, and part of the Ouachita Range, this park is on the spot of an 1890s resort hostelry named in honor of the Queen of the Netherlands. Now there's a modern lodge with thirty-six guest rooms, a restaurant, golf course, forty campsites, picnic areas, trails, an animal park, and a miniature scenic train that takes passengers on a ten-to fifteen-minute, 1½-mile trip around the grounds. The Deer Forest animal park is an "exotic" petting zoo, with llamas, pygmy goats, fallow deer, emus, and the like. Various interpretive programs (sometimes with live animals) take place on some summer weekends. One-third of the park's campsites may be reserved.

On the Caddo River, 28 miles west of Hot Springs at **Caddo Gap,** enjoy tubing, fishing, and canoeing. **Arrowhead Cabin and Canoe Rentals,** 191 Peppermint Terrace (501–356–2944), rents cabins (you supply linens and blankets) and also leads float trips for both amateurs and pros down the Caddo River.

Eureka Springs and the Ozarks

If you have more time to explore Arkansas, head up to **Eureka Springs,** 200 miles northwest of Hot Springs, near the Missouri border. Nestled in a valley, this town and the surrounding Ozark Mountains are popular vacation destinations offering folk culture, natural beauty, and lots of recreation.

Put on your walking shoes and do some exploring. A guide that divides the city into six walking routes is available from the **Chamber of Commerce office,** Scenic Highway 62; (501) 253–8737 or (800) 6EUREKA—tourist literature. Tours #1–5 are all under a mile; all involve "ups and downs." If your kids get tired, the guide also lists the routes for the replicas of old-fashioned trollies and open-air trams that stop at or near most town lodging. Single-ride or all-day tickets are available. Here are some highlights: **Tour One,** a popular route, begins and ends at the historic **Grand Central Hotel,** 37 North Main Street. It passes Victorian homes, limestone rock formations, a view of West Mountain, the last home of temperance leader Carrie Nation, and two scenic springs.

While strolling, browse the crafts sold in shops throughout town, and sample some local restaurants. Try **Myrtie Mae,** Highway 62 West, in the Best Western Inn of the Ozarks; (501) 253–9768. It has solid American fare, including chicken fried steak, soups and salads, and a kids' menu.

At the **Historic Depot** on North Main Street (Highway 23), the ES&NA (Eureka Springs and North Arkansas Railway) runs vintage trains every hour from 10:00 A.M. to 4:00 P.M., spring through mid-December; (504) 253–9623. The journey, more than 4 miles round-trip (about 45 minutes), chugs past lush mountain scenery, and if you want, lunch or dinner is available in the elegant dining car. Back in the yard, kids will be interested in the display of handcar, coaches, and railway motorcars.

Another worthwhile attraction is **Abundant Memories Heritage Village,** Highway 23 North; (501) 253–6764. In twenty-six authentically decorated buildings, the village displays toys, antiques, tools, military items, sleighs, and carriages dating from Revolutionary to Civil War times. For memories from an even earlier era, sample **Dinosaur World,** 8 miles west on Highway 287, open March–December; (501) 253–8113. This facility displays more than one hundred life-size dinosaurs—and a four-story replica of King Kong. Outside there are picnic tables and miniature golf; inside is a cafe.

There's also **Eureka Springs Gardens,** 5½ miles on Scenic Highway 62 West; (501) 253–9256—recording, or 253–9244. Wooden walkways lead to forsythia, lilies, wildflowers, and other flora that bloom on thirty-three acres of hillside, meadow, and woodland. Strolling is easy with benches and pavilions along the trails. In the works: a garden of First Lady Hillary Clinton's preferred flora, a limestone statue honoring President Bill Clinton, and a wedding garden. All trails are handicapped-accessible. In 1994, the garden plans to open year-round.

With **Eureka Springs Duck Tours,** junction Highways 62 and 23 North (501–253–7879), you get a watery look at the scenic countryside on your way to a splashdown in Lake Leatherwood when you board these amphibious vehicles (seasonal operation).

Onyx Cave is 3 miles east on Highway 62, then left; (501) 253–9321. Self-guided tours lead to fascinating underground formations with exploration proudly topped with narration. Ramp access leads to the cave entrance; this cavern is "doable" with young kids. Another plus: the free button and doll museum.

The **Christ of the Ozarks Statue** that overlooks the city is on the grounds of the **Great Passion Play** (501–253–9200 or 800–882–PLAY), the world's largest open-air drama. The story of Christ's resurrection takes place from late April until late October (closed Monday and Thursday) and includes a cast of 200 actors plus live camels, doves, donkeys, horses, and sheep. Several other religious related attractions include a Bible Museum and a 10-foot section of the Berlin Wall with Psalm 23 lettered in German.

About 10 miles west of Eureka Springs is 28,000-acre **Beaver Lake.** At this end there's a swimming beach with lifeguards; additional beaches and lodgings are around the shoreline. Take a relaxing seventy-five-minute cruise aboard *Belle of the Ozarks,* which departs daily May–October, from the dock at Starkey Marina, just off Scenic Highway 62 West; (501) 253–6200.

A unique Ozark attraction several hours east of Eureka Springs is worth the trip. The **Ozark Folk Center State Park** (501–269–3851 or 800–264–FOLK—lodge) is a mile north of Mountain View on Spur 382 off Highways 5, 9, and 14 and spreads out on eighty mountaintop acres. During the season (April through early November), twenty-five crafts-people perform traditional Ozark skills such as wood carving, broom making, quilting, and blacksmithing. Upon arrival, kids can sign up for the **Young Pioneer Program**. This entitles them to join a workshop or team up for a one-on-one learning experience with a particular craftsperson. Sessions last anywhere from one day to one week. Adults have similar options. During the season, concerts are staged in the music hall six nights a week with Sunday gospel concerts. Combination tickets (crafts and music) are available. The center has a lodge with sixty units, a restaurant, and gift shop with handcrafted items. Special musical performances and craft fairs are held on Thanksgiving and Christmas; special events take place year-round.

For more underground treasures, take a guided tour of **Blanchard Springs Caverns** (501–757–2211), 9 miles north of Mountain View via Routes 9 and 14. It's the only underground attraction operated by the U.S. Forest Service. The caverns, open year-round, feature modern elevators that take visitors down to huge rooms filled with formations.

For more mountain fun, visit during festival times. For the free *Ozark Visitor's Guide*, which includes special events, contact **Arkansas' Ozark Mountain Region**, P.O. Box 579T, Flippin 72623; (501) 453–8563 or (800) 544–MTNS.

WHERE TO STAY

Eureka Springs has the largest number of bed and breakfasts and inns in the state. The Association of Bed and Breakfasts, Cabins and Cottages of Eureka Springs, P.O. Box 13 (501–253–6657), serves as the area's largest reservation service.

Here are a few lodging choices.

Crescent Cottage Inn, 211 Spring Street; (501) 253–6022. Children are welcome at this Victorian inn where charming rooms all have private baths.

Downtown is home to several historic hotels where families are welcome, including **Grand Central Hotel**, 37 North Main; (501) 253–6756. The hotel has fourteen suites with complete kitchens, in-room whirlpool spas, cable TV, and free hotel parking. **Basin Park Hotel**, 12 Spring Street (800–643–4972), has fifty-five units, some suites, and a gift shop and restaurant.

Contemporary choices include **Best Western Eureka Inn**, 1 Van

Buren; (501) 253–9551 or (800) 528–1234. It has a restaurant, outdoor pool, and video games. **Ozarka Lodge** is at Route 6 (junction Highways 23 South and 62 East); (501) 253–8992 or (800) 321–8992. It features forty-four rooms, all connecting, including several oversized family rooms; there's an outdoor pool, complimentary morning coffee, and nearby restaurants.

An Ozark family favorite, some 90 miles east of Eureka Springs: **Scott Valley Resort & Guest Ranch**, P.O. Box 1447, Mountain Home; (501) 425–5136. A playground, pets, heated pool, horseback riding, canoeing, tennis, hayrides, three meals a day, and more are what make this place so popular.

FOR MORE INFORMATION

Hot Springs Convention and Visitors Bureau, 134 Convention Boulevard; (501) 321–2835 or (800) SPA–CITY. They provide helpful literature and lodging information. In town, stop by **Fordyce Visitor Center and Museum**, Bathhouse Row (501–623–1433) or the **Hot Springs National Park Visitor Center**, Central Avenue and Reserve Street (501–321–9763). **The Ouachita National Forest** headquarters in Hot Springs is at 100 Reserve Street; (501) 321–5202. Call the **Arkansas Department of Parks and Tourism** at (501) 682–7777 or (800) NATURAL.

Emergency Numbers
Ambulance, fire, police: 911
AMI National Park Medical Center, 1910 Malvern Avenue, (501) 321–1000, where there is also a poison control center; (501) 624–1121.
Although there is no twenty-four-hour pharmacy in Hot Springs, **Consumer's Discount Pharmacy**, 531 West Grand Avenue, is open 7 days a week; (501) 624–2538.

4 and 5
MINNEAPOLIS AND ST. PAUL
Minnesota

The license plates—"Land of 10,000 Lakes"—are misleading. It's actually closer to 12,000. Throw the Mississippi River into the equation, and you can see how the preponderance of water dominates life in the Twin Cities. With thirty-one large lakes lying within the metropolitan area of Minneapolis and St. Paul, outdoor recreation is an important part of people's daily routines. There is an estimated acre of parkland for every forty-three Twin Citians, ranging from grassy city oases and the famed Minnehaha Falls in south Minneapolis to public parks that contain everything from Indian burial mounds to botanical gardens.

The abundant natural beauty that enthralls both visitors and residents of Minneapolis–St. Paul also tantalized seventeenth-century French explorer Jean Nicolet, who traveled south from Canada along the Northwest Passage seeking a route to China. Instead, Nicolet found Dakota and Ojibwa tribes, eager to exchange fur pelts for blankets, knives, tobacco, and tools. The area became a major trading post and, after being fought over during the French-Indian War, eventually became part of Minnesota.

Minneapolis–St. Paul is truly the Midwest—situated midway between the Atlantic and the Pacific. The two cities are quite different in style and design. St. Paul is the older, more traditional city, its European, East Coast feel accentuated by historic buildings, city parks, a wide boulevard called Summit Avenue stocked with breathtaking mansions. Minneapolis is often called "the first city of the West," an aggressively hip place filled with contemporary architecture, a cutting-edge renovated warehouse district, and an overall atmosphere that is quicker paced and grittier than quiet St. Paul.

The winters are severe, but Minneapolis and St. Paul have Skyway systems—enclosed and climate-controlled walkways two levels above the street that connect people to downtown office buildings, restaurants, and attractions. Snow and ice removal is efficient. Summers can be quite humid, but unpredictable summer storms can also bring cool spells. For spring and fall trips, bring jackets and other warm clothing.

Both cities welcome families, so much so that the area is often cited as one of the top ten places in America to raise children.

GETTING THERE

Minneapolis–St. Paul International Airport, (612) 726–5848, located 10 miles from downtown Minneapolis and eight miles from St. Paul, serves more than two dozen airlines. Car rental companies include **Enterprise Rent-A-Car** (800–325–8007), **Budget** (800–527–0770), **Hertz** (800–654–3131), **Avis** (800– 331–1212), and **Thrifty** (800–367–2277).

Amtrak passengers pull into the St. Paul/Minneapolis Midway Station, 730 Transfer Road in St. Paul, (800) 872–7245, which is about a fifteen-minute drive from downtown St. Paul and twenty-four minutes from downtown Minneapolis. The **Greyhound/Trailways** bus terminal in Minneapolis is at 29 N. Ninth St., (612) 371–3320, and the St. Paul location is at Ninth and St. Peter, (612) 222–0509.

GETTING AROUND

Unless you plan to spend all your time in one downtown area or at the Mall of America in nearby Bloomington, it's advisable to rent a car. The Twin Cities operate an excellent transit system, notably with express buses running between the Twin Cities and to and from the Mall of America. Call the **Metropolitan Transit Commission** (612–827–7733) for routes and fares.

There are cabs in the Twin Cities, but it's not really a taxi kind of place. Expressway I–94 connects the Twin Cities, I–35W leads you to most Minnesota sites, and cultural and historical attractions are clearly marked along the streets and highways. Both places are laid out in an easily understood grid with a few idiosyncrasies tossed in to make life interesting.

WHAT TO SEE AND DO

Museums

DO NOT TOUCH signs are nowhere to be found at the **Minnesota Children's Museum**, 1217 Bandana Boulevard North, St. Paul; (612) 644–5305. This museum is a big hit with the eight and under set. There's an area reserved for toddlers with blinking traffic lights and other colorful stimuli. Four- to seven-year-olds revel in the child-size Main Street, where they whip up imaginary desserts in the ice cream parlor, learn about money at the bank, or cut a record in the recording studio. A historic train is there for the climbing, and visitors also operate a crane and other construction equipment. In the warm months, you can explore the lovely garden, with its topiary dragon, giant robin's eggs, and clearly marked plant and flower specimens.

Upstairs, there's a kite-colored maze and a multilevel landscape where kids crawl in and around a mountain vista, an urban expanse, and a seaside village. Throughout the day, the Children's Museum shows movies and schedules art and cooking classes, workshops, and performing arts events. There are also revolving exhibits, which in the past involved exploring China's culture and experiencing the world through touch.

The Minnesota History Center, 345 Kellogg Boulevard, St. Paul; (612) 296–6126. An architectural masterpiece made of Minnesota materials—Rockville granite and Winona limestone—the History Center is both an innovative museum and a state-of-the-art research center. The world's largest collection of materials on the State of Minnesota is housed in the Center, including a circa 1890 fire engine, vintage Betty Crocker radio broadcasts, buffalo horns, and Native American artifacts. The hands-on museum is organized around themes such as family, work, community, and place. The historic interpreters in period clothing bring an immediacy to the past, while special events make history anything but musty and dull. The Research Center features a microfilm room with forty-two self-service microfilm stations and a special collections room for fragile items. This spectacular museum has something for all ages, and the friendly staff is superbly trained to dispense boredom-free information. There's a gift shop that will appeal to families, as well as the Cafe Minnesota, a surprisingly good eatery specializing in regional food.

Science Museum of Minnesota, 30 East Tenth Street, St. Paul; (612) 221–9488. Educational entertainment is the motto of this huge, wonderful museum dedicated to hands-on, interactive exhibits dealing with natural history, science, and technology. The museum's 1.5 million natural history and science specimens include dinosaur exhibits, an Egyptian mummy, an authentic all-wood Hmong house, and other exhibits designed for science enthusiasts, from pre-school to high school age.

The newly expanded Paleontology Hall offers up-close and personal looks at dinosaurs, including the 82-foot-long Diplodocus. At Anthropology Hall, you can learn about the food, shelter, clothing, and rituals of the world's cultures.

Pause before entering the Science Museum to gawk at "Izzy," the 40-foot steel iguana created by a sixteen-year-old St. Paul schoolboy. Then walk immediately to the information desk and purchase tickets for the

Science Museum Omnitheater. Shows quickly fill up, and you don't want to miss the awesome movies projected upon a titled dome that is 76 feet in diameter. The shows engross all ages, but the film *Search for the Great Sharks* may frighten younger children.

Minneapolis Institute of Art, 2400 South Third Avenue; (612) 870–3131. Adjacent to the Children's Theater Company, the Minneapolis Institute of Art houses more than 70,000 works spanning 25,000 years of history in a structure combining classic revival and contemporary steel-and-brick architecture. The complex, situated in lovely Fair Oaks Park, also contains the Minneapolis College of Art and Design, as well as the Children's Theater Company (see Theater).

The museum's diverse collection includes antiquities from around the world, a lustrous collection of Chinese jade, African masks, Impressionist and Postimpressionist works, photography, and a Rembrandt. Popular period rooms, which display the museum's decorative arts collection, are gaily festooned for the holidays. A major magnet for children is the 2,000-year-old mummy, as well as rooms dedicated to pre-Columbian gold objects crafted by the Incas.

Other Attractions

Mississippi Mile, Plymouth and Hennepin avenues, Minneapolis; (612) 348–9300. Downtown Minneapolis is bordered by the Mississippi Mile, a riverfront parkway offering walking, jogging, and biking paths and scenic river views. Points of interest include **Nicollet Island,** home to the historic Nicollet Island Inn, the Nicollet Island Pavilion, and many examples of nineteenth-century architecture that look small-town perfect. **Our Lady of Lourdes Church,** the oldest Minneapolis church in continuous use, and **St. Anthony Main and Riverplace** are historic structures that have been converted to a nightclub, shopping, restaurant, and movie complex. **Mississippi Live** is a massive nightclub complex that features everything from local bands to national acts and often hosts alcohol-free, all-ages shows on weekends. Tour the **Ard Godfrey House,** the oldest home in Minneapolis, built in 1849, and visit one of the city's loveliest spots, the **Upper St. Anthony Falls Lock and Dam** (at Portland Avenue and the Mississippi River), the uppermost of a series of twenty-nine locks connecting Minneapolis with the Gulf of Mexico. View barges and other watercraft from the lock's observation deck.

The Raptor Center, 1920 Fitch Avenue, St. Paul; (612) 624–4745. Located on the St. Paul campus of the University of Minnesota, the Raptor Center annually receives more than 500 injured birds of prey for treatment. This offbeat, thought-provoking museum starts with an audiovisual presentation introducing the medical and educational focus of the facility, followed by a live bird demonstration of hawks, owls, falcons, and eagles, and a tour.

Minnesota Valley Wildlife Refuge, 3815 East Eightieth Street, Bloomington; (612) 854–5900. Operated by the U.S. Fish and Wildlife Service, this center features many hands-on exhibits and computer games that allow children to explore such jobs as wildlife manager, refuge manager of a deer herd, or fire boss on a prescribed forest burn. A spectacular twelve-projector slide presentation is shown regularly in the center's auditorium, and naturalist-led programs are also available.

Special Tours

Padelford Packet Boat Company, Plymouth Avenue and the Mississippi River at Boom Island Park (in the Mississippi Mile complex); (612) 227–1100. Take a breather from hectic sight-seeing and take a languid trip down the Mississippi aboard one of the old-style riverboats. Excursions, accompanied by a colorful narrative about the area, leave from both downtown St. Paul and downtown Minneapolis daily at 10:00 A.M., noon, and 2:00 P.M. Minneapolis riverboats leave from Boom Island and travel through the upper lock for a view of St. Anthony Falls and James J. Hill's Old Stone Arch Bridge. The St. Paul cruise leaves from Harriet Island, a short walk across the river from downtown, and follows the mouth of the Mississippi River to old Fort Snelling. In the summer, there are baseball cruises, Sunday brunch excursions, and Dixieland dinner cruises.

Artvantage Tours, 7304 Clarendon Drive, Edina 55439; (612) 941–1334. Artvantage Tours help visitors connect with the area's burgeoning artistic community. Trips include excursions to corporate art collections, public art installations, galleries, studios, architectural landmarks, and museums—and all tours are staffed by art specialists.

Landmark Center, 75 West Fifth Street, St. Paul; (612) 296–6126. Tour the restored Old Federal Courts Building and site of the famous gangster trials of the 1930s. The docents recreate mobster history so vividly you will swear you can see the pinstripes. The old courtrooms have been elegantly renovated. A ground floor cafe serves toothsome fare (especially desserts), and an added attraction outside is **Rice Park**, St. Paul's oldest and prettiest city park.

Theater

More than eighty professional theater companies thrive in the area, not to mention numerous community, experimental, and dinner theater troupes.

One child-oriented choice is **The Children's Theater Company**, 2400 Third Avenue South, Minneapolis; (612) 874–0400. This award-winning theater, located in a mammoth white brick building attached to the Minneapolis Institute of Arts, appeals to both kids and adults.

First and foremost are the children, who are accommodated in the 746-seat auditorium with seats specially raked so that smaller theatergoers can see the stage. There's even a crying room for children to sob freely without hampering the enjoyment of other audience members. Shows are lavish and vividly staged, ranging from children's classics—*The 500 Hats of Bartholomew Cubbins* and *Babar*—to innovative renderings of new works—*Strega Nona Meets Her Match* and *Crow and Weasel*.

The **Guthrie Theater**, 725 Vineland Place, Minneapolis, (612) 377–2224, was founded in 1963 by the legendary Sir Tyrone Guthrie to prove that classical repertory could exist, and indeed flourish, outside of New York and Chicago. Shakespeare, Chekhov, Ibsen, Moliere, Miller, and Euripides are well represented here, and in case you fear your children are not ready for the classics, there are pretheater symposiums before selected performances. Children's guides are available at the box office. Get to the Guthrie early for a pretheater stroll through the **Walker Art Center's sculpture garden**, one of the largest public sculpture gardens in the world. It features works by Claus Oldenberg, Frank Gehry, Henry Moore, and George Segal.

The Guthrie is situated in the same complex as **The Walker Art Center**, Hennepin Avenue and Vineland Place; (612) 375–7600. The center houses one of the nation's finest permanent collections of modern art, both American and European. There are representative works from many famous twentieth-century artists working in the media of painting, sculpture, photography, mixed media, video, and film. The Walker also boasts an enormous print collection. Children's programs are unusual and fun, with most taking place on the weekends. Past events have involved puppet making with local performance artists and a make-your-own video class.

Touring companies of Broadway shows land at one of three locations: **The Ordway**, 345 Washington Street, St. Paul, (612) 224–7661; **The State**, 805 Hennepin Avenue, Minneapolis, (612) 339–7007; or **The Orpheum**, 910 Hennepin Avenue, Minneapolis (612) 339–7007. The Ordway is a beautiful new theater with impeccable acoustics, while the State and the Orpheum are historic playhouses renovated right down to the gilt trim and painted bucolic murals. Many Broadway productions have passed through the Twin Cities here.

Visitors to the Science Museum in St. Paul may want to drop into the **Great American History Theatre, Crawford Livingston Theatre, Science Museum**, 30 East Tenth Street, St. Paul; (612) 292–4320. Past productions at this cozy, child-friendly theater include dramatizations of F. Scott Fitzgerald's *The Great Gatsby* and a countrified version of *A Christmas Carol*.

Purchase tickets for theater events at individual box offices, or call TicketMaster at (612) 989–5151.

Sporting Events

The Twin Cities offers a wide variety of sports events. **The Minnesota Vikings** professional football team plays through December at the climate-controlled H.H.H. Metrodome, 501 Chicago Avenue, Minneapolis; (612) 989–5151. Also at the Metrodome, **The Minnesota Twins** run the bases April through October; (612) 375–1116. Over at the Target Center, 600 First Avenue, Minneapolis, (612) 673–1600, catch the court action of the **Minnesota Timberwolves**, the state's exciting NBA team.

Outdoor baseball returned to the Twin Cities in the summer of 1993 with the Northern League **Saint Paul Saints** playing to capacity crowds at the Municipal Stadium in St. Paul, 117 Energy Park Drive, St. Paul; (612) 644–6659. A Saints game means affordable fun—tickets cost $3.00 for general admission and $6.00 for reserved seats. In addition to watching the game, patrons can get a haircut, receive a $5.00 massage from a group of massage therapist nuns, or watch the antics of the team mascot, a pig in a baseball cap.

Shopping

Mall of America and Camp Snoopy, Interstate 494 and Highway 77, Bloomington, Minnesota; (612) 851–3500. Think of your local mall multiplied by six, and you have the overwhelming Mall of America. Many tourists come from all over the world and never leave the mall to explore the Twin Cities. More than 25 million visitors have traipsed through the state's newest attraction, an enormous complex that features 400 specialty shops, eight nightclubs (including Planet Hollywood), 12,750 parking stalls, fourteen movie theaters, a miniature golf course, and anchor stores Nordstrom, Bloomingdale's, Macy's, and Sears.

Children and adults will be equally flabbergasted by the Lego Imagination Center, which features larger-than-life displays of dinosaurs, a fully-operational circus, firehouse, birthday party, and spinning globe and spacecraft—all made out of Legos.

Plopped down in the middle of the mall is **Knott's Camp Snoopy**, a seven-acre indoor amusement park complete with a roller coaster and twenty-two other rides, seven shops, three entertainment theaters, and fourteen eateries. Admission is free, and the park operates on a point pass system where you purchase paper tickets at booths or at automated ticket machines placed throughout the park. Be sure to set a spending limit. Parents on a budget should limit their children's rides. Camp Snoopy contains attractions for all ages.

Avoid the games of skill and other carnival attractions and the pricey **Ford Playhouse** dinner theater. Worthy attractions at Camp Snoopy include Pearson's Wilderness Theater, featuring live animals, and the Northwood Stage, which hosts live musical performances throughout the day.

Exercise caution about excessive spending at the mall too. Sensory

With its 400 stores surrounding an amusement park, the Mall of America offers something for everyone. (Courtesy Minnesota Office of Tourism)

overload—all the bright lights, welcoming sights, and sounds and noises—wear you down after awhile, and you might be tempted to run up your credit card. Take frequent breaks for drinks or snacks at the mall's restaurants, rather than the two chaotic food courts. Taking time out for a movie or to explore the quieter (during the day) fourth level is also an option. Don't try to take in the entire structure in one day.

The crowds can also be daunting, and it's advisable to visit the mall in either early morning or late afternoon. The crowds are smaller during the week than on the often bedlam-like weekends.

SPECIAL EVENTS

January–February: The festival season kicks off in winter's deep freeze with the St. Paul Winter Carnival; (612) 297–6953. It runs for twelve days during the end of January through early February.

More than one hundred events make up the festival, including parades, fireworks, skating, ice-carving contests, an indoor carnival complete with rides and games of chance, treasure hunts, hockey tournaments, fancy dress balls, and the crowning of the Carnival's King Boreas and his Queen of the Snow.

If you're in the Twin Cities in June, don't miss the Institute's annual June Fete, a fair of food, crafts, and entertainment.

July: In mid-July, it's Minneapolis's turn to get silly, with the Minneapolis Acquatennial, (612) 377–4621, an annual summer salute to water, fun, and families. The ten-day festival draws more than a million spectators and participants with seventy-five events taking place in and around Lake Calhoun, Lake Nokomis, and Nicollet Island. Festivities include a sand castle/sand sculpture competition; a sailing regatta; bass fishing, skateboard, and volleyball tournaments; as well as arts and crafts, music, pontoon boat rides, special foot races, and other events.

On Independence Day weekend, St. Paul hosts Taste of Minnesota, (612) 228–0018, on the grounds of the State Capitol, Aurora and Constitution avenues in St. Paul. Tour the Capitol, which contains the largest unsupported marble dome in the world. Eat your way through the Taste of Minnesota with vittles from dozens of Twin Cities restaurants.

August–September: The end of August through Labor Day is the Minnesota State Fair, (612) 642–2200, more than one hundred years old and the largest twelve-day state fair in the country. Held at the meticulously maintained and landscaped State Fairgrounds at Snelling and Larpenteur in St. Paul, the State Fair is a two-week extravaganza of livestock and crops judging, a midway, a juried art show, crafts, food, parades, and well-known musical entertainers.

City children who think that food comes from supermarkets will be wowed by the fair demonstrations, the agricultural exhibits, and the barns filled with cows, pigs, poultry, rabbits, and horses. If your family has never been to a big midwestern state fair, this is the one to try.

WHERE TO STAY

The Twin Cities have myriad places to rest your travel-wearied head, from big-name chain hotels to all-suite complexes and more modest accommodations. On the high-end, there's the **St. Paul Hotel**, 350 Market Street, St. Paul; (612) 292–9292. This expertly renovated hotel offers superb accommodations, one of the best restaurants in the Twin Cities— **the St. Paul Grill**—and a lovely view of Rice Park, the Ordway Music Theatre, and the Landmark Center.

In Minneapolis, indulge yourself at the subdued opulence of the **Marquette Hotel**, IDS Center, Seventh and Nicollet; (612) 332–2351. You can eat at the hotel restaurant, the same one where Mary Tyler Moore used to dine on her TV show. Two more pricey hotels, but worth it, are **The Whitney**, 150 Portland Avenue, (612) 339–9300, and **The Hotel**

Luxeford, 1101 Lasalle, (612) 332–6800, luxurious suite hotels. Minneapolis also has a **Hyatt Regency Hotel,** South 13th Street at Nicollet; (612) 370–1234 or (800) 223–1234.

Moderate prices and good value can be found at the **Raddison Hotel St. Paul,** 11 East Kellogg Boulevard; (612) 292–1900. The hotel boasts an indoor pool with a panoramic view of the St. Paul skyline; it is connected to the Skyway system and is within walking distance of the city's most popular attractions. Its counterpart in Minneapolis is the **Radisson Hotel Metrodome,** 615 Washington Avenue East; (612) 379–8888. **Best Westerns** are also a sure thing, and two of the nicer ones are at the **Kelly Inn—State Capitol,** 161 St. Anthony, St. Paul, (612) 227–8711, and in Minneapolis, the **Best Western Regency Plaza,** 41 North Tenth Street, Minneapolis; (612) 339–9311.

Suite hotels are sanity savers for families, and a terrific complex is the **Crown Sterling Suites,** 175 East Tenth Street, St. Paul; (612) 224–5400. Here you will find tastefully appointed rooms with balconies offering great views of the city, complimentary breakfast and beverages, and satellite television. There are also some quite attractive weekend package deals.

If you really want to have an unusual hotel experience, check into the **Burnsville Fantasuite Hotel,** 250 N. River Ridge Circle, Burnsville, (612) 890–9550, where you can pick out special suites decorated in futuristic, tropical, prehistoric, and other fantasy motifs.

WHERE TO EAT

People take their chow seriously in Minnesota, with an emphasis on rib-sticking fare such as steaks, wild rice soup, humongous sticky buns, and walleye pike. Vegetarians and connoisseurs of lighter fare will like **Cafe Brenda,** 300 North First Avenue, Minneapolis; (612) 342–9230. The café features luscious and low-fat seafood dishes, pasta, and desserts flavored with honey or maple syrup.

Hearty German cuisine can be found at **Gastof zur Gemutlichkeit,** 2300 Northeast University Avenue, Minneapolis; (612) 781–3860. Specialties include wienerschnitzel, sauerbraten, spaetzle, glorious apple strudels, and black forest torte. Teenagers love hanging out at the unspeakably hip **Loring Cafe,** 1624 Harmon Place, Minneapolis, (612) 332–1617, where the elite meet to drink espressos and recite poetry. Parents and children admire the Loring's funky decor and great food, including artichoke dip, designer pizzas, and filling pasta dishes; and it's so noisy in there, unruly children are just part of the scene.

A casual place in Minneapolis where you can kick back and dine is **Market Bar-B-Que,** 1414 Nicollet Avenue, Minneapolis; (612) 872–1111.

It's home of some of the most righteous barbecued ribs in the country. Another casual option is **Mick's City Center,** 40 South Seventh Street, Minneapolis; (612) 376–0560. Mick's is an art deco cafeteria turned unpretentious American restaurant. Families are welcome at Mick's, which is famous for its hamburgers, grilled shrimp, and huge, gooey desserts.

In St. Paul, families love the old world specialties at **Cossetta's,** 211 West Seventh Street; (612) 222–3476. They are known for cheesy pizza, imported meats and cheeses, and monstrous calzones. The **Heartthrob Cafe,** Seventh and Wabasha, (612) 224–2783, is a zany place where kids are encouraged to be rambunctious. This fifties and sixties inspired diner sports gregarious waitpersons on rollerskates who urge you to try the quesadillas, guacamole-topped hamburgers, and many-flavored malts and milkshakes.

Cafe Latte, 850 Grand Avenue, St. Paul, (612) 224–5687, features innovative and delicious salads, homemade soups and breads, coffee drinks, and an irresistible spread of pastries and cakes. For steaks, you can't beat the **Cherokee Sirloin Room,** 886 South Smith Avenue, St. Paul; (612) 457–2729. The steaks are the size of Buicks, and the baked potatoes are big too.

DAY TRIPS

Grand Casino Hinckley, Interstate 35 at the Hinckley exit; (612) 449–0057. Gambling is legal in Minnesota and abundant, so if you want to see the state's casinos—which are less glitzy than Vegas or Atlantic City—this is probably the best one suited for families. A beautiful hour-and-a-half ride from the Twin Cities, this 90,000-square-foot casino features more than 1,500 loose video slots with individual progressive payouts frequently in excess of $50,000. Also featured for the avaricious types are keno, poker, and blackjack machines, fifty-two blackjack tables, bingo, and the Royal Ascot video derby, a horse racing game. What separates this casino from others is the **Kids Quest Activity Center,** a 7,800-square-foot professionally supervised children's activity center. The casino also hosts **Powwows** and other **Native American events** on weekends. There's also a video arcade for teens and two restaurants, a 360-seat Grand Casino buffet and the Grand Grill American, both featuring tasty regional fare and live nightly entertainment.

FOR MORE INFORMATION

Visitor Information Centers
City of St. Paul: (612) 298–4012

St. Paul Convention and Visitors Bureau: (612) 297–6985
Minneapolis Convention and Visitors Bureau: (612) 348–4313
Metropolitan Regional Arts Council: (612) 291–6303
Ramsey County Parks and Recreation: (612) 777–1707
Hennepin County Parks and Recreation: (612) 348–4313.
Parks and recreation information: (612) 348–2142 in Minneapolis; (612) 777–1707 in St. Paul.

Other Useful Information and Numbers
Road condition information: (612) 296–3076
Traveler's Aid: (612) 726–5500
Metropolitan Transit Commission: (612) 827–7733
St. Paul area Chamber of Commerce: (612) 223–5000
Greater Minneapolis Chamber of Commerce: (612) 370-9132
The *Twin Cities Reader* and the *City Pages* feature comprehensive guides to what's happening.

Emergency Numbers
Ambulance, fire, police: 911.
Poison Center: (612) 347–3141.
Children's Hospital of St. Paul Children's On-Call Line: (612) 220–6868
Abbott Northwestern Hospital of Minneapolis Emergency Room: (612) 863–4233
Twenty-four-hour pharmacy: Walgreen Drug Stores, 1550 University Avenue, St. Paul; (612) 646–6165

6
OKLAHOMA CITY
Oklahoma

Oklahoma City (or OKC, as it's known in these parts) went from a frontier wilderness to a busy town of 10,000 in just one afternoon, when unassigned lands were opened to the first takers in the Great Land Run of April 22, 1889. The legacy of the early pioneers and an identification with Native American culture are still evident throughout Oklahoma's capital (now a city of one million) and in surrounding towns and villages. Exploring this heritage via museums, historic sites, and festivals (including the country's largest celebration of Native American culture) is a fascinating experience for visiting families. OKC, sitting on top of one of the country's largest oil fields, is a friendly, inexpensive city and, thanks to its central location, a gateway to the state's many recreational areas. Oklahoma, by the way, has more man-made lakes than any other state and boasts sixty-two state parks.

GETTING THERE

Will Rogers World Airport, south of I–40 on South Meridian, is a fifteen-minute drive from downtown. **Airport Express** (405–681–3311 or 800–225–5652) provides transportation downtown and to any location in the state. Car rentals and taxis are also available.

There is no **Amtrak** service to OKC.

Greyhound (405–235–6425 or 800–231–2222, has a terminal at 427 West Sheridan. Interstate highways I–40, I–35, I–44, I–244, and I–235 connect Oklahoma City to the rest of the country.

GETTING AROUND

Since most of the major attractions are not within walking distance of each other, a car is a necessity.

Metro Transit (405–235–7433) has frequent bus service to all major attractions.

WHAT TO SEE AND DO

Museums and Historical Sites

The city's museums and galleries are numerous, so we've narrowed the choices to the most appealing for kids. One is actually **seven** museums under one roof.

Enterprise Square, USA, 2501 East Memorial (between Broadway Extension and I–35); (405) 425–5030. This Disneyesque, high-tech tribute to free enterprise is full of electronic gadgetry that will tickle your family's collective fancy. As you enter amidst music and lights, three "alien" puppets emerge from a silver spaceship to guide you through a two-and-one-half-hour journey. Economics Arcade has video games where you and the kids drill for oil, operate a lemonade stand, build a home—in short, pursue the American Dream. Kids love the talking dollar bills that explain the delicate balance between prices, wages, and profits. A multimedia presentation and massive 3-D graphics of Americans who changed the way we live (including Ford, Bell, and Edison) are also part of the experience. This place is educational, entertaining—and the only one of its kind in the country.

Kirkpatrick Center Museum Complex, 2100 N.E. Fifty-second Street; (405) 427–5461 or (800) LEARN–KC. This must be heaven: seven kid-friendly museums under one roof (a total of ten acres worth) for one reasonably priced admission. Make a day out of it, with lunch in the Garden Cafe or an outdoor picnic. Here are the highlights.

Omniplex Science Museum. Come here first, as your kids will want to spend the most time in this colorful, inviting space. Surrounding a two-story dinosaur are some 330 hands-on exhibits, such as a twenty-four-foot diamond molecule that kids can climb inside and a Green Arcade and Weather Station, a fun way to learn about the environment. Toddlers have their own KIDSPACE with an office and computer area, water play, and the chance to construct a building, plumbing and all.

The **Oklahoma Air Space Museum** features more than 500 exhibits ranging from a vintage 1914 aircraft to a mock space shuttle cockpit. Memorabilia honoring famous Oklahoma pilots and astronauts are also on display.

In **Red Earth Indian Center,** kids are particularly interested in the Dwellings of the Earth exhibit, featuring to-scale early Native American homes. Also appealing: the colorful art from Oklahoma Indian artists and handcrafted work, such as beaded moccasins and colorful toys.

Kirkpatrick Galleries. An eclectic collection of interesting objects includes a portion of the Berlin Wall; toy trains; and a fascinating collection of more than 700 hats, from military to football helmets from the personal collection of naval Admiral Crowe, an Oklahoma native and former Chairman of the Joint Chiefs of Staff.

At the **Kirkpatrick Planetarium** see dazzling star shows in the Star Theater with sophisticated special effects and a state-of-the-art sound system.

The beautiful, wraparound photo mural of the Grand Canyon, the largest photo mural in the world, at the **International Photography Hall of Fame** intrigues even tiny tots. Traveling and permanent photography exhibits round out the displays.

As a last stop in this complex, visit the **Kirkpatrick Conservatory and Botanical Gardens**, a perfect place to sit down and relax. Six different gardens include a conservatory, miniature fruit orchard, tropical garden, and life-size elephant topiary.

The museum store has a good supply of museum-related toys, crafts, and experiments plus books, art, and other items. Weekend showcases and summer programs are part of the fun.

If you've ever hummed a cowboy tune or romanticized the Old West, come to the **National Cowboy Hall of Fame and Western Heritage Center**, 1700 N.E. Sixty-third; (405) 478–2250. This is more than a western art museum, though the extensive collection of paintings and sculpture by noted contemporary masters is one of the finest in the country. One highlight: the striking, 18-foot sculpture *The End of the Road*, portraying a dead Indian warrior slumped in his saddle. This sprawling facility also pays tribute to real and fictional cowboys and rodeo stars. The kids like the authentic replica of an Old West town where they can step inside a marshall's office, an authentic sod house, a mine, and other establishments. In the Western Performers Hall of Fame, an area is devoted to the John Wayne collection, an impressive cache of guns, knives, kachina dolls, art, and movie memorabilia and films donated by the late actor. If you come in October, catch the **National Children's Cowboy Festival** (see Special Events).

At the **State Capitol**, N.E. Twenty-third and Lincoln Boulevard, (405) 521–3356, free tours are conducted hourly from 8:00 A.M. to 3:00 P.M. If that doesn't interest you, there are still two good reasons why you should stop by: It's one of the few U.S. state capitol buildings without a dome, and it's the only capitol with several oil wells on the grounds. (Take a camera.)

Parks and Zoos

Myriad Botanical Gardens, Reno and Robinson, downtown; (405) 297–3995. Step inside this soothing, seventeen-acre retreat in the middle of downtown where you'll find a sunken, spring-fed lake filled with giant

Kids love the hands-on exhibits at the Oklahoma Air Space Museum. (Photo by Fred W. Marvel/courtesy Oklahoma Tourism and Recreation Department)

goldfish and Japanese Koi, surrounded by landscaped rolling hills. The garden's centerpiece is the seven-story Crystal Bridge, a covered glass and steel greenhouse-type structure with exotic plants, palm trees, and flowers. Take the Adventure Walk under a 35-foot cascading waterfall or enjoy the view from the suspended Skywalk. The Water Stage frequently has live entertainment. Admission charged; free guided tours can be arranged in advance.

Ranked as one of the best and largest in the country, the **Oklahoma City Zoo**, 2101 N.E. Fiftieth, (405) 424–3344, features more than 2,000 animals inhabiting 110 acres. The facility is in the midst of a long-term period of expansion. The newest exhibit is Great EscApe, featuring gorillas, orangutans, and chimps living in a natural habitat, with cliffs, streams, pools, and clearings. Another new installation, Aquaticus, one of the most popular exhibits, has aquariums, dolphin and sea lion shows, and marine life displays. At the Children's Zoo and Discovery Area, kids see and touch animals up close. A Sky Safari offers a panoramic overview, and there's also a narrated Safari Tram. Frequent evening entertainment takes place in the amphitheater.

The **Will Rogers Park**, N.W. Thirty-sixth Street and North Portland; (405) 297–2211. This 130-acre parks department facility is the city's finest for families, with grassy slopes, freshwater ponds, and a beautiful rose garden. For fun, there's an olympic-sized pool, frisbee golf course, picnic tables, and the lighted OKC Tennis Center.

Other Attractions

Frontier City Theme Park, 11601 N.E. Expressway; (403) 478–2412. It has come a long way from its beginnings years ago as an Old West town, complete with gunfights. That section, since renovated, is still going strong, but over the years they have added more than sixty rides, shows, and attractions. Fireworks are held nightly, Memorial through Labor Day. Open daily June to August; weekends April, May, September, and October.

White Water Bay, 3908 West Reno; (405) 943–9687. It's wet, wild and has everything a family water park should have, including a wave pool, chutes, flumes, slippery slides, and a play area for kids under six.

Theater, Music, and the Arts

Lyric Theatre, (403) 528–3636, a professional company, performs musicals June through August at Kirkpatrick Fine Arts Auditorium, 2501 North Blackwider Avenue, on the Oklahoma City University Campus. Ballet Oklahoma, (403) 843–9898, and the Oklahoma City Philharmonic Orchestra (405–843–0900) perform at the Civic Center Music Hall, 201 Channing Street. And don't forget the Oklahoma Opry, 404 West Commerce, (405) 632–8322, with weekly, Saturday night country western performances. Oklahoma Children's Theatre, (405) 948–6408, appears year-round at City Arts Center, State Fair Park, west of downtown, just north of I–40.

Shopping

Penn Square Mall, Northwest Expressway at Pennsylvania, (405) 842–4424, boasts several large department stores, specialty shops (including The Disney Store), the largest cinema complex in town, and a farmers' market that sells fresh local produce from April through October. Choctaw Indian Trading Post (405–947–2490) has three stores at two locations in town. The main store at 1500 Portland has a huge selection of Native American jewelry, pottery, sand paintings, kachina dolls, and "kid stuff." Next door, Half-Breed Trading Post sells handmade Indian goods from native areas worldwide. A smaller store is in Crossroads Mall at the junction of I–240 and I–35.

Sports

Three professional teams bring out the fans. The Oklahoma City 89ers AAA baseball team plays at All Sports Stadium, State Fairgrounds, I–44 and N.W. Tenth; (405) 946–8989. Oklahoma City Cavalry team, members of the Continental Basketball Association, play all home games at Myriad Convention Center, downtown on Sheridan. Call (403) 232–DUNK for information. **The Oklahoma Blazers,** Central Hockey League team, alternates games between the Myriad Convention Center and State Fair Grounds arena. Call (403) 235–PUCK for information.

SPECIAL EVENTS

Contact the Oklahoma City Convention and Visitors Bureau for specifics on the following annual events.

January: International Finals Rodeo, competition to determine world championships.

April: Festival of the Arts, a five-day celebration featuring over 160 visual, culinary, and performing artists; Centennial Horse Show.

June: Stockyard Stampede, with western arts, crafts, and entertainment, barbecue and fajita cook-off, rodeo demonstrations, and more; Red Earth, country's largest celebration of Native American culture, featuring art, crafts, powwow dance competition; Aerospace America, "aerobatic" performances with military, specialty, antique, and classic aircraft; Festival of the Pig, barbecue cook-off features food stands.

Mid-September–Early October: State Fair of Oklahoma, with Walt Disney on Ice and Ringling Brothers circus.

October: National Children's Cowboy Festival, hands-on activities and special events, Cowboy Hall of Fame.

November: World Championship Quarter Horse Show, state's largest out-of-state visitor attraction.

December 31: Opening Night, downtown celebration with music, dance, art, food, and kids' activities.

WHERE TO STAY

Consult the *Visitors Guide* for accommodations information. There is no bed-and-breakfast reservation service because bed and breakfasts are scarce in OKC. Lodging choices range from four **Motel 6s** (national reservations: 505–891–6161) to **Holiday Inns,** four in the area (national reservations: 800–465–4329), to luxury hotels. There's also a selection of all-suite hotels that are ideal for families. **Embassy Suites,** 1815 S. Meridian, (405) 682–6000 or (800) EMBASSY, has one- and two-bedroom suites and a pool. The more moderately priced **Governors Suites Hotel,** 2308 S. Meridian, (405) 682–5299, features free full breakfast, indoor jacuzzi and sauna, outdoor pool, and free airport transportation.

Centrally located downtown, the **Sheraton Century Center,** One North Broadway, (405) 235–2780 or (800) 285–2780, keeps the kids happy with its outdoor pool and adjacent shopping mall.

WHERE TO EAT

The *Visitors Guide* has a restaurant listing. Choose from a wide variety of eateries in **Bricktown**, the city's renovated warehouse district one block east of downtown's Myriad Convention Center, on Sheridan. One that's fun for families: **The Spaghetti Warehouse**, 101 East Sheridan, (405) 235–0402, featuring a wide selection of Italian and American dishes. The Meridian Avenue area also has many of the city's restaurants, from fast food to fine dining. **Applewoods**, 4301 S.W. Third, (405) 947–8484, features down home cooking (pot roast is the specialty).

Oklahomans like their beef—and if your family does, too, head to **Cattlemen's**, two blocks south of I–40 on Agnew and Villa in Stockyard City; (405) 236–0416. This restaurant specializes in tasty, reasonably priced steak with all the trimmings. Don't expect anything fancy: The place caters mainly to "working cowboys" who come to sell their cattle at the stockyards. A breakfast buffet is served on weekends.

DAY TRIPS

Today, more American Indians live in Oklahoma than anywhere else: Thirty-seven federally recognized tribes maintain headquarters in the state. A wide variety of attractions, festivals, and events pay tribute to Native American culture—and many are just a day trip away from OKC.

The town of **Anadarko**, about an hour's drive southwest, is tribal headquarters for the Apache, Wichita, and Western Delaware tribes. **Indian City U.S.A.**, 2 miles southeast of the town on Highway 8, (405) 247–5661, is a fascinating, outdoor restoration of Native American dwellings, showing the Native American way of life before the arrival of white settlers. Indian guides lead daily tours through seven life-size villages. **The American Indian Exposition**, a colorful, six-day show attended by 10,000 Plains Indians from fourteen tribes, is held here in August. **Fort Cobb Reservoir**, (405) 643–2249, twenty-five minutes northwest, is a good place to stop for a swim.

Guthrie, thirty-five minutes north of OKC on I–35, has retained almost all of its original eighteenth-century architecture. Along with numerous shops and galleries are a number of interesting museums and historical sites, such as the grand **Scottish Rite Masonic Temple**, Capitol and Oklahoma streets, (405) 282–1281, a 1929 design inspired by ancient Egyptian, Greek, and Roman civilizations. The huge **Lazy E Arena**, 4 miles east of Seward off I–35, (405) 282–3004, hosts numerous rodeos, equestrian, and other events year-round. Loads of fun festivals make this a worthwhile day trip destination. Contact the Guthrie Chamber of Commerce, 202 West Harrison, Guthrie, OK 73044; (405) 282–1947 or (800) 299–1889.

If you have older kids, consider taking a 150-mile round-trip journey to **Wewoka**, southeast of OKC, stopping at Shawnee (about 30 miles northwest of Wewoka) and Norman (about 12 miles west of Little River State Park) on the way back. Wewoka, the capital of the Seminole Indian tribe, is home to the **Seminole Nation Museum**, 524 South Wewoka; (405) 257–5580. Kids like the replicas of a Florida Seminole House, dioramas of a stickball game, and artifacts from pioneer through oil boom days. The free museum is closed in January; open daily from 1:00 to 5:00 P.M. the rest of the year.

Thirty miles northwest of Wewoka, **Shawnee** is the home of a tribal complex of the **Pottawatomie** and the **Citizen Band Pottawatomie Indians**. To prearrange a tour, contact the tribal office at (405) 275–3125. There's an arts-and-crafts shop at the complex. Also in town: the **Mabee-Gerrer Museum**, St. Gregory's Abbey and College, 1900 West MacArthur Drive, (405) 878–5100, where the big attraction is more than 6,000 Egyptian Dynasty items, including the mummy of a princess. Continuing west on Highway 9, you come to **Little River State Park**, (405) 360–3572, the closest to OKC (a forty-five-minute drive). Stop to stretch, play, hike—or go for a swim on Thunderbird Lake. Twelve miles west of Little River or OKC is **Norman**, home of the University of Oklahoma, which has a good **Museum of Science and Natural History**, 1335 Asp Avenue; (405) 325–4711. The museum houses dinosaur fossils, Native American items, and artifacts from Greece and Rome.

FOR MORE INFORMATION

Oklahoma City Convention and Visitors Bureau: 4 Santa Fe Plaza; (405) 278–8912 or (800) 225–5652

For a statewide vacation guide: **Oklahoma Tourism and Recreation Department**, 505 Will Rogers Building, OKC; (405) 521–2409 or (800) 652–6552

State parks information: (800) 654–8240.

Emergency Numbers
Ambulance, fire, police: 911
Poison Control: (800) 522–4611—OK
Twenty-four-hour emergency room: Baptist Medical Center, 3300 Northwest Expressway; (405) 949–3011
Twenty-four-hour pharmacy: Regional Hospital Pharmacy, 2825 Parklawn Drive, Midwest City (a suburb just east of downtown); (405) 736–1330

7
ST. LOUIS
Missouri

Among cities, St. Louis is a rare breed. Characterized by the 630-foot-high Gateway Arch, St. Louis is one of a handful of cities with a great urban park. Forest Park, site of the 1904 World's Fair, is a sweet expanse of greenery, just fifteen minutes from the Gateway Arch. Forest Park's 1,300 acres offer families a new age mix of nature and nurture—art, history, theater, science magic for kids, a well-landscaped zoo, and plenty of sports: tennis, biking and hiking trails, and nine- and eighteen-hole golf courses.

GETTING THERE

The **Lambert-St. Louis International Airport**, 10701 Lambert International Boulevard, is 13 miles northwest on I-70; (314) 426–8000. Most major airlines serve the airport, including **American** (800–433–7300 or 314–231–9505), **Northwest** (800–225–2525), **United** (800–241–6522 or 314–454–0088), and **TWA** (800–221–2000). Taxis and rental cars are available. Rental car companies include **National** (800–227–7360 or 314–426–6272), **Hertz** (800–654–3131 or 314–426–7555), and **Avis** (800–331–1212 or 314–426–7766).

Greyhound/Trailways, 1450 North Thirteenth Street (800–231–2222), and the **Amtrak Station**, 550 South Sixteenth Street (314–331–3300), also offer convenient transportation to St. Louis. For train ticket reservations and information, call (800) USA–RAIL.

GETTING AROUND

Taxis include **Yellow** (314–361–2345), **County** (314–991–5300), and **Allen** (314–241–7722). **Bi-State Transit,** 707 North First Street

(314–231–2345), offers inexpensive bus transportation. St. Louis's relatively new **Metro Link** (314–231–2345), a light-rail mass transportation system, connects most major attractions within the city, including the airport, Union Station, Busch Stadium, the Cervantes Convention Center, and even the north St. Louis suburbs. Metro Link conveniently offers free transportation in the metropolitan area weekdays from 10:00 A.M. until 3:00 P.M. Rental cars, however, are still a good option for getting around.

To explore downtown, park your car and take the **Levee Line**. These free buses painted like riverboats transport you to such major attractions as St. Louis Union Station and the Riverfront.

WHAT TO SEE AND DO

Museums

Take your children to the **St. Louis Science Center**, 5050 Oakland Avenue (314–289–4444). Let your kids loose for some hands-on science fun at the Science Center's two connected buildings. Kids' eyes grow wide at the sight of the life-size Tyrannosaurus Rex who moves and roars menacingly in the atrium. Wind your way through his world and the changing habitats to see what the land looked like when these giants roamed it, and when dragonflies swooped down on the St. Louis area. At the Human Adventure gallery, explore perception and senses by creating patterns in a kaleidoscope, find out why "pretzels" in your ears help hearing, and how your hands can conduct an electric concert. The Discovery Room is a hands-on place to finger such objects of interest as skeletons, sandboxes, tepees, wheelchairs, and stethoscopes. At the Computer Connection (book space in advance) school-age children learn programming possibilities or probe hall exhibits like *Sonic Six*, an aluminum sound sculpture by Howard Jones where your hands moving over holes create alluring tones.

The tunnel between the two buildings leads you into an underground domain of pipes and wires. Walk through a coal mine, complete with shoveling noises and canary songs, and a simulated sewer where water pipes emit swishing noises and live—but caged—rats run. Exhibits pose ethical questions about medical research and behavior. When you get hungry, eat at Einstein's Food for Thought Cafeteria, where the snacks are relatively good.

Star-studded skies come alive at the planetarium shows in the **McDonnell Star Theater** (children over five admitted; try to purchase tickets in advance, if possible). Browse the exhibits around the theater, which illustrate the Gemini space capsule, Mars probes, properties of gravity, and the brilliance and power of the sun.

Outside is **Science Park**, a kid-size, hands-on educational play park. Here children image themselves in a human kaleidoscope and a giant prism, crawl through thermal tubes, switch giant gears, toss echoes down a 100-foot chamber, and roll balls across a looping track.

The **St. Louis Art Museum**, 1 Fine Arts Drive, Forest Park; (314) 721–0072. Originally the Palace of Fine Arts, the museum is the sole remaining building from the Louisiana Purchase Centennial Exhibition of 1904. Greek columned, eagle crowned, and sited by a reflecting pool, the palace once mirrored East Coast standards of sophistication.

With 1990s renovation adding 30,000 additional feet of gallery space, more of the museum's permanent collection came out of the closet, including ancient Egyptian statues of gods and goddesses, mummies, and gold jewelry dating from 600 B.C. Other interesting features of the museum's permanent collection include dazzling works by Claude Monet and Edgar Degas. There is an exhibit on decorative arts, furniture, and household items as they evolved through history. On occasional Sunday afternoons, the museum holds special festival days for children and families. Call ahead to check.

For aviation history, and a sample of life in the American West, visit the **History Museum**, in the Jefferson Memorial Building in Forest Park, Lindell and DeBalivier; (314) 746–4599. The legendary exhibit Charles Lindbergh's Spirit of St. Louis is of popular interest. Backed by nine St. Louis businessmen, Charles Lindbergh bet his stamina against the tediousness of a 33½-hour trans-Atlantic crossing. The museum's one-room gallery evokes Lindbergh's May 20 and 21, 1927, record-breaking flight. There's an eight-minute film and a collection of memorabilia, including flight suit, arm cup for water, hip chronometer, and diary. Logged at eighteen hours: "I've lost command of my eyelids . . . I've got to find some way to keep awake. There's no alternative but death or failure." For musical firsts, peruse Ragtime to Rock N'Roll, a small exhibition of sheet music, photographs, and memorabilia of St. Louis' ragtime, blues, gospel, and jazz musicians including Chuck Berry, Miles Davis, and Ike Turner.

Also in Forest Park is the **Zoological Park** (314–781–0900), a well-kept eighty-three-acre landscaped treat. Board the miniature train pulled by a small-gauge engine. Your children will love the ride under a waterfall and through a tunnel (warn the little ones of several minutes of darkness). The four strategically placed stops allow you to see most everything and still not have to carry a walk-weary child.

Be sure to allow at least an hour for the zoo's **The Living World**, two halls whose interactive, high-tech exhibits, computers, and video screens portray the biological world. In the animal hall, you'll be amazed at the dazzling display of four viewing levels—tanks of coral, screens that flash images of spawning salmon, a look at live quail hatching, and a computer that defines such terms as "anthropod." In the Ecology Hall follow your fancy as computers inform you about such natural subjects as bird feeding habits or extinct animals.

If you have limited time, pay a short but rewarding visit to the birds. They swoop and chatter in a free-flight cage, built in 1904 and claimed to be the world's largest. Stop by at the Jungle of the Apes and see Fred, a 330-pound silverback lowland gorilla, the zoo's primate pride. The habitat of the Jungle of the Apes was developed to study great ape behavior; it offers banyan trees, black-haired chimps sunning on rocks like satisfied Buddhas, wizened-faced orangutans, and shy gorillas striking poses behind gray-limbed, ersatz trees. Raja, a baby elephant born in 1992, is also quite a crowd-gatherer.

Then end your day with a stunning sunset stroll along **Forest Park's** windy lanes and expansive lawns. This special green space educates with museums and learning centers, entertains with eighty-three acres of zoo critters, and, like all great city parks, Forest Park allures and pampers us with space and grace. Forest Park also offers lots of recreational activities including seasonal golf, tennis, and ice skating. Call (314) 535–0100.

More Attractions

What's a city without a symbol? St. Louis is synonomous with **the Gateway Arch,** at Market Street on the riverfront; (314) 425–4465. This 630-foot-high stainless steel curve glinting along the riverfront marks the city's gateway position for the pioneers heading west to possibility.

For a bird's-eye view, ride the tram to the arch's top, but only if you can tolerate tight places. Make reservations when you arrive at the arch, and be prepared for a two-to-three-hour wait.

There is plenty to do while you wait. You may watch *Monument to the Dream,* a twenty-eight-minute film detailing the arch's building trials. Or, meander through the nearby **Museum of Westward Expansion**, beneath the Gateway Arch (314–425–4465), and admire such pioneer artifacts as the Native American peace medals, wooden stagecoaches, and recipes for buffalo stew.

One of St. Louis' newer attractions is the **Arch Odyssey Theater**, underground at Gateway Arch; (314) 425–4465. This high-tech theater, with a four-story-high screen, will surround you with sight and sound during the twenty-seven-minute, 70 mm film *To Fly,* the current film being shown every forty-five minutes.

Just north of the arch **Laclede's Landing,** between Eads and King bridges on the Riverfront (314–241–5875), is named for Pierre Laclede, who came ashore here in 1763 to establish a fur trading post. Now, these cobbled walkways and reclaimed warehouses sport shops, bars, and restaurants.

Just downriver, and across from the arch, commercialism floats a more tacky existence. Here paddleboats are turned into moored Burger

The busy St. Louis riverfront is a popular family attraction. (Courtesy St. Louis Convention and Visitors Commission)

Kings, pizza parlors, and casinos (which don't welcome those under twenty-one). You may want to climb aboard the *Belle of St. Louis,* the *Huck Finn,* the *Tom Sawyer,* or the *Becky Thatcher* and enjoy dinner on the Mississippi. You can enjoy a one-hour harbor cruise aboard a paddle wheeler, or two-and-a-half-hour dinner/dance cruises with **Gateway Riverboat Cruises,** 500 North Leonor K. Sullivan Boulevard; (314) 621–4040.

Green Spaces

At the **Missouri Botanical Gardens,** 4344 Shaw Boulevard (314–577–5100), find a still point and a stunning vista from the meditation huts and tranquil stone paths in the Japanese Garden. With fourteen acres, this is the largest formal Japanese gardens in the U.S. Then, tour the Climatron, the first geodesic dome greenhouse, and the blooming rose gardens, lily ponds, and flower bedecked paths. Dozens of individual gardens delight the senses, particularly the Scented Garden. It features flowers noteworthy for their fragrance and texture, sculptures and fountains that fill the garden with the sounds of water and chimes, and braille markers that make this garden especially appreciated by blind visitors.

At the **Laumeier Sculpture Park,** 12580 Rott Road (314–821–1209), a ninety-six-acre outdoor park, the landscape blooms with modern sculpture, some of huge proportions such as the red 100-foot-long Alexander Lieberman statue *The Way*. On these rolling hills among the pines and oaks, the angles, lines, and massive size of these innovative modern sculptures delight your eye.

Other Attractions

Just a few minutes from Laumeier is **The Magic House**, 516 South Kirkwood Road (Lindbergh Boulevard); (314) 822–8900. This is a fun house of interactive exhibits. Here kids (and adults) explore sensory and scientific awareness by dancing with their shadows, tapping morse code, trying computers, and crawling through tunnel mazes. Tots one to seven especially enjoy A Little Bit of Magic, their own place for sliding, climbing, jumping, turning steering wheels, and sand painting with colored lights.

Tour the **Anheuser-Busch Brewery**, I–55 and Arsenal Street (314–577–2626), whose claim to fame is being the largest brewer in the world. See everything from the packaging plant to the lager cellar to the Budweiser Clydesdale Stables. Parents can enjoy free samples of Anheuser Busch beers. The gift shop caters to the whole family, with items ranging from beer mugs to Budweiser T-shirts.

St. Louis has another claim to fame: offbeat museums. The **National Bowling Hall of Fame and Museum**, 111 Stadium Plaza (301–231–6340), has actual bowling alleys you can use; compare old-time alleys to modern-day lanes. Let the folks at the Hall of Fame bowl you over with tours, exhibits, parties, and dinners.

If you've ever collected toy trains, and wished for miles of track, visit the fifty-acre **Museum of Transport**, 3015 Barrett Station Road; (314) 965–7998. Here you'll be dwarfed by the yardful of big engines like the Union-Pacific steam locomotives, the 1890s Black Diamond, and Big Boy, a 600-ton steam locomotive from the forties.

Do you have a canine among your best friends? If so, you won't want to miss a visit to **The Dog Museum**, Queeny Park, 1721 South Mason Road; (314) 821–DOGS. Paintings, figurines, a dog-specific video theater, and a gift shop are all on the grounds of the Jarville House, a Greek revival mansion. Bring home a souvenir for your fuzzy pal.

Sports

Bring the kids to a **Cardinals** baseball game, Busch Memorial Stadium; (314) 421–3060. They can sit, if seats are available, in the special Kids Corner with the team mascot, Fredbird. Admission. Also check for hockey games and times for the sports arena. Come early to **Busch Stadium**, 250 Stadium Plaza (314–421–3060), and tour the **St. Louis Cardinal Hall of Fame**, 100 Stadium Plaza (314–421–FAME), which features films and sports memorabilia, and the National Bowling Hall of Fame, 111 Stadium Plaza (314) 231–6340.

More Recreational Spaces

Creve Couer Park, Dorset Road (314–889–2863), invites you to sail or canoe, camp, hike, and picnic. Winter brings ice skating and sledding; and in the spring, call about fishing and boating in the park. For more outdoor activity, Queeny County Park, 550 Weidman Road (314–391–0900), features the Greensfelder Recreational Complex with skating rinks, outdoor pool, and tennis courts. The park also hosts the St. Louis Symphony Pops in the summer.

Shopping

The shopping in St. Louis is as much an attraction as an activity. Plaza Frontenac, 97 Plaza Frontenac, Clayton and Lindbergh (314–432–5800), features ritzy apparel at Saks, Gucci, Montaldo's, and Rodier. The St. Louis Union Station, Market Street, between Eighteenth and Twentieth streets (314–421–6655), offers scores of shops in a century-old renovated train station. The St. Louis Center, 515 North Sixth Street (314–231–5522), is a large, enclosed shopping center with four floors. Shops of interest in the Saint Louis Galleria, I–170 and Highway 40 (314–863–6633), include FAO Schwartz, Godiva, Crayola Kids, and Ann Taylor.

Nightlife and Performing Arts

Take a walk along Laclede's Landing to find some lively nighttime entertainment in St. Louis. It won't be long before you begin to hear the swinging brass of the dixieland jazz and ragtime bands playing in bars and restaurants. *The Riverfront Times,* distributed at no charge in restaurants and offices throughout the city, and the *St. Louis Magazine,* 612 North Second Street (314–231–7200), list calendars of events and nightly entertainment.

St. Louis also has a thriving performing arts scene. At Powell Symphony Hall, 718 North Grand (314–533–2500), listen to the St. Louis Philharmonic and the St. Louis Symphony Orchestra, one of the oldest symphony orchestras in the country, led by Maestro Leonard Slatkin. Dance St. Louis is located at 634 North Grand, (314) 534–5000; The Muny on Forest Park at the Riverport Performing Arts Center, 14141 Riverport Drive, Maryland Heights, (314) 298–9944; and the West Port Playhouse, 600 West Port Plaza, (314) 576–7100.

The Fox Theater, 527 North Grand Boulevard (314–534–1678), an ornate Siamese-and-Byzantine-style theater, opened in 1929 and was restored in 1981. Today it features Broadway productions, such as *Phantom of the Opera,* comedians such as Seinfeld, as well as concerts and dance.

Entertain the entire family with **Bob Kramer's Marionnettes**, 4143 Laclede Avenue; (314) 531–3313. These puppet shows delight the child in everyone. See demonstrations of puppet making Monday through Saturday at 10:00 and 1:00, and the show Puppet Follies happens every Saturday at 11:15 and 2:15. The store sells great puppets. There is an admission fee, and call in advance for specific shows.

Gambling: Not for Kids

The **Casino Queen**, 200 Front Street (800–777–0777), offers gambling excursions on the Illinois side of the river six times daily. Breakfast, lunch, and dinner cruises are available, but plan your child care in advance with a hotel or service because guests must be twenty-one years or older to board.

The **Admiral**, 802 North First Street (800–878–7411), a large dockside casino, is scheduled to open in early 1994 with slots, blackjack, and craps, and a restaurant and delicatessen.

SPECIAL EVENTS

January: The Missouri Botanical Garden features the Annual Orchid Display.

February: Historic Soulard hosts a Mardi Gras Celebration, with a charity ball, Creole cook-off, jazz music, and parade.

March: Downtown turns green for a day, and comes alive with the luck and spirit of the Irish, during the St. Patrick's Day Parade. Near the end of the month, jazz talent from across the land unites in St. Louis for the Mid-America Jazz Festival.

April: Six Flags Over Mid-America reopens, and the St. Louis Cardinals kick off their new season. The Storytelling Festival offers professional tales from early May.

May: Riverboat races between modern day Huck Finn and Tom Sawyer commemorate National Tourism Week. See the clowns, acrobats, and zany circus antics reminiscent of the travelers of the 1800s, at Circus Flora. Jefferson Barracks Park hosts American Indian Days, featuring food, dancing, and celebration at an intertribal powwow. The Children's Zoo opens its outdoor area to visitors.

June: Zoo and Aquarium Conservation Day, at the zoo. Get a Taste of West Port as you sample foods from more than fifteen different restaurants. At the month's end, the Sand Castle Festival, Laumeier Sculpture Park, features huge sand castles.

July: The Veiled Prophet (VP) Fair is said to be one of the largest Independence Day celebrations in the United States, each year attracting millions to the Gateway Arch and to the St. Louis waterfront. From July

3–5, festivities include hot air balloons, sky diving, jet fighters, and fireworks, plus more than 150 international craft and food vendors.

August: Artisans and craftspeople strut their stuff at the Festival of the Little Hills.

September: Early fall brings the Annual Bevo Day. A parade, plenty of food, rides, markets, and arts-and-craft shows take this festival into the night. Downtown hops during the St. Louis Blues Heritage Festival, featuring live rhythm-and-blues, jazz, rock-and-roll, and gospel music. Also, the St. Louis County Fair and Air Show features exhibits, demonstrations, and other attractions.

October: Faust Park hosts the Faust Folk Festival, with nineteenth-century-style performing arts and a crafts sale. Missouri Chili Cook-Off and the Applebutter Festival, in Historic Kimmswick (20-minute drive from downtown St. Louis), invite with homemade apple butter, carriage rides, and entertainment.

December: During the holidays, St. Louis jumps into the season with the Light Up Ceremony, the Christmas Parade (314–851–1441), and the Annual Way of Lights (314–397–6700). Keeping with tradition, the Nutcracker plays at Fox Theatre.

WHERE TO STAY

For a luxury hotel stay look into the **Hyatt Regency St. Louis Union Station**, One St. Louis Union Station; (314) 231–1234. Other hotels include **Courtyard by Marriott**, 2340 Market Street, (314) 241–9111, **Hampton Inn Union Station**, 2211 Market Street, (314) 241–3200, **Holiday Inn Downtown Convention Center**, 9th Street at Convention Plaza, (314) 421–4000, **Holiday Inn Downtown Riverfront**, 200 North 4th Street, (314) 621–8200, **Regal Riverfront Hotel**, 200 South 4th Street, (314) 241– 9500, and **Days Inn at the Arch**, 333 Washington Avenue, (314) 621–7900. **Doubletree, Mayfair Suites**, 806 St. Charles Street, (314) 421–2500, features a bar and grill, rooftop pool, wide variety of rooms and easy access to all the attractions of St. Louis, making this a popular lodging choice. Families take priority at the **Summerfield Suites Hotel**, 1855 Craigshire Road; (314) 878–1555 or (800) 833–4353. A spacious living area complete with television and VCR joins two separate bedrooms with their private baths. Fully equipped kitchens make feeding little ones easier and cheaper.

Resort

To combine a St. Louis visit with a resort stay, try the **Tan-Tar-A Resort and Golf Club**, Osage Beach, (800) 826–8272, about three hours from St. Louis. The resort features championship golf courses, five pools, tennis, racquetball, and dozens of other activities plus the Lake of the Ozarks. Children's programs offered in season.

WHERE TO EAT

Tony's, 410 Market Street, (314) 231–7007, is one of only a few Mobil five-star rated restaurants in the U.S. Come early—by 6:00 P.M. if you can. No reservations are taken; but the wait is worth it. Dinners come with three bread courses, attentive service, and scrumptious food. Among the specialties: veal, rigatoni, quail.

For the best burgers in St. Louis, munch at **O'Connell's Pub,** 4652 Shaw Street; (314) 773–6600. For dinner with a view and nightly entertainment, make reservations at **Top of the Riverfront Restaurant,** top of the Clarion Hotel, 200 South 4th Street; (314) 241–3191.

Find a more relaxed setting at the **Old Spaghetti Factory,** 727 North 1st Street, (314) 621–0276, where pasta and special sauces dominate the menu. **Ozzie's Restaurant and Sports Bar,** 645 West Port Plaza, (314) 434–1000, provides comfortable atmosphere, wood furnishings, twenty-two televisions, and many hockey, baseball, and other jerseys adorning the walls.

Fitz's Bottling Company, 6605 Delmar, (314) 726–9555, is a root beer microbrewery where customers can see the root beer being brewed and watch the old bottling line. Daily specials often feature barbecue and burgers. For Italian cuisine, try **Zia's,** 5256 Wilson Avenue, (314) 776–0020, and taste the St. Louis specialty of toasted raviolis. For Nouvelle American cuisine, make reservations for **Faust's,** in the Adam's Mark-St. Louis, 4th and Chestnut streets; (314) 342–4690. For the best bakery in town, try **Amighetti's Bakery and Cafe,** 3151 Wilson; (314) 776–2855. Voted one of the best in St. Louis, the breads, pizza, ice cream, and more will satisfy the whole family.

DAY TRIPS

Plan a day to visit **Six Flags Over Mid-America,** P.O. Box 60, Eureka, Missouri; (314) 938–5300. Secure your stomach for the mind blowing Ninja—the black belt of roller coasters—and cool off from the summer heat on the Log Flume or the rapids of Thunder River. Looney Tunes Town gives the kids a chance to meet Bugs and other characters, and at the end of the day, you enjoy Batman Nights with lasers and fireworks. Take I–44 to exit 261, about 30 miles from St. Louis.

Among the 5,000 caves that gave Missouri the nickname the "Cave State," the **Meramec Caverns,** one hour west of St. Louis by way of I–44, in Stanton, are the most well-known. Discovered more than 200 years ago, the Caverns feature rock formations that are more than 70 million years old. You'll be amazed at the colors, the formations, the "onyx mountain," the natural pools of water, and the enormous size of the Cavern. Kids marvel at the "Jungle Room," named for it's resemblance to a swampy jungle full of rocky "vegetation." Outside, restaurants and gift shops await.

Instead of grabbing a bite at the crowded concession, make a stop at **La Jolla Natural Park**, adjacent to the Caverns, along the banks of the Meramec River and enjoy a picnic or barbecue. This will get you geared up for your drive back to the city.

FOR MORE INFORMATION

The St. Louis Convention and Visitors Bureau: (314) 421–1023; (800) 325–7962; (800) 888–FUN–1 for free information about lodging, restaurants, and important numbers.

Fun Phone: (314) 421–2100, for information about special events.

Missouri Information Center: Interstate 270 in North St. Louis, Riverview exit; (314) 869–7100

St. Louis County Department of Parks and Recreation: 41 South Central Avenue, 63105; (314) 889–2863

St. Louis Visitors Center: 308 Washington Avenue, 63102; (314) 241–1764; open 9:30 A.M. to 4:30 P.M. daily.

Emergency Numbers

Ambulance, fire, police: 911

For Highway Patrol: (314) 434–3344

Children's Hospital: The **Cardinal Glennon Children's Hospital**, 1465 S. Grand St.; (314) 577–5600

Twenty-four-hour pharmacy: Walgreens, 4 Hampton Village Plaza Shopping Center; (314) 351–2100

Poison Control: The Cardinal Glennon Children's Hospital features a poison control center. Call the hotline: (314) 772–5200.

8
WICHITA
Kansas

Wichita, the largest city in Kansas and a major aviation and agriculture center, is cosmopolitan without being too slick; residents sport a friendly, open manner and are happy to help tourists. There are plenty of attractions in town, and Wichita also makes an excellent base from which to explore such exciting sites as a Cosmosphere and Space Center just a day trip away.

GETTING THERE

Mid-Continent Airport, (316) 946–4700, 5 miles west of downtown on Highway 54, is served by a number of major airlines. Car rentals, taxis, and shuttles (many hotels run their own) are available at the airport.

Amtrak (800–USA–RAIL) doesn't stop in Wichita (the closest stop is in Newton, 30 miles north).

Greyhound/Trailways provides transportation nationally from the depot at 312 South Broadway; (316) 265–7711 or (800) 231–2222.

GETTING AROUND

Metropolitan Transit Authority buses (316–265–7221) run regular daytime routes in Wichita, except for Sunday. Three nineteenth-century-style trolleylike buses serve downtown and major tourist destinations.

WHAT TO SEE AND DO

Children's Museum of Wichita, 435 South Water; (316) 267–2281. This museum truly has something for all ages. The Tot Tug for toddlers comes complete with preschool toys and a model train. Younger kids love the colorful three-story maze that looks like a small village from the outside; inside are challenging crawling and climbing spaces. Playacting is encouraged: Kids can be judges, doctors, or fire fighters, thanks to true-to-life costumes and props. Kids can time travel in the Prairie House with its miniature furniture, tepee, and chuck wagon. Older kids like the challenging, science-related exhibits, such as the Infinity Chamber, where they see hundreds of their own images. Weekends are lively, with original puppet shows on Saturday and a Sunday Concert Series. Also on Sunday, kids can talk to other youngsters around the world (some in other children's museums) at the Ham Shack, with the help of local licensed amateur radio operator volunteers. Frequent traveling exhibits add spark to this already dynamic facility.

Omnisphere and Science Center, 220 South Main; (316) 264–6178 for current show lists or 264–3174 for information. There is a nominal admission to this museum of hands-on exhibits that teach kids the basics of physics, chemistry, and astronomy. There's an extra fee for the changing planetarium shows and live science demonstrations with audience participation. In the summer, the museum's magician and illusionist performs, and other kids' programs are offered.

Sedgwick County Historical Museum, 204 South Main; (316) 265–9314. Inside this imposing 1892 City Hall building (a National Historic Site) are some delightful exhibits that kids enjoy, including the Child's World area with doll and toy collections, a 1910 drugstore, a Victorian home, and a Wichita-built Jones Six automobile.

Five minutes west of downtown are three riverside museums that, along with the botanical gardens listed below, comprise the **Museums on the River:**

The Indian Center Museum, 650 North Seneca; (316) 262–5221. The museum is inside the arrow-shaped Mid-American All Indian Center, a Bicentennial gift to all Native Americans from the people of Wichita. The location: at the confluence of the Big and Little Arkansas (pronounced "arKANSAS" in these parts) rivers where the Wichita tribe camped more than one hundred years ago. At this meeting point stands a striking, 44-foot-tall sculpture, *The Keeper of the Plains*, that kids find quite impressive. The center displays changing exhibits of traditional and contemporary Native American works. Try to come on Tuesday when volunteers prepare American Indian cuisine, including Indian tacos, meat pies, and fry bread. An annual powwow (see Special Events) is held here, with some events usually held at the town park.

Lake Afton Public Observatory, 247th Street West and Thirty-ninth Street South; (316) 794–8995. Located 15 miles southwest of Wichita, this place is a lovely spot to spend an evening (open Friday and Saturday after sunset and Sunday evenings during the summer). See Saturn's rings, the moon, star clusters, and galaxies through the 16-inch telescope. Kids can make their own telescope and play astronomy computer games. The Observatory is across from **Lake Afton Park** (316–794–2774) where there's fishing, boating, and camping.

Old Cowtown Museum, 1871 Sim Park Drive; (316) 264–0671. Relive Wichita's frontier days at this historic village museum, a circa 1865–1880 town with authentically furnished homes and businesses. Located on seventeen acres along the Arkansas River, Old Cowtown includes original buildings, such as the Munger House, built in 1869, the town's first log house/hotel. There's lots for kids to like, including a main street straight out of a Western movie, a fully stocked General Store, the town's first jail, a one-room schoolhouse, a blacksmith at work, and a livestock area with Texas longhorn cattle. Costumed interpreters answer questions, and on selected days in July and August, Girl Scouts in period clothing reenact childhood activities, from attending school to helping with washboard laundry.

Summer weekends bring activities including reenactments, nineteenth-century music, theatrical performances, or cooking demonstrations. The museum, open weekends year-round and daily March through October, also holds several special events (see Special Events). On Thursday through Sunday evenings, the museum's Empire House Restaurant and Dinner Theatre serves a buffet dinner followed by an old-time, family oriented melodrama; a musical review; and comedy skits. Lunch is served Monday through Friday, and on summer Saturdays. Call (316) 269–0900.

The Wichita Art Museum, 619 Stackman Drive; (316) 268–4921. This museum is worth a stop if you have time—it's free except during selected traveling shows. The beautiful mother and child paintings by Mary Cassatt invariably appeal to youngsters. Other American works by such artists as Charles Russell, Winslow Homer, and Edward Hopper are also on display. A changing interactive gallery of art experiences is intriguing for both kids and adults.

Parks, Gardens, and Zoos

Botanica, 701 Amidon; (316) 264–0448. At this "living museum of plants" your senses will be delighted by nine-and-one-half acres of colorful tulips, irises, daylilies, mums, wildflowers, and other flowers. From spring to fall, more than 300 varieties of roses bloom in the Rose Garden. Reflecting pools, streams, and a pond of goldfish and Japanese Koi add kid appeal to this fragrant facility. The Woodland Walk, a one-quarter-mile wood chip trail laid out by Boy Scouts, is full of native plants, birds, and small wild animals. A natural area with poisonous plants is a good place to show kids how to identify poison ivy, poison hemlock, and other no-no's. Special events, including festivals, parties, concerts, plus seasonal flower shows, are held throughout the year. Catered lunches are sold on Wednesdays and Fridays, and guided tours are offered April through October; both require reservations.

Sedgwick County Zoo and Botanical Garden, 5555 Zoo Boulevard (northwest edge of town, just off I–235); (316) 942–2212. This fine zoo, open 365 days a year, allows compatible groups of animals to roam within natural barriers in habitats resembling different geographic areas of the world. The newest exhibit is the North American Prairie, with a skywalk over a habitat where bison and antelope roam. Elsewhere, birds fly free in a tropical rain forest, nocturnal creatures scamper through a dark herpetarium, and tigers, rhinos, zebras, elephants, lions, and monkeys roam. Have lunch or a snack at the restaurant on the premises.

Other Attractions

Barnacle Bill's FantaSea Water Park, 2220 North Woodlawn; (316) 682–7031 for taped information, or 682–8656. The only water-oriented theme park in the state, Barnacle Bill's runs the gamut from small wading pools with slides for tiny tots to large water slides and a giant wave pool. Grab a bite at the concession stand, or bring your own cooler (no glass or alcohol allowed). The park is open May through Labor Day; call for specific days.

The **Joyland Amusement Park,** 2801 South Hillside; (316) 684–0179. This typical amusement arena has adult and kids' rides, arcade, picnic grounds, bumper cars, and a miniature train tour. The park is open April through October.

The **21st Century Pyradomes,** 3100 North Hillside; (316) 682–3100. Drive by to see the eight distinctive geodesic domes designed by H. Buckminster Fuller and a 60-foot pyramid inspired by (what else?) the pyramids of Egypt. Should you desire, tours are offered on weekday afternoons.

Tree Trunk Art, as it's known, can be found at numerous spots throughout town. Artist Gino Salerno has recycled old tree trunks into delightful pieces of art that kids adore, including Wizard of Oz characters, which can be found at **Watson Park,** 33044 South Old Lawrence Road. For other locations, call the parks department at (316) 268–4361.

Wichita Boat House and **Arkansas River Museum,** 335 West Lewis; (316) 267–9235. The Boat House, on the east bank of the Arkansas River, is scheduled to open spring 1994. Along with boat rentals (mostly sailboats and rowboats), you can tour the Jay Hawk, an America's Cup–winning racing yacht.

Theater, Music, and the Arts

The **Convention Center's Fun Fone** (316–262–7474) offers daily updates of entertainment and special events. The downtown Century II

History comes alive at the Old Cowtown Museum. (Courtesy Old Cowtown Museum)

complex is where most cultural activities take place, including Metropolitan Ballet, (316) 687–5880, which performs the Nutcracker each Christmas season; Music Theatre of Wichita, (316) 265–3107, staging five
different productions each summer; Wichita Symphony Orchestra, (316)
267–7658, whose performances include Young People's Concerts; and
Wurlitzer Pops, (316) 263–4717, featuring the grand old organ from
New York's Paramount Theater in several concerts throughout the year.
The Wichita Children's Theatre, 201 Lulu, (316) 262–2282, performs
both here and at their own theater.

Shopping

Dorothy and Toto hailed from Kansas, so it's only natural that Wizard
of Oz artifacts are sold at shops throughout the town and state. At **The
Best of Kansas** at the Hay Market, 5426 East Central, (316) 685–0611,
you'll find Oz memorabilia as well as native arts, crafts, and food products.
Get yourself and your pardners outfitted with boots, jeans, and cowboy
hats at **Shepler's,** the world's largest western store, 6501 West Kellogg;
(316) 946–3600. Wichita is also the home of Coleman products, an extensive line of camping items. The **Coleman Factory Outlet Store and Museum,** 239 North St. Francis, (316) 264–0836, offers a wide assortment
of discounted products as well as a display of vintage Coleman items.

Sports

The **Wichita Wings**, a Major Soccer League team, play at the Kansas Coliseum, I–135 at Eighty-fifth Street North; (316) 262–3545. **Wichita Wranglers**, an AA minor league baseball team, go to bat at Lawrence-Dumont Stadium, 300 South Sycamore; (316) 267-3372. The new **Wichita Thunder** hockey team (316–264–GOAL) also plays at the Kansas Coliseum.

SPECIAL EVENTS

Contact the Wichita CVB for details on the following annual events.

April: Renaissance Faire, with arts and crafts, dramatic and musical performances, authentic games and activities.

May: Wichita River Festival, ten days of parades, bike and bathtub races, old-fashioned socials, hot air balloons, and the grand finale—Wichita Symphony's *1812 Overture* (young kids might not like the cannons, but they will like the fireworks that follow); Kansas Polkatennial, with three days of nonstop polka music and dance.

July: Indian Powwow, with traditional Indian dancing.

August: National Baseball Congress, with top-quality nonprofessional teams playing at Lawrence-Dumont Stadium.

September: Wichita Arts Festival, a weekend of dance, theater, music, and art; Mexican Independence Day Celebration, with music, food, games, and sport tournaments; Kansas State Fair, Hutchinson.

October: Wichita Asian Festival, with traditional costume fashion shows, dances, skits, karate demonstrations, and Asian food; Old Sedgwick County Fair, first weekend, at Old Cowtown Museum, recreates an 1870s fair with music, craft demonstrations and sales, antique buggies, wagon rides, steam-operated carousel, traditional foods, costumed reenactments, and theatrical performances.

Late November–December: Old-Fashioned Christmas, Cowtown, Monday through Saturday evenings after Thanksgiving, with music, programs, and refreshments.

December: Wichita Winter Fest, a weekend of strolling carolers, roasted chestnuts, cider, activities, and entertainment.

WHERE TO STAY

The Wichita CVB has a Lodging Guide that lists a few bed-and-breakfast inns, though there is no B&B reservation service. A wide assortment of reasonably priced accommodations range from budget motels, including **Super 8 Motel**, 527 S. Webb Road, (316) 686–3888 or (800) 848–8000, to full-service hotels. Be sure to ask about weekend packages. Some choices: **Wichita Royale**, 125 North Market; (316) 263–2101 or (800) 876–0240. This hotel has a cafe, free cribs, an indoor pool, and airport van. **Wichita Suites**, 5211 East Kellogg (US 54); (316) 685–2233 or (800) 243–5953. Choose from eighty-nine studio or one- and two-bedroom suites, all with refrigerators. There's also a heated pool, exercise equipment, and free cribs (but no rollaways). The **Wichita Marriott**, 9100 Corporate Hills Drive, (316) 651–0333 or (800) 228–9290, has good-sized rooms and an indoor and outdoor pool. The **Residence Inn**, 411 South Webb Road; (316) 686–7331 or (800) 331–3131. This all-suite hotel offers lots of space with equipped kitchens and complimentary breakfasts.

WHERE TO EAT

The Wichita CVB has a helpful restaurant guide. An interesting note: Wichita is the world headquarters of **Pizza Hut**, and the chain sometimes opens up prototypes in town to test new architecture or new menu items. Check locations with the CVB.

A few family friendly selections: **Pasta Mill**, 808 East Douglas, (316) 269–3858, serves Italian and American lunch and dinner, with a kid's menu available. Youngsters like the tableside hibachi cooking at **Kobe Steak House of Japan**, 650 North Carriage Parkway, (316) 686–5915, open for dinner seven days a week and offering a kid's menu. Reservations are suggested.

DAY TRIPS

The Kansas Travel and Tourism Division's *Attractions Guide* has a helpful listing divided by geographical areas and other tourist literature.

For swimming and other water sports, head thirty minutes northeast of town to **El Dorado State Park**, Highway 177, (316) 321–7180, which sports the state's largest recreational lake. Enjoy fishing and swimming at two beaches (no lifeguards) as well as a marina (no boat rentals), hiking trails, and picnicking. The town of El Dorado is also the home of the **Flint Hills Overland Wagon Trips**, 120 South Gordy; (316) 321–6300. Trips leave on selected spring, summer, and fall weekends for picturesque overnight rides on horses, covered wagons, and stage coaches. Meals, campfires with singing and tall tales, plus hearty pioneer meals and snacks, are included. All ages are welcome, but we wouldn't advise this with very young or fussy kids who might find the trip bumpy and boring once the novelty wears off.

Hutchinson, 45 miles northwest of Wichita (and the site of the annual State Fair in September) is a must. There's lots to see, but the real star is the **Kansas Cosmosphere and Space Center**, 1100 North Plum; (316) 662–2305 or (800) 397–0330. Tourists frequently are surprised to find such a comprehensive collection of NASA space artifacts housed in The Hall of Science, which features hands-on exhibits and the world's largest public display of space suits. An Omnimax Theatre shows larger-than-life films daily (sometimes too realistic for very young children), and a Planetarium offers sky shows on weekends year-round, summer weekdays, and certain holidays. Your kids may want to return someday for their five-day Future Astronaut Training Program for students entering the seventh, eighth, or ninth grade.

Hutchinson is also home to the **Dillon Nature Center**, 3002 East Thirtieth; (316) 663–7411. This thirty-acre site has woods, prairie, marshes, and ponds that attract hundreds of different wildlife species. Two miles of trails, picnic areas, a fishing pond, and garden make this a pleasant stop. Admission is free, although there are sometimes fees for special programs. Just west of Hutchinson on Highway 96 is another treat for kids: the **Hedrick Exotic Animal Farm**; (316) 422–3296. Joe and Sondra Hedrick raise and train animals for petting zoos and camel, ostrich, and pig races throughout the country. The assortment of animals on this working farm also includes zebras, llamas, goats, kangaroos, and exotic birds. Open daily, the farm offers tours for a fee.

There's lots more in the Hutchinson area, including two state parks, a small zoo, and the nearby **Yoder Amish Community**, with shops selling handicrafts, furniture, and baked goods. Contact The Greater Hutchinson Convention/Visitors Bureau for more information; (316) 662–3391 or (800) 658–1777.

Winfield, 60 miles south of Wichita, is the home of **Binney & Smith Crayola Factory**, 2000 Liquitex Lane; (316) 221–4200. Your kids will be fascinated by the plant tour, which shows how crayons are created, from the beginning right to the final packaging. This is an extremely popular tour for kids, and during the school year, groups book as much as a year in advance. Summer visitors will find it easier to get in—but we advise reserving as soon as you know your travel plans.

Another interesting tour for kids: **Country Critters Puppet Factory** in Burlington, 95 miles northeast of Wichita, 217 Neosho; (316) 364–8623. See how the puppets are created, sewn together, decorated, and packaged for shipment. The tours are offered twice daily on weekdays; call first to reserve. And if you're in Burlington on Saturday night, stop by the **Flint Hills Opry**, 404 Neosho, (316) 364–5712, for down-home performances by local (and occasionally Nashville) singing talent.

FOR MORE INFORMATION

Wichita Convention and Visitors Bureau: 100 South Main, Suite 100; (316) 265–2800 or (800) 288–WICHITA. Two satellite offices on I–35 are open summers only, both inside Hardee's Restaurants: Towanda Service Area, 20 miles north of town, and Belle Plaine Service Area: 20 miles south of town

The Kansas Travel and Tourism Division: 700 S.W. Harrison, Suite 1300, Topeka 66603-3712; (800) 2–KANSAS.

Emergency Numbers

Ambulance, fire, police: 911

Twenty-four-hour Poison Control Information Center: (316) 688–2277

Hospital: Medical Center, 550 North Hillside; (316) 688–2468

Pharmacy: Cumming's Pharmacy, 501 North Hillside, near Wesley Medical, (316) 682–4565, is open every day of the year from 8:00 A.M. to midnight

9
BOISE
Idaho

Families feel welcome in Boise, Idaho, a small, friendly metropolis in the foothills of the Rocky Mountains. Boise, the state's capital and largest city, appears like a green oasis in the middle of the surrounding brown hills, earning it the nickname the City of Trees. The Boise River cuts through the center of town, and the Greenbelt bicycle and pedestrian path that follows it offers year-round recreation. Boise also is a convenient gateway to fun and adventure: An abundance of white-water rivers, mountain slopes and lakes, forest trails, and dramatic desert landscapes offer families a variety of ways to enjoy the great outdoors.

GETTING THERE

Boise Municipal Airport (208–383–3110), 8 miles southwest of downtown off I–84, is served by several airlines, including **Delta, Empire, Horizon, Morris Air, Sky West,** and **United.** Car rentals are available at the terminal.

Amtrak (800–USA–RAIL) is at 1701 Eastover Terrace. For bus transportation, **Greyhound's** station is at 12212 West Bannock Street; (208) 343–7531 or (800) 231–2222. By car, Boise is reached by I–84.

GETTING AROUND

A car is really a necessity to explore Boise and the surrounding area. **Boise Urban Stages** (208–336–1010) offers public bus transportation around town, with schedules available at City Hall or by calling the company.

Spring through fall, the **Boise Tour Train**, a narrated tour aboard a replica of an 1890s locomotive, departs from Tour Train depot in **Julia Davis Park** between Myrtle Street and the Boise River (208–342–4796 or 800–999–5993) and travels to the city's historical sights.

WHAT TO SEE AND DO

Museums

Julia Davis Park (208–384–4240), in the heart of town between Myrtle Street and the Boise River, contains museums, the zoo, botanical gardens, and more (see Parks, Zoos, and Gardens).

Idaho Historical Museum, 610 Julia Davis Drive; (208) 334–2120. Two floors of exhibits reveal the colorful history of Idaho and the Pacific Northwest. Among the reconstructed interiors are a Chinese apothecary shop, an Old West saloon, a blacksmith forge, and a vintage kitchen. Among the period pieces on display are beaded moccasins and Native American clothing.

The ten galleries of the **Boise Art Museum**, 670 Julia Davis Drive (208–345–8330), feature works by notable artists. Permanent exhibits revolve around an extensive collection of American Realist art on loan from Sun Valley collector Glenn C. Janss. Kids should have no trouble picking out things they like from the watercolors, drawings, and other media portraying animals, urban scenes, flowers, and portraits by such artists as Georgia O'Keeffe, Red Grooms, and Edward Hopper. Because the collection is so large, exhibits change seasonally. Sign up for one of the twice-weekly tours or browse on your own. Be sure to visit the Museum Store, which has a good selection of jewelry and books.

Visit the **Discovery Center**, 131 Myrtle Street (208–343–9895), on the end of the park. Here you can play with magnetic sand, see your shadow on the wall, and create giant bubbles. These are some of the more than one-hundred hands-on exhibits that teach kids about science. An echo tube and after image, for example, explain about delayed perception. A sun tracker brings a beam of sunlight into the museum for solar experiments.

Elsewhere in town is **The Basque Museum**, 607 and 611 Grove Street (208–343–2671), at the Cyrus Jacobs-Uberuaga House (the oldest brick house in Boise, built in 1864). This building—the only Basque museum in the U.S.A.—served as a boardinghouse for newly arrived immigrants from northern Spain during the 1900s who came to central Idaho's rocky terrain to work as sheepherders. Black-and-white photographs collected from local families and original furniture create the era, as do the traditional dance nights held throughout the year and upon request.

The State Capitol, Jefferson Street and Capitol Boulevard

(208–334–2470), constructed of Idaho sandstone and marble from Vermont, Alaska, and Georgia, offers free self-guided tours and exhibits on gems and timber products. Several statues may interest kids: a replica of the *Winged Victory of Samothrace*, a gift from Paris; *The Patriot*, a tribute to a 1972 disaster in which many miners died; and a dignified commemorative depicting George Washington atop a horse.

The **Old Idaho Penitentiary** is at 2445 Old Penitentiary Road (1½ miles east on Warm Springs Avenue, then left); (208) 334–2844. It grew from a single-cell building in 1870 into an Old West complex that served as a regional prison until 1973. A tour of the museum reveals portraits of famous inmates and lawmen, as well as captured contraband weapons and artifacts. An eighteen-minute slide show tells about this penitentiary's colorful past. Inside the compound, view the effects of a riot, see several cell houses, a punishment area nicknamed Siberia, the Women's Ward, Death Row, and the Gallows. A former dormitory houses several history of electricity hands-on exhibits. A former prison shirt factory now sports a transportation display of a 1903 steam fire pumper, buggies, and other vehicles.

Parks, Zoos, and Gardens

Along with museums, **Julia Davis Park**, spanning more than ninety acres, features playgrounds, tennis courts, boat rentals, picnic facilities, amusement rides, a rose garden, free summer entertainment at the band shell, and kid-pleasing attractions.

Visit **Zoo Boise**, 355 North Julia Davis Drive; (208) 384–4260. It's noted for the Northwest's largest display of birds of prey, such as bald and golden eagles and hawks. Bengal tigers and Idaho's native elk, deer, and bighorn sheep delight kids, as does the petting zoo. The zoo is only one of five in North America to feature a moose habitat.

Ever expanding, the **Idaho Botanical Garden**, 2355 Old Penitentiary Road (208–343–8649), now features a ¾-mile nature trail plus nine theme gardens. Among the greenery highlights: the children's, Basque, Chinese and meditation, and native plant gardens.

Boise's **Greenbelt** links a network of five parks along the Boise River. **Ann Morrison Park**, between Americana Boulevard and the river, is the city's largest, with 153 acres complete with playgrounds, picnic areas, tennis courts, and skate and bicycle rentals at Shoreline Park, on the west end. For further information on the city's parks, call the Park System (208–384–4256).

Morrison-Knudsen Nature Center (208–334–2225), a 4½-acre habitat between Warm Springs Avenue and the river, has outdoor viewing windows where visitors observe different facets about the underwater life of a mountain stream. A new interpretive center features hands-on exhibits revolving around wildlife and the flow of the river. There's an indoor aquarium, an outdoor lagoon with sturgeon, bass, and rainbow trout, and an outdoor nesting ground for ducks and geese.

The **Peregrine Fund World Center for Birds of Prey** is off I–84 on South Cole Road, on the outskirts of town; (208) 362–8687. This endangered species center recently added a new interpretive center with a number of hands-on activities. At the Tropical Raptor Building, see such birds as the giant Harpy eagle, with a wing span nearing 7 feet. In spring, watch, via one-way mirrors, as incubated eggs hatch into young Peregrine falcons. Enraptured and want more? Visit the **Snake River Birds of Prey Natural Area,** another raptor center; (208–334–1582). It's one hour from Boise near Swan Falls Dam off Highway 69, south of Kuna. This area boasts the world's largest concentration of nesting eagles, hawks, and prairie falcon. Access to the area is gained via some fairly rough gravel roads. Although you can see the area on your own, the best way to tour is via guided boat trips (see Outfitters).

Adventures

Beyond Boise, there's the great outdoors: snow-packed mountains, raging rivers, lush forests, and rugged canyons. Some of the following make perfect day trips, while others, farther afield, are suitable for a weekend (or longer) jaunt.

Mountain Pleasures

Bogus Basin, 2405 Bogus Basin Road, 18 miles north; (208) 332–5100 or (800) 367–4397. Sister mountains, Deer Point and Shafer Butte, offer 2,000 skiable acres, six chair lifts, and extensive night skiing. Day care is available for infants and up (no strict age limit). There are Mogul Mouse ski lessons for ages three to five, Mogul Mites for ages six to eight, and Junior Beginners for ages eight and up. Snowboarding is available for ages eight and older. Nordic skiing abounds along trails that glide through some breathtaking scenery.

Sun Valley, a mile north of Ketchum on Sun Valley Road, is a year-round resort 154 miles (about three hours) northeast of Boise (or thirty minutes by air from Boise to Hailey, 12 miles south of the resort). In winter, Bald Mountain's 3,400-foot vertical drop is inviting to experts, while kids and beginners favor Dollar/Elkhorn, where the Sun Valley Ski School is located. Kids seventeen and under (one per parent) ski free during selected periods. Non-Alpine devotees enjoy cross-country skiing, snowboarding, and sleigh rides, as well as ice skating. When the snow melts, the area offers tennis, golf, hiking, biking, and white-water rafting. Accommodations range from condos to hotels to resorts to bed-and-breakfast cabins.

The **Elkhorn Youth Activities Center,** P.O. Box 6009, Sun Valley 83353 (208–622–4511 ext. 1014), provides both full- and half-day child care for ages six months to three years, as well as ages three to ten. It may also be possible to arrange for nighttime babysitting. The **Sun Valley Resort Playschool**, Sun Valley Mall behind the Post Office (208–622–2133), offers full-day child care for ages six months to six years. Check with the care givers about after-hours babysitting.

Call the **Sun Valley–Ketchum Chamber Central Reservations** for lodging and activities throughout the area; (208) 726–3423 or (800) 634–3347.

Summer visitors to Sun Valley often head 7 miles north to **Sawtooth National Recreation Area** in the state's Central Rockies, for the alpine lakes, dense forests, and nearly 600 campsites. If you come from Boise, access the area via the Ponderosa Scenic Byway, State Highway 21. At mile #125, stop to see the spectacular views of Stanley Lake Overlook. You'll soon come to the point where this scenic highway converges with State Highway 75 (Sawtooth Scenic Byway) at the town of **Stanley,** headquarters for several Salmon River outfitters. If you stop at the **Stanley Ranger Station** (208–774–3681), pick up a cassette and player that tells you about the sites as you travel south. The tape and recorder may be returned at the **Sawtooth Visitor Information Center** (208–726–8291), just north of Ketchum and Sun Valley on Highway 75 (or pick up the tape at Sawtooth and drop it off at Stanley if you're coming from Sun Valley). The Visitor Center has year-round information on camping, hiking, biking, and campfire programs.

Closer to Boise, the verdant forests surrounding the **Cascade and Payette rivers,** 1½ hours north of Boise via Highway 55 (Payette River Scenic Route), offer more recreation. Outfitters take you down the Payette River, a popular white-water destination (see Outfitters), on half-, full-, or three-day outings.

Desert Dunes

At **Bruneau Dunes State Park,** one hour south of Boise on Highway 51 (208–366–7919), you'll find North America's tallest dune, 470 feet. A 5-mile, self-guided nature trail explains the desert habitat. Stroll in the early morning or late evening, the best times for observing the desert wildlife, and you might see a rabbit dart by or an eagle soar. Get your camera ready; sunrises and sunsets are spectacular. There's a campground and environmental education center with area wildlife and natural history displays.

Hell's Canyon

In a class by itself, **Hell's Canyon National Recreation Area** encompasses more than 650,000 acres. Straddling the Snake River in Idaho and Oregon (two to three hours north of Boise), it features rugged outdoor river country. The gorge is more than a mile deep in some locations, making Hell's Canyon the deepest river gorge on the continent. This is an area of desert slopes, rugged mountain peaks, cool lakes, and clear streams. Cougars, bobcats, elk, deer, mountain goats, and bighorn sheep live within the forests and ridges. The more than 1,000 miles of trails range from easy to difficult, though access roads to trailheads are often narrow, steep, and rocky.

Most people concur that **Heavens Gates Overlook** offers the best view into the canyon from Idaho. To reach this spot, drive a half-day from the south end of Riggins via an extremely steep and winding gravel road, Forest Road 517. A strenuous one-half-mile trail, open from July to September, provides an access to the overlook. A better and easier way to explore the canyon is via an aluminum jet boat or a float trip. More than thirty outfitters offer various trips (see Outfitters), many of them center on a one-mile stretch in Riggins, located in a steep canyon at the confluence of the Salmon and Little Salmon rivers. For more information, contact the **Hells Canyon National Recreation Area**, P.O. Box 832, Riggins 83549; (208) 628–3916.

Outfitters

Idaho has literally hundreds of outfitters that offer adventurous excursions, some of them offering combination trips. For a free directory, contact the **Outfitters and Guides Association**, P.O. Box 95, Boise, Idaho 83701 (208–342–1919); or **Idaho Tourism** (800–473–3543). Here's a sampling.

Boise Tours, P.O. Box 5723, Boise; (208) 342–4796 or (800) 999–5993. They have jet boat trips to Hell's Canyon, overland trips to Snake River Canyon Birds of Prey, Payette River Rafting, and Oregon Trail Expedition.

Two companies that cover Idaho rivers offer special family expeditions along the Lower Salmon: **River Odysseys West (ROW)**, P.O. Box 579, Coeur d'Alene (800–451–6034), and **Outdoor Adventure River Specialists (OARS)**, P.O. Box 67, Angels Camp, California (800–346–6277). Programs are flexible and allow ample time for exploring such shore findings as caves, mines, and waterfalls. Lower Salmon runs glide by otters, eagles, and bighorn sheep. Camp out on sandy beaches where kids wade in shallow water. Age limits vary, though generally the trips are best with ages five and up.

Rocky Mountain River Tours, Dave and Sheila Mills, P.O. Box 2552, Boise, 83701; (208) 345–2400; in summer (208) 756–4808. They offer four-, five-, and six-day white-water raft trips on the Middle Fork of the Salmon River. This river cuts through scenic and rugged areas. The Mills welcome families. When the water is high in early season, the trips are better suited to experienced rafters and teens.

Theater, Music, and the Arts

In season, **Ballet Idaho** (208–343–0556) performs at the Morrison Center of Boise State University (BSU), 1901 University Drive. Look for classic holiday performances such as *The Nutcracker.* The **Boise Philharmonic** (208–344–7849) also plays at the Morrison Center, sometimes accompanied by **Boise Master Chorale** (208–375–2948), which also presents a series of their own concerts. The **Idaho Shakespeare Festival** performs a full summer season, including one contemporary play, in an open-air amphitheater along the Boise River at ParkCenter; call (208) 336–9221 for tickets and information.

Sports

Boise Hawks semiprofessional baseball team plays mid-June through early September at Memorial Stadium, 5600 Glenwood, at the edge of the Fairgrounds; (208) 322–5000.

Shopping

Boise Towne Square Mall, on the west edge of the city, I–84 at Franklin and Cole roads (208–378–4400), has more than 170 specialty shops, larger stores such as J.C. Penney and Sears, plus a fast food court. At **Made in Idaho USA** (208–378–1188), at the mall, browse a majority of products made or grown in Idaho. Downtown shops include **Toycrafters World**, 1020 West Main (208–345–2971), featuring handcrafted toys from around the world, with an emphasis on those made of wood.

SPECIAL EVENTS

Contact the Boise Convention and Visitors Bureau for information on the following or call (800) VISIT–ID.

January: Winter Carnival Week, Sun Valley; Winter Carnival, McCall (about 100 miles north of Boise), nationally acclaimed week-long event with giant ice sculptures and races.

March–April: Drag racing season at Boise's Firebird Raceway.

May–August: Wednesday entertainment, food, and music at Alive After Five, The Grove, downtown pedestrian mall.

June: Idaho Shakespeare Festival through August, Boise. Boise River Festival, four-day event includes River Parade with lit floats and music, Hot Air Balloon Rally, food, a jazz concert, fireworks finale, and Women's Challenge Bicycle Race between Boise and Sun Valley. Old Time Fiddlers' Contest, third full week of June, Weiser, about ninety minutes west of Boise; call (800) 437–1280 for tickets.

July: Fourth celebrations throughout the city parks; Boise Music Festival through end of August.

Boise's famous family-oriented festivals hold something special in store for everyone.
(Courtesy Boise Convention and Visitors Bureau)

August: Western Idaho Fair, Boise, ten-day event.
September: Julia Davis Park Art in the Park displays arts and crafts.
October: Idaho Botanical Gardens' Oktoberfest.
November: Festival of the Trees, Boise Convention Center, four- or five-day event; volunteers decorate then auction off trees, and sell crafts.
December: Festival of the Night Skies, Toy for Tots event, ParkCenter Pond, includes fireworks.

WHERE TO STAY

Boise Visitors Guide has a lodgings listing, including several bed-and-breakfast inns. Here are a few choices for families.

The Owyhee Plaza Hotel, 1109 Main Street; (208) 343–4611, (800) 821–7500—ID, or (800) 233–4611. The hotel has a convenient downtown location, one hundred guest rooms, plus a courtyard swimming pool. Airport shuttle is free.

Marriott Residence Inn, 1401 Lusk Avenue; (208) 344–1200 or (800) 331–3131. It has penthouses with a bedroom and bath on the second floor, a full kitchen, and complimentary breakfast buffet.

Red Lion Inn Downtowner, 1800 Fairview Avenue, and **Red Lion**

Inn Riverside, Twenty-ninth and Chinden streets; (800) 547–8010. Both have outdoor pools, coffee shops, and laundry service.
Idaho Heritage Inn, 109 West Idaho; (208) 342–8066. This five-room bed and breakfast close to downtown offers complimentary newspapers, in-room breakfast, plus bicycles.
Families staying in **Sun Valley** might try the **Idaho Country Inn**, 134 Latego Lane, Sun Valley 82340; (208) 762–1019. This log-and-rock lodge offers such modern amenities as a jacuzzi and rooms with TVs and refrigerators.

WHERE TO EAT

The *Boise Visitors Guide* features a dining guide.
The **Brick Oven Beanery**, 801 Main Street on the Grove (208–342–3456), serves up roasted chicken and crusty bread. **Red Robin Burger and Spirits Emporium**, 267 North Milwaukee (208–323–0023), gets Boise's vote for the best burgers. There's also one on the lake at Park-Center, east on Beacon off Broadway; (208) 344–7471. Parents appreciate the children's menu and outdoor patio. For deep-dish pizza, pasta, sandwiches, and salads—kid pleasers, all—try **Chicago Connection Pizza**, at two locations: 7070 Fairview (208–377–5551) and 3931 Overland (208–344–6838). Sample the Basque cuisine at **Onati**, 3544 Chinden Boulevard (208–343–6464), where specialties include lamb and seafood dishes.
For tasty lunches and yummy desserts, try **Cristina's**, corner of Fifth and Main streets; (208) 385–0133. Pastries, breads, and gourmet coffees are among the treats offered by this bakery, a local favorite.

DAY TRIPS

In addition to the adventurous possibilities above are some shorter, tamer side trips, many of them accessible via the state-designated Scenic Byways. A popular swimming area with Boise residents is **Lucky Park**, 10 miles northeast on Highway 21 (208–344–0240), comprised of Sandy Point, a swimming beach with lifeguards located below the dam, and a picnicking and marina area. Continue on Highway 21 northeast to **Idaho City** (about 45 miles from Boise), a well-preserved Gold Rush town with many structures from the 1860s. Walk along the planked boardwalks that lead past the old jail where criminals carved their names on the wooden walls; Boise Basin Museum, with a collection of Gold Rush artifacts; an old schoolhouse; the Idaho World building; The Boise Basin Mercantile, the state's oldest general store; and other landmarks. The city of 50,000 boasts thirty-nine parks, including the largest, **Tautphaus Park.** Visit the **Greater Idaho Falls Chamber of Commerce, Bureau of Land Management and Forest Service** visitor and information center, 505 Lindsay Boulevard, just off I–15 and Highway 26, or call (208) 392–4290 for more information. One-and-one-half miles away is **Warm Springs Resort,** where you can swim in geothermally heated pools.

The entire Boise Basin is surrounded by **Boise National Forest** (208–364–4100), encompassing more than 2½ million acres including 900 miles of hiking trails, the headwaters of the Boise and Payette rivers, ghost towns, and abandoned mines. Big game roam through large areas of the forest in the summer. Cross-country skiing and snowmobiling are popular winter activities.

FOR MORE INFORMATION

For Boise travel information: **Boise Convention & Visitors Bureau/ Southwest Idaho Travel Association,** 168 North Ninth Street, Suite 200; (208) 344–7777 or (800) 635–5240.

Emergency Numbers
Ambulance, fire, police: 911
Hospital: St. Luke's Regional Medical Center, 190 East Bannock, (208) 386–2222, twenty-four-hour emergency service
Twenty-four-hour pharmacy: The pharmacy in the twenty-four-hour Anderson's Grocery Store (208–344–8660), 1650 West State, has the latest hours in town.
Poison Control Hotline: (800) 632–8000

10
DENVER AND ROCKY MOUNTAIN NATIONAL PARK
Colorado

The Mile High City is a green, tree-lined metropolis that, you may be surprised to know, is not *in* the mountains—but rather on high, rolling plains (flatter than Manhattan) *near* the mountains. With the edge of the Rocky Mountains just 30 miles west, Denver is a year-round recreational mecca—and with a rich selection of museums, plus the largest performing arts complex outside of New York's Lincoln Center, Denver is a cultural mecca as well. Add to that more than 300 days of bright sunshine a year, a summer that's comfortably dry, a winter where the snow comes and goes (the heavy snows usually fall in the mountains and you can frequently golf in January!), and you have the makings for a family vacation paradise.

GETTING THERE

The new **Denver International Airport** (scheduled to open in summer 1994) takes the place of Stapleton International. DIA is the world's largest airport, covering 53 square miles (twice the size of Manhattan Island). This state-of-the-art facility, 24 miles from downtown, has a new baggage-handling system to get baggage to the terminal before passengers arrive. Public buses (see Getting Around) transport passengers into town, and private shuttle services, taxis, and car rentals are available. Be sure to seek out KidsPort, installed by the Denver Children's Museum—a great place for kids of all ages, accompanied by parents, to play before take-off. KidsPort will be opening mid-June 1994 on the airport's mezzanine level and will feature a toddler area and a variety of educational and recreational activities, including an interactive geography computer game to keep older kids (up to early teens) occupied. There's a small admission; children under two years are free.

Amtrak, Union Station, Seventeenth and Wynkoop, (800) USA–RAIL, is a hub on the major east-west routes, with three arrivals and three departures daily. (The basement of the station contains one of the largest model railroads, which can be viewed the last Friday of every month.)

Greyhound (800–231–2222) is at Denver Bus Terminal, Nineteenth and Arapahoe.

Denver is at the crossroads of several major highways: I-70 from the west and east, I–25 from the north and south, and I–76 from the northeast.

GETTING AROUND

Beyond downtown, you will need a car, or public transportation.

Regional Transportation District (RTD) (303–299–6700) provides public transit for metropolitan Denver/Boulder. The RTD Cultural Connection Trolley (303–299–6000) goes to Denver's top cultural attractions (leaving every thirty minutes) for an all-day fare of $1.00. The shuttle buses on the Sixteenth Street Mall are free and take visitors for one mile through the heart of downtown on the pedestrian promenade.

The Ski Train, 555 Seventeenth Street, (303) 296–I–SKI, makes a two-hour journey through the Rockies, through twenty-six tunnels, stopping at the foot of Winter Park's major lifts. The train operates Saturdays and Sundays throughout the ski season.

WHAT TO SEE AND DO

Museums and Historical Sites

The Children's Museum of Denver, 2121 Children's Museum Drive, I–25 and Twenty-third Avenue; (303) 433–7444. Be prepared to have a ball (literally—there are 80,000 balls to dive into) at this top-notch facility. Older kids are invariably drawn to the miniature TV studio, where they read the news or work the camera. The Bank on It area is a superb way for kids to learn that money doesn't grow on trees. At KidSlope, a mountain made out of plastic, kids learn to ski year-round (in fact, every fifth grader in Denver must take a ski lesson here). Admission is free during Friday Night Live, 5:30 to 8:00 P.M. Ask about special workshops and programs.

Take the Denver Trolley along the South Platte River from the museum to the **Forney Transportation Museum**, 1416 Platte Street, (303) 433–3643, where antique and classic automobiles, plus a steam locomotive, are on display.

The **Colorado History Museum**, Thirteenth and Broadway, (303) 866–3682, is a wonderful place to learn about this state's colorful past. Dioramas, photos, artifacts, and exhibits portray the rich western heritage of covered wagons, Indian dances, buffalo hunts, miners, pioneers, fur trappers, and cowboys—stuff that most kids love.

At the **Colorado Railroad Museum**, 17155 W. 44th Avenue, Golden, (303) 279–4591 or (800) 365–6263, train lovers enjoy viewing the more than fifty historic locomotives and cars exhibited on eleven acres. Inside are model railroads and other train memorabilia.

Colorado State Capitol, Broadway and Colfax; (303) 866–2604. While younger kids may be bored stiff at the Colorado State Capitol, older kids should appreciate a visit to this building, modeled after the U.S. Capitol in Washington, D.C. Free tours are offered weekdays from 9:00 A.M. to 3:00 P.M. The fifteenth step on the west side is exactly one mile high. The dome is covered with 200 ounces of 14K gold, but the building's really valuable material is the rare Colorado rose onyx. The entire world's supply was used as wainscoting in the building. The Rotunda offers a splendid panorama.

The **Denver Art Museum**, Fourteenth Avenue and Bannock Street; (303) 640–2793. The largest in a fourteen-state radius, this museum is a work of art itself, resembling a medieval fortress, with twenty-eight sides and ten stories covered with more than a million Corning gray glass tiles that each reflect light in different ways. The museum recently incorporated a number of interactive learning tools during the renovation and reinstallation of all its galleries, making the museum especially appealing to younger visitors. Kids like the Western and American Indian galleries, complete with dugout canoes, totem poles (housed in a two-story atrium), toys and games, and what many consider to be the world's finest examples of Native American art. Try to visit on Saturday, when admission is free. Twice a month, there's a Saturday for Families program.

Many black cowboys helped settle the West as Paul Stewart, founder and curator of the **Black American West Museum**, the Dr. Justina Ford House, 3091 California Street, (303) 292–2566, discovered. At this museum, which contains one of the best collections of western black memorabilia, listen to the oral histories of wranglers, miners, and entrepreneurs. Learn how rodeo star Bill Pickett came to invent the art of "bulldogging" (steer wrestling). Find out about freed slave Clara Brown who traveled to California on a wagon train, became a laundress of miners' shirts, and saved and invested wisely to amass a small fortune, which she used to buy freedom for her friends and relatives in Kentucky.

The **Denver Museum of Miniatures, Dolls and Toys,** 1880 Gaylord Street; (303) 322–3704. There's a delightful assortment of tiny treasures housed in the historic Pearce-McAllister Cottage, an 1899 Colonial revival house. Although the building itself and the period furnishings may bore kids, the upstairs rooms filled with period toys and dollhouses won't. Pick up a "treasure hunt" sheet so your kids can answer the questions and receive a small token from the gift shop. Saturday Art Workshops are held on the first Saturday of each month.

The **Denver Museum of Natural History,** 2001 Colorado Boulevard, City Park; (303) 322–7009. This is the top visitor attraction in town, and this family spot deserves its popularity. The dioramas are especially appealing in the renovated Explore Colorado: From Plains to Peaks Hall, with eleven scenes depicting the state's diverse plants and wildlife. Kids light up discovery boxes in front of each scene to reveal such things as a quail nest with eggs—plus information on how many eggs are laid each year and how many chicks are hatched. Interactive videos explore subjects such as animal families and Colorado weather patterns. The Hall of Life is another winner: Visitors use a magnetic "life card" to activate exhibits and store information on height, weight, blood pressure, and pulse rate. Seventeen of the thirty-eight exhibits (which range from nutrition and fitness to substance abuse) are programmed to encode information on the card. At the end of the tour, visitors receive a printout of their basic health information, fascinating info for kids. At the Navaho Hall there's an authentic hogan (a Navaho dwelling) that shows how Native Americans live.

The Dinosaur and Fossil Mammal Halls are always popular. Here, the state fossil, an original Stegosaurus specimen, is displayed with four other dinosaur skeletons and more than ninety other prehistoric animals. The museum is constructing a new permanent display, slated to open fall 1995, called Prehistoric Journey: New Dinosaur and Fossil Exhibits; it is said to be the nation's most elaborate paleontology exhibit.

Don't leave without visiting the Schlessman Family Earth Sciences Laboratory, where scientists prepare and study fossil specimens, magnified to one hundred times their size so visitors can view them via a live color television monitor. There's also an open storage area where the museum's collection of fossils can be viewed.

Stop for a snack at the restaurant before proceeding on to the IMAX Theater or Gates Planetarium (separate admission for each)—or save them for a separate visit.

United States Mint, West Colfax at Cherokee Street; (303) 844–3582. Don't miss a chance to show your kids how coins are made: more than five billion coins are produced here each year; this is the second largest storehouse of gold bullion in the nation, after Fort Knox. The free tours weekdays from 8:00 A.M. to 3:00 P.M. reveal the fascinating process, from stamping to counting and bagging. Your chances of gaining admission are better if you line up in the morning; if possible try to be in line before 1:30 P.M. Chances are you won't leave without buying a unique coin souvenir (not sold elsewhere) from the gift shop.

Amusement Centers and Parks

Celebrity Sports Center, 888 South Colorado Boulevard; (303) 757–3321. Walt Disney built it so, as you might guess, it's great fun: a huge swimming pool, three water slides, bowling, and more.

Elitch Gardens Amusement Park, 4620 West 38th Avenue; (303) 455–4771. This hundred-year-old park boasts three roller coasters (including the all-wood Twister), a carousel, Kiddieland, live entertainment, and a high dive show. Elitch is planning a move to downtown Denver sometime in 1995 (though it might not be until 1996) and will dismantle the roller coaster board by board and reconstruct it in its new home. The new seventy-acre park will boast formal flower gardens, shops, games, food pavilions, and restaurants along the banks of the South Platte River, as well as twenty-five major rides and entertainment such as gunfights, circus acts, musical revues, and concerts.

Lakeside Amusement Park, I–70 and Sheridan Boulevard; (303) 477–1621. Lakeside is the area's largest, with fifteen kiddie rides, Cyclone Roller Coaster, forty rides, plus a scenic miniature train.

Tiny Town, 6249 South Turkey Creek Road; (303) 790–9393. This teeny, tiny town will tickle tykes, with a steam train ride around one hundred handcrafted miniature structures, including newly added Old West buildings. It's open May through October and decorated with Christmas lights during the holiday season.

Water World, Eighty-eighth Avenue at Pecos Street; (303) 427–SURF. Water World has everything from twisting water slides and oceanlike wave pools for the older crew to Wally World for younger folks. It's open Memorial through Labor Day.

Parks and Zoos

Denver has the largest city park system in the nation, with 205 parks in the city and 20,000 acres of mountain parks. The most prominent is **City Park,** Seventeenth Avenue and Colorado Boulevard. Here you'll find the Museum of Natural History as well as two lakes, picnic sites, playgrounds, playing fields, tennis courts—and the beautifully landscaped **Denver Zoo,** East Twenty-third and Steel Street; (303) 331–4100. The zoo's seventy-three acres house more than 1,300 exotic animals in barless enclosures (imagine staring a Bengal tiger in the eye). A highlight: the Northern Shores exhibit, where polar bears and sea lions can be viewed from glass-walled underwater areas. The zoo, consistently rated as one of the country's top ten, is open every day of the year. The newest addition,

Tropical Discovery, is an entire ecosystem under glass, with exotic venomous snakes, alligators, crocodiles, piranhas, leopards, and anacondas. Another Denver park: **Buffalo Bill's Memorial Museum and Grave,** Top of Lookout Mountain, I-70 exit 256; (303) 526-0747. This famous frontier scout and showman wanted to be buried in Wyoming, but because he died in Denver, he is buried on this site, some twenty minutes west of town. Along with the gravesite are guns, outfits, and posters from his Wild West Show and exhibits on the Pony Express and frontier life. If everyone has taken his or her Dramamine, hold on as you leave the museum for a drive on the curving Lariat Loop Trail to Golden.

Stop and smell the roses at **Denver Botanic Gardens,** 1005 York Street; (303) 331-4000 or 4010 (recorded information). There are also Japanese and Rock Alpine plant gardens and a tropical rain forest along with other exotic species, located both indoors and outdoors on twenty-one lovely acres. Seasonal flower shows are held at this year-round facility. The garden is undergoing a twenty year, $40 million redevelopment and will soon start construction on a Children's Exploration Garden with mazes, a tree house, and interpretive gardens.

Shopping

Downtown at the **Sixteenth Street Mall,** with its pedestrian promenade, you find dozens of shops, outdoor cafés, and plenty of restaurants. Larimer Street, particularly **Larimer Square** (between Fourteenth and Fifteenth streets), is the most interesting area, with art galleries, cafés, and crafts shops reflecting the Victorian flavor of the city's past. Take a horse-drawn carriage ride from here for a trip up the mall or throughout lower downtown (also called LoDo), the old section where Victorian warehouses have been converted into art galleries, discos, pubs, restaurants, and condo lofts.

The 140 upscale stores of **Cherry Creek Mall,** 1000 East First Avenue, (303) 388-3900 or (800) 424-6360, include Saks, Neiman Marcus, and—hold on to your wallets—F.A.O. Schwarz. A number of shops around town sell Native American and southwestern art, jewelry, and furnishings. If you like to hunt for bargains, head to the outdoor **Mile High Flea Market,** (303) 289-4656, held weekends and Wednesdays on eighty paved acres at I-76 and Eighty-eighth Avenue. Along with the hundreds of vendors, there are food stalls and amusement and pony rides for the kids.

Theater, Music, and the Arts

There's always something entertaining going on in Denver—from evening concerts at the Botanic Gardens and the Zoo to big-name tours at the city's two large amphitheaters (**Red Rocks** and **Fiddlers Green**). *The Denver Events Guide,* published biannually by the Convention and

The whole family will have fun on a horse-and-carriage ride along Denver's 16th Street Mall, a mile-long pedestrian plaza lined with shops, departments stores, and outdoor cafés. (Courtesy Denver Metro Convention and Visitors Bureau)

Visitors Bureau, is a comprehensive listing. Tickets for many events can be purchased at the **Ticket Bus** on the Sixteenth Street Mall at Curtis Street.

Cultural events abound at the **Denver Performing Arts Complex** (The PLEX), Fourteenth and Champa Street. Call (303) 893–4100 for tickets and show schedules. Second only to New York's Lincoln Center in capacity, this complex, with 9,000 seats in ten theaters, offers symphony, opera, theater, and dance performances year-round.

Sports

Denver's new National League baseball team, the **Colorado Rockies**, will play their 1994 season in Mile High Stadium before moving to their new baseball-only home, **Coors Field**, in 1995. Purchase tickets by calling (303) ROCKIES (762–5437).

The **NBA Denver Nuggets** play from November to April at the McNichol Sports Arena; call (303) 893–6700. The American Professional Soccer League team, the **Colorado Foxes**, plays at Englewood High School Stadium, 3800 South Logan, from May to August. Call (303) 840–1111 for information. The **NFL Broncos** play at Mile High Stadium, 1700 Federal Boulevard, (303) 433–7466.

SPECIAL EVENTS

Check with the Convention and Visitors Bureau for details on these events:

January: National Western Stock Show and Rodeo, includes Children's Ranchland, junior show and sale, buffalo, goats, and lots more.

March: Powwow brings Native American tribes to the Denver Coliseum.

June: Cherry Blossom Festival, Sakura Square; Juneteeth, celebration commemorating the end of slavery with food and events, parade, open stage, Gospel Extravaganza.

July: Buffalo Bill Days, Golden, with parade, crafts fair, and Wild West Show; Denver Black Arts Festival features African American artists and entertainers in City Park.

Late August–Early September: Colorado State Fair, the state's largest single event.

September: Octoberfest, Larimer Square.

WHERE TO STAY

A listing of accommodations, ranging from bed-and-breakfast inns to all-suite hotels, can be found in the *Official Visitor's Guide.* Three packages designed by the Convention Bureau feature discounted hotel rooms, tickets, and car rentals; call (800) 489–4888. **Bed and Breakfast—Rocky Mountains,** 639 Grant Street, 80203, (303) 860–8415, is a free reservation service for inns and home stays throughout the state.

Downtown hotels include a number of well-known chains. The all-suite **Residence Inn by Marriott,** 2777 Zuni, (303) 458–5318, offers free breakfast daily and free light dinner and cocktails on weekdays. **Embassy Suites Hotel and Athletic Club** at Denver Place, 1881 Curtis, (303) 297–8888 or (800) 733–3366, also offers complimentary breakfast and cocktails. **The Hyatt Regency Denver,** 1750 Welton Street, (303) 295–1234 or (800) 233–1234, has an outdoor pool, jogging track, and tennis courts. **The Westin Hotel,** 1692 Laurence Street, (303) 572–9100 or (800) 228–3000, offers large rooms and heated indoor and outdoor pools. A bargain downtown, **Comfort Inn-Downtown,** Seventeenth Street and Tremont, (303) 296–0400 or (800) 4-CHOICE, was once part of Brown Palace, the city's Victorian landmark, and shares the hotel's distinctive atrium lobby. Complimentary breakfast is included. The **Westin's Tabor Center,** 1672 Lawrence Street, Denver, Colorado 80202, (303) 572–9100 or (800) 228–3000, offers the new Westin Kids Club amenities. These include child-friendly rooms, children's sports bottle or tippy cup upon check-in, as well as a safety kit with a night light, Band-Aids, and emergency phone numbers. Rooms feature bath toys and bath products for kids, and parents can request—at no charge—jogging strollers, potty seats, bicycle seats, and step stools. Restaurants and room service also feature children's menus.

WHERE TO EAT

Denver's *Official Visitor's Guide* offers a descriptive listing of restaurants. Don't be surprised if you find buffalo steaks on the menu: The city, considered the buffalo capital of the U.S., serves more of the meat (said to be lower in fat, calories, and cholesterol than beef) than any other city. A restaurant, **Denver Buffalo Company**, 1109 Lincoln Street (three blocks from the State Capitol), (303) 832–0880, serves their own ranch-raised buffalo along with seafood, poultry, pasta, and other dishes. The complex also has a trading post and art gallery.

For something completely different, take the kids to **Casa Bonita**, 6715 West Colfax (at Pierce); (303) 232–5115. This huge facility seats 1,200 and serves Mexican and American food in a Mexican village setting, complete with strolling mariachis, high divers, gunfights—and a volcano.

DAY TRIPS

Colorado is ski country, and Denver is a fairly short drive from a variety of top notch areas. Winter Park, about 70 miles northwest of Denver, is a popular ski destination. (The Ski Train, detailed in Getting Around, delivers skiers right to the base of the mountain.) Winter Park (303–726–5514 or 800–453–2525) features more than 130 trails of diverse terrain.

For parents who want to catch up with their kids' ski skills, and for kids who want to learn, Winter Park offers an excellent kids' ski school and special workshops. Discovery Park, with 20 acres of trails, terrain gardens, gentle slopes, and three chairlifts, gives even the most skittish beginner enough space to learn. In addition, Winter Park has a nursery for infants two months and up and a nonski program for ages through five. Most kids ages three and four enjoy the ski-and-play programs on their own little "mountain." Older kids and teens perfect skills in day-long kids' classes.

In Summit County, ninety minutes west of downtown Denver, there are several ski areas, all with goods kids ski programs: Keystone Resort/Arapahoe Basin (303–468–2316 or 800–222–0188), Copper Mountain (303–968–2882 or 800–458–8386), and Breckenridge (303–453–5000 or 800–800–BREC). (For summer vacationers, golf, tennis, horseback riding, mountain biking, and sailing, on nearby Lake Dillon, are the main attractions.)

Vail/Beaver Creek (303–949–5750 or 800–622–3131) is 100 miles west of town. For details on area ski resorts, contact Colorado Ski Country at its airport booth or in town at 1560 Broadway, Suite 1440, Denver 80202; (303) 837–0793.

Denver Convention Bureau's Ski Lift Line, (800) 489–4888, can arrange transportation from your hotel to the lifts, lift tickets at ten area resorts and ski equipment rental (including clothes, if you need them).

FOR MORE INFORMATION

The Denver Visitor Information Center, (303) 892–1112, 225 West Colfax (across the street from the U.S. Mint), offers more than 500 free brochures and maps. Wheelchair Getaways of Colorado, (303) 674–1498 or (800) 238–6920, rents accessible full-size luxury vans by the day, week, or month.

Emergency Numbers
Ambulance, fire, police: 911
Poison Control: (800) 332–2073
Pharmacy: Clay Drug, 9297 Federal Boulevard, (303) 426–8901, is open
    until midnight.
Hospital: Saint Joseph Hospital, 1835 Franklin Street; (303) 837–7240

11
GRAND TETON NATIONAL PARK AND JACKSON
Wyoming

Jagged, snow-capped, and glistening in the sun, Grand Teton's mountain peaks, rising as high as 13,770 feet, fulfill the vision of the American West as both rugged and beautiful. The Gros Ventre and Shoshoni tribes called the 40-mile range *Teewinot*, a word meaning "many pinnacles." The mountains ascend sharply on the park's western side, above mirror-like glacial lakes and a deeply forested valley. Grand Teton National Park, stretching for 310,000 acres across fields, mountains, and lakes and cut through by a river, is often bypassed on the way to the more famous, and more crowded, Yellowstone National Park to the north.

But don't pass this beauty by. While sharing much of Yellowstone's larger-than-life scenery, Grand Teton is less crowded and less well-known. As a result, on a visit here, families leave the throngs behind to hike along often quiet trails, gently float down the Snake River, canoe on pristine lakes, and enjoy the frequent sightings of moose, deer, and elk.

GETTING THERE

The **Jackson Hole Airport**, 1250 East Airport Road (307–733–7682), hosts about ten daily flights from connecting Salt Lake City and Denver. The **Grand Teton Lodge Company**, Box 240, Moran 83013 (307–733–2811), offers a shuttle from the airport to Jackson Lake Lodge. Among the taxicab companies are **Caribou Cab** (307–733–2888) and **Tumbleweed Taxi** (307–739–7167).

Autumn is a magical time among the majestic Grand Tetons. (Courtesy Wyoming Travel Commission)

A car is important in order to easily get around the park at your own pace. Among the airport rental car companies: **Avis** (307–733–3422 or 800–331–1212), **Budget** (307–733–2206 or 800–268–8900), and **Hertz** (307–733–2272 or 800–654–3131). Note: Reserve a rental car well in advance. In tourist season cars become scarce, and you don't want to be stranded without one.

When driving to the Grand Teton National Park from the south, pass through Jackson and continue north on U.S. 26/89/191, a highway that is open year-round, covers the length of the park, and continues to Yellowstone. From the east enter the park at Moran Junction, on U.S. 26/287.

Public transportation is minimal. **Greyhound** services Rock Springs, Wyoming (nearly 200 miles away); (307) 362–2931. They also go to Idaho Falls in neighboring Idaho, about one hundred miles from Grand Teton; (208) 522–0912. The nearest **Amtrak** station is in Pocatello, Idaho, about 150 miles away from the park.

GETTING AROUND

A car is a must. If you want to tour the park by mountain bike or canoe, rent these in Moose, just outside the eastern park entrance.

WHAT TO SEE AND DO

Getting Oriented

Your first venture should be to the **Moose Visitor Center**, Drawer 170, Moose, Wyoming 83012; (307) 739–3300. It's 13 miles north of Jackson Hole near the park's southern border. Talk to the rangers about trails, sites, and activities that appeal to your family. Pick up a free map, songbird guide, and the *Teewinot*, the park newsletter. The newsletter lists hikes, lodgings, and naturalist programs (including summer campfire programs and full-moon walks), ranger-led hikes, and children's programs. Be sure to obtain a copy of the *Young Naturalist*, a brochure that sparks kids' interest with park information, nature questions, and a list of activities necessary to earn a Young Naturalist souvenir badge. (While kids must earn this, parents must pay a nominal fee for this award.)

Browse the Visitor's Center bookstore. *Short Hikes and Easy Walks in Grand Teton National Park*, available for a small fee, is a great resource as it offers suggestions to families, especially those with small children, and those who want to experience the wilderness without the hard work. The park's department also has handouts with hiking information. *Short Trails* lists the less strenuous and time-consuming walks that take anywhere from thirty minutes to four hours. *Day Hikes* lists more involved and often more strenuous treks that could keep you on the move from four to fourteen hours.

Grand Teton's many wonderful recreational pleasures—from easy scenic drives to simple hikes, boat rides, or peaceful canoeing to difficult backpacking treks—suit families with diverse outdoor temperaments.

Scenic Drives

If pressed for time on this family push, you could just drive through the park by entering at Moose and continuing north along **Teton Park Road**. This windy stretch continues for about 50 miles, becoming U.S. 287/191/89 near the park's northern border, as the road heads into Yellowstone. Some scenic places to stretch your legs: about 8 miles north at **Cottonwood Creek** and **Lupine Meadows**. If your visit can only be brief but does allow for time out of the car—a necessity—continue north to pristine **Jenny Lake** where a brief boat ride and a short walk lead to a picnic spot by a waterfall. Be aware of the schedule for the return boat rides; after the last trip, you must either spend the night or take a long hike back, about 2½ hours (see the hiking section later in this chapter).

Back on Teton Park Road, the trip north leads you by the 7,593-foot **Signal Mountain** and **Jackson Lake**, an impressive stretch of clear waters with wooded shores. At **Colter Bay Visitor Center**, take time to check out the educational programs and to browse in the **Indian Arts Museum**, where Native American artists demonstrate their crafts daily from June through early September.

Hiking and Canoeing: the Southern Park

One of the most popular hikes is the 2½-mile trek to **Hidden Falls**, a cascade of water on the south shore of Jenny Lake. But an easier way to reach these falls —especially if you have young children—is to board the ten-minute shuttle boat ride across Jenny Lake. From the dock follow the sound of rushing water about ¼ mile to **Inspiration Point**, 400 feet above Jenny Lake, for a scenic view. Continue along the trail for .2 mile to the falls. This spot may be crowded, but for solitude continue to hike 3½ miles along level ground to the glacier-carved boulders of **Cascade Canyon**, habitat of the yellow-bellied marmot and golden-mantled ground squirrel. You're sure to see some of these scurrying around as you admire the wildflowers that bloom throughout the summer.

Just north of Jenny Lake lie two nearly connected bodies of water: **String Lake** and **Leigh Lake** both offer easy hikes, easy canoeing, and scenic views. The **String Lake Trail** circles this body of water for an easy 3½ miles (allow about three hours), and the **Leigh Lake Trail** (park at the String Lake parking lot) leads 2 miles (about one hour) to the lake's south shore. For some extra fun combine a canoe and hiking trip. Put in your canoe at String Lake and paddle to the northern edge; then portage about 100 yards to Leigh Lake. Paddle along this pristine lake, pausing to hike along the shores. You can picnic at almost any spot along this trail and be sitting pretty with a scenic view of 12,605-foot **Mount Moran**, a peak partially covered by Skillet Glacier. Let your kids dangle their toes in the lake and look for deer in the woods.

Note: You can rent canoes from **Dornans' Moose Enterprises**, 10 Moose Street (307–733–2522), as well as from several park concessions. Dornans' also sells groceries and sandwiches.

Hiking and Canoeing: the Northern Park

Jackson Lake, nearly 20 miles long and fed by the Snake River, dominates the northern section of the park. This lake, more heavily forested and generally somewhat quieter than the lakes in the southern section, affords easy access to canoe rentals at **Signal Mountain Marina** on Jackson Lake; (307) 733–5470.

The rangers at the nearby **Colter Bay Visitor Center** offer helpful information and nature programs, including slide shows on such local denizens as coyote and bald eagles. To see live animals head out along the nearby **Hermitage Point Trail**, which begins at the visitor center and loops for 3 miles around **Swan Lake** and **Heron Pond** through pine forests, meadows, wetlands, and lakes. Because this path is less traveled, you are likely to catch sight of beaver, otter, elk, and moose, and listen for the hornlike sounds of the hard-to-find trumpeter swans that can sometimes be spotted here. Be careful of the turnoffs. A round-trip hike of the entire 8.8-mile Hermitage Point trail takes about four hours. For very young children and bird lovers, the **Lunchtree Hill Trail**, a half-mile hike beginning at Jackson Lake Lodge, winds through marshy meadows that are home to songbirds and hummingbirds. For a moderate hike that rewards you with a climb through woods to a summit with a panoramic view, opt for the **Grand View Point Trail**, a 2.2-mile, two-hour round-trip trek that pleases older children (and parents too).

Swimming

Swimming is allowed in **Jenny**, **Leigh**, and **String** lakes, but with these glacier-fed lakes' waters hovering at about 54 degrees Fahrenheit, only those impervious to cold go for the plunge. Most people settle for toe dangling. For the intrepid, String Lake offers the shallowest water, and Leigh Lake invites with quartz sand and a beautiful view. While fishing is allowed on **Bradley** and **Taggert** lakes, as well as the **Snake River**, swimming is not.

River Float Trips and Fishing Trips

A float trip down the Snake River gently weaves you through the spectacular landscape, providing ample opportunity for wildlife viewing. Especially nice are the dinner trips with **Barker-Ewing Float Trips**; (800) 365–1800. These leave the Moose Visitor Center at 6:00 P.M. for a 10-mile drive upstream. Your float downstream on a twelve-person raft takes about three hours (dress warmly). While no wildlife sightings are guaranteed, you're more likely to see animals at dusk than during the day. Often great blue herons dance above the water, and eagles nest in the tall pines. Look sharply and you might even see a moose. After 5 miles the guides pull in to an encampment where you dine and watch the sun set over the Teton peaks. Other companies offering float trips include **Grand Teton Lodge Co. Float Trips** (307–543–2811) and **Triangle X Float Trips** (307–733–5500), which offers trips with overnight accommodations in a tepee.

If you're angling to do some fishing, call **Snake River Fishing and Float Trips** (800–325–8605), which has trips down this scenic river. For a listing of other outfitters and the best fishing sites, contact **Wyoming Game and Fish**; (800) 423–4113.

Mountain Biking

The hearty can take to their fat wheels for a scenic foray through the park. Rent some two-wheelers from **Mountain Bike Outfitters**, P.O. Box 303, Moose 83012; (307) 733–3314. But be careful; don't pedal along the often crowded park roads. Instead, be safe and bike along a designated mountain trail.

Horseback Riding

For horseback riding, the area east of Jackson Lake is a good place. At the **Jackson Lake Lodge Corral**, Jackson Lake (307–543–2811), saddle-up for a guided breakfast or evening excursion. The **Grand Teton Lodge Company** (307–543–2811) operates one- and two-hour treks for riders ages eight and up. **Teton Trail Rides, Inc.**, Jenny Lake (307–733–2108), has similar hour-long trips as well as overnight pack trips. With **Wilderness Trails Outfitters' Bedroll and Breakfast** (307–733–7860) sleep under the stars (or in a tent) after a ride to their base camp and a cookout.

Hot-Air Ballooning

Less demanding, but equally pretty, is an aerial journey with **Rainbow Balloon Flights, Inc.** (307–733–0470), which has you floating over the Snake River and Jackson Valley.

Jackson Attractions

On this vacation allow some time to explore **Jackson**, sometimes called **Jackson Hole**, a cowboy town 13 miles south of Grand Teton National Park's Moose headquarters. Jackson's small-town, Old West flair and friendliness intrigue kids. With little kids, hop aboard the **stage-coach**, at the corner of the town square next to the ticket booth, for a short spin through town.

You'll notice right away that the town square differs from most local parks as it's adorned at all four corners with arches made of real elk antlers collected by the local boy scouts who gather these after the local herd sheds them. Be around this square in the summer on a Monday through Saturday night at 6:30 P.M. when the town's good guys shoot it out with the bad guys, a special treat for elementary school kids. (Warn little ones of the guns' noise, and assure everyone of their safety. No real bullets are fired.)

There's more rough riding at the **Jackson Hole Summer Rodeo**, Rodeo Grounds, Snow King Avenue (307–733–2805), every Wednesday and Saturday evening through Labor Day. Kids love the steer roping, barrel racing, and quick horsemanship.

The **National Wildlife Art Museum**, 110 North Center Street, P.O. Box 2984 (307–733–5771), features 250 works by well-known painters and sculptors, plus a private collection of big game wildlife art. The **Jackson Hole Museum**, 105 North Glenwood Street (307–733–9605), focuses on Jackson's history with archaeological artifacts, fur trade exhibits, as well as mounted game heads (which often scare little kids and annoy environmentally concerned adults).

Golf. Jackson Hole sports two championship golf courses, both with scenic views: The **Jackson Hole Golf and Tennis Club**, P.O. Box 250, Moran 83013 (307–543–2811—winter and 307–733–3111—summer); and the **Teton Pines Golf Club** (307–733–1733). Apparently the high altitude (6,209 feet above sea level) carries golf balls 10 percent farther than at sea level. For younger kids **Alpine Golf**, Snow King Resort (307–733–7680), offers eighteen holes of miniature golf.

Scenic Mountain Views. Get a bird's eye view of the summer and fall scenery even if you don't ski by riding the **Snow King Scenic Chairlift**, Snow King Resort; (307) 733–5200 (see Skiing). If you hike up, the ride down is free. **Teton Village's Aerial Tram**, Teton Village 83025 (307–733–2292), offers splendid views as well.

Winter Fun
Alpine (Downhill) Skiing
The Jackson Hole area offers excellent skiing at several facilities. The slopes at **Snow King Ski Resort** (307–733–5200), Wyoming's original ski area, nearly swoop down into town. Open to skiers from mid-December to April, with night skiing available Wednesday to Saturday, Snow King has a 1,571-foot vertical drop and lots of beginner and intermediate trails.

Outside of town, skiers have both **Grand Targhee Ski Resort** (800–TARGHEE) and **Jackson Hole Ski Area**, Box 290, Teton Village; ski area (307) 733–2292. On the sunny west side of the Teton mountains is **the Grand Targhee Ski Resort**, Box Ski, Alta, Wyoming, via Driggs, Idaho 83422; (307) 353–2300 or (800) TARGHEE. It offers 3,000 acres of terrain, about 70 percent of it intermediate.

Grand Targhee has nursery facilities for tots six months to seven years. Children age three can have private lessons, while ages five to seven take a learn-and-play program. The ski school also has ski programs for ages five through twelve. Children five and under always ski free, and children twelve and under generally ski free when one adult purchases a three-day or more lodging package.

Skier and family travel expert, Dorothy Jordon, in *Skiing With Children: An Information Guide for Families USA/Canada* available from Travel With Your Children, 45 West Eighteenth Street, N.Y., N.Y. 10011 (212–206–0688), notes Grand Targhee's layout is a plus for skiing families. "It's virtually impossible for a child to get lost while skiing since terrain and trails funnel into the base area," says Jordon. "It's a real advantage and mind easer for parents when older kids go skiing alone."

The **Jackson Hole Ski Resort** (307–733–2292 or 800–443–6931) may be the area's most well-known area. Twelve miles from Jackson, located at Teton Village, P.O. Box 290 83025, this ski area boasts a 4,139-foot vertical rise, among the steepest in the United States. Jackson Hole, while offering some top-notch, difficult terrain, also has more than 22 miles of groomed beginner and intermediate trails. Rendezvous Mountain is a challenge; most families start and even keep to the less demanding trails on Apres Vous.

At the **Jackson Hole Ski School** classes are available for adults, kids ages three to five, and six to fourteen. A nursery is available for ages two months to eighteen months, and child care is provided for ages nineteen months to five years. Children six and under ski free.

Teens aren't forgotten either with Teenage Clinics, for ages thirteen to seventeen, at holidays—Christmas, Presidents Weekend, and spring break—so these intermediate skiers can perfect their form while hanging out and having fun.

Nordic (Cross-Country) Skiing

For those who like the easy, gliding pace of cross-country skiing, the **Jackson Hole Ski School Nordic Center**, P.O. Box 290, Teton Village 83025, (307) 733–2292, rents cross-country skis and offers several kilometers of groomed trails. A variety of cross-country programs are offered for children and families.

The **Grand Targhee Nordic Center**, Box SKI, Alta, (307) 353–2300 or (800) TARGHEE, has 12 kilometers of groomed trails. The **Teton Pines Nordic Ski Center**, next to the J.H. Racquet Club, (307) 733–2292, features between ten and thirteen kilometers of trails plus lessons for children and adults as well as day-care facilities and rentals. The **Spring Creek Nordic Center**, Box 3154, (307) 733–8833, offers fourteen kilometers of trails that wind through a nature reserve making it likely you'll spot some deer, elk, maybe even moose. Rentals and lessons are available.

In **Grand Teton National Park**, check with the rangers for trail conditions, but generally when there's snow, favorite cross-country trails include the beginner's 3-mile **Swan Lake-Heron Pond Loop**, near the Colter Bay Visitor Center, and the longer 9-mile **Jenny Lake Trail**.

Off-the-Slopes Winter Recreation

Nonskiers and those who want a break from the moguls have plenty of choices. At the **National Elk Refuge** east of Jackson, thousands of elk come to feed during the winter. A sleigh ride through the refuge with **National Elk Refuge Horse Drawn Sleigh Rides**, Box C, Jackson 83001, (307) 733–9212, is available from mid-December through April. The whole family, even little ones, will like seeing these majestic animals close-up.

For more wildlife head out on a guided safari with naturalists from the **Great Plains Wildlife Institute**, Box 7580, 83001; (307) 733–2623. Use the van's telescopes and binoculars for up-close looks at bighorn sheep, moose, and bald eagles. Full-day tours include the extra fun of lunch at a local ranch plus a snowshoe nature walk. Half-day tours are offered too. Call ahead to book.

For a special treat you and the kids are not likely to forget, take a **dog sled** trek. This is a cozy and easy way to get into the backcountry. The huskies do the work while you savor the woodland peace and the wildlife. For this tour all you'll hear are the wind in the trees, the swoosh of the sled, and the panting of the dogs. Among the area's companies, **Jackson Hole Iditarod Sled Dog Tours**, Box 1940, 83001 (307–733–7388), is led by Frank Teasley, a professional musher and veteran of Alaska's grueling Iditarod. His guided runs take you east to Granite Hot Springs, past wildlife trails and to a 108-degree hot springs soak (wear a suit), through Grand Teton National Park, or through the Gros Ventre Wilderness. **Washakie Outfitting** (307–733–3602) is another choice.

Ask about the size of the sled. For most runs two smaller kids or one adult and one small child can usually snuggle in the sled, while another adult, if the guides permit, can stand on the back of the sled. Ask how many sleds will be required for your group.

The south entrance to **Yellowstone National Park** (see chapter Yellowstone National Park) is about two hours away. In winter, most of the roads are closed to public vehicles, but the animals are out. With young children opt for a tour by heated park snowcoach (a bus equipped for the deep snow). Call **TW Recreational Services, Inc.** (307–344–7311).

With teens or preteens try a snowmobile run from Yellowstone's south entrance to Old Faithful. Pass by bison and elk, track coyotes, and watch out for the mule deer as you roar up to this steamy geyser surrounded by snow—quite a sight in winter.

Outfitters include: **Rocky Mountain Snowmobile Tours**, (307) 733–2237 or (800) 637–7147; **Flagg Ranch Village**, (307) 543–2861 or (800) 443–2311; **Heart Six Snowmobile Tours**, (307) 739–9477 or 543–2477; and **Jackson Hole Snowmobile Tours**, (307) 733–6850 or (800) 633–1733.

Theater and the Arts

Yes, Jackson has theater, but the fare tends to be good old western family goings-on. From Memorial Day through Labor Day, **Dirty Jack's Wild West Theatre**, north of the Town Square on Cache (307–733–4775), puts on slapstick cowboy comedy. Check out the musical comedy at the **Jackson Hole Playhouse**, Deloney Street between Millward and Glenwood streets; (307) 733–6994. The **Pink Garter Theatre**, P.O.Box 3210 (307–733–3670), at times, also sports what they call "elegant and rowdy family fun."

Shopping

Boutiques, western wear shops, and more than forty art galleries, specializing in western landscapes and paintings of cowboys and Native

Americans, ring the town square and adorn the side streets. Pop in and out of the galleries until you find one that appeals to you; you won't have a problem. Other good bets: **Trailside America**, Town Square and Center Street, Drawer 1149 (307–733–3186); and **Gallery of the West**, Chet's Way, upstairs King and Broadway streets (307–733–9211). Many stores offer Native American jewelry and crafts. Know what you're buying and comparison shop. The **Valley Bookstore**, Gaslight Alley, Town Square (307–733–4533), features a good selection of maps, mountaineering books, field guides, and children's books.

SPECIAL EVENTS

Check with the Visitors Bureau for more specific information about these events in the Grand Teton and Jackson areas.

April: The Pole-Pedal-Paddle, a ski-cycle-canoe relay race starts at Jackson Hole and finishes at the Snake River.

May: The Elk Antler Auction, Jackson town square; Old West Days with Native American dancing, cowboy poetry, and mountain-man rendezvous.

June–September: Wednesdays and Saturdays see the Jackson Hole Summer Rodeo near downtown Jackson.

July–August: Nightly concerts at the famed Grand Teton Music Festival, Teton Village.

August: Targhee Bluegrass Festival with musicians from the Rocky Mountain region, children's entertainment, and crafts.

September: Jackson Hole Arts Festival of gallery shows, artist's workshops, and dance.

October: Quilting in the Tetons, exhibits and workshops.

December–April: Ski races for amateurs.

WHERE TO STAY

Lodging is limited within Grand Teton but widely available in nearby Jackson. Within the park, one of the best lodges for families is **Signal Mountain Lodge**, Box 50, Moran; (307) 543–2381. They offer lakefront cabins, apartments, and motel units. **Jackson Lake Lodge**, Box 240, Moran, is also lakefront and a good family choice with motel-style units; (800) 628–9988. **Colter Bay Village**, Box 240, Moran (307–543–2855), rents log cabins.

Grand Teton National Park has five campgrounds. **Jenny Lake**, with only forty-nine sites, is the most popular; this campground tends to fill before 8:00 A.M., so arrive early. Another popular spot is **Lizard Lake** with sixty sites; this tends to fill by 2:00 P.M.

Outside the park grounds there are several facilities. **Snake River KOA**, 12 miles south of Jackson Highway 89–191, Box 14A Star Route (307–733–7078), features showers and also arranges horseback riding and float trip departures. Trailers and tents are welcome. For familiar chain lodgings, try **Best Western Executive Inn Motel**, P.O. Box 1101, in Jackson (307–733–4340 or 800–528–1234); or **Best Western Inn at Jackson Hole**, in Teton Village (307–733–2311 or 800–842–7666). **Days Inn**, which offers free continental breakfast, is a mile south of downtown Jackson, 1280 West Broadway; (307) 739–9010, (800) 833–5343, or (800) 325–2525.

In Jackson Hole the **Wildflower Inn** (307–733–4710), a bed and breakfast 10 miles from the park's south entrance, welcomes families. This hand-hewn log home sports pleasing country decor, a glass-enclosed hot tub, and friendly hosts. Stay here for a real western welcome. For additional bed-and-breakfast options, call **Bed and Breakfasts Western Adventure**, a reservation service, P.O. Box 20972, Billings, Montana 59104; (406) 259–7993.

Another option is **Teton Village**, Teton Village Property Management, Teton Village; (307) 733–4610 or (800) 443–6840. Twelve miles northwest of Jackson on Wyoming 390, they offer 125 condominiums spread out at the base of 10,536-foot Rendezvous Peak, with easy access to the Jackson Hole Ski Area (described earlier). Besides condominiums, Teton Village has other lodgings, including the **Inn at Jackson Hole**, P.O. Box 348; (307) 733–2311. Twenty-nine of the seventy-six units have cooking facilities.

In summer Teton Village sports a good children's recreational program, **Cowboy Kids Summer Camp**, P.O. Box 290, Teton Village 83025; (307) 739–2691. Open from mid-June through Labor Day, it keeps kids ages four through ten busy with hiking, tram rides, nature programs, field trips, and barbecues from 8:00 A.M. to 5:00 P.M. Kids bring their own lunch, but snacks are provided. Visitors and locals can take advantage of this program because no minimum number of days is required, but do reserve in advance.

Snow King Resort, P.O. Box SKI, Jackson 83001 (307–733–5200 or 800–522–5464), has hotel rooms, suites, and condominiums. For more Jackson Hole accommodations, call **Jackson Hole Central Reservations**, Box 510, Teton Village 83025; (307) 733–4005 or (800) 443–6931.

Another ski resort that makes an ideal summer spot for families, especially those with tots, is **Grand Targhee**, about an hour's drive from Grand Teton National Park, Box Ski, Alta 83422; (307) 353–2300 or (800) TARGHEE. The Babies Club offers child care for little ones, and the Kids Club Day Camp has activities for ages four to ten from 9:00 A.M.

to 5:00 P.M. Although the weekly **Targhee Institute Science Explorers** program for grades four through seven fills up with locals, check to see if space is available for your visit. Grand Targhee's accommodations include motels and condominiums.

Spring Creek Resort Hotel & Conference Center, Box 3154, Spring Gulch Road, (307) 733–8833 or (800) 443–6139, is situated on a 1,000-acre nature preserve atop a butte. This casually upscale resort is both family friendly and rated four-diamond from AAA. With a pool, studio rooms and condominiums, great views and some of the area's best dining, Spring Creek is a treat. Kids especially like looking out the dining room windows to count the wildlife that roams by. The resort also provides transportation to the ski areas as well as its own cross-country center. In summer the resort can arrange day forays from white-water rafting to hiking and horseback riding.

Go western with a dude ranch stay. The **Triangle X Ranch,** P.O. Box 120T, Moose 83012 (307–733–2183), is a **dude ranch** complete with nature hikes, scenic float trips, western dancing, and cookouts. Winter activities include cross-country skiing and wildlife viewing. **Lost Creek Ranch,** 25 miles northeast of Jackson, P.O. Box 95, Moose 83012 (307–733–3435), has two-bedroom cabins, outdoor heated pool, tennis court, and a children's program. Ride the range or head off to a secluded fishing spot. **R Lazy S Ranch,** a mile north of Teton Village, P.O. Box 308, Teton Village 83025 (307–733–2655), has twelve cabins and separate riding programs for adults and kids over six, as well as pack trips, hikes, and boating.

WHERE TO EAT

Before setting out to explore the park, stock up at **Dornans' Deli,** 10 Moose Street (307–733–2415), with muffins, sandwiches, and drinks, or sit down at an outdoor picnic table and enjoy sandwiches and a cup of homemade soup as you gaze over the Teton peaks. In the park, take a meal break at the **Jackson Lake Lodge Pioneer Grill,** Jackson Lake Lodge; (307) 543–2811.

Jackson, like any town that swells in season with tourists, serves up a variety of eateries. The tourist map of town lists most of the restaurants, including the familiar fast food places just like the ones back home.

For some western pizzazz with your plateful of baked beef and chicken, go to **the Bar J Chuckwagon Supper and Original Western Show,** off Wyoming 390; (307) 733–3370. After your meal, go country with a medley of cowboy singing, poetry, foot stompin' fiddle playing, and dancing. In town, **Bubba's Bar-B-Que,** 515 West Broadway (307–733–2288), dishes up moderately priced ribs, chicken wings, and a salad bar. In winter go to dinner by horse-drawn sleigh with the **Bar-T-Five Outfitters**, P.O. Box 2140, Jackson 83001; (307) 733–5386. Layer-up for this moonlight-and-stars ride to a pioneer cabin for barbecue and chicken followed by foot stompin fun with the Bar-T-Five Singin' Cowboys.

DAY TRIPS

For more river adventures, contact **Barker-Ewing River Trips**, 45 West Broadway, Box 3032B, Jackson 83001; (307) 733–1000 or (800) 448–4202. They offer a white-water overnight raft trip down the Snake River, on a section that is scenic but not in the Grand Teton National Park. Minimum age is six. This trip is a delight, but remember to dress warmly and bring rain gear and gloves just in case. (You're not in Kansas anymore.)

Even with little tots you can recreate the pioneer days with **wagon train trips** lasting two to six days. Families ride in renovated wagons that have cushions to soften the bounce (an amenity not available to our stalwart pioneers). You can also ride horseback alongside. The trips include campfire cookouts and, with some outfitters, staged "Indian" attacks just to simulate the frontier fears and create some excitement. Among the outfitters: **Wagons West**, Peterson-Madsen-Taylor Outfitters, P.O. Box 1156A, Afton 83110; (307) 886–9693 or (800) 447–4711.

FOR MORE INFORMATION

The **Moose Visitor Center** (307–733–2880), 12 miles north of Jackson Hole, is at the park's southern end. **Colter Bay Visitor Center**, near Jackson Lake (307–543–2467), is in the north area of the park. **Grand Teton National Park**, Drawer 170, Moose, Wyoming 83012. **Wyoming Division of Tourism**, I–25 at College Drive, Cheyenne, Wyoming 82002; (307) 777–7777 or (800) 225–5996. **Wyoming State Museums and Historic Sites**, 2301 Central, Barrett Building, Cheyenne 82002; (307) 777–7014. **Wyoming Recreation Commission**, 122 West Street, Herschler Building, 2 West, Cheyenne 82002; (307) 777–7695.

For a *Jackson Hole Vacation Planner*, call (800) 782–0011. **Jackson Hole Visitors Council**, P.O. Box 982, Jackson 83001; (800) 782–0011. **Jackson Chamber of Commerce**; (307) 733–3316. **Jackson Hole Visitors Council**, P.O. Box 982, Jackson 83001; (800) 782–0011. **Weather** and **road** conditions, (307) 733–2220.

Before your trip obtain a copy of the sixteen-page *The Kids Guide to Jackson Hole*, available from Nancy Brumsted and Jan Segerstrom, Teton

County Schools, P.O. Box 568, Jackson County 83001. The guide, written by local school children, gives other kids inside tips.

Emergency Numbers
Ambulance, fire, police: 911
Local sheriff: (307) 733–4052
Local police: (307) 733–1430
Local fire department: (307) 733–2331
Hospital: St. John's Hospital, 625 East Broadway in Jackson; (307) 733–3636
Twenty-four-hour pharmacy: Albertson's Grocery Store, 520 West Broadway; (307) 733–9222
Poison Control Hotline: (800) 422–2704

12 and 13
YELLOWSTONE NATIONAL PARK, CODY, AND BIG HORN NATIONAL FOREST
Wyoming

No family member will ever be bored in a national park as spectacular as **Yellowstone**. This important and impressive geothermal region continues to display some of the powerful forces deep within the earth. Old Faithful erupts spraying steam hundreds of feet into the air. But this well-known geyser with a habit of spouting on schedule is just one of many that mark the landscape. Yellowstone offers much more than geysers. Admire the canyon, hike through forests along trails that lead to waterfalls, take scenic boat trips on the lake, fish for trout, ride horseback, and just look out your car window to see bison, moose, and bighorn sheep in their native habitat.

GETTING THERE

The **Yellowstone Regional Airport** (307–587–5095), Cody, serves the Big Horn Basin and is serviced by **Continental Express** and **Mesa Airlines/United Express**. **Jackson Hole Airport** (307–733–7695) is larger and serviced by **Delta, Skywest, American Airlines, Continental Express,** and **United Express**. Hertz and Avis rental car companies have airport facilities.

    Greyhound (406–587–3110) offers bus service to Bozeman, Livingston, and West Yellowstone, Montana. **Karst Stage** (406–586–8567 or

406–587–9937) offers connecting bus service from Bozeman and Livingston to the park's north entrance. The **Rock Springs Bus Line** (406–669–3208) serves Jackson, Wyoming; the **Cody Bus Line** (307–587–4181) serves Cody. From most of these towns you can take bus transportation to Yellowstone National Park. **Powder River Transportation** (307–344–5555 or 800–442–3682) provides bus service from Cody to Yellowstone's east entrance. There is no direct rail service to the park.

To enter Yellowstone National Park by car coming from Montana in the north, take U.S. 89; from the northeast, take U.S. 212; from Cody, which is east of Yellowstone, take U.S. 20/40/16. If traveling from the south, take U.S. 287/191/89; if arriving from the west, take U.S. 20 to the park's west entrance. The park entrance fee, good for seven days, is $10.00 per vehicle, and $4.00 per person for bus passengers, hikers, bicyclists, motorcyclists, and snowmobilers between the ages of sixteen and sixty-two. If you plan to stay longer, have a disability, or are over sixty-two years of age, look into an annual **Yellowstone Passport, Golden Eagle, Golden Access,** or **Golden Age Passport.**

GETTING AROUND

A **Grand Loop Road** that cuts a figure eight, stretching for 142 miles through the park, takes you by most of the major attractions. Those who prefer that others do the driving should contact **TW Recreational Services,** the park's concessionaire, Yellowstone National Park 82190; (307) 344–7311. They offer bus tours that cover the Grand Loop, or choose either the Lower Loop or the Upper Loop. These drive-by tours, however, don't do much more than literally allow you to "glimpse" Yellowstone.

The best way for families to experience Yellowstone is by spending time here. Let the family vehicle lead you to some of Yellowstone's wonders, and allow yourself to savor these at your own pace. Be sure to get out of the car: stroll, hike, horseback ride, and walk. Only by getting off the road can you truly gain a sense of Yellowstone's grandeur.

WHAT TO SEE AND DO

Spring, summer, and early fall before the snows arrive are the best times for families to visit Yellowstone; to avoid the thickest crowds, however, schedule your arrival in late spring or early June. Because Yellowstone is most popular for families in warm weather, particularly when school's out, the hiking, driving, and sight-seeing information listed below applies to the warm seasons unless otherwise stated.

If you can get away in late spring or in early autumn, your visit may be more satisfying. Not only do the crowds dissipate at these times, but so does the heat. In spring wildflowers dot the meadows, and in fall the aspens turn the color of spun gold creating fairy-tale vistas of mountains and ridges.

Winter in Yellowstone brings a special rustic peace. The park's vast fields of snow make Yellowstone a haven for cross-country skiers and snowmobilers. In places icicles arch over the falls while elsewhere a meadow remains perennially green thanks to the warmth of a nearby hot spring. Eagles float overhead gliding on an updraft of air warmed by the boiling geysers. Winter does, however, make for some closed roads and deep snow. Snowmobiles are available, and the cross-country skiing on groomed trails or in the backcountry is superb—if you know what you are doing. TW Recreational Services offers a day trip by heated snow coach to accessible park highlights. (See In Winter and Where to Stay).

Yellowstone can be divided into five different regions: **Geyser Country**, full of fumaroles, mud pots, hot pools, and home to Old Faithful; **Mammoth Country**, a thermal area of hot springs; **Roosevelt Country**, where the park offers stagecoach rides and rugged scenery; **Canyon Country**, made dramatic by the Grand Canyon of Yellowstone; and **Lake Country**, where moose, and sometimes bear, roam the shores of Yellowstone Lake, where the native cutthroat trout is plentiful.

Geyser Country

In Geyser Country the star is **Old Faithful**, named for its regular schedule of eruptions; check the chalkboards at the visitors center, the local shops, and ice cream parlors for the expected time or simply watch the crowd getting thicker. Ask the rangers at the **Old Faithful Visitor Center** (307–344–7381, ext. 2109) for tips on trails to take.

Old Faithful won't disappoint, splashing steamy water 100 to 180 feet into the air; it's a reminder of earth's primal forces. The area around Old Faithful, however, is disappointing, overbuilt, and overcrowded. With all the parking lots, lodging, eateries, and traffic jams, this bit of the park often seems more reminiscent of a mall than a majestic natural wonder.

Don't settle for just a view from the benches surrounding Old Faithful. Obtain a map of the **Upper Geyser Basin** from the Visitor Center, and select any number of easy boardwalk trails that wind past forty steamy geysers, and hot bubbling pools. **Note:** Be careful to stay on the boardwalk. Do not walk on the ground as the crust around these thermal areas can be dangerously thin. Visitors have been burned, and some killed, by the scalding water. Also tell your kids ahead of time to resist the urge to throw pennies, sticks, or anything else into the boiling springs. This is not good for kids or the thermal attractions. Hold little ones by the hand, or put them in the stroller as the boardwalk makes for a perfect pathway.

Some popular and not-too-long trails include the **Geyser Hill Loop**, a 1.3-mile track, that takes you over bubbling ground. Look for **Beehive Geyser**, which can spray more than 100 feet in the air, but alas, not as predictably as Old Faithful, and **Doublet Pool**, which is a beautiful blue color.

As you meander along the boardwalk past these geothermal wonders, keep an eye out for bison. Often several will simply sit near the boardwalk. Admire them from afar, and don't attempt to create a catchy photograph of your child next to the big bison—for that could be the last photo. However peaceful these animals may look, they are wild, unpredictable, and potentially dangerous.

Back on the road from **Old Faithful** toward **Mammoth Hot Springs**, stop at **Midway Geyser Basin** and explore the colorful pools. A nearby interesting spot is the **Three Senses Trail**, where blind as well as sighted visitors focus on the sounds of the geysers and hot springs.

Allow at least one-half hour to visit **Fountain Paint Pot**, a colorful area where the algae and bacteria surrounding these muddy water holes have turned them to shades of pastel pinks and blues.

Near here, the road north from Geyser Country to Mammoth Country takes you past great sweeps of plains, often with herds of bison grazing, especially near **Gibbons Meadows**.

Mammoth Country

Near the northern border of Yellowstone and just minutes away from Gardiner, Montana, is **Mammoth Hot Springs**, where even in high season, the crowds thin out a bit. We prefer staying here for its rustic, but serviceable lodging and the long scenic stretches of road that lead here.

As the acidic waters of Mammoth Hot Springs pass through the limestone, calcium carbonate remains. Eventually the build up causes the unusual-shaped terraces you see. The springs, which continue to grow, cover an entire hillside.

Also in Mammoth Country are the park headquarters. At the **Albright Visitor Center** (307–344–7381, ext. 2263), look at the films, slides, and photographs of the park.

In the Mammoth area several day hikes and walking trails are worth the trouble, but these are not for beginning hikers. The **Beaver Ponds Trail**, for example, puts you to the test, gaining 500 feet in elevation.

As this area is less crowded, Mammoth is a good place to go horseback riding. With luck you may come upon a herd of elk. Even a brief foray off the road does much to enliven your sense of Yellowstone's wonders.

Roosevelt Country

Roosevelt Country drew the first tourists here with its lodging facilities. Less dramatic than the geyser or canyon areas, Roosevelt Country has the simple serenity and peaceful good looks of forests, meadows, streams, lakes, and marshes. A rewarding and not too difficult hike, especially with young children, is **Tower Fall Trail**. This waterfall cascades 132 feet and then flows into the Yellowstone River. Admire the setting of white water and mountain peaks from the visitor's platform, then hike the half mile of switchback trails down to the falls. Deer often rest on the rocks at the river bottom, where the tumbling waters create a thunderous display. Rest awhile before you attempt the half-mile hike back uphill. Horseback and stagecoach rides can be arranged at the lodge. (See Special Tours.)

If you continue from the center of Roosevelt Country toward the northeast entrance of the park, you'll see the **Lamar Valley** and **Lamar River**, known for its good viewing of bison, elk, and mule deer. Small ponds for fishing are nearby and so is the **Yellowstone Institute**, Box 117, Yellowstone National Park, Wyoming 82190; (307) 344–7381. This nonprofit organization offers a variety of summer classes.

Canyon Country

Don't miss **Canyon Country**; many think of this as Yellowstone's most dramatic feature. The canyon, 20 miles long and 4,000 feet across, captivates with its bands of pink, yellow, and orange. Two waterfalls, the **Lower Falls** and the **Upper Falls**, cascade into the misty canyon. During your exploration, bypass **Canyon Village**, a touristy spot, but check out maps at the **Canyon Visitor Center** (307–242–2550, ext. 6205).

Popular overlooks include **Inspiration Point**, a short, paved walk to a spectacular overlook of the canyon, and **Grandview Point**, another short walk to a canyon view. Simply admire the view. Along the South Rim stop at **Upper Falls Overlook**, handicapped accessible, and try the **Clear Lake Trail**, a hike through large rolling meadows and forested areas to **Clear Lake**.

Just a few miles south of the canyon lies the **Hayden Valley**, an expanse of wild grass and sage that attracts elk, bison, and bears. Be careful as you are in bear country.

Lake Country

Over 100 miles of shoreline surrounded by the natural landscape of tree-covered mountains and blue skies make **Yellowstone Lake** not only North America's largest mountain lake, but another park highlight. Look for Canada geese and trumpeter swans. Stop at the **Fishing Bridge Visitor Center** (307–242–2450, ext. 6150) to find out about fishing areas. Ask about **Elephant Back Mountain Trail** that leads you on a 4-mile hike to a panoramic view of the lake and into **Pelican Valley**.

Lake Yellowstone Hotel, a nearby lodge, surprises with beautiful lake views. From June to September, sign up for a one-hour narrated, scenic cruise. Remember to watch for bear and moose that graze along the shoreline and bald eagles as they swoop down to catch trout

Head to **Steamboat** and **Lake Butte** for a sunset picnic.

Beyond these five areas lie the **backcountry**. You need a permit if you plan to trek through this area, and you will have to inform the various ranger stations of your exact plans. The wilderness can be beautiful, but take proper precautions. Ask the rangers for information about campsites, trails, hiking guides, and bears.

Special Tours

In warm weather. **TW Recreational Services,** Yellowstone National Park, 82190 (307–344–7311), the park's concessionaire, offers a variety of exciting off-the-road trips. Call TWR well before your visit to book any of these trips.

With limited time, go for the one- or two-hour guided **horseback rides.** While limited to easy "walks," these trail trips take you through the woods and into the hills, where herds of elk or deer may be plentiful. Instead of hearing car engines and the chatter of other tourists, on these rides listen to the yells of female elk, the wind rustling the leaves, and the birds. **Roosevelt, Canyon,** and **Mammoth** offer guided trail rides in the summer. Beginning and ending dates vary a bit, so check each location. Minimum age is generally eight; check with the reservationists or stable hands. With kids too young for horses, sample a pioneer journey with a scenic, but short, ride in a replica of a **Concord stagecoach**. These depart from the Roosevelt Lodge corrals early June through August and tour the Roosevelt-Tower region.

Something different for dinner? Climb aboard a horse-drawn wagon for a western-style campfire steak dinner with **Old West Dinner Cookouts**, early June through August, Roosevelt.

Other possibilities include **cruises** on Yellowstone Lake, **boat rentals** from the marina, and **guided fishing trips** at Bridge Bay Marina from Yellowstone Lake. To fish, anglers twelve years and older must obtain a fishing permit. These are available throughout the park at Ranger Stations, visitor centers, and the Hamilton general store. For information and reservations, call (307) 344–7311.

In winter. Covered with snow, Yellowstone in winter serves up a special kind of peace. In winter, park roads are restricted to over-the-snow vehicles. The elk, bison, deer, and coyotes still roam the park, but the majority of tourists do not. From the **Mammoth Hot Springs Hotel** (see Where to Stay), you can rent snowmobiles, go ice skating, or rent skis. If cross-country skiing is your prime interest, book a stay at **Old Faithful Snow Lodge,** near the famous geyser. The ski shop rents equipment including snowshoes, and nearby 40 miles of relatively short trails glide through the Old Faithful area, taking you past steaming hot springs, shooting geysers, and some big game—elk and bison. Additional short trails are available in the Blacktail Deer Plateau area and the Lamar Valley. To get to some of the trailheads, hop aboard a snow coach or the van shuttles. Warming huts are spaced throughout the park for snowmobilers, skiers, and snow coach passengers. But dress appropriately. This is real winter. **The Heart Ski Ranch**, Moran (307–543–2477), offers family friendly snowmobile trips in winter.

WHERE TO STAY

Book your park accommodations as soon as you know the dates of your stay. Especially in season, Yellowstone is busy, and lodgings fill up fast. For reservations, call (307) 344–7311.

The park cabins and lodges offer a range of family friendly rooms for a variety of budgets. There are ten accommodations in six locations within the park. Most of these are basic, without televisions, radios, and telephones; some are without private baths.

Mammoth Hot Springs Hotel, open December to early March and late May through late September, offers hotel rooms and cottage-style cabins, some with full bath, and some without. This is the only park lodging fully accessible by automobile in winter. From here you can rent snowmobiles.

Roosevelt Lodge Cabins, open June through the end of August, has rustic charm and simplicity. Limited number of family cabins.

Canyon Lodge Cabins, open June through the end of August, is half a mile from the Yellowstone's canyons, and cabins are simple but have private baths.

Fishing Bridge R.V. Park, open at the end of May until September, allows RVs up to 40 feet in length, hard-sided only—no pop-ups or tents. Electric, water, and sewer hookups and laundry and shower facilities are available.

Lake Yellowstone Hotel & Cabins, open mid-May until the end of September, was renovated in 1991 and is among the park's best. New suites are available, but rooms in their annex building are less expensive.

Lake Lodge Cabins, open beginning of June until September, offers both Western and Frontier cabins with laundry facilities and restaurant at the main lodge.

Grant Village, open June 1 through September, is situated on the shore of Yellowstone Lake and provides the southernmost overnight accommodations in the park. Private baths, a steak house, laundry, and lounge are provided.

Old Faithful Inn, open May 8 through early October, is a National Historic Landmark standing near Old Faithful. This stately log hotel has a dining room, lounge, and gift shop.

Old Faithful Lodge Cabins, open late May through mid-September, also has complete view of Old Faithful and accommodates visitors with simple cabins with or without private baths.

Old Faithful Snow Lodge, open mid-May through mid-October, and again in winter, is popular with skiers. While the rooms do not have baths, the cabins do. In winter this lodging is accessible only by over-the-snow vehicles. TW Recreational Services' snow coaches arrive here daily for excursions.

All reservations can be made through the **Reservations Department,** TW Recreational Services, Inc., Yellowstone National Park, Wyoming 82190-9989; (307) 344–7311. Rooms at Yellowstone book quickly, so it's best to make reservations at least four months in advance. About twelve campgrounds are also available, most on a first-come basis.

Outside the park near the eastern entrance is Buffalo Bill's original lodge (with a few modern changes), the **Pahaska Tepee,** 183 Yellowstone Highway, Cody 82414; (307) 527–7701. The lodging is in cabins, and fishing, overnight pack trips, and trail rides can be arranged.

WHERE TO EAT

Yellowstone offers a variety of dining choices. Dress is always casual, and cafeterias and fast food are easy enough to find. The restaurants at **Mammoth Hot Springs, Lake Yellowstone Hotel, Old Faithful Inn, Grant Village,** and **Canyon Lodge** offer a variety of choices on their menus, including children's meals. Breakfast and lunch are served, and reservations are required for dinner; call (307) 344–7901. Family style restaurants are located at **Roosevelt Lodge** and **Old Faithful Snow Lodge.** Roosevelt Lodge offers an Old West barbecue. **Lake Lodge, Old Faithful Lodge,** and **Canyon Lodge** all offer cafeterias with choices of salads, sandwiches, pasta, chicken, and more, all à la carte. If your stay is short and every minute counts, fast food is available at **Mammoth Hot Springs, Old Faithful,** and **Canyon Lodge.** A convenience for hikers and fishers, box lunches can be ordered from any dining room or cafeteria to be picked up the next morning.

DAY TRIPS: CODY AND THE BIG HORN NATIONAL FOREST

Situated conveniently between Big Horn and Yellowstone, on Route 14/16/20, is the town Colonel William "Buffalo Bill" F. Cody founded in 1898. A day trip, or better yet an overnight, in **Cody,** 52 miles from Yellowstone National Park's east entrance, is a must. First of all, the drive that parallels the river, leads through the scenic **Shoshone National Forest**, and the **Wapiti Valley**, an area President Teddy Roosevelt once dubbed "the most scenic 52 miles in the U.S." Not much has changed along this route since Roosevelt's era; in the Wapiti Valley, cottonwoods line the riverbanks, and the road cuts through gorges surrounded by yellow and pink mesas, buttes, and bluffs. This is the landscape of pioneer treks and movie westerns.

In the **Bighorn National Forest**, which encompasses more than a million acres in north-central Wyoming near the Montana border, the activities are as great as all outdoors: fishing, hiking, camping, and exploring the backcountry. As some areas restrict vehicles, park the car and hike in to sample this forest.

GETTING THERE

To Cody
From Yellowstone the easiest way to reach Cody is to drive east for 52 miles along U.S. 14/16/20. (See What to See and Do). The **Yellowstone Regional Airport**, Cody, serves the Big Horn Basin and is serviced by **Continental Express** and **Mesa Airlines/United Express**. The **Jackson Hole Airport**, 1250 East Airport Road, Jackson (307–733–7682), is serviced by **Delta, Skywest, American Airlines, Continental Express**, and **United Express**. From the Jackson Hole Airport, which is located near the southern end of the **Grand Teton National Park**, Yellowstone is about a two-hour drive, or much more if you go leisurely and plan to sightsee. Head north along Highway 287/191/89 from the Grand Teton National Park to the Yellowstone's south entrance. Rental car companies are located at the airports.

To the Big Horn National Forest
The closest regional airport is the **Yellowstone Regional Airport**. The most common way to see the **Big Horn National Forest** is by car. From Cody continue east. The road splits into 14 and 14A (alternate). Along 14 you drive through canyon and forest. The cliffs along the roadside may seem intimidating, but this is the most manageable road, especially for trailers or during winter weather. Highway 14A is a more open, alpine route with great overlooks, but the 10 percent grade makes this road difficult for some vehicles and drivers.

GETTING AROUND

A car is really a necessity, especially if you are continuing from **Yellowstone** to **Cody** to the **Big Horn National Forest**. A handy booklet is

Wyoming Loop Tour, available from the Chamber of Commerce, which outlines routes to and through such scenic sites as the Big Horn Mountain Scenic Byway, the Black Hills, Thermopolis and Hot Springs State Park, Sheridan, and Buffalo.

WHAT TO SEE AND DO

Cody

Spending the night in Cody gives you ample time to enjoy the drive to town as well as time to savor two of the town's very different must-sees. The first one you'll come to is **Historic Trail Town**, Highway 14/16/20, 2 miles west of the Buffalo Bill Historical Center (307–587–5302), open mid-May to mid-September. Set on a strip of land just off the main drag, Historic Trail Town looks like a cowboy movie set, but this is the real thing. On this site near where western legend Buffalo Bill Cody and friends first surveyed "Cody City," archaeologist Bob Edgar has collected and placed twenty-six authentic nineteenth-century log buildings that face each other on two sides of a "street." Scores of wagons and wheels line the middle.

The weathered wood and simple furnishings create a haunting feel, evoking the West as it really was. The structures offer up such legends as the Hole in the Wall Cabin where Butch Cassidy and the Sundance Kid plotted, a saloon with bullet holes in the door, and Trail Town Cemetery, where among others Jeremiah "Liver Eating" Johnston, a mountain man, hunter, and trapper whose life became a movie legend, lies buried. As you peer in these fragile-looking homes and feel the wind in your face, you can imagine the toughness of pioneer living.

Plan to spend several hours at the **Buffalo Bill Historical Center**, P.O. Box 1000, Cody 82414; (307) 587–4771 or (800) 553–3838. It's aptly labeled the "Smithsonian of the West." Spend an afternoon at this facility's four museums, and you'll come away with an enhanced sense of both western myth and reality. From the artifacts of showman Buffalo Bill Cody and his Wild West Show, you understand the larger-than-life panache of mountain men, rodeo riders, and sharp shooters such as Annie Oakley.

The extensive holdings of the Firearms Museum include muskets dating to 1590, as well as eighteenth-century Flintlock rifles, Civil War pistols, and nineteenth-century percussion revolvers. Browse the Whitney Gallery of Western Art to see the land and its people, sometimes idealized, through the eyes of such artists as Frederic Remington, Charles Russell, and Albert Bierstadt.

The **Plains Indian Museum** presents the clothing, religious objects, and daily artifacts of the Sioux, Crow, and twenty-five other tribes who lived from the Mississippi River to the Rocky Mountains, and from Texas to mid-Canada. Children delight in the intricately beaded moccasins, shirts, and dresses. Take time to sit in a real tepee with your kids and discuss its symbolism and practicality, and experience the world from this vantage point.

The **Cody Nite Rodeo** is the event that has earned Cody its nickname "Rodeo Capital of the World." After dinner follow the crowds to the rodeo grounds, P.O. Box 1327–A, Cody; (307) 587–5155. Every evening from June through August cowboys rope calves, race barrels, and ride broncos. Purchase tickets in advance at the ticket booth wagon, City Park, from the Cody Country Chamber of Commerce, 836 Sheridan Avenue (307–587–2297), or at the gate after 7 P.M.

WHERE TO STAY

Cody

The historic **Irma Hotel**, 1192 Sheridan (307–587–4221), a town grande dame that has lost a bit of her "glow," offers forty original rooms in the historic hotel, plus annex rooms in a motel. Children eight and under stay free. The **Historic Buffalo Bill Village Resort**, Seventeenth and Sheridan Avenue (800–527–5544), is a complex of three hotels: a **Holiday Inn**, a **Comfort Inn**, and the **Village**, plus a camper village. There's a pool as well. In Cody, the **Center for Environmental Adventures** (307–587–2076 or 800–356–9965) offers a combination of ranch activities plus trekking, backpacking, sailing, and rock climbing. Call for more details.

For a listing of eighty bed and breakfasts in the Wyoming area, contact **Bed & Breakfast Western Adventure**, P. O. Box 20972, Billings, Montana 59104; (406) 259–7993.

WHERE TO EAT

In **Cody** dine at **The Buffalo Bill Bar** and the **Irma Restaurant**, the Irma Hotel, 1192 Sheridan (307–587–4221), a hotel built in 1902 by Buffalo Bill Cody, and named for his daughter. Belly up to the elaborate cherry wood back bar, a gift to Cody from an appreciative Queen Victoria, who delighted in Buffalo Bill's Wild West Show. Despite the tin ceiling and ornate bar, this place is far from fancy. Locals with muddy boots and dusty chaps come here for the prime rib.

The **Sunset House Family Restaurant**, Sunset Motor Inn (307–587–2257), serves three meals daily and has take-out lunches. Kids like the piano music. **Franca's Italian Dining**, 1421 Rumsey Avenue

(307–587–5354), requires reservations. Try the house specialty *Tortelloni Verdi al Mascarpone*, prepared by Franca herself.

SPECIAL TOURS

For a different but delightful perspective on the area's canyon and rivers, sign-on for a family-friendly raft trip through the Shoshone National Forest. Most of the trips combine easy paddling with just enough rapids for some thrills, but always ask about the suitability given the ages of your children. With **Wyoming River Trips**, P.O. Box 1514B, Cody 82414 (307–587–6661), excursions range from ninety-minute floats through scenic red rock canyons to half-day (to five hours) wildlife viewing trips where the rapids and the wildlife add excitement. **River Runners**, P.O. Box 845, Cody 82414 (307–527–RAFT), has a similar range of excursions.

WHAT TO SEE AND DO

Bighorn National Forest

On the way to the **Bighorn National Forest**, 23 miles east of Cody on Alternate Route 14, is **Powell**, in the heart of the Shoshone reclamation area. An agricultural center, Powell grew green as a result of the Buffalo Bill Reservoir irrigation project. Look west for a glimpse of **Heart Mountain**—a geological phenomenon, as this mountain's top is older than its base.

Scenic Drives and Hikes

Just beyond **Lovell**, which is at the junction of U.S. 14A and 789/310, stop by the **Bighorn Canyon National Recreational Area Visitor Center**, U.S. 14A; (307) 548–2251. It's open daily in summer, on Saturdays and Sundays other times. Ask about summer guided hikes, and nature talks, and obtain a copy of *Canyon Echoes*, the forest newsletter. For more western canyons and wildlife, turn north on Route 37 just before the visitors center for views of **Bighorn Canyon** and the **Pryor Mountain Wild Horse Range** where more than 120 wild horses roam free. About 17 miles from the turnoff, enjoy the views from the **Devils Canyon Overlook** of Bighorn Lake below and the many-hued canyon walls.

While hiking you might see bighorn sheep and black bear, although the latter are rarely seen by tourists. No grizzlies reside in the Big Horn.

Medicine Wheel, 27 miles east of Lovell, is a controversial attraction within Big Horn National Forest. This prehistoric 74-foot stone circle with twenty-eight spokes radiating from a central cairn is said to be a sa-

A llama trek is a fun and unique way to experience Big Horn National Forest. (Courtesy Wyoming Travel Commission)

cred place of worship for Native Americans. Although tourists are not supposed to enter the area, non–Native Americans may park in a nearby lot and hike the mile to the observation area. As the trail is strenuous, a shuttle is available in summer to transport people who may have difficulty making the climb. The information booth provides literature about the significance of this area to Native Americans.

Continue on 14A to **Burgess Junction** where this road joins U.S. 14. About 5 miles south of this junction, take Forest Road 26 to the **Big Goose Falls Ranger Station**. From here continue on route 296 to **Big Goose Falls**. This 5-mile one-way hike from the ranger station crosses the East Fork four times, providing wonderful views, plunge pools, and water-sculpted rocks. But beware: This 10-mile round-trip may be best for older children and teens who are hearty hikers (parents too should be in shape). As always bring plenty of water, food, and appropriate clothing—T-shirts, sweatshirts, and rain gear.

An easy hike is the 2.4-mile **Blue Creek Loop Trail**. The trailhead begins at Sibley Lake, Highway 14, near the campground. Follow the creek and, if you like, venture onto another loop, the **Deadhorse Park Loop**. While the terrain remains easy, the two loops together amount to 6 miles. Bring your camera for some photographs of the often-seen moose, deer, and elk in the meadows and the lodgepole pines.

On Route 14, the **Shell Falls Trail** in the Paintrock district offers some more easy hiking. Walk through the forest on a path that treats you to some wonderful views of the falls. Spend time at the novelty shop you'll pass, managed by a couple who give a singing/talking introduction to the falls. After hearing the stories and fun facts, the falls are even more fun. Look around for the bighorn sheep who like the steep cliffs and fresh water.

WHERE TO STAY

Camping areas within the forest are divided into five districts: Buffalo, Tensleep, Paintrock, Medicine Wheel, and Tongue. Each has picnic grounds, grocery facilities, cabins or motels, and restaurants. **Bear Lodge** on 14A (write 1643 Seventeenth Street, Sheridan 82801; 307–655–2444) and **Arrowhead Lodge** (P.O. Box 267, Dayton 82836; 307–655–2388) are two good picks. Both offer modern motel units and rustic cabins. (Be sure to specify which type of lodging you prefer.) Bear Lodge has a stock pond for fishing, and snowmobiling in winter. Arrowhead has nearby rivers and streams for fishing, as well as snowmobiling and skiing in the winter.

WHERE TO EAT

In the Bighorn National Forest

Most cabin lodging comes with meals for guests. A few, such as **Arrowhead**, have a café that may be open to walk-ins depending on the hour and the season. Call ahead. Day trippers should buy ample provisions, including water and food, in Cody before heading out to hike.

SPECIAL EVENTS

April: Cowboy Songs and Range Ballads, Buffalo Bill Historical Center.

June: At the Plains Indian Powwow, one the nation's largest gatherings of Plains tribes from the United States and Canada, members sing and dance in competition wearing tribal dress, Buffalo Bill Historical Center.

July: Cody Stampede, which draws crowds for the rodeos, parades, street dances, fireworks, and western entertainment.

July: The Yellowstone Jazz Festival stages outdoor concerts in Yellowstone National Park as well as in Cody and Powell.

MORE DAY TRIPS

Include time in your Yellowstone vacation to explore nearby, and often less crowded, Grand Teton National Park, Wyoming. While it's possible to sample the park in a day, try to at least spend one overnight. In season the Jackson area, the southern gateway to Yellowstone, offers good skiing with short lift lines on relatively uncrowded slopes. (See the chapter Grand Teton National Park and Jackson, Wyoming.)

Combining a Yellowstone tour with a dude ranch stay is sure to be a family favorite. Whether you're a greenhorn beginner or a saddle savvy wrangler, Paradise Guest Ranch, P.O. Box 790, Buffalo, Wyoming 82834 (307–684–7876), has a ride to suit you. This ranch offers custom rides twice daily for adults and kids six and older. Feel free to choose a scenic, slow-paced trail ride through the woods, a trot across a ridge top, or an adventuresome all-day trek that has you jumping ravines and galloping across high mountain meadows. Unlike many other guest ranches, Paradise allows you to ride with your kids or send them on with their own group. When not on horseback kids six and older and preschoolers ages three to five enjoy nature-oriented children's programs from 8:00 A.M. to 5:00 P.M. Nonriders (and the saddle-sore) can join a guided mountain walk, fish for trout, or soak in a hot tub. Evening activities bring the family together at talent shows, chuck wagon barbecues, and square dances. The accommodations are first-rate in modern cabins with kitchen, fireplace, and laundry facilities.

FOR MORE INFORMATION

Yellowstone Information

Park and camping (307–344–7381, ext. 2107), dining (307–344–790 or 344–7301), lodging (307–344–7311), Lost and Found (307–344–7381 or 344–7301, ext. 2107), and the RV Park (307–344–7311). The Grant Village Visitor Center (307–344–7381, ext. 6602). The Yellowstone Association, P.O. Box 117, Yellowstone National Park 82190. For information for the physically challenged: Handicapped Access, Yellowstone National Park, Wyoming 82190; (307) 344–7381, ext. 2108.

Handy publications about Yellowstone include *Yellowstone Today* and the *Yellowstone Guide*. For information about surrounding cities, contact the Wyoming Division of Tourism, I–25 at College Drive, Cheyenne 82002; (307) 777–7777 or (800) 225–5996.

Shoshone National Forest

Contact the Wapiti Ranger District, Shoshone National Forest, 203A Yellowstone Avenue, P.O.Box 1840, Cody 82414; (307) 578–1202. Shoshone National Forest, P.O.Box 2140, 888 Meadow Lane, Cody 82414; (307) 527–6241.

Cody. Cody Country Chamber of Commerce, visitor information and central reservations, P.O. Box 2777, 836 Sheridan Avenue, Cody 82414; (307) 587–2297. **Buffalo Bill's Yellowstone Country**, 836 Sheridan Avenue, P.O. Box 2777; (307) 587–2297.

Bighorn National Forest

Bighorn National Forest, 1969 South Sheridan Avenue, Sheridan 82801; (307) 672–0751. Big Horn Mountain Sports, 334 North Main, Sheridan 82801 (307–672–6866) and the U.S.D.A. Forest Service, Tongue District, Bighorn National Forest, offer a pamphlet on area day hikes.

General

Wyoming Division of Tourism, I–25 at College Drive, Cheyenne 82002; (307) 777–7777 or (800) 225–5996.

Emergency Numbers

Yellowstone and Cody
Ambulance, fire, police: 911
For rangers in **Yellowstone**: (307) 344–7381
Hospital, emergency room, and pharmacy: In Yellowstone National Park, **Yellowstone Medical Services** offers twenty-four-hour emergency room and ambulance service from the end of May through mid-September at **Lake Clinic**, in Lake, on Yellowstone Lake, (307) 242–7241. Other medical facilities are located at **Old Faithful Clinic**, Old Faithful area (307–545–7345), from the end of May through mid-October; and at **Mammoth Family Clinic**, Mammoth Hot Springs (307–344–7965), year-round, Monday through Friday. **West Park Hospital**, 707 Sheriden Avenue, Cody; (800) 654–9447 or (307) 527–7501 in Cody.
Pharmacy: Cody Drug, Eastgate Shopping Center, 1813 Seventeenth Street (307–587–2283), provides an after-hours emergency pharmacy and has delivery service.
Poison Control: (800) 442–2702

14
ALBUQUERQUE
New Mexico

Albuquerque, New Mexico's largest city (metropolitan area population is about 480,000), was founded as a Spanish colony in 1706 along a wide curve of the Rio Grande. Today, the sprawling city dominated by the Sandia Mountains spreads far beyond the small adobe buildings of what is now called Old Town, a tree-lined historic area of shops, restaurants, and galleries. The Spanish and Native American influences in cooking, music, architecture, and other areas blend with Anglo American, African-American, and Asian cultures, adding zest to Albuquerque life.

There's a lot to see and most of the time the weather's fine, with sunny days and low humidity. Summers are hot but bearable, brisk winters bring snow to the surrounding mountains, autumns and spring are simply delightful.

GETTING THERE

Albuquerque International Airport (505–842–4366) is 5 miles south of downtown. **Airport Fast Park** (505–242–5181) operates a shuttle. Taxi service and car rentals are also available. **Amtrak** (800–USA–RAIL) serves Albuquerque Station, 314 First Street S.W.

Greyhound Bus Lines (505–243–4435) is at 300 Second Street S.W. By car, enter town from the north or south on I–25, or from the east or west via I–44.

GETTING AROUND

Since the city is spread out, a car is virtually mandatory. **Sun Tran** is the public bus system; call (505) 843–9200 for information.

WHAT TO SEE AND DO

Museums

Old Town, the picturesque historic plaza at Rio Grande Boulevard and Route 66, features these nearby museums of special interest to families.

New Mexico Museum of Natural History, 1801 Mountain Road, N.W.; (505) 841–8837. The state's most visited museum is devoted to the natural and physical sciences of New Mexico and the Southwest and is a favorite with kids. A highlight: the Evolator time machine, a one-of-a-kind stand-up theater that simulates an elevator but travels through 38 million years of the state's geologic history.

Other appealing attractions include the Bone Zone, where the impressive fossils of New Mexico's extinct inhabitants include a 25-foot brachiosaurus leg and three life-size skeletal casts of dinosaurs. Hands-on activities take place at the Naturalist Center, where kids are attracted to the active beehive and ant farm. In the New Mexico Seacoast Exhibit, small sharks prowl in a saltwater aquarium. The Dynamax Theater shows larger-than-life films on a 26-foot-tall screen. Check for special exhibits, events, and workshops.

The Albuquerque Museum of Art, History and Science, 2000 Mountain Road N.W.; (505) 243–7255. It's free, so stop in for a peek. Although it's a good way to expose school-age kids to the area's 400 years of local history, from the Spanish Conquistadors to modern times, children either find this place interesting or boring depending on their interest in armor and art. The galleries exhibit authentic arms and armaments from the sixteenth century plus traditional and contemporary art.

The American International Rattlesnake Museum, 202 San Felipe N.W.; (505) 242–6569. Your kids will be either repulsed or delighted (or a little of both) as you walk through a glass-enclosed exhibit featuring the largest live collection of rattlesnake species on public exhibit. Everyone who makes it through gets a certificate of bravery.

The Albuquerque Children's Museum, 800 Rio Grande Boulevard N.W., Suite 10, in the Sheraton Old Town Place; (505) 842–5525. Kids age two to twelve enjoy five categories of hands-on exhibits. At Creating/Imagining, kids dress up, stage puppet shows, and practice weaving on a giant loom. Weekly Make-It-Take-It art activities allow kids to create their own projects. How Things Work includes zoetropes, where kids draw their own cartoons, a Capture Your Shadow Wall, and a freshwater fish tank, with chameleons and the museum's pet, "Snakey." At Heritages, kids examine real artifacts—coins, rocks, feathers, and clothes—to learn about different cultures and time periods. When a volunteer is present at the Communications Exhibits area, kids use a medieval printing press to compose a message. They will love trying out different ways to communicate, such as using the Oscilloscope, which displays their voice patterns on a screen; the Whisper Disks, which transport their whispers across the room; and in Ship's Communication, which has them shout commands into a pipe. At the Toddler Area, tykes play with foam blocks in a safe environment. Call about ongoing and special activities.

Elsewhere in town:

Indian Pueblo Museum, 2401 Twelfth Street N.W.; (505) 843–7270 or (800) 766–4405—outside New Mexico. Part of the Indian Pueblo Cultural Center, this nonprofit organization is owned and maintained by the nineteen area Indian pueblos. The building is patterned after Pueblo Bonito, a well-known ruin in Chaco Canyon in northwestern New Mexico. On the lower level, ancient artifacts reveal the history of the Pueblo Indians. The upper level has alcoves, one for each of the nineteen tribes, which feature changing exhibits, murals, and contemporary art. An area for kids offers a chance to dress up in traditional clothing, grind corn, and take part in other hands-on activities. Each weekend, traditional dance performances and art demonstrations are free to the public. Ask about special events and workshops. Their restaurant serves only Native American food. The two most popular items (most kids love them): Indian baked bread and Indian fry bread. Another treat: Their shop features authentic Indian crafts—especially jewelry—at fair prices.

The Maxwell Museum of Anthropology, University of New Mexico, Redondo Road at Ash Street, (505) 277–4404, depicts the history of Native Americans. This museum is ranked as one of the finest of its kind. Ancestors, one of the permanent exhibits, shows the evolution of humans using life-size models that compare Neanderthal and Cro-Magnon man with modern man. Frequently changing exhibits, mainly highlighting Southwestern culture, recently included the role of women over the past two centuries and colorful Mexican folk art. Free admission.

Older kids may enjoy strolling around the campus of the **University of New Mexico,** founded around 1889. Some buildings feature distinctive Pueblo Native American architecture, and there are almost 700 acres of gardens, plus several art museums. Call or visit the UNM Visitor Center, 1700 Las Lomas N.E.; (505) 277–1989.

To visit the **National Atomic Museum,** Kirkland Air Force Base at Wyoming Boulevard, about 7 miles south of the center of town, (505) 845–6670, you must get a pass from the military guards at the visitor's center. Whether you're for or against nuclear energy and/or weapons, you and your school-age kids should find this museum both educational and intriguing. Operated by the Department of Energy, the museum—the only one of its kind in the country—has exhibits and films on energy and its many sources, particularly atomic energy. The Manhattan Project that developed, produced, and tested the first atomic bomb, and was centered

Spectacular ceremonial dances take place throughout the year at the Indian pueblos of the Rio Grande Valley. (Courtesy Albuquerque Convention and Visitors Bureau)

in New Mexico, is highlighted. Not everything is portrayed through rose-colored glasses. A fifty-one-minute documentary, *Ten Seconds That Shook the World,* shown four times daily, includes newsreels of the 1930s and 1940s, and concludes with Japan's unconditional surrender after the two atom bombings by the United States. The museum also includes a solar-powered TV, interactive exhibits and games, and a tour that explores the development of nuclear weapons. Outside, an ungainly 280mm atomic cannon, the F1015D Thunderchief, is on display. Admission is free; the museum is open daily, except major holidays.

Other Attractions

If your kids aren't afraid of heights, consider a scenic ride up the rugged west side of the Sandia Mountains on the **Sandia Peak Tram,** #10 Tramway Loop N.E.; (505) 856–6419. Up, up, up you go on over Domingo Baca Canyon on the world's longest continuous cable tramway. You may spot bear, bighorn sheep, and mule deer on the slopes below. It's 2.7 miles to the 10,378-foot observation deck on Sandia Peak, where there's an awesome view of Albuquerque and beyond. In the summer, tram riders take the Sandia Peak Ski Area chairlift down the other side of the mountain. The 7,500-foot-long double chairlift to the Sandia Peak Ski Area (a popular winter ski facility) goes through spruce, ponderosa pine, and aspen forests. Rentals are available at the ski lift base for the mountain bike trails across Cibola National Forest. The chairlift stops running in late afternoon, while the tram continues until sunset. If you take the tram back down, you can purchase packages that include dinner at the High Finance Restaurant atop the peak or at the Firehouse Restaurant, which overlooks the city from the tram base.

No child fails to be impressed by the more than 15,000 petroglyphs (ancient Indian drawings) on the 17-mile-long West Mesa escarpment that comprises **Petroglyph National Monument**, 6900 Unser Boulevard N.W., 8 miles west of the city; (505) 897–8814 or 873–6620. It's estimated that the petroglyphs were carved somewhere between 1100 and 1600 A.D. by hunting parties who camped at the base of the lava flow of the five now extinct volcanos. Four easy walking trails wind through the petroglyphs.

Coronado State Park and Monument, 22 miles north of Albuquerque, a mile west of Bernalillo on Highway 44, (505) 867–5351, preserves the ruins of the Kuaua Pueblo. Although normally off-limits to non-Indians, the restored kiva (sacred ceremonial chamber) is open to the public. A number of paintings were discovered on the walls; some are reproduced in the kiva, while the originals are in the visitor's center, which offers a superb panorama of the Rio Grande and the Sandia Mountains. There's also a good interpretative trail to follow.

Albuquerque is considered the **Hot Air Balloon Capital** of the World, and its weather makes year-round ballooning both a spectator and participant sport. If you get an urge to take off, there are a number of hot-air-balloon-ride companies (consult Albuquerque Convention and Visitors Bureau—ACVB—for a listing). Be aware that most companies have a minimum age of eight or so, mainly because younger children often get antsy, scared—or simply bored. But older children often love the easy sensation of floating with the breeze.

Parks and Zoos

The **Rio Grande Zoological Park**, 903 Tenth Street S.W., (505) 843–7413, is the largest zoo in the state, and worth a visit to see more than 1,200 animals in natural-looking habitats. The African savannah, tropical rain forest, and primate island are among the highlights of this top-notch facility. The **Rio Grande Nature Center State Park**, on the east bank of the Rio Grande at Candlearia Road, (505) 344–7240, contains over seven acres of woods and park. A partially underground glass visitor's center features exhibits on the Rio Grande's history, ecology, and geology. Nature trails wind through the bosque—or cottonwood trails—along the river.

Theater, Music, and the Arts

Friday and Sunday's *Albuquerque Journal* and Thursday's *Albuquerque Tribune* list cultural happenings in town, or call the twenty-four-hour Events Line tape; (505) 243–4577 or (800) 284–2282. Catch a performance at **The New Mexico Repertory Theater**, (505) 243–4500, the only resident professional theater group in the state; the **Southwest Ballet**, (505) 294–1423; or the **New Mexico Symphony Orchestra**, (505) 843–7657. Ticketmaster at Smith's is a citywide computerized ticket agency for all major entertainment events; call (505) TIC–KETS.

Sports

Albuquerque Dukes are the professional baseball Triple-A farm team of the Los Angeles Dodgers and the Pacific Coast League; call (505) 243–1791 for information.

Shopping

Native American arts and crafts are the specialty here. In the shops of Old Town you'll find a variety of jewelers and trading posts, art galleries, and gift shops. Kids especially enjoy **La Pinata**, #2 Patio Market, (505) 242–2400, with bright piñatas, paper flowers, and porcelain dolls. Another favorite is **Rug Rats and Ruffles Children's Shop**, 309 Romero N.W., (505) 243–9691, with toys, gifts, dolls, piñatas, and southwestern gear. Don't forget to browse the jewelry and crafts at the **Indian Pueblo Cultural Center.**

At the Wyoming Mall, 2266 Wyoming, a stop at **Planet Fun**, (505) 294–1099, gives kids ages one to twelve the chance to romp on an acre of life-size toys. There's a special crawling area for toddlers, while older kids can climb and crawl through a huge jungle gym or create a tune on a jumbo piano keyboard like the one from *Big*. There's a glassed-in area for parents, complete with snack bar and TV.

SPECIAL EVENTS

Albuquerque hosts a variety of fairs and festivals.

April: Gathering of Nations, cultural festival and Powwow of more than 5,000 Native American dancers, and singers representing more than 300 tribes.

May: Magnifico! Albuquerque Festival of the Arts. First full seventeen days of the month. Hundreds of events, including Kidfest, a hands-on family festival.

June: New Mexico Arts & Crafts Fair.

Late July: Mountain Discovery Days, Sandia Mountains. Entertainment and arts and crafts.

Early August: Summer festival with food and historical re-enactments at El Rancho de las Golondrinas, an old Spanish colonial village, halfway between Albuquerque and Santa Fe.

September: New Mexico State Fair, one of the top ten such fairs in the country.

October: International Balloon Fiesta, a nine-day spectacular from the first through the second weekend of October. Storytellers International, second full week in October, features ghost stories, workshops, and storytelling for all ages.

Late October–Early December: Arts and Crafts fairs throughout the area.

Christmas Eve: Luminaria tour of Albuquerque. The neighborhood streets are lighted with luminarias.

WHERE TO STAY

The Official Tourist Guide has a comprehensive lodging section, including bed and breakfasts and guest houses. **Accommodations Unlimited, Inc.**, (505) 291–0215, rents fully furnished luxury apartments and townhouses on a daily basis, complete with linens, phones, and dishes. You'll also find a wide choice of familiar chain motels and hotels.

Casas de Sueños, 310 Rio Grande Boulevard Southwest, (505) 247–4560, is one block from Old Town and adjacent to the Albuquerque Country Club. Some of the casitas in this "House of Dreams," which calls itself a B&B inn, come with a kitchen and fireplace. All have private courtyards.

Fairfield Inn by Marriott, 1760 Menual N.E., (505) 889–4000 or (800) 228–2800, is an excellent choice in the economy range. The new property, formerly part of the Hilton, has an indoor pool and sauna (and an outdoor pool shared with the Hilton). They serve a complimentary continental breakfast and offer complimentary airport transportation.

Hyatt Regency Albuquerque at Albuquerque Convention Center, 300 Tijeras N.W., (505) 842–1234 or (800) 233–1234, is one of the state's newest luxury hotels. The property has 395 large guest rooms, fourteen suites, an outdoor pool, health club and spa, a restaurant, and two lounges. Complimentary airport transportation is offered.

If you want to combine a stay in town with some additional New Mexico fun, book the **Bishop's Lodge,** 3 miles north of Santa Fe on Bishop's Lodge Road, P.O. Box 2367, Santa Fe; (800) 732–2240 or (505) 983–6377. They offer family-style accommodations with horseback riding. Near town, the lodge is close to all the sites and also offers a kids' program from June through Labor Day and over Christmas break, for kids four to twelve.

WHERE TO EAT

Check the official ACVB brochure for a comprehensive restaurant listing.
Three nostalgic eateries are sure to appeal to kids and adults. **Owl Cafe,**
800 Eubank N.E., (505) 291–4900, a fifties-style diner has a soda fountain, jukebox, and patio, plus excellent burgers and sandwiches. **66
Diner,** 1405 Central Avenue N.E., (505) 247–1421, a former transmis-
sion shop, serves up art deco decor plus burgers, ribs, and sandwiches.
Yester-Dave's Grill, 10601 Montgomery, (505) 293–0033, has a live disc
jockey plus vintage cars, and offers ribs, burgers, and sandwiches.

By all means sample the local cuisine, keeping in mind that in New
Mexico, the sauce—made with green and red chili peppers grown in the
southern part of the state—is what distinguishes local cooking from standard Tex-Mex fare. A good place for enchiladas and other authentic food
is at one of the three Gardunos of Mexico locations: 10551 Montgomery,
(505) 298–5000; 5400 Academy, (505) 821–3030; or 8806 Fourth Street
N.W., (505) 898–2772. There's live mariachi music to add to the fun.

Bella Vista, North Highway 14, Cedar Crest, (505) 281–3370 or
281–3913, in the foothills of the Sandia Mountains, has a bountiful luncheon buffet. Dinner is served, too.

DAY TRIPS

A visit to this area wouldn't be complete without a trip to an Indian
pueblo. The ACVB recommends visiting on a feast day and also recommends being aware of varying rules and restrictions concerning photography, sketching, and tape recording. *The Official Guide Book* lists the
phone numbers of the various pueblos. Isleta Pueblo, fifteen minutes
south on I–25, (505) 869–3111, has the church of San Augustin, one of
the oldest mission churches in the Southwest (1613–1630). The pueblo
runs Isleta Lakes Water Recreation area with picnic grounds and camping facilities.

The pleasures of Santa Fe are only some 55 miles away from Albuquerque, via I–25. A longer, but more scenic, route is the popular
Turquoise Trail that travels along Route NM-536 (National Scenic
Byway) to Sandia Crest (described earlier) and North NM-14 to Santa Fe.
Along the way, stop at **The Tinkertown Museum,** 121 Sandia Crest Road,
(505) 281–5233, open April through October, to see carvings and collections that include a miniature Western town, circus exhibit, and a house
made of glass bottles. You can take a detour off the trail south to **Sierra
Farms,** corner of Cardinal Road and New Mexico 337 South, Tijeras;
(505) 281–5061. It's fifteen miles south of I–40, exit 175, about forty-five

minutes from Albuquerque. This cheese-making company welcomes visitors year-round. Sundays from 1:00–4:00 P.M. is officially Children's Afternoon when kids help feed baby goats, and families picnic on the grounds. Children are also invited to come after 2:00 P.M. on weekdays, weather permitting, although this visit is more informal than the one on Sunday. Back on the **Turquoise Trail**, restored ghost towns include Golden, once a gold-and-turquoise-mining town, and Cerrillos, often used as a setting for Western films and filled with small shops selling antiques and other interesting items. While driving the Trail, look for a roadrunner—New Mexico's state bird.

Santa Fe, extremely popular (and crowded) with tourists in July and August, is situated at an altitude of 7,000 feet. Trendy and gentrified, Santa Fe has a great deal to offer. Start your exploring at the Santa Fe Plaza, which dates from the early 1600s. At one time this area served as a bull ring and the unloading spot for the freight wagons. Now art galleries, shops, and restaurants line the streets. There are several museums in town, but kids may prefer the colorful **Museum of International Folk Art**, about 2 miles from the Plaza, 706 Camino Lejo; (505) 827–6350. Here a fascinating assortment of objects, ranging from toys to religious images, is presented in a pleasant, kid-pleasing setting. Check out the special museum events offered as part of the Saturdays Are for the Kids Program.

If the kids are still game, right behind the museum is another of interest: **Wheelright Museum of the American Indian**, 704 Camino Lejo (505–982–4636), exhibiting works from all Native American cultures. (Kids will like the fact that the building is shaped like a Navajo hogan.) And don't forget the **Santa Fe Children's Museum**, 1050 Old Pecos Trail (505–989–8359), for those hands-on experiences that kids love.

The **Southwest Adventure Group** (800–766–5443) offers more first-hand fun for kids and parents. Their children-only tour of Indian cliff dwellings, for example, comes with permission to climb into the ancient Anasazi homes. The family raft trip on the Rio Grande features regional tales by a Native American storyteller and a taco lunch in the shade of a cottonwood tree.

Call the Santa Fe Visitors and Convention Bureau at (505) 984–6760 or (800) 777–2489 for complete tourist information.

FOR MORE INFORMATION

A number of helpful publications, including the semiannual *Official Albuquerque Visitors Guide*, can be obtained from the **Albuquerque Convention and Visitors Bureau**, 121 Tijeras N.E., 1st Floor; (505) 243–3696 or (800) 284–2282. There are two other tourist information centers: one at the airport, lower level at the bottom of the escalator, open daily from 9:30 A.M. to 5:00 P.M.; and one in Old Town, on Romero N.W., across from the church, open Monday through Saturday at 10:00 A.M. and Sunday 11:00 A.M. to 5:00 P.M.

Emergency Numbers

Ambulance, fire, police: 911

Twenty-four-hour emergency room: University Hospital, 2211 Lomas N.E., (505) 843–2111 (center of town); or Lovelace Medical, 5400 Gibson Boulevard (southern part of town), (505) 262–7000 or (800) 877–7526.

Poison Control: (505) 843–2551

Handicapped Transportation Information: (505) 764–6165

Twenty-four-hour pharmacy: Walgreen's, with branches throughout town, including 5001 Montgomery Plaza N.E., (505) 881–5210 (Northeast Heights section)

15
ARCHES NATIONAL PARK AND CANYONLANDS NATIONAL PARK
Utah

Arches National Park, just 5 miles north of Moab, features the world's largest concentration of natural red and golden sandstone arches. This is a sight your children will long remember. Over 1,500 majestic arches plus red rock canyons, fins, spires, and balancing rocks give this landscape an extraterrestrial aura. The fascinating formations were created from the erosion of the Entrada Sandstone, a thick layer of rock deposited as sand some 150 million years ago.

The park comprises 73,000 acres; you could easily get an "eyeful" after a few hours, but plan to spend at least a day, hopefully more, exploring. The early morning and early evening light are dramatic times to view the arches' red desert, with the peaks of the La Sal Mountains in the background. Open year-round, the park has a high season from mid-March to October. **Canyonlands National Park** is quite close, and certainly worth a visit, although it's more rugged and not as accessible for families, particularly those with young children. (In fact, it's the state's least visited national park, albeit the largest.)

GETTING THERE

Canyonlands Field Airport, 21 miles west of Moab on Highway 191 (801–259–7421), offers regular commuter service from Salt Lake City via **Alpine Aviation.** The nearest major airport is **Walker Field** in Grand Junction, Colorado, two hours east (303–244–9100), which is served by

Continental, **Mesa** (a United Express connection), **SkyWest** (a Delta connection), and **Alpine**. Major car rental companies are located at the airport.

The nearest **Amtrak** (800–USA–RAIL) is in the town of Thompson, 45 miles north. By car, the park is 5 miles north of Moab off U.S. 191.

GETTING AROUND

A car is a necessity. Rental cars and jeeps are available in the area. A 41-mile (round-trip) paved road in the park leads to the major sights. There are also unpaved roads for four-wheel-drive vehicles.

WHAT TO SEE AND DO

The **visitor center**, just inside the park entrance, is open year-round and features exhibits and a slide program detailing the arch formations. Obtain a trail guide here that shows the distances for hiking and the approximate times to allow.

Follow the paved road from the visitor center. While you can see many of the major arches from the road, short trails (as well as more strenuous hikes) lead to many others. *Best Hikes With Children in Utah* by Maureen Keilty (The Mountaineers) details several trails in Arches, Canyonlands, and other Utah parks, and tells how to stimulate your kids' imaginations as you proceed. On your hike, take the opportunity to teach your children to respect the area's ecology, and remind them not to walk on the cryptobiotic crust, an important feature of the Colorado Plateau. This black, knobby surface frequently seen growing on the soil is comprised of organisms that have an important function in the desert; they hold moisture, prevent erosion, and contribute nitrogen and carbon to the soil. They are easily recognized and shouldn't be stepped or driven on; stay on the trails and the roads.

Note: In the summer, temperatures can climb to 110 degrees, so it's best to do your hiking early in the day or in the evening; carry plenty of water and wear wide-brimmed hats and sunscreen.

Two miles from the visitor center, the paved road passes the **Park Avenue Viewpoint**, where you can follow a moderate 2-mile hike (best with older kids) that starts at **South Park Avenue** and follows a red-rock canyon bottom to **North Park Avenue**—about ninety minutes away. The high vertical walls resemble a city skyline.

Back in the car, follow the road for 10 miles along the foot of the salmon-colored **Great Wall**. **The Balanced Rock**, approximately at the center of the park, fascinates kids: This massive 50-foot boulder appears to be precariously balanced atop a slim 75-foot pedestal! The .4-mile loop that leads to the rock takes about fifteen minutes and is an easy hike. East of here, off the main paved road, a spur road leads to the "Windows section." An easy .9-mile trail loop to North and South Windows and Turner Arch takes about forty-five minutes.

After continuing your drive on the main road for several miles, you will come to an unpaved road that leads to Wolfe Ranch, an 1888 homesteader's creation, with an old log cabin and corral. This serves as the trailhead for a 3-mile round-trip to a park landmark, Delicate Arch. The hike takes about three and one-half hours and is moderately strenuous. The trail climbs up slick rock to the arch—making it unsuitable for very young kids and definitely challenging for older siblings. The suspension bridge that crosses Salt Wash at .1 mile may intimidate younger kids; if so, you can turn around. If you cross the bridge (older kids will be right in their element), look for petroglyphs on the left cliff. Once you reach the arch, don't walk under it because it's quite steep. You also can see the arch from a viewpoint a half mile to the southeast (at the end of a gravel road).

The main road ends at The Devil's Garden area, where there are about a dozen significant arches, some without names. The only one visible from the road is Skyline Arch, which can also be accessed by an easy .5 mile hike that leads to the base. Hopefully, your kids will have the stamina for the easy 2-mile hike to Landscape Arch, the largest natural arch in the world at 288 feet high and 306 feet across. If you must limit your hike, this is a good one to take.

Ranger-led programs take place from mid-March until mid-October. Check the visitor's center for current schedules. There are no programs specifically for children.

Pack Creek Ranch, Mountain Loop Road, Moab (801–259–5505), operates two-hour horseback trips on the outskirts of the park from mid-March to the end of October. Kids under five can't ride alone; if doubled-up with a parent, then the pair can go out for a one-hour ride. Depending on the season, there are other off-road rides. The ranch also has room for guests in units with kitchenettes; and, for added convenience, enjoy the restaurant and pool.

See Adventures, following the Canyonlands listing, for other outfitters and activities in and around Arches.

SPECIAL EVENTS

The communities around Arches and Canyonlands offer a variety of year-round activities. Contact the Utah Canyonlands Region (801–587–3235 or 800–574–4FUN) for more information.

January: Winter Festival, Monticello.

February: Quarter Horse Show, Moab.

March: Canyonlands Half Marathon/5-mile Race, Moab; U.S. Mail Trail Ride equestrian event, Green River.

April: Easter Jeep Safari; Bicycle Stage Race; Quarter Horse Show—all in Moab. Jeep Jamboree, Blanding.

June: Rodeo; Butch Cassidy Days, Moab.

July: Frontier Days, Blanding; Pioneer Days celebrations, Moab/Monticello; Little Buckaroo Rodeo, Green River.

August: County Fairs, Moab/Monticello; Rodeo, Monticello; Dead Horse Point Square Dance Festival, Moab; Hispanic Folk Festival, Monticello.

September: White Mesa Annual Ute Indian Bear Dance, Blanding; Melon Days, Green River; Utah Navajo Fair, Bluff.

October: Canyonlands Fat Tire Bike Festival; Rock, Gem, and Mineral Show, Moab; Jeep Jamboree, Blanding.

November: Western Poetry Writers Party and Reading, Moab.

December: 10K Winter Sun Run, Moab.

WHERE TO STAY

The park's **Devil's Garden** campground is open on a first-come, first-served basis, with water available from mid-March to mid-October. Facilities include tables, grills, and flush toilets. Because the campground is normally full by late morning or early afternoon during peak season, plan to arrive early.

Area accommodations are listed in the brochure *Utah's Canyonlands,* available from **Grand Country Travel Council,** and in the *Utah Travel Guide,* available from the Utah Travel Council (see For More Information). Lodging includes a variety of motels and several bed and breakfasts. One possibility is **Comfort Suites,** 800 South Main (801–259–5252 or 800–221–2222), with fifty-two rooms, a pool, hot tub, and kitchens. **Cottonwood Condos,** 338 East 100 South, in a residential area right off Main Street; (801) 259–8897 or (800) 447–4106. This former apartment house has eight one-bedroom units that come with stocked kitchens and a queen-sized sofa in the living room. Linens and towels are provided. **Circle A Ranch B&B,** 128 West 200 North (801–259–7632), rents two sides of a duplex, each sleeping six and each with a full bathroom and kitchen. There's a big yard where kids can play, and vegetable and flower gardens. For a change, wake up to the ranch's all-organic breakfast.

WHERE TO EAT

There is no food served or sold in the park. **Moab** is where you'll satisfy your appetite. **The Moab Information Center** supplies a restaurant guide. **Bar M Chuckwagon**, 541 South Mulberry Lane, (801) 259–2276, serves hearty cowboy-type vittels, followed by a one-hour Western show with a live band, Native American and clog dancers, and more. It's held every night except Sunday from April through September in an outdoor tent with a retractable canopy top. The restaurant closes the rest of the year.

Some local favorites include: **The Rio-Colorado Restaurant and Club**, 2 South 100 West; (801) 259–6666, serves Southwestern cuisine, some Mexican, special desserts, and Sunday brunch with full buffet. **Cafe Ruisseau**, 125 South Main, (801) 259–2599, serves traditional American cuisine, full breakfast menu with early bird specials, and daily lunch and dinner specials. **Golden Steak Restaurant**, 540 South Main, (801) 259–7000, is a family style restaurant that serves steaks, hamburgers, and home-style meals. They offer breakfast and daily specials.

DAY TRIPS

Canyonlands

Canyonlands is an immense 527-square-mile wilderness comprised of three very different areas. The northern Island in the Sky district is a towering, level mesa between the Green and Colorado rivers. The Needles district, east of the river's confluence, has the densest concentration of arches, rock spires, canyons, potholes, prehistoric Indian ruins, and petroglyphs—plus the Needles, enormous rock pinnacles of orange and white. The Maze district, west of the rivers, is wild, remote, and generally inaccessible, with canyons, tall standing rocks, and colorful sandstone fins.

Popular seasons in this high desert country are from March to May and August to October. Services are very limited: You won't find food, gasoline, stores, lodging, or drinking water (except seasonally in the **Squaw Flat Campground** in the Needles). **Needles Outpost**, just outside the Needles park boundaries, off U.S. 211, has gasoline, food, and limited supplies available seasonally.

From Moab, the **Island in the Sky Visitors Center** (801–259–4351) is 32 miles southwest, while the **Needles Visitors Center** (801–259–6568) is 76 miles away. Both are open seven days a week, with reduced winter hours. Rangers offer information, maps, brochures, and, during the summer, guided walks and evening campfire programs.

You can explore the park in several ways. Drive on paved and two-wheel-drive roads to the Needles and Island in the Sky districts, which lead to overlooks, trailheads, picnic areas, and developed campgrounds. There are also rugged, four-wheel-drive trails throughout the park. These are steep and rocky sometimes, and in the park's own words, "tortuous."

Short walks and long hikes lead to some of the park's most outstanding features. Certain trails have wayside exhibits or brochures, available at trailheads or visitors centers. Because this is a desert area, *the park advises taking a number of precautions:* Carry a gallon of water per person per day (active people may require more); drink water frequently; protect yourself from intense sun by wearing a hat, sunglasses, sunscreen, long pants, and a long-sleeved shirt. Save strenuous activity for early morning or late afternoon. Be wary of climbing slick rock because it's often easy to climb up but impossible to climb down. Use special caution near cliff edges, and keep younger children in hand and older children in sight at all times.

Families who have visited **Arches National Park,** but would like to spend at least a half day exploring **Canyonlands,** should head straight to **The Island** district where they will find "possibly the world's greatest exposure of red rock canyons." This area is particularly suited to families with younger kids and/or those with limited time. It features short walks and spectacular overlooks of the **White Rim** below, **the Needles,** and **the Maze.** If you have just a half day to spend, drive the 12 miles from the visitors center to **Grand View Point Overlook,** making stops at **Shafer Canyon** and **Buck Canyon overlooks.** You can also take the 1.5-mile dirt road to **Green River Overlook.** All provide different vantage points and superb vistas, which might include such wildlife as bighorn sheep, coyotes, or foxes on the ledges below.

Then drive 6 miles to **Upheaval Dome**—the Canyon's most spectacular formation, a 2-mile-wide crater filled with various colored spires and boulders. The **Crater View Trail** offers an easy-to-moderate hike for kids. The trail starts at a picnic area, which has water and toilet facilities, and offers two options: a 500-yard (one-way) walk up slick rock to an (unfenced) view of the crater—good for young and/or beginning hikers—or a more challenging 0.8-mile (one-way) hike to a second, fenced-in vantage point.

The Needles District, 49 miles northwest of the town of Monticello, can be accessed by U.S. 191. **Newspaper Rock State Historical Monument,** 13 miles off U.S. 191 on Scenic Byway U-211, displays petroglyphs spanning 1,000 years. Although paved access roads in the Needles area lead to a number of viewpoints, you must be touring in a four-wheel-drive vehicle to do any in-depth exploring. The main road ends at **Big Spring Canyon Overlook,** where there is a large assortment of mushroom-shaped hoodoos.

Adventures

Moab, the only city in the state on the **Colorado River,** is the headquarters for a number of jeep, raft, canoe, jet boat, and airplane tours of the region. The **visitor's office** (see For More Information) provides a list

The Druid Arch is just one of the magnificent formations located in Canyonlands National Park. (Photo by Jim Marie/courtesy Utah Travel Council)

of outfitters as well as lots of other area information. There are miles and miles of scenic federal land around Moab that actually have fewer restrictions than the national parkland. Therefore, many of the outfitters, even those licensed to operate in the parks, take advantage of the surrounding areas to schedule adventure activities. Here are some possibilities.

Sherri Griffith Explorations, 2231 South Highway 191, Moab; (801) 259–8229 or (800) 332–2439. They offer a number of trips on the Green and Colorado rivers, including three specialty trips each summer for families. A recent offering, The Family Goes to Camp—Expedition Style, is a five-day/four-night journey to the majestic canyons of the Green River, with hiking, bouldering, water games, playing in the sand, and camping on sandy beaches; it's recommended for kids as young as five.

Tagalong Expeditions, 452 North Main, Moab (801–259–8946 or 800–453–3292), offers a variety of adventures. Rafting trips range from a one-day Colorado River trip north of Moab, to three to four days through Canyonlands (minimum age six). Canoe 120 miles down the Green River, then take a jet boat trip back on the Colorado. Enjoy four-wheel-drive trips through Canyonlands and the miles of jeep trails around Moab. The company stresses that the four-wheel trips, though they do cover rugged terrain and can be bumpy, are not meant to be "high adventure," but rather entertaining narrated guided trips that include short walks. They have taken kids as young as four, although usually ages ten and up enjoy the trips most. In the winter, the company runs combination trips featuring Nordic skiing in the La Sal Mountains and one- or two-day land trips in or around the national parks.

Canyonlands Field Institute (CFI), P.O. Box 68, Moab; (801) 259–7750. This nonprofit organization explores the ecology, geology, and archaeology of Arches and Canyonlands National Park, the canyons of the Green and Colorado rivers, and the wilderness of the Colorado plateaus. CFI is a licensed river outfitter in Utah and Colorado, and they run a variety of **Eco-River Trips**, many of which provide educational experiences for families. Among their trips, led by naturalist instructors: a two-day/one-night Colorado River journey to the **Westwater Canyon**, on the Colorado-Utah state line near Moab; you can spot bald and golden eagles as you float in an open canyon bounded by red sandstone cliffs. There are two sets of rapids. CFI is also known for its in-depth weekend field seminars that detail natural and cultural history. Several are family oriented. Canyonlands also arranges a variety of programs custom-made for families, lasting from one half day to one week or more, all with an educational aspect. You choose the place and focus. Sample programs include Arches National Park and/or BLM Wilderness Study Areas near Moab, and one-day naturalist guided explorations, where you can determine how much walking is involved. CFI offers discounted rates for those under sixteen.

Dinosaur Discovery Expeditions, P.O. Box 307, Fruita, Colorado; (800) DIG–DINO. They sponsor a **Dinosaur Diamond Safari** for nondiggers (children must be sixteen years), touring significant dinosaur sites in Grand Junction, Colorado, and Moab, Price, and Vernal, Utah—cities that form "**The Dinosaur Diamond**." The trip, held in late September, includes museum visits, dinosaur locations, and national monuments in these fossil rich areas, including a stop at Arches National Park. In summer, Dinosaur Discovery Expeditions offers a variety of family oriented educational trips about dinosaurs.

The Moab area is also a favorite of mountain bikers. There's a popular half-day route, the **Slickrock Bike Trail**, which starts about 3 miles east of town and follows an extremely challenging, clearly marked 10-mile loop. This is not for beginners—and be sure to pack plenty of water. Bike shops that offer daily rentals and guided tours include **Rim Tours**, 94 West 100 North Street (801–259–5333 or 800–626–7335), which rents bikes and camping gear. They also run guided tours with no strict age limits, including three- to six-day spring and fall outings to Canyonlands National Park. Call for a brochure, which also details summer trips to western Colorado.

DAY TRIPS

Take some time to explore Moab, a pleasant town with some interesting attractions.

Dan O'Laurie Museum, 118 East Center Street; (801) 259–7985 (closed Sundays). Archaeological, geological, and historical exhibits detail the area's history from the prehistoric Ute Indian days to the uranium boom of the 1950s.

Hollywood Stuntman's Hall of Fame, 11 East 100 North Street (801–259–6100), was transplanted from California to Moab some twenty years ago by its founder, who has been collecting memorabilia for more than forty years. The fascinating exhibits include costumes, weapons, and other stunt equipment, as well as more than 50,000 photos and cement footprints of movie stars and stunt people.

The Moab area has been a popular filming location since 1949, and the visitors center provides you with a movie location guide. Locations are accessible with a two-wheel-drive vehicle. Inside **Arches National Park,** for instance, scenes for *Indiana Jones and the Last Crusade* were shot in **South Park Avenue** and **Windows** areas; the scene where Thelma and Louise of that movie lock an officer in his patrol car trunk was shot at **The Courthouse Towers** area.

The small town of **Monticello,** 21 miles north of Blanding on U.S. 191, close to the turnoff for the Needles section of Canyonlands, has a cinema, a strip of inexpensive motels, and several eateries. Situated on the edge of the **Abajo** or **Blue Mountains** at 7,050 feet, it provides superb panoramas of the surrounding countryside. This is the seat of San Juan County, so you can pick up lots of information about the region. For example, pamphlets about the many **Anasazi** sites in southeastern Utah may be obtained from the **county tourist office,** 117 South Main (801–587–2231); the **National Park Service,** 32 South 100 East Street (801–587–2737); or the **Bureau of Land Management (BLM),** 435 North Main Street (801–587–2141).

FOR MORE INFORMATION

National Parks: **Arches National Park,** Box 907, Moab 84532 (801–259–8161); **Canyonlands National Park,** 125 West 200 South, Moab 84532 (801–259–7164).

Area Tourist Information: **Grand County Travel Council** (Moab Information Center), corner of Main and Center, Moab (801–259–8825 or 800–635–6622); **San Juan County Travel Council,** 117 South Main, Monticello (800–574–4386); **Utah Travel Council,** Council Hall/Capitol Hill, Salt Lake City, Utah 84114–1396 (801–538–1030).

Emergency Numbers

The only phones are at the visitor center. The park has qualified emergency medical personnel who can help the injured, or can transport them to **Allen Memorial Hospital**, 719 West 400 North, Moab (801–259–7191).

City Market Pharmacy, 425 South Main, Moab (801–259–8971), is open from 9:00 A.M. to 7:00 P.M. Monday through Friday, until 6:00 P.M. Saturday, and from noon to 4:00 P.M. Sunday; on most holidays it's open from 9:00 A.M. to 4:00 P.M.

Poison Control: (800) 456–7707

16
GRAND CANYON NATIONAL PARK
Arizona

Indescribable beauty, awesome vistas, fascinating natural and cultural history: The Grand Canyon must be seen to be believed. Created by the uplifting of the Colorado Plateau and the erosion caused by the Colorado River, the canyon stretches 277 miles across northern Arizona and is approximately a mile deep. Most visitors experience the canyon by traveling along its rim, stopping to take in its majesty via different vantage points. The South Rim, which includes Grand Canyon Village and Desert View, receives 90 percent of park visitors and is open year-round. The North Rim, a thousand feet higher in elevation, receives far fewer visitors and closes for winter because of heavy snows. The Inner Canyon can be reached only on foot, by mule, or via the Colorado River and is a favorite with hikers and backpackers.

Yes, your children will find the canyon "awesome"—but first a warning. Be careful near the edge of the canyon and on the trails. Guardrails are intermittent, and accidents, unfortunately, happen. This is one area where it's imperative to keep small children firmly in hand; even where there are barriers, unattended kids have been known to climb over them. Some canyon rims, more than 7,000 feet above sea level, can cause dizziness and shortness of breath. Also, because the North Rim is more than a hundred miles from a fully staffed hospital, we don't recommend it for families (it's briefly described later). Enjoy the scenery, but remember to hold on to small children, and be sure the older ones know the rules.

GETTING THERE

The best connections to the Grand Canyon are through **Sky Harbor International Airport**, Phoenix; (602) 273–3300. Connecting flights leave from here, from Flagstaff's **Pulliam Airport** (602–774–1422), and from Las Vegas' **McCarran International** (702–739–5743), to **Grand Canyon Airport** (602–638–2446) on the South Rim. Free van transportation is available to lodges in Tusayan, 7 miles south of the park and, for a fee, to Grand Canyon Village, on the South Rim, via **Tusayan/Grand Canyon Shuttle**, (602) 638–2475. Taxi service is also available. Those making the 200-mile trip to the North Rim can take a **Trans Canyon Shuttle** (602–638–2820) in season, or rent a car at the Grand Canyon Airport.

Greyhound/Trailways services Flagstaff and Williams, Arizona. **Nava-Hopi** Tours (602–774–5003 or 800–892–8687) handles scheduled bus connections from Flagstaff (about 80 miles south) and Williams (about 58 miles west) to Grand Canyon Village and Tusayan.

Amtrak (800–USA–RAIL) serves Flagstaff and, from April through October, runs a bus from Flagstaff to Williams. At Williams you may take the historic **Grand Canyon Railway** (602–635–4000 or 800–THE–TRAIN), a two-and-three-quarter-hour trip to the South Rim on a turn-of-the-century steam train. Enjoy on-board entertainment and complimentary snacks. After exploring the canyon, reboard the train at 3:15 P.M. for the ride back to Williams.

By car from Flagstaff's I–40, the best approach to the South Rim is via U.S. 180 (about 80 miles) or try the more scenic Route 64 (107 miles). From I–40 in the west, take Route 64 from Williams. For the North Rim from Flagstaff, take U.S. 89 to Bitter Springs, then U.S. 89A to Route 67, then south to the North Rim, a 210-mile drive.

GETTING AROUND

If you're staying at Grand Canyon Village, a car is a convenience but not a necessity because the village is eminently walkable. There are free shuttles from late May to late September along the South Rim and West Rim Drive. You can also get taxis and bus tours at the Village, as well as in Tusayan and at the North Rim. A car, however, will allow you to drive the scenic East Rim.

You can reach the Inner Canyon, which includes Phantom Ranch, only by foot, mule, or via the Colorado River from April to October on trips that range from one to twenty-two days. Except for one-day trips, it's advisable to make river reservations one year in advance. Minimum age requirements vary. For a complete listing of bus, horseback, and river tour operators, check the Grand Canyon Chamber of Commerce *Visitor's Guide* (see For More Information).

Transportation Desks providing information on wheelchair accessible vehicles, taxis, coaches, tours, mule and horseback rides, Phantom Ranch facilities, and air tours are located at lodge lobbies.

If you drive your own car, a number of scenic overlooks afford breathtaking views. The East Rim Drive (Highway 64), open to vehicles year-round, follows the canyon rim for 26 miles east of Grand Canyon Village to Desert View (the park's east entrance). The West Rim Drive, closed to private vehicles from late May through September, follows the rim for 8 miles west from Grand Canyon Village to Hermits Rest.

WHAT TO SEE AND DO

The South Rim

If you come to the South Rim in summer, as most tourists do, be prepared for crowds at the more popular spots. Entrance fees at press time were $10.00 for each private vehicle or $5.00 per bus/tour van passenger, pedestrian, or cyclist. The admission is good for seven days and includes both rims.

If you're not on a tour, what you see depends on how much time you allot for your trip. The first view of the canyon is usually from the scenic overlook at Mather Point. Each overlook provides a different perspective of this vast canyon, so take advantage of as many as you can. Ideally, you will come at different times of day. Sunset at the canyon, especially at Taki Point and East Rim Drive, is a not-to-be-missed treat; if you can rouse the kids, sunrise is also special, particularly at Hopi Point and West Rim Drive.

First stop: the visitor center, (602) 638–7888, 6 miles north of the park's south entrance station, open daily from 8:00 A.M. to 7:00 P.M. A ranger is stationed here and can dispense information along with maps and brochures. *The Guide,* a free park newspaper, is full of basic tourist information. Also free: *Young Adventurer,* featuring activities and information for kids. The park offers a series of four Junior Ranger patches ($1.50 each) to different age groups, from preschool to thirteen years, who are committed to learning more about the park and protecting its resources. Inquire at the visitors center, Yavapai or Tusayan Museum, or the North Rim information desk.

The visitor center's bookstore offers a good supply of books, slides, and postcards. Its exhibit hall features natural and cultural history displays, including dioramas that the kids will like. At the auditorium, a variety of brief audiovisual presentations are shown throughout the day; check the schedule for times and topics. The lobby's bulletin board lists ranger-led rim walks, talks, and evening events. The courtyard has an interesting display that shows different types of vessels that have run the Colorado River, including the oldest—a 1909 Cataract Boat.

Less than a mile northeast, the recently renovated **Yavapai Museum** (602–638–7888) offers sensational canyon views from its picture win-

Hopi Point lookout is a great place to take in a view of the Grand Canyon. (Courtesy United States Department of the Interior National Park Service)

dows. Panels identify the buttes, points, and tributary canyons that are visible. The exhibits present the canyon's geologic history in a way that school-age and older kids can appreciate: via rock samples, ancient fossils, and a geologic clock that tells the time (in millions of years) it takes to form the rock layers revealed by the Colorado River. Educational videos and Indian lore about the canyon make this a worthwhile stop. Here you can also buy books, postcards, maps, and slides.

From the museum—if your kids are old enough and hardy—consider walking the easy, paved, flat, self-guided 2.7-mile nature trail that travels west leading to Maricopa Point, with vistas of the Colorado River. The trail passes the Hopi House, a well-stocked gift shop, and the grand old log-and-stone El Tovar Hotel. You can buy inexpensive brochures on the trail's biology and geology at the visitor's center, Yavapai Museum, or at Verkamp's Curios, next to the El Tovar.

East Rim
If you budget enough time—at least one day or more—take a drive

along the **East Rim to Desert View.** The 25-mile, one-way drive takes forty-five minutes. We suggest saving the lookouts for the drive back. One exception: **Buggeln Picnic** area, about 1.2 miles east of **Grandview Point.** The scattered picnic tables are shaded by ponderosa pines, and there are some scenic canyon views. As you are rimside, watch the kids carefully.

At the end of East Rim Drive is **Desert View** with its superb overlook and famous 70-foot Watchtower, built in 1932 by the Fred Harvey Company. There's a nominal entrance fee that entitles you to see reproductions of petroglyphs, wall paintings, a Hopi altar, and the tower. Climb the windy stairs for spectacular 360-degree vistas of the canyon and beyond, to the Painted Desert and the San Francisco Peaks. The odd-looking wooden boxes with slits that are set into the wall at intervals are reflectoscopes. Look down into the black glass for intensified canyon views. Desert View has a small visitors center as well as a general store, snack bar, service station, and campground.

Three miles west of Desert View, you'll find the **Tusayan Museum and ruin,** constructed by Anasazi Indians in approximately A.D. 1185. The small museum has artifacts and models of the Anasazi tribes as well as those of modern day tribes of this region. (Today, the Havasupai people inhabit the inner canyon in a remote village accessible only by foot, pack animals, or from the river. The Navajo live on a reservation to the east of Grand Canyon.)

Inexpensive leaflets describe Anasazi farming and foraging methods. Walk along the short paved trail (one-eight mile round-trip) that leads to the ruins where about thirty Anasazis lived for some twenty years before they moved on. Thirty-minute guided tours are offered several times a day.

Inner Canyon

If your kids are older, if the whole family is fit, and if time allows, consider hiking a short way into the canyon for a totally different perspective. A number of caveats are in order: Be aware that it takes about twice as long to hike up as it does to go down. Canyon hiking is the reverse of mountain climbing, so save your energy for the return trip. Increase your calorie intake by bringing along plenty of nutritious food. As you descend, you enter a desert environment (except for the river corridor). The temperature at the bottom of the canyon can be as much as 30 degrees Fahrenheit higher than rim temperatures: Summertime highs along the Colorado River can reach 120 degrees. For any trip longer than thirty minutes, take along plenty of water (at least a gallon per person) and drink frequently. Wear a hat and clothing that covers your legs, arms, and body in order to avoid excessive water loss and prevent sunburn. You may encounter wildlife on your hike: Don't feed, touch, or disturb the animals. Day hikers account for 60 percent of the search-and-rescue efforts along Grand Canyon trails: Never, ever, hike farther than your family's stamina (and your supplies) permit. Finally, don't think you can hike to the Colorado River in one day: It's a two-day trip and hikers actually have died trying to make it in less time.

Obviously, the message is clear: Inner canyon hiking is not for the neophyte, or for younger children. If you have older school-age kids with hiking experience, and if you are a veteran hiker, you may want to consider the **Bright Angel Trail.** A hike down the trails gifts you with an up-close view. The park maintains two trails—the **Bright Angel Trail,** which begins west of the Bright Angel Lodge in the Village, and the **South Kaibab Trail,** which begins near Yaki Point on the East Rim Drive. Try hiking at least a portion, however small. The trail wary should go on the **Bright Angel Trail** since from May to September the resthouses along the way provide water. But still tote your own as you most certainly on a hot day will want to quench your thirst before the first water fountain at the 1½ mile marker. (Round-trip: 3 miles; time to allow: 2½–4 hours.) Another popular destination is **Indian Gardens,** 4.6 miles from the trailhead (allow 6–9 hours roundtrip), which features picnic tables, and toilets as well as water. Only attempt to trek to **Plateau Point,** 7.1 miles from the rim, and to **Bright Angel Creek,** 9.1 miles from the top and where **Phantom Ranch** offers rustic lodging, if you have older children and teens who are experienced and hearty hikers. Remember, as you descend into the canyon the temperatures become hotter, as high as 100 degrees plus, and the most difficult part of the trek occurs at the end—going uphill when you are tired. This is not a place to have to carry an exhausted child.

Along the Bright Angel trail, well before the mile-and-a-half resthouse, the trail rewards you with marine fossils of branchipods (ancient shelled animals), corals, sharks, and sponges. As you walk through the first tunnel look for Indian pictographs.

The **South Kaibab Trail,** also park maintained, is another good option. Along the 1¼-mile trip to **Cedar Ridge** you pass different rock layers including Kaibab, Tarroweap, Coconino, and Hermit. Enjoy a "treasure hunt" for shell and bird fossils. From Cedar Ridge, it's 3 miles to the **Tonto Trail,** a desert region of shrubs, cacti, and, in summer, home to the black-throated sparrow.

To get off the beaten path for backcountry camping, obtain an overnight permit, preferably in advance by mail, from the **Backcountry Office,** Box 129, Grand Canyon 86023.

North Rim

North Rim elevations are higher, the temperatures are lower, and there's much more rainfall (some 60 percent more). Approach this area through the Arizona Strip (the land between the canyon and the Utah border), which leads to a forty-five-mile drive south on Route 67. The vistas are superb here, along the Kaibab Plateau. If you're staying at the lovely **Grand Canyon Lodge** (see Where to Stay)—even if you're not—go inside, or outside on the viewing deck, for exceptional canyon vistas. On the hotel grounds is the trailhead to Bright Angel Point, a one-half-mile round-trip along the crest of a rock jutting into the canyon. (This is not recommended with young children because of the sheer drop on each side of the trail!)

The North Rim's most popular overlooks include **Point Imperial**, the highest point on either rim at 8,803 feet, 11 miles from Grand Canyon Lodge, with views of the countryside surrounding the canyon. Fifty miles south, **Cape Royal** is another popular stop, with views of Angel's Window, a natural arch. There are rest rooms and a scenic picnic spot near the parking area. Take the nearby **Cliff Springs Trail**, a one-mile round-trip trail that descends to a forested ravine, past a small Indian ruin, to the creek and spectacular views of the canyon.

Tours

A scenic air tour is an expensive but breathtaking way to see the canyon. Several airplane and helicopter tour operators are located in Tusayan, just south of the park's south entrance, or at Grand Canyon Airport. You can obtain a list from Grand Canyon National Park (see For More Information). Indulge with a helicopter flight-seeing tour. **AirStar** (602–638–2622; 800–962–3869) and **Papillon** (602–638–2419; 800–528–2418) both offer thirty-minute flights. While AirStar has no price reduction for kids, Papillon flies kids 2 through 12 for 30 minutes for about a 15 percent discount. Many others operate out of California, Nevada, Utah, New Mexico, and other parts of Arizona. Be sure to inquire about children's rates and safety records.

Horseback tours are offered by **Apache Stables**, located at Moqui Lodge. Choose from short rides through Kaibab National Forest to the longer East Rim and other excursions. Call (602) 638–2424.

Mule rides may be easier than hiking, but require a good deal of fortitude. You must sit in the saddle for hours, control your mount, and descend into steep terrain. Obviously, this is for older kids only (height requirement is four foot seven inches) and not for heavy parents (weight limit is 200 pounds). You should make reservations at least nine months—preferably a year—before your trip. Call (602) 638–2401 or 638–2631, extension 6576.

The following motor coach tours are available from **Fred Harvey Transportation Company**, (602) 638–2401: a two-hour trip that travels 8 miles along the rim to Hermit's Rest, a native stone building created in 1914, with stops at viewpoints along the way; Desert View, covering some 52 miles in three and three-quarter hours, venturing east along the rim, stopping at Yavapai Museum and Lipan Point—a spectacular overlook; and Desert View and the Sunset Tour, a ninety-minute orientation that heads to the rim for the fading light of sunset. Outbound tours explore surrounding areas, such as Monument Valley and Anasazi ruins.

You can also float and raft this territory. For day-long adventures try a 12-hour **float trip** along the Colorado River, which includes a 3-hour ride to the put-in spot and a picnic lunch. While scenic, this journey glides through the Glen and Marble canyons and not the Grand Canyon. Outfitters include **Fred Harvey Tours** (602–638–2401) and **ARA Wilderness Adventures** (602–645–3279).

The **raft trips**, which last from three days to three weeks, gift you with a bottoms-up view of the canyon and a taste of white water. Remember though, that for many of the shorter trips, you raft into the Phantom Ranch and, alas, must hike back out, a journey of several hours. The park service has a list of more than twenty companies that offer Colorado River raft trips. Family-friendly outfitters include **OARS**, P.O. Box 67, Angels Camp, CA 95222 (800–346–6277; 209–736–4677), which sets a minimum age of twelve; **Canyoneers**, P.O. Box 2997, Flagstaff 86003; (800–525–0924; 602–774–4559), with a minimum age of ten; and **Hatch River Expeditions**, P.O. Box 1200, Vernal, Utah 84078 (800–433–8966; 801–789–3813), which has a minimum age of 9.

Entertainment
There are a variety of ways to keep the kids entertained in the evenings.

Grand Canyon, Hidden Secrets at the IMAX theater, shown daily on a 70-foot-high screen, is a wonderful, larger-than-life film that will keep the whole family enthralled. The theater is located at Highway 64/U.S. 180 at the south entrance to the park; call (602) 638–2203 for show times. **Over The Edge Theatre,** in the village at the community building, presents a multimedia canyon orientation show that uses twelve projectors to create a sensational spectacle. Call (602) 638–2229 for schedules.

Squire Fun Center at the Best Western Grand Canyon Squire Inn, Highway 64 in Tusayan, has a six-lane bowling alley, billiards, game room, and big screen TV. And don't forget the day and evening ranger presentations at the canyon; check at the visitor center for schedules, or call (602) 638–7888.

Shopping
If you're looking for the basics—groceries, camping supplies, clothing, souvenirs, books—check out **Babbitt's General Store** in Grand Canyon Village next to the post office; (602) 638–2262. Fine arts is the specialty at **Gallery Grand Canyon,** Highway 64, Tusayan, (602) 638–9201, where you'll find top-quality Indian pottery, jewelry, Hopi kachina, Navajo rugs, paintings, and the like.

SPECIAL EVENTS

Contact the Grand Canyon Chamber of Commerce for more information on the following area events.

Easter: Sunrise Services (nondenominational)—Mather Point.
Late April: Moqui Chili Cook-Off.
September weekends: Grand Canyon Chamber Music Festival.
Early October: Arizona Governor's Cup Antique Car Rally.

WHERE TO STAY

Listings of lodgings are available from the Chamber of Commerce and National Park (see For More Information). Fred Harvey operates the hotels and lodges on the South Rim; all are open year-round and are within the park, except for Moqui Lodge.

El Tovar, Village Loop Drive, was built in 1905 and is a National Landmark. It has the most deluxe accommodations—and truly breathtaking surroundings as it's perched on the edge of the canyon. Food is continental.

Bright Angel Lodge, West Rim Drive, is rustic, more affordable, and has two restaurants and a limited number of private cabins by the rim.

Thunderbird and **Kachina,** Village Loop Drive, are both modern, two-story lodges at the rim's edge.

Maswik Lodge, U.S. 180 West, west end of village, in the Canyon Village, has a cafeteria, lounge, and gift shop.

East and West Yavapai Lodge, Mather Center, set in pine and juniper groves minutes from the rim, has a gift shop, cafeteria, and lounge.

Moqui Lodge, Arizona 61, park entrance, is just outside the park in the Kaibab National Forest. It is moderately priced, has a dining room and cocktail lounge, and on-site horseback riding and cooking out areas.

Trailer Village, near the visitor center, has campsites with full hookups and nearby bath and laundry facilities.

Phantom Ranch, built in 1922, can be reached only by foot, rafting, or by mule. It features western-style cabins and dormitories, a dining hall, beer hall, and fishing and swimming in Bright Angel Creek.

It's important to make reservations as far in advance as possible, either through your travel agent or by calling (602) 638–2401 or contacting **Grand Canyon National Park Lodges,** P.O. Box 699, Grand Canyon, Arizona 86023; (602) 638–2474. In addition to Trailer Village (described earlier), the following campgrounds are located in the South Rim area: **Grand Canyon Camper Village,** (602) 638–2887, 1 mile south of the U.S. 180 park entrance, is considered the best in the area with 200 RV sites with full hookups, water, and electricity, and sixty tent sites, tipi rentals, flush toilets, coin-operated showers, grills, and picnic tables; reservations are accepted. **Mather Campground,** (602) 638–7888, with 319 RV and tent sites, flush toilets, coin-operated showers, water, laundry, grills, and picnic tables, can be reserved up to eight weeks in advance through MISTIX at (800) 365–2267 or by writing P.O. Box 85705, San Diego, California 92186-5705. **Desert View Campground,** 26 miles east of Grand Canyon Village, operates on a first-come, first-serve basis.

In Tusayan, family choices on Highway 64 include the following: **Best Western Grand Canyon Squire,** with 150 units, dining room, heated pool, and tennis courts (602–638–2681 or 800–622–6966); and the **Quality Inn Grand Canyon** with 185 units, heated pool, dining room, and coffee shop (602–638–2673 or 800–221–2222).

If you can't book lodging in Grand Canyon Village or in Tusayan, try the town of Williams, 60 miles south on Highway 64 (Chamber of Commerce number: 602–635–4061), and Flagstaff, 80 miles south on Highway 180 (602–774–4505 or 800–842–7293).

WHERE TO EAT

The finest (and most expensive) dining in the area is at the **El Tovar Hotel,** although they have a nice children's menu and off-season lunch specials. Elsewhere, area restaurants serve reasonably priced American food. For the most inexpensive meals, head for the cafeterias at **Maswik Lodge** and **Yavapai Lodge** (602–638–2360) in Grand Canyon Village, and **Desert View Trading Post** (602–638–2360). There's a **McDonald's** in town, too.

DAY TRIPS

A good beginning for your Grand Canyon adventure lies 80 mile southwest of the national park in **Flagstaff.** Not only does this city serve as the most accessible airport gateway and the easiest place to pick up your rental car, but the **Museum of Northern Arizona,** Route 4 (602–774–5211), presents a comprehensive exploration of the Colorado plateau, a 130,000-square-mile province of sedimentary rock that, eons ago, forces uplifted a mile or more above sea level. Now encompassing parts of Utah, Arizona, New Mexico, and Colorado this region sports the Grand Canyon as its crown jewel. If articulating geological phenomena leaves your mouth as dry as the arid areas you're trying to explain, then you'll especially appreciate the museum's colorful charts that trace the earth's changes. The exhibits also describe the region's wildlife and culture. Small by big city standards, the galleries are just about the right size for grade-schoolers who want to learn but not everything. Even the most blase child will go wide-eyed at touching the petrified femur of a duck-billed dinosaur, learning rock facts from the computer station, and eyeing the skeletal model of Dilophosaurs, a dinosaur known only to have inhabited northern Arizona, but who recently gained star status as a creature in "Jurassic Park."

The **bookstore** presents an admirable collection of adult and children's guides and the **Museum Shop** offers authentic Native American crafts, including small, flat kachinas suitable for Christmas ornaments.

On the 1½-hour drive from Flagstaff to **Tusayan**, the gateway town for the park's south entrance, the road leads you through ponderosa pine groves and fields dotted with creosote and sagebrush.

Outside of the Grand Canyon National Park, State Route 64 intersects with U.S. 89 at Cameron, an interesting historic trading post, hotel, and Indian art gallery. Here, head south for about 20 miles on U.S. 89, and turn left to the ancient Indian ruins at **Wupatki National Monument**. This area was once thriving, full of cosmopolitan villages inhabited by several Native American cultures. By 1300, all that remained were ruins, and today some 2,000 archeological sites are located within the monument. The better ones have paved roads and are accessible to tourists. The Wupatki Visitor Center (602–556–7040) is 14 miles east of the U.S. 89 turnoff between Flagstaff and Cameron. Here are exhibits of various artifacts of this vanished culture, including pottery, jewelry, and tools. Kids particularly enjoy the Wupatki (Hopi for "Tall House") room, a reconstruction of what living quarters probably looked like. Rangers give lectures and tours of the nearby ruins, or you can take a self-guided trail from behind the visitor center. Archaeologists have reconstructed a ball court; there's also an open-air amphitheater, and a series of blowholes, which are thought to have had religious significance. A short drive away are other major ruins. The Lomaki—a small, two-story pueblo some 9 miles northwest of the visitor's center—is the best preserved.

If you came to the Grand Canyon expecting to see the **Painted Desert** (as many do), you're in for a disappointment—it's simply too far. But if you are determined, you will have to travel some to see this landscape where trees have turned to stone over eons. Here striations of purple, red, pink, and blue run through large rock mounds that were carved ages ago by the Little Colorado River. It is a display of eerie and breathtaking beauty. The most famous part of the Painted Desert is at Petrified National Park, 190 miles from the canyon's south rim. A more restricted expanse is found at Little Painted Desert County Park, 15 miles north of Winslow (140 miles from South Rim). Closest to the canyon: a narrow band of the Painted Desert along U.S. Highway 89 from about 3 miles north of Cameron to the small village of The Gap. (You could take a detour on your way to the Wupatki ruins. See Petrified Forest chapter.)

After the ruins, you might decide to proceed onto **Flagstaff** (82 miles south of the Grand Canyon National Park entrance). Don't miss the **Lowell Observatory** on Mars Hill, (602) 774–3358, a mile from downtown. Founded by astronomer Dr. Percival Lowell in 1894, this is the site where Pluto was discovered in 1930 by an observatory worker using Lowell's calculations. See exhibits in the domed visitor's center. On selected summer evenings view a slide show, and then gaze through the telescope. Contact the Flagstaff Visitor Center, (602) 774–9541 or (800) 842–7293, for more tourist information.

FOR MORE INFORMATION

Grand Canyon Chamber of Commerce, P.O. Box 3007, Grand Canyon, Arizona 88023, (no phone), will send you an informative visitor's guide. For park information, contact **Grand Canyon National Park**, Box 129, Grand Canyon, Arizona 86023.

Not all park facilities meet accessibility standards, though the numbers are increasing. Request the *Accessibility Guide* from the visitor center or from the park at the address just given. The National Park Service provides free wheelchairs for park visitor's temporary use. Usually, a wheelchair is available at the Yavapai Museum and the visitor center. A temporary permit for wheelchair access to West Rim Drive in the summer is available from the visitor center. Inquire at the center or at Yavapai and Tusayan Museums about temporary parking permits for designated parking.

Emergency Numbers

Dial 911 for twenty-four-hour emergency medical service; from hotel rooms, dial 9–911. A twenty-four-hour emergency phone is located to the left of the visitor center. Park rangers patrol the canyon and serve as fire fighters and police officers.

Pharmacy: The South Rim has a clinic and pharmacy open all year; although it's not open twenty-four hours, rangers and clinic staff provide around-the-clock emergency service. Call (602) 638–2551 or 638–2469 for the clinic, (602) 638–2460 for the pharmacy.

North Rim medical services consist of a clinic staffed by a nurse practitioner from May through October. Rangers perform emergency medical services.

17
HOUSTON
Texas

Houston, the fourth largest city in the U.S.A., was recently chosen by *Money* magazine as the fourth most livable city in the nation. It's also a nice place for a family to visit, with much to offer: a special vitality, friendliness, lots of cultural events, and some exceptional museums, including a new children's museum, plus a spectacular Space Center. Not too far beyond the urban sprawl are the sandy beaches and Victorian charm of Galveston Island.

GETTING THERE

There are two airports. Some airlines use both; ask when reserving. **W.P. Hobby Airport** (713–643–4597) is 9 miles southeast of downtown; **Houston Intercontinental Airport** (713–230–3000) is 15 miles north. **Airport Express** (713–523–8888) offers shuttles between Intercontinental and Hobby airports and the four downtown passenger terminals.

The **Amtrak** station (800–USA–RAIL) is at 902 Washington Avenue at Bagby. **Greyhound/Trailways** (800–231–2222) is at 2121 Main. By car, I–10 passes through the middle of Houston; U.S. 59 runs northeast to southwest, and I–45 runs northwest to southeast.

GETTING AROUND

A car and a map are helpful for exploring this sprawling city. The maze of highways can be confusing, especially if you stop to ask for directions: Local nicknames for major freeways (such as the Katy for I–10 west of town, and the East Freeway for I–10 east of town) don't appear on maps.

The **Metropolitan Transit Authority** (Metro) buses, 401 Louisiana, (713) 635–4000, can take you to many—but not all—places on your agenda. Minibuses serve downtown routes.

WHAT TO SEE AND DO

Museums and Historical Sites

Houston boasts about its truly excellent museums. Some of the best for families include.

The Children's Museum of Houston, 1500 Binz (713) 522–1138. It will be love at first sight once your kids see this new $10 million facility with its brightly colored exterior, featuring thirteen giant cut-out figures of boys and girls seemingly holding up the building. Inside, nine galleries house top-notch interactive exhibits. Some highlights: At The KID-TV Studio, youngsters create sound tracks, use video equipment to manipulate images, and choose costumes to role play in front of the camera. At the New Perspectives Gallery, a Mexican mountain village and a Taiwan market town, among other sets, illustrate other cultures. Along with showcasing art by and for kids, The Inspirations Gallery includes an art activity room; be sure to spend some creative time here. The Experimentations Lab in the Meadows Environmental Gallery teaches about science firsthand. Tykes three years and under have their own Tot*Spot Gallery, with age-appropriate activities. In the outdoor courtyard, play the challenging Buckminster Fuller's Junior World Game played on a giant map, and explore plants and water in the Greenhouse and Babbling Bayou. Something special is always going on, so check the schedule.

Located in the northern section of Hermann Park is the **Museum of Natural Science,** 1 Hermann Circle, Hermann Park; (713) 639–4600. This is the largest such facility in the Southwest—and quite an interesting place. Each of the eighteen halls involves a different natural science, and many have interactive exhibits. Yes, there are dinosaur skeletons (considered one of the best displays in the country), plus other interesting collections, such as seashells, rocks, and minerals, and North and South American Indian artifacts (including shrunken heads from Ecuador). The Hall of Petroleum and Technology tells the story of how oil is formed via fossils, models, electronic boards, and touchable displays, including a model of an offshore oil rig. Kids become part of a mission control crew at the Challenger Center or see models of future space vehicles at the Arnold Hall of Space Science. Save enough time for the daily star (or weekly laser) shows at the Burke Baker Planetarium (713–639–4600) and/or a giant-screen film on natural science topics at the Wortham IMAX Theatre (713–639–IMAX).

The **Museum of Fine Arts,** 1001 Bissonnet; (713) 639–7300. With 27,000 outstanding works of art, this museum may be a little daunting for some kids, so be selective. The museum's bookstore has a list of twenty items you shouldn't leave without seeing, which is a helpful way to narrow the choices. (Also obtain a map at the entrance.) The fine Re-

A visit to the Houston Children's Museum is a must for all families. (Courtesy Greater Houston Convention and Visitors Bureau)

naissance collection leaves most kids cold, but the Impressionist and Postimpressionist paintings by van Gogh, Cassatt, Braque, and Matisse usually spark interest. Major traveling exhibits are also showcased.

San Jacinto Museum of History and Monument, 1800 Park Road 1826, LaPorte; (713) 479–2421. Located in San Jacinto State Park 21 miles east of downtown, the museum is in the base of a monument on the spot where Sam Houston defeated Mexican General Santa Anna to win independence for Texas in 1836—just weeks after the Alamo massacre. There is no charge to enter the museum, where there are exhibits on the development of Texas from Native American civilization to statehood. Take the elevator to the 489-foot Observation Floor (fee) for a great view of Houston. Then come back down and see the exciting film *Texas Forever! The Battle of San Jacinto,* shown in the museum's theater, where forty-two projectors create an unforgettable multi-image production (fee). Right across the street is the *Battleship Texas* (713–479–4414), a dreadnought built in 1914 that saw action in both world wars. Kids enjoy scrambling around the decks.

The Orange Show Foundation, 2401 Munger (713–926–6368), is a change of pace from the usual. This folk art environment dedicated to the orange amuses most kids. The artwork was made from found objects and created over a twenty-five-year period by a retired postman and amateur artist. The foundation is open from March to mid-November. Weekly art workshops are held for kids.

Don't miss **The Space Center Houston**, 1601 NASA Road 1, Clear Lake, 25 miles south of downtown Houston; (713) 244–2105 or (800) 972–0369. This new facility, on 123 acres on the southwest corner of the Space Center, has the feel of a theme park—and for good reason. Walt Disney Imagineering designed it, and BRC Imagination Arts, the company that designed Epcot Center, produced it.

Space Center Plaza is the central hub of activity, where visitors are directed to various attractions. Kids will want to head straight to the Feel of Space, a hands-on interactive area where a wall of computer simulators enables them to land a shuttle or retrieve a satellite. A walk-in shuttle mockup shows how astronauts eat, sleep, shower—and, yes, go to the bathroom—in space. Tethered space helmets can be tried on. There's usually a line of volunteers waiting to be strapped into recliner-type chairs to experience the difficulties of maneuvering in simulated zero gravity. (This can be frustrating, and it is best suited for older kids.)

In Starship Gallery, after an eleven-minute film entitled *On Human Destiny*, which highlights great moments in space exploration, visitors enter a darkened gallery lighted by tiny "stars" to see historical space artifacts. View the original Mercury capsule, Lunar Roving Vehicle trainer, and Apollo 17 command module (distinguished by a charred bottom from its fiery reentry to Earth's atmosphere after a 1972 moon voyage). A walk-in vault houses the largest exhibit of moon rocks on earth, and visitors can actually touch a 3.8-billion-year-old chip of rock brought back by Apollo 17.

Much is going on elsewhere: The IMAX Theatre shows space-related films on a five-story-high screen. At Mission Status Center, visitors listen in on communications between Mission Control and astronaut crews, or view live closed circuit broadcasts of astronauts in training (and sometimes at work). NASA Tram Tours go behind the scenes to the Weightless Environment Training Facility; the famed Mission Control Center; the new Space Station Control Center; simulated environments where astronauts train; and the outdoor Rocket Park, where oversized, retired flight hardware is stored. Eating choices include a sit-down café and fast food eatery. And, of course, there's a gift shop with all sorts of "out of this world" souvenirs.

Parks and Zoos

Hermann Park, at the intersection of Fannin and Montrose (between downtown and the Astrodome), is comprised of 400 acres filled with family fun. Attractions include the **Museum of Natural Science** (described earlier), picnic grounds, a miniature train, pedalboat rides, lovely gardens (including a 6.5-acre Japanese garden), the beautiful **Macom Rockwell Fountain** (between Fannin and San Jacinto streets), **the Miller Outdoor Theater**, where free concerts are held, and the **Houston Zoological Gardens** at 1513 North MacGregor (713–525–3300), which locals call the Hermann Park Zoo. It's free and quite appealing, with a fine children's petting zoo, a walk-through aviary, and an aquarium—in all, 3,000 animals represent more than 700 species. Among the latest additions is the Alligator Texas Wetlands Exhibit, which features a walk-through alligator habitat. At the Small Mammals World, the highlight is a complete ecosystem enclosed in a twenty-five-inch glass container, where shrimp, algae, sea grass, and microorganisms are kept alive with just the right balance of light and temperature—and no outside oxygen, food, or filter. (NASA designed the model to study long-range support systems.)

The park is just on the edge of what's considered the museum district, with the Children's Museum and Museum of Fine Arts within walking distance.

Other Attractions

Astroworld, A Six Flags Theme Park, off Loop 610 at the Fannin exit; (713) 799–1234. This seventy-five-acre park has something for everyone, with more than one hundred rides, including roller coasters, white-water river rapids rides, and a children's section. The newest offering, not for the young or the timid, is Batman: The Escape, a stand-up ride. Astroworld is open daily in the summer, and weekends mid-March to October 31. Next door **WaterWorld**, a fifteen-acre Six Flags water park (same phone as Astroworld), offers a children's play area and the usual wet and wonderful water rides; open weekends in May and September and daily in the summer months.

Theater, Music, and the Arts

Houston is rich in cultural offerings, with permanent companies in the performing arts. *The Post* and *The Chronicle,* the city's two daily newspapers, and *Know Houston,* a free monthly publication available around town, are good sources of information about cultural events. **Houston Ticket Company,** 2707 Chimney Rock at Westheimer (Galleria), (713) 877–1555, sells tickets to concerts, theater, sports, and other events. Tickets are also available from **Ticketmaster** (713–629–3700), which has more than seventy-five ticket centers in the greater Houston area. Free music, dance, theater, and festivals are held year-round at the **Miller Outdoor Theater,** 100 Concert Drive, Hermann Park; (713) 520–3290. Special shows are held on selected Saturdays for kids and their families.

Shopping

The glass-domed, three-level **Galleria,** 5075 Westheimer

(713–621–1907), has department stores, 300 shops, plus restaurants, movies, and ice skating on the ground floor.

Sports

Houston Astros step up to bat at The Astrodome, 6400 Kirby Drive. Call (713) 799–9555 for ticket and schedule information. **The Houston Rockets** NBA action takes place at the Summit, 10 Greenway Plaza; (713) 627–0600. Football fans root for the **Houston Oilers** at the Astrodome; call (713) 797–1000 for schedules and ticket information. If you can't attend a game at the Astrodome, consider taking a tour of the facility, which includes an eighteen-minute video ("The Astrodome Experience"), a glimpse into the owner's lounge and the TV and radio production areas—even a walk on the AstroTurf. Call (713) 799–9544 for information.

SPECIAL EVENTS

Contact the HCVB for more information on the following special events.

February: Mardi Gras celebration, twelve days of festivities, including nighttime parade, Galveston.

Late February–early March: Houston Livestock Show and Rodeo.

Spring: Westheimer Art Festival.

March: Houston Azalea Trail, first two weekends.

April: Houston International Festival, dance, food, and music in various locations in downtown.

May: Blessing of the Shrimp Fleet, first Sunday after Easter, Galveston; Historic Homes Tour, Galveston.

June: Sandcastle Competition, Galveston.

July: Fourth of July Freedom Festival; Ringling Brothers Barnum and Bailey Circus (month may vary).

Fall: Multicultural outdoor festivals reflecting the city's ethnic diversity, including Greek Festival in October.

October: Westheimer Arts Festival.

Thanksgiving: Foley's Annual Thanksgiving Day Parade.

Christmas: Dickens on the Strand, Victorian-style celebration, Galveston Island; Christmas Boat Lane Parade, Clear Lake; Candlelight Tour, Sam Houston Park.

WHERE TO STAY

The Official Visitors Guide has an accommodations listing. **Downtown Houston Bed and Breakfast**, 1200 Southmore Avenue, (713)

523–1114/(800) 553–5797, provides information on area inns that welcome kids. The best rates usually are offered on weekends, so book well in advance. Familiar budget and moderately priced chains include several **Days Inns**, (800) 325–2525; **Comfort Inns**, (800) 228–5150; and **Quality Inns**, (800) 228–5151.

Embassy Suites Hotel, 9090 South West Freeway; (713) 995–0123/(800) 362–2779. The two-room suites with sofa sleeper and galley kitchen are ideal for families, as are the pool and complimentary breakfast. Five miles south of the Astrodome, the **Radisson Suite Hotel Houston**, 1400 Old Spanish Trail, (713) 796–1000/(800) 333–3333, has separate living area with kitchenette and sleep sofa, plus a bedroom, and free transportation to the Astrodome, and WaterWorld.

Westin has two hotels in the Galleria Mall, both on the expensive side, that have great benefits: shops, department stores, restaurants, an Olympic-sized ice-skating rink, and lighted tennis right at your doorstep, plus the new Westin Kids Club. Staff are trained to be sensitive to the needs of parents and kids. Rooms, if requested, can be child safe and child friendly (already equipped with necessary cribs, etc.). Upon registering parents receive a safety kit complete with night light, Band-Aids, and identity bracelets. Kids get their own amenity—a soft drink cup or laundry bag with crayons. You can request such niceties as a jogging stroller, emergency diapers, potty seats, bicycle seats, refrigerators, and step stools. Call ahead about babysitting services.

Westin's Oaks, 5011 Westheimer Road, (713) 960–8100/(800) 288–3000, is the older of the two, with 406 rooms and some suites in a 21-story building, a pool, cafe, and free parking garage. Westin's **Galleria**, 5060 West Alabama (same phone as Oaks), has similar offerings, with 492 rooms and suites in a 23-story complex.

The Houston Marriott Astrodome, 2100 South Braewood at Greenbriar, (713) 797–9000 or (800) 228–9290, likes families—so much so that, at the time of this writing, they were offering a summer promotion with special rates and extras including kids activities, a poolside barbecue, and Kids Eat Free privileges to ages twelve and under.

WHERE TO EAT

Houston's Official Visitors Guide has a restaurant listing. Along with the expected Tex-Mex and Mexican fare, Houston has a surprising variety of diverse eateries—there's a total of 7,000. Here are a few possibilities.

The Great Caruso, 10001 Westheimer at Briarpark in Cariloon Center; (713) 780–4900. Super service and good food abound at this establishment, where singing waiters, Broadway performers, and concert pianists entertain nightly in an opera house setting.

Some like their barbecue sauce spicy, but many, including kids, like it sweet. Apparently, so does former president Bush, who has stopped by **Otto's Bar-B-Que**, 5502 Memorial Drive; (713) 864–2573. This casual eatery dishes up East Texas–style ribs, brisket, sausage links, and ham for lunch and dinner, with kids' meals available.

Hard Rock Cafe, 1801 Kirby Drive; (713) 520–1134. This is preteen and teen heaven, although the rest of the family will also enjoy the rock memorabilia and music, good burgers, steaks, and salads.

DAY TRIPS

Galveston Island, 51 miles south of Houston on the Gulf of Mexico, is a leading summer resort with 32 miles of sandy beaches, fishing piers, and a variety of interesting sites. If your image of Galveston is the faded one of years gone by, you will be pleasantly surprised by the new Galveston: gussied up, refurbished, and packed with attractions. From Houston, drive via I–45 or take a Texas Limited excursion train (713–864–9991), which features restored cars from the 1930s through 1950s. The train stops at the Railroad Museum, Twenty-fifth and The Strand, (409) 765–5700, one of the nation's largest, located in the restored Galveston Union Depot.

Galveston hosts more than six million tourists a year, so be prepared for company. Stewart Beach, (409) 765–5023, Seawall Boulevard at Broadway Boulevard, at the east end of the island, is the island's most popular, with a new pavilion, bath houses, restaurants, concessions, rides, arcades, water slides, bumper boats, go-carts, and miniature golf.

A fun way to explore the island is aboard the diesel and electric town trolley, designed to look like a turn-of-the-century streetcar, which travels a 4.7-mile track from Seawall Boulevard to The Strand, the historic Victorian district. A recorded narrative details points of interest on the one-hour round-trip ride. Tickets and information are available at Moody Terminal South, 2100 Seawall, (409) 763–4311, and Strand Terminal North, The Strand Visitors Center, 2016 Strand, (409) 765–7834.

A must see: **Moody Gardens**, One Hope Boulevard; (409) 744–1745 or (800) 582–4673. This is part of an ongoing project that is transforming the former marshlands into a 142-acre botanical garden. The gardens boast Palm Beach, the state's only (imported) white sand beach, complete with freshwater "lagoons" and waterfalls, volleyball courts, and paddleboats. Kids play aboard the Yellow Submarine, which has giant octopus tentacle slides, a periscope, portholes with built-in aquariums, and simulated submarine sounds. Other attractions include an entertainment complex, an IMAX theater (one of only three in the world with 3–D capability), and The Rainforest Pyramid, a ten-story glass structure housing more than a thousand species of plants found in the rain forests of Asia, Africa, and South America. The habitat includes waterfalls, cliffs, caverns, forests—plus thousands of butterflies, hundreds of tropical fish, and a large section of exotic birds.

For a free discount coupon book and brochures on area attractions, contact the Galveston Island Convention and Visitors Bureau, 2106 Seawall Boulevard; (409) 763–4311, (800) 351–4237, or (800) 351–4236—Texas.

FOR MORE INFORMATION

The **Houston Convention and Visitors Bureau:** Market Square, 801 Congress, Third floor, Houston 77002; (713) 227–3100 or (800) 365–7575.

Emergency Numbers
Ambulance, fire, police: 911
Poison Control: (713) 654–1701
Hospital: The Texas Medical Center, Ben Taub General Hospital, 1502 Taub Loop; (713) 793–2000.
Twenty-four-hour pharmacy: Eckerd's, 6011 Kirby Drive; (713) 522–3983

18
LAKE TAHOE
Nevada and California

This beautiful alpine body of water, which bisects California and Nevada (two-thirds is in California), lures visitors with winter skiing; summer swimming, boating, and hiking; and year-round casino gambling on the Nevada side. This distinctively blue lake at the northern end of the Sierra Nevada mountains, 22 miles long and 12 miles wide with 72 miles of shoreline, is the second deepest lake in the U.S.

Whether you stay on the north or south shore (the lake's most developed areas) is a matter of personal preference. Both offer access to the great outdoors; however, the north shore is convenient to more ski areas. While both have Nevada casinos, the north shore has less neon. The lake's largest city, South Lake Tahoe, California (population 22,000), is in the midst of a long-range, multimillion dollar upgrading. Just northeast, the city of Stateline, Nevada, is known for its strip of famous casinos.

GETTING THERE

Reno Cannon International Airport (702–328–6400) is served by nine major carriers. Some major hotels offer free shuttles. Ground transportation to the south shore's five major hotels is via Tahoe Casino Express (702–785–2424 or 800–446–6128), which has fourteen round-trips daily. The trip takes one hour and twenty minutes. Aero Trans (702–786–2376) provides shuttles to the north shore. It's 29 miles to the north shore communities of Incline Village and Crystal Bay, Nevada. Car rentals are available at the airport.

Alpha Air has daily flights from Los Angeles to Tahoe Valley Airport (916–544–5810), on Highway 50, South Lake Tahoe. Car rentals and taxi, shuttle, and limousine service are available for the fifteen-minute drive into town.

Amtrak (800–USA–RAIL) services the area, with stops at East Commercial Row and Lake Street in Reno, and at Railroad Street and Commercial in Truckee, California.

Greyhound stations (800–231–2222) are at 155 Stevenson Street, Reno, and 10065 Donner Pass Road, Truckee.

Two major freeways, U.S. 50 and I–80, link Lake Tahoe with the rest of the country. North shore communities are on Highway 28, which connects with California Highway 89 on the west shore and Nevada Highway 50 on the east shore. The point where Highways 89 and 50 connect on the south shore is called the "Y."

GETTING AROUND

A car is helpful, but not imperative. Skiers can take the free shuttles offered by many ski areas (see Winter Pleasures). The roads are often congested, particularly on weekends. Note that Highway 89, which traverses the western shore, is full of zigs, zags, and 10 mph zones—though it is more scenic than the eastern route.

Visitors are encouraged to use public transportation whenever possible. (At press time, many hotels were offering free bus passes.) North shore buses are run by **Tahoe Area Regional Transit** (TART); (916) 581–6365 or (800) 736–6365. **South Tahoe Area Ground Express** (STAGE) serves the city of South Lake Tahoe; call (916) 573–2080. Check out their discount transfer coupons to the summer Bus Plus Van (916–541–6368) to south and west shore beaches, as far as Meeks Bay, where TART buses leave for the north shore.

WHAT TO SEE AND DO

No matter what time of year you visit, the outdoors will be your focus. In summer, enjoy the beaches, boating, hiking, and biking; in winter, take to the hills for good family skiing. *Lake Tahoe: A Family Guide* by Lisa Gollins Evans (Mountaineer Press) offers detailed information on hiking trails and other outdoor activities.

Beaches

Among nearly thirty beaches ringing the lake, the following have family appeal:

Northeast Shore: **Sand Harbor**, in Lake Tahoe Nevada State Park, 8 miles south of Incline Village on Highway 28, features white sand, picnic areas, nature trail, a boat launch, and rest room with showers. There is a parking fee. The amphitheater here is the scene of summer concerts (see Special Events).

South Shore: **Baldwin Beach**, Baldwin Beach Road, about a mile west of the Lake Tahoe Visitor Center, Highway 89, is scenic, quiet, accessible to bikers along the South Shore Bike Trail and has shallow water (see Biking).

West Shore: **D.L. Bliss State Park**, almost 17 miles south of Tahoe City on Highway 89, is considered by many to have the finest beach on the lake, with sparkling white sand and coves for snorkelers. The park is also noted for some of the area's best trails. Arrive early; parking is limited.

Boating, Kayaking

Boat rentals are available throughout the north and south shore. **Tahoe Paddle & Oar** runs guided kayak tours from the North Tahoe Beach Center, King's Beach, 7860 North Lake Boulevard (off Highway 89 between Tahoe City and Truckee), weekdays from June to October; call (916) 581–3029 for information.

Sight-seeing boats provide a leisurely way to see the lake, but some kids find them boring. *M.S. Dixie* paddlewheeler (702–588–3508 or 882–0786) offers narrated scenic cruises daily from April to October, leaving from Zephyr Cove, Nevada, 4 miles north of south shore casinos on Highway 50. Breakfast, brunch, and sunset dinner cruises are possible as are day trips to glacier-carved Emerald Bay, one of the state's most photographed sites. The Bay is also the destination of the glass-bottomed *Tahoe Queen*, which leaves daily, year-round from Ski Run Marina, South Lake Tahoe. Call (916) 541–3364 or (800) 23–TAHOE for reservations. At the north shore, take the new *Tahoe Gal* from North Tahoe Cruises from the Lighthouse Center in Tahoe City. Call (916) 583–0141.

Nature and Hiking Trails

You don't have to be a survivalist to enjoy hiking around the lake. For the hearty, the **Tahoe Rim Trail**, with 115 miles cleared and maintained by volunteers (it will soon increase to 150 miles and encircle the lake), is a good choice. Spooner Lake, Highway 28 near the intersection of U.S. Highway 50, is one of the most popular accesses.

Squaw Creek Meadow starts at the bridge behind the Olympic Village Inn at Squaw Valley, off Highway 89 between Tahoe City and Truckee. At first the beginners' trail is steep, but soon the terrain levels. (Pick the more gentle left path at the fork.) In summer (mid-July is peak season), meadows bloom with colorful wildflowers.

At the **Lake Tahoe Visitor Center Trails**, Highway 89, South Shore (916–573–2674), the National Forest Service offers some interesting self-guided tours, but first go inside to learn about the area's history. In summer, Monday through Friday, a one-hour Woodsy Ranger program for ages five to thirteen features environmental games and a ranger-led nature walk. Families with young children should opt for the short (0.15-

mile loop) **Smokey's Trail**, just south of the Center, that stresses campfire safety. Kids who remember what they learned receive a patch or comic book. The **Rainbow Trail**, another good bet, travels a half-mile loop through pine forests to meadows, with a stop at the Stream Profile Chamber on Taylor Creek. The building is partly underwater, so you can look out windows to see trout, salmon, and other fish swim by.

The **Tallac Historic Site Trail**, a mile one way, passes the Kiva Beach picnic area and several turn-of-the-century summer estates of some of San Francisco's richest and most famous citizens. Reserve tours of the posh Pope House in advance through the Visitor's Center. There's no admission to enter the **Tallac Museum** (916–541–5227), located inside another grand home where an elegant room has been restored. **Trail of the Washoe**, a 0.75-mile loop, features information about the history and culture of the Washoe tribe, members of which came from the mountains to spend their summers here before white settlers arrived.

The **Tahoe Meadows Handicapped Access Trail** was designed for those in wheelchairs, the blind, and families with small children. The leveled trail, a 1.3-mile loop around the meadow, includes ten bridges over gullies and meadow streams and is marked with signs. The trailhead is about a half mile below the Mt. Rose Highway summit (10 miles from Incline Village on Mt. Rose Highway 431) at the Tahoe Rim Trail trailhead. The **Lake Tahoe Visitors Center Trails** and **South Lake Tahoe Bike Path** (described earlier) are also accessible to those in wheelchairs.

Biking

Biking is big in Tahoe where there are 5 miles of unpaved biking trails for every mile of paved roads. A number of bike rental concessions are located throughout the area. Call or visit early on weekends to avoid being disappointed.

The **South Lake Tahoe Bike Path**, a 3.4-mile easy trail that parallels Highway 89, is so lovely that your family won't be alone, but the pedaling is still fun, especially if you have little kids who delight in being pulled in a baby trailer or sitting in a canvas-topped surrey. Most cyclists ride from east to west: The eastern end is about 1.5 miles north of the Highway 89 and 50 intersection. From here, it's about a 1.5-mile ride northwest to the long expanse of Pope Beach. If you're renting a bike, access the trail 0.3 miles west at Camp Richardson Resort and Marina (916–541–1801); baby trailers and four-person surreys are for rent. Pedal a half-mile west to Kiva Beach, a lovely place for a swim. From the pine-shaded picnic area, cyclists link up with trails along the lake to the Tallac Historic Site (described earlier). (Bikes aren't allowed on nature trails.) Push on for 0.7 miles to rest at beautiful Baldwin Beach (see Beaches).

Mountain bikers also can have their sport here. The most popular trail, the challenging **Flume Trail**, starts at Spooner Lake, east of Incline

Village, and travels up a high ridge affording splendid lake views. Call Lake Tahoe Visitor's Center at (916) 573–2674 for information.

At **Northstar at Tahoe**, 6 miles southeast of Truckee on California State Highway 267 (916–587–0215 or 800–GO–NORTH), you can rent mountain bikes from the Mountain Adventure Shop in Northstar Village, where you can get trail maps and ask about guided tours. Mountain bike school packages are offered on selected weekends. Chairlifts carry bikers and hikers to midmountain and to the top of Lookout Mountain. Other attractions: a ropes course 50 feet in the trees near the Village lets those age ten and up pursue mentally and physically challenging games and exercises. The course is open Thursdays through Sundays. There's also a climbing wall and an orienteering course (register at Mountain Adventure Shop). Trail and pony rides, tennis, golf, swimming (with lessons), and Minors' Day Camp for ages two (potty trained) to ten round out the summer fun.

Squaw Valley, off Highway 89 between Tahoe City and Truckee; (916) 583–6985 or (800) 545–4350. This self-contained village boasts more than 30 miles of single tracks and roads for all levels. Rent bikes at the mountain bike store and repair center at the base (elevation 6,200 feet). The Cable Car whisks you and your bike up 2,000 vertical feet to the center of the resort's trail network. Choose trails that wind through meadows of wildflowers, or, if your gang is up to it, attempt a more challenging uphill push. **High Camp Bath and Tennis Club** (elevation 8,200 feet) is the center of summer fun and offers numerous activities. Plans for a hotel adjacent to the Bath and Tennis Club are in the works.

Winter Pleasures

Northstar and **Squaw Valley** are two of about two dozen area downhill and cross-country ski areas. In the winter, **Northstar** has all-day child care and learn-to-ski options for ages two to six (reservations advised: 916–587–0278). Starkids lessons are for ages five to twelve. Squaw Valley typically offers skiing into June. Options for kids under thirteen range from day care to structured ski lessons, either half- or full-day. Other popular ski resorts include the following.

North Shore: **Alpine Meadows**, 6 miles northwest of Tahoe City, off Highway 89; (916) 583–4232. They offer free shuttles from the Tahoe Basin, Snow School for ages three to six, and the longest season in the area (until July 4th). **Diamond Peak**, 1210 Ski Way, Incline Village, (702) 831–3249, has ski programs for ages four to twelve and free shuttles from areas throughout the north shore.

South Shore: **Heavenly**, straddling the state line; (702) 586–7000 or (800) 2–HEAVEN. They run an aerial tram in the summer for scenic vistas and access to a 2-mile round-trip hiking trail. Winter ski lessons are offered for ages four to twelve. Heavenly hopes to open a day-care center in the near future. Two favorites with locals: **Kirkwood**, 30 miles south of South Lake Tahoe on Highway 88 (209–258–6000), with a ski school for ages four to twelve; and **Sierra at Tahoe**, 12 miles west on Highway 50 (916–659–7535), offering lessons to ages four to six.

There are miles of marked cross-country ski trails and rentals around the lake as well as designated snow-play areas.

Kids as young as seven can ride along on the guided snowmobile tours, which cover 14 miles of groomed trails offered by **Zephyr Cove Snowmobile Center**, 760 Highway 50, Zephyr Cove, Nevada, 4 miles north of the south shore casinos; (702) 588–3833. In the summer, Zephyr Cove opens its marina for boat rentals, and has a nice beach, plus volleyball and horseback riding. It also offers lodge rooms, cabins, and a campground with hookups for RVs.

Museums and Historical Sites

Ehrman Mansion, Sugar Pine Point State Park, 10 miles south of Tahoe City on Highway 89; (916) 525–7982. Tour this elegant 1900 summer home led by rangers who sometimes don period costumes. Also on the grounds is an 1860 log cabin built by one of the area's first white settlers. An old water tower adjacent to the mansion houses a nature center with interactive exhibits on plants and animals. Open late summer through Labor Day.

Emigrant Trail Museum, Donner Memorial State Park, just off I–80 at Donner Lake exit west of Truckee; (916) 582–7892. A tribute to the emigrant movement of the mid-1800s, this small museum houses a covered wagon and homestead. Exhibits tell about the natural history of the Sierra Nevada and the construction of the Central Pacific Railroad. Walk along the self-guided nature trail, then enjoy the park's natural wonders, with camping, picnicking, boating, and fishing among the possibilities. The museum is closed Thanksgiving, Christmas, and New Year's Day.

Gatekeepers Log Cabin Museum, south end of Fanny Bridge, Tahoe City; (916) 583–1762. This hand-crafted building houses a collection of Native American (Washo) baskets, tools, clothing, pictures, early railroad and logging equipment, and other area memorabilia of the region's nineteenth and early twentieth century. Open summers only.

Vikingsholm (916–525–7277 or 525–7232) is a replica of a hundred-year-old Norse castle constructed in 1929 on Emerald Bay (south shore) as a summer retreat. Costumed rangers give tours from July to September. Arrive by cruise boats (see Boating) or hike in about a mile from Highway 89. (Although swimming is allowed at Emerald Bay, be forewarned that there's lots of boat traffic.)

Other Attractions

Ponderosa Ranch, 100 Ponderosa Ranch Road, Highway 28, North

Children and adults will enjoy a day on the slopes at Squaw Valley. (Photo by Hank deVre/ courtesy Squaw Valley Ski Corporation)

Shore at Incline Village; (702) 831–0691. This is where "Bonanza," the legendary TV show and the TV movie *Bonanza: The Next Generation* were filmed. Although the inside of the Cartwright's home may not mean a thing to your kids, they will still enjoy this recreated town. The fun-filled ranch is open mid-April through October.

The north shore's new **Incline Village Recreation Center**, 980 Incline Way (702–832–1310), includes a pool, gym, dance studio, game room, sport shop, and on-site child-care center. The center plans year-round family-oriented activities, classes, and programs, including special children's nights and teen dances, and visitors are welcome.

Theater, Music, and the Arts

The visitor's bureaus listed below are your best sources for what's going on. Don't miss the **Valhalla Festival of Arts and Music** on the south shore, a summer-long cultural celebration featuring outdoor concerts (such as a jazz concert on top of Heavenly Mountain), performances, and events, including children's activities. Tickets are available through the **Lake Tahoe Visitors Authority** (800–AT–TAHOE) or **Tahoe Tallac Association** (916–541–4166).

The Reno area is home to a ballet company, the Reno Philharmonic, the Nevada Opera, the Reno Little Theater—plus lots of splashy casino shows. Remember, however, that those under twenty-one are not welcome in the gaming areas of the casinos. Call ahead to be sure. The Reno/Tahoe Visitor's Information Center can supply dates, times, and locations: (800) FOR–RENO.

Shopping

Many stores have souvenirs of the friendly, green, lake "monster," Tahoe Tessie. At Tahoe Tessie's Museum and Gift Shop, 8612 North Lake Boulevard, Kings Beach, north shore (916–546–TSSI), Tessie herself appears on weekends (summers only). A forty-eight-page adventure book, *The Story of Tahoe Tessie, the Original Lake Tahoe Monster,* includes a history of Lake Tahoe.

SPECIAL EVENTS

March: Snowfest, ten-day winter carnival, North Lake Tahoe; day and night activities include opening torchlight parade, ski races, snow-boarding and snow-sculpturing contests, spaghetti feeds, "crazy" events, street dances, fireworks, and children's theaters.

April: Cinco de Mayo Celebration, Reno and Sparks, a giant outdoor fiesta with music, dance performances, authentic foods, and arts and crafts.

June: Annual Wagon Train, south shore, featuring parade of authentic wagons, buggies, and riders on horseback; Valhalla Renaissance Festival, Richardson's Resort, south shore.

June–September: Valhalla Festival of Arts and Music, south shore.

June: Truckee-Tahoe Air Show, with stunts, displays, and hot air balloons.

July: Music at Sand Harbor, Sand Harbor State Park amphitheater (8 miles south of Incline Village).

July–August: Wa She She E Deh Fine Arts Festival and Arts Market, with Native American culture, crafts, and fine arts, Tallac Historic Site, south shore; Lake Tahoe Summer Music Festival.

August: Shakespeare at Sand Harbor, Lake Tahoe Nevada State Park amphitheater; Great Gatsby Weekend, Tallac Museum, includes kids' activities; Truckee Championship Rodeo.

October: Snow Dance, Preston Park, Incline Village, authentic ceremony by Sierra Nevada Miwok Indians. Weekend activities also feature craft fair, salmon specialties, traditional food. Kokanee Salmon Festival, U.S. Forest Service Center, south shore.

November: Great Reno Balloon Race.

December: Sparks Hometowne Christmas; this Victorian-style celebration includes tree lighting, parade, carolling, theatrical events, crafts, entertainment, and food.

WHERE TO STAY

Tahoe North Convention and Visitor's Bureau (800–TAHOE–4–U) has a computerized **Central Reservation Service**, which represents lodging properties in their Travel Planner. Ask about summer and winter packages. On the south shore, the **Lake Tahoe Visitors Authority's** (800) AT–TAHOE number directs your call to appropriate properties and offers a free lodging guide. There's a high concentration of condos and vacation home rentals in the posh **Incline Village** and **Crystal Bay** area, a good bet for families. Call (800) GO–TAHOE for information. All of the visitor's bureaus supply campground information (see For More Information). (The wide selection includes three national forests: Tahoe to the north, Toiyabe to the east, and Eldorado to the southwest.)

Besides Northstar, these lodgings in Tahoe and the Squaw Valley areas offer something special for families.

North Shore: **Resort at Squaw Creek**, 400 Squaw Creek Road, Olympic Valley, California; (916) 583–6300 or (800) 583–6300. This pretty property features 405 accommodations, including rooms, suites, and bilevel penthouses with kitchens. Enjoy three pools, tennis, outdoor ice skating, ski in/ski out access to Squaw Valley, an equestrian center, hiking and mountain bike trails, and a Mountain Buddies program for ages five to thirteen. Summer day care and year-round babysitting are available for children under five.

Hyatt Lake Tahoe, Incline Village; (702) 831–1111 or (800) 327–3910. Mom and dad can try their luck in the big casino while kids ages three (potty trained) to twelve have fun at Camp Hyatt (daily Memorial to Labor Day; Friday and Saturday year-round).

South Shore: **Embassy Suites Resort**, 4130 Lake Tahoe Boulevard, Highway 50, South Lake Tahoe; (916) 544–5400 or (800) EMBASSY. The 400 suites—each with a refrigerator, microwave, and coffeemaker—include some that are child proofed. Swim in an indoor pool, and enjoy free continental breakfast.

WHERE TO EAT

Lake Tahoe features a number of restaurants (North Lake Tahoe alone has more than one hundred), so your choices are many. Call (800) TAHOE–4–U for north shore restaurant suggestions, and the South Lake Tahoe Chamber of Commerce (916–541–5255) for recommendations in their area. Here are a few possibilities.

Incline Village/Crystal Bay: Locals like the **24 Hour Coffee Shop** at the Crystal Bay Club, Highway 28, Crystal Bay; (702) 831–0512. The food is good and the prices are reasonable.

Tahoe City/West Shore: **Grazie!**, Roundhouse Mall, 700 North Lake Boulevard; (916) 583–0233. They offer Italian food in a lovely lakeside setting. Lunch is served weekdays; dinners nightly.

South Shore: **Red Hut Waffle Shop**, 2723 Lake Tahoe Boulevard, South Lake Tahoe; (916) 541–9024. (There's also one in Stateline, Nevada.) They serve breakfast and lunch—big helpings at good prices.

DAY TRIPS

Virginia City, about one hour northeast of the north shore, was once a thriving mining town. The silver mined here aided in financing the Union during the Civil War, in building San Francisco, and in bringing statehood to Nevada. Take a thirty-five-minute trip through the historic **Comstock mining district** aboard the **Virginia and Truckee Railroad**; (702) 847–0380. Tour an underground mine and the nearby Victorian mansions. Contact the Virginia City Chamber of Commerce for more information; (702) 847–0311.

The Reno/Tahoe Tourist Information Center (702–827–RENO or 800–FOR–RENO) can tell you what to see and do in and around **Reno**, a fifty-minute ride from Incline Village and an hour-and-ten-minute drive from south Lake Tahoe. The Reno/Sparks Visitors' Centers are located at the Reno Cannon International Airport and downtown at 275 North Virginia Street.

Because Tahoe, about 30–40 miles away, offers more of the outdoors plus gambling, with less of Reno's intensity, Tahoe is most likely the place for most of your stay. Because most flights arrive and depart from Reno, however, you might consider staying in town for a night or two. Generally, hotel rooms are less expensive here than in Tahoe. Many of the casinos here have Las Vegas counterparts, including **Circus, Circus**, 500 North Sierra Street; (702) 329–0711 or (800) 648–5010. Decorated to look like a giant circus tent, it, like its sister hotel, offers circus acts.

Wilbur D. May Great Basin Adventure in Rancho San Rafael Park, 1502 Washington Street; (702) 785–5961. This child-oriented theme park features mining exhibits, a discovery room, petting zoo, and play area. Planned for completion in January 1995: **Reno's National Bowling Stadium**, the nation's first, topped by a geodesic dome housing an Omnimax Theater with "sensor seats."

Other attractions with family appeal include the **National Automobile Museum**, 10 South Lake Street at Mill Street; (702) 333–9300. It houses over 200 rare, restored old vehicles, some experimental, others that belonged to presidents and celebrities. **Fleishmann Planetarium**, 1650 North Virginia Street (702–784–4811), is on the University of Nevada-Reno campus, and offers star and laser shows and telescope viewing. Reno's cultural offerings are listed under Theater, Music, and the Arts.

The neighboring town of Sparks has **Wild Island** amusement park, I–80 East and Sparks Boulevard; (703) 331–WILD. Enjoy the water slides, wave pool, miniature golf, and grand prix mini–auto racing.

FOR MORE INFORMATION

North Shore: **Tahoe North Visitors and Convention Bureau**, P.O. Box 5578, Tahoe City, California 96145; (916) 583–3494 or (800) TAHOE–4–U.

Incline Village/Crystal Bay Visitor's and Convention Bureau, 969 Tahoe Boulevard, Incline Village, Nevada 89451; (702) 832–1606.

South Shore: **Lake Tahoe Visitors Authority**, 1156 Ski Run Boulevard, South Lake Tahoe, California 96150; (916) 544–5050 or (800) AT–TAHOE.

Reno/Tahoe, P.O. Box 837, Reno, Nevada 89504; (800) FOR–RENO.

Emergency Numbers
Ambulance, fire, police: 911

North Shore:
Call the hospital for poison control information and for medicine in an emergency after pharmacy hours.

Twenty-four-hour emergency medical services (including pharmacy and poison control): **Tahoe Forest Hospital**, Pine Avenue and Donner Pass Road, Truckee, California; (916) 587–6011

South Shore:
Twenty-four-hour emergency medical services: Barton Memorial Hospital, South Avenue and Fourth Street, South Lake Tahoe, California; (916) 541–3420

19
LAS VEGAS
Nevada

It's glitzy, gaudy, and gauche. So why pick Las Vegas for a family vacation? Several good reasons. First, the price. Because gambling pays the bills, most of the hotels charge about half the tab of other cities, making it possible for nongamblers to stay—and eat—in style at bargain rates. This adult playground, minus the gambling, makes a fun-filled family vacation spot that your kids won't soon forget. (You must be twenty-one to gamble in a casino.) A day or two here, amidst the neon and synthetic extravaganzas, balanced with some down-to-earth day trips, can be just the ticket to alleviate those boring vacation blues.

GETTING THERE

McCarran International Airport (702–739–5743) is 5 miles southeast of the city. An inexpensive limousine shuttle service, **Bell Trans** (702–739–7990 or 800–274–7433), operates to the strip hotels; **Gray Line Tours** (702–384–1234) operates airport express service to and from all hotels and motels. Taxis and rental cars are also available.

Amtrak (800–USA–RAIL) serves the city daily. Las Vegas is the only city in the world where the train station is inside a casino resort (Jackie Gaughan's Plaza Hotel, site of the city's original Union Pacific Railroad depot).

The Greyhound Terminal is at 200 South Main Street; (702) 384–8009 or (800) 231–2222. By car, the major artery is I–15 (south to Los Angeles and north to Salt Lake City). U.S. 93 connects Las Vegas to Reno in the north and Phoenix to the south.

GETTING AROUND

You'll find it easy to drive around this compact city. The major hotels and casinos are located in two areas. The downtown area, fondly called, Glitter Gulch, includes the four blocks of Fremont Street between Main Street and Las Vegas Boulevard. The other area, the Strip, is a three-and-one-half-mile section of Las Vegas Boulevard. Every hotel offers free parking.

The **Las Vegas Transit System** (702–384–3540) operates public buses. The **Las Vegas Strip Trolley** (702–382–1404) runs daily every thirty minutes from 9:30 A.M. to 2:00 A.M., stopping at all major hotels along the Strip.

WHAT TO SEE AND DO

Attractions

When is a hotel not a hotel? When it's a Las Vegas mega-theme resort, complete with casino plus much more. Start sightseeing at these spectacular showplaces.

Three relatively new (opened in late 1993) strip hotel casinos offer spectacular stays:

Luxor, 3900 Las Vegas Boulevard South, (702) 795–8118, for example, is not just another casino. This Egyptian-themed resort comes complete with a River Nile, and reproductions of murals and hieroglyphics from such sites as the Valley of the Kings as well as a full-scale model of King Tut's Tomb. While adults game at a 100,000-square-foot casino, kids (or adults) play at Sega VirtuaLand, an 18,000-square-foot area in which Sega, that marvel of computer wizardry, debuts its largest virtual reality technology. This includes Virtua Formula, an interactive racing game with 3D technology, in which you feel as if you are zooming around the track, competing for the checkered flag.

Treasure Island, 3650 Las Vegas Boulevard South, (702) 894–7111, which has appropriated the nickname "the Adventure Resort," is the latest Vegas property of Mirage Resorts Incorporated. There are hourly cannon battles, complete with actors and muskets, between the priate ship *Hispaniola* and H.M.S. *Sir Francis Drake* at Buccaneer Bay fronting the hotel. (Hint: the pirates win—after all, this is Vegas.) The entertainment continues inside with the French-Canadian troupe, Cirque du Soleil, performing a specially designed show twice nightly. The casino, of course, has a booty-and-plunder decor.

But perhaps even Luxor and Treasure Island might be eclipsed by the city's largest entry, **The MGM Grand Hotel and Theme Park,** 3799 Las Vegas Boulevard South; (702) 891–1111. This hotel not only has 5,005 rooms and a casino but also comes with a 33-acre theme park featuring twelve major attractions, theme streets, four theaters, and a host of rides. This entertainment complex is the largest of its kind, with thirty-story towers, spas, pools, five tennis courts, eight theme restaurants, and a special events arena.

The Las Vegas Strip comes alive with superstar entertainment, show spectaculars, and dazzling lights. (Courtesy the Las Vegas News Bureau)

In addition, the Wizard's Midway & Arcade features games of skill plus a video arcade. King Looey's Youth Activity Center, for ages three to sixteen, offers activities from 8:00 A.M. to midnight, including escorted outings to the theme park, behind-the-scenes hotel tours, swimming and tennis lessons, and crafts.

Other family pleasing favorites include:

Circus Circus, 2880 Las Vegas Boulevard South, (702) 734–0410/ (800) 634–3450, is cleverly designed to look like a Big Top: inside is a free carnival midway with food stands and rides plus circus acts. The sight of trapeze artists gliding through the air above the gambling casino is a bit surreal, but most kids (permitted in the observation gallery on the circus level, but not in the casino) love it. A brand new climate-controlled theme park, **Grand Slam Canyon**, opened adjacent to the hotel-casino August 23, 1993. A takeoff on the Grand Canyon, the park features 140-foot sandstone cliffs, tunnels, grottos, a waterfall, and a number of rides, including the only indoor double-loop, double-corkscrew roller coaster in the U.S.

At the **Mirage**, 3400 Las Vegas Boulevard South, (702) 791–7111, a computer-driven volcano erupts every fifteen minutes in the evening, starting at dusk. There's also a giant man-made waterfall and a natural habitat that houses rare Royal Siberian white tigers, which can be viewed for free behind a glass safety screen. Five Atlantic bottle nose dolphins frolic in a 1.5-million-gallon pool; they can be viewed both above and below water level (fee).

Caesar's Palace, 3750 Las Vegas Boulevard South, (702) 731–7110/ (800) 634–6661, has a moving walkway that carries visitors through a brief diorama of Ancient Rome. There's also an Omnimax Theatre, (702) 731–7900, with larger-than-life films that most school-age kids love. At the enormous **Excalibur,** 3850 Las Vegas Boulevard South, (702) 597–7777/(800) 937–7777, a first-floor Fantasy Fair features craft booths, medieval games, gypsy carts, and two forty-eight-seat motion simulator adventure rides. The third-floor Medieval Village boasts shops, seven theme restaurants, and strolling costumed singers, jugglers, and musicians.

Wet 'n Wild, 2600 Las Vegas Boulevard South, on the Strip just south of Sahara Avenue; (702) 734–0088. This water park offers everything from the tame—Children's Water Playground with miniature water slides, bouncing Lily Pads, and water cannons—to wild—rides such as Bomb Bay, which drops you feet first from a capsule, creating a free-fall sensation.

In nearby Henderson (about 15 minutes from the Strip) the following make pleasantly sweet stops on the way to Hoover Dam (see Day Trips).

Ethel M. Chocolates Factory and Cactus Gardens, Mountain Vista and Sunset Road; (702) 433–2500 or (800) 438–4356. Daily free tours show chocolates being made (free sample at the end). Outside, a lovely two-and-a-half-acre Cactus Garden with more than 350 species awaits. Ethel's last name was Mars, and she was the mom of Forest Mars, creator of Mars Bar, M&Ms, and Milky Way.

A free factory tour of **Kidd's Marshmallow Factory,** 8203 Gibson Road (702–564–5400), reveals all you ever wanted to know about how to make these puffy, white confections. You receive a free bag of the goodies at the tour's end.

Museums

Las Vegas is not all "mega" extravaganzas, as evidenced by the following interesting museums (a word used loosely in some cases).

Guinness World of Records Museum, 2780 Las Vegas Boulevard South; (702) 792–3766. This collection of world records covers the biggest, smallest, fastest—stuff that kids love. Browse the videos of world records being set, and the life-size replicas. Interactive computers feature a World of Sports data bank with thousands of sports records brought to the screen at the touch of a button. The World of Arts and Entertainment rocks with a jukebox that plays popular songs. Animal World recounts such oddities as the oldest monkey and the most poisonous jellyfish.

Imperial Palace Auto Collection, fifth floor of Imperial Palace Hotel,

3535 Las Vegas Boulevard South; (702) 731–3311. The more than 200 antique and classic cars on display include many formerly owned by famous personalities—such as a 1939 Mercedes Benz custom built for Adolph Hitler and President Dwight D. Eisenhower's 1952 Chrysler Imperial limousine parade car.

Las Vegas Natural History Museum, 900 Las Vegas Boulevard North; (702) 384–3466. While not huge, this museum is interesting. Three animated dinosaurs, fairly new acquisitions, are popular. The shark room, highlighted by a mounted 14-foot great white shark, has smaller, live versions swimming in a 300-gallon tank. A large hands-on room offers a variety of do-it-yourself activities, such as digging for a fossil or rubbing a dinosaur. Mounted international wildlife (lions, tigers, bears, and cheetahs) and a flight room with mounted birds, such as raptors, geese, and swans, round off the bill of fare. Ask about special programs and workshops.

Liberace Museum, 1775 East Tropicana Avenue; (702) 793–5595. Even kids who haven't the slightest idea who this popular entertainer was enjoy some of the kitschy offerings here. One of the museum's three buildings houses his pianos (including ones once owned by Chopin and George Gershwin) and his spectacular cars. Another building is devoted to the dazzling sequined costumes and jewelry that Mr. Showmanship wore on his worldwide tours. Still another building features the extensive memorabilia collected by Liberace during his lifetime. A sizable part of the admission goes to fund scholarships for deserving students.

Lied Discovery Children's Museum, 833 Las Vegas Boulevard North; (702) 382–KIDS. It was voted "Best Museum" in the *Las Vegas Review Journal's* annual "Best of Las Vegas" poll. Even before you enter, you know it will be fun: The outside resembles a playhouse, with a tepee-shaped structure on the left. Kids let loose at this hands-on place, where there's a Toddler Towers to crawl and slide through, a Space Shuttle and Gyrochair to maneuver, a Musical Pathway to tap a tune on, a KKID radio station to play disk jockey at, and much more. Traveling exhibits, workshops, performances, and demonstrations happen throughout the year.

Parks and Zoos

Southern Nevada Zoological Park, 1775 North Rancho Drive; (702) 648–5955 or 647–4685. This small zoo appeals most to younger kids. They like the petting zoo and the more than fifty species of reptiles and small animals of the southwestern deserts. Other animals not indigenous to the area—monkeys, a lion, and a tiger among others—also please.

Theater, Music, and the Arts

Just about every hotel has some kind of entertainment, though not all is suitable for kids. For listings of current shows and cultural events, check the entertainment pages of the daily *Las Vegas Review Journal* and

Las Vegas Sun, or call the Chamber of Commerce at (702) 735–2451. **Ticket Time** (702–597–1588 or (800) 597–SHOW) specializes in all Las Vegas shows, concerts, golf, and special events.

A note about casinos and shows: Remember that no one under twenty-one is allowed in the casinos. If you want to gamble, choose a hotel with a supervised children's activity center, or take turns being with your kids while the other parent tries his or her luck.

The entertainment in Las Vegas can be relatively inexpensive, and glitzy, but not always appropriate for children. Each show has its own restrictions. Topless shows are obviously not suitable for kids, but some other types of song-and-dance extravaganzas might be delightful. Often individual performers set their own rules about not admitting children younger than a certain age. Check with the box office and the Convention and Visitors Bureau before purchasing tickets.

Sports

The AAA **Las Vegas Stars** baseball team, a farm club for the San Diego Padres, plays at Cashman Field Center from April through September; (702) 386–7201. Championship boxing is also held regularly, as is PGA championship golf.

Shopping

Two malls are located on the Las Vegas Strip: **Fashion Show Mall**, just north of the Mirage, 3200 Las Vegas Boulevard South, has name stores such as Saks, Bullocks, and Neiman Marcus along with 145 specialty shops and eateries—plus a celebrity walk of fame. **Forum Shops at Caesars,** on the ground floor of the hotel-casino, 3570 Las Vegas Boulevard South, is filled with upscale boutiques and restaurants; it recreates ancient Roman streetscapes, with ornate fountains, classic statues, and huge columns and arches.

The Boulevard Mall, a short cab ride from the Strip, 3528 Maryland Parkway, is the largest shopping center in Nevada, with scores of specialty stores and Sears and J.C. Penney as anchors. Bargain hunters may want to try the **Belz Factory Outlet World Mall**, Las Vegas Boulevard South and Warm Springs Road, about 3 miles south of the Hacienda Hotel. This mall, the only nonsmoking facility in Las Vegas, has seventy-two outlets including twenty-five children's stores. **The Las Vegas Factory Outlet Stores of America,** 9115 Las Vegas Boulevard South, offers 30 acres of open-air shopping and fifty outlets.

SPECIAL EVENTS

April: Giant Picnic Land, Lied Discovery Children's Museum, food and fun festival with picnic games and activities, music, and entertainment.

End of May or early June: Helldorado Festival with rodeos, parades, beauty contest.

July: Fourth of July Jamboree, Boulder City.

September: Jaycee State Fair with carnival, entertainment, livestock shows; Art in the Park Fair, Boulder City.

October: Las Vegas Invitational PGA Golf Tournament.

December: National Finals Rodeo.

WHERE TO STAY

With approximately 86,053 surprisingly affordable guest rooms, your family has a large selection of accommodations: everything from inexpensive motels to a penthouse suite on the Strip. It's imperative, however, to reserve well in advance. This is a convention paradise, and sometimes every last room will be booked. **Las Vegas Reservation Systems** (800–233–5594) claims to offer the lowest rates to all Las Vegas hotels. **City Wide Reservations** books rooms as well as hotel packages; call (800) 733–6644. The *Official Visitor's Guide* has a good listing of area accommodations.

If you're prepared for the hustle and bustle of Las Vegas, the megaresort **Circus Circus, Treasure Island, MGM Grand Hotel and Theme Park,** and **Luxor** (described earlier) will do quite nicely. Not too far from the action is the **Mardi Gras Inn,** a Best Western, at 3500 Paradise Road; (702) 731–2020 or (800) 528–1234. It offers 300 minisuites with separate living area, refrigerator, in-room movies, outdoor pool, and free airport shuttle. **Gold Coast Hotel and Casino,** 4000 West Flamingo Road (702–367–7111 or 800–331–5334), a mile west of center Strip, has a bowling center, two movie theaters, outdoor pool, and free child care until midnight for ages two (potty trained) to eight years.

WHERE TO EAT

The *Las Vegas Official Visitor's Guide* contains a descriptive listing of restaurants. Try at least one of the legendary, lavish hotel buffets—the best bargain going. (Though prices vary, an average is about $2.50 for breakfast, $3.50 for lunch, and $4.00 or $5.00 for dinner.) The Circus Buffet at **Circus Circus Hotel/Casino,** 2880 Las Vegas Boulevard South (702–734–0410 or 800–634–3450), is served at breakfast, brunch, and dinner (the latter two offer a sundae bar, as well). Prices are rock bottom. Don't expect to be alone: There are four serving lines that accommodate between 12,000 and 13,000 persons daily—more than 4 million a year. Try the Round Table Buffet at the **Excalibur**, 3850 Las Vegas Boulevard South; (702) 597–7777 or (800) 937–7777. Hot and cold entrées are served from 7:00 A.M. to 10:00 P.M. daily while knights in armor add to the atmosphere. Try some of the restaurants at Luxor, MGM Grand, and Treasure Island.

If the kids crave fast food, take them to the **Mardi Gras Food Court**, Riviera Hotel and Casino, 2901 Las Vegas Boulevard South; (702) 734–5110 or (800) 634–6753. The nine quick-serve restaurants here include Burger King, Tico Riko, Forenza Pizza, Orient Express, and Baskin Robbins. For something more substantial away from the slot machines, try the **Bootlegger Ristorante and Lounge**, 5025 South Eastern Avenue; (702) 736–4936. They serve tasty, moderately priced Italian-Continental meals. Pasta, chicken, veal, and other continental fare are on the menu of **Cafe Michelle**, 1350 East Flamingo Road (702–735–8686), a sidewalk café in the Mission Center.

DAY TRIPS

Lake Mead, a welcome blue oasis in the middle of the desert, is about 30 miles southeast of Las Vegas. The largest man-made body of water (by volume) in the United States, created by the construction of Hoover Dam, the lake extends 110 miles when filled to capacity. More than 550 miles of shoreline, and six marinas, mean plenty of boating, water skiing, and fishing. For campers, there are six developed campgrounds. Open daily from 8:30 A.M. to 4:30 P.M., the Lake Mead Visitor's Center (702–293–4041) is 4 miles northeast of Boulder City on Boulder Highway, U.S. 95. Take a tape for a self-guided tour of the lake's Northshore and Lakeshore roads. Come aboard the paddlewheeler *Desert Princess* (702–293–6180), a tour boat that offers a pleasant way to see the dam, especially with young children. Narration, food, and beverages are offered.

Hoover Dam, considered one of the world's great engineering achievements, is a popular tourist destination. Guided, thirty-five-minute tours leave the top of the dam every few minutes and take visitors inside the structure to see its inner workings. The Hoover Dam Visitors Bureau, 1228 Arizona Street, Boulder City (702–294–1988), shows a free movie daily, every half-hour, about the history of the dam's construction.

Red Rock Canyon, 15 miles west of Las Vegas, is a favorite setting for TV and film Westerns. Enjoy the sculptured sandstone outcroppings and the magnificent geological formations. Follow the scenic, 13-mile, one-way loop for splendid vistas of the blazing-red rock formations. Take time to walk some of the several short trails, which afford glimpses of wildlife as well as streams, springs, and seasonal waterfalls. Picnic sites are located at Red Spring and Willow Spring. Call the Visitors Center at (702) 363–1921 for more information.

Nearby, **Bonnie Springs Ranch/Old Nevada**, West Charleston Boulevard (702–875–4191), is a restored pioneer village with gunfights in the street, train rides on weekends, cactus gardens, two museums, a shooting gallery, restaurant, and ice cream parlour. The Ranch has a petting zoo and horseback riding.

From Thanksgiving to Easter, you can ski at **Lee Canyon Ski Area**, Mt. Charleston, Toiyabe National Forest (702–646–0008), about forty minutes northwest of Las Vegas. **Mt. Charleston Recreation Area**, on U.S. 95 (702–873–8800) also offers summer diversions, such as picnic and campground sites, lookout points, and hiking trails.

If you have never visited the **Grand Canyon**, consider taking a one-day or two-day/one-night air tour from Las Vegas, 200 miles from the attraction. **Scenic Airlines** (702–739–1900 or 800–634–6801) offers a number of packages to the area, including a flight without a tour. Ask about their kids' rates for ages two to eleven.

FOR MORE INFORMATION

Las Vegas Convention and Visitors Authority, 3150 Paradise Road, Las Vegas 89101 (702–892–0711), operates a Visitors Information Center on the Main Concourse of the Convention Center seven days a week from 8:00 A.M. to 5:00 P.M.

Emergency Numbers
Ambulance, fire, police: 911
Poison Information Center: (702) 732–4989
White Cross Drugs, 1700 South Las Vegas Boulevard, is open 24 hours, although the pharmacy is open from 7:00 A.M. to 1:00 A.M.; (702) 384–8075.
Twenty-four-hour emergency room at **Humana Hospital Sunrise**, 3186 South Maryland Parkway; (702) 731–8000

20
NEW ORLEANS
Louisiana

New Orleans is a city of contrasts. A party place and the birthplace of jazz, this city is known for wild Mardi Gras celebrations and the lively nightlife of the French Quarter. Yet New Orleans is also a terrific family destination full of fascinating museums, a world-class aquarium and zoo, and historical sights—not to mention some of the best food around. A visit to this port city on the Mississippi—a mixture of eighteenth-century charm, Old South graciousness, and lively good times—makes for a memorable family vacation.

GETTING THERE

New Orleans International Airport, U.S. 61 in Kenner, about 12 miles west of downtown (504–464–0831), is about a half hour drive. **The Airport Shuttle** (504–522–3500) departs every fifteen minutes for major downtown hotels. Purchase tickets from the Airport Shuttle Information desks. Car rentals are available.

 Greyhound (504–525–9371 or 800–231–2222) and Amtrak (504–528–1610 or 800–USA–RAIL) are neighbors at 1001 Loyola Avenue.

 New Orleans is the point of embarkation for several passenger ships, including Carnival's *Enchanted Seas.* Starting October 1994, the *Tropicale* (800–237–5361), the *Delta Queen* and the *Mississippi Queen* steamboats (504–586–0631 or 800–458–6789), and (in late fall to early winter) Holland America's *Noordam* (800–544–0443) will also depart from New Orleans.

 By car, arrive via I–59 and U.S. 11 from the north; I–10 and U.S. 90 from the east and west.

GETTING AROUND

Much of New Orleans is best seen on foot; self-guided walking tour brochures are available from the Convention and Visitors Bureau. Public bus and streetcar service is provided by the **Regional Transit Authority** (RTA), 101 Dauphine Street; (504) 569–2700. Transfers from the 5-mile-long **St. Charles Streetcar** line to public buses cost 10 cents. The vintage **Riverfront Streetcars** connect the cultural and commercial developments along the riverfront. (New expansion is planned.) Obtain a **VisiTour Pass** for unlimited rides on all buses and streetcars from hotels and shopping areas. RTA's **RideGuide Map** is available at their office or the New Orleans Welcome Center, 529 Ann Street; (504) 566–5068.

New Orleans is on a 5-mile land strip between the Mississippi River and Lake Pontchartrain. Because streets twist in this crescent-shaped city, locals usually give directions indicating riverside, lakeside, uptown (or upriver), and downtown (or downriver)—which is the location of both the Central Business District (CBD), where Canal Street meets the river, and the French Quarter.

Taxis are abundant, and usually you can hail one with little difficulty in the CBD and French Quarter.

A free **ferry system** connects with the West Bank, offering great skyline views. Leave from the Canal Street and Jackson Avenue docks for the twelve-minute trip.

You can hire a mule-drawn surrey carriage by the hour on the Decatur Street side of Jackson Square. If you drive, downtown has short-term metered parking, but read the signs because towing is enforced.

WHAT TO SEE AND DO

The people, sights, and sounds (there's music everywhere) are what make a visit here unique. Here are some of the attractions your family won't want to miss.

The French Quarter

The French Quarter (*Vieux Carre*), considered the heart and soul of the city, is the site of New Orleans' original settlement. The approximately 90-block area is bordered by Canal on the west, Rampart on the north, Esplanade on the east, and the Mississippi River on the south. This is the area most people associate with New Orleans. Besides family sites, the French Quarter also has many tawdry attractions. It might be wise to talk with your children ahead of time about what they may see as they walk along—scantily clad women dancing in bar entranceways, for instance. State your opinion, answer questions, and initiate any relevant conversations before you stroll. All of this is much better dealt with ahead of time rather than as you drag your fourth-grader away from a doorway. Nevertheless, there are family attractions in the French Quarter that your whole family will enjoy.

Visit **Preservation Hall**, 726 St. Peter Street; (504) 522–2841—day or 523–8939—night. It's a great way to introduce kids to the city's incomparable jazz. There's no alcohol or food served. Seating is minimal. Be prepared to wait in line outside the door for the evening shows. Doors open at 8:00 P.M. Admission is $3.00.

Jackson Square, 700 Chartres, is a lively pedestrian mall bordered by St. Ann, St. Peter, and Decatur streets; it's the heart of the Quarter. Along with an equestrian statue of General Andrew Jackson, you'll find mimes, portrait artists, tap dancers, and reggae musicians. Some of the city's most distinguished buildings are here, including the beautiful Spanish-style **St. Louis Cathedral** (504–525–9585), where tours are given daily except Sundays. Two historic buildings are the **Presbytere**, home of the Supreme Court during Spanish colonial times, and the **Cabildo** (scheduled to re-open late February 1994 after renovation), built in 1795 as the **Spanish Governor's Palace** and site of the ratification of the Louisiana Purchase. Both are part of the Louisiana State Museum Complex (504–568–6968), which houses its valuable historical collections in these and several other buildings—including the **Old U.S. Mint**, 500 Esplanade Avenue (504–568–8213), devoted to the history of jazz and including instruments once belonging to Louis Armstrong and other famous musicians, as well as a Mardi Gras exhibit.

Musee Conti Wax Museum, 917 Conti Street; (504) 525–2605. Here historical, costumed Louisiana figures ranging from Napoleon to Louis Armstrong are recreated in wax. Even if you've been disappointed by other wax museums, give this one a chance. Young kids may find the Haunted Dungeon scary, particularly the sound effects (shrieks and wails), though older kids will like this.

Mardi Gras (Fat Tuesday), the day before Lent, is the culmination of at least two weeks of elaborate parades, with the largest occurring the weekend before. On Mardi Gras, parades wind through the narrow streets, and the mostly costumed, mostly rowdy crowd lives it up. Disorderly conduct is commonplace, madness is everywhere, and it's generally not an event for kids. (Besides, the hotels charge more!)

From the French Market district, you can take a Riverfront Trolley to Julia Street, just a few blocks from the **Louisiana Children's Museum**, 428 Julia Street; (504) 523–1357. At press time, the museum was quadrupling its size. Plans include adding the only interactive math exhibit in a children's museum involving hands-on experiences with money, graphics, statistics, and problem solving. The space, scheduled to open in

All hands reach for beads during a Mardi Gras parade. (Photo by Christine Degon)

June 1994, will also feature a physics-oriented science area, theater, art shop, cooking area, and exhibit fostering sensitivity toward people with disabilities.

Zoos, Aquariums, and Nature Centers

Make a day of it visiting the **Audubon Park and Zoo** and the **Aquarium of the Americas**, both run by the nonprofit Audubon Institute. After a visit to the uptown zoo, take a free shuttle bus to the St. Charles Avenue Streetcar, which stops downtown near the Aquarium at 1 Canal Street. Or hop aboard the *John James Audubon* riverboat, which travels back and forth several times a day; (504) 586–8777 or (800) 233–BOAT. Call the Audubon Institute (504–861–2537) for information.

The zoo is at 6500 Magazine Park, just south of Audubon Park, which borders the Mississippi between Exposition Boulevard, Walnut Street, and St. Charles Avenue. It's acclaimed as one of the top zoos in the country. At the Louisiana Swamp Exhibit, you'll be greeted by the world's only white alligators who inhabit a cypress marsh along with otters, raccoons, and other creatures. (Try the Cajun food here.)

Pathways to the Past offers hands-on ways to discover the ancient link between reptiles and birds. Colorful birds in the Tropical Bird House; Suri, a rare white tiger, in the Asian Domain; and the frolicking monkeys and apes in the World of Primates never fail to amuse kids. Other fascinating exhibits include African Savanna, North American Grasslands, and South American Pampas. Don't miss the newly remodeled Californian sea lion pool and amphitheater.

Aquarium of the Americas, 1 Canal Street, on sixteen acres along the riverfront, is a truly outstanding facility that recreates the Western Hemisphere's saltwater and freshwater habitats. As you walk through a 30-foot acrylic tunnel at the Caribbean Reef, you'll be surrounded by parrot fish, angelfish, cownose rays, and hundreds of other specimens. A walk along the treetops of the lush and misty Amazon Rain Forest offers sumptuous views of cascading waterfalls, rare orchids, colorful birds, and such exotic species as poison arrow frogs, red-bellied piranha, and giant Anaconda. In the Gulf of Mexico, a 400,000-gallon exhibit demonstrates how an oil rig can actually become a thriving artificial reef. Watch prowling sharks, Southern sting rays, giant groupers, and 200-pound tarpons swim in the rig's shadows. The Mississippi River Delta, complete with Cajun trapper's station, has rare white alligators, longnose gar, and other native species. The shark exhibit, here through fall 1994, features nearly fifty species, plus a petting pool with baby nurse sharks.

The adjacent **Woldenberg Riverfront Park** (also managed by the Audubon Institute) covers thirteen landscaped acres along a river bend between Toulouse and Canal streets. From here watch ships, tug boats, and paddlewheelers on the Mississippi. The park has more than 300 shady oaks, magnolias, willows, and crepe myrtle trees, and a large green lawn. Call (504) 861–2537 for information.

The **Louisiana Science and Nature Center,** 11000 Lake Forest Boulevard, in Joe Brown Memorial Park (eastern New Orleans); (504) 246–5672. This eighty-six-acre wildlife preserve comes complete with nature trails, a planetarium with IMAX theater, and a greenhouse. Kids can try on a giant turtle shell for size, watch a laser beam show set to music, and follow nature trails through wetlands and forests.

Parks

City Park, 1 Palm Drive, at the city's northern edges (504–482–4888), is on 1,500 acres dotted with majestic oaks draped with Spanish moss. Here you'll find tennis courts; picnic tables; four golf courses; a miniature train ride; 8 miles of lagoons with ducks, geese, and canoe and paddleboat rentals; a Botanical Garden; and Storyland, a nursery rhyme–themed amusement park complete with nineteenth-century carousel and two miniature trains. (If you come during the humid summer, bring bug repellant!) **New Orleans Museum of Art,** Lelong Drive, is in the southern section of the park; (504) 488–2631. Newly renovated and doubled in size, it now houses 35,000 pieces. Among those with kid appeal: the bejeweled imperial eggs of Peter Carl Faberge, Mayan artifacts in the Art of the Americas collection, and the impressionist works of Edgar Degas.

Jean Lafitte National Historical Park and Preserve (504–589–3882) is comprised of several units throughout the city, including the French Quarter, Garden District, Chalmette, St. Bernard, and Barataria, about an hour from town. All offer ranger-led programs, tours, and exhibits. The French Quarter Unit, 916 North Peters (504–589–3719), has free tours, including a daily *Tour du Jour* highlighting such topics as African American heritage, architecture, and women's landmarks. The visitor's center features programs about local history and culture; every other weekend, see demonstrations of ethnic crafts, music, and cooking.

Chalmette Unit, 8606 West St. Bernard Highway; (504) 589–4428. Take a 1½-mile self-guided tour along a road linking key positions on the field where the 1815 Battle of New Orleans took place. Exhibits and an audiovisual program in the visitors center explain the city's role in the War of 1812.

The Barataria Unit, 7400 Highway 45, Marrero (504–589–2330), 15 miles south of town, features the marshy flora of the Louisiana coastline. Walk on boardwalks through oak, palmetto, and cypress trees. Watch a film that introduces visitors to life in south Louisiana; then set out on a nature trail to see the wetlands creatures: alligators, egrets, and ibises among them. In spring, native wild irises bloom.

A number of tour companies in town offer everything from visits to the town's above-the-ground cemeteries to walking tours. One such company is New Orleans Tours, Inc., 4220 Howard Avenue; (504) 592–1991 or (800) 543–6332. Options include a complete city tour and an afternoon of plantation visits (see Day Trips). The CVB sight-seeing brochure features others.

By the time you read this, gambling may have come to New Orleans (although at press time the picture was still unclear, and politically complicated). Harrah's New Orleans plans to open a temporary casino in March 1994 in the New Orleans Municipal Auditorium while constructing the world's largest gaming facility on the site of the Rivergate Exhibition Hall, scheduled to open in 1995. Meanwhile, riverboat gambling on the Mississippi River is also in the works. Hilton Hotels is scheduled to open a casino aboard a riverboat, with plans to premiere the 2,400-passenger *Queen of New Orleans* in 1995 adjacent to the riverwalk and the New Orleans Hilton. Although kids won't be allowed in the gaming area, the plans include a video arcade and gift shop. Call (504) 587–7777 or (800) 587–LUCK for the latest info. The law requires boats to cruise, though their operators would prefer to keep them docked. The first gaming boat is the *Star Casino* on Lake Pontchartrain in Orleans parish. Contact the CVB for an update.

The *Steamboat Natchez,* run by the same company that operates the

John Jay Audubon (the zoo/aquarium ship), offers twice daily river cruises leaving from the Jax Brewery in the French Quarter as well as evening dinner/jazz cruises; (504) 586–8777 or (800) 233–BOAT. *Cajun Queen Riverboat,* leaving from the Aquarium of the Americas dock, and *Creole Queen Paddlewheeler,* departing from Poydras Street Wharf, offer narrated cruises; (504) 529–4567 or (800) 445–4109.

Theater, Music, and the Arts

For information on cultural events, see the entertainment sections of the morning and evening newspapers, *Times-Picayune* and *States-Item,* as well as tourist publications such as *Where* and *This Week in New Orleans,* available around town and at hotels. Ticketmaster (504–522–5555) supplies tickets for most events.

Among the theater troupes: **Pontalba Historical Puppetorium,** 514 St. Peter Street, Jackson Square (504–522–0344), features animated puppets telling the story of legend Jean Laffite. **Le Petit Theatre Du Vieux Carre,** 616 St. Peter Street (504–522–9958), has a Children's Corner with humorous and traditional plays from October through May. Musical comedies and dramas are also performed here in the city's oldest theater, built in 1797. **The Saenger Theatre,** Rampart at Canal (504–524–2490), features touring Broadway shows and pop and rock shows.

Theatre of Performing Arts, North Rampart near corner of Dumaine (504–529–2278), is home to the city's opera and ballet companies. **Louisiana Philharmonic** (504–523–6530) performs at several locations, including the Orpheum Theater, 129 University Place; call for schedule.

Sports

The NFL **Saints** play at the Superdome, 1500 Poydras Street, Sugar Bowl Drive (504–587–3810), from August to December. Site of the Sugar Bowl, this is one of the largest buildings in the world, spanning over fifty-two acres and twenty-five stories high. Tours are offered several times daily, except when events are in progress.

Denver Zephyrs, a AAA minor league farm team for the Milwaukee Brewers, moved to New Orleans in 1993 when major league baseball moved to Denver; they are now the **New Orleans Zephyrs.** In 1994 they will play at University of New Orleans' Privateer Park, corner of Press Drive at Leon C. Simon Boulevard. In 1995 they will move to a stadium (unnamed at press time) in Jefferson Parish at David Drive and Airline; call (504) 282–6777 for tickets.

Shopping

Canal Street is the center of a downtown shopping thoroughfare that is highlighted by **Canal Place,** 365 Canal Street (504–522–9200), with some fifty upscale shops such as Gucci, Saks, and Brooks Brothers. Riverwalk Complex, between Canal and Poydras streets, features some 200 shops (including the Disney and Warner Bros. stores) and eateries along the Mississippi on the site of the 1984 World's Fair.

Antiques hunters venture down to Royal and Chartre streets in the French Quarter to seek out remnants of the Old (and wealthy) South. In the arcades of the over 250-year-old **French Market**, along Decatur Street, you'll find a variety of shops, open-air produce stands, and casual restaurants. **Jax Brewery**, 600-610 Decatur Street, across from Jackson Square (504–586–8015), has over seventy-five specialty shops and restaurants.

SPECIAL EVENTS

Contact the CVB for more information on the following events.

January: Sugar Bowl on New Year's Day at the Superdome.

February–March: Masquerade balls, parades, and festive music of Mardi Gras.

March: St. Patrick's Day Parade; Earth Fest, with games, entertainment, and activities for kids, Audubon Zoo; Crescent City Classic 10,000-meter race beginning at Jackson Square.

April: Crescent City Classic Jr. race for ages four to twelve at East Jefferson Stadium; French Quarter Festival with historic home visits, food sampling, and cruises on the Mississippi.

April/May: New Orleans Jazz and Heritage Festival at the Fairgrounds, ten-day event; Zoo-To-Do at Audubon Zoo features live entertainment, face painters, and a petting zoo.

June: Great French Market Tomato Festival showcases food, entertainment, and tomato tasting; Reggae Riddums Festival, with African and Caribbean crafts, food, and concerts, City Park.

July: Fourth on the River features family entertainment and fireworks.

October: Swamp Festival, Audubon Zoo and Woldenberg Riverfront Park; costume parties and scary stories for kids during Boo-at-the-Zoo.

November: Fall Festival at Destrahan Plantation features food tents; Bayou Classic, college football at the Superdome.

November–January: City Park's Celebration in the Oaks includes caroling and decorations.

December: Creole Christmas, with restaurant specials and open houses.

WHERE TO STAY

The CVB publishes a lodging guide that indicates which hotels provide babysitting referrals. Rates are higher during Mardi Gras, the Jazz Festival, and Sugar Bowl, when it's wise to reserve up to a year in advance.

Because New Orleans hotels are pricey, bed and breakfasts are a good alternative. Call **Bed and Breakfast Inc.**, 1021 Moss Street; (504) 488–4640 or (800) 749–4640. This reservation service books rooms and suites in various neighborhoods; some inns welcome children. Although the French Quarter is fine for exploring, families with young kids probably are better off elsewhere: either uptown or in the city's Garden District (around St. Charles Avenue, with charming nineteenth-century homes) where the atmosphere is less intense.

If you desire to stay in the French Quarter, however, choose a lodging in the quieter part, such as the **Chateau Motor Hotel**, 1001 Chartres Street; (504) 524–9636. They have reasonable prices, free garage, pool, and a coffee shop. Ask for a room overlooking the courtyard. Another good choice is **The Lafitte Guest House**, 1003 Bourbon Street (the quiet, residential part of the street); (504) 581–2678 or (800) 331–7971. They welcome families, supply cribs for infants, and accommodate young children in this antiques-furnished French manor house.

For a big splurge that's worth it, try one of the following. The **Pontchartrain Hotel**, 2031 St. Charles Avenue, near downtown; (504) 524–0581 or (800) 777–6193. It offers one hundred charming rooms and suites with period furniture. Free cribs provided. **Windsor Court**, 300 Gravier Street, (504) 523–6000 or (800) 262–2662, offers rooms and suites, some with kitchenettes.

Centrally located, the **Inter-Continental**, 444 St. Charles Avenue, (504) 525–5566 or (800) 327–0200, offers nicely appointed rooms (under twelve stay free with adults) and a heated pool. **Hyatt Regency**, 500 Poydras Plaza; (504) 561–1234 or (800) 233–1234. The Hyatt is connected to the New Orleans Centre shopping mall. It's big, with 1,200 rooms, some overlooking the heated outdoor pool. Camp Hyatt kids' menus are available. The **Radisson Suite Hotel**, 315 Julia Street, (504) 525–1993 or (800) 333–3333, offers families space.

Some moderately priced, downtown hotels include the **Clarion New Orleans**, 1500 Canal Street, (504) 522–4500 or (800) 252–7466; the **Comfort Inn-Downtown**, 1315 Gravier St., (504) 586–0100 or (800) 228–5150.

Although it's out of the way (5 miles east of the central business district), the free parking, free breakfast, kitchenettes, and special weekly rates at **Family Inns of America**, 6303 Chef Menteur Highway, make up for the inconvenience; (504) 246–2400 or (800) 348–2299.

The **Westin Canal Place**, 100 Rue Iberville, (504) 566–7006 or (800) 228–3000, offers the new Westin Kids Club amenities. These include child-friendly rooms, children's sports bottle or tippy cup upon check-in, as well as a safety kit with a night light, Band-Aids, and emergency phone numbers. Rooms feature bath toys and bath products for kids, and parents can request—at no charge—jogging strollers, potty seats, bicycle seats, and step stools. Restaurants and room service also feature children's menus.

WHERE TO EAT

Restaurants are featured in the tabloid section of the Friday *Times-Picayune*.

Louisiana cooking is a combination of the delicate creole (French, Spanish, and African), with its subtle seasonings, and cajun (Acadian), known for its hearty spices: hot peppers, sausage, and roux (brown sauce). Adventurous eaters will discover some delicious dishes, and even fussy kids will usually find something on the menu to suit their taste-buds. Try the huge local specialty sandwiches, po-boys and muffulettas, big enough to share. What kid wouldn't like puffy, light beignets, covered with powdered sugar? They make a great breakfast or dessert treat. New Orleans also loves pralines (pronounced *praw-leens* here). As for street food, keep an eye out for the Roman Candy Man; he sells taffy from his mule-drawn cart. Also watch for the colorful Lucky Dog hot dog–shaped carts throughout the French Quarter.

Ralph and Kacoo's Seafood Restaurant, 519 Toulouse Street (and several suburban locations); (504) 522–5226. This place is known for its cajun dishes, such as charcoal-broiled redfish, shrimp, crawfish, and large crab. No reservations at this popular, casual spot, so you might have to wait. **The Gumbo Shop**, 630 St. Peter Street (504–525–1486), serves creole cuisine, including gumbo (a thick, spicy soup made with seafood, poultry, or sausage). Enjoy lunch or dinner in this casual atmosphere. They will prepare milder versions of spicy food for younger palates upon request.

Cafe du Monde, 800 Decatur Street (also at Esplanade Mall, Lakeside Mall, and New Orleans Centre); (504) 581–2914. Home of beignets and cafe au lait, the French Market location is open twenty-four hours.

Mother's, 401 Poydras Street; (504) 523–9656. This restaurant is noted for its yummy po-boys and creole dishes, including red beans and rice with sausage. It serves three meals daily, but expect long lines at lunch.

DAY TRIPS

The saltwater Lake Pontchartrain, north of town, is 40 by 25 miles, and a popular place for water sports and sunning on the many beaches. (The water is too murky for swimming.) You can rent a sailboat at **Sailboats South**, 300 Sapphire Street; (504) 288–7245. If you have the time, take a scenic ride over the Lake Pontchartrain Causeway, a toll road that consists of two separate, parallel 24-mile highways that connect the lake's two shores: It's the longest highway bridge in the world.

Several area companies offer tours through the Louisiana swamplands where visitors can observe fascinating plant and animal life. **Swamp Monster Tours,** 108 Indian Village Road, Slidell, about an hour east of the city (504–641–5106), features narrated two-hour voyages on a covered boat through Honey Island Swamp. Alligators may bump their snouts against the side of the boat, and you may spot snakes and white-tailed deer along the banks. The tours are offered daily year-round, weather permitting; reserve in advance because a minimum of six passengers is required.

A visit to a sugar cane plantation can be interesting history, revealing the genteel past of the Old South's privileged classes and the harsh realities of slavery. The closest to the city (22 miles away) is **Destrahan Plantation,** 9999 River Road, Destrahan; (504) 764–9315, the lower Mississippi Valley's oldest plantation house, built in 1787. A fall festival is held the second weekend in November.

Undoubtedly the most impressive is **Oak Alley Plantation,** 3645 Louisiana Highway 18, Vacherie (60 miles from New Orleans, on the river's west bank); (504) 523–4351—New Orleans or (504) 265–2151. The Greek Revival–style mansion has twenty-eight white columns and exactly twenty-eight oak trees outside whose branches form an arch over the wide passageway to the mansion's entrance; it's quite a sight!

FOR MORE INFORMATION

Greater New Orleans Tourist and Convention Commission, Inc., 1520 Sugar Bowl Drive (504–566–5011), has helpful literature. *New Orleans For Kids,* a handy guide for families, is available from them for $5.00, including shipping and handling. A **Welcome Visitor Center** at 529 St. Ann Street (504–566–5031) is open seven days.

Emergency numbers
Ambulance, fire, police: 911
Hospitals with twenty-four-hour emergency rooms include **Tulane University Medical Center,** 220 Lasalle Street (504–588–5711; and **Touro Infirmary,** 1401 Foucher Street (504–897–8250).
Poison Control: (800) 256–9822—Louisiana
A **twenty-four-hour pharmacy** is located at **Walgreen's Pharmacy,** 1429 St. Charles Avenue; (504) 561–8331.

21
PETRIFIED FOREST NATIONAL PARK AND THE PAINTED DESERT
Arizona

A visit to northeast Arizona's 147-square-mile **Petrified Forest National Park** is a fascinating trip back in time. Despite the name, don't expect to find a forest: The semiarid desert and shortgrass prairie landscape contains little vegetation. The main attraction: the remains of what was a forest some 225 million years ago and is now petrified wood, some of it small brightly colored chips, and some of it enormous prone logs. The Petrified Forest National Park presents the largest collection of petrified wood in the world.

How did this come about? Most of northeast Arizona was a floodplain 225 million years ago. When these huge trees (much like sequoias) died, they fell to the ground and began to rot. Then, rivers and streams washed these dead trees into oxygen-deprived swamps, where the trees sank and were covered with mud, clay, and silt. At the same time, widespread volcanic eruptions jettisoned silica-containing volcanic ash into the air that settled on the land. When the silica was absorbed into the swamp water, tiny quartz crystals formed inside the sunken wood, thus "petrifying" it forever. The wood's colors—which include blazing oranges, rusts, deep reds, and yellows, blended with dark white, grey, and tan—shine in the desert.

In the northern part of the park, the **Painted Desert** affords more eye-catching terrain. Here millions of years of erosion have sculpted the sandstone, shale, and clay into colorful pastel layers, many of which reveal fossils of animals that lived millions of years ago. The park service recently approved a twenty-year plan, placing new emphasis on interpretive programs on the fossil beds dating back to the Triassic Period, and the life of early man.

This region of Arizona also offers easy access to **Navajoland** (featured later under Day Trips) and other interesting sites.

GETTING THERE

The closest airport to the area, about 110 miles northeast, is the **Pulliam Municipal Airport**, 6200 South Pulliam Drive, Flagstaff; (602) 556–1234. Car rentals are available at the airport and downtown.

The Flagstaff bus station is **Greyhound/Trailways**, 399 South Malpias Lane (602–774–4573), with connections to the Holbrook station, 2106 Navajo Boulevard (602–524–3832).

Arrivals at the **Amtrak** station, 1 East Santa Fe Avenue, Flagstaff (602–774–8679 or 800–USA–RAIL), can connect to the Winslow station, 300 East Second Street, a little more than 30 miles west of the Park. In Winslow, car rentals are available from **Ames Ford**, 1001 East Third Street (602–289–3354); or **Cake Chevrolet**, 1200 East Second Street (602–289–4681).

By car, enter the Petrified Forest National Park's south entrance by following U.S. 180, about 25 miles from Holbrook. The north entrance is off I–40, 22 miles east of Holbrook.

GETTING AROUND

A car is a must. Driving along the windy, paved 28.6-mile road from either the north or the south is the best way to experience the park. But be sure to get out of your car to look around and explore. Winter storms sometimes close the road.

WHAT TO SEE AND DO

We're starting our journey from the south entrance of the **Petrified Forest National Park** (with mileages indicated), though these sights can be accessed from the north as well. There are visitor's centers at both entrances.

Begin at the **Rainbow Forest Museum and Visitor Center**; (602) 524–6228. Kids marvel at the casting of a gigantic phytosaur skeleton from the Triassic period and other exhibits that show evidence of bizarre amphibians, ferns, and creepy-crawlies that scampered here some 225 million years ago. The museum also exhibits a few prehistoric Native American artifacts, but the main focus is on ancient animal life. The Conscience Wood exhibit contains stolen petrified wood returned with apologies from tourists. Note: Petrified wood is a protected treasure. Each year, the park loses thousands of pounds of it to souvenir-seeking tourists. Don't give into temptation; you may purchase pieces that come from private lands outside the park in most of the area gift shops. Your family should do some exploring on foot. The trails near the visitor's center offer easy strolling. Obtain a pamphlet about the **Giant Logs Trail** from the visitor's centers. This self-guided trail, which begins behind the visitor's center, winds in a half-mile loop past huge rainbow colored logs.

The **Long Logs Trail** starts directly across from the museum. This easy half-mile nature trail gets you close to lots of petrified logs. The mile-long **Agate House Trail**, which branches off from the Long Logs Trail, leads to the Agate House. Ancient Native Americans built this lodging in 1150 A.D. using "bricks" made of petrified wood. Two reconstructed rooms enable you to visualize the house's original size.

From here, head back to the car and drive along the park's northbound road. Keep an eye out for the **Flattops** (mile 5.2), oddly shaped remnants of sandstone that frame this wilderness portion of the park. As you continue, several worthwhile turnoffs offer both scenic views and welcome chances to stretch your legs. Among them: the **Crystal Forest Interpretive Trail** (mile 8.1), a paved ¾-mile trail that features some of the most beautiful wood in the park, and the **Jasper Forest** (near mile 9.9) whose overlook provides great views to the west and north. The **Agate Bridge** turnoff (mile 10.1) leads to a petrified log under which the earth has washed away, leaving a natural bridge, which has since been braced with concrete. At the **Blue Mesa** turnoff (mile 12.9, 2½ miles to parking), an overlook and a 1-mile looping interpretive trail show how the now eroding hills were formed.

Bring binoculars to examine the petroglyph-covered **Newspaper Rock** (mile 12.1). From an observation point above, observe this huge sandstone rock, about 30 to 40 feet tall and wide. Petroglyph markings of spirals, snakes, birds, and other figures create a magical effect.

Puerco Indian Ruins (mile 17.4) contain the remains of tribes who inhabited the area between A.D. 1100 and 1200 and again between around 1300 to 1400. This site, which has undergone some restoration, once contained a one-story pueblo with more than seventy rooms and two kivas. This apparently was one of the first Indian efforts at large-group living. Archaeologists believe that the nearby river, rich soil, birds, and deer attracted more than one tribe to this settlement. Visitors walk along the trail for an up-close look at the petroglyphs and the pueblo's foundations.

Starting at mile 23.6, several overlooks reveal the **Painted Desert**. The desert appears to change color throughout the day, from red-clay to brown to hazy blue and gray tones. Minerals in the sandstone and clay

A walk along the Long Logs Trail affords great opportunites to see petrified trees. (National Park Service photo)

create this dreamy, yet eerie effect. At mile 26.2, **The Painted Desert Inn** (602–524–2550) offers eight breathtaking viewpoints of the desert. The inn was built in 1924 with local materials and Native American labor, and it closed in 1962. Now it's a National Historic Landmark housing a Native American cultural museum, with artifacts and historical explanations, a bookstore, and a park service information desk.

Stop at the **Painted Desert Visitor Center** (mile 28.1); (602) 524–6228. A 17-minute film details the process by which the wood became petrified, and rangers answer questions. Other conveniences: a cafeteria, gas station, and gift shop.

Shopping

Desert Oasis sells such souveniers as Hopi Indian kachina dolls, turquoise Navajo neckpieces, and tomahawks next to the Painted Desert Visitors Center; (602) 524–3756. In Holbrook, find more specialized (and sometimes pricey) Indian boutiques, such as **McGee's Beyond Native Tradition**, 2114 Navajo Boulevard (602–524–1977), which sells Indian jewelry, rugs, and paintings; and **Nakai's Indian Cultural Trade**

Center, 357 Navajo Boulevard (602–524–2329), offering a wide range of Native American pottery, rugs, artwork, and dolls. Many shops also sell petrified wood.

SPECIAL EVENTS

For more details on the following, consult the individual tourist bureaus under For More Information.

February: Flagstaff Winterfest, with snow games, Frozen Buns Fun Run, dog sled races, and a carnival.

March: Arizona Ski and Golf Classic, Flagstaff.

June: Holbrook: Old West Days Celebration, with arts and crafts and a Junior Indian Rodeo. Those who do not dress western may get "arrested." Also, Indian Dancing every weekday, Memorial Day to Labor Day. Flagstaff Route 66 Festival with fajitas and chili cook-offs.

July: Fourth of July Holbrook Fire Department Barbecue and fireworks show. The Native American Arts and Crafts Show, Holbrook, features silver work and paintings; Flagstaff Festival of the Arts.

July/August: Navajo County Southwestern Quilt Festival and Doll Show, Holbrook.

August: Navajo County Fair, Holbrook, has a rodeo, midway, and talent shows. Flagstaff Festival in the Pines displays the handiwork of more than two hundred craftspeople, plus offers a kid's fun area, live entertainment, and international cuisine.

September: Navajo Nation Tribal Fair, Window Rock, the largest Indian fair in the world, featuring intertribal powwow, rodeo performance, competition, and dance, plus a talent show, midway, and food.

October: The Snow/Bowl Ski Extravaganza Fair, Flagstaff.

December: Flagstaff Symphony's Holiday Spectacular.

WHERE TO STAY

The town of **Holbrook**, once a popular stop for those heading out west along Route 66, is the closest city to the **Petrified Forest National Park** in which to find accommodations.

Family choices in Holbrook include the following.

The Comfort Inn, 2602 East Navajo Boulevard; (602) 524–6131. Conveniently located at the exit of I–40, it has a restaurant, pool, and in-room movies. Another familiar name, the **Ramada Inn**, recently opened at 2408 Navajo Boulevard; (602) 524–2566.

For a welcome change from typical motels, try the **Wigwam Motel**, 811 West Hopi Drive; (602) 524–3048. Stay in small buildings shaped like wigwams, complete with brightly patterned blankets, old furniture, and air conditioning.

There are no camping facilities in the national park. However, **wilderness camping** is allowed with a permit from the Rainbow Forest Museum or Painted Desert Visitor Center. Campers should park vehicles at either the **Flattops** (near the Rainbow Forest Museum) or at Kachina Point (near the Painted Desert Visitor Center).

Holbrook campgrounds include **Holbrook Hilltop KOA Campgrounds**, 102 Hermosa Drive (602–524–6689), which offers a pool, showers, cabins, and tent sites, and **O.K. RV Park**, 1576 Roadrunner Road (602–524–3226), with tent sites, showers, and full hookup.

For bed-and-breakfast accommodations, contact the **Arizona Association of Bed and Breakfast Inns**, 3661 North Campbell Avenue; (602) 231–6777 or 622–7167. At press time, the only nearby, family-welcoming bed and breakfasts were in Flagstaff, but call for an updated listing. In Flagstaff, consider **Inn at Four Ten**, 410 North Leroux Street; (602) 774–0088. This recently renovated 1907 building offers nine rooms and moderate rates.

WHERE TO EAT

Inside the park, the **Painted Desert Oasis** has a cafeteria-style restaurant next to the Painted Desert Visitor Center; (602) 524–3756. The **Rainbow Forest Curio** (602–524–3138) offers snacks, ice cream, and sandwiches.

In Holbrook, dining choices include Chinese noodles and stir fry at the **Sundown Restaurant**, 915 West Hopi Drive; (602) 524–3785. Try the salad bar and baked goods at the **Roadrunner Cafe**, 1501 East Navajo Boulevard; (602) 524–2787. For burgers, pizza, and chicken wings, head to **Kody's Dugout**, 405 West Hopi Drive; (602) 524–1888. The Mexican food is worth the wait at **Romo's Cafe**, 121 West Hopi Boulevard (602–524–2153), a local favorite.

DAY TRIPS

Travel northward to the Navajo Nation, which spans more than 25,000 square miles of Arizona, Utah, and New Mexico, forming the largest Native American reserve in the U.S.A. The area contains some spectacular desert scenery and the huge Lake Powell. The Navajos, who administer this territory themselves, are generally tolerant of tourists. But visitors must respect the laws and customs of the Navajo people, and not treat the Indian reservation as a tourist stop. Photography, for example, is restricted. It is completely forbidden, for instance, to snap shots of the devoutly religious Hopi Indians, who reside within the boundaries of the Navajo nation; advance permission must be granted for other photos, including taking snapshots or videos of the homes of Native Americans. This territory operates on Mountain Standard Time. Have your questions answered in advance of a visit by calling the **Hopi Cultural Center;** (602) 734–2401.

The following are several of Navajoland's highlights. Choose your day trip opportunities from among these selections, or set aside several days to explore this area. For lodging and other information about Navajoland, contact **Navajoland Tourism Department,** P.O. Box 663, Window Rock, Arizona 86515; (602) 871–6659 or 7371.

From Holbrook, drive northeast on I–40 to U.S. 12N, to the junction of Highway 264 to **Window Rock,** which has been the capital of the Navajo nation since the 1930s. The city gets its name from the doughnut hole–shaped space in the middle of the towering sandstone rock just northeast of Junction 264 and Indian Highway 12. Visit the **Navajo Tribal Museum,** in the Arts and Crafts Enterprise building, next to the **Navajo Nation Inn.** Here you can see elaborate Navajo craftwork displays and learn about the tribe's origins. Visitors may also sit in on the **Navajo National Council Chamber** meetings when in session, or tour the circular chambers where colorful murals adorn the walls. For information call Mr. Harold Morgan; (602) 871–8417 or 6419. Also in town: **Navajo Nation Zoo and Botanical Park,** near the New Mexico state line on Highway 264 (602–871–6574), contains birds of prey, large mammals, and other animals of cultural importance to the Navajo. The area also includes an exhibition center, trails, and examples of traditional dwellings. **The Navajo Nation Inn,** 48 West Highway 264 (602–871–4108 or 800–662–6189), offers comfortable lodging and guided tours of the immediate area and of such day trip destinations as Canyon de Chelly.

About 30 miles westward, the town of Ganado is the home of the **Hubbell Trading Post,** at the crossroads of U.S. 191 and Highway 264; (602) 755–3254. The nation's oldest known trading post still in operation, established in 1876, is named after the man who traded coffee, sugar, and supplies with the Native Americans in exchange for their thickly woven blankets and handy trinkets. At this National Historical Monument, many Navajos still purchase groceries and other dry goods. Scheduled guided tours and self-guided tours are available.

U.S. 191 takes you north to the **Canyon de Chelly National Monument** (602–674–5436), near the city of Chinle (60 miles west of Window Rock). You'll be amazed by the 1,000-foot sandstone walls that shoot up from the ground as you enter. The National Monument encompasses more than 100 miles of these canyons, prehistoric sites, and Navajo cliff dwellings. The Anasazi Indians lived here for years, and now the area is home to Navajos who reside between the canyon walls. The Monument includes the beautiful, red sandstone, 26-mile long **Canyon de Chelly**, adjoining the 35-mile-long **Canyon del Muerto** and **Black Rock** and **Moment Canyons**. The entrance to Canyon de Chelly is on Navajo Route 64, just past Chinle and a few miles east of U.S. 191. The north and south rim drives incorporate many spectacular overlooks. (Allow about two hours for each rim.) The visitor's center (602–674–5500), at the intersection of the rim drives, sells guidebooks. Here you'll also find information on summer ranger-led activities that might include a daily morning canyon hike, an afternoon archaeology/nature walk, daily talks, and campfire programs.

Jeep tours are the only way to thoroughly explore the canyon's interior, which is rich in prehistoric ruins, plant life, and ancient art. From late spring to early fall, **Thunderbird Lodge**, ½ mile from the visitor's center (602–674–5841), provides loding as well as half- and full-day tours. Horseback rides give you another perspective. Two National Park Service authorized outfitters offer hourly guided horseback tours (extended and overnight rides also available): **Justin's Horse Rental**, at the mouth of Canyon de Chelly (602–674–5678); and **Twin Trail Tours**, North Rim Drive, 9 miles north of the visitor's center (602–674–8425).

The Monument Valley, northwest of Canyon de Chelly, near the Utah border and 23 miles north of Kayenta on U.S. 163 (167 miles north of Flagstaff), is the highlight of Navajoland. This landscape of towering buttes and red-tinted desert is spectacular. The red sandstone monoliths, some almost 2,000 feet high, have been the setting for numerous westerns, such as *Stagecoach* and *Fort Apache*. The valley, which has been preserved by the Navajo, features a 14-mile drive that starts at the visitor's center (801–727–3287), where you'll also find an information desk, exhibits, and crafts. For accommodations and jeep tour information, call **Goulding's Lodge**; (801) 727–3231.

East of the Valley, take advantage of the view at the **Four Corners Monument**, ½ mile northwest of U.S. Highway 60 junction in Tee Nos Pos. From here you can see four states: Arizona, Colorado, Utah, and New Mexico.

Glen Canyon and Lake Powell, 122 miles west of the Valley along U.S. 160 and AZ 98, is a 196-mile-long man-made canyon lake complete with miles of beach, tucked-away coves, marinas, and lots of water activities. At the Glen Canyon Recreation Area, most of it in Utah, families picnic, scuba dive, water and jet ski, hike, and take a number of excursions to area attractions. Call (602) 645–2471 for more information. (See the Arches National Park and Canyonlands chapter for more of Utah's sight-seeing.)

The massive **Meteor Crater**, 35 miles east of Flagstaff and 20 miles west of Winslow, off I–40 via a 5-mile paved road (602–289–2362), is worth a stop. A plummeting meteorite formed this gigantic hole in the earth 49,000 years ago. The Apollo astronauts trained at this exceptionally well-preserved National Landmark. After taking in the view from the observation tower, visit the **Astronaut Hall of Fame** and enjoy a picnic lunch at Astronaut Park. For longer stays, try the on-site RV park; (602) 289–4002. It's complete with rest rooms and private showers, full hookups, country store, recreation room, and playground.

FOR MORE INFORMATION

Petrified Forest National Park, Office of the Superintendent, Box 217, Petrified Forest National Park, Arizona 86028; (602) 524– 6228. **Holbrook Chamber of Commerce,** 100 East Arizona Street; (602) 524–6558. **Flagstaff Visitors' Center,** 101 West Santa Fe Avenue; (602) 774– 9541 or (800) 842–7293. **Canyon de Chelly National Monument,** P.O. Box 588, Chinle, Arizona 86503; (602) 674–5436. **Arizona Office of Tourism,** 1100 West Washington Street, Phoenix, Arizona 85007; (602) 542–8687. **Navajoland Tourism,** P.O. Box 663, Window Rock, Arizona 86515; (602) 871–6659 or 7371.

Emergency Numbers
Ambulance, fire, police or rescue in most areas: 911
Poison control for these areas: (800) 362–0101

In Holbrook
Fire: (602) 524–3131
Police: 524–3991
Hospital: Community General Hospital, 500 East Iowa, (602) 524–3913
Navajoland Tourism (see above) has literature containing emergency numbers, hospitals, and ranger information for different sections of their territory.

In Flagstaff
Ambulance, fire, police: 911
Hospital: Flagstaff Medical Center, 1200 North Beaver Street; (602) 779–3366

In Canyon de Chelly
Ambulance: (602) 674–5464
Twenty-four-hour emergency pharmacy: Winslow Memorial Hospital, 1501 Williamson Street, Winslow; (602) 289–4691

22
PHOENIX
Arizona

Phoenix lures you with much more than golf, although the area's green fairways and those in nearby Scottsdale offer some of the best putting and driving anywhere. But in the city, and just beyond, the legends and colors of the Sonoran desert beckon, with Native American lore, pastel bluffs and buttes, and bold red mountains. Nearby on the Reservation, the trails fill with the green of creosote against wheat-colored rocks, and the scent of sagebrush. Phoenix is an especially charming winter getaway with mild temperatures—no record-breaking summer highs—and a palette of colors and textures to soothe a dreary winter soul.

GETTING THERE

Just minutes from downtown Phoenix is the **Sky Harbor International Airport.** More than twelve major airlines service Sky Harbor, including **Alaska Airlines** (800–426–0333), **America West** (800–247–5692), **Delta** (800–221–1212), and **Trans World Airlines** (800–221–2000).

    Courier Transportation, 1602 South Second Street, Phoenix 85004, (602) 232–2222, and **SuperShuttle,** (800) 331–3565, can take you to your hotel with twenty-four-hour service. **Yellow Cab Co.,** 156 East Mohave Street, Phoenix, (602) 275–8501, offers taxi service.

GETTING AROUND

A car makes getting around convenient. Because there are more than sixteen car rental agencies, shop around and be choosy. Your options include **Hertz** (800–654–2132); **Advantage Rent-A-Car,** Airport 204 South Street, (602) 244–0450 or (800) 777–5500; **Courtesy Leasing and Rent-A-Car,** 101 North Twenty-fourth Street, (800) 368–5145; and **Thrifty**

Car Rental, 4144 East Washington Street, (602) 244–0311 or (800) 367–2277.

The **Transit System** (602–253–5000) runs buses Monday through Saturday, and operates the **DASH** shuttle Monday through Friday.

WHAT TO SEE AND DO

Museums and Attractions

Start exploring this odd-but-captivating coupling of city and desert with a trip downtown to the **Heard Museum**, 22 East Monte Vista Road; (602) 252–8848. The museum offers one of the U.S.A.'s best collections of native Southwest artifacts. In this Spanish-style building of courtyards and intimate galleries, the rooms are cool, the colors hot, and the voices and visions clear.

Don't skip the introductory, thirty-minute slide show, a blend of Native American stories set against spectacular countryside shots. In the rooms that follow, the baskets, tapestries, pottery, and jewelry weave these peoples' histories by presenting the art of their lives. Like the Arizona landscape, the textures and designs are both earth-hued subtle and suddenly dramatic. Be sure to browse the second-floor gallery of Navajo rugs, whose geometric patterns echo the earth's contours.

The **kachina gallery**, many of whose Hopi dolls were donated by Senator Barry Goldwater, exudes a special magic, and appropriately so. Kachinas, after all, represent the Native American spirit essences of all the natural things in the world. The room has an eerie quality, enhanced by a background of taped ancient chants. Some of these kachinas, brightly painted and feathered, are sprightly figures; others, intricately carved from cottonwood roots and bearing elaborate headdresses and masks, appear more formidable. By sitting on the benches and studying these figures, you sense the Native American way of seeing the world through the rhythms of ritual and nature.

Before you leave the Heard, stop at the gift shop, an interesting melange of southwestern items from pricey eagles carved by Native American sculptors, to buckles, rugs, and even chili lovers' cookbooks. The children's collection offers an especially nice assortment of native stories.

Explore the halls of the **Phoenix Art Museum**, 1625 North Central Avenue, Phoenix 85004; (602) 257–1222. The museum is the largest of its kind in the Southwest. From Renaissance to contemporary works, the museum offers hours of viewing pleasure, including paintings, photographs, sculptures, and special exhibits. At times there are Cowboy Artists Shows. Little ones enjoy the children's gallery made just for them.

The **Arizona Museum of Science and Technology**, 147 East Adams

Street; (602) 256–9388. Interactive science exhibits teach kids about a wide range of science from physics to health.

Allow some time to stroll through **Heritage Square**, Sixth and Monroe streets, (602) 262–5071, a three-square-block park, with restored Victorian buildings. Plan your visit on a Wednesday, and you can skip the sit-down meal and munch on fresh veggies from local farmers who sell their produce at stalls surrounding the courtyard.

Green Spaces and Zoos

Visit the **Desert Botanical Gardens**, 1201 Galvin Parkway; (602) 941–1225. At these gardens within city limits, the Sonoran flora, and desert habitats worldwide, come alive with a thirty-five-acre display of 10,000 plants. All outdoors, this living museum, is one of only ten accredited by the American Association of Museums. One visit here dispels the myth that deserts are boring and barren. In the two-hour self-guided walking tour, you discover not only how many shades of green color the desert, but how many shapes flourish there.

The three-acre Sonoran desert display, heralded by a red rock and a huge acacia, presents such distinct habitats as a saguaro forest, a desert stream area, and a mesquite thicket where the air smells lightly sweet. Look quickly to catch the lizards darting from plant to plant.

You can spend hours roaming around with the lions, tigers, and bears at the **Phoenix Zoo**, 455 North Galvin Parkway, Papago Park; (602) 273–1341. With 123 acres and more than 1,200 animals, this is the largest privately owned, self-supporting zoo in the United States. Features include an African Savanna, a children's zoo, and a tram ride to see Indonesian Sumatran tigers.

Special Tours

With your cacti-spotting skills honed and your desert eyes widened, venture into the Sonoran expanse. Go through it by jeep, or glide over it in a hot air balloon. Whatever your angle, the desert boulders, sagebrush, and feathery palo-verde cast a spell as old and potent as the one that lured the prehistoric Hohokam Indians here, the tribe who first settled this river valley centuries ago.

Many companies operate jeep tours and balloon flights. **Cowboy Desert Tours**, (602) 941–2227 and 941–1555, claims exclusive rights to motor through the Salt River Indian Reservation, which borders the city and belongs now to the Pima/Maricopa tribes.

For a roomful of Indian tradition, tour the **Hoo-Hoogam Ki Museum**, Route 1, Box 216, Scottsdale; (602) 941–7379. Alice Santo, frequently present, is the most interesting part of this one-room display of Pima kitchen ware and current children's drawings. Santo sits patiently demonstrating the centuries-old skills of Pima basket weaving; she is one of only six Reservation women who still weave. She painstakingly splits willow reeds with her teeth—it took her three years to master just this— then she twines these thin threads with Devil's Claw to create the ancient black pattern of her tribe.

Next, take to the hills, with its view of **Superstition Mountain**, sacred to the Apache. On these brown hills the Cavalry chased Geronimo and Cochise. From the top of a flat rock, you can imagine the red dust flying as the spirited appaloosas bore these proud Indians in quick pursuit.

A jeep tour reveals up close this beautiful but dusty, and sometimes dastardly, desert. On the nature walk, guides demonstrate how to extract water from a fish-hook cactus, and they caution you to step around the holes that house some of the eleven species of resident rattlesnakes.

But on a desert stroll, you get eye level to a flowering cactus and feel the smooth tops of the boulders. Walk past giant saguaro 30 feet high and 400 years old, and peer at squat hedgehog cactus brightened by pink flowers, jojoba bushes, and prickly pears with pieces munched by wild pigs.

Hot Air Balloon Tours

From a hot air balloon, the Sonoran floats for miles, taking on a fairy-tale softness. The desert appears like a broad bowl rimmed by the city's skyscrapers, urban sprawl, and the red mountains. This bird's eye view is worth the 6:00 A.M. pickup, and thirty-minute drive to a dirt field. Wake up in time to watch the spectacular inflation of these huge balloons, 100 feet tall and 75 feet wide. Mos accommodate eight people; some smaller ones hold four.

The flight itself is magical, as the balloon leaves the earth so smoothly that you won't be aware of the moment of liftoff unless you look down. All of a sudden you're wafting airborne. The glide is as good as the view. And at 2,000–3,000 feet the desert unfolds delicately, and quietly, becoming a smooth stretch of green cacti-dotted earth. Below catch sight of jackrabbits hopping for shelter from the balloon's dark shadow.

The trip, expensive at about $150 per person for an hour's flight, is definitely worth the cost when taken with a reputable company. **Unicorn Balloon Company**, 15001 North Seventy-fourth Street, Scottsdale Airport, Scottsdale, (602) 991–3666, is just one of Phoenix's reputable balloon companies. Sunrise and afternoon flights are available during the winter. Sunrise flights are offered in fall and spring. Check the local tourist board and the hotel's concierge for other recommendations. And be wise. Although some operators take two-year-olds aloft, a wicker basket hanging in the sky is no place to hold a squirming kid. Winds change quickly, and balloons land with a bounce and a thud. Board only those children who are unafraid of heights and who, when standing, can see clearly over the basket's rim. At the journey's end, enjoy the traditional champagne toast.

Sports and Recreation

Those who love race cars will want to find out what's going on at the **Phoenix International Raceway**, 1313 North Second Street, #1300; (602) 252–3833.

In Phoenix sports fans catch up with the **California Angels** on their **Official Spring Training Tour**, 2068 First Street, Livermore, California 94550; (510) 447–1122. Choose a package with lodging, exclusive functions with team members and coaching staff, and preferred game tickets. The **Oakland A's** offer a similar training tour, 2068 First Street, Livermore, California 94550; (510) 373–2432. In season, don't miss seeing the **Phoenix Cardinals**, P.O. Box 888; (602) 379–0101. Basketball fans head to the America West Arena, One Phoenix Suns Plaza, 201 East Jefferson Street, (602) 379–7900, to see the champion NBA team and pride of the town, the **Phoenix Suns**. Pick up tickets at the box office or at **Select Ticket Service**, 540 West McDowell Road; (602) 254–3300.

Golf lovers have scores of immaculate greens and fairways from which to choose. **Cavecreek**, 15202 North Nineteenth Avenue, (602) 866–8076; **Encanto**, 2705 North Fifteenth Avenue, (602) 253–3963; and **Papago**, 5595 East Moreland Street, (602) 275–8428, are some of the area's public courses. A number of private clubs and hotels offer golf, including **Arizona Biltmore Country Club**, Twenty-fourth Street and Missouri Avenue, (602) 955–6600; the **Ritz-Carlton**, 2401 Camelback Road, (602) 468–0700; **Marriott's Camelback Inn Resort, Golf Club and Spa**, 5402 Lincoln Drive, Scottsdale, (602) 948–1700, which has a championship course; and the **Hyatt Regency Ranch Scottsdale**, 7500 Doubletree Ranch Road, Scottsdale, (602) 991–3388 and (800) 233–1234.

Performing Arts and Entertainment

In season, venture down to **Patriot Square Park**, Washington and Central avenues, where you can picnic and enjoy the performances on the outdoor stage.

The **Arizona Theater Company** (602–256–6899), **Arizona Opera** (602–226–7464), **Ballet Arizona**, and the **Actors Theater of Phoenix** all make their home at the **Herberger Theater Center** (602–381–0184). Undergoing renovation, the 1929 **Orpheum Theatre**, near city hall in downtown Phoenix, was once considered one of the West's most luxurious theaters. When completely renovated, this 1,450-seat playhouse will stage performing arts, film festivals, and children's theater. The **Sundome Center for the Performing Arts**, R.H. Johnson Boulevard, Sun City West, (602) 584–3118, seats 7,169, making it the largest single-level theater in the U.S. Celebrities and various performing art groups regularly take to the stage here. At the **Phoenix Civic Plaza Convention Center and Symphony Hall**, 225 East Adams Street, (800) AT–CIVIC, the **Phoenix Sym-**

phony Orchestra plays, and a variety of other events take place. Call for a schedule.

Need more excitement after dark? **America's Original Sports Bar/ Phoenix Live!**, 455 North Third Street, offers 40,000 square feet of games. Another Phoenix area winner for after-five entertainment, **The Improvisation**, 930 East University Drive, Tempe, (602) 921–9877, offers dinner and a comedy revue.

SPECIAL EVENTS

January: Phoenix Open Golf Tournament, (602) 870–0163, usually hosted by the Tournament Players Club golf course.

April: Photo Extravaganza—Carefree/Cave Creek, (602) 488–3381. Capture the blossoms and wildflowers of the desert's spring.

May: Cinco De Mayo Festival, (602) 262–5025, which celebrates the Mexican victory over French troops in 1862, is a lively and colorful fiesta.

September/October: Jazz on the Rocks (602–282–1985) draws crowds from across the Southwest to hear their favorite musicians play.

November: At the Hot Air Balloon Race and Thunderbird Balloon Classic, (602) 978–7208, world competitors compete for prizes.

WHERE TO STAY

The Phoenix/Scottsdale area has a variety of accommodations. Here are some good choices.

The **Hyatt Regency Scottsdale**, 7500 Doubletree Ranch Road, Scottsdale; (602) 991–3388, or for reservations, (800) 233–1234. The Hyatt is a desert oasis with ten swimming pools and championship golf, and it also hosts a children's program on weekends year-round for three- to twelve-year-olds. Program operates Friday 5:00 P.M.to 9:00 P.M., Saturday 9:00 A.M. to 9:00 P.M., and Sunday 9:00 A.M. to 5:00 P.M., and daily in the summer and on holidays. Various package plans are available. Regency club rooms come with complimentary breakfast, afternoon snacks, cocktails and hors d'oeuvres, and one hour of free tennis.

The deluxe **Scottsdale Princess**, 7575 East Princess Drive, Scottsdale, (602) 585–4848 or (800) 223–1818, offers weekly Super Team Sports Camps for locals and guests ages five and older Monday through Friday from June to mid-August. Kids play tennis, enjoy pool games, and do arts and crafts. On major holidays, the Princess Kids Klub offers activities for ages five to twelve from 9:00 A.M. to 12:30 P.M. and from 5:30 P.M. to 8:30 P.M.

One of the best ways to explore the many hidden wonders of the Sonoran desert is on a guided tour on horseback. (Courtesy Phoenix and Valley of the Sun/Convention and Visitors Bureau)

Red Lion's La Posada Resort, Scottsdale, (800) 547–8010, rests under the shadow of Camelback Mountain and offers a pool with cascading waterfalls.

The Boulders, P.O. Box 2090, Carefree, Arizona 85377; (800) 553–1717. On 1,300 acres in the Sonoran foothills at Carefree, outside Phoenix, this spacious resort offers desert ambiance, fine dining, and a top-rated golf course. All rates include modified American plan. Various packages are available.

The Pointe has three locations in the Phoenix area. Tapatio Cliffs, 11111 North 7th Street, Phoenix 85020, (602) 866–7500; South Mountain, 7777 South Pointe Parkway, Phoenix 85044. For both locations, call (800) 528–0428. Accommodations at these pleasant hotels with a Spanish influence are suites clustered around interior courtyards. Various rates and packages.

The newly renovated all-suite **Pointe Hilton Resort at Squaw Peak,** 7500 North Dreamy Draw Drive (602–977–7777 or 800–934–1000), comes with a complex of kid-pleasing pools and a year-round children's program for ages four to twelve from 9:00 A.M. to 5:00 P.M.

The newly opened **Holiday Inn SunSpree Resort Scottsdale**, 7601 East Indian Bend Road (800–HOLIDAY) offers affordable prices and a children's program.

At press time the **Ritz-Carlton Phoenix**, 2401 East Camelback, (602) 468–0700 or 800–241–3333, was in the process of extending its Ritz Kids program and standardizing family friendly amenities at all Ritz hotels. Call for the latest information.

The 1929 classic, **The Arizona Biltmore**, is at Twenty-fourth St. at Missouri; (602) 955–6606 or (800) 228–3000. Partially built under the direction of Frank Lloyd Wright, the hotel is situated on thirty-nine acres and has two PGA golf courses and eight tennis courts. The Kids Kabana, a supervised play program, is offered year-round, daily from 8:00 A.M. to 6:00 P.M. for ages four to twelve. Special programs are added at holidays and in the summer.

In downtown Phoenix, the **Holiday Inn Crowne Plaza**, (602) 257–1625 or (800) HOLIDAY, offers moderate rates at a location convenient to the American West Arena, the convention center, and the Algora Center.

Just minutes outside of the city is **The Wigwam**, Litchfield Park, Arizona 85340; (800) 327–0396. They provide you with privacy and comfort in guest casitas hidden among an orange-and-palm-tree oasis. A true Southwest luxury resort, The Wigwam has tennis courts, a pool, a health club, horseback riding, and seasonal kids' programs.

WHERE TO EAT

Try **The Good Egg**, 2957 West Bell Road, Phoenix 85023, (602) 993–2797, and 906 East Camelback Road, Phoenix 85014, (602) 274–5393. They serve up fresh breakfasts and lunches straight off the griddle. Omelets and frittatas are some of their specialties. For dinner, try the barbecue landmark of Arizona, **Bill Johnson's Big Apple**, 3757 East Van Buren Street, Phoenix 85008, (602) 277–6291, or 3101 West Indian School Road, Phoenix 85017, (602) 863–7921. Over three decades of experience make this restaurant an oldie but goody. Authentic Mexican cuisine begins at **Garcia's Mexican Restaurants**, 5509 North Seventh Street at Missouri Avenue, Phoenix 85014, (602) 274–1176, or 4420 East Camelback Road, Phoenix 85018, (602) 952–8031. For thirty years this has been a top pick in Phoenix for south-of-the-border dishes and atmosphere at reasonable prices. The **Compass Restaurant**, 122 North Second Street, Phoenix 85004, (602) 252–1234, offers a menu of southwestern dishes with a breathtaking view of the Valley of the Sun. For a special dinner before you go, visit **Christopher's Bistro**, 2398 East Camelback Road, Phoenix 85016; (602) 957–3214. Voted 1989's Best New Chef by

Food and Wine magazine, Christopher Gross will lure you in with exciting American specialties with a French flair.

DAY TRIPS

For more desert beyond Phoenix, don't miss **Sedona**, 120 miles north of Phoenix on I–17 and Route 179. It is an easy day trip to a dramatically different landscape of red rock mountain ranges. But the road to Sedona, about two hours from Phoenix, is part of the fun.

At 4,000 feet, as you pass **Prescott National Forest**, brackish colored bushes cover the ground, and yellow "prairie grass" grows in patches. Nearby, make a quick stop at **Montezuma Castle National Monument**, I–17 north to exit 289 (about 25 miles south of Sedona). These well-preserved, four-tiered, limestone cliff dwellings started in the twelfth century offer insight into the Hohokam life by the river.

Back on the road, the canyons and cliffs on the Coconino National Forest come into view, as do the buttes surrounding Sedona. Rising in fantastical shapes, separated by stretches of pine, piñon, and sycamore trees, these singular rock formations amaze, and their hues dazzle. Salmon, wheat, rust, and red, these towering mesas and buttes flash with brash streaks of pinks, purples, and grays. This is sheer delight.

Sedona, a town in the heart of Arizona's Red Rock country, is a funky match of old-time western polyester stores, Native American trading posts—try Gordon Wheeler's for some of the more authentic Native American jewelry—and art galleries, complete with an upscale, but ersatz Spanish-style shopping plaza, Tlaquepaque. In the three tiers of shops radiating out from a central plaza, you will find leather, pottery, crafts, and hand-woven clothes. Browsing is good fun, and when you tire, just sit and enjoy the view of Sedona's fabulous rocky slopes fronted by green forests.

Venture further to experience one of the great natural wonders, the **Grand Canyon**, about five hours drive from Phoenix. The range of colors along the canyon walls carved into the earth by the Colorado River offers amazing views year-round. Take a hike through the mighty basin, ride down on the back of a mule, or drive the scenic rim. Take Interstate 17 north to Flagstaff, then Route 180 northwest to the Canyon.

Play cowboy on a six-day backpacking and horseback riding tour of the Superstition Mountains. **American Wilderness Experience**, P.O. Box 1486, Boulder, Colorado 80306, (800) 444–0099, offers this trip for ages eighteen and older. Visit cliff dwellings, look for coyote, deer, and rattlesnakes, and camp in tents under the stars.

FOR MORE INFORMATION

Phoenix and Valley of the Sun Convention and Visitors Bureau, One Arizona Center, 400 East Van Buren Street, Suite 600, Phoenix 85004–2290; (602) 252–5588 or (800) 992–6005 in Arizona.

Flight Guides West, Inc., 1635 East Myrtle Avenue, Suite 300, Phoenix 85020; (602) 943–4493; monthly flight guide and airline schedule information.

A Taste of Phoenix, 3370 North Hayden Road, Suite 123-289, Scottsdale 85251; (602) 998–5810 for dining guide.

The Arizona Office of Tourism (602–542–TOUR), the Phoenix Chamber of Commerce (602–254–5521), the Visitor Hotline (602–252–5588), and Arizona State Parks (602–542–4174) all offer visitor information.

Emergency Numbers

Ambulance, fire, police: 911

Phoenix Fire Department: (602) 253–1191

Air Evac Medical Air Transportation: 2630 Sky Harbor Boulevard, Phoenix 85034; (502) 244–9327

Phoenix Police Department: (602) 262–7626

Poison Control: (602) 253–3334

Hospitals: St. Joseph's Hospital and Medical Center, 350 Thomas Road, Phoenix 85013; (602) 285–3000. Phoenix Memorial Hospital, 1201 South Seventh Avenue, Phoenix 85007; (602) 258–5111

Doctor Referral: (602) 230–CARE

23
SALT LAKE CITY
Utah

Salt Lake City, the capital of Utah, takes its name from the 92-mile-long Great Salt Lake, 15 miles north of town. The lake features white-sand beaches, beautiful pink-streaked sunsets, and many species of migratory birds. The sprawling city, surrounded by the Wasatch Mountains in the east and north and the Oquirrh Mountains to the west, is a safe area where families can enjoy a relaxed vacation at a slower pace than in most other cities. The city is world headquarters of the Mormon religion, whose first settlers arrived in the valley in 1847. Today more than half of the city's population are practicing Mormons, members of the Church of Later Day Saints (LDS). The city's Mexican American, Greek, and Japanese communities add some cultural diversity to this clean, inviting city.

GETTING THERE

Salt Lake International Airport, 776 North Terminal Drive (801–539–2400), serves most major airlines and is fifteen to twenty minutes west of downtown. Car rentals, cabs, city bus #50 (with hourly departures), and courtesy vans from some of the better hotels provide transportation into the city.

The **Amtrak** station (800–USA–RAIL) is at 320 South Rio Grande. **Greyhound** is at 160 West South Temple; (801) 355–9589 or (800) 231–2222. Interstates 15 and 80 intersect in Salt Lake City.

GETTING AROUND

A car isn't absolutely necessary, thanks to the public transportation system and the fact that most of the main tourist activities cluster right in the heart of town. The streets run at right angles to each other, numbered in a grid scale starting at the center point of Temple Square.

The **Utah Transit Authority's** bus system (801–287–4636) is extensive and runs throughout the valley. A free fare zone helps visitors tour the downtown area. Call the transit authority for information. An old-fashioned trolley, with pickup points at Trolley Square and Temple Square, circles downtown and major hotels.

Among the taxicab companies: **City Cab** (801–363–5550), **Ute Cab** (801–359–7788), and **Yellow Cab** (801–521–2100).

WHAT TO SEE AND DO

Historical Sites

The center of the city, and the heart of the Mormon religion, historic **Temple Square**, 50 West North Temple, encompasses ten acres enclosed within a 15-foot wall. Inside are the six-spired **Mormon Temple**, the **Tabernacle** (which is the concert hall), **Assembly Hall**, gardens, monuments, and information centers; (801) 240–2534. Several types of free guided tours are given throughout the day.

Completed in the 1890s, the temple, constructed from granite and hardwood, took Mormon pioneers forty years to construct. It rises more than 200 feet above ground at its highest point. Only confirmed Mormons may enter the Temple, but millions of visitors are allowed in the Tabernacle across the plaza.

The **Tabernacle's** unusual design catches attention with its domed roof and red sandstone piers. The building's acoustics are amazing; kids, seated in the rear, "ooh and aah" when they hear the "cling" of a pin as it hits the floor near the front podium. Public organ recitals take place daily. The public may attend Thursday evening rehearsals of the world famous **Mormon Tabernacle Choir** and their Sunday morning performances at 9:30 A.M. (when they're in town). Visitors also are invited to the Tuesday and Wednesday evening miniconcerts by the Mormon Youth Choir and Symphony.

At the **Joseph Smith Memorial Building**, just east of Temple Square, 15 East South Temple (801–240–1266), sit down at one of the 150 family research stations and find out about your ancestors by accessing the computer base. It's open Monday through Saturday from 8:00 A.M. to 10:00 P.M. For more in-depth research, head to the main library around the corner, the **Family History Museum**, 35 North West Temple; (801) 240–2331. It has the world's largest collection of genealogical information, including registers, passenger lists, local histories, and much more. You do not need to be a Mormon to access these records or find them useful. The archives cover information on many generations of individuals in more than fifty countries.

Beehive House, 67 East South Temple, a block east of Temple Square;

(801) 240–2671. Here city founder Brigham Young made his home in the mid-1800s. See how pioneers conducted their daily lives through displays that include hand-stitched quilts and rugs, butter churns, and iceboxes. Free twenty-minute tours take place regularly throughout the day. The beehive, a symbol of the Mormon's work ethic, is on the building's small tower and is also part of the Utah state seal.

The **State Capitol**, North State Street and Capitol Hill (801–538–3000), is quite impressive, with an ornate interior and great views from Capitol Hill. Admission is free.

Museums

While not exactly teeming with museums, Salt Lake City has some kid-friendly places the whole family will enjoy.

At the **Hansen Planetarium**, 15 South State Street (801–538–2014), you can see not only stars, but also 3-D shows with laser beams that dance in sync with popular music, three floors of exhibits, including a rock brought back from the moon, and educational science presentations. Kids spin in the Gyro Rings, and make their hair stand on end by touching the Van de Graaf generator. In the domed theater participate in the frequent star-identification lectures and shows that allow you to push buttons and decide which journey through the starry skies you embark upon.

The **Pioneer Memorial Museum**, 300 North Main Street (801–538–1050), has an extensive collection of pioneer artifacts. Step back in time to prairie days as you peruse old-fashioned dolls, wooden clocks, and hand-stitched clothing of the period. The Carriage House is a separate building with the covered wagon used by Brigham Young to cross the plains as well as a mule-drawn streetcar and a blacksmith shop.

The **Children's Museum of Utah**, 840 North 300 West; (801) 328–3383. Here kids have a chance to play surgeon and implant an artificial heart, experience what it's like to get around in a wheelchair, and be a TV anchor or a 747 jet pilot. Regularly scheduled seminars and workshops explain everything from how to make a clay pot to how a cow produces milk.

Utah Museum of Natural History, University of Utah campus, Wasatch Drive; (801) 581–4303. *Jurrasic Park* fans will be impressed by the almost-complete dinosaur skeletons unearthed in the state. Other worthy collections such as the Hall of Minerals also intrigue kids.

Great Salt Lake

The 92-mile-long **Great Salt Lake** is quite marshy and somewhat sticky. Kids are fascinated by the tiny brine shrimp that live in the lake and the "thick" water, which has a salinity rate as high as 27 percent, though the salt concentration is not as high as it used to be. Floating in the lake is still a unique experience. Warning to kids: Don't get a mouth-ful of this water because it tastes terrible. And if you get it in your eyes, you'll wish you hadn't. The water stings quite badly. Be sure to wear eye goggles for swimming.

One of the most accessible points to the lake is **Saltair Beach State Park,** 16 miles west of the city on I-80; (801) 250-4400. Here you'll find white-sand beaches, camel rides, picnic areas, paddleboats, food conces-sions, and a parking lot. At the **Saltair Pavilion** summer concerts take place.

Amusement Parks

Cool off in the huge freshwater pools and nineteen water slides of **Raging Waters,** 1700 South 1200 West; (801) 973-9900.

Lagoon Amusement Park and Pioneer Village, 17 miles north on I-15 in Farmington (801-451-8000), is the largest amusement park be-tween Kansas City and the West Coast. Get an all-day passport for access to 125 rides, ice show, pioneer village, music, games, food courts, and the water park. There's an adjacent campground and RV park.

The 49th St. Galleria, off 700 West; (801) 263-2987. This entertain-ment mall has an 80-foot bungee tower (but we don't recommend jump-ing; just watch if you must), bowling, video games, roller skating, and a food court with lots of choices.

Parks and Zoos

Hogle Zoo, 2600 Sunnyside Avenue (801-582-1631), is home to more than 1,200 furry, feathered, and scaly creatures from around the world. Those with special kid-appeal: the Great Apes exhibit, the African Savannah, and the tropical rain forest. Don't miss the hands-on Discovery Land, where kids experience what it feels like to be an animal, sliding down the middle of a hollow tree or "burrowing" under the earth. Tiny tots might like to touch the critters at the Small Wonders Barn.

Stroll through fifteen acres of gardens at the **Red Butte Garden and Arboretum,** the University of Utah, off South Campus Drive on the east-ern edge of Fort Douglas; (801) 581-5322 or (801) 581-IRIS for recorded information. This is a pastoral, take-a-break place with duck ponds, water lilies, abundant floral displays, and rare plants. Free tours are offered, or guide yourself through the well-labeled gardens. Outside of the main garden, another one hundred acres remain in their natural state, except for the easy hiking trails that are open to visitors. On sum-mer Saturday mornings, a Canyon Kids Concert might include Scottish or Greek dancing, and a demonstration of symphony instruments. Sun-day evening summer concerts bring top local and national talent. En-trance to the gardens, open year-round from 9:00 A.M. to sunset, is free.

Located on sixteen wooded acres in the southwest corner of Liberty

Park is **Tracy Aviary,** 59 East 1300 South; (801) 596–5034. A leader in nature education and the oldest public aviary in the world, it features more than 1,000 bird species, from vultures to eagles to tropical varieties. Free bird shows held twice daily (except Monday) delight all. **Liberty Park,** 1000 South and East streets (801–972–7800), has kiddie rides and boat rides on a pond.

Pioneer Trail State Park, 2600 East Sunnyside Avenue (801–584–8391), below the mouth of Emigration Canyon on the east side of the city, marks the end of the Mormon Trail, used for twenty-two years by 68,000 pioneers migrating from Illinois. Facilities include a recreated pioneer town where costumed hosts greet visitors in buildings (some reconstructions, most relocated original dwellings) with authentic furnishings. At the visitor's center, a mural and audio presentations detail the migration of the Mormon pioneers. The park is also the site of **This is the Place Monument,** 2601 Sunnyside Avenue, commemorating the site where Brigham Young first explained, "This is the place," referring to a safe refuge for Mormons. From here, enjoy a breathtaking view of the valley.

Go country at **Wheeler Farm,** 6351 South Ninth East; (801) 264–2212. At this horse-powered seventy-five-acre dairy, visitors can help milk cows, feed chickens, and gather eggs each afternoon. Nature walks, fishing, wagon rides, farming and weaving demonstrations, songs, and pioneer stories are part of the fun. December brings Christmas on the Farm, with wagon rides, Santa, nativity play, and homemade decorations.

Special Tours

Old Salty (801–359–8677 or 800–826–5844) is a two-hour, summer tour of Salt Lake's main attractions aboard canopied open-air rail cars that leave from Temple Square. Just because of the vehicle, these tours have more kid appeal than the city bus tours provided by companies such as **Gray Line Tours,** 353 West 100 South; (801) 521–7010.

Theater, Music, and the Arts

Salt Lake City Visitors Bureau provides information on cultural attractions, or consult the morning *Salt Lake City Tribune* or evening *Desert News.* The city hosts several theaters, including the **Pioneer Theater Company** at the University of Utah (801–581–6961 or 581–5682), a well-respected regional theater with equity actors in leading roles. **Salt Lake Repertory Theatre** (City Rep), 148 South Main Street (801–532–6000), stages musical comedies.

Ballet West (801–393–9318), **Riroe-Woodbury Modern Dance Company** (801–328–1062), and **University of Utah's Repertory Dance Theater** (801–581–6702) all perform at the Capitol Theatre, 50 West 200 South (801–534–4364), as does the **Utah Opera Company.**

Salt Lake City's Trolley Square holds much in store for visitors. (Courtesy Salt Lake City Convention and Visitors Bureau)

The **Utah Symphony** gives concerts year-round at Symphony Hall, 123 West South Temple; (802) 533–6407 or 533–5626.

Sports

Salt Lake Trappers minor league baseball team plays from mid-June to Labor Day at Derks Field, 65 West 1300 South; (801) 484–9900. The popular NBA **Utah Jazz** basketball games are held at Delta Center, 301 West South Temple (801–325–SEAT or 800–358–SEAT), where **Golden Eagles Hockey** games also take place.

Shopping

Trolley Square, 600 South 700 East, is a complex of fashionable shops, eateries, and theaters in buildings that used to house the town's electric trolleys. Just south of Temple Square, you'll find two enormous downtown shopping malls—**Crossroads Plaza**, 50 South Main (801–531–1799), with four floors of shops and restaurants; and **ZCMI Center Uptown**, 36 South State (801–321–8743), with two floors of stores, including the ZCMI Department Store and a food court.

Gardner Historic Village, 1095 West 7800 South, West Jordan; (801)

566–8903. The village features old-style shops and the 1877 Gardner Mill, converted into a country store. In the village, **Archibald's Restaurant** (801–566–6940), a former grain silo, serves up teriyaki chicken, fish, salads, and other dishes. The builder of the silo, Archibald Gardner, was a Mormon during the time when polygamy was still accepted. Each booth has a portrait portraying one of Gardner's eight wives, along with a brief history of her life.

SPECIAL EVENTS

Contact the Salt Lake Visitors Bureau for more information on the following events.

March: Music in the Mountains offers a variety of musical talents.

June: Utah Arts Festival with performing artists, crafts, children's art yard, and environmental exhibitions.

July: The Days of '47 Celebration honors the arrival of the pioneers in 1847, with square dancing, fireworks, rodeos, and one of the biggest parades in the U.S.A.

August: Belly Dancing Festival, with Middle Eastern food and festivities; Nature Fair at Tracy Aviary.

September: Utah State Fair; Greek Festival, three days of dancing, performances, and plenty of baklava.

November: Historic Temple Square Christmas Lighting Ceremony electrifies 250,000 lights that decorate the square; a Dickens Festival with Christmas shops and entertainment operates from late November to mid-December at the Utah State Fair Park; Buffalo Round-up, Antelope Island in Great Salt Lake.

December: Candlelight Christmas Tour, Pioneer Trail State Park features caroling, and costumed pioneer families who welcome visitors to their period-decorated homes and share stories and cookies.

WHERE TO STAY

The *Salt Lake Visitors Guide* has a comprehensive listing of lodgings, including several bed and breakfasts. Because tourism is Utah's number one industry, expect a wide choice of reasonably priced accommodations. If you plan to visit in April or October when Mormons from other regions congregate here, be sure to reserve well in advance.

Downtown: **Peery,** 110 West 300 South Street; (801) 521–4300 or (800) 331–0073. The city's oldest lodging is an elegant, renovated seventy-seven-room hotel with in-room movies, free breakfast, free cribs, and two restaurants. **Red Lion Hotel,** 255 South West Temple

(801–328–2000), is large and modern, with 495 rooms and nineteen suites (some with refrigerators), a pool, free airport shuttle, restaurant, and coffee shop. The **Quality Inn City Center**, 154 West Sixth Street (801–521–2930 or 800–4–CHOICE), offers well-priced, comfortable accommodations.

Elsewhere: The **Residence Inn by Marriott**, 765 East 400 South (801–532–5511 or 800–331–3131), is 8 blocks from downtown and one block from Trolley Square. Suites sleep up to six, and there's an outdoor pool, complimentary continental breakfast, and free airport shuttles. **Embassy Suites Hotel**, 600 S.W. Temple (801–359–7800 or 800–362–2779), offers another suite option for families, plus an indoor pool.

Budget accommodations are available at **Travelodge**, 524 South West Temple Street (801–531–7100 or 800–255–3050), and the **Shilo Inn**, 206 South West Temple (801–521–9500 or 800–222–2244). Both are near numerous restaurants, and the Shilo Inn has a pool.

WHERE TO EAT

Salt Lake Visitor's Guide has a restaurant section with maps and descriptions. Here are some good family choices.

Ruth's Diner, 2100 Emigration Canyon Road; (801) 582–5807. About ten minute from downtown, the diner is known for their great breakfasts (lunch and dinner also served) presented amidst 1940s decor. Right next door is the **Santa Fe Restaurant**, 2100 Emigration Canyon Road; (801) 582–5888. It has a romantic Southwest lodge setting and serves a Sunday brunch buffet, plus daily lunch and dinner.

The **Cafe Pierpont**, 122 West Pierpont Avenue; (801) 364–1222. Located in a renovated school, it welcomes families with Mexican fajitas, enchiladas, fresh tortillas, and nachos. **Brackman Brothers Bagels**, 147 South Main (801–537–5033), the best place for New York–style bagels, also sells sandwiches and snacks.

Check out the elaborate setting, as well as the Mexican and American food at **Totem's Club and Cafe**, 538 South Redwood Road; (801) 975–0401. Wooden pillars, wagon wheels, spouting fountains, and live entertainment add to the western-lodge feel. Because the restaurant is a bit out of the way, many of the downtown hotels provide shuttle service.

DAY TRIPS

Salt Lake City is the gateway to nine ski resorts, all located within an hour of downtown. This is a skier's paradise as the season runs from November until May or June. The UTA (801–BUS–INFO) provides daily buses to Alta, Brighton, Solitude, and Snowbird. (Note: Salt Lake City is a hopeful for the 2002 Winter Olympics. See the Wasatch chapter for additional information on Utah ski areas as well as the recreational opportunities of the **Wasatch National Forest**.)

In summer, these slopes offer families great hikes and a variety of recreational opportunities. Snowbird (801–521–6040) and Solitude (801–534–1400) offer weekend mountain bike clinics for all levels. In addition, in summer take the aerial tram to the summit of Hidden Peak for splendid views of Heber Valley and the canyons of the Wasatch Mountains. Two trails lead back to the base, about a two-hour hike. Guided hiking tours can be arranged.

Kennecott's Bingham Canyon Mine, U-48, Copperton; (801) 322–7300. Located 22 miles west of Salt Lake City, the canyon is the largest man-made excavation on earth—2½ miles from rim to rim. A visitor's center houses an exhibit explaining the pit's geology and open-pit copper-mining operations, and a theater features a twelve-minute video on the mine. The center provides a bird's eye view into the huge open pit where trucks and shovels appear to be toy sized. Open April to October, it's worth seeing.

Adventure

A number of Salt Lake outfitters offer rafting trips on the Green, Colorado, San Juan, and other rivers from May to September. Try **Holiday River Expeditions**, 544 East 3900 South (801–266–2087 or 800–624–6323), which also heads to the Yampa River in Dinosaur State Park. Another option is **Moki Mac River Expeditions**, 1821 East Fort Union Boulevard; (801) 268–6667 or (800) 284–7280. Minimum ages vary with the trips, which range from one day to two weeks.

Salt Lake City is a good starting point for heading to the state's five national parks, all a day's drive away: Arches and Canyonlands (see the Arches chapter), Capitol Reef, Bryce Canyon, and Zion. Contact the Utah Travel Council for more information.

FOR MORE INFORMATION

Salt Lake Convention and Visitors Bureau, 180 South West Temple; (800) 541–4955 or (801) 521–2686. **Utah State Travel Council**, 300 North State Street, Capitol Hill Council Hall, Salt Lake City 84114; (801) 538–1030 or (800) 222–UTAH. **Visitor Information Center**, Temple Square at South Temple Street (801–240–2534), has information on the Mormon church.

Emergency Numbers

Ambulance, fire, police: 911

Hospitals: Holy Cross Hospital, 1045 East 100 South; (801) 350–4111. Primary Children's Medical Center, 100 North Medical Drive; (801) 588–2233; main number 588–2000

Poison Control twenty-four-hour hotline: (801) 581–2151 or (800) 456–7707

A twenty-four-hour pharmacy is located inside the grocery store Harmon's, 3200 South 1300 East; (801) 487–5461

24
SAN ANTONIO
Texas

Yes, San Antonio is a big city—but it doesn't have that hectic, congested feeling. What this town near the south central tip of Texas does have is loads of charm, personality—and lots of appealing, family-friendly attractions. San Antonio will open up your kids' eyes to different cultures and life-styles as well as to some significant moments in U.S. history. Everyone will remember the Alamo long after they return home. They will also remember taking a boat ride right through downtown on the San Antonio River. Parents will never hear those discouraging words— "I'm bored."

GETTING THERE

San Antonio International Airport, (210) 821–3534, about fifteen minutes from downtown, is serviced by a number of major airlines. The **Star Shuttle** (210–366–3183) provides twenty-four-hour service to major downtown hotels. Taxis and car rentals are available at the airport.

Amtrak (800–USA–RAIL) has a station at 1174 East Commerce; the local phone number is (210) 223–3226.

Greyhound/Trailways is at 500 North St. Mary's Street; (800) 231–2222.

By car, you can reach San Antonio via one of four major interstates leading into it from every direction: I–35, I–10, I–37, and I–410. The city is surrounded by an outer loop; each freeway leads into the central business district.

GETTING AROUND

The **Metropolitan Transit Service's** ninety-four regular VIA bus routes and four downtown streetcar routes go to every major tourist attraction and business in the central district. Express bus routes operate from downtown to Sea World and Fiesta Texas, and there are two cultural tour routes. The streetcars, reproductions of those used a half century ago, are a special treat—and the fare is only a dime. VIA's downtown information center is at 112 North Soledad; (210) 227–2020.

WHAT TO SEE AND DO

Museums and Historical Sites

The Alamo, 300 Alamo Plaza; (210) 225–1391. Smack in the heart of the city is the best-known tourist site in Texas. All of the 189 patriots who fought for Texas's independence from Mexico died here on March 6, 1836, after thirteen days of repeated attacks by Mexican General Santa Anna and 4,000 men. Eventually, Santa Anna was captured and the Texas revolutionists were led to victory by Sam Austin.

Start your visit at the **IMAX Theatre** in Rivercenter, (210) 225–4629, immediately adjacent to the southeast corner of the Alamo complex. A forty-five-minute film entitled *Alamo: The Price of Freedom* is shown five times daily and offers a good introduction to what went on here and will help put your visit into perspective.

Cowboy Museum and Gallery, 209 Alamo Plaza; (210) 229–1257. Wild West aficionados will like the authentic cowboy, Indian, gunfighter, and trail driver outfits displayed at this fun museum, along with carriages, wagons, buggies, and other Wild West memorabilia—including a Sioux necklace made out of human finger bones (the kids will be talking about this for months). There's a replica of a western town, a western art gallery, and a great gift shop.

Hertzberg Circus Museum, 210 Market Street (corner of South Presa and West Market streets); (210) 299–7810. Appealing exhibits include a miniature model of a three-ring circus, complete with animals and performers, Tom Thumb's carriage, a priceless antique circus poster collection, plus lots of other Big Top memorabilia.

Institute of Texan Cultures, 801 South Bowie at Durango, HemisFair Park; (210) 226–7651. The name may not do it justice, but this is quite an interesting place to explore the state's ethnic diversity and pioneer heritage. The institute encourages visitor participation, so you don't have to worry if your kids head to the loom to try out weaving or climb inside the Indian tepee. In the middle of the exhibit floor, the Dome Theatre shows *Faces and Places of Texas*.

After your visit, head over to **HemisFair Urban Water Park**, 200 South Alamo Street; (210) 558–2300. This is not a traditional water theme park; however, lots of water spurts and cascades from the fountains here, so the appellation is technically correct—and nobody said you can't get wet. The park also has a creative playground where your tykes can let loose. The park's 750-foot-high **Tower of the Americas** (210–299–8616) provides the best vantage point of the city. HemisFair Park was the site of the 1968 World's Fair.

Ripley's Believe It Or Not! and **Plaza Theatre of Wax**, 301 Alamo Plaza; (210) 224–9299. At the wax theater, more than 200 lifelike characters loom in four theme sections: Hollywood, Texas History, Religion, and Horror (very young kids may be frightened by these ghouls, but it's all in good fun). Ripley's exhibits include 500 one-of-a-kind oddities from around the world. You can buy a single or combination ticket.

San Antonio Museum of Art, 200 West Jones Avenue; (210) 829–SAMA. The building this museum is housed in—formerly the site of the Lone Star Brewery—is a treat in itself. It's a castlelike structure with glass elevators, skylights, and skywalks. There's something for everyone, from Greek and Roman sculpture to art most kids can relate to, particularly the extensive folk art collection. Kids' workshops are frequently held in the Start Gallery.

The Witte Museum, 3801 Broadway (adjoining Brackenridge Park); (210) 820–2111. This institution, more than sixty years old, is full of hands-on exhibits of Texas history, natural science, and anthropology. Steer the kids toward Texas Wild: Ecology Illustrated, a permanent exhibit showing the ecological diversity of the state's seven natural areas. Walk through the diorama recreating the southern Texas thornbush and its wildlife—armadillo, javelina, and the endangered jaguar. There are also many other exhibits and family programs here.

Still in the planning stages at press time, the **San Antonio Children's Museum** is slated to open downtown at 305 East Houston Street in the fall of 1994. Designed primarily for ages two to ten, exhibits and interpretive materials will be in both Spanish and English, and are planned to foster understanding of the multi-cultural diversity of modern urban life. The visual centerpiece of the museum is to be a climbing structure featuring composite elements and reminders of San Antonio landmarks and attractions. Call (210) 21–CHILD.

Attractions

Fiesta Texas, at the junction of I–10 and Loop 1604, northwestern San Antonio; (210) 697–5050. This new theme park (actually a "musical showpark") is great fun, with rides, food, performers, a water park, and four major theme areas: Rockville, an area that lovingly recreates life in the fifties and early sixties; Spassburg, the German village—a homage to nearby Texas Hill Country—recreates Oktoberfest with sing-alongs, oompah bands, and authentic foods and features five special children's rides; Crackaxle Canyon, a 1920s boom town, is highlighted by the fa-

The Rivercenter is the heart of San Antonio's famed River Walk. (Courtesy San Antonio Convention and Visitors Bureau)

mous Rattler—the highest and fastest wooden roller coaster in the world; and Los Festivales, the Mexican theme area, which features Latin American music and dance, plus major productions showcased in the 2,000-seat theater. Bring your bathing suit for Splashwater Springs water park, with wet attractions for all ages. The park operates daily from Memorial Day weekend through Labor Day and is open weekends from March through Memorial Day weekend and from Labor Day weekend through Thanksgiving weekend.

Paseo Del Rio (River Walk), in central downtown, is San Antonio's heartbeat. A narrow slice of the San Antonio River gently winds for 2½ miles through the city some 20 feet below tree-lined cobblestone walkways lined with restaurants and shops. River Walk stretches from the Municipal Auditorium on the north end to the King William Historic District on the south, with its restored Victorian buildings. Take a riverboat ride along the Paseo's twenty-one blocks—especially nice at night, when the lively walk twinkles with lights, and music fills the air. Narrated tours are offered by Paseo del Rio boats, (210) 222–1701, or take

The River Limo, a black boat with flags, which stops at major establishments along the walk. Purchase tickets on board or in advance at several downtown hotels, restaurants, and ticket locations.

Sea World of Texas, 10500 Sea World Drive; (210) 523–3000/(800) 527–4757—Texas or (800) 722–2762—nationwide. This 250-acre park (currently the largest of the Sea World Parks) thrills all ages with more than twenty-five shows, exhibits, rides, and concerts. Of course, there's Shamu, the gentle killer whale.

The dolphin and beluga whale show is another winner, but chances are your family's favorite will be the hilarious sea lion, walrus, and otter performance entitled Spooky, Kooky, Castle. All kids love the penguins, who "do their thing" quite naturally behind a glass partition as guests glide by on a slow moving conveyer walkway. Prepare to get wet at two water theme rides: the Texas Splashdown flume (a roller coaster–type ride with a five-story drop) and Rio Loco, a wild, churning six-person circular raft ride. Both are a bit turbulent for the average young child, but the park's newest water adventure, Lost Lagoon, has something for all ages: a huge wave pool with surf as high as 3 feet, a 40-foot tower with four twisting slides, children's water play area; and an adult activity pool with tube slide and waterfall. The centrally located Shamu's Happy Harbor is a youngster's dream come true: a three-acre play area with net climbs, sway bridges, sand play areas, and more—plus fast food and shaded seating for grown-ups. Summer brings special evening shows and laser light and fireworks demonstrations. A special treat within the park is Cypress Gardens West, a twelve-acre haven featuring a variety of foliage, flower beds, lawns, and waterways. The park is open weekends and some holidays during the spring and fall, daily during the summer, and is closed December through February.

You can also take the plunge at **Splashtown,** 3000 North Pan Am Expressway (three minutes north of downtown on I–35N); (210) 227–1400. This family water park features a dozen major water rides, a huge wave pool, and Kids Kove for tykes.

Parks, Gardens, and Zoos

Brackenridge Park, 2800 block of Broadway (main entrance); (210) 229–8480. This 433-acre park is a gem. The idyllic setting includes the San Antonio River, which originates from underground springs north of the park and then winds through groves of ancient oaks and the Japanese Tea Garden with its floral displays, irregularly shaped ponds with giant goldfish and water lilies, pebble pathways, bridges, and a waterfall. The park is also good fun: You'll find a golf course, polo field, bike trail, paddleboats, and picnic area. On North St. Mary's Street, ride a carousel at number 3910, a miniature railway at number 3810 (it runs on a 3½-mile track through the park), and a scenic Skyride at number 3910. Also visit both the highly respected **Zoological Gardens** and **Aquarium**, home to more than 3,600 animals and birds in barless cages and open pits resembling their natural habitats. Children's Zoo highlights include a Tropical Tour boat ride, playground, Everglades exhibit with alligators and water birds, and an educational center with a rain forest.

San Antonio Botanical Gardens, 555 Funston; (210) 821–5115. Feast your eyes (and nose) on this thirty-three-acre garden of flowers found throughout the state. A third of the facility is devoted to formal gardens including an aquatic, herb, and biblical garden, with fig trees, date palms, and other plant life mentioned in the Holy Book. A garden for the blind emphasizes touch and scent. After entering the conservatory, descend into a tunnel 16 feet below ground where ecosystems blossom in tent-like glass pavilions.

Theater, Music, and the Arts

Consult the Friday "Weekender" section of the *San Antonio Express News* for cultural and special events, or call the San Antonio Convention and Visitors Bureau. Tickets for a variety of major events and concerts, including those held at the new Alamodome, can be obtained from Ticketmaster at (210) 224–9600.

The unique **Arneson River Theatre**, in La Villita on the River Walk, (210) 299–8613, has its stage on one side of the river and its audience on the other. Something entertaining is bound to be going on during your stay: Fiesta Nacho del Rio and Fiesta Flamenco are two popular shows being performed regularly at press time. **Majestic Theater**, 212 East Houston Street, (210) 226–3333, hosts touring Broadway shows and the San Antonio Symphony Orchestra. Summer children's theater is offered by the **Guadalupe Cultural Arts Center Theater**, 1300 Guadalupe Street; (210) 271–3151.

Sports

For information on schedules and tickets, contact the following: **San Antonio Missions** baseball, April through August, (210) 434–9311; **San Antonio Spurs** basketball (NBA), November through April, (210) 224–9578; **San Antonio Racquets** team tennis, July, (210) 732–1223; **Houston Oilers** summer training camp (NFL), July and August, (210) 736–1105. The new Alamodome is the site of **The Alamo Bowl**, featuring major college football on New Year's Eve as well as occasional Houston Oiler games; call (210) 207–3651.

Shopping

Market Square is a Mexican-style market that comprises two square blocks downtown at I–35 and Commerce Street. Vendors sell fruits and vegetables at the farmers market building (soon to be renovated). The indoor market, El Mercado, features more than thirty-five specialty shops selling locally made arts and crafts; jewelry; and Mexican, South American, and southwestern Indian products. Some shopkeepers will bargain with you, others won't. Restaurants and shops line the plazas outside El Mercado, and the patios host frequent fiestas.

Another appealing shopping area is **La Villita**, a historic district on the east bank of River Walk. Visitors can browse through shops of twenty-five artists and craftspeople and watch many of them at their work. For more information, call (210) 299–8610.

SPECIAL EVENTS

It seems there's always a fiesta or two going on in San Antonio. Contact the SACVB for more information on the following events.

February: Carnival Del Rio, a long weekend of entertainment and food along River Walk.

March: Alamo Memorial Day; St. Patrick's Street Parade downtown and St. Patrick's River Dyeing, includes Irish dancing and music; Spring Renaissance Fair, La Villita.

April: Fiesta San Antonio, the biggest of the year, features ten days of parades, festivals, sporting events, music, arts shows, and other events.

Late April–early May: Cinco De Mayo, festival at Market Square celebrating Mexico's independence from France.

May: Tejano Conjunto Festival features the music of South Texas (a mixture of Mexican and German).

Memorial Day: Return of the Chili Queens, celebration (and eating) of chili.

August: Texas Folklife Festival celebrates the history and heritage of more than thirty ethnic groups who settled in Texas with four days of song, dance, food, and crafts.

October: Shrine Circus (month may vary).

November: San Antonio Marathon; Lighting Ceremony and Holiday River Parade; Holiday River Festival.

December: Christmas festivities include Rivercenter Pageant; Fiesta De Las Luminarias, where thousands of candles illuminate the River Walk; Fiestas Navidenas, with piñata parties, blessing of the animals, and a visit from Pancho Claus in Market Square; and Las Posados, with singers moving along the River Walk.

WHERE TO STAY

The SACVB publishes a lodging guide and map. A lodging reservation line (800–858–4303) gives you information about the hotels they service. The city has accommodations in all prices, including a number of inexpensive motels in the airport area, as well as large national chains located throughout the city. For bed and breakfasts, contact **Bed and Breakfast Hosts of San Antonio** reservation service; (210) 824–8036 or (800) 356–1605.

The ideal location to be, of course, is along River Walk. Here are a few selections in this area.

If you're looking for charm versus chain hotels, here are two hotels that exude personality. **La Mansion Del Rio**, 112 College; (210) 225–2581/(800) 292–7300—Texas or (800) 531–7208—U.S., Mexico, and Canada. This hotel (a law school in another incarnation) overlooks the River Walk and is tastefully decorated with a Spanish Colonial flair. There's an excellent on-site restaurant and lovely garden courtyards. **The Fairmount Hotel**, 401 South Alamo, (210) 224–8800 or (800) 642–3363, only has thirty-six rooms, but its reputation is large. Originally built in 1906, the hotel was scheduled to be demolished in 1985 when conservationists saved it from the wrecking ball, arranging to have the hotel moved to its present location, just opposite HemisFair Park (2 blocks from the River Walk). The luxurious hotel, with seventeen suites, is listed in the *Guiness Book of World Records* as the largest building ever moved intact on wheels—a "factoid" that kids love!

The city's largest hotel, the **Marriott Rivercenter**, 101 Bowie, (210) 223–1000 or (800) 648–4462, offers 1,000 rooms, plus an indoor/outdoor pool, the largest health club in town, a full-service restaurant, and a fine dining restaurant open for dinner only. The hotel is connected to the Rivercenter Mall.

Embassy Suites has two locations. One is at the airport, **Embassy Suites Hotel-Airport**, 10110 Highway 281 North, (210) 525–9999; and the other is **Embassy Suites Northwest**, 7750 Briaride; (210) 240–5421 or (800) 362–2779.

Don't forget the Hyatt, with two area locations. **Hyatt Regency San Antonio**, 123 Losoya, (210) 222–1234 or (800) 223–1234, built over an extension of the San Antonio River, has 631 rooms and water cascading through the lobby, linking the river and the Alamo. Kids get a Welcome Kit and specially priced menus. The new **Hyatt Regency Hill Country Resort**, 9800 Resort Drive, is located some 20 miles north of town; phone (210) 647–1234 or (800) 223–1234. The 500-room luxury hotel features a four-acre water park with two swimming pools (one a Ramblin' River floating waterway) separated by a waterfall—plus Camp Hyatt children's program for ages three to twelve during holidays, weekends, and daily throughout the summer. Rock Hyatt for teens thirteen to seventeen offers excursions, sports, and social events as well as a Rock Zone meeting place. Call for schedules.

WHERE TO EAT

The Friday "Weekender" section of the *San Antonio Express News* contains a dining guide; the Convention Bureau also provides a listing of restaurants. It's most fun to eat along River Walk; many eateries here are fine for families and relatively inexpensive. **Kangaroo Court Restaurant,** 512 River Walk, (210) 224–6821, serves American fare (burgers, fries) and is known for its yummy cheesecake. Try Texan favorites (BBQ, chicken fried steak) at **Republic of Texas**, 526 Riverwalk; (210) 226–6256. Sample Tex-Mex food at **Rio Cantina**, 421 Commerce; (210) 226–8462.

At Market Square, **Cafe Y Panaderia Mi Terra**, 218 Produce Row, (210) 225–1262, is a local institution with a bakery in the lobby and a dining room where tamales and tacos are served to a constant flow of appreciative diners twenty-four hours a day.

DAY TRIPS

Take a ride to Hill Country: Fredericksburg and Kerrville are two charming historic German communities north of San Antonio. Kerrville, 65 miles away, is an arts and crafts mecca and home of the **Cowboy Artists Museum**, 1550 Bandera Highway, (210) 896–2553, with changing exhibits of paintings, drawings, and sculptures by members of the Cowboy Artists of America. Fredericksburg, 71 miles from San Antonio and settled by German immigrants in 1846, has wide streets lined with century-old gingerbread houses and many antiques shops. You can still hear German spoken occasionally here. **The Museum of the Pacific War**, 340 East Main Street, (210) 997–4379, is dedicated to those who served in World War II with Fleet Admiral Chester W. Nimitz.

You won't be far from the **LBJ Ranch**, 75 miles from San Antonio on U.S. 290. Former president Lyndon B. Johnson and his wife Lady Bird donated 200 acres of their ranch to the National Park Service. The **LBJ State Park**, just off 290, includes a visitor center with museum and theater, picnic sites, swimming pool, wildlife enclosures, and the Johnson family cemetery where LBJ is buried. The ranch is located 15 miles west of Johnson City on Highway 290 near the town of Stonewall. This is also where the LBJ State Park is located, (210) 644–2252, with the museum and visitor's center. Bus tours to the ranch (you can't go on your own) from the visitor's center are run by the LBJ National Historical Park; call (210) 868–7128 for tour information.

A quick trip to Mexico is another possibility. **Nuevo Laredo** is only 150 miles south of San Antonio and features colorful shops.

A statement to Mexican customs that you intend to visit only the border city is all that is required. If you are driving, it's also recommended you purchase short-term Mexican auto insurance that's available from several agencies and travel services on the U.S. side of the border. Most U.S. car insurance is not valid in Mexico.

Note: When only one parent (whether that parent is married or divorced) is entering Mexico with a child or children, Mexico requires a notarized statement from the other, non-traveling parent indicating that the traveling parent has permission to take the child into Mexico for a specified amount of time. This rule is designed to cut down on child kidnappings by disgruntled non-custodial parents. Obtain a similar letter when you are traveling with children who have a different last name from yours.

FOR MORE INFORMATION

The **Convention and Visitors Bureau** operates three information sites. The main center: 317 Alamo Plaza (directly across from the Alamo), open every day (except Thanksgiving, Christmas, and New Year's Day) 8:30 A.M. to 5:00 P.M.; (210) 299–8155 or (800) 447–3372

Satellite centers: terminals number one and two at the San Antonio Airport, (210) 821–3421 or 821–3448, open every day from 10:00 A.M. to 6:00 P.M.

VIA Metropolitan Transit provides transportation for the handicapped. Call their VIA TRANS line at (210) 227–5050 or TDD 227–7744. Most San Antonio attractions are wheelchair accessible. The River Walk, however, has only limited accessibility.

Our Kids Magazine, 8400 Blanco Road, (210) 349–6667, features a monthly calendar of events for families and other interesting news; it's free at various locations throughout town, or call for a sample copy.

Emergency Numbers
Ambulance, fire, police: 911
Poison Control (Galveston): (713) 654–1701
Twenty-four-hour pharmacies: Eckerd's Drug Stores at 6900 San Pedro Avenue, (210) 824–3237, and 9832 Wurzback, (210) 690–1616
Twenty-four-hour clinic: Nix River Walk Clinic, 408 Navaro, (210) 271–1841

25
TUCSON
Arizona

In Tucson, just after a rainfall, the desert smells like creosote and sage. Explore higher in the red rock mountains that ring this city, and the towering saguaros point the way into a landscape where jackrabbits and prairie dogs cool off in the shade of mesquite trees, javelinas leave tracks in the sand, and the wind carries the scent of pine and the buzzing of bees. Here the boulders reveal ancient petroglyphs, the age-old secrets of the Hohokam Indians, "the vanished ones" who disappeared leaving behind only cliff dwellings, rock designs, and pottery shards.

Tucson's landscape is like that. The subtle shades and variations pull you into its legends and lore. In this town you will learn of cowboys, cactus, Native American culture, and enjoy some special museums.

GETTING THERE

The **Tucson International Air Terminal** (602–573–8100) is 10 miles south of the city and is served by eleven major airlines, including **Alaska Airlines** (800–426–0333), **America West** (800–247–5692), **Delta** (800–221–1212), and **Trans World Airlines** (800–221–2000). The **Tucson Airport Information Centers** (602–290–9191), located at the airport, provide tourist information.

For ground transportation, buses come into the **Greyhound/Trailways** station, 2 South Fourth Avenue; (602) 231–2222. Trains arrive at the **Amtrak Station**, 400 East Toole; (800) 872–7245. The transcontinental route I–10 offers an east-west highway approach to the city; this route joins I–19 and follows the west side of Tucson, offering convenient access to major streets. From San Diego in the west, take I–8, which joins I–10. From the Canadian border use U.S. 89 to Tucson.

GETTING AROUND

Avis (800–331–1212 or 602–294–1494) and **Hertz** (602–294–7616 or 800–654–3131) are among the car rental agencies. **Sun Tran** (602–792–9222) provides buses throughout Tucson. Some taxi services include **Allstate Cab** (602–624–6611) and **Checker Cab** (602–623–1133), but the locals advise visitors to rent a car. Sites are spread out, and taxis at times are hard to find.

WHAT TO SEE AND DO

Museums and Green Spaces

Start your Southwest tour 14 miles west of town at the **Arizona-Sonora Desert Museum**, 2021 North Kinney Road; (602) 883–2702. Part zoo and part botanical garden, this mostly outdoor facility displays more than 200 live animals and 1,000 species of plants. You find that far from being a boring or barren place, the Sonoran desert features such diverse habitats as grasslands, riparian (streamside) regions, and mountainous areas.

Highlights to explore include a recreated limestone cave complete with mineral room (kids love the phosphorescent glow-in-the-dark quality of these gems) and a Mexican oak pine woodland thick with hopbrush, mesquite, and mountain yucca, and home to black bear and mountain lions.

Kids love gawking at the ocelots, jaguarundi, and vultures as well as marveling at the myriad shapes of cactis. Allow time to tour the aviary, a soothing place to rest for awhile and spot the birds.

With your eyes and ears sharpened to the desert's variety, enjoy more of the real thing by driving through the **Saguaro National Monument** (602–296–8576 or 602–883–6366) whose western section abuts the desert museum. To reach the western section, drive west on Speedway; to reach the eastern section, drive east on the Old Spanish Trail. In each area endless groves of towering saguaro dot the landscape. These cacti serve as the quintessential symbol of the Old West.

Old Tucson Studios, 201 South Kinney Road (602–883–0100), is just a whoop and a holler away from the western section the Saguaro National Monument. Since 1939, when Columbia Pictures built this western town as a set for *Arizona*, this red rock and cactus country has served as the backdrop in scores of Hollywood movies and television westerns such as *Gunfight at the O.K. Corral* and "Little House on the Prairie." Nighttime brings special events such as rodeos, concerts, and musical shows. Call for daily show schedules, filming, and other special events.

The International Wildlife Museum, 4800 West Gates Pass Road;

(602) 629–0100. Some people may enjoy this museum of mounted displays and dioramas, but after experiencing the real desert, some people see these exhibits as stilted. There are also films and presentations that show hundreds of species of mammals, birds, and reptiles, and an interactive video display of the world's game parks and wildlife refuges. Guided tours offered hourly Wednesday through Sunday, 9:00–5:30.

For a beautiful display of plants and flowers, visit **The Tucson Botanical Gardens**, 2150 North Alvernon Way; (602) 326–9255. Covering more than five acres of land, the indigenous plants include wildflowers, cactus, and herb gardens. Kids enjoy the interactive Children's Multicultural Garden, and the new Sensory Garden, complete with a sensory treasure hunt. Special events from classes to concerts are frequently scheduled, so be sure to call.

Just outside town, the **Pima Air and Space Museum**, 6000 East Valencia Road (602–574–0462), features more than 180 vintage and contemporary aircraft. Even if you can't tell a Cessna Skymaster from a Lockheed Neptune or a Learjet, all of which are on display, you will be impressed with these flight legends. Particularly interesting are the vintage World War II planes, including gliders and bombers. On the field as well is the Airforce One used by Presidents Kennedy and Johnson. You could spend all afternoon here, but count on at least two hours.

Before you head back to town, 9 miles southeast of Tucson is the **Mission San Xavier del Bac**, 1950 West San Xavier Road; (602) 294–2624. The Jesuits founded this mission, which is on the Tohono O'odham Indian Reservation, in the 1600s. Walk around this "White Dove of the Desert," visit the school, and admire the Spanish mission architecture. If you visit during the spring, try to catch the San Xavier Pageant and Fiesta.

In town, on the University of Arizona campus, the **John P. Schaefer Center for Creative Photography** (602–621–7968) offers visual treats of a different nature. Aside from the photographers' archives, galleries, library, and research facility, a rare collection of more than 50,000 photographs makes this center a delight. By prior appointment enjoy a private viewing of the original prints of such noted masters as Ansel Adams, Richard Avedon, Linda Connor, Edward Weston, and dozens more.

Star gaze at the **Flandrau Science Center and Planetarium** (602–621–4515), which is also at the university. Check out the star show, laser light show, and 360-degree movie.

Before you leave campus, allow some time to explore **The Arizona State Museum**, Park Avenue and University Boulevard; (602) 621–6302. The museum displays collections of pottery and artifacts used in the daily activities of the Native Americans, including the region's ancient Native Americans.

If you are interested in art, browse through the **Tucson Museum of Art**, 140 North Main Avenue (602–624–2333), and **The University of**

A trip to Old Tucson Studios provides something for everyone. (Photo courtesy Old Tucson Studios/Arizona Office of Tourism)

Arizona Museum of Art (602–621–7567). Both offer a variety of exhibits from Renaissance and pre-Columbian work to contemporary collections, and traveling exhibitions.

Parks and Recreation

The **Tohono Chul Park**, 7366 North Paseo del Norte (602–742–6455), is a natural desert park with rabbits, birds, and lizards. On a self-guided tour, discover demonstration gardens that illustrate water conservation, an ethnobotanical garden that recounts some desert history, and a geology wall that recreates the Catalina Mountain range, which looms nearby. After your stroll, relax with tea or dinner in the Spanish Colonial tearoom. **The Sentinel Peak Park**, off Broadway, west of I–10 on Cuesta, offers a far-reaching view of Tucson and its surrounding area.

For horseback riding and hiking, follow the trails at **Tucson Mountain Park**, 8 miles west on Speedway Boulevard and Kinney Road (602–883–4200), an enclave of 17,000 acres.

When the long days and the Arizona heat begin to make you wilt, cool off at **The Breakers Waterpark**, 9 miles north to exit I–10, then east 1½ miles to 8555 Tangerine Road; (602) 792–1821. Frolic in the water slides, pools, and a playground; volleyball, basketball, horseshoes, picnic facilities, showers, lockers, and food are all available. Call for information about discounts.

Pima County Parks and Recreation (602–740–2690) provides information about local facilities, including swimming pools, tennis and racquetball courts, picnic areas, playgrounds, and ball fields.

Sports

Baseball fans will find the Cleveland Indians spend their spring training season at Hi Corbett Field (602–325–2621 or 327–9467), East Broadway and Randolph Way, beginning in March. The University of Arizona has seasonal football and basketball games at McKale Center. Call the University of Arizona ticket office (602–621–2411) for details. Horse Racing at Rilloto Downs, 4502 North First Avenue (602–293–5011), begins in November and continues to early May. If you can't stay away from the greens, the PGA marks the beginning of its tournament in February with the Northern Telecom Tucson Open. Call the Tucson Activity Line at (602) 544–4424 for more information.

Theater and Performing Arts

The Arizona Theater Company, Brady Court, 40 East Fourteenth Street (602–622–2823), plays during the October-through-May season at the Temple of Music and Arts, 330 South Scott Avenue; (602) 884–4875. The Invisible Theater, 1400 North First Avenue (602–882–9721), performs contemporary plays between September and June. The Gaslight Theater, 7010 East Broadway (602–886–9428), offers audience participation theater. During the summer months, the University of Arizona's resident company (602–621–1162) hosts a colorful Summer Art Festival.

Classical music fans should get tickets for The Tucson Symphony Orchestra (602–792–9155), which performs classical and pop music in the Tucson Convention Center Music Hall. In the spring and fall, relax outdoors at the Reid Park Bandshell and enjoy the sounds of the Tucson Pops Orchestra; (602) 791–4873. Tucson also boasts two major opera companies. Supported by a full orchestra, the Southern Arizona Light Opera Company (602–323–7888) performs at the Tucson Community Center's Music Hall from October through May. From October to March, the Arizona Opera Company (602–293–4336) presents four operas at the same location.

Shopping

El Mercado de Boutiques, Broadway and Wilmot, keeps shoppers busy with more than twenty shops offering Native American and Latin folk art, Asian and local arts and crafts. In the Foothills Shopping Center, The Old Pueblo Museum offers gems and art for display and for sale.

Flea markets, swap meets, antiques and souvenir shopping can be found within Tucson's shopping district along Fourth and Seventh streets.

SPECIAL EVENTS

February: La Fiesta do los Vaqueros Rodeo, the Rodeo Grounds, has food, horses and cowboys, and a rodeo.

March: The Tucson Festival features dances, operas, and exhibits honoring the multicultural groups that contribute to Tucson's culture.

October: Oktoberfest at Mt. Lemmon Ski Valley (602–576–1400) features German food, drinks, dances, and music.

November: The most colorful event around takes place in mid-November when more than fifty hot air balloons from all over North America join the Tucson Balloon Festival, which kicks off at the Tucson Hilton, 7600 East Broadway.

WHERE TO STAY

Resorts

The Westin La Paloma, 3800 East Sunrise Drive, Tucson 85718; (800) 876–3683. This four-star, four-diamond resort offers golf, a spa with quality treatments, and a year-round children's program. In summer the program expands to become the Kactus Kids Camp, offering swimming, nature walks, and arts and crafts for ages five to twelve from 9:00 A.M. to 3:00 p.m, Monday to Saturday. Other times, the program offers supervised babysitting by the hour at the Children's Lounge for ages six months to twelve years, Sunday through Thursday 8:00 A.M. to 5:00 P.M., Friday and Saturday 8:00 A.M. to 9:00 P.M. Call and ask about seasonal packages. A junior tennis camp is available from June to mid-August. Families can get into the scoring with a family golf clinic for ages five and older.

Tanque Verde Ranch, 14301 East Speedway, Tucson 85748; (602) 296–6275. Guests stay in comfortable casitas and soothe their saddle-sore muscles in the hot tub or by swimming laps in the pool. This dude ranch offers a good riding program for adults as well as kids from November to May. Rates include three meals.

For family-friendly lodgings at an inn, call **The Arizona Association of Bed & Breakfast Inns,** 3661 North Campbell, Box 237, Tucson, Arizona, 85719; (602) 231–6777. Listings are offered throughout the state.

La Posada del Valle, 1640 North Campbell, Tucson; (602) 795–3840. This inn offers five guest rooms furnished with antiques and pieces from the twenties and thirties. The inn prefers that children be over twelve.

El Presidio Bed and Breakfast, 297 North Main Avenue; (602) 623–6151. Located in the historic El Presidio district and within walking distance of craft shops and the Tucson Museum of Art, this bed and breakfast offers three suites and a guest house. Children over twelve are welcome only in the guest house, which has a living room and kitchenette. Rates range from $85–$105.

WHERE TO EAT

Don't leave Tucson without trying some of the city's authentic cuisine. El Charro Cafe, 311 North Court Avenue (602–622–5465), has been serving up Mexican food in one location or another for more than seventy years. House specialties, at reasonable prices, include the green corn tamales, caldo de queso (cheese soup), and a variety of enchiladas. Janos, 150 North Main Avenue, offers creative New Southwestern cuisine at more upscale prices. For a steakhouse with live entertainment, stop by Gus & Andy's Steak House, 2000 North Oracle Road.

DAY TRIPS

To really understand the fascination with the local flora, fauna, and bold red buttes, get out into the desert with a jeep tour. These trips literally take you off the beaten path, over trails and up boulders into the Santa Catalina Mountains. Your guide leads short walks to observe ancient petroglyphs or examine such finds as "fish hooks" on barrel cactus or the "straw" of the yucca. By reservation Mountain View Transportation (800–594–9644) can arrange customized, overnight jeep trips that take you to Tombstone and other nearby attractions.

You won't want to miss Tombstone, "the town too tough to die," 70 miles from Tucson; (602) 457–3929. This historic American landmark was the roughest mining town in the West during the 1800s. Take pictures of such famous places as the O.K. Corral, Boothill, Bird Cage Theater, and the Crystal Palace Saloon, and look for the ghosts of such old regulars as Doc Holliday, Wyatt Earp, and Johnny Ringo. While you're there, explore nearby ghost towns.

For some more history, visit the Tumacacori National Historical Park, 48 miles south of Tucson, off I–19; (602) 398–2341. Here the abandoned Mission, San Jose de Tumacacori, has been preserved. Its thirty-six acres contain a historical park, a modern museum of the local history, a church, and a patio garden.

Get a glimpse of the future at the famed Biosphere 2, 35 miles north of Tucson; (602) 825–6200. Several scientists resided in this glass-enclosed system. Tour the grounds, watch the multi-image slide show, and visit the viewing gallery next to the ocean biome to see the extensive coral exhibit. Call for information and reservations.

Spend another day cooling off in the mountain streams and waterfalls of **Sabino Canyon**, 5900 North Sabino Canyon Road, Tucson; (602) 749–2861. You can view this desert oasis in the Catalina National Forest from a guided tram ride that takes you around the canyon to explore, but you will probably want to spend additional time picnicking, hiking, and admiring the natural rock walls, pools, and animals that abound nearby.

No visit to Tucson would be complete without a day roaming the trails through the desert on horseback. Try **Pusch Ridge Stables**, 13700 North Oracle Road, Tucson; (602) 297–6908. They offer numerous rides designed for visitors of various riding abilities.

FOR MORE INFORMATION

The Arizona Office of Tourism: 1100 West Washington Street, Phoenix, Arizona 85007; (602) 542–TOUR.

The Metropolitan Tucson Convention & Visitors Bureau: 130 South Scott Avenue, Tucson, Arizona 85701; (800) 638–8350 or (602) 624–1817.

The Tucson Chamber of Commerce: Post Office Box 991, Tucson, Arizona, 85702; (602) 792–1212.

OASIS (Older Adult Service and Information System): 3435 East Broadway Boulevard; (602) 882–3114 (offers special events and day trips for people over age fifty-five).

Tucson Activity Line: Post Office Box 35026, Tucson, Arizona, 8574; (602) 544–4424 (provides information about restaurants, attractions, and events).

Road information: (602) 573–7623; **Police** information: (602) 791–4452 **Weather**: (602) 881–3333.

Emergency Numbers

Ambulance, fire, police: 911

Poison Control: 1501 North Campbell Avenue, Room 1156; (602) 626–6016

Hospitals: **El Dorado Hospital**, 1400 North Wilmot Road (602–886–6361); **Tucson Medical Center**, 5301 East Grant Road (602–324–1950 or 800–533–4TMC); and **University Medical Center**, 1501 North Campbell Avenue (602–694–0111). All offer twenty-four-hour emergency and trauma services.

26
WASATCH-CACHE NATIONAL FOREST AND SKI VACATIONS
Utah

The **Wasatch-Cache National Forest**—more than a millon acres of lakes, forests, canyons, and mountains located north, east, and southeast of Salt Lake City—provides families with a variety of year-round vacation possibilities. The Wasatch Mountains, part of the Rocky Mountain range, are home to several ski areas, some considered among the best in the country, with slopes for every age and ability. Many ski resorts stay open all year, offering hiking, mountain biking, and other fair weather recreation.

GETTING THERE

Salt Lake International Airport, 776 North Terminal Drive (801–575–2400), is served by most major airlines. Car rentals are available. Salt Lake City's **Amtrak** is at 320 South Rio Grande; (800) USA–RAIL. **Greyhound** is at 160 West South Temple; (800) 231–2222.

GETTING AROUND

On a ski vacation, you may not need a car if you plan to spend most of your time at the resort or on the slopes. Shuttle buses transport skiers from the airport and downtown Salt Lake City to the ski resorts. Call **Canyon Transportation** at (801) 255–1841 or (800) 255–1841. **Lewis Brothers Stages** (801–359–8677 or 800–826–5849) operates buses from the airport and downtown, plus **Canyon Jumper** buses from Park City to Alta, Snowbird, Solitude, and Sundance. **Share-A-Ride Van Services** is available upon request from the airport or downtown to all locations along the Wasatch Front. There's also **Park City Transportation**, 1555 Lower Ironhorse Loop, Park City 84060; (801) 649–8567 or (800) 637–3803. **Utah Transit Authority's Ski Bus** (801–262–4636) operates to and from most downtown hotels, with several stops around the valley.

WHAT TO SEE AND DO

Skiing

The Wasatch Mountains, with an average of 460 inches of light and fluffy snow each year, feature some of the country's best skiing. One of the following ski areas located within an hour of downtown Salt Lake City promises an exhilarating experience for the whole family. (Distances are from downtown Salt Lake City.)

Big Cottonwood Canyon. **Brighton** is 31 miles southeast on Star Route 152; (801) 532–4731 or 943–8309—recording, or (800) 873–5512. Known as "the place where Salt Lake learns to ski," this is a great place for beginners. KinderSki classes lasting one hour and forty-five minutes are offered to ages four to six three times daily. Ages seven and up take group lessons and can opt for a new program that allows beginners to stay all day for additional instruction. Two children up to ten years ski free with one paying adult. A cafeteria and restaurant-pub are on premises.

Solitude Ski Resort is 23 miles southeast on Star Route 152; (801) 534–1400 or (800) 748–4754. Rated as one of the top forty North American ski resorts, Solitude has a Moonbeam Learning Center offering instruction and full-day supervised skiing through their nationally recognized program, Skiwee, for ages four to seven, and Quad Squad for ages eight to twelve. Solitude's Nordic Center offers 11 miles of groomed trails through the canyons, forests, and fields.

Little Cottonwood Canyon. **Alta** is 25 miles southeast on Utah 210; for lodging, call (801) 742–3333 or 942–0404. Known as a superb expert slope, Alta also has terrain for beginners and intermediates. **Alta Children's Center** (801–742–3042) provides child care for ages three months to twelve years. The Ski School (801–742–2600) features two-hour group lessons twice daily for ages four to twelve, as well as half- and full-day programs including lunch and day care, if needed.

Snowbird adjoins Alta on Utah 210; (801) 742–2222—snow report, or (800) 453–3000—reservations. Snowbird is known for its steep and rugged trails, although it has a separate novice slope. Infant and toddler care is provided for ages six weeks to three years. Camp Snowbird, for toilet-trained kids three to twelve, provides day care, outdoor play, crafts, and movies, either hourly or by the half and full day. The Children's Ski School starts with ages three to four, who have ninety-minute lessons.

Child/Teen Super Classes, for ages five to fifteen, are organized by age and ability. Half days are available for beginners; full days include lunch.

Provo Canyon

Laid back, environmentally conscious, and just plain beautiful, **Sundance**, RR3, Box A-1, Sundance, Utah 84604, (800) 892–1600 or (801) 225–4107, is on 5,000 acres of protected wilderness at the base of Utah's mighty 12,000-foot Mount Timpanogos. This relatively small resort offers 450 acres of downhill skiing and 14 kilometers of cross-country trails. About an hour from Salt Lake City's airport, this retreat was created by Robert Redford in 1969. The property features eighty-two cottages and ten mountain homes tastefully accented with Native American crafts and western hand-hewn furniture. Inquire about a supervised kids' ski school for ages six and older.

Park City. Located about forty-five minutes east of Salt Lake on I–80 and U-224, the former mining town of Park City sports three resorts that offer something for every level of ability. If Salt Lake City wins its bid to host the 2002 Winter Olympic Games, this area will be the site of a number of competitions, including bobsled/luge, ski jump, and freestyle events. A new $35 million Winter Sports Park in Bear Hollow, 4 miles west of Park City on Route 224 (801–649–5447), has four nordic jumps, a freestyle jump, and a snowboard half-pipe, open to the public.

The Park City Ski Area, 1345 Lowell Avenue (Highway 224); (801) 649–8111, (800) 227–2754—ski school reservations, or (800) 222–PARK. This is Utah's largest ski area, featuring eighty-three designated trails, 650 acres of open-bowl skiing, and a mixture of beginner, intermediate, and expert terrain. Kids ages seven to thirteen take full- or half-day (afternoons only) group lessons. Kinderschule, for ages three to six (toilet trained), includes snack, lunch, and lessons. For après-ski fun the Resort Center has an outdoor ice skating rink.

Park West Ski Area, 4000 Park West Drive (Highway 92); (801) 649–5400. This resort starts them young with a Skiers in Diapers program for ages three or younger. Experienced instructors work with babies on skis—with bottles and stuffed animals along for the ride! Kids Central also offers half- and full-day state-licensed day care for eighteen months up to about twelve years. A variety of packages include day care and group lessons for various ages. The resort has a snowboard park and offers evening sleigh rides.

Deer Valley, 2250 Deer Valley Drive South (Highway 224); (801) 649–1000 or (800) 424–3337. This upscale resort offers half- and full-day care to infants two to twenty-four months and children two to twelve years. Half days can't be reserved; reservations are recommended for full days during holidays. Children's Ski School offers a variety of programs, including group lessons to kids in first grade through twelve years, a full-day Reindeer Club skiing program for ages four and one half through kindergarten, and a full-day Bambi Special for ages three to five with lessons, snow play, and indoor activities. Teen Equipe workshops for ages thirteen to eighteen feature a full day of challenging skiing.

Summer Slopeside

Several of these area resorts also offer warm weather pleasures. **Snowbird's** aerial tram stops at the top of Hidden Peak, offering mountain bikers a spectacular 11,000-foot view of canyons and valleys. The tramway, open to sightseers, is open daily year-round except in May and late October to late November. Snowbird's summer sizzles for kids with Camp Snowbird Day Camp for ages four to twelve, featuring activities such as panning for gold, hiking, tennis, nature studies, movies, and crafts. It's held weekdays from early June through the Friday before Labor Day. Overnight camps and workshops for older kids, held on selected dates, include swimming, tram rides, nature studies, and more. For further information and reservations, call (801) 521–6040, ext. 5026.

At **Sundance** summer's bonuses include hillsides of wildflowers, horseback trail rides and day trips, guided hikes, hot air balloon flights, fly fishing forays, hayride dinners, waterskiing clinics, outdoor theater, free movies, and low lodging rates. The Sundance Kids Day Camp, complimentary from 9:00 A.M. to 4:00 P.M. Monday through Saturday for ages six to twelve, features Native American myths and crafts, hiking and horseback riding, and a theater workshop. Deluxe rooms come with a kitchenette, and summer rates include breakfast and the kids' program, which operates with a minimum of four children.

Strap your mountain bikes to the chairs of **Solitude's Moonbeam Lift** for the ride that leads to 25 miles of trails for all levels of cycling. Ed Chaunder, author of the book *Mountain Bike Techniques*, offers weekend clinics here and at Snowbird. Bike and accessory rentals are also available. Call Snowbird or Solitude for more information.

Deer Valley's new Sterling Lift near Silver Lake Lodge carries mountain bikers up to thirteen trails totaling 20 miles for beginner to advanced rides (more terrain planned soon). Open Wednesday through Friday afternoons, with extended hours weekends and holidays, the lifts can be accessed with an all-day pass. Bike and helmet rentals are available at the Silver Lake ticket office at the base; call (801) 645–6733 for more information. Children must be accompanied by a paid adult eighteen or older. The resort also has a 4.8-mile primarily single-track course—the former site of World Cup mountain bike action! More summer fun: a swim and tennis club open Memorial through Labor days, where everyone is welcome; call (801) 649–1000 for information. Deer Valley hosts summer-long outdoor Utah Symphony Orchestra performances, as well as several pop music concerts and a Bluegrass Festival.

Guided meal or trail horseback rides provided by Park City Stables leave from both **Deer Valley** and **Park City** resorts. For reservations and information, call Rocky Mountain Recreation; (801) 645–7256. (This company operates fishing and pack trips and winter snowmobile tours; minimum age is six for all trips.) The horseback rides are offered from Memorial Day through mid-October. **Park City Resort** also has a pony corral for younger kids, an Alpine Slide (younger kids slide down with a parent), a Little Miners Theme Park, with scaled down rides for ages six and under, and a terrific miniature golf course.

The town of **Park City** is part of a nationwide Rails to Trails program that converts abandoned rail lines for multi-use recreation. The town's 29-mile rail trail is great for biking as well as easy nature walks. To find out more about bike rentals from local shops and hotels, or to get a free *Park City Bike Guide*, call the Chamber Bureau at (801) 649–6100 or (800) 453–1360.

ABC Reservations Central, Park City (801–649–2223 or 800–523–0666), books a number of area adventures including hot air ballooning, historic tours, glider flights, and backcountry snowmobile tours; they also book lodging and transportation.

Aside from ski resort trails, the Wasatch Mountains have fat-tire trails, some as close as ten minutes from Salt Lake. The Wasatch Crest Trail, for instance, branches off Millcreek Canyon (3800 South and Wasatch Boulevard). This experts-only challenging trail features spectacular alpine views, steep climbs, stream crossings, and rocky stretches. Call the Salt Lake Ranger District, 6944 South 3000 East, (801) 943–1794, for maps and tips if planning a fat-tire trek through the Wasatch.

Backcountry Adventures

Wasatch-Cache National Forest also offers unlimited opportunities for family excursions. A great deal of planning should go into a back-country outing. Even the forests get crowded on holidays and in summer. Wasatch-Cache is one of the country's most heavily used forests for recreation. To avoid crowds and temperature extremes, visit in autumn and spring. Contact a National Forest Service Office (see For More Information) for specific advice and information.

Logan District

Logan, home of Utah State University and about 90 miles north of Salt Lake, is just southwest of **Logan Canyon Highway**, U.S. 89, a National Scenic Byway, most of it traveling primarily through the forest's Logan Ranger District. The byway, just over 39 miles long, runs from the mouth of Logan Canyon to Bear Lake.

This scenic byway tour starts at the **Logan District Ranger Office**, where you'll find information, rest rooms, picnic tables, and pleasant canyon views. Some highlights of the drive include the following.

The scenery in Wasatch National Forest's Logan Canyon is nothing short of spectacular. (Courtesy Utah Travel Council)

Logan Wind Cave, 5 miles from Ranger Office, can be found high above Logan Canyon. A 1.5-mile trail, moderately difficult for kids, leads to the cave. Spring visitors are treated to clusters of blooming wildflowers, while fall brings spectacular autumn foliage. The cave is part of the rock formation you'll pass midway up the canyon wall, called the China Wall. *Best Hikes With Children in Utah* by Maureen Keilty (The Mountaineers) details this and other hikes in the Wasatch National Forest. On this hike, Keilty advises that you watch out for rattlers.

At **Wood Camp Campground** and **Jardine Juniper Trail**, 10.3 miles from Lady Bird, campers find only seven individual family units with no water. The big attraction here is west of the campground, where the Jardine Juniper trailhead is located. This moderately strenuous and long (5 miles one-way) trail climbs over 2,000 vertical feet through glacier-carved moraines and green forests. With older, hardy kids, it's worth the hike to the end to see to the tree thought to be more than 2,000 years old—and one of the largest living junipers anywhere.

Accessed by a paved but winding 7-mile road that climbs 2,300 feet to the lake, at 8,100 feet elevation, is a popular thirty-nine unit campground, **Tony Grove Lake Area**, 19.2 miles from the Ranger Office, usually open July 4 to October 1. From here try a self-guided nature trail around the perimeter of the lake, which passes ancient glacial deposits and fields of wildflowers. Spruce and fir trees stand in the wetter areas of the shore and spread into a thick forest beyond. See fauna such as mountain chickadees, ground squirrels, yellow-bellied sapsuckers, and muskrats. As for flora, the lake is home to gooseberry shrubs, pink coralbells, tangled willows, and mountain sunflowers.

Beaver Mountain Ski Road Junction, 24.2 miles from the Ranger Office, leads to the ski resort (801–753–0921), via Road 243. From late November to mid-April the resort has three chair lifts and a day lodge. The road leads to camping spots in the Sink Hollow and Beaver Creek areas.

The Limber Pine Nature Trail, 30.3 miles from LB, is an excellent spot for an family hike. The 1¼-mile loop, which starts from a picnic spot, is easy for kids and takes about an hour to complete. A guide available at the trailhead points out the geological history and different wildlife species. You'll hear (and maybe even see) the nuthatches, woodpeckers, and mountain chickadees that fly through the treetops, and witness the quaking aspen trees, bent over in arches by heavy snows.

The scenic byway ends at **Bear Lake**, 20 miles long and from 4 to 8 miles wide, one of the state's most popular for water recreation. Half of the lake is in Utah, the other half in Idaho. Year-round fishing from shore is excellent on the east side. (Legend has it that the lake is home to the mythological Bear Lake Monster.) Raspberries grow wild all around the lake, and several small stands sell raspberry milk shakes.

Bear Lake State Park (801–946–3346), the final stop, is comprised of three state-operated facilities: **Bear Lake Marina**, 2 miles north of Garden City; **Rendezvous Beach**, which has a sandy beach and is 2 miles west of Laketown; and **Eastside**, 20 miles north of Laketown.

For a brochure detailing things to see and do on this scenic byway, contact Logan Ranger District, 860 North 1200 East, Logan, Utah 84321; (801) 753–2772. For more information, you can also contact Bridgerland Travel Region, 160 North Main, Logan; (801) 752–2161 or (800) 882–4433. More than forty hiking trails are listed in the book *Cache Trails,* available at area sporting good stores.

The Ogden District

A scenic byway, U-39, starts in **Ogden**, some 30 miles north of Salt Lake, and stretches for 44 miles through the narrow **Oden Canyon**. It climbs through the Wasatch-Cache National Forest to some of northern Utah's most breathtaking vistas. Along the way, you may catch glimpses of wildlife such as mule deer, ground squirrels, and marmots. If you venture onto back roads that lead away from the traveled route, you find breathtaking overlooks, picnic areas, fishing, and campgrounds.

The byway also leads to a highlight of this district, the **Pineview Reservoir**, a popular summer recreation area with two designated swim areas with lifeguards, two campgrounds, two boat ramps, and two trail-heads, including the 22-mile **Skyline Trail** (also open to mountain and motor bikes). This is a part of the **Great Western Trail**, which, once completed, will stretch from Canada to Mexico, incorporating various hiking, biking, horseback, and vehicle trails.

This region features twelve developed campgrounds. For more on this area, contact the **Union Station Information Center**, 2501 Wall Avenue, Ogden; (801) 625–5306. It has detailed recreation maps showing roads, trails, and campgrounds. Information is also available from Ogden Ranger District, 507 Twenty-fifth Street, Ogden, Utah 84401; (801) 625–5112.

Wasatch Mountain State Park

About 45 miles east of Salt Lake City, 2 miles northwest of Midway, and 22 miles from Park City, Wasatch Mountain State Park is a popular destination; (801) 654–1791. It features a twenty-seven-hole golf course, more than 135 camping/picnicking areas, modern rest rooms, hot showers, utility hookups, and plenty of recreation areas. Nature trails are used by cross-country skiers and snowmobilers (rentals available in the park) in the winter, and by hikers in the summer. This is Utah's most developed state park and, as you might expect, summers are crowded—and hot.

SPECIAL EVENTS

See the Salt Lake City chapter for more festivities. For more information on the following, contact one of the visitor's bureaus listed under For More Information, or the individual ski area.

January: Treats await as you ski from station to station at Solitude Ski Resort's Chocolate Lover's Tour and Chocolate Tasting Extravaganza.

March: Winterfest Snow Sculpture; Music in the Mountains, both in Park City.

April: Easter Egg Hunt, Park City Ski Area.

June: Savour the Summit, Park City's food festival, features samples from over thirty area restaurants.

July: The nation's best cowboys take part in the Oakley Rodeo.

August: Park City Art Festival; Summit County Fair, Coalville Fair Grounds.

September: Autumn Aloft, thirty hot air balloons ascend from Park City; Miner's Day Celebration, with parade down Main Street, fun, and games, Park City.

October: Oktoberfest at Snowbird Mountain features polka dancing, German beer, and live entertainers.

November: America's Opening, Main Street, Park City, kicks off ski season with Men's World Cup Ski Races, fireworks, on-snow parades, music, food, and more.

December: On Christmas and New Year's eves, many ski resorts have visits from Santa complete with on-slope parades and more.

WHERE TO STAY

The Utah Travel Guide, published by the Utah Travel Council, is a helpful reference, which includes lodging and other state information.

A wide variety of accommodations exist in and around the **Salt Lake City** and **Park City** areas. Most of the major ski resorts listed above offer their own lodging and/or chalet arrangements; ask for reservations when you call. *The Utah Winter Vacation Planner*, available from the **Utah Travel Council**, lists ski area lodging. There are several reservation services that book entire packages, including **Park City Ski Holidays** (801–649–0493 or 800–222–PARK) representing more than 3,000 units in town including private homes and condos.

Moderately priced family lodging is available in Park City. Try **Best Western Landmark Inn**, 6560 North Landmark Drive; (801) 649–7300 or (800) 548–8824. It features rooms with refrigerators, twenty-four-hour restaurant, free shuttle to the slopes, and a convenient location just minutes from the mountain and next to a factory mall. You will find moderate rates at the **Chamonix Lodge**, 1450 Empire, only 150 yards from Park City Ski Area; (801) 649–8443 or (800) 443–8630. Rooms have small refrigerators and coffee makers. Third and fourth persons in room cost an additional $10 each. The **Edelweiss Haus**, 1482 Empire Avenue, (801) 649–9342 or (800) 438–3855, offers moderate motel-style rooms, some of which are suites with kitchenettes.

The ten-room, renovated, 1893 former miners' boardinghouse, the **Old Miners' Lodge**, 615 Woodside Avenue, (801) 645–8068 or (800) 648–8068, is fun. Families are welcome, and cribs are $5 extra. The **Prospector Square Hotel**, 2200 Sidewinder Drive, (801) 649–7100 or (800) 453–3812, offers one- and two-bedroom condominiums, indoor pool, and free shuttle service to the ski area. See the Salt Lake City chapter for accommodations in the city.

For lodging in the **Ogden area**, contact the **Ogden/Weber Convention and Visitors Bureau**, 2501 Wall Avenue, Ogden; (801) 225–8824 or (800) ALL–UTAH. For the Logan area, contact **Cache Chamber of Commerce**, 160 North Main; (801) 752–2161 or (800) 657–5353.

Some of the **National Forest** campgrounds can be reserved calling **Mistix**; (800) 280–2267. Other sites book on a first-come basis. The most popular (read "crowded") camping areas are in Ogden and near Salt

Lake City. A few choices: **Perception Park**, on the shore of the Ogden River, features about fifty sites, lots of nature trails, and good fishing. It's also one of the few campgrounds equipped with flushing toilets, and is handicapped accessible. **The Spruces**, in the mountains east of Salt Lake City off I–215, is an expansive camping area with rest rooms.

WHERE TO EAT

In **Logan**, typical American-style eats are served up at the **Bluebird Cafe**, 19 North Main; (801) 752–3155. Kids love the almost twenty-foot-long counter where the cafe's famous chocolates are displayed.

People come from miles around to the town of **Perry**, about 20 miles north of Ogden, to eat steak, prime ribs, BBQ, and other tasty dishes at the five-star **Maddox Ranch House Restaurant**, 1980 South Highway 89; (801) 723–8545 or (800) 544–5474.

In Ogden, dinner (steak, shrimp, prime ribs) is an experience at the **Prairie Schooner**, 445 Park Boulevard; (801) 392–2712. Eat inside a covered wagon, with a campfire and howling coyote sounds.

Enjoy a local specialty, freshly harvested peach milk shakes, at the **Peach City Drive-In**, 306 North Main; (801) 723–3923. Located north of Ogden in **Brigham City**, this eatery also offers chicken baskets, steak sandwiches, and cheeseburgers.

Park City has more than fifty restaurants serving everything from continental cuisine to hearty western fare. Contact the **Chamber/Bureau** at (801) 649–6100 or (800) 453–1360 for dining information.

DAY TRIPS

The booklet *Utah's Scenic Byways and Backways* contains descriptions of popular touring routes in the state, including several in and around the Wasatch area. Obtain the guide from the chamber of commerce and regional travel offices listed under For More Information. The drives last from forty-five minutes to several hours, and the routes are also denoted by rainbow-colored signs throughout the state. Included is one of the most popular mountain routes in the state, **the Mirror Lake Scenic Byway**, U-150 from Kamas through the Wasatch-Cache National Forest to the Utah/Wyoming border. Scenic viewpoints, picnic areas, lakes, meadows, and rugged peaks and cliffs can be accessed from this high mountain byway, much of which parallels the Provo River.

For more day trip ideas, see the chapters on Arches and Canyonlands, near Moab, and Salt Lake City.

FOR MORE INFORMATION

Visitor Information: **Salt Lake Convention and Visitors Bureau,** 180 South West Temple; (801) 521–2868. **Utah State Travel Council,** 300 North State Street, Capitol Hill Council Hall, Salt Lake City 84114; (801) 538–1030. **The Utah County Travel Council,** 51 South University, Suite 111; (801) 370–8393 or (800) 222–UTAH. For a copy of the *Ski Utah Winter Vacation Planner,* contact **Ski Utah,** 150 West 500 South, Salt Lake City, Utah 84101; (801) 534–1779.

Forest Service and Ranger Districts: The USDA Forest Service (800–332–4100) distributes a pamphlet called *Leave No Trace! An Outdoor Ethic,* which provides helpful advice and rules of the forest. The main office of the Wasatch-Cache National Forest is located at 8226 Federal Building, 125 South State, Room 8103, Salt Lake City 84138; (801) 524–5030. You may also contact individual district offices, some of them listed above.

Contact the **Wasatch Cache National Forest's** main office for information on handicapped accessible campgrounds and trails. **The Ogden Ranger District** (801–625–5112), for one, has an accessibility program that encourages the disabled to be involved in an outdoor experience.

Emergency Numbers

Ambulance, police, fire: 911

Hospitals: Salt Lake City—**Holy Cross Hospital,** 1045 East 100 South (801–350–4111); or **Primary Children's Medical Center,** 100 North Medical Drive (801–588–2000). Ogden—**McKay-Dee Hospital,** 3939 Harrison Boulevard; (801) 627–2800. Park City—**Park City Family Health and Emergency Center,** 1665 Bonanza Drive; (801) 649–7640. Logan—**Logan Regional Hospital,** 1400 North 500 East; (801) 752–2050.

Poison Control twenty-four-hour hotline: (800) 456–7707 or (801) 581–2151

Smith's has **twenty-four-hour pharmacies** in locations including 442 North 175 East in Logan (801–753–6570); and 4275 Harrison Boulevard in Ogden (801–479–0700). In Park City, a twenty-four-hour pharmacy is located inside **Albertson's Food Store,** 1800 Park Avenue; (801) 649–6134. In Salt Lake, there's a pharmacy open until midnight inside a grocery store, **Harmon's,** 3200 South 1300 East; (801) 487–5461.

THE PACIFIC NORTHWEST AND CALIFORNIA

27
ANAHEIM/ ORANGE COUNTY
California

Anaheim/Orange County has been called Southern California's playground—and for good reason. Anaheim's future as a dream vacation destination for families was sealed in 1955 when Walt Disney opened the Magic Kingdom in Disneyland. Ten minutes away, Knott's Berry Farm has attracted families for generations. Orange County also offers families many other reasons for coming, including 42 miles of coastline often dubbed the "American Riviera." Their tourist and convention bureau is quick to point out that Anaheim is *not* a suburb of Los Angeles, which is 28 miles north, but rather a destination unto itself. Still, if you have time, do take in some of the bountiful attractions that Los Angeles offers (highlights follow).

GETTING THERE

The four area airports are served by major airlines. **Los Angeles International** (LAX), (310) 646–5252, 31 miles northwest of Anaheim (approximately fifty minutes), is the major international gateway into Southern California. **John Wayne/Orange County Airport,** (714) 252–5006, 16 miles southeast of Anaheim (about 25 minutes), offers direct nonstop service to nineteen U.S. destinations. **Ontario Airport** (909–983–8282) is 27 miles northeast of Anaheim (about 45 minutes). The smallest airport is at Long Beach, (310) 421–8293, 20 miles west (about thirty minutes). **SuperShuttle** is among several companies providing service from hotels to airports twenty-four hours a day; phone (714) 517–6600/(800) 554–6458—outside California.

Greyhound is at 2080 South Harbor Boulevard, Anaheim; call (714) 999–1256 for information.

Amtrak (800–USA–RAIL) has a station at Anaheim Stadium, a mile from the Anaheim Convention Center, and makes several other Orange County stops.

Two major freeways, I–405 and I–5, run north and south through Orange County.

GETTING AROUND

A car is a necessity in this land of freeways, but if you would rather not drive, many hotels operate shuttle services to popular attractions. The **Orange County Transit District** (OCTD), (714) 636–7433, runs buses throughout the county. **Southern California Rapid Transit District** (RTD) serves Los Angeles County and some areas of Orange County. Call (213) 626–4455.

WHAT TO SEE AND DO

Theme Parks

Let's face it: You didn't come here for culture (although it is available). The following attractions are the reasons families flock to this area.

Disneyland, 1313 Harbor Boulevard; (714) 999–4565 or (213) 626–8605, ext. 4565. Before leaving home, purchase a good guidebook, and plan your tour strategy. If you can avoid peak park times, do so. (These include weekends, Memorial through Labor Day, Christmas Day through New Year's Day—the busiest of all—and other school holidays.) Opening hours vary; call in advance. Then arrive as early as possible (about a half hour before opening) to beat the crowds—and the heat. The park is huge—eighty-five acres in all—so don't try to see too much, too soon. If you can, tour the park in portions (one-, two-, and three-day passports are available).

Disneyland has eight theme areas: Adventureland, Critter Country, Fantasyland, Frontierland, Main Street U.S.A., New Orleans Square, Tomorrowland, and Mickey's Toontown. The latter, the newest theme land (the first addition in more than twenty years), is a cartoon character community where Disney stars, including Roger Rabbit, interact with guests. Yuu can rent strollers by the main entrance (even small kids beyond stroller age may welcome the ride because touring the park is wearying). There's a Baby Center for preparing formulas, warming bottles, and changing infants.

Knott's Berry Farm, 8039 Beach Boulevard, Buena Park; (714) 220-5200 or 827-1776. Started in 1940, this nonglitzy park has grown to 150 acres and six theme areas containing over 165 rides, attractions, live shows, shops, and restaurants (including the still-going-strong Famous Chicken Dinner). A favorite with the younger set: Camp Snoopy, a six-acre wooded area with waterfalls, streams, and lakes. Attractions include the Bear-y Tales Playhouse with slides, giant sawdust-filled punching bags, and a mirror maze; scaled down rides; interactive scientific experiences at Thomas Edison Inventors Workshop; and trained forest animals. The newest attractions include the world's largest inflated Snoopy figure—a 38-foot-tall structure where kids bounce and bump on air-filled cushions—and a soaring, spinning Camp Bus ride for the entire family. Older kids thrill to Montezuma's Revenge Roller Coaster and the Sky Tower parachute jump. Ghost Town is still here to amuse the younger kids with its jail, blacksmith shop, general store, and stagecoach rides. Stroller rentals and two baby stations, with changing tables and a microwave for bottle heating, are available.

If you still have time or energy, you're close to **Movieland Wax Museum**, 7711 Beach Boulevard (714–522–1155), just east of Knott's. More than 280 costumed wax stars pose in scenes from famous movies—including Macaulay Culkin in *Home Alone*.

Raging Waters, 111 Raging Waters Drive, San Dimas; (909) 592–6453. Located in southeast Los Angeles County, Raging Waters is close to Anaheim and at forty-four acres is the largest water park west of the Mississippi. With slides, rides, sandy beaches, a man-made river, and a wave pool, there's something for everyone, including tiny tots. Bring lots of sunscreen, take plenty of shade breaks, and plan on spending the better part of the day.

Universal Studios, 100 Universal City Plaza, Universal City (between Hollywood and the San Fernando Valley); (818) 508–9600. Families do bring very young kids here, but most attractions are designed for school-age and older kids. Some rides have special effects younger children may find frightening. Two favorites are **Earthquake—The Big One**, which "traps" riders in a subway as an earthquake occurs, complete with collapsing earth, shooting flames, and a huge flood; and in the **King Kong Encounter**, guests sit on the Brooklyn Bridge while a 30-foot Kong comes too close for comfort, breaking suspension cables and power lines in the process. Most older kids love this, but younger kids may find them a bit too realistic. **Back to the Future** is not for the faint of heart, but this attraction is great fun, combining a ride, a Delorean, high-tech video thrills, and the sensation of a super-duper roller coaster.

Fortunately, there are gentler alternatives, including the delightful **E.T. Adventure**, where guests enjoy a ride on a sky-bound bicycle. Stage shows include **The Rocky & Bullwinkle Show; Animal's Actors Stage,** where more than sixty trained animals perform; and the fifteen-minute **Beetlejuice Graveyard Revue,** featuring famous horror figures gyrating to rock 'n' roll hits. **An American Tail: Fievel Goes West** offers a live stage show and a wonderful interactive playground where everything is oversized, as seen from a mouse's eye view. There's a 15-foot-high banana peel to slide down and an 11-foot slice of Swiss cheese to crawl through. A new streamlined backlot tram tour takes riders through locations and settings from *Home Alone 2* and *E.T.,* as well as television show sets.

Six Flags Magic Mountain, 26101 Magic Mountain Parkway, Valencia (Santa Clarita Valley); (805) 255–4111. For preteens and teens who crave excitement, this 260-acre theme park offers plenty. The specialty: roller coasters, with such daunting names as Psyclone, Flashback, Revolution, Ninja, and Colossus, which is rated as one the top 10 in America. There's lots more, too: water flume rides; shows; and for the younger set, a petting zoo and Bugs Bunny World, a six-acre area with mini–roller coaster and other scaled down rides. The newest addition is High Sierra Territory, a depiction of the California woods, with a water ride, rock maze, and the world's tallest artificial walk-through tree. The park has a baby-care center and stroller rentals.

Museums

Orange County is home to **The Richard Nixon Library and Birthplace,** 18001 Yorba Linda Boulevard, Yorba Linda (about 7 miles north of Anaheim); (714) 993–5075. Families with school-age kids, no matter what their political persuasion, may find this place surprisingly interesting. Interactive exhibits allow visitors to summon Nixon's recorded opinions on various issues, listen to the famous "smoking gun" tape from Watergate days, and view life-size statues of world leaders. Across the pond, Nixon's birthplace, a small farm, has been restored and includes original furnishings and family photos. **The Ronald Reagan Presidential Library and Museum,** 40 Presidential Drive, Simi Valley (805–522–8444), which includes a chunk of the Berlin Wall, is 20 miles north of downtown Los Angeles.

George C. Page Museum, 5801 Wilshire Boulevard, Los Angeles; (213) 936–2230. Located in Hancock Park, this twenty-three-acre property is in the midst of the La Brea Tar Pits (overland explorers found the bubbling asphalt pools on this site in 1769). It features Ice Age fossils, discovered in the early 1900s, of mammals, birds, plants, insects, and reptiles. Behind glass windows, workers in the museum's paleontology labs dust and identify fossils from the still oozing pits. Along with two short films (*Dinosaurs, the Terrible Lizards* and *The La Brea Story*), there are more than one million fossils and reconstructed skeletons of creatures who got stuck in the pits. Try to pull large poles out of sticky asphalt, and you will realize how hard it was to escape.

If you have time, explore the **Los Angeles County Museum of Art,** also in Hancock Park at 5905 Wilshire Boulevard; (213) 857–6111. This large complex includes the Ahmanson Gallery with paintings by Rembrandt and Picasso. The newer Robert O. Anderson Building features traveling exhibits and twentieth-century art. The museum sponsors frequent cultural activities, and programs for parents and kids. Stop for lunch at the indoor/outdoor Plaza Cafe, then stroll through the park—a lively place with mimes, street musicians, and vendors.

Los Angeles Children's Museum, 310 North Main Street in the Los Angeles Mall downtown; (213) 687–8800. Aimed at ages two to twelve, this museum's interactive, educational exhibits are guaranteed to please. Highlights include Sticky City, featuring giant foam shapes with velcro tapes; a storehouse of LEGO blocks for young builders; and a recording studio where kids create music with studio instruments and synthesizers, or radio dramas with sound effects. Weekend performances by mimes, actors, and storytellers and weekday theatrical games and dance workshops are held at the Louis B. Mayer Performance Space, the area's only theater designed exclusively for kids. Special family events are held throughout the year.

Another primarily-for-kids place is the **Children's Museum,** 301 South Euclid Streett, La Habra; (310) 905–9793. Many of the exhibits are in the waiting, baggage, and freight rooms of the historic, renovated Union Pacific Depot. Permanent exhibits include a Touch Table with a rotating collection of birds' nests, feathers, shells, and the like; a Bee Observatory; LEGO city, where kids can build to their heart's content; an indoor carousel; a Preschool Playpark; a Science Station where elecetricity, images, and reflections are explored; and a Kids on Stage area with costumes, props, sets, lighting, and sound. Call to find out about special workshops, Saturday programs, and preschool storytelling hours.

California Museum of Science and Industry, 700 State Drive, Exposition Park (downtown Los Angeles); (213) 744–7400. It's free, it's fabulous, it's the country's second-largest science/technology museum (the Smithsonian is the first). Unfortunately, at press time there was a dramatic staff cutback and talk of closing this splendid facility completely— call to find out. Hopefully, you will be able to enjoy the wide variety of interactive exhibits.

Natural History Museum, also in Exposition Park at 900 Exposition Boulevard; (213) 744–3414. Everything you might expect to find at a natural history museum is here (including dinosaurs). The fourth largest of its kind in the country, this vintage museum (circa 1913) has a sparkling Gem and Mineral Hall; a taxidermy exhibit of North American and African mammals in natural surroundings; a Hall of American History that includes old cars; a lively Hall of Birds, with sounds and animation; and—tops with younger kids—the Ralph M. Parsons Discovery Center, a huge room where kids from age two are encouraged to touch fossils and other objects, examine insects through a magnifying glass, listen to the ocean from a seashell, and explore various discovery boxes. This museum is a winner.

Simon Wiesenthal Center's Museum of Tolerance, 9786 West Pico Boulevard; (310) 553–8403. The message this museum conveys is a crucial one for kids: understanding among all people. The Tolerancenter explores the dynamics of racism and prejudice in American life via thirty-five participatory installations. At Understanding The Los Angeles Riots, visitors input personal profiles (age, gender, ethnicity) and are asked questions about social justice and responsible citizenship. A wall-sized computer map pinpoints more than 250 hate groups around the country. At the Holocaust Section, each visitor gets a different photo passport with the story of a child whose life was changed by the Holocaust. As the visitor proceeds through the tour, the passport is updated, and the child's fate is revealed at the end—an extremely moving experience. At the second-floor Multimedia Learning Center, more than thirty workstations give visitors, via touch screen technology, access to a huge amount of information on World War II and the Holocaust.

Barnsdall Art Park, 4800 Hollywood Boulevard, Los Angeles; (213) 485–4474. Included in this eleven-acre park and arts center is a Junior Arts Center that offers free Open Sunday family art workshops on forty Sundays a year. Some are held at the center; others are at various community service centers around the city. In August, the Center sponsors a Children's Festival of the Arts in the park.

Parks and Zoos

Griffith Park, north of Hollywood (213–664–1181), with 4,100 acres of wooded land, is the largest park within the boundaries of any U.S. city. At the Park Ranger Visitors Center, 4730 Crystal Springs Drive, (213) 665–5188, obtain directions to a miniature open air train, a simulated roller coaster and plane adventure, pony and wagon rides, and an antique carousel. At Travel Town, on Zoo Drive, a small outdoor museum displays old vehicles: fire engines, a Union Pacific steam engine, and old city streetcars. Hiking trails, tennis courts, golf courses, guided horseback rides, nature trails, and a swimming pool are among the other offerings. The park is also home to **Griffith Observatory,** 2800 East Observatory Road (213–664–1191), with sky shows and astronomy exhibits. Solar telescopes operate by day; at night, view the moon and planets via a Zeiss refractory. Also in the park: **Gene Autry Western Heritage Museum,** 4700 Western Heritage Way; (213) 667–2000. The museum displays the

A hard day at the beach may be just what you need on a vacation to Anaheim. (Courtesy Anaheim Area Visitor and Convention Bureau)

history of the American West through art and artifacts, such as authentic weapons of Western heroes and costumes and props from radio, movie, and television Westerns. Noteworthy is the museum's famed collection of cowboy boots. Films are shown in the 222-seat theater.

Nearby is the **Los Angeles Zoo**, 5333 Zoo Drive; (213) 666–4090. Spread out over 113 acres, it's home to more than 2,000 mammals, birds, reptiles, and amphibians, grouped into respective geographical areas. (Don't miss the cuddly koalas in the Australia environment.) Adventure Island, the children's zoo, highlights animals of the American Southwest through interactive exhibits. A tram ride circles the zoo, with stops at strategic areas (the hilly terrain can be tiring for young—and old—feet). Treat the kids to an elephant or camel ride.

Beaches

Orange County's 42-mile coastline includes beach communities reached via the Pacific Coast Highway: Seal Beach, Huntington Beach, Newport Beach, Laguna, Corona del Mar, Balboa, Dana Point, San Clemente, and San Juan Capistrano. A popular choice for families is **Balboa**, with its 919-foot fishing pier that ends in a public beach with rest rooms and showers nearby. Lifeguards keep watch during summer and post flags when the tide is coming in. The waves here are fairly gentle compared to the popular surfing beaches, such as Huntington. From January through March, outfitters such as **Whale Watching Excursions** (714–695–9444) offer outings from the Newport Beach area.

Los Angeles County has 72 miles of shoreline, from Malibu in the north to Long Beach (where you can board the *Queen Mary*) in the south. Colorful street performers ply their trade along Venice Beach's Oceanfront Walk. Santa Monica Pier and its famous boardwalk feature carnival games, carousel rides, and free summer concerts.

Theater, Music, and the Arts

Orange County has ten theaters and amphitheaters, including Anaheim's **Celebrity Theater**, 201 East Broadway (714–535–2000), which hosts top entertainers, Broadway plays, and sporting events. The Sunday Calendar in the *Los Angeles Times* features weekly events or call (213) 688–ARTS. *Destination Los Angeles,* published by the LAVCB, lists ticket agencies and addresses for TV show tickets. Many don't admit kids under ten years; the "Tonight Show" refuses anyone under eighteen years.

Studio tours: NBC Studios in Burbank offers weekday backstage tours, including a walk through a newsroom and a chance to see the "Tonight Show" crew rehearsing. Call (818) 840–3537. The **Warner Brothers VIP Tour**, 4000 Warner Boulevard, Burbank, (818) 954–1744, emphasizes the technical and the behind-the-scenes aspects of movie and television production. Limited to those over age ten. **Paramount Studios**, 860 North Gower Street, Hollywood (213–956–5575), gives out free tickets weekdays at 8:00 A.M. for TV show tapings—most require audience members to be sixteen or older. For the Paramount two-hour studio walking tour, visitors should be age ten or older.

Sporting Events

Anaheim has three professional sports teams. The California Angels baseball (714–634–2000), and the Rams football (714–535–5800), games are played at Anaheim Stadium, 2000 Gene Autry Way. The new Mighty Ducks professional hockey team plays at The Pond in Anaheim, 2695 East Katella; (714) 704–2428. Head to Los Angeles for Dodgers baseball at downtown's Dodger Stadium (213–224–1491), basketball with the Lakers at the Forum (310–419–3100) and the Clippers at the L.A. Sports Arena (213–748–8000), or hockey with the Kings at the Forum (310–673–6003).

Shopping

Fashion Island Shopping Center, 600 Newport Center Drive, Newport Beach, (714) 721–2022, is on a hill overlooking the ocean and is Orange County's only open-air regional shopping center. There are movie theaters, summer weekly music concerts, kids' activities—even a koi pond. **The Irvine Ranch Farmer's Market**, on the first level of the Atrium Court, is a wonderful place to buy produce and other culinary delights.

Hobby City, 1238 South Beach Road, Anaheim (714–527–2323), has a doll and toy museum, miniature train ride, and lots more, including a restaurant. It's 2 miles south of Knott's Berry Farm.

For something completely different in greater Los Angeles, head to Beverly Hills to window and people shop along the posh Rodeo Drive.

SPECIAL EVENTS

ACVB can provide a current listing of events and contacts, or call their visitor information line at (714) 635–8900. For more information on Los Angeles area events, call (213) 689–8822.

January 1: Tournament of Roses Parade and Rose Bowl Game, Pasadena.

February: Festival of Whales, Dana Point, held weekends in late February, features concert series, sporting competition, street fair, and film fest.

March: Fiesta de las Golindrinas (Return of the Swallows), Mission San Juan Capistrano. Month-long celebration of the annual arrival of the swallows from Argentina on St. Joseph's Day.

Easter: The Crystal Cathedral in Garden Grove, adjacent to Anaheim, puts on The Glory of Easter.

April: Air Show at El Toro Marine Corps Air Station features the famed Blue Angels flight demonstration team. Knott's Berry Farm's Country Fair includes shows and country bands.

May: Cinco de Mayo on Olvera Street, Los Angeles, features mariachis and Spanish dancers. Strawberry Festival, Garden Grove, includes a carnival, arts and crafts, and parade.

June: Surfing Championship, Huntington Beach Pier, the world's largest surfing contest.

July: Orange County Fiesta, Mile Square Park, Fountain Valley, offers carnival rides, sports, music, fireworks, and more. Orange County Fair, Costa Mesa Fairgrounds, with rides and rodeo.

July–August: Laguna Canyon holds its huge Festival of Arts and Pageant of the Masters, with nightly re-creations of artworks featuring live models and a full orchestra.

August: Ringling Brothers Barnum and Bailey Circus, Anaheim Arena.

September: Sand Castle and Sand Sculpture Contest, Corona del Mar State Beach. Newport Seafest at Newport Beach spans two weekends.

October: Anaheim Harvest Festival with crafts, foods, and family entertainment.

November: The Glory of Christmas Pageant, Crystal Cathedral, Garden Grove.

December: Christmas festivities include Tree Lighting at Mission San Juan Capistrano and Las Posados candlelight processions on Los Angeles's Olvera Street.

WHERE TO STAY

Anaheim/Orange County has 45,000 rooms (18,000 in Anaheim) in everything from budget motels to luxury hotels. Ideally, families should stay as close to Disneyland as possible. For lodging in greater Los Angeles, consult the *Destination Los Angeles* guide available from the LAVCB (see For More Information).

Here are a few choices.

The **Disneyland Hotel**, 1150 West Cerritos Avenue, Anaheim; (714) 956–6400. Connected to the park by the monorail, this recently refurbished hotel offers 1,131 rooms, eleven restaurants and lounges, three swimming pools, ten tennis courts, a tropical beach, marina (with pedalboats, remote control tugboats, and a miniature *Queen Mary*), Fantasy Waters shows twice weekly, and Disney character meals at breakfast and weekend dinners year-round, and daily during summer and holidays. Expensive, yes—but worth the splurge. Call to see if the children's program has been revived.

Anaheim Hilton Hotel and Towers, 777 Convention Way; (714) 750–4321. Two minutes from Disneyland, the Hilton has 1,600 rooms and suites, a year-round pool, several jacuzzis, and a game center. The summer Vacation Station daily kids' program is for ages five to thirteen.

In the budget range, try **Raffles Inn and Suites**, 2040 South Harbor Boulevard, Anaheim; (714) 750–6100. It's two blocks south of Disneyland, has family suites that sleep six, an outdoor pool and jacuzzi, free Disney shuttle, and complimentary continental breakfast. A bit more upscale **Summerfield Suites West Hollywood**, 1000 Westmount Drive, West Hollywood (310–657–7400 or 800–833–4353), offers suite rooms, a complimentary buffet breakfast, and laundry facilities. The property is about twenty minutes from Universal Studios and popular beaches. Ask about their summer family specials. The **Century Plaza Hotel and Tower**, 2025 Avenue of the Stars, Los Angeles (310–277–2000), offers surprise gifts at check-in for children three through twelve. Car seats, changing tables, and bottle warmers are available.

The **Westin South Coast Plaza**, 686 Anton Boulevard, Costa Mesa, California 92626, (714) 540–2500 or (800) 228–3000, offers the new

Westin Kids Club amenities. These include child-friendly rooms and children's sports bottle or tippy cup upon check-in as well as a safety kit with a night light, Band-Aids, and emergency phone numbers. Rooms feature bath toys and bath products for kids, and parents can request—at no charge—jogging strollers, potty seats, bicycle seats, and step stools. Restaurants and room service also feature children's menus. Just minutes away by car are Disneyland, Knott's Berry Farm, and Newport Beach.

WHERE TO EAT

The ACVB publishes a *Best Places Guide to Dining, Services and Shopping in Orange County*. The kids will get a kick out of **The Overland Stage Restaurant**, Inn at The Park Hotel, 1855 South Harbor Boulevard, Anaheim; (714) 750–1811. The decor is Old West (complete with stagecoach) and the food is hearty American, with a children's menu available.

Two dinner theater experiences for kids: **Medieval Times Dinner and Tournament**, 7662 Beach Boulevard, Buena Park (800–899–6600), serves a four-course dinner (no utensils allowed) to guests who sit in an arena while knights joust on horseback. **Wild Bill's Western Extravaganza**, 7600 Beach Boulevard, Buena Park, (714) 522–4611 or 800–883–1546), puts on a two-hour Western show as guests dine on a four-course meal.

DAY TRIPS

Could you really go home without exploring **Hollywood**? It "ain't what it used to be," but a walk down Hollywood Boulevard is a must. Look for the famous fifty-foot Hollywood sign that graces the Hollywood Hills, on the town's northern end. Storefronts along the boulevard showcase movie memorabilia, including Dorothy's ruby red slippers from The Wizard of Oz. At **Mann's** (formerly Grauman's) **Chinese Theater**, 6925 Hollywood Boulevard (213–464–8111), celebrities' feet, heads, signatures (and even a nose—Jimmy Durante's) have been immortalized in cement since 1927. As you walk through downtown, you'll tread on the Hollywood Walk of Fame, containing the names of celebrities framed by terrazzo and brass stars, including Marilyn Monroe at 1644 Hollywood Boulevard, Elvis Presley at 6777, and John Lennon at 1750 Vine Street.

Memories of the 1992 riots—and visions of traffic and parking headaches—may result in tourists shying away from downtown L. A. The ACVB suggests that those staying in Anaheim take an Amtrak ride into downtown. It's easy and convenient: the Children's Museum (described earlier) is across the street from the station. Afterwards, take a stroll on the colorful cobblestoned walkways of Olvera Street in Old Los Angeles. A Mexican-style marketplace sells piñatas, crafts, sombreros, and other gifts and crafts. Restaurants range from fast food to sit-down Mexican eateries.

San Diego, 90 miles south of Anaheim, makes for a perfect day or two, thanks to Sea World, Balboa Park and its fabulous museums, San Diego Zoo, historic Old Town, beaches, and more. See the San Diego chapter for more information.

FOR MORE INFORMATION

The **Anaheim Visitor and Convention Bureau** is located across from Disneyland at the Anaheim Convention Center, 800 West Katella Avenue, Anaheim 92803; (714) 999–8999. The **Los Angeles Convention and Visitors Bureau** operates two visitor information centers: the Downtown Los Angeles center at 695 South Figueroa Street (213–689–8822) is open Monday through Saturday from 8:00 A.M. to 5:00 P.M., and the Hollywood Visitor Information Center is at The Janes House, Janes Square, 6541 Hollywood Boulevard; (213) 689–8822, open Monday through Saturday, 9:00 A.M. to 5:00 P.M. Helpful publications include *Destination Los Angeles*, which also has extensive listings for Southern California.

L.A. Parent, Box 3204, Burbank 91504 (818–846–0400), is a monthly newspaper featuring family events and relevant news.

The **Los Angeles County Commission on Disabilities** publishes a free brochure on services by public and private agencies, including transportation, recreational facilities, and equipment. Write or call them at 383 Hall of Administration, 500 West Temple Street, Los Angeles 90012; (213) 974–1053 or 974–1707 (TDD). The Junior League offers Around the Town with Ease, listing wheelchair facilities of over one hundred of the area's most popular destinations. Send $2.00 for postage and handling to them at Farmers Market, Third and Fairfax, Los Angeles 90036, or call (213) 937–5566.

Emergency Numbers

Ambulance, fire, police: 911
Poison Control: (800) 544–4404
Twenty-four-hour pharmacy: Sav-On, 1021 North State College (at La Palma); (714) 991–9161
Twenty-four-hour emergency room: Anaheim Memorial Hospital, 1111 West La Palma; (714) 774–1450.

28
CRATER LAKE NATIONAL PARK
Oregon

Crater Lake, Oregon's only national park, is in a remote area, 140 miles south of Eugene, the nearest major city. While not a national park "superstar" (and fortunately lacking the crowds that this status brings), this park does have enough majestic, placid beauty to be considered an "undiscovered gem." The highlight is Crater Lake—the deepest lake in the U.S. at 1,932 feet—created by the fiery eruption of Mt. Mazama more than 7,000 years ago. The eruption buried Indian communities as far as 70 miles away. As the mountain collapsed inward, it formed a caldera that filled with rain and snowmelt until it became the pure, deep blue it is today. The lake, along with the somewhat eerie, volcano-created landscape around it, makes for fascinating sight-seeing. Since the Cascade Mountains rise above 7,000 feet, summer is short, with snows often arriving in October.

GETTING THERE

The nearest airport of any significant size is **Jackson County Airport** (503–772–8068) in Medford, about 80 miles southwest of the park, with daily service from United and Horizon airlines. Major car rental companies are at the airport.

Amtrak (800–USA–RAIL) stops at South Spring Street Station, in the town of Klamath Falls, 64 miles southwest, where car rentals are also available.

Greyhound (503–779–2103 or 800–231–2222) has a station at 1200 Klamath Avenue, Klamath Falls.

I–5, the state's main north-south route, is about 82 miles west of the park's west entrance (take the Crater Lake/Highway 62 exit in Medford). State Route 62 also connects with points south and the park's southern entrance. State Route 138 leads to the park's northern entrance, open summers only. Note: It's a good idea to tank up before entering the park. Once in the park, gas is available at Mazama Village, during summers only.

GETTING AROUND

A car is a necessity. Because of heavy snow (common as late as May and June), most roads in the park are open only in July, August, and September. At other times, when chains or traction devices may be required, the only access is the road from the western and southern entrances to park headquarters at Rim Village.

WHAT TO SEE AND DO

Start your visit at the main park visitor center, **Steel Center**, in the headquarter's area southwest of the lake, 3 miles below Rim Village. Open year-round from 9:00 A.M. to 5:00 P.M., the center shows an eighteen-minute video about the lake. The film retells the eruption of Mt. Mazama from the eyes of the local Native Americans, the Maklaks. **The Rim Visitor Center**, Rim Village, is open June through September. At the **Sinnot Memorial Overlook**, near Rim Village, rangers hold fifteen-minute talks on the lake's formation from July 4th through Labor Day. Besides offering a good view of the lake, the small museum here provides a helpful overview with photos of the park at different seasons, a scale model of the lake, and other displays about the lake's history. After getting oriented, enjoy the park's wonders in the following ways.

Scenic Drives

In the summer, the 33-mile drive around **Crater Rim Road** provides access to more than a dozen scenic viewpoints, most along the side of the road. Start driving clockwise at either of the visitor's centers. A drive all the way around the meandering road without stopping takes about an hour, but plan to get out of the car and sightsee, so allow several hours to enjoy this scenic route, and take along snacks or lunch as there are several nice picnic areas.

It's worth the drive out to the **Pinnacles**, a rather eerie landscape of fascinating volcanic spires, accessible by a 7-mile dead-end road off Rim Drive near Kerr Notch. Reached via a ¾-mile paved spur road, **Cloudcap**, another "must see" on the east rim, treats you to the highest viewpoint accessible by car.

The awe-inspiring beauty of Crater Lake will stay with you and your family for a long time. (Courtesy Oregon Tourism Division)

Note: Stay away from the edge of the caldera, and keep behind rock walls at all points along the caldera rim. Keep a tight grip on young children at all times. Footing can be difficult on the steep and unstable volcanic rock and soil of the rim and inner caldera walls. Bring jackets and warm clothing as the winds sweeping through here can make it quite chilly.

Hiking

A number of day hikes are well-suited to families. With younger kids, try one—or both—of the following easier and shorter treks. **Castle Crest Wildflower Trail** is a 0.4-mile loop from the trailhead on East Rim Drive, a half mile from park headquarters, or a 1-mile loop from across the headquarters' parking lot. The trails are usually covered with snow from early October to early July. The easy hike (watch out for patches of uneven ground and rocks) takes from thirty to forty-five minutes and leads to a small brook, lush vegetation, and, in the summer months, clusters of fragrant wildflowers. Another easy thirty-minute hike is **Godfrey Glen**, a one-mile stretch, 2.4 miles south of headquarters, that travels through ancient forests and affords views of **Annie Creek Canyon**, wildflowers in season, and, with luck, some deer. The park urges visitors not to feed any animals.

An easy but longer hike of about one hour starts west of Rim Village parking area, and leads to **Discovery Point**. This 1.3-mile, one-way trek affords great lake views; at the point a plaque commemorates John Wesley Hillman's 1853 discovery of Crater Lake.

With older children accustomed to hiking, try the moderately strenuous 1.6-mile round-trip trek to **Watchman Peak**, a 8,035-foot-high precipice with a lookout tower that provides a spectacular lake view. The hike leaves from the parking lot ("the corrals") between Watchman and Hillman peaks on West Rim Drive. Good news: There are chemical toilets here.

Boat Touring

In summer don't miss the two-hour ranger-narrated boat tour of Crater Lake; call (503) 594–2511. During peak season, boats leave nine times a day from the Cleetwood Cove dock, which is at least a one-hour drive and hike from Rim Village. Be forewarned: It's necessary to hike from the parking area down a very steep one-mile trail, which climbs 700 feet. This trail, the only safe access to the shore and boat docks, is recommended only for those in good physical condition and *not* for anyone with heart, respiratory, or leg problems. Visitors are advised to take along jackets (the temperature on the lake may be considerably colder than that on land), water (none is available at the Cove), snacks, sunglasses, sunscreen, sturdy hiking shoes—plus cameras and binoculars. A composting toilet is available at the docks.

The boats, which carry up to sixty passengers, cruise around the lake into hidden coves, along towering cliffs, and by the **Phantom Ship**, a rather odd-looking basalt island that in certain light looks like an early battleship. There's a stop at **Wizard Island**, a miniature cinder cone that rises 760 feet above the lake's surface. If you want to stay and explore, hike the one-mile trail to the cone's top and picnic. Some hardy souls swim in the lagoon (temperatures usually range from 45°F to 50°F and never get higher than 60°F). Those who stay can take a later boat back, but the return will depend upon available space on subsequent boats; you're not guaranteed a ride back until the final tour of the day, which arrives at the dock after 5:00 P.M. (Don't forget the return requires you and the kids to have enough energy to hike back up the trail).

Programs

The Junior Ranger programs, usually one hour long, offer enjoyable ways for ages six to twelve to learn about the park. In 1993, the summer programs were held at 6:00 P.M. at **Mazama Campground Amphitheater;** check at the visitor's center. At the end of the program, each child receives a Junior Ranger book. After completing four exercises, plus attending another ranger program, your child receives a Junior Ranger badge.

Evening campfire programs at Mazama Campground Amphitheater, southwest of the Steel Center, feature a different ranger talk each night. In the winter holiday season, ranger-led informative snowshoe walks usually are offered.

Biking

Bicycles, including mountain bikes, are allowed only on paved roads, the Grayback motor nature trail, and the dirt road to the park on the east side of the Pinnacles.

Fishing

Although fish are not native to Crater Lake, as a result of stocking in past years, healthy amounts of Kokanee salmon and rainbow trout await anglers. Fishing is allowed at Cleetwood Cove (see Boat Touring) and Wizard Island.

Skiing

Cross-country skiing, a winter draw for the park, is allowed on trails and roads that aren't plowed during the winter. These include Rim Drive, but not on the 3-mile stretch of road from Park Headquarters to Rim Village. Ski and snowshoe rentals are available at Rim Village Gift Shop, usually starting the second week of November. The closest downhill skiing to Crater Lake National Park is at Williamette Pass, 50 miles north on Highway 58 (503–484–5030), and Mt. Ashland, 18 miles west of Ashland (follow signs from I–5); (503) 482–2897 or (800) 547–8052— Southern Oregon Reservations.

SPECIAL EVENTS

August: The Rim Run, with some 500 runners following the 33 miles around Rim Drive, takes place the second Saturday in August. As the park's only special event, it's popular enough to strain lodging and eating facilities. Beware. Either book early for the fun, or avoid the crowds by visiting another time.

Area events include the Oregon Shakespeare Festival in Ashland (see Day Trips) and Horse and Buggy Days, July 4th, downtown Klamath Falls.

WHERE TO STAY

At present, the only accommodations in the park are those at **Mazama Village** (503–594–2511), open until mid-October, weather permitting. Each of the forty rooms has two queen beds and private baths in motel-type cabins. **Crater Lake Lodge**, under renovation for the past few years, should be completed by 1995, with additional guest rooms available from May to October as well as dining room facilities.

Crater Lake National Park has two campgrounds: **Mazama Campground** has 198 wooded sites, flush toilets, potable water, pay showers, laundry facilities, and telephones. It is operated on a first-come basis, generally closing for the season in mid-October, weather permitting. **Lost Creek Campground**, off the East Rim Drive on Pinnacles Road, is a small, sixteen-site, tent-only campground that usually closes for the season in mid-September. Reservations are not available. Arrive early in the day, as camp sites fill quickly. If these campgrounds are filled, try the National Forest campgrounds to the west of the park.

Lodging options within a 25-mile radius of the park are limited as well, though there are a handful of inexpensive motels. The visitor's center can supply you with a listing of nearby lodging, including **Fort Klamath Lodge Motel**, Highway 62, Fort Klamath (503–381–2234), 6 miles from the southern entrance to the park. Fort Klamath also sports a grocery store and a coffee shop. **Diamond Lake Resort** (503–793–3333 or 800–733–7593) is on a mountain lake 13 miles northwest of the park's northern rim. It has forty plain but modern motel rooms, ten housekeeping studios with kitchens, and forty-three rustic cabins, plus three restaurants, as well as fishing and boat rentals. The **Ashland** area, 89 miles southwest, has the highest number of bed-and-breakfast inns in the state, approximately four dozen. Contact the **Ashland Bed and Breakfast Reservation Network**, P.O. Box 1051, Ashland 97520; (503) 482–2337. Also try **Southern Oregon Reservations** (800–547–8052), which books accommodations and packages. The *Oregon B&B Directory*, 230 Red Spur Drive, Grant Pass 97527 (800–841–5448), lists bed-and-breakfast homes throughout the state, including some in the Crater Lake area.

WHERE TO EAT

At Rim Village the **cafeteria** adjacent to the gift shop serves breakfast, lunch, and dinner, plus a salad bar, snacks, desserts, and deli sandwiches year-round. Upstairs, the **Watchman Deli Lounge** has burgers, sandwiches, pizza, snacks, beer, wine, and spirits (families welcome) in summer only. Also, the **camper services building**, at Mazama Village, near the Annie Springs entrance station, 4 miles south of park headquarters, sells convenience store items, and also has a coin laundry, shower facilities, and unleaded gas.

Dining options near the park are limited. The Medford/Ashland area has the highest concentration of restaurants. In Ashland, try **Omar's**, at the intersection of Siskiyou Boulevard and Highway 66; (503) 482–1281. In business for almost fifty years, this local favorite gains praise for steak and fresh seafood and has a children's menu.

DAY TRIPS

Ashland, 89 miles southwest, is worth a visit, especially because it's the home of the **Oregon Shakespeare Festival**; (503) 482–4331. The festival, which runs from mid-February through the end of October, is among the oldest and largest in the country. From mid-June through September, period English dances precede outdoor performances of the Bard's classics. The theater offers work by other playwrights as well. Kids also enjoy the two-hour backstage tour of dressing rooms, costumes, props, and stagehands at work, plus a visit to the Shakespeare Festival Exhibit Center where costumes can be tried on. The festival's Elizabethan Theatre overlooks charming **Lithia Park** in the town center, which has a duck pond, playground, band shell, nature trail, and creek. In June, the park hosts a Renaissance dinner, Feast of Will, that serves up food, period music, and dancing. (Reserve through the festival number above, or through Southern Oregon Reservations, 800–547–8052, which has festival packages including tickets and accommodations.)

Ashland also has its share of art galleries and antiques shops, as does its neighbor, **Medford**, where the **Main Antique Mall**, 30 North Riverside (503–779–9490), is the largest in southern Oregon.

The Oregon Caves National Monument is worth a stop, particularly if you are continuing on to the Pacific Coast. It's two hours west of Medford, at the end of Highway 46, 20 miles east of Cave Junction; (503) 592–2100. The marble cave high in the Siskiyou Mountains is the state's largest—perhaps the largest on the West Coast—and is filled with stalactites, stalagmites, flowstone, and other formations. The seventy-five-minute guided tours operate frequently, year-round, though on busy summer days you may have a wait of an hour or more. Because exploring the caves involves a certain amount of coordination (there are 200 steps to climb), small children must meet a height requirement before being allowed on the tours. Above ground, explore the area's scenic trails. The Oregon Caves Chateau offers lodgings and meals from June to September.

Closer to the national park, the town of **Klamath Falls** offers a forty-five-minute historical trip in a restored 1906 trolley. Board the trolley at the

Baldwin Hotel Museum (summer only), 31 Main Street (503–883–5207), or at the Klamath County Museum, 1451 Main Street; (503) 883–4208. Both feature historical and archeological exhibits. One more museum stop: The Favrell Museum, 125 West Main Street (503–882–9996), has an extensive arrowhead collection that fascinates some kids.

Although there is no river rafting in the park, the nearby Rogue River is famous for its white water and scenery. Among the river runners who offer family-friendly and/or just-for-family trips: OARS (Outdoor Adventure River Specialists), Box 67, Angels Camp, California 95222 (209–736–4677 or 800–346–6277), features four- and five-day Rogue River trips for kids seven and older. For a list of additional outfitters, contact Oregon Guides and Packers, Box 10841, Eugene, Oregon 97440; (503) 683–9552.

FOR MORE INFORMATION

Crater Lake National Park: Box 7, Crater Lake, Oregon 97604; (503) 594–2211.

Ashland Chamber of Commerce and Visitor Center: 110 East Main Street, Ashland, Oregon 97520; (503) 482–3486.

Handicapped information: Most viewpoints are wheelchair accessible. There are ramps at Rim Village Visitor Center, and at its cafeteria/gift store. Mazama Village campground amphitheater has paved walkways. Also accessible are the rest rooms at Mazama Village, Steel Information Center, and Rim Village.

Emergency Numbers

Ambulance, fire, police: 911 from public phones or from concession phones

First aid stations: Steel Information Center and Rim Village Visitors Center, or any patrol ranger in a park service vehicle. For serious injuries, the park dispatcher will summon an ambulance to a hospital in Medford.

Hospitals: Medford's Rogue Valley Medical Center, 2825 East Barnett Road; (503) 770-4144, with twenty-four-hour emergency room and trauma center. Klamath Urgent Care Center, 2655 Shasta Way, Klamath Falls; (503) 882–2118. 9:00 A.M. to 7:00 P.M., Monday through Saturday; 11:00 A.M. to 4:00 P.M. Sunday.

Pharmacies: Phoenix Pharmacy, 700 North Main Street, Phoenix; (503) 535–1561. 9:00 A.M. to 6:00 P.M. weekdays, until 5:00 P.M. Saturday

Poison Control: (800) 452–7165

29
OLYMPIC NATIONAL PARK
Washington

Snowcapped mountains, ocean shores, and temperate rain forests await visitors to **Olympic National Park**, encompassing some 900,000 acres in the center of the Olympic Peninsula in northwest Washington State. The sharp contrast in surroundings, unusual wildlife, and overall lack of commercialization make for a down-to-earth, back-to-basics vacation. Your family can venture into the misty rain forest, where Sitka spruce and Douglas fir loom over mossy footpaths; view majestic Mt. Olympus; explore tide pools on Pacific beaches; and see some outstanding scenery, including wildlife. (However, you probably won't see the Roosevelt Elk, whose protection was one of the main reasons the park was created. The species is shier than elk found farther east.)

GETTING THERE

Port Angeles, some 75 miles west of Seattle, is the main entry point for **Olympic National Park. William Fairchild International Airport** is 1 mile west of Port Angeles, off Highway 101; (206) 452–5095. It's served by **Horizon Airlines** (800–547–9308), with daily flights from Seattle, Victoria, and Portland. Rental cars are available. The closest major airport is **Seattle-Tacoma International Airport,** 120 miles away.

Amtrak has no service to the Olympic peninsula.

Because the Olympic Peninsula is connected on the east by the Kitsap Peninsula, which projects north between Hood Canal and Puget Sound, you may have to travel on a ferry or cross a bridge to arrive here. Coho Ferry, at the foot of Laurel Street, Port Angeles (206–457–4491), provides daily, year-round passenger and auto services to and from Victoria,

British Columbia. **Victoria Express,** 115 East Railroad Avenue at Landing Mall on the waterfront, provides passenger service in summer only; call (206) 452–8088, (800) 633–1589— Washington, or (604) 361–9144— Canada. **Washington State Ferries,** based in Seattle (800–84–FERRY), has year-round service across Puget Sound and between Port Townsend and Whidbey Island, Edmonds and Kingston, and Seattle and Bainbridge Island.

The bus system is **Clallam Transit,** 2417 West Nineteenth, Port Angeles; (206) 452–4511. It provides limited service to Lake Crescent, Forks, and other nearby areas, as well as winter weekend trips to Hurricane Ridge.

By car, all three areas of the park (mountains, forest, and coast) are accessible by Highway 101, with spur roads leading to many areas inside the park.

GETTING AROUND

A car and good hiking boots are necessary. An option to driving is one of the sight-seeing tours offered by **Olympic Van Tours;** (206) 452–3858. They leave from the Coho ferry terminal, Port Angeles. Journeys to **Hurricane Ridge** and the **Hoh Rain Forest** can be made by reservation only.

Port Angeles is the site of the **Olympic Visitors Center,** the largest in the park. From here, **Heart o' the Hills Road,** an 18-mile paved road, begins its ascent to Hurricane Ridge Visitors Center (not always reachable in winter). No roads pass through the rugged heart of the rain forest. The few secondary roads that do penetrate the interior are mainly trailheads for the vast network of trails.

A number of the trails in the park are handicapped accessible. Contact any visitor's center for information.

WHAT TO SEE AND DO

First, come prepared. Summer months bring less rainfall, but rain gear is essential for the occasional downpours. Much of the backcountry here remains snowed in until the end of June. Carry your own water supply, and never drink any untreated backcountry water, no matter how clear it may appear! The visitor's center sells water purification tablets.

Because the park is so vast, we've divided it into sections. Some of the visitor's centers and ranger stations listed have naturalist programs that the entire family will enjoy. Because of recent budget cuts, however, programs have been curtailed. The children's section of the park's newspaper contains a list of activities (including ranger-led walks, talks, or campfire programs) that, when completed, entitle a child to a Junior Ranger Badge.

It takes at least two days to sample the park's major sites: ocean beaches, rain forest, and Hurricane Ridge. Here are some of the highlights.

Northern Rim

Start at the major entrance, **Olympic Park Visitor Center,** 3002 Mt. Angeles Road (off Race Street); (206) 452–0330. Pick up free maps, and tour the **Pioneer Memorial Museum,** which displays aspects of the early loggers' lives, as well as exhibits on the park's flora.

Highway 101 west of Port Angeles skirts the southern shore of 8½-mile-long, glacier-carved **Lake Crescent.** This scenic drive offers fjordlike views. Self-guided hikes are possible around Lake Crescent, on the park's northwest boundaries. Obtain trail booklets, such as *Ever Changing, Ever Green,* at trailheads at **Storm King Ranger Station** (206–928–3380), where there's an information booth and interpretive programs; at **Lake Crescent Lodge,** also on the south shore; and at the Fairholm Ranger Station, on the north shore. From these points, embark on trails rated easy to moderate that visit such sights as the 90-foot-high **Marymere Falls** (where the last part of the trail is fairly steep).

The Fairholm Station features an easy .75-mile nature trail perfect for youngsters. Experienced hikers may want to tackle the difficult **Mt. Storm King Trail,** which covers 4.2 miles and climbs 1,700 feet. The trail can be accessed from either Lake Crescent Lodge or the Storm King Ranger Station.

If you've brought your bikes, the **Spruce Railroad Trail** on the northeast shore of Lake Crescent offers the best opportunity for a bike tour. The trailheads are located at the North Shore and Lyre River, and the 4-mile trail follows the World War I era Spruce Railway Bed.

From Lake Crescent, it's about a 13-mile ride (west, along Highway 101 then south via a spur road) to **Sol Duc Hot Springs Resort,** U.S. 101, 40 miles west of Port Angelos; (206) 327–3583. Here you can soak in hot tubs (fee), if you so desire; the tubs are located about 12 miles south of Highway 101. After kids get accustomed to the sulfur smell, they may like the soothing waters. **Salmon Cascades,** 6 miles along Sol Duc Road, can be reached by a short trail. From a viewing platform, autumn visitors watch the annual migration of salmon returning from the sea to spawn. **The Ancient Groves Nature Trail,** a 0.5-mile loop, is another good, short trail, and is located 8.3 miles along Sol Duc Road.

Hurricane Ridge, 17 miles south of the Olympic Visitors Center in the subalpine meadows of Olympic high country, is the northern rim's most popular area. Hurricane Ridge affords splendid views of Mt. Olympus, the park's southern interior, and, to the north, the Strait of Juan de

Fuca and British Columbia (on a clear day). Naturalist programs and guided walks, exhibits, hiking trails, and picnic areas are available. **Obstruction Point Road,** a steep 8.4-mile dirt road leading east from the Ridge, offers the best views of Mt. Olympus.

A good hike for families: the **Meadow Loop Trail,** beginning at the visitor's center, and weaving for 2 miles through flower-filled meadows and mountain vistas. Deer and bear populate the woods and alpine meadows around here. Some of the deer have become bold enough to graze in the frequently crowded parking lot. As with any wildlife you may encounter, keep your distance, and never feed any animals in the park.

In the winter, **guided snowshoe walks** (snowshoes provided free of charge) take place every weekend from late December through March. In the heart of ski season, this area offers two rope tows and one Poma lift for downhill skiers. Rentals are available. **Cross-country skiers** make good use of the snow-covered nature trails. Dress warmly. Winter storms are common along Hurricane Ridge, which is often subjected to high winds and low temperatures. The park warns that hypothermia is the leading cause of death in the park.

Northwest Area

If you approach the park from the northwest along the spur road leading from Route 112, you arrive at **Lake Ozette,** the most westerly lake in the contiguous United States. Two trails leave from the Ranger Station for the ocean beaches. The northernmost, **Cape Alava Trail,** 3.3 miles, leads through lowland coastal forest to the beach; a second trail stretches 3 miles to **Sand Point.** You can take the Cape Alava Trail, hike for 3 miles on the beach, and then return via the Sand Point trail—if your kids can walk 9.3 miles. Many kids enjoy both the challenge and the scenery. Cedar walkways on the trails make footing easier for smaller feet, but hiking shoes, tennis, or soft-soled shoes are recommended because the wood is slippery when wet or frosty. Besides exploring tide pools for marine life, hikers can see unusual sea stacks, those eerie eroded remains of coastal cliffs that rise from the water, and pass by Indian Petroglyphs.

Western Area

The **Hoh Rain Forest,** the only temperate rain forest in North America, is 91 miles from Port Angeles (turn off 12 miles south of Forks). Each year this forest receives 150 inches of rainfall, creating a beautiful, lush landscape (including some of the world's largest trees) that you won't find anywhere else in this country. At the **Hoh Ranger Station Visitor Center** (203-374-6925), Highway 101, check the bulletin board for notices, campground activities, and guided walks.

The beauty of Olympic National Park will captivate every member of the family. (National Park Service photo)

Trailheads for two nonstrenuous trails kids enjoy begin right behind the visitor's center. **The Hall of Mosses,** a .75-mile trail, passes through moss draped maples, while the **Spruce Nature Trail,** 1.5-miles, ventures along the Hoh River. You may forget that you are actually in Washington and not in the Amazon as you wander through humid air, under towering trees, past lush greenery and over fern-covered floors. Don't forget your camera.

A number of trails wind down to deserted beaches along the more than 57 miles of wild, rugged coastline in the western area. Before hiking to or on any of the beaches, obtain the "Strip of Wilderness" folder at any ranger station, as there are certain precautions you should take. Either write down or carry a tide table (available at visitor's centers) to avoid being trapped by high tides: People have lost their lives thinking they could beat incoming waters as they hiked around a point or headland. Always use overland trails where they exist. Moreover, be careful as sudden high waves can pick up and hurl beach logs.

If you're driving to the coast from the Hoh Rain Forest, you'll first come to **Ruby Beach,** with scenic views, deep red sand made of tiny garnet crystals, and spectacular sunsets. Certain points of the beach trail can only be passed at low tide.

From Ruby Beach, only the south 14 miles of 101 (known as the **Kalaloch-Ruby Beach Highway**) are accessible by car. The six beaches along this stretch can be reached by paved roads that lead to trails that range from .25 to 3.5 miles long. Exploring tide pools at low tide is a wonderful way to teach children about the ecology of this area.

At the end of this stretch, on the park's southwest boundary, is the **Kalaloch Information Station**. This area serves as a center for beach vacationers, with a general store, lodge, gas station, ranger station, and campground. Enjoy several beach and coastal walks here, as well as nightly campfire programs at the Campground Amphitheater from late June to early August.

Southern Area

Quinault, on the park's south central boundaries, is the home of the Quinault Indians. (Travel to the reservation is prohibited without permission.) Wander onto the **Maple Glade Rain Forest Trail**, which runs for .5 mile, beginning across from the Quinault Ranger Station; (206) 288–2444. Yet another rain forest adventure awaits along the nearby 1-mile **Graves Creek Nature Trail**. These lesser known areas are less crowded alternatives to the Hoh Rain Forest trails.

Adventure

Active families enjoy the park to the fullest with the help of outfitters.

Try **Olympic Raft and Guide Service**, 464 Highway 101 West, Port Angeles; (206) 457–7011 or 452–1443. They offer river-rafting trips in the Olympic National Park that are recommended for all ages, including a Class II, half-day beginner's trip down the Elwha River and two Class I trips—one through the Queets Corridor, the other down the Hoh River.

Nootka Jack Adventures, P.O. Box 1492, Forks (206–374–5831 or 800–348–8735), offers completely outfitted backpack trips in the park. Trips include three-day parent/child camps for ages five to ten and five-day parent/child camps for ages eight and up. On these five-day excursions, guides lead you through the rain forest to the ocean coast, talk about how to survive in the wilderness, and teach skills such as how to build your own campfire. Nootka Jack Adventures also tailors trips for families.

Olympic Park Institute, 111 Barnes Point Road, Port Angeles, has family field seminars exploring the wonders of the park. Call (206) 928–3720 or (800) 775–3720 for a free catalog.

Uncle Dave's Guide Service, near milepost 178 on Highway 101 (206–374–2577), offers guided float trips and fishing excursions along the Hoh River.

Other delightful day adventures, depending on the age of your child, include llama treks, guided berry-picking tours (a popular summer pastime), sea kayak tours around Port Townsend, scenic flights, and mountain bike trips. For details contact the **North Olympic Peninsula Visitor and Convention Bureau**, Highway 101 South, Forks; (206) 374–9845 or (800) 942–4042. The bureau has a free visitor's guide.

Olympic National Forest

Much of the **Olympic National Forest** that borders the eastern edge of the park is more accessible and more developed than much of the park's interior. Pick up information on forest trails at one of the two ranger stations: **Hoodsport** (206–877–5554) and **Quilcene** (206–765–3368), U.S. 101 South. **North Olympic Peninsula Visitor and Convention Bureau**, Highway 101 South, Forks (206–374–9845 or (800) 942–4042), sends a free visitor's guide.

SPECIAL EVENTS

Neighboring communities liven things up on the Olympic Peninsula with a variety of events.

January: Polar Bear Dip, Port Angeles; Centrum's Chamber Music Festival, Port Townsend.

February: Discovery Bay Salmon Derby; Hot Jazz, Port Townsend.

March: Clallam Bay/Sekiu's Spring Fling.

April: Rain Fest, Forks; Audubon Society's Bird-A-Thon, Sequim.

May: Irrigation Festival, Parade and Music Festival, Sequim; Juan de Fuca Festival of the Arts, Port Angeles.

June: Community Clambake and International Days, Port Townsend.

July: Fork's Old Fashioned Fourth Celebration, with frog pulls, arm wrestling, and fireworks; Wine and Food Festival, downtown Port Angeles; Clambake, Sequim; Jazz, Port Townsend; Port Angeles annual Salmon Derby.

August: Jefferson County Fair, Port Townsend; Clallam County Fair, Port Angeles; Derby Days and Kiddie Parade, Port Angeles; Makah Days, Neah Bay.

September: Sekiu Salmon Fishing Derby and Coast Week Celebration.

November: Festival of Trees, Port Angeles.

December: Christmas Fair Arts and Crafts and BazArt, fine art sale, Port Angeles.

WHERE TO STAY

There are a number of lodging choices within the park, including sixteen campgrounds operating on a strictly first-come, first-serve basis. Most are relatively primitive, with only two having hookups and showers. These are **Sports Center & RV Park**, near milepost 178 on Highway 101 (206–374–9288); and the **Hoh River Resort & RV Park**, between milepost 175 and 176 on Highway 101 (206–374–5566). Year-round campgrounds with summer naturalist programs are located at **Heart O' the Hills, Hoh, Kalacoch,** and **Mora.**

Accommodations within the park range from beachside cabins to historic lodges. Be sure to reserve well in advance for the summer season.

Kalaloch Lodge, U.S. 101, 36 miles south of Forks (206–962–2271), is open year-round. Accommodations range from forty modern cabins with kitchenettes (fifteen on a coastal bluff overlooking the ocean), plus eight lodge rooms or ten motel units. While there is no TV or phone in rooms, there is a coffee shop and cocktail lounge as well as a grocery store and service station.

Lake Crescent Lodge, U.S. 101, 21 miles west of Port Angeles (206–928–3211), is open late April to late October. Choose from five rooms in the main lodge (none have private baths), thirty modern guest rooms, and several cottages (four with fireplaces). Roll-away beds and cribs are provided for a small fee. Services include a dining room, cocktail lounge, and rowboat rentals.

Lake Quinault Lodge, on the shore of Lake Quinault (206–288–2571 in Washington State or 800–562–6672), is a rustic timber lodge built in 1926. F.D.R. stayed here in the 1930s and so liked the area and a particular type of elk that he took steps that eventually resulted in the creation of the park. Lake Quinault's main lodge has thirty-two rooms, two suites, and thirty-six lakeside rooms, all with private baths.

Log Cabin Resort is at 6540 East Beach Road on the northeast end of Lake Crescent; (206) 928–3245. It is open mid-May to October and offers lodging ranging from rustic one-room log cabins to lodge rooms, most with private baths, except for the four rustic cabins that share a bathhouse. The "resort" also has a forty-site RV campground.

Sol Duc Hot Springs Resort, U.S. 101, 40 miles west of Port Angeles (206–327–3583), is open mid-May to late September. There are thirty-two cabins, all with private bath and six with full kitchens, plus a swimming pool and three hot springs pools. The lodging features a dining room, snack bar, and grocery store, but no TV or phones in the room.

Nearby communities have a variety of hotels, motels, and bed and breakfasts. For information, write the **Olympic Peninsula Resort and Hotel Association,** Colman Ferry Terminal, Seattle 98104. Here are a few choice examples.

Port Townsend
Diamond Point Inn, 241 Sunshine Road, Port Townsend (206–797–7720), is a bed and breakfast that welcomes kids to stay in

one of their six rooms (suites available). **Anapurna Inn**, 538 Adams (206–385–2909), accepts children of all ages (and pets). They feature suites with kitchen facilities. The **Bishop Victorian Guest Suites**, Washington and Quincy streets (206–385–6122), has some two-bedroom suites. **The Harborside Inn**, 330 Benedict Street (206–385–7909 or 800–942–5960), offers comfortable waterfront rooms. A few feature kitchen facilities.

Port Angeles
   Red Lion Bayshore Inn, 221 North Lincoln (206–452–9215 or 800–547–8010), is right on the waterfront. It has 185 rooms on two levels, an outdoor pool and jacuzzi, and adjacent coffee shop.
   The **Best Western Olympia Lodge**, 140 Del Guzzi Drive (206–452–2993), is another good choice; as is the **Uptown Motel**, 101 East Second (206–457–9434 or 800–858–3812), which has a great view, and suites and rooms with refrigerators and microwaves.

WHERE TO EAT

All the lodges and resorts within the park have on-site restaurants, which serve breakfast, lunch, and dinner, except at Sol Duc, where breakfast and dinner are served in the main dining room, with lunch at the Poolside Deli. Buy sandwiches, snack foods, and supplies from the **Fairhold General Store** (206–928–3020) on the western end of Lake Crescent; it's open April 1 through October 1 (except Memorial and Labor days). The **Hurricane Lodge Visitors Center** serves sandwiches and light meals.
   Port Angeles has a fair share of family-friendly restaurants. For breakfast and lunch, **The Joy of Eating**, 903 West Eighth Street (206–457–2069), is known for its fresh, homemade bread, which accompanies lunch sandwiches and omelettes. At the **Bushwhacker Restaurant**, 1527 East First Street (206–457–4113), the menu includes prime rib, clam chowder, shrimp, and a salad bar. For Italian food, stop in at **Gordy's Pizza and Pasta**, 1123 East First Street; (206) 457–5056. Choose from an array of salads, pastas, pizzas, and sandwiches. Homemade cheesecake is their dessert specialty.

DAY TRIPS

Convenient to the Lake Ozette area of the park is a day trip to **Neah Bay**, a small fishing village off Route 112, where the **Makah Cultural and Research Center**, 8 miles south of Makah Reservation on the Pacific Ocean near Cape Alava (206–645–2711), is well worth a visit. The driving time to cover the 72 miles from Port Angeles to the cultural center is about two hours. Along the way near the coast, you might catch sight of trumpeter swans and bald eagles that frequent this region. A mud slide in the coastal village of Ozette, 15 miles south, uncovered a site containing hundreds of perfectly preserved Makah Indian artifacts more than 500 years old. The subsequent archaeological dig was one of the largest in North America, and many of the finest objects are on display here, including trinkets, tools, ceremonial pieces, and whaling and sealing instruments of these ocean-dependent Indians. A longhouse replica features soft voices speaking the Makah language.

In the summer on the **Makah Reservation**, guided horseback tours are offered on the Tsoo-Yess Beach and River area, 6 miles west of Neah Bay. At other times of year, tours may be arranged by reservation daily. Call Tsoo-Yess River Ranch; (206) 645–2391. While the ranch has no official age limit, discuss with the guides if the ride is appropriate for your age children, and whether you may have young kids sit in the saddle with you for a trail walk.

Returning east from Neah Bay, take Highway 112 to Pysht to visit the **Merrill & Ring Pysht Tree Farm**, Highway 112; (206) 963–2382 or (800) 998–2382. This "managed tree farm" offers guests a slide show, forestry trails that teach harvest cycles, and weekly guided tours (call for schedules).

You can also take a ferry ride to the attractions of charming Victoria, British Columbia. (See the chapter Victoria.)

Although the town of Port Angeles is a convenient gateway to the park, some may find it rather dreary. A more appealing option: **Port Townsend**, on the Puget Sound, has lots of Victorian charm and an active cultural life, including a number of summer music festivals (see Special Events), art galleries, historical sights, and a scenic coastline. Contact the Port Townsend Chamber of Commerce, 2437 Sims Way (206–385–2722), for visitor information.

West of **Port Townsend** are several worthwhile attractions in the Sequim area. **The Dungeness Spit National Wildlife Refuge**, 3 miles north of Highway 101 near Sequim (206–683–5847), is home to 150 species of wildlife and approximately 250 different bird species. This 6-mile arc is the longest natural sand spit in the world, growing 34 feet in length a year. From here you are treated to fabulous views of the **Strait of San Juan de Fuca, Mount Baker**, the **San Juans, Vancouver Island**, and the **Olympic Mountains**. Frolic in the sand at the pit's base, or if your kids are energetic, take a 5.5-mile hike to the coast guard lighthouse, open to visitors Thursday through Monday. Remember though that the hike requires about two hours one-way. Look for harbor seals on your journey. Bring plenty of water, a lunch, and jackets because the weather here changes suddenly.

Also in the Sequim area is the **Olympic Game Farm**, 1423 Ward Road (follow the signs from Sequim); (206) 683–4295. You can drive through or take a summer guided walking tour to see a wide assortment of animals including jaguar, rhino, timber wolves, cougar, and buffalo. An extra summer treat: a stocked pond (poles and bait supplied). A map and more information are available from the **Sequim/Dungeness Chamber of Commerce**; (206) 683–6197 or (800) 737–8464.

FOR MORE INFORMATION

Park Information: Olympic National Park, Office of the Superintendent, 600 East Park Avenue; (206) 452–0330. **The Olympic Park Visitor Center,** 3002 Mt. Angeles Road, Port Angeles (206–452–0330), is the park's largest.

Area information: Port Angeles Chamber of Commerce and Visitor Center, 121 East Railroad Avenue; (206) 452–2363. **North Olympic Peninsula Visitor and Convention Bureau,** Highway 101 South, Forks; (206) 374–9845 or (800) 942–4042.

Emergency Numbers

Park emergencies or to report a crime: 911 or (206) 452–4501, 7:00 A.M. to midnight during the summer, until 5:30 P.M. off-season. After hours, in Clallam County (northern peninsula from Forts to Port Angeles and Sequim), dial 911. In other areas, call (206) 452–4545. You may also contact a park ranger at the **Hoh Ranger Station;** (206) 374–6925.

Hospital: Olympic Memorial Hospital, 939 Caroline, Port Angeles, has twenty-four-hour emergency services; (206) 457–8513.

Twenty-four-hour pharmacies: Jim's Pharmacy, 424 East Second Street, Port Angeles (206–452–4200); **Sequim Plaza Pharmacy,** 933 North Fifth Avenue, Sequim (206–683–1122).

Poison Control: (800) 542–6319

30
PORTLAND
Oregon

Portland seems to have it all: clean air (thanks to strict legislation); a cheerful, uncongested downtown with fountains, statues, shops, and places for pedestrians to linger; a lively cultural life; good restaurants; a fine selection of museums; plus a superb location, with ocean beaches to the west and some of the Northwest's most spectacular scenery to the east. All of this combines to deliver a postcard perfect family vacation.

GETTING THERE

Portland International Airport (PDX) is 9 miles northeast of downtown (503–335–1234) and served by some fourteen airlines. Car rentals, cabs, shuttle service, and public bus transportation are available. **Amtrak** (800–USA–RAIL) is at 800 Northwest Sixth Avenue. **Greyhound** (800–231–2222) is at 550 Northwest Sixth Avenue.

By car. The main north-south route to Portland, I–5, originates in southern California, extending through Seattle. Most traffic from the east comes from I–84, which becomes Banfield Expressway before intersecting with I–5 and Burnside Street, a main downtown artery. East-west thoroughfares are U.S. 26 and U.S. 30.

GETTING AROUND

Tri-Met, 701 Southwest Sixth Avenue (503–233–7433), provides excellent bus and trolley transportation. An extensive part of downtown is a fareless ride zone. Nearly all of the seventy-four bus lines run through the downtown transit mall along Southwest Fifth and Sixth avenues. Tickets and information are available at **Tri-Met's Customer Assistance Office** in Pioneer Courthouse Square, on Southwest Sixth between Morrison and Yamhill. **Metropolitan Area Express** (MAX) light rail line travels a 15-mile route from downtown east to Gresham, gateway to Mount Hood. Construction is currently underway to expand service west to the communities of Beaverton and Hillsboro, with completion expected in 1998.

The Willamette River divides the compact city in two, with downtown on the west bank and a mostly residential Lloyd District on the east bank. Much sight-seeing can be done on foot in the downtown area.

WHAT TO SEE AND DO

Museums

American Advertising Museum, 9 Northwest Second Avenue; (503) 226–0000. This small museum is best appreciated by middle school and older kids because it's "text heavy"—though it does have a monitor playing an hour's worth of 1980s commercials that invariably appeal to the younger set. Kids also can join their parents in watching early television commercials, including looking at the Burma Shave signs and watching Arthur Godfrey sell Lipton Soup.

If your kids like cowboys, visit the **Cowboys Then and Now Museum,** 729 Northeast Oregon Street; (503) 731–3200. This small but comprehensive museum, three blocks east of the Oregon Convention Center, has some interesting things to offer. A time line traces the evolution of the cattle industry from the days of Columbus to the present and includes items such as Wild West Show posters and original barbed wire. One highlight is a real chuck wagon, more than one hundred years old, with a talking "Cowboy Zack" who tells about life on the trail in the 1880s. A continuous video in the thirty-seat auditorium shows cowboys past and present. Several interactive exhibits, such as the Box Office Buckaroos, display photos of famous Western stars, whom visitors try to identify. There's a Western saddle to climb on, too, and a tack room to browse through.

Oregon Museum of Science and Industry, OMSI, 1945 Southeast Water Avenue; (503) 797–4000 or (800) 955–6674 (advance tickets and taped schedule of events). This fabulous facility shows kids that science is fun. Six Halls of Wonder feature computer games, tornado and earthquake simulators, space adventures, sailboats, and more. At the futuristic-looking Hello World station, kids send signals into outer space. Check out the exhibits, which have included a look at Leonardo da Vinci's futuristic concepts, as well as the annual Snakes, Frogs, and Lizards show in October. Sit back and enjoy the OMNIMAX theater, with its five-story dome, and the Murdock Sky Theater, with its laser and astronomy shows. Combination tickets are available.

Portland Art Museum, 1219 Southwest Park Avenue at Jefferson Street; (503) 226–2811. This comprehensive museum covers thirty-five centuries of art—European, Asian, African, and Native American. The baskets, masks, canoes, and totem poles of the Northwest Coast Indians particularly please younger kids. Family Days, which occur five or six times a year, usually are linked to a special exhibit. On these days, children enjoy free admission, hands-on activities, and entertainment.

The Portland Children's Museum, 3037 Southwest Second Avenue (503–823–2227), presents hands-on exhibits designed for children from tots to age ten. Kids make a splash with water play, cook in a bistro, or weigh and ring up food at the Kid City Grocery Store. Long recognized as a leader in ceramic education, this museum's Clayshop, free with museum admission, allows kids to pound, pull, and roll out clay into something artistic or functional (a gift to take home costs $1.00, or $2.00 if fired). Through 1994, the theme of multicultural diversity, A World of Touch, features the Omokunle Village in the new Children's Cultural Center. At this imaginary town, somewhere in southwest Nigeria's countryside, kids learn by touching artifacts and clothing.

If your kids grow wide-eyed at a big house, visit Pittock Mansion, 3229 Northwest Pittock Drive; (503) 823–3623. This huge manor house, built between 1909 and 1914 by the founder of The Oregonian newspaper, has tours. Allow time to stroll among the forty-six acres of gardens—great for picnics—where you'll find splendid city and mountain views.

Parks, Zoos, and Gardens

Washington Park, encompassing 332 acres on the west end of downtown (entrance at the head of Park Place), offers picnic areas, forested hiking trails, and tennis courts. (Note: The park was designed by the Olmsted brothers, who also created New York's Central Park and San Francisco's Golden Gate Park.) The excellent Metro Washington Park Zoo, 4001 Southwest Canyon Road (503–226–1561), is here. Dedicated to the conservation of rare, threatened, and endangered species, the zoo has more than one thousand animals representing 192 species. Highlights include the Cascade Exhibit, featuring the fish and wildlife that inhabit this region; a Penguinarium; the African rain forest; and four species of endangered bears: the Kodiak, the Polar, the Malayan Sun, and the Asiatic Black. Newest additions are a one-and-a-half-acre Elk Meadow exhibit, featuring four native Roosevelt elk; and a Maasai goat kraal where kids can hug cute pygmy goats. Check the special activities for the frequent keeper talks, birds of prey and reptile shows, summer family concerts, family overnights, and one-day family programs and excursions. Be sure to ask for a free children's Trail Journey at the zoo admission gate, which points the way to six "trails" that depict wildlife seen by the pioneers.

The **Washington Park and Zoo Railway** (fee additional) not only gets you off your feet for a bit, it takes you to the noted **International Rose Test Gardens**, Southwest Kingston in the park, Washington Park Station. See just some of the many hundreds of roses that earned Portland the nickname "City of Roses." Just uphill on Southwest Kingston, the peaceful **Japanese Gardens** (503–223–1321) charms with an Oriental Tea Garden, complete with an authentic Tea House. Still further uphill is the **Hoyt Arboretum**, 4000 Southwest Fairview Boulevard; (503) 823–3655. It contains the largest collection of conifers in the U.S., spread out on 200 acres with 10 miles of trails. For kids who like to walk, this is a scenic delight.

Next to the Zoo is the **World Forestry Center**, 4033 Southwest Canyon Road; (503) 228–1367. The center's forestry exhibits include a model of a paper mill, a re-creation of a forest fire, a 70-foot talking tree, and the multimedia presentation "Forests of the World." Just north of the Center is the **Oregon Vietnam Veterans Living Memorial**, where simple black granite slabs mark each year's losses.

Downtown's **Tom McCall Waterfront Park** is a 2-mile greenway, formerly an expressway, on the west bank of the Willamette River, Front Avenue between the Steel Bridge and the River Place Marina, (503) 222–2223. It is popular with joggers, walkers, and cyclists. In the summer kids frolic in the **Salmon Street Springs**, Front Avenue and Salmon Street, where there are one hundred jet sprays to keep them cool.

Other Attractions

Check out **Pioneer Courthouse Square**, a single block public plaza in the heart of Portland. Among the public art works appealing to the younger set is the *Weather Machine*, a 25-foot mechanical sculpture that tells the atmospheric conditions via lights, symbols, and figurines. Be there for the daily noon forecast, when lights flash, plumes of steam billow, and trumpets herald the hour. On clear days, Helia, a sun, shines; in stormy weather a dragon appears; and when there's mist or drizzle, you'll see a blue heron (chances are he'll appear at least once during your stay, as it rains often in Portland). Pioneer Courthouse Square also hosts concerts, festivals, special events, and floral displays. (Another bonus: public rest rooms are nearby.)

Ira Keller Memorial Fountain, Third Avenue and Southwest Clay Street, directly across from the Civic Auditorium, entertains onlookers— and delights kids—as 13,000 gallons of water a minute flow in the form of waterfalls, fountains, and basins.

Tours

The sternwheeler *Columbia Gorge* departs from Waterfront Park at Southwest Front and Stark streets for two-hour narrated cruises of the harbor area from early October to mid-June. During the summer, the boat cruises the Columbia Gorge (see Day Trips). Call (503) 223–3928 for schedules.

Theater, Music, and the Arts

To find out what's happening, see the Friday Arts & Entertainment insert of *The Oregonian* daily newspaper, or the free weekly tabloids, *Willamette Week* and *The Downtowner*. Ticketmaster (503–224–4400) has tickets to most major entertainment events. Tickets are available by phone, at Ticketmaster outlets, and at all G.I. Joe's stores.

The **Portland Center for the Performing Arts** complex is the focus of the city's cultural life. The jewel of the complex is **Arlene Schnitzer Concert Hall**, a renovated vaudeville house of the 1920s, 1037 Southwest Broadway, where the Oregon Symphony performs classical, pops, family, and kids' concerts. Across the brick plaza is the **New Theatre**, with two performance spaces for plays. A few blocks away, at 222 Southwest Clay Street, the **Civic Auditorium** hosts performances by the Portland Opera and the Oregon Ballet Theater. For ticket and schedule information for the complete complex, phone (503) 248–4496.

The **Carousel Company Theater for Children**, 630 Northeast Pacific Street (503–238–0012), puts on original musical comedies just for kids on Saturdays and weekdays, from October to June. The forty-five-minute shows usually contain a "message." In summer, the theater generally hosts a traditional children's show. Reservations are a good idea because many school groups attend performances. **Ladybug Theater**, Oaks Park, at the foot of Southeast Spokane Street (503–232–2346), features improvisational children's theater for ages three to ten (but it's also appreciated by older kids and adults). Performances are weekends during the school year and weekdays during the summer.

Shopping

Portland's retail core is located downtown. Just off Pioneer Courthouse Square, you'll find **Mier & Frank**, 621 Southwest Fifth (503–223–0512), the city's oldest department store; and **Nordstrom**, 701 Southwest Broadway (503–224–6666). Just to the east, **Pioneer Place**, 700 South West Fifth Avenue (503–228–5800), an eighty-store pavilion, includes the only **Saks Fifth Avenue** in the Northwest. Preteens and teens love **Nike Town**, corner of Sixth and Salmon streets; (503) 221–6453. The store/"museum" displays Michael Jordan's shoes, John McEnroe's broken tennis racquet, and other sports memorabilia. The younger set will adore the multi-video screens in the floor and the fish tanks in the walls.

The outdoor **Portland Saturday Market** in downtown's Skidmore District, at the west end of the Burnside Bridge, is a lively place where

artists, craftspeople, entertainers, farmers, and cooks sell locally produced goods from open-air booths. It's open Saturday and Sunday, March
through Christmas.

The recently opened **Lloyd Center**, on the east bank between Multnomah and Weidler, (508) 282–2511, has glass-enclosed walkways between 150 shops, restaurants, and an indoor ice skating rink.

Sports

The popular NBA **Portland Trail Blazers** basketball team plays at the
Memorial Coliseum, 1401 North Wheeler Street. Also at the Coliseum:
Portland Winter Hawks Hockey, part of the Western Hockey League,
and **Portland Pride**, indoor soccer. Call the Coliseum's ticket office
(503–235–8771) for information.

SPECIAL EVENTS

For exact dates of the following events, contact the Portland/Oregon Visitors Association. For twenty-four-hour events information, call (503)
233–3333.

April: Oregon Trails Blossom Festival, entertainment, food, and historical tours and demonstrations, Hood River.

May: Mother's Day Weekend Annual Rhododendron Show, Crystal
Springs Rhododendron Gardens.

June: Portland Rose Festival/Grand Floral Parade, a three-week festival of over seventy events, including a carnival, air show, rose parade,
boat races, and more.

July: Waterfront Blues Festival.

August: The Bite: A Taste of Portland features Northwest bands and
food from Portland's restaurants.

September: Portland Marathon includes a kids' run; Artquake street
fair has performances, crafts, foods, visual arts.

December: Festival of Trees, Memorial Coliseum; Zoolights Festival
at Metro Washington Park Zoo; Portland Parade of Christmas Ships.

WHERE TO STAY

The *Portland Book* contains lodging information. **Northwest Bed &**
Breakfast, 610 Southwest Broadway, Suite 609 (503–243–7616), has
hundreds of listings in cities, mountains, and the coast. Another agency,
Oregon Bed & Breakfast Guild (800–944–6196), will send a free directory of participating properties.

There's also the **Oregon Bed and Breakfast Directory**, 230 Red Spur

Drive, Grants Pass 97527, (800) 841–5448, which has descriptions of 150 lodgings in the state. To receive a copy, call or send $2.00 and a self-addressed stamped business envelope.

The **Westin's Governor Hotel**, South West Tenth at Alder, (503) 224–3400 or (800) 228–3000, offers the new Westin Kids Club amenities. These include child-friendly rooms, children's sports bottle or tippy cup upon check-in, a safety kit with a night light, Band-Aids, and emergency phone numbers, and bath toys and bath products for kids. Parents can request—at no charge—jogging strollers, potty seats, bicycle seats, and step stools. There's also a kids menu in restaurants and for room service.

The **Heathman Hotel**, South West Broadway at Salmon, (503) 241–4100 or (800) 551–0011, another first-class hotel, is a registered Historic Place. This renovated first-class 1920s Beaux Arts hotel charms with tastefully decorated rooms and suites, a complimentary video movie library, and a top-notch restaurant, all just steps from the Performing Arts Center.

Though a bit on the pricey side, the **Portland Marriott**, 1401 Southwest Front Avenue (503–226–7600 or 800–228–9290), is the only downtown hotel with an indoor pool (which, to some traveling families, is a necessity). This is a large hotel with more than 500 rooms, some with refrigerators.

The more moderately priced **Mark Spencer Hotel**, 409 Southwest Eleventh Avenue, is also downtown; (503) 224–3293 or (800) 548–3934. It offers standard and one-bedroom suites with kitchens. Though the clientele is predominantly businesspeople, this hotel works well for families too. The **Holiday Inn Portland—Downtown**, 1021 Northeast Grand Avenue, is another moderate choice; (503) 235–8433 or (800) HOLIDAY. You might also try the **Comfort Inn-Lloyd Center**, 431 Northeast Multnomah; (503) 233–7933 or (800) 4–CHOICE.

Rose Manor Inn, 4546 Southeast McLoughlin Boulevard (503–236–4175 or 800–252–8333), is in the city's Southeast neighborhood. It has an outdoor pool, seventy-six motel-style rooms, some with kitchenette, and some adjoining two-bedroom duplex townhouses.

For suite space, try **Shilo Inn Suites-Airport**, 11707 Northeast Airport Way, (503) 252–7500 or (800) 222–2244, or **Embassy Suites**, 9000 Southwest Washington Square Road (about 8 miles from downtown); (503) 644–4000 or (800) 772–3897.

WHERE TO EAT

The city's official visitor's guide, *The Portland Book*, contains a listing of restaurants, as does the Friday Arts & Entertainment insert of *The Ore-*

gonian. Fresh Oregon-grown produce highlights many restaurant dishes. For some kid-pleasing options, try the following.

Old Wives' Tales, 1300 Southeast Burnside (503–238–0470), is a trendy place for a tasty bite. The menu ranges from vegetarian to Italian to Middle Eastern. Kids romp in the playroom while parents linger over coffee, accompanied by live jazz. **Original Pancake House**, 8601 Southwest Barbur Boulevard (503–246–9007), is a Portland institution (particularly on weekends, when the crowds are thick). They serve pancakes plain and simple or embellished with an endless variety of toppings. For something a little different, head to **Greek Cusina**, 404 Southwest Washington; (503) 224–2288. Evenings include tasty dinners, folk music, belly dancing—even plate breaking (a Greek tradition your kids will like)! The restaurant also serves breakfast and lunch. If you don't mind being serenaded by an accordion player, go to **Der Rheinlander**, 5035 Northeast Sandy Boulevard (503–249–0507), for large portions of hearty German food at reasonable prices.

DAY TRIPS

Mount Hood National Forest and the Columbia River Gorge

The great outdoors is an easy day trip away from Portland. With 1,200 miles of trails, a river, and mountains, **The Mount Hood National Forest** offers excellent recreational opportunities. For specifics about winter sports such as skiing, snowshoeing, and hiking, contact the Forest Office at 2955 Northwest Division Street, Gresham 97030; (503) 666–0771.

About 20 miles east of Portland, on Oregon's northern border, the spectacular **Columbia River Gorge** carves its way through the steep Cascade Mountains. Don't miss driving the **Columbia River Scenic Highway**, which offers some of the most beautiful scenery in the Northwest. From Portland, access the gorge via I–84, or take the more scenic U.S. 30. Thirty miles of this road—from Troutdale east to Dodson—is a designated scenic highway. After this stretch, the narrow, two-lane highway, which passes along trails, picnic spots, and seven major waterfalls, merges back and forth into I–84. Off exit 31 is the spectacular **Multnomah Falls**, the state's top tourist attraction and the country's second highest falls, cascading 620 feet to the gorge. Take a paved trail to the viewing platform for fabulous views. The base area has a visitor center (opening May 1994) and a restaurant (503–695–2376).

For water wonders of a different sort, visit the huge hydroelectric **Bonneville Dam**; (503) 374–8820. The Bradford Island Visitor Center, off exit 40 of I–84, features an underwater observatory where you can watch salmon make their way upstream on the dam's ladder. Walk along the canal side to watch the boats and barges. Tour the large fishery on your own. In the neighboring town of Cascade Locks, the beautiful **Cascade Locks Marine Park** (503–374–8619) has picnic grounds, a playground, and camping; it's also the launching site for the sternwheeler *Columbia Gorge* (see Tours), which cruises the gorge in the summer and heads to Portland in the late fall.

The next town is **Hood River**, known as the "sailboarding capital of the world" (events held at the Waterfront Center Event Site), and also noted for the region's many apple orchards.

Besides admiring the smooth gliding of the sailboarders, and the scenery from your car, from May to September you can board the **Mt. Hood Railroad**, 110 Railroad Avenue; (503) 386–3556 or (800) 872–4661. It employs vintage 1906 railcars to travel through the gorge and the foothills of Mt. Hood. Sometimes these splendid views are enhanced by reenactments of old-fashioned western train robberies. Another stop of interest might be **Children's Park**, Ninth and Eugene streets (503–386–5153), an adventure park for all ages, designed with input from local kids.

Phil Zoller's Guide Service, 1244 Highway 141 (at what is known locally as B.Z. Corner), White Salmon, Washington (509–493–2641), 14 miles north of the town of Hood River, runs white-water rafting trips through the gorge on the White Salmon River year-round. The spring-fed river's temperature remains at 45 degrees throughout the year; wet suits are available, including kids' sizes. While there is no minimum age for children, use common sense and ask the guides about appropriateness. The half-day trip includes a narration of the gorge's history, wildlife, and folklore.

In season, be sure to get some fresh fruit at the roadside stands. **Rasmussen Farms Pumpkin Funland** (503–386–4622), Hood River, has storybook characters and animals created from pumpkins, gourds, and vegetables, plus a Halloween Hut decorative maze. For more information on the gorge area, call the **Columbia River Gorge Visitors Association** at (503) 269–6616 or (800) 366–3530.

From Hood River, you can head south on Route 35 to **Mt. Hood** (about 40 miles) over **Barlow Pass** where you can hike parts of the last portion of the Oregon Trail, then loop west to Portland on U.S. 26. However, covering the gorge *and* the mountain—particularly with kids—is a very full day, almost too full; consider staying overnight or visiting on separate days.

Mt. Hood, the tallest of the Oregon Cascades at 11,239 feet, and one hour southeast of Portland, offers skiing (three major ski areas twist down the mountain) as well as a summer alpine slide at **Mt. Hood Skibowl** (503–222–BOWL) near the quaint village of Government Camp. **Timberline Ski Area**, the summer training ground of the U.S. Ski Team

A day at the Oregon Coast Aquarium is a day well spent. (Photo by Kent Kerr/courtesy Oregon Tourism Division)

(503–272–3311 or 800–547–1406—lodge reservations, or 231–7979 from Portland), has winter and summer skiing. The U.S. Forest Service has free daily tours of the huge wooden lodge built in the 1930s as a WPA project, and now a National Historic Landmark. The **Mount Hood Visitors Information Center,** 65000 East Highway 26, Welches (503–622–4822), is open daily.

The Oregon Coast

Another refreshing day trip possibility is the Oregon Coast, with its rugged scenery and sandy beaches for strolling and picnicking. The **North Coast** stretches from Astoria, 95 miles northwest of Portland, where the Columbia River meets the Pacific Ocean, to Newport, 135 miles south. **Astoria,** the first American settlement west of the Rockies, sports Victorian homes, historic landmarks, and interesting sights. Murals depicting the area's settlement adorn the **Astor Column;** (503) 325–6311. From atop the 125-foot column on Coxcomb Hill, enjoy vistas of the Columbia River and surrounding countryside. **Fort Clatsop National Memorial,** Route 3, 5 miles southwest of Astoria (503–861–2471), is a reproduction of the fort where the Lewis and Clark

Expedition passed the winter of 1805. In the summer, rangers in period clothing demonstrate frontier skills. Year-round at the visitors center is an audiovisual presentation.

Seaside, the Pacific Northwest's largest beach resort community, sports a 2-mile promenade for strolling, which features an antique carousel and the Seaside Aquarium, Second Avenue at the Promenade; (503) 738–6211. If you're planning on continuing south to Newport, one of the largest Oregon Coast ports, skip the small Seaside Aquarium and instead visit the newer, bigger, and better twenty-three-acre Oregon Coast Aquarium, 2820 Southeast Ferry Slip Road, Newport; (503) 867–3123. This winner's aquarium pools, cliffs, caves, and dunes replicate those of coastal Oregon and feature a number of animals, including seals, sea lions, and three sea otters rescued from Exxon's Valdez Alaska oil spill. At the Touch Pool, kids hold starfish and other little creatures. Many of the animals here play with toys—from frisbees to plastic balls referred to as "environmental enrichment devices." These "toys" are part of a new movement—with this aquarium at the forefront—that maintains that such play challenges animals and promotes curiosity and dexterity.

Newport's flat, wide beaches are a perfect place to explore tide pools during low tide. Ona Beach State Park, 7 miles south of Yaquina Bay Bridge, is a favorite sandy spot.

FOR MORE INFORMATION

The Portland/Oregon Visitors Association, 26 Southwest Salmon, can provide you with helpful tourist information; (503) 222–2223 or (800) 962–3700.

Emergency Numbers
Ambulance, fire, police: 911
Hospital: Twenty-four-hour emergency room, pharmacy, and pediatrics care: Emanuel Hospital & Health Center, 2801 North Gantenbein Avenue; (503) 280–3200
Pharmacy: Safeway Pharmacy, 1025 Southwest Jefferson Street, is open until 8:00 P.M. on weekdays, and until 4:00 P.M. on weekends; (503) 223–3709.
Poison Control: (503) 494–8968

31
SAN DIEGO
California

Glorious weather, a beautiful bay, plus green expanses, lively arts, and festivals combine to make San Diego alluring. Free beaches stretch 70 miles, from Oceanside in the North County south to the Mexican border, just 17 miles away.

GETTING THERE

San Diego International Airport—Lindbergh Field (619–231–5221) is 3 miles northwest of downtown. Shuttles (including complimentary hotel shuttles), car rentals, and taxis are available. San Diego Transit Route 2 buses leave every half hour for downtown.

Amtrak (800–USA–RAIL), Santa Fe Depot, C Street and Kettner Boulevard, provides service to and from Los Angeles.

Greyhound/Trailways, 120 West Broadway (800–231–2222), operates daily service to Los Angeles, connecting to cities throughout the U.S.

By car, San Diego is about 120 miles south of Los Angeles, two-and-one-half hours via freeway Interstate 5. Interstate 8 leads drivers from Yuma, Arizona, and from the East Coast. Interstate 15 provides access from Riverside County, Nevada, and the west.

GETTING AROUND

Metropolitan Transit Corporation buses (619–233–3004) serve the metro area. **San Diego Trolley** (619–233–3004) services the downtown area, south to the Mexican border at Tijuana, and San Diego's East County. The Transit Store at Broadway and Fifth Avenue downtown has free transit maps and sells MTS tickets, including Day Tripper passes for unlimited rides on all MTS buses, trolleys, and the Bay Ferry to Coronado, and discounts to Sea World.

The **San Diego–Coronado ferry** (619–234–4111) leaves from the Broadway pier off Harbor Drive.

The San Diego area stretches 30 miles, from the northern suburb of Del Mar to the Mexican border, so a car is extremely helpful. Main downtown thoroughfares are Harbor Drive, which runs along the waterfront; Broadway, which goes through downtown; and Sixth Avenue to Balboa Park. Stay off the freeways at rush hour.

WHAT TO SEE AND DO

Because San Diego is so spread out, attractions are grouped according to location. Many of the following involve at least one full day.

Balboa Park

Located just north of downtown, this 1,200-acre park is reached by crossing the Cabrillo Bridge (also called the Laurel Street Bridge) toward the California Tower (which has a carillon that chimes the hours) onto El Prado, the park's main pedestrian thoroughfare. The park is adorned with green lawns, fountains, palms, and majestic eucalyptus trees, and features museums, a huge zoo, sports facilities, restaurants, and a performing arts complex, plus weekend street entertainers. Weekend **Punch and Judy** shows are held at the **Marie Hitchcock Puppet Theater**, the Palisades Building; (619) 685–5045. A free tram makes twelve stops through the central core of the park. The **Balboa Park Visitors Center**, in the House of Hospitality, 1549 El Prado (619–239–0512), provides a free map and sells discounted passports to several museums (which also sell the passports). Many offer free admission on the first Tuesday of the month. There are thirteen museums, so be selective. Here are some top choices.

San Diego Museum of Man, 1350 El Prado; (619) 239–2001. Exhibits at this museum, located just under the California Tower, deal mainly with anthropology and archeology, centering around Early Man, pre-Columbian Maya, and the Southwest Indians. Costumes and customs of San Diego's widely diverse ethnic communities are part of the Lifestyle and Ceremonies exhibit, which also includes a video on reproduction suitable for most school-age kids (even groups of preschoolers come to watch it). At press time, the museum was planning an Egypt exhibit that should remain for several years. (Their most spectacular exhibits are often traveling ones.) (See Special Events for other information.)

Reuben H. Fleet Space Theater and Science Center, 1875 El Prado; (619) 238–1233. Watch exciting films projected on the giant OMNIMAX theater screen, but be sure your kids are prepared for the potentially frightening realism. Everyone seems to like the 3-D laser light shows held Wednesday through Sunday evenings. Sky Show and Star Gazing parties are held the first Wednesday of every month at 7:00 P.M. A Space Theater ticket also buys admission to the hands-on Science Center, where more than fifty exhibits demonstrate the principles of science by allowing kids to do such things as peek through periscopes and listen to heart beats through stethoscopes.

San Diego Natural History Museum, 1788 El Prado; (619) 232–3821. Your kids will love this venerable institution. (It's more than one hundred years old.) Steer them toward the Desert Discovery Lab, with live reptiles, and the Scripps Hall of Mineralogy, where there's a walk-through mine tunnel and twelve hands-on learning centers. All kids automatically gravitate toward the dinosaur skeletons. Ask about nature walks, films, and other special happenings.

San Diego Zoo, 2920 Zoo Drive; (619) 234–3153. This is one of the best. Some 3,900 animals of 800 species, many rare and endangered, live in this hundred-acre, world-renowned facility. Arrive as early as possible, as this place is extremely popular. Two of the newest bioclimatic habitats simulating natural surroundings include Pygmy Chimps of Bonobo Road and Wings of Australasia—both guaranteed to please all ages. The chimps are the second phase of Gorilla Tropics, a setting of thick vegetation that includes African trees, shrubs, and grasses, a waterfall, boulders, and twisted palms and vines. In the Wings of Australasia, more than twenty rain forest aviaries include dozens of colorful birds native to Australia and Southeast Asia: cockatoos, Tahitian blue lorries (the only breeding flock in captivity), parrots, and sixty-five species of pigeons and doves—most threatened in the wild and rare in captivity.

Zoo admission includes the aerial tramway (a 3-mile guided bus tour costs extra) and the Children's Petting Zoo, with its goats, sheep, guinea pigs, bunnies, and an animal nursery. The baby monkeys and other cuties behind the glass viewing area delight kids and adults. Strollers, a good idea, are available at the zoo entrance. Southeast of the zoo, behind the Spanish Village Art Center, where arts and crafts are exhibited, a miniature railroad and a carousel await.

If you still have time and energy, consider these other Balboa Park attractions: **San Diego Aerospace Museum**, 2001 Pan American Plaza (619–234–8291), with a collection of aircraft, spacecraft, and related artifacts; **San Diego Automotive Museum**, 1030 Pan American Plaza (619–231–AUTO), featuring more than sixty classic and collectible cars; **San Diego Model Railroad Museum**, 1649 El Prado (619–696–0199), with six giant model railroad exhibits, Lionel toy trains, and working semaphore; **San Diego Museum of Art**, 1450 El Prado (619–232–7931), featuring Egyptian and pre-Columbian through twentieth century artists—plus a Sculpture Garden cafe; and **Timken Museum of Art**, 1500

El Prado, a free museum displaying European art by such notables as Rembrandt and Cezanne as well as a collection of eighteenth- and nineteenth-century American paintings and Russian icons.

Old Town

Old Town San Diego State Historic Park, a twelve-acre park just north of downtown at Juan Street, and bounded by Wallace, Juan, Twiggs, and Congress streets, is the site of the state's first permanent Spanish settlement. Historic buildings grace the Old Town Plaza, a pleasant place to linger and people watch. The best way to explore this 6-block area is on foot: San Diego Avenue turns into a pedestrian mall. Cars are allowed on Juan and Congress streets, both lined with shops and restaurants. The Visitors Information Center at Robinson Rose House, 4002 Wallace Street, on the south side of the plaza (619–220–5422), has videos, maps for a self-guided tour, and ranger-led tours daily at 2:00 P.M.

Your kids' age and interests will determine how many places to visit. Some of the more interesting buildings: the one-room Mason Street School (on Mason Street) is the city's first schoolhouse, with vintage desks and a pot-bellied stove; San Diego Union Newspaper Historical Building, San Diego Avenue, is restored to its 1868 appearance, the date of the the first issue. The Seeley Stables, on Juan Street, the city's stagecoach stop features Western and Native American memorabilia, including toys, musical instruments, and a collection of horse-drawn vehicles. An hourly slide show features scenes of early California (admission).

The Seaside

The beautiful San Diego Harbor bustles with activity: pleasure crafts, commercial and cruise ships, sportfishing and navy ships. A sight-seeing cruise affords one of the best ways to savor the harbor. If your kids won't be bored, consider a one- or two-hour narrated tour offered by San Diego Harbor Excursion, 1050 North Harbor Drive (619–234–4111), and several other companies. For a shorter cruise, board the San Diego ferry (at the foot of Broadway) for a fifteen-minute ride to Coronado. At the dock, Old Ferry Landing, consider renting bikes. Quiet and flat Coronado, at about 12 square blocks, affords easy family cycling. If you're not staying at the Hotel del Coronado (see Where to Stay) stop by this National Historic Landmark. (Trolleys run between the landing and the hotel.)

If your kids are landlubbers, don't fret. Along San Diego's Harbor Drive, the Embarcadero waterfront walkway is a lovely place to stroll. It unofficially starts at Ash Street at the Maritime Museum, 1306 North Harbor Drive; (619) 234–9153. There you board the 1904 luxury steam yacht Medea; the turn-of-the-century ferryboat Berkeley (which carried passengers to Oakland during the earthquake of 1906); and the Star of

India, the oldest (over 125 years) square-rigged merchant sailing vessel still afloat. Several of the ship's cabins have been restored (including one with an old dollhouse and little high-button shoes). Below deck are interesting displays of knot tying, sail rigging, and other nautical skills. The *Berkeley* has exhibits on oceanography and naval history, including models of several well-known ships.

Less than a mile south is **Seaport Village**, West Harbor Drive at Kettner Boulevard (619–235–4014), a lively shopping, dining, and entertainment complex. Let the kids take a spin on the restored **1890 Looff Carousel**, once a Coney Island fixture, featuring delightful hand-carved animals. Fast food emporiums and snack bars are plentiful. A grassy section in the middle of the village attracts skaters, sun bathers, kite fliers, and street performers and hosts frequent celebrations.

If you take Harbor Drive north around the bay, you arrive at **Point Loma**, a large promontory at the end of Catalina Boulevard, which features the **Cabrillo National Monument** (619–557–5450) at the Point's tip. The paths around the monument's visitors center afford spectacular views of San Diego. Take a trail south to the **Old Point Loma Lighthouse**, in service from 1855–1891, which has the restored family quarters of the last lighthouse keeper. To the delight of all, from late December to the end of March, Point Loma is a terrific place to watch the annual migration of Pacific gray whales.

San Diego's other bay, **Mission Bay Park** on Mission Boulevard, north of downtown and south of La Jolla, offers lots of activity as well. This man-made 4,600-acre waterfront recreation area is three-fourths public land. Your first stop should be the Visitor Information Center, 2688 East Mission Bay Drive (619–276–8200), directly off the Mission Bay Drive exit off Route 5. Pick up free brochures on the park's facilities.

Cyclers, rollerskaters (rentals available), joggers, and skateboarders take to the **Mission Boulevard boardwalks**. The 2-mile stretch of **Mission Beach**, on the Pacific side of the peninsula, is one of the area's oldest. The water is rougher and the beach narrower in the north end, near **Belmont Park**, 3145 Mission Boulevard (619–488–1549), a shopping and entertainment center along the boardwalk. Once an abandoned amusement park, the Plunge, a 1925 indoor pool, and the Giant Dipper wooden roller coaster have been restored. A new indoor Pirate's Hideaway features soft, modular recreational playground equipment for children ages two to twelve. **Bonita Cove**, southeast of Belmont Park, is a good family bayside beach with calm waters, grassy knolls for picnicking, and a playground.

The highlight of Mission Bay: **Sea World of California**, 1720 South Shores Road; (619) 226–3901. This place is big, so consider a stroller, which you can rent near the entrance. Most kids like Baby Shamu and mom (the summer Night Magic performances have particular charm),

Paper flowers are always in bloom in San Diego's Old Town section, which is considered California's birthplace. (Photo by Bob Yarbrough/courtesy San Diego Convention and Visitors Bureau)

but chances are the antics of Clyde and Seamore, the sea lion duo, will appeal even more. In all, five shows, which include the bird, whale, and dolphin and water-ski shows, keep kids busy. In addition, tour the four aquariums for a fascinating glimpse of sea life. Shark Encounter, with a submerged viewing tube, allows visitors to walk through the sharks' habitat. While fascinating, this may frighten the very young who may not realize they are not in danger.

Standouts among the park's more than twenty major educational exhibits include the park's Rocky Point Preserve, a two-part habitat for bottlenose dolphins and Alaska sea otters, and Dolphin Bay, the world's largest interactive habitat for bottlenose dolphins. Buy the trays of fish and squid sold at the park so that your kids can take part in the animals' daily feeding. (Hand-washing stations are nearby for after feeding.) For a touch of magic your kids won't soon forget—reach down and feel the dolphin's smooth skin. Another popular exhibit is the Otter Outlook with its underwater viewing area.

Let the kids loose at Cap'n Kid's World, a play area with interactive games for children 37 to 61 inches tall. A 320-foot Southwest Airlines Skytower offers panoramic views, as does a Skyride, enclosed gondola cars that ascend to a height of 100 feet on the half-mile round-trip over Mission Bay.

Other Attractions

The **Children's Museum of San Diego** (619–233–8792) was setting up shop at press time in temporary headquarters at 200 West Island, downtown across from the convention center. The hands-on museum plans to relocate to a permanent home in Balboa Park sometime in 1996.

La Jolla

A posh suburb 12½ miles (about fifteen minutes) north of San Diego, La Jolla offers several attractions.

The **Scripps Institute of Oceanography** recently opened the **Stephen Birch Aquarium Museum**, 2300 Expedition Way; (619) 534–FISH. It displays more than thirty large tanks of colorful saltwater fish. A 70,000-gallon tank simulates a La Jolla kelp forest, complete with sea anemones, starfish, crabs, and lobsters. This aquarium offers a fabulous view of the La Jolla coastline and easy acess by pathways to the popular La Jolla Shores beach. Be sure to come early.

Ellen Browning Scripps Park, at the La Jolla Cove, along Coast Boulevard below Prospect Street, features a children's pool at the south end, where a seawall protects the waters from strong waves and currents. It's a great place to teach the kids snorkeling—though, as you might expect, it's frequently crowded.

North of La Jolla, don't miss **Torrey Pines State Reserve**, North Torrey Pines Road (Old Hwy 101) (619–755–2063), a preserve for the world's rarest pine trees, *Pinus torreyana*. Thousands of these unusual, gnarled trees—more than half of the world's total—grow on cliffs 300 feet above the ocean. The Visitors Center (make a left after entering the park's gate and proceed up the hill) has a video presentation and area information.

Theater, Music, and the Arts

San Diego is an important center for regional theater productions that often end up on Broadway or off-Broadway. For half-price day-of-performance or full-price advance sale tickets to theater, music, and dance events, call TIMES ARTS TIX at (619) 238–3810, or visit their booth at Horton Plaza, Broadway at Broadway Circle, downtown. The bimonthly *San Diego Performing Arts Guide*, available around town, lists all current performances of the sixty-member San Diego Theatre League. These include puppet performances and theater for young audiences. Also consult the Thursday "Night & Day" section of the *San Diego Union Tribune* or the weekly San Diego *This Week*.

Music offerings: **San Diego Symphony Orchestra** (619–699–4205) has outdoor SummerPops concerts at the Embarcadero, Marina Park South.

From mid-June to mid-August, the Spreckels Organ Pavilion in Balboa Park (619–239–0512 or 235–1105) features free family twilight concerts.

Sports

For **San Diego Chargers** professional football (619–280–2111) and **San Diego Padres** professional baseball (619–283–4494) head to San Diego Jack Murphy Stadium, 9449 Friars Road. **San Diego Gulls** ice hockey team of the U.S. International Hockey League (619–225–PUCK) skate at San Diego Sports Arena, 3500 Sports Arena Boulevard. **San Diego Sockers** (619–224–GOAL), members of the new Continental Indoor Soccer League, also play at the Sports Arena. **The Aztecs**, the city's major college team, kick off at San Diego State University; call (619) 594–4549.

Shopping

Downtown **Horton Plaza**, between Broadway and G Street and First and Fourth avenues (619–239–8180), is a multilevel, postmodern maze of large and small shops, fast food emporiums, restaurants, a farmers' market, and more. Old Town's **Bazaar del Mundo**, a Mexican-style shopping center at 2754 Calhoun Street, offers colorful, handcrafted wares. The historic **Gaslamp Quarter**, a 16-block downtown historic district, has Victorian buildings and renovated warehouses that house antiques dealers, specialty shops, and art galleries.

Walking tours are available on Saturdays (donation required) from the headquarters at 410 Island Avenue; (619) 233–5227.

SPECIAL EVENTS

Contact the San Diego CVB for more information on the following annual events.

March: Ocean Beach Kite Festival, with kite building, decorating, and flying contests.

April: Fightertown Festival at Miramar Naval Air Station features classic car show, carnival midway, craft fair, military displays, and stages with music, dancing, and martial arts.

Early Spring: Art Alive, floral interpretations of paintings and sculptures from San Diego's Museum of Art.

May: Cinco de Mayo celebrations throughout the area; International Children's Festival, five days of professional music, storytelling, comedy, and puppetry performances plus arts and crafts; American Indian Cultural Days, with singers and dancers, traditional food, exhibitions, and arts and crafts, Balboa Park.

June: Old Town Heritage Festival; Indian Fair, Balboa Park; Threshing

Bee and Antique Engine Show, Vista, two consecutive weekends of early American crafts, farming, log sawing, blacksmithing, food, entertainment, and daily antique tractor parade.

July: Ringling Brothers and Barnum and Bailey Circus, San Diego Sports Arena; Sand Castle Days at Imperial Beach Pier includes children's contest, parade, and fireworks at dusk.

August: Street Scene, the state's largest music festival, transforms 18 blocks of the historic Gaslamp Quarter into a music and food festival.

September: American Indian Day features arts and crafts, singers and dancers, food and entertainment, Balboa Park.

October: Haunted Museum of Man, Balboa Park; Escondido Downtown Street Faire, with arts and crafts vendors, bands, international food, and children's rides; Kidzartz Festival, a celebration held in various locations at Balboa Park; Threshing Bee and Antique Engine Show (see June); Underwater Pumpkin Carving Contest, La Jolla.

November: Mother Goose Parade with floats, clowns, bands, and equestrians, El Cajon.

December: Del Mar Holiday Faire, with man-made snow, children's rides, entertainment, and Santa; Old Town events include Las Posadas and Holiday Open House; San Diego collegiate Holiday Bowl and downtown parade; Christmas on the Prado events, Balboa Park; San Diego Harbor Parade of Lights.

WHERE TO STAY

THE SDCVB has an accommodations directory. **San Diego Hotel Reservations** (800–SAVE–CASH) features discounted rates to more than 250 area resorts and hotels. Contact **Bed & Breakfast Directory** for San Diego, P.O. Box 3292, San Diego 92163 (619–297–3130), for referrals and information on the thirty inns and homes throughout the county, or order their complete directory for $3.95. Here are some lodging choices for families in varied locations.

Downtown: **Harbor Hill Guest House**, 2330 Albatross Street (619–233–0638), is an inexpensive bed and breakfast with harbor views and kitchenettes. **Embassy Suites Downtown**, 601 Pacific Highway (619–239–2400 or 800–362–2779), has refrigerators, pool, and some rooms with harbor views.

Mission Bay: **The Hyatt Islandia**, 1441 Quivira Road (619–224–1234 or 800–233–1234), has over 400 units; some in a seventeen-story tower with bay and ocean views, and others in marina suites in a three-story building. The huge pool is a hit with kids. Camp Hyatt activities for ages three to twelve are held weekends from Memorial to Labor Day from 4:00 to 10:00 P.M.

Coronado: The grand **Hotel del Coronado**, 1500 Orange Avenue; (619) 435–6611 or (800) 468–3533. This has long been favored by the rich and famous (and shown in several movies). There's a beach, Olympic-size pool, poolside video arcade, bike rentals, tennis courts, and full spa. In summer, the hotel offers afternoon Camp Oz for ages four to six and Camp Breaker for seven to twelve, an evening kids' program several evenings a week, plus tennis programs for all ages, and organized family activities.

San Diego County North: **Rancho Bernardo Inn**, 17550 Bernardo Oaks Drive; (619) 487–1611, (800) 542–6096—CA, or (800) 854–1065. The inn is a half hour from Sea World, the Zoo, Wild Animal Park, and the airport. This resort has 287 units, with golf, tennis, fitness center, pools, free bikes (and five miles of trails), and an activity program for ages five to seventeen in August and during major holidays, from 9 A.M. to 9 P.M.

WHERE TO EAT

A dining guide is available from the SDCVB. Much of the time, you'll grab a bite by the bay or give in to fast food convenience. "Cool" preteens and older siblings can check out the **Hard Rock Cafe** in La Jolla, 909 Prospect Street; (619) 454–5101. Go to **Hob Nob Hill**, 2271 First Avenue (619–239–8176), for inexpensive but satisfying meals; try the Canadian blueberry pancakes for breakfast. **The Old Spaghetti Factory**, 275 Fifth Avenue (619–233–4323), serves ample portions of pasta in a real trolley car.

DAY TRIPS

If the San Diego Zoo hasn't satisfied your craving to see animals, head to Escondido, 30 miles northeast of downtown, to **San Diego Wild Animal Park**, 15500 San Pasqual Valley Road; (619) 557–3966. At this 2,100-acre preserve, endangered and rare animals roam freely in areas that replicate their native habitats. Hidden Jungle, among the park's newest exhibits, recreates an 8,500-square-foot Central American rain forest with sloths, turtles, tropical hummingbirds, spiders, ants, and—most fascinating—2,000 butterflies. Board the fifty-minute guided monorail tour, free with admission, for an easy view of the park. Young children like the Petting Kraal, with its gentle deer, sheep, and goats. Check the park's schedule for the animal shows, and don't miss the bird show at the amphitheater.

With the border city of **Tijuana** only 17 miles south of downtown, why not pay a brief visit to Mexico? Although you can drive, and many visitors park on the U.S. side and walk into Tijuana, consider using the San Diego trolley. There are several tourist information booths after you cross the border. **The Tijuana Cultural Center,** Paseo de los Heroes y Mina has an OMNIMAX theater and museum of Mexican History and Art. **Mexitlan,** Ocampo and Second streets, is an outdoor museum with hundreds of miniature buildings plus folk dance demonstrations. And don't miss those duty-free bargains. No passport or visa is required for a stay of less than 72 hours within 75 miles of the border.

Note: When only one parent (whether that parent is married or divorced) is entering Mexico with a child or children, Mexico requires a notarized statement from the other, nontraveling parent indicating that the traveling parent has permission to take the child into Mexico for a specified amount of time. This rule is designed to cut down on child kidnappings by disgruntled noncustodial parents. Obtain a similar letter when you are traveling with children who have a different last name from yours.

FOR MORE INFORMATION

San Diego Convention and Visitors Bureau: First Interstate Plaza, 401 B Street, Suite 1400, San Diego 92101; (619) 232–3101.

International Visitor Information Center: Hornton Plaza , First Avenue and F Street; (619) 236–1212.

Information center on East Mission Drive (off Route 5): (619) 276–8200.

San Diego Family Press (619–685–6970), a monthly publication containing events, is free at museums, supermarkets, and libraries, or send $2.50 to cover postage and handling to Box 23960, San Diego 92123.

Emergency Numbers

Ambulance, fire, police: 911

Poison Control: (619) 543–6000

Twenty-four-hour pharmacy: Savon Escondido, 318 West El Norte Parkway; (619–489–1505)

Hospital: UCSD Medical Center, 225 Dickinson Street; (619) 543–6400

32
SAN FRANCISCO
California

It's easy to fall in love with San Francisco: Surrounded on three sides by shimmering water, the city has rolling hills, a lively waterfront, charming Victorian homes, as well as lofty skyscrapers, great restaurants, loads of entertainment—and, of course, those fabled cable cars. The weather can be superb. Summer foggy mornings are frequent, but when the sun is bright and the sky clear, the year-round temperate climate is appealing. (Summer daytime temperatures average 54 to 65 degrees. Bring along long pants, light jackets, and sweaters because the winds frequently whip up, both on the ocean and bay sides.)

GETTING THERE

San Francisco International Airport (415–761–0800), 14 miles south of the city off U.S. 101, is served by more than forty major scheduled carriers. A $1.7 billion expansion project should be completed by 1995. Shuttle services to town, taxi service, and car rentals are available. Some passengers prefer the convenience of the smaller **Oakland International Airport** (510–577–4000) across the bay.

Greyhound Bus Lines is at Transbay Terminal, 425 Mission Street at First; (800) 231–2222. Interstate lines headquarters at Transbay Terminal include **AC Transit** (510–839–2882), which goes to the East Bay via the Oakland Bay Bridge; **Golden Gate Transit** (415–332–6600), which goes to Marin and Sonoma counties; and **SAMTRANS** (San Mateo County Transit), which heads to San Mateo and the San Francisco International Airport; (800) 660–4287.

Rail service is provided by **Amtrak** (800–USA–RAIL) to the Oakland depot at Sixteenth and Wood streets, with shuttle service to the San Francisco Transbay Terminal. **Caltrain**, Fourth and Townsend streets (800–660–4287—northern California) operates daily trains to San Jose.

Shuttle buses transport passengers to and from the Transbay Terminal.
By car, most travelers from the east enter via I–80, which ends at the
Bay Bridge, linking Oakland to San Francisco. Scenic U.S. 101 runs
north-south through the state and enters the city via the Golden Gate
Bridge. The faster north-south route, I–5, runs east of the city, connecting
to the Bay Bridge via I–580 and I–80 from both the north and south.

GETTING AROUND

With a good city map in hand, walking is the best way to see the 46-
square-mile city—although the hills can be tough on youngsters. San
Francisco Municipal Railway (Muni) runs the city's cable cars, buses,
and five metro lines, which go underground downtown and on the
streets in the outer neighborhoods; (415) 673–6864. One-, three-, or
seven-day Muni Passports are good on every regularly scheduled Muni
vehicle and are valid for reduced fares to ball games at Candlestick Park
and discounted admission to two dozen museums and attractions. Passports are sold at the San Francisco Visitor Information (see For More Information) and other outlets; call (415) 673–6864 for specific locations.

A ride on a cable car is a must. Purchase tickets before boarding at
self-service ticket machines at all terminals and major stops. There are
three lines. Twenty-six cars begin at Powell and Market streets: the Powell-Hyde Line (No. 60), considered the most scenic, terminates at Victorian Park near the Maritime Museum and Aquatic Park; the
Powell-Mason Line (No. 59), ends near Fisherman's Wharf. The eleven
California Street Line cars (No. 61) start at the foot of Market Street and
run through Chinatown to Van Ness Avenue.

BART (Bay Area Rapid Transit) runs speedy, aluminum trains that
connect eight San Francisco stations with Daly City to the south and
with 25 East Bay stations; call (415) 788–BART.

Golden Gate Ferry (415–332–6600) travels between the San Francisco Ferry Building, at the foot of Market Street, and downtown Sausalito and Larkspur.

WHAT TO SEE AND DO

Museums and Zoos

The Exploratorium, 3601 Lyon Street (415–563–7337), is in the Marina district, within the walls of the Palace of Fine Arts, the only remaining structure from the 1915 Panama Pacific Exposition. This hands-on
museum is frequently hailed as the best science museum in the world.
Others have borrowed ideas and exhibits from the Exploratorium, which
was founded in 1969 by physicist Dr. Frank Oppenheimer.

More than 700 displays encourage all ages (some 60 percent of visitors are adults) to push, pull, talk, look through, feel, and listen to exhibits that are based on light, sound, vision, hearing, touch, motion, waves, animal behavior, heat, and temperature. You and the kids will learn about phenomena that exist everywhere in nature. Step inside the Distorted Room, where nothing is exactly as it appears. Stand in front of the Anti-Gravity Mirror, where you take flight without leaving the ground. Move a 400-pound pendulum with a tiny magnet. Freeze water with a vacuum. Outside, enjoy views of San Francisco's skyline across the bay, and, at the Wave Organ exhibit, listen to the wave-activated "liquid" music emanating from twenty pipes that extend into the bay.

When it's time to reenergize, there's a café for sandwiches and light snacks. Inquire about special activities and workshops. You must reserve in advance and pay extra to enter the Tactile Dome, a pitch-black, crawl-through experience recommended for adults and kids over seven; call (415) 561–0362 to reserve.

Several worthwhile museums for families are located in the eastern section of the Golden Gate Park (a must-see, must-do stop that is described further under Parks and Zoos). The **M.H. de Young Memorial Museum,** near Tenth Avenue and Fulton Street (415–750–3600), has twenty-two galleries of American art, from the seventeenth to nineteenth century, by such artists as Whistler, Cassat, Homer, Copley, and Sargent. The large gallery of landscapes, *trompe l'oeil,* and still life pieces from the turn of the century is a fine place to introduce youngsters to American art. Colorful and dramatic tribal art from Africa and Oceania is also visually appealing to kids. Frequent traveling exhibitions require extra admission and advance tickets. Studio workshops for ages seven to thirteen are offered by artist-teachers. There are tours of current exhibits every Saturday. Admission also allows entry to the adjacent **Asian Art Museum,** Tea Garden Drive, a facility with more than 10,000 pieces of Asian sculpture, paintings, and ceramics from various periods. Call (415) 668–8921 or 688–7855 for information on daily tours and on films and storytelling hours for children.

California Academy of Sciences (415–221–5100 or 750–7145—tape), directly across from the de Young Museum, includes both an aquarium and planetarium. At the Steinhart Aquarium, kids can touch creatures from the deep in a hands-on tidal pool, then gaze wide-eyed at the schools of fast-swimming fish darting about the 100,000-gallon Fish Roundabout Tank. There's also a living coral reef tank and lots of other marine creatures—14,000 to be exact—to delight the kids. Feeding times for dolphins, seals, and penguins are especially popular with youngsters. The Morrison Planetarium presents daily sky shows and, on selected evenings, Laserium light shows (415–750–7141; 750–7138 for Laserium). The museum itself has lots to appeal to kids: the glimmering Gem and Mineral Gallery (with a giant quartz stone); the Wild California hall, which shows the state's diverse habitats; The Far Side of Science Gallery, featuring more than 160 cartoons by Gary Larson (a big hit with the preteen and teen set); Life Through Time, a three-and-one-half-billion-year exploration of the evidence for evolution; and The Space and Earth Hall, with its simulated "earthquake floor." Call ahead to check hours for the Discovery Room, where kids are welcome to touch and explore such objects as birds nests and shark teeth.

Bay Area Discovery Museum, 557 East Fort Baker, Sausalito; (415) 289–7268. Located beneath the Golden Gate Bridge at East Fort Baker, just south of Sausalito, this vibrant hands-on museum is geared to ages two to twelve, but even older kids will be intrigued by many of the exhibits. The museum was in the process of doubling in size at press time. New additions include a transportation exhibit in a renovated 1930s gas station on the museum's grounds. The exhibit includes a computer command center where kids try to solve traffic problems; an Interactive Media Center, with a broadcast studio and computer work stations; an Interactive Science Laboratory; and an ever-changing Maze of Illusions. In addition to special workshops, arts and science programs, and festivals, the museum runs a number of field trips, including family camping and hiking trips.

If you have time, a visit to one the following will be entertaining. **The Mexican Museum,** Fort Mason Center, Building D, Laguna Street and Marina Boulevard South (415–441–0445), offers special free art activities, music, theater, dance, and exhibition tours one Sunday each month. **Josephine D. Randall Junior Museum,** 199 Museum Way off Roosevelt Way (415–554–9600), includes a petting corral, working seismograph, mineral and fossil displays, and special classes most Saturdays. **San Francisco Cable Car Museum,** Washington and Mason streets (415–474–1887), shows a film about how these vehicles work. There are also scale models of cable cars and vintage photos. But the real attraction is watching the exposed machinery pull the cables under the city's streets. This facility is the working powerhouse and repair shop of the entire motorless cable car system. Visitors can watch the fascinating cable-winding process from a mezzanine gallery and visit a room where the cable can be observed under ground.

Parks and Zoos

Along with the two museums above, **Golden Gate Park** (415–666–7200) offers 1,017 acres full of family fun: playgrounds, several lakes, twenty-one tennis courts, a polo field (where you can watch matches), nine-hole golf course, horse stables for riding (lessons offered—415–668–7360), and, at the park's southeast corner, off Kezar Drive, a charming 1912 carousel and children's playground. There's even

The sights, sounds, and excitement of San Francisco lie on the other side of the famous Golden Gate Bridge. (Photo by Carl Wilmington/courtesy San Francisco Convention and Visitors Bureau)

a small herd of bison that grazes just off Kennedy Drive. **The Conservatory of Flowers**, John F. Kennedy Drive; (415) 666–7017. In the northeast corner, the conservatory is the oldest building in the park. (Shipped in pieces from England, it was completed in 1879.) It's home to rare orchids, a tropical garden, and seasonal flower displays. **Huntington Falls**, on Strawberry Hill, a small island surrounded by Stow Lake in the eastern end, is the tallest artificial falls in the West. You can rent motorboats, paddleboats, and rowboats by the hour at the boathouse on Stow Lake Drive; (415) 752–0347. A city map with an overview of the Golden Gate Park is available from the Convention Bureau or from park headquarters in McLaren Lodge, corner of Stanyan and Fell.

Families congregate around the **Music Concourse**, the heart of the park (right around the de Young Museum), where the Golden Gate Park Band performs on Sundays. In this area, you'll find the **Japanese Tea Garden**, Tea Garden Drive; (415) 752–1171. This serene five-acre area constructed for the 1894 Midwinter International Exposition, features ponds, Japanese greenery, a pagoda, arched moon bridge, Buddha, and, in the spring, fragrant Japanese cherry blossoms. Women in kimonos serve tea and cookies at the Tea House.

Because the park is so vast, a car is helpful, although parking can be a problem. On Sundays, roads are closed to all vehicular traffic to accommodate bicycle riders and skaters. (You can rent roller skates throughout the park.) You may opt to take a Muni bus; call (415) 673–MUNI. Friends of Recreation and Parks (415–221–1311) conduct walking tours of the park on weekends from May to October. At press time, a discounted adult pass to five of the park's attractions (three museums, Tea Garden, and Conservatory of Flowers) was available. Call the SFCVB for information at (415) 391–2000.

The San Francisco Zoological Gardens and Children's Zoo, Sloat Boulevard and Forty-fifth Avenue (415–753–7061 or 753–7083 for tape), is ranked among the country's top city zoos. It's home to more than 1,000 animals and birds who live in attractive landscaped enclosures. Along with the expected, more unusual inhabitants include pygmy hippos, snow leopards, and a rare white tiger named Prince Charles. The $2 million Gorilla World is the world's largest gorilla habitat. There's also a Koala Crossing and, adjacent to the main zoo, near the carousel, a Children's Zoo (separate admission) where your kids can pet and feed gentle barnyard animals. At the Insect Zoo the scorpions, ants, honeybees, and other creepy crawlies, including the world's largest centipede, wow the kids. A weekend afternoon insect show is sure to please.

On the Waterfront

You and your family will probably spend much of your time on San Francisco's vibrant waterfront. Golden Gate National Recreation Area (GGNRA) comprises approximately 28 miles of California coastline and is the largest urban park in the world. It's also the most popular U.S. National Park, attracting some seventeen million visitors a year. The park stretches from San Mateo in the south through parts of the San Francisco waterfront to the Cliff House and Fort Point, to Alcatraz, and across Golden Gate Bridge north to a portion of Marin County.

Fort Point, a brick formation completed in 1861 at the base of the Golden Gate Bridge, affords scenic views of the city. (Yes, you can walk across the two-mile stretch. The walkway is free, but bundle up—it can be chilly.)

If your kids are up to it, walk along the shoreline for nearly 4 miles by following the Golden Gate Promenade footpath. This stroll, which begins at Fort Point, provides scenic views as you wind by bocce ball courts, the yacht harbor, and Fort Mason Center. GGNRA park headquarters are at the Fort Mason Center, Bay and Franklin streets; (415) 979–3010 or 556–0560. Obtain maps and park information at the center, formerly a surplus military property, now a lively arts and recreation complex offering more than 1,000 activities monthly—and superb picnic facilities.

The footpath terminates at **Aquatic Park**, the lagoon adjacent to the Hyde Street Pier, at the foot of Polk Street, the location of the **National Maritime Museum**; (415) 556–3002. This musuem features ship models, painted figureheads, shipwreck photos, and other artifacts. Admission is free.

Near **Fisherman's Wharf**, which includes Piers 43–47 at Taylor and Jefferson streets, several historic ships are open to the public—including the *Balclutha*, a steel-hulled, square-rig vessel built in 1886 in Scotland and the last of the Cape Horn fleet; the 1895 lumber schooner *C.A. Thayer*; and the 1890 ferryboat *Eureka*. Only U.S. ranger-guided tours are allowed to board the scow schooner *Alma*; call (415) 556–3002. On the third Saturday of every month, kids can take afternoon tours of the historic ships at Hyde Street Pier. Reservations are required; (415) 556–1871.

Fisherman's Wharf, Piers 43–47 at Taylor and Jefferson streets—and the northern waterfront, off Jefferson Street (at the end of the Powell-Hyde cable car line from Union Square)—is one of the city's top tourist attractions. Here you'll find dozens of seafood restaurants and sidewalk stands, vendors selling souvenirs, street performers, fishing vessels, and nearby attractions such as **Ripley's Believe it or Not! Museum**, 175 Jefferson Street; (415) 771–6188. Recently remodeled, it contains such oddities as a cable car made from 275,000 matchsticks, a walk-through kaleidoscope, rotating tunnels, and more. The **Wax Museum at Fisherman's Wharf**, 145 Jefferson Street (800–439–4305—CA), features four floors of more than 270 celebrities from Eddie Murphy to a recreation of King Tut's treasure-filled tomb. The **Guiness Book of World Records**, 235 Jefferson Street (415–771–9890), records the biggest, the smallest, and most bizarre, plus videos of world's records being set and fun hands-on exhibits.

Sight-seeing cruises of the bay by the **Red & White Fleet** (415–546–BOAT or 800–BAY–CRUISE—CA) are available at Piers 41 and 43½. Along with forty-five-minute cruises under the Golden Gate Bridge and around Alcatraz, the line offers a number of other cruises. One option is a fifty-five-minute trip to **Marine World Africa USA**, Marine World Parkway, 30 miles northeast of San Francisco in Vallejo (707–643–ORCA), an exciting oceanarium and wildlife park. The **Blue and Gold Fleet** (415–705–5444) leaves from **Pier 39** (Embarcadero and Beach Street) for a seventy-five-minute cruise, sailing under both the Golden Gate and Bay Bridges and offering close-up views of both sides of Alcatraz (see Other Attractions).

Pier 39—a two-level complex featuring loads of shops, restaurants, and video arcades—is a real hit with kids. On the second level, the **San Francisco Experience** (415–982–7550), a half-hour multimedia spectacular, tells about the city's past and present in an entertaining way. The lobby houses an interesting earthquake exhibit and antique amusement devices.

Another Pier 39 hit is the **Marine Mammal Interpretive Center**, J on level 2 for docents, (415) 289–7339, established after a herd of California sea lions took a fancy to the locale. Depending on the season and weather, up to several hundred of these blubbery, barking sea denizens may be sunning themselves near K dock, Level 1.

On the GGNRA's western (Pacific) shoreline, **Cliff House** and **Seal Rocks**, 1090 Point Lobosa (415–386–3330), offer spectacular views. The house, the third on the spot, is on the site of the elaborate estate of inventor Adolph Sutro. Today the building combines an eatery, pub, and gift shop. The lower restaurant is a great place to watch the sea lions and shorebirds that usually congregate at Seal Rocks, 400 feet offshore. (If you have binoculars, bring them along.) If the day is clear, you may also be able to see the Farallon Islands, about 30 miles away. You can also see the remains of the historic Sutro baths, an enormous swimming and restaurant complex that burned down in 1966. Below Cliff House is **Ocean Beach**, a 4-mile stretch of sandy shoreline, great for walking or jogging (though it's windy here), but not swimming because the current is dangerous. One of the few swimming beaches in the city is **China Beach**, at Twenty-eighth Avenue and Sea Cliff, on the city's northern edge, where lifeguards are on duty during the summer. Be prepared for the bay's chilly water.

Other Attractions

Alcatraz Island, 1½ miles from shore, is an extremely popular attraction that most kids enjoy. "The Rock," a maximum security federal prison phased out in 1963, was once home to such famous criminals as Al Capone and Machine Gun Kelly. Red and White boats leave from Pier 41 (415–546–BOAT) daily every half hour starting at 9:30 A.M. Tickets are available daily beginning at 8:00 A.M.; it's a good idea to buy them at least one day in advance in the summer. Dress warmly and wear comfortable shoes. On the island, you can take self-guided trail walks (the terrain here is steep), audiocassette tours narrated by former inmates and guards through the main cell block, and ranger-led programs.

Among the city's diverse neighborhoods, **Chinatown**, with its gateway at Grand and Bush, is a favorite with kids. Stroll through the gateway, bedecked with dragons and stone lions, and meander 24 blocks crowded with people and exotic sights and smells—restaurants, food markets, temples, and small museums. The **Chinese Culture Center**, 750 Kearney, on the third floor of the Holiday Inn (415–986–1822), offers rotating exhibits of arts and crafts along with educational and cultural programs.

Several blocks to the north of Chinatown in the Russian Hill neighborhood, take a slow (very slow) drive down Lombard Street, called the "world's crookedest." There are nine (count them) hairpin turns as the street descends Russian Hill on the block between Hyde and Leavenworth. The view from Hyde Hill is superb. It's also possible to walk the street, up and down staircases—if your kids (and you) have the energy.

Shopping

Visiting one of the city's lively retail and restaurant complexes is an experience in itself. A family favorite is **Ghirardelli Square**, 900 North Point Street; (415) 775–5500. Bordered by North Point, Polk, Beach, and Larkin streets, it has more than seventy shops and restaurants. The oldest building, the Woolen Mill, dates back to 1854. From 1893 to the early 1960s, the Domingo Ghirardelli family produced chocolate here. Some of the original vats and ovens are in operation at the Ghirardelli Chocolate Manufactory on the plaza level of the Clock Tower.

Japan Center, Post and Buchanan Square (415–922–6776), occupies 3 square blocks just south of the city's small Japanese quarter. The complex houses restaurants and sushi bars, Japanese baths, theaters, and various shops. In the spring, the center and the surrounding Japantown area are the site of the Cherry Blossom Festival.

The Cannery, ½ block from the Hyde Street cable car turnaround at 2801 Leavenworth and Beach (415–775–7104), was once a Del Monte peach cannery. The 1906 buildings were renovated into a three-level complex with shops, galleries, restaurants, a comedy club, and street performers. **The Anchorage**, 2800 Leavenworth (415–775–6000), a 2.6-acre site in the heart of Fisherman's Wharf, has specialty shops, restaurants, and a courtyard where street performers entertain.

Theater, Music, and the Arts

The Visitor Information Center's twenty-four-hour phone hotlines have updates on arts events; call (415) 391–2001. BASS/Ticketmaster centers can be found in several locations, or you can charge tickets by phone. Call (510) 762–2277 for information. TIX Bay Area, on the Stockton side of Union Square (415–533–7827), has selected day-of-performance tickets for theater, dance, and music events. Cash only; no reservations or phone orders accepted. Call for opening hours (closed Sunday and Monday). They also sell full-price tickets to many events in the neighborhoods and outlying areas through BASS tickets.

Kidshows offers a variety of musical, theatrical, and storytelling performances during the school year. They're located in the Cowell Theatre, Landmark Building A, Fort Mason, Marina Boulevard and Buchanan Street. Call (415) 392–4400 for information.

Sporting Events

Baseball fans can watch the **San Francisco Giants** play at Candlestick Park, 8 miles south of San Francisco; call (415) 467–8000 or (415) 674–MUNI for Ballpark Express bus information. **The Oakland Athletics** play at the Oakland Coliseum, off I–880; call (510)-762–BASS for ticket information. The **San Francisco 49ers** football team plays at Candlestick Park. Games are usually sold out well in advance; call (415) 468–2249 for ticket information. **San Francisco Bay Blackhawks** pro soccer team plays at Spartan Stadium in San Jose, about forty minutes from San Francisco. Call (408) 295–4295 or (800) 677–HAWK for information. The **Golden State Warriors** play NBA basketball at the Oakland Coliseum; call (510) 638–6300. The annual **Volvo Tennis Tournament** takes place in early February at the Civic Auditorium, 90 Grove Street; (415) 239–4800.

SPECIAL EVENTS

The Datebook, a pink insert in Sunday's *San Francisco Examiner,* is an excellent source of weekly events, including fairs and festivals. For a detailed quarterly events SFCVB calendar, request the *San Francisco Book,* $2.00. (See For More Information.) Among the highlights are these events.

January–February: Chinese New Year Celebration includes Miss Chinatown USA pageant, outdoor festivities, cultural programs, and Golden Dragon parade on final Saturday night. (Be prepared for noise!)

April: Cherry Blossom Parade: More than 2,000 Californians of Japanese descent and performers from Japan participate in an elaborate offering of Japanese culture and customs.

May: Cinco de Mayo Parade/Celebration, includes two days of outdoor cultural festivities and live entertainment; Carnival, in the Mission District, is a Mardi Gras–like celebration that includes a parade, street festival, and costume contest.

July: Fourth of July Celebration, Crissy Field in the Presidio, features family festivities and fireworks display.

September–October: Renaissance Pleasure Faire, weekends, in Blackpoint Forest features thousands of costumed participants who stage an Elizabethan harvest festival.

October–November: Grand National Rodeo, Horse and Stock Show, Cow Palace.

December: Pickle Family Circus Holiday Show, Palace of Fine Arts.

WHERE TO STAY

A lodging guide is available from the SFCVB. Bed-and-breakfast reservation services include **Bed and Breakfast International** (415–696–1690 or 800–872–4500), for stays in private homes throughout the state; and **Bed** and Breakfast San Francisco (415–479–1913 or 800–452–8249), for inns, home stays, apartments, houseboats, and yachts in San Francisco and beyond. Hotel reservation services include **Golden Gate Reservations** (415–252–1107 or 800–423–7846) and **San Francisco Reservations** (415–227–1500 or 800–677–1550).

Other lodging possibilities include the following.

Four Seasons Clift, 495 Geary Street; (415) 775–1700 or (800) 332–3442. This stately hotel in the Union Square area is "grand" in every sense of the word. Expensive, yes—but if you're going to splurge, this is the place to do it. The hotel is kid friendly, with toys for toddlers, pint-size terry robes, magazines for teens, bedtime snacks of milk and cookies, and, if you need them, high chairs, diapers, and strollers. There's a pediatrician on call twenty-four hours—and a kids' menu available on twenty-four-hour room service. You'll also get a list of child-friendly attractions. A family plan offers two rooms (connecting whenever possible) at a single-room rate.

The **Westin St. Francis**, 335 Powell at Union Square, San Francisco, California 94102, (415) 397–7000 or (800) 228–3000, offers the new Westin Kids Club amenities. These include child-friendly rooms, children's sports bottle or tippy cup upon check-in, as well as a safety kit with a night light, Band-Aids, and emergency phone numbers. Rooms feature bath toys and bath products for kids, and parents can request—at no charge—jogging strollers, potty seats, bicycle seats, and step stools. Restaurants and room service also feature children's menus.

Also in the Union square area, **The Savoy**, 580 Geary Street, (415) 441–2700 or (800) 227–4223, is a smaller property with eighty-three rooms, and moderately priced. Families are welcome, and cribs, and children under fourteen are free.

The **Hyatt Fisherman's Wharf**, 555 North Point Street, (415) 563–1234 or (800) 233–1234, is conveniently located and offers Hyatt's family-friendly amenities of kid's menus and room service plus a heated pool.

Columbus Motor Inn, 1075 Columbus Avenue (415–885–1492), is several blocks from Fisherman's Wharf. It's comfortable enough, with color TV, air conditioning, and in-room coffee—and works well for a family on a budget. Ask about their family units: two adjoining rooms with shared bath.

Hyde Park Suites, 2635 Hyde Street; (415) 771–0200 or (800) 227–3608. This attractive facility is 6 blocks from the Wharf, with small suites that include fully equipped kitchens.

About 4 miles from San Francisco's International Airport and about twenty minutes from downtown, **Summerfield Suites San Francisco**, 1350 Huntington Avenue, San Bruno (415–588–0770 or 800–833–4353), offers two-bedroom suites, a bonus for families.

WHERE TO EAT

The San Francisco Book (see For More Information) contains a comprehensive listing of restaurants. In many cases, you'll find yourself grabbing a bite while on the go. There are a number of fine fast food places in Pier 39: **Apple Annies** (415–397–0473), for pizza and sandwiches; **Boudin Sourdough Bakery and Cafe** (415–421–0185), serving sandwiches made with the city's famous French sourdough bread. Boudin also has branches in Ghirardelli Square, Fisherman's Wharf, and several other locations citywide. For a casual sit-down meal, **Charley Brown's** in The Cannery, 2801 Leavenworth (415–776–3838), is a good, moderately priced choice because of their bountiful children's burger platters. (Parents can indulge in the prime ribs.) The preteen and teen set will be happy at the **Hard Rock Cafe**, 1699 Van Ness Avenue at Sacramento Street; (415) 885–1699. For burgers, ribs, chicken, and sandwiches, the **Alcatraz Bar and Grill**, Pier 39 (415–434–1818), is a hoot. The decor is "early prison"—and there are related exhibits, artifacts, and a jail cell. The back room has spectacular bay views.

DAY TRIPS

The Greater Bay area offers loads of kid-pleasing sights. Don't miss a trip to **Muir Woods National Monument** in Mill Valley, 17 miles north via U.S. 101; (415) 388–2595. This 550-acre preserve is home to majestic redwoods, some as high as 252 feet and up to 1,000 years old. At the new visitor's center, kids can get a Junior Ranger Pack with a variety of activities they can complete to earn a patch. The majority of the main trails are fairly level and paved for easy walking.

On the East Bay, the city of **Berkeley** is home campus for the University of California. Strolling around this city of 100,000 is an experience your preteens and teens will enjoy: The counterculture of the 1960s is still very much in evidence. Street performers, shops, cafés, and vendors abound on Telegraph Hill, just south of the campus. Take a self-guided walk around the campus: The Visitors Center, in University Hall, University Avenue and Oxford Street, is open weekdays; call (510) 642–5215. Maps and brochures are available.

FOR MORE INFORMATION

San Francisco Convention and Visitor Bureau, P.O. Box 429097, San Francisco 94142–9097, will send you the comprehensive guide *The San*

Francisco Book ($2.00) and lodging information. Their Visitor Information Center is in Benjamin Swig Pavilion on the lower level of Hallidie Plaza at Market and Powell streets; (415) 391–2000. A twenty-four-hour recorded message lists daily events and activities: (415) 391–2001.

San Francisco Peninsula Parent Newsmagazine, P.O. Box 1280, Millbrae, California 94030 (415–342–9203), includes area events for families. Disabled visitors may obtain information from the Disability Coordinator in the Mayor's Office of Community Development (415–554–8926), or from The Easter Seal Society (415–752–4888). For public transportation information, request the *Muni Access Guide,* Muni Elderly and Handicapped Programs, 949 Presdio Avenue, San Francisco 94115; (415) 923–6142—weekdays.

Emergency Numbers
Ambulance, fire, police: 911
Poison Control: (800) 523–2222
Twenty-four-hour pharmacy: **Walgreens,** 3201 Divisadero Street at Lombard; (415) 931–6415
Hospital with twenty-four-hour emergency rooms: **San Francisco General Hospital Medical Center,** 1001 Potrero Avenue; (415) 206–8000 or 206–8111 for emergencies. **The Medical Center at the University of California,** 505 Parnassus Avenue at Third Avenue; (405) 476–1000.

33
SEATTLE
Washington

Seattle ranks prominently on most top ten lists of splendid U.S. vacation destinations. The city is in a superb location, surrounded by mountains (the Cascades to the east and the Olympics to the west), by evergreen forests, salt water (Puget Sound, an arm of the Pacific), and by fresh water (Lake Washington). Sight-seeing and recreational opportunities abound.

Originally built on seven hills (one has since been leveled), the city sports a lively waterfront and a multitude of family-friendly attractions. Yes, the mild climate is also moist (bring rain gear), but the locals have adapted to the inclement weather (which one resident says is more like a steady drizzle than real downpours).

GETTING THERE

Seattle-Tacoma (Sea-Tac to the locals) **International Airport**, (206) 433–4645 or (800) 544–1965, about 16 miles from downtown, is served by more than forty airlines. Airport shuttles include a motor coach and a van service; taxi service and car rentals also are available.

Amtrak (800–USA–RAIL) is at Third and Jackson.

The **Greyhound** bus station is at Eighth Avenue and Stewart Street; call (206) 624–3456.

By car, those coming from the north or south enter Seattle from I–5; those from the east via I–90.

GETTING AROUND

Although some of downtown Seattle's hills are steep, walking is a good way to see the city (wear comfortable shoes). You will want a car if you plan to explore Metropolitan Seattle's attractions.

Metro buses (206–553–3000) are free between 4:00 A.M. and 9:00 P.M. in the city's core area between Battery and South Jackson streets and Sixth Avenue and Alaskan Way.

The elevated Monorail travels a mile from downtown Seattle to Seattle Center.

Vintage trolleys run frequently along the waterfront to Pioneer Square and the International District; call (206) 553–3000.

WHAT TO SEE AND DO

Museums and Attractions

Seattle Center, 305 Harrison; (206) 684–8582 or 684–7200. This seventy-four-acre park built for the 1962 Seattle World's Fair includes landscaped grounds with fountains and trees, theaters, an amusement park called Fun Forest, and, next door, The Center House with a variety of shops and restaurants—as well as **The Seattle Children's Museum**, 305 Harrison; (206) 441–1767. Tykes "work" and play in a mini-neighborhood, with kid-size doctor's office, grocery store, public buses, and fire engines. In the Little Lagoon, toddlers play with a giant busy board, crawl through a friendly whale, and watch colorful fish swim in the aquarium. Frequently changing cultural exhibits feature costumes, games, and musical instruments from around the world. A professional artist at the Imagination Station helps kids and adults create masterpieces in paper, textiles, and clay. Ask about special events and workshops.

Another kid pleaser located within the Seattle Center is the **Pacific Science Center**, 200 Second Avenue North; (206) 443–2001. This modern structure, also called "The Cathedral of Science," boasts pools and fountains and more than 200 hands-on exhibits, plus dinosaurs, a planetarium with sky and laser shows, and an Imax Theater. Kids especially like the giant fiberglass moon and the Native American longhouse.

Seattle Center surrounds **The Space Needle**, Fifth Avenue North and Broad Street; (206) 443–2100. From the top level observation deck of the city's 605-foot landmark, you have a superb view of the city, Puget Sound, and—if the weather is clear—Mt. Rainier, Mt. Baker, and the Cascade and Olympic ranges. Save this for a sunny day. The observation deck is open from 10:00 A.M. to midnight.

Museum of Flight, 9404 East Marginal Way South (on Boeing Field); (206) 764–5720. Located within "The Red Barn," the original Boeing airplane factory, this museum retells the history of flight, from Leonardo da Vinci to the Wright Brothers to today's space age. Most kids are fascinated by aircraft: They will be intrigued by the more than forty aircraft on display, including a flying ambulance (C-45 Mercy Plane), Boeing B-47 Bomber, and barnstorming *Curtiss Jenny*.

Seattle's landmark Space Needle dominates the downtown skyline. (Photo by Jim Bell/ courtesy Seattle-King County News Bureau)

The **Museum of History and Industry (MOHAI)**, 2700 Twenty-fourth Avenue East; (206) 324–1126. The museum features exhibits about Native Americans and immigrants from Europe, Asia, and Africa who have made unique contributions to Seattle since the city's inception in the 1800s. Among the 70,000 artifacts are many that children relate to: a large costume collection, hundreds of dolls and toys, plus the carpenter's glue pot that started the great Seattle fire of 1899 and many artifacts of the fire's destruction. At the Hands-on History section, kids play with puzzles, games, and toys, and try on period clothes. There's even a video produced just for kids about the heritage of the Pacific Northwest. Special programs for kids and families coincide with current exhibitions. Each summer, Super Wednesdays! workshops present special programs.

The **Seattle Aquarium**, Pier 59, Waterfront Park, 1483 Alaskan Way; (206) 386–4300 or 386–4320—tape. Head to the underwater viewing area, and be transfixed by creatures—including sharks and octopus—gliding through the enormous tank. A new tide pool exhibit recreates the sealife of the Washington State Coast. Kids enjoy handling the starfish and anemones in the touch tanks. Helpful staff members answer questions. Next door to the aquarium, is the **Omnidome Film Experience**, Alaskan Way, Pier 59, Waterfront Park; (206) 622–1868. The theater has been featuring a film about the eruption of Mount St. Helens, shown on their 180-degree dome screen. (Warning: Very young children are sometimes frightened by the "you are there" realism.)

The **Hiram M. Chittenden Locks** (more commonly called The Ballard Locks), 3015 North West Fifty-eighth Street; (206) 783–7059. Another popular attraction is on this 8-mile canal that connects saltwater Puget Sound with freshwater Lake Washington. Depending on the tide, boats are raised or lowered from six to twenty-six feet. Hour-long tours take place twice daily. Another kid pleaser is the fish ladder on the south side of the locks. Here watch salmon or trout (depending on the season) jump over twenty-one concrete steps from the sea to fresh water. The locks and grounds, which include the seven-acre Carl English Gardens, are open to the public daily from 7:00 A.M. to 9:00 P.M.

Parks and Zoos

Seattle boasts an extensive park system. Across from Pike Place Market, First Avenue at Pike Street, **Victor Steinbrueck Park** is a nice place to watch ferries sail across Puget Sound and to listen to the street musicians. The waters of the Sound are chilly, but if a beach is on your mind, the sandiest and largest is at **Alki Beach Park**, Alki Avenue Southwest, in west Seattle. There's a popular bicycle/jogging trail (nearby shops rent bikes) and great views of passing ferries and the Olympic Mountains.

Woodland Park Zoo, 5500 Phinney Avenue North, 10 miles north of downtown; (206) 684–4800. Considered one of the ten best in the U.S.A., the zoo is particularly known for its natural habitats. Kids' favorites include the five-acre African Savanna, where hippos, zebras, lions, and giraffes roam, separated from viewers by hidden natural barriers. In addition to elephants, the huge Elephant Forest also has a tropical forest, Thai temple, and a working Thai logging camp. The newest attraction is the Tropical Rain Forest, complete with lush trees and vegetation, orchids, and waterfalls.

Special Tours

Four water sight-seeing companies offer tours from the waterfront, including **Seattle Harbor Tours**, which departs daily from Pier 55 for one-hour cruises in the harbor; (206) 623–1445. That's just about right for younger kids, who tend to get antsy on tour boats. With older kids, you might consider the two-and-one-half-hour tour of Seattle's Elliot Bay and Lake Washington Ship Canal via the Ballard Locks, which is offered by **Gray Line Water Sightseeing**; (206) 623–4252. **The Spirit of Puget Sound** has lunch, dinner, and midnight cruises that include a live Broadway Review. These cruises depart from Pier 70; call (206) 443–1442 to reserve. **Tillicum Village and Tours** has a cruise from Pier 56 to Blake Island State Park for a salmon-bake dinner cooked over an open-pit alder fire in a North Coast Indian cedar longhouse. The meal is followed by costumed tribal dancing. Call (206) 443–1244 for information.

Shopping

Shopping in Seattle is a many splendored thing. Have your pick of colorful wares, admire the scenery, and munch on tasty bits of food at the **Pike Place Market**, First Avenue at Pike Street, (206) 682–7453, one of the city's top tourist attractions. This colorful market, begun in 1907, is a great place to buy produce, cheese, fresh seafood (packed in dry ice for transport home), crafts, flowers, baked goods, coffee, spices in bulk, and even "junk." Stairs or an elevator lead to the harbor.

The waterfront stretches from Pier 51 on the south to Pier 70 on the north, where there is a complex of shops and restaurants in a restored wharf. Pioneer Square (which adjoins the Kingdome sports arena, 201 South King Street) spans some 18 blocks and includes a variety of art galleries (more per square foot than in any other U.S. city), shops, restaurants, and the **Klondike Gold Rush National Historical Park**, 117 South Main Street; (206) 553–7220. This national park inside a storefront offers five free films on the Gold Rush of 1897.

In the International District, east of the Kingdome, are exotic Asian shops and restaurants, including **Uwajimaya**, 519 Sixth Avenue South, (206) 624–6248, a large Japanese supermarket, bazaar, and delicatessen.

Theater, Music, and the Arts

Seattle Weekly, on newsstands every Wednesday, offers extensive listings of cultural events. **Ticketmaster Northwest** has tickets to concerts, sports, and fine arts events. Call (206) 628–0888 to charge or to find out their locations about town. For half-price day-of-performance tickets for theater, music, and dance events, head to **Ticket/Ticket's** two locations: at the Broadway Market, 401 Broadway East; or at Pike Place Market Information Booth, First and Pike streets (206–324–2744). Seattle has more equity theaters than any U.S. city outside of New York, including **Seattle Children's Theatre**; (206) 633–4567.

Sports

The **Seattle Mariners** American League baseball team plays at the Kingdome from April through early October; call (206) 628–3555. The **Seattle SuperSonics** basketball team shoots hoops at Seattle Center Coliseum from October through April; call (206) 283–DUNK. The NFL **Seahawks** are at the Kingdome from August through December; (206) 827–9777. And the **Seattle Thunderbirds** play hockey at The Seattle

Center Coliseum or Seattle Arena; call (206) 448–PUCK. University of Washington football is also a popular fall attraction; call (206) 543–2230.

SPECIAL EVENTS

Contact the Seattle Convention and Visitors Bureau for more information on the following:

May: Seattle International Children's Festival, a six-day event featuring more than one hundred performances by professional companies from six continents.

Memorial Day weekend: Northwest Folklife Festival features scores of musicians and artists performing on twenty stages.

Mid-July: Bite of Seattle, a large food fair offering culinary specialties from some of the city's best restaurants.

Late July–early August: Seafair, the city's largest festival, includes a variety of community celebrations culminating in hydroplane races, a giant parade, and "crazy events," such as milk carton boat derbies.

Labor Day Weekend: Bumbershoot, an arts festival ranked among the top five festivals nationwide, offers kids' activities, music, dance, theater, comedy, visual and literary arts.

WHERE TO STAY

Seattle has a wide variety of lodging in different price ranges. Information on bed and breakfasts can be obtained from **Pacific Bed and Breakfast Agency,** 701 North West Sixtieth Street, Seattle 98107, (206) 784–0539, or the **Washington State Bed-and-Breakfast Guild,** 242 North West Market Street, Seattle 98107, (509) 548–6224.

Families may prefer staying in the Seattle Center area because it's more economical than downtown (and within easy reach via the Monorail). Some modest but perfectly acceptable choices are **Sixth Avenue Inn,** 200 Sixth Avenue, (206) 441–8300; **Park Inn,** 225 Aurora Avenue, (206) 728–7666, which has an indoor pool; and **Quality Inn City Center,** 2224 Eighth Avenue, (206) 624–6820 or (800) 4–CHOICE, which features some family suites with kitchenettes.

For the big splurge, try the elegant **Four Seasons Olympic Hotel,** 411 University Street, (206) 621–1700 or (800) 223–8772, with an indoor pool, health club and several restaurants.

The Westin Hotel, 1900 Fifth Avenue, (206) 728–1000, or (800) 228–3000, which sports great city views, a fitness center, and an indoor heated pool, also has the recently begun Westin Kids Club. Rooms, if requested, can be child safe and child friendly (already equipped with necessary cribs, etc.). Upon registration parents receive a safety kit complete with night light, Band-Aids, and identity bracelets. Kids get their own amenity—a soft-drink cup or laundry bag with crayons. You can request such niceties as a jogging stroller, emergency diapers, potty seats, bicycle seats, refrigerators, and step stools.

WHERE TO EAT

The *Seattle Visitors Guide* has a listing of restaurants. Chances are you'll be noshing a lot, particularly at the **Pike Place Market,** where goodies range from warm sourdough bread to crisp Washington State apples.

Fresh seafood is a specialty of this area, and there are many fine seafood restaurants along the waterfront. (Fortunately, most kids at least like fish and chips). **Ivar's Acres of Clams,** Pier 54, (206) 604-6852, is an informal place that serves much more than clams.

Red Bobin, 1100 Fourth Avenue, (206) 447-1909, has other locations, but this one downtown is the most convenient. They're known for their gourmet burgers, but there's also other kid-pleasing fare.

Parents shouldn't miss a stop at one of the city's ubiquitous coffee bars for espresso. Ask for hot chocolate for the kids.

DAY TRIPS

Puget Sound has hundreds of islands, and exploring at least one makes an ideal day trip. **Washington State Ferries,** 801 Alaskan Way, (206-464-6400 or 800-843-3779—WA) offers ten routes with twenty-five vessels. From the Seattle Waterfront, among the most popular, short scenic day trips for families are the car ferries to Bainbridge Island. In thirty-five minutes, you arrive at a small, rural island with one main street. Take your bike and a picnic lunch aboard the ferry and pedal around this scenic island.

The beautiful **San Juan Islands**—with their small towns, rolling countryside, and tiny harbors—are the state's most popular offshore destination. Automobile ferries, which leave from Anacortes, some 90 miles north of Seattle, serve four of the islands. **Lopez** is popular with bicyclers because it's level and relatively traffic free, and **Shaw** is pretty but has no visitor facilities. On Orcas, drive to Mt. Constitution, the highest point in the San Juan chain, where the observation deck offers superb vistas. If you have time only to visit one, the best family island is **San Juan,** where there are a variety of restaurants, small resorts, motels and bed and breakfasts, beaches, a whale-watching museum, bald eagles, and Friday Harbor—the largest town in the San Juan chain.

Note: these islands are very popular in the summer. Call to see how early you should arrive at the ferry. If you're planning on overnighting, reserve in advance. For more information on the islands, call the **State of Washington Tourism**; (206) 753–5600 or (800) 544–1800.

Mt. Rainier, at 14,411 feet, has a National Park that's 98 miles southeast of Seattle. That makes it rather long for a day trip with young children: You might opt to stay overnight at Paradise Inn in Ashford, (206) 569–2275, 20 miles east of the Nisqually entrance. The park and surrounding Cascades offer hiking trails, lakes and rivers for fishing, horsepack tours, and miles of scenic beauty. The Henry M. Jackson Visitor's Center, located at Paradise, (206) 569–2211, features exhibits, films, and splendid wraparound views.

If your kids need a theme park in their lives, **Enchanted Village**, 36201 Enchanted Parkway, Federal Way, (206) 661–8000, 27 miles from Seattle, will do. This amusement park has roller coasters, carousels, musical shows, and other rides, and, next door, Wild Waves Water Park has the things you'd expect from giant slides to artificial surf.

In winter, skiers will find four ski areas on **Snoqualmie Pass**, 54 miles from downtown.

FOR MORE INFORMATION

Seattle-King County Convention & Visitors Bureau, 520 Pike Street, Suite 1300, Seattle, WA 98101; (206) 461–5840. There's a Visitor Information Center at Washington State Convention and Trade Center, ground level, 800 Convention Place; (206) 461–5840.

Seattle's Child is a parent's publication listing events and other information of interest to families. Call (206) 441–1091.

Emergency Numbers
Ambulance, fire, police: 911
Poison Control: (206) 526–2121
There is no twenty-four-hour pharmacy; some of the larger **Pay Less Drug Stores**, with locations around town, are open until 9:00 P.M.; call (206) 223–1128.
Hospitals with twenty-four-hour emergency rooms include: **Northwest Hospital**, 1550 North 115th Street (206–364-0500), or **Virginia Mason Hospital**, 925 Seneca Street (206–583–6433). Call the hospitals to inquire about prescriptions when the pharmacies are closed.

34
YOSEMITE
NATIONAL PARK
California

Yosemite National Park, on the eastern border of central California, is comprised of 1,170 square miles that includes towering sequoias, huge granite boulders, toppling waterfalls, hidden lakes, and unspoiled forest. This area affords families truly breathtaking scenery and myriad ways to enjoy it. Although the park is open all year, summer attracts the most tourists: some three million. If you visit then, expect crowds, traffic, and difficulty in finding lodging (unless you've booked well in advance). The 7-mile stretch of the **Yosemite Valley**, the most frequented section of the park, is eye-catching any time of the year. If possible, visit in the off-season; however, summer is the only time you can be guaranteed passage into the eastern high country, which is often snowed in from late autumn until late spring.

GETTING THERE

Fresno Air Terminal, 97 miles south (209–498–4095), is the closest airport; it is served by **Delta, United, USAir,** and **American.** Many Yosemite-bound tourists also arrive at **San Francisco International**, 13 miles south of San Francisco (415–876–7809), a four- to five-hour drive; or **Los Angeles International**, Century and Sepulveda (310–646–5252), six hours away. Rental cars are available at all three airports.

Yosemite Gray Line (209–443–5240 or 800–640–6306—California) offers daily bus service to and from Yosemite and the Fresno airport, the Merced and Fresno **Amtrak** stations (800–USA–RAIL), and Merced and Fresno **Greyhound** stations (800–231–2222). Connections are also possible via Amtrak and express bus from Oakland to Merced and from San Diego and Los Angeles to Fresno; call Amtrak for information. **Via Bus**

Lines (209–384–1315) also goes to Yosemite from Merced, connecting with Amtrak, Greyhound, and Trailways.

Three highways come to Yosemite, all intersecting with Highway 99, which runs north-south through the Central Valley. There are four entrances to the park. West: The **Big Oak Flat** entrance is 98 miles east of Manteca via Route 120, the most direct route from San Francisco (however, this area can be snowy in winter). The **Arch Rock** entrance is 75 miles northeast of Merced via Route 140, and is considered the major route. South: **Wawona**, 64 miles north of Fresno, is accessed by Route 41, the shortest route from Los Angeles. East: **Tioga Pass**, open Memorial Day through October, is 10 miles west of Lee Vining, off Route 120. Winter visitors are advised to take Route 140 through Mariposa, the least mountainous route, which may not require chains, although it's wise to carry them when traveling through the Sierra Nevada.

GETTING AROUND

Yosemite National Park has about 200 miles of roads and 840 miles of hiking trails. Almost 95% of the park is undeveloped. Consult the map on the back of the *Yosemite Guide*, a newspaper detailing current park events, available from any entrance station or visitor center. (Note: On your journey, you may see burn areas, remnants of the 1990 fires. Along with the black tree trunks are new patches of colorful plants, a sign of rebirth.)

Free shuttle buses service the more populated sections of the park, making a car unnecessary for getting around. However, with children, a car is undoubtedly more convenient. Bus routes covered include: eastern **Yosemite Valley** (all year), **Mariposa Grove** and **Tuolumne Meadows** (summers only), and **Badger Pass Ski Area** (winter only). The shuttle stops at museums, natural areas, historical sites, shops, and lodges.

Bike rentals are available in the Valley at **Yosemite Lodge** (209–372–1208) all year, and during the summer at **Curry Village** (209–372–1200—summer). Although children's bikes (and helmets, required for all riders) are available, child carriers are not, and only one rider per bike is allowed. Rental bikes are not permitted outside Yosemite Valley and are prohibited from pedestrian and hiking trails and the last ½-mile section of the Mirror Lake Road.

Saddle trips for ages seven and older, ranging from two hours to a full day are available from Yosemite Valley, Easter to mid-October, and during summer in Wawona, White Wolf, and Tuolumne Meadows. Reservations recommended; call (209) 372–1248 for information. Helmets, available free at the stables, are required.

River rafts can be rented, along with life jackets and paddles, in early summer at Curry Village for rafting on the Merced River. If the previous winter is severe, causing fallen trees, rafting might be suspended, but at press time it was planned for summer 1994. Rafting is not allowed on Merced River above Yosemite Valley Stables or below El Capitan Bridge because of hazardous rapids and park regulations.

A variety of sight-seeing tours, most by bus, are also offered by the park's new concessionaire, **Yosemite Concession Services Corporation.** Reserve by calling (209) 372–1240. Information is available at hotel tour desks or next to the **Village Store** in Yosemite Village. If you're staying in the park, you can order pack lunches the night before from either your hotel or from one of the park shops.

WHAT TO SEE AND DO

The **Yosemite Valley,** 7 miles long and 1 mile wide, includes **Yosemite Village,** the center of the park's activities, offering lodgings, shops, and restaurants. Come here to get oriented, particularly if you are entering from the west. However, you may want to stop at some of the notable vistas you'll pass *before* arriving at the **Yosemite Valley Visitor Center** (209–372–0299) because the circle road around the valley is one-way.

At the visitor center, the auditorium behind the center has a multimedia presentation that will familiarize you with the park's offerings. There's also a short slide show in the center entitled "One Day in Yosemite," showing visitors how to make the most out of a brief stay. Chat with park rangers, who will suggest hiking trails and touring routes, and explore natural history displays. Behind the center, an authentic recreation of an **1872 Ahwahnichee Indian village** offers a short, self-guided trail.

Next door, the **Yosemite Museum's Indian Cultural Exhibit** (209–372–0291) features a **Fine Arts Gallery** with rotating exhibits of historical paintings, photos, and resident artist interpretations, and displays of the park's first inhabitants, the Miwok and Paiute people, from 1850 to the present. Kids like the displays of leather clothing and hand-woven baskets, augmented with demonstrations of basket weaving, bead work, and traditional games.

Here are some of the park's most famous attractions that your family won't want to miss.

Bridalveil Fall is off Southside Drive (the Valley Road). Park your car, then follow a paved .75-mile trail (there's a small, 100-foot rise) to the base of the 620-foot cascade.

El Capitan, a gigantic, granite mass—the largest single granite rock on Earth—towers nearly 4,000 feet in the air. The rock is on your left as you drive further into the valley. There are several turnouts where you can stop for fabulous views: You may even see daring rock climbers inching up the stone walls. (Don't do this unless you are an excellent rock climber.)

Nearby are two of the valley's ten waterfalls: **Vernal Fall** and **Nevada Fall.** Families with older children accustomed to hiking may follow a moderately steep trail that starts from the day-use parking lot at Curry Village to the footbridge overlooking 300-foot **Vernal Fall** (it's 2½ miles round-trip). If you're really hale and hardy, it's another 2 miles to **Nevada Fall**, then on to the top of another park landmark, **Half Dome**, a famous 5,000-foot-tall rock.

A much easier way to sightsee, especially with younger kids, is to sign up for a park tour. Or, if you're driving, you get an excellent view of the Dome by taking a left across Sentinel Bridge, parking your car, and walking to the center of the bridge. Eighty-seven million years old in plutonic rock years, this huge domed, sliced-in-half beauty is the symbol of Yosemite, reaching a height of 8,842 feet.

Yosemite Falls, a short walk from the visitor's center, is the highest waterfall in North America. It's comprised of three cascades: **Upper Fall** drops 1,430 feet; **Cascades** (Middle Fall) goes another 675 feet, pouring into **Lower Fall**, with a 320-foot drop. View the falls from the parking lot, or, for a closer perspective, walk along the .25-mile path that begins near Yosemite Lodge and leads to the base.

An easy trail with kids is the self-guided nature trail that starts in front of the visitor's center. Pick up the pamphlet *A Changing Yosemite* at the trailhead. The 2-mile paved loop circles through Cook's Meadow. As you proceed up Highway 41 leaving the valley, don't miss **Tunnel View** (park just before the Wawona Tunnel) where you can look below into the valley for an unforgettable panorama of **El Capitan**, **Half Dome**, **Sentinel Rock**, and **Bridalveil Fall**. As you continue on Highway 41, you'll come to the turnoff road to **Glacier Point**, with more spectacular vistas. This road, however, is closed in winter.

Wawona

Highway 41 heads through the mountains south to **Wawona** (a Native American word for giant sequoia). Here you'll find **Wawona Pioneer History Center** (209–375–6514), with historic Yosemite buildings from the 1800s and early 1900s. Rangers conduct tours, and volunteers wear period costumes from late spring until mid-fall. The **Wawona Stables**, next door, offer a variety of scenic rides through this corner of the park. Younger children can be strapped on a friendly lead pony. Call (209) 375–6502 for information. **The Wawona Hotel** is on State Route 41, 27 miles from Yosemite Valley; (209) 252–4848. This National Historic Landmark, built in 1879, is a good stop for breakfast, lunch, or dinner; try a Sunday brunch or summer Saturday western barbecue.

The *Yosemite Guide* lists the interpretive programs held in this park section.

Six miles south of Wawona is the **Mariposa Grove of Big Trees.**

While you can view a number of giant sequoias from the parking lot, get an up-close view by following the .75-mile self-guided nature trail to the huge **Grizzly Giant**, thought to be 2,700 years old. You can take a narrated **Big Trees Tram Tour** that departs right from the grove several times daily, spring through fall. Reservations are not required.

Tuolumne Meadows

The alpine **Tuolumne Meadows**, on the park's eastern edge, offers a high-country experience. This pristine area is filled with sparkling lakes, granite domes, and rolling meadows where wildflowers bloom in spring and summer. **The Tuolumne Meadows Visitor Center**, open summers only, is a little more than an hour and a half drive from the valley on Route 120 East; (209) 372–0263. It features geological exhibits, wildflower species, and displays on John Muir, the naturalist who founded Yosemite in the late 1800s.

In summer, spend an awesome day on the **Tuolumne Meadows Tour**. Photo opportunities range from **Tioga Road** (the highest auto pass in the Sierra) to the overlook at **Mono Lake** (nesting grounds for 90 percent of the California gull population and notable for the **tufa towers**—calcium carbonate formations that line its shores) to the summit of **Lee Vining Canyon**. Horseback tours are also available.

Note: The high elevations may cause some people to experience altitude sickness, particularly young children or those who have heart and lung diseases. Altitude sickness frequently affects people at elevations above 8,000 feet. Although the valley's elevation is 4,000 feet, Tioga Pass is 9,945. The sickness is characterized by headache, nausea, irritability, insomnia, shortness of breath, general malaise, and fatigue. Acclimate yourself, if possible, by attempting higher elevations gradually over a period of two or more days; and avoid alcohol, sugar, and high-fat meals. Drink plenty of water. Those who develop altitude sickness should descend to a lower elevation as soon as possible and, if symptoms persist, go to the **Yosemite Medical Clinic**, which specializes in treating this illness.

Family Fare

Kids love the **Happy Isles Nature Center**, 1 mile southeast of Curry Village (209–372–0287), open daily from late spring until October. This museum and exhibit area include numerous dioramas, interactive exhibits, wildlife displays, a display of Yosemite at night, and books for kids. Films are also shown periodically.

Junior (ages eight to nine) and **Senior Rangers** (ages ten to twelve) spring into action from June through August. Park rangers lead programs several days a week, including exploring "secret" places in Yosemite Valley and Tuolumne Meadows. A child earns a certificate for each day he or she attends; after three days a patch is awarded. Sign up one day ahead of time at **Happy Isles Nature Center** (see later listing).

Families with older kids may want to take advantage of what many consider some of the world's best rock climbing and the best rock-climbing school: **Yosemite Mountaineering School and Guide service**, headquartered at Tuolumne Meadows from June to October and at Curry Village from October to May. Participants, who don't have to be especially athletic, must be fourteen for a regular class; kids under fourteen can arrange group lessons in advance; call (209) 372–1244. Free art classes for all ages are offered at the **Art Activity Center** next to the post office at Yosemite Village every day from spring through fall; sign up at the center.

The **Yosemite Theater**, Valley Visitor Center, holds several musical shows perfect for families, including **Yosemite by Song and Stories**. Older children enjoy actor Lee Stetson's interpretations of **John Muir** one-man shows (no babies allowed). Tickets may be purchased at the visitor center.

Free evening programs feature interpretive talks, slides, and movies at campgrounds and hotel amphitheaters; consult the Yosemite Guide for schedules.

Le Conte Memorial Lodge, shuttle stop #12, on the way to Curry Village (209–372–4542), offers a children's center with special programs for ages five to twelve led by the Sierra Club on Wednesdays and Thursdays in July to the first week of August.

Family campfires with songs and stories take place several times a week in all major areas from late June to early September.

Winter Activities

Snow season usually begins in November and lasts through March, with an average snowfall of 180 inches, making Yosemite a skier's haven—yet, at 4,000 feet, Yosemite Valley's temperatures remain mild. More winter perks: It's easier to spot wildlife—coyotes, raccoons, mule deer, and perhaps even a bear—when the trees are barren of leaves. (Never feed the park's animals in any season.) Moreover, the dramatic winter light offers a different perspective of the mountains. And, naturally, the crowds are thinner. Winter offers many family possibilities.

Family skiing is popular at the **Badger Pass Ski Area**, 23 miles from Yosemite Valley on Highway 41; (209) 372–1330. Families have been coming here for generations, attracted to the relatively small mountain, with one triple chair, three doubles, one surface lift, and nine ski runs. The **Yosemite Ski School**, the first in California, has an excellent reputation. Babysitting for ages three (toilet trained) to nine is available in the Badger Pup Den. From January to March, bargain midweek ski packages are available. The park also has 350 miles of cross-country ski trails, many in the Badger Pass area.

The outdoor ice skating rink in Curry Village, on the valley's eastern

The Badger Pups ski program will delight kids during a winter vacation to Yellowstone's Badger Pass. (Courtesy Yosemite Concession Services, Yosemite National Park)

edge, provides a perfect view of Half Dome behind the trees. The rink and concessions are open from late November to March. Rentals are available, and there's a warming hut and snack bar, where you can buy hot cocoa. Call (209) 372– 1441 (winter).

Take a family-oriented **Discover Yosemite** daytime naturalist program on Wednesdays. Guides point out animal tracks, identify trees, and explain how humans and animals differ in the way they adapt to the cold. Tours depart from the Yosemite Lodge lobby; call (209) 372–1445 for more information.

See the **Sierra Nevada** from a vantage point unreachable by mechanized means on a winter snowshoe walk. You can rent snowshoes for kids ten years and older at Badger Pass. Naturalists lead the two-hour journey from the Badger Pass Ski Area to Clark Range. Call the **Badger Pass Ranger station** (209–372–0409), or sign up in advance at **Valley Visitor Center.** Tours take groups of about thirty-five five days a week.

Children who participate in any winter outdoor National Park program may ask a ranger for a Junior Snow Ranger certificate. Two certificates enable him or her to purchase a Junior Snow Ranger patch for a nominal fee.

SPECIAL EVENTS

While the park has some annual events, most of the fairs and festivals take place in the communities of southern Yosemite, a short drive south of the park on Highway 41. See Day Trips for other activities in these areas, and call the local visitors bureaus.

January: Chefs' Holidays, a month-long festival of free daytime cooking demonstrations and evening banquets by America's best chefs, Ahwahnee Hotel.

March: Western Artists Art Show, Ahwahnee.

April: The Great American Chili Cook-Off, Madera, with special events, food, and entertainment; Family Day Parade, Raymond, includes children's carnival and craft fair; Yosemite Winterfest, Badger Pass, costume contests, races, barbecue, and torch-light parade ends the ski season.

Easter Holidays: Special activities for adults and kids at Badger Pass include Easter egg hunt on the slopes.

May: Fishing Derby, Bass Lake; Chowchilla-Madera County Fair.

July: Boat parade and fireworks, Bass Lake.

August: Three-day Warbird Airshow displays former military aircraft from North America and abroad, Madera; Sierra Mono Indian Fair Days, North Fork, with foods, traditional dances, and games.

September: Madera County Fair, Madera; Sierra Mountaineer Days, Oakhurst, with parade, carnival, barbecue, and dance.

October: Mountain Apple Fest and Craft Fair, Oakhurst, with orchard samples, cider, and handmade artwork incorporating apples!

November: Yosemite Western Artist Christmas Boutique, Oakhurst, arts and crafts sale.

December: Yosemite Pioneer Christmas, caroling, candlelight tours, and stagecoach rides, Wawona; Holiday events at Badger Pass include Santa Skis, movies, crafts, caroling; Christmas at Fresno Flats, Oakhurst, nineteenth-century open house.

WHERE TO STAY

In-park lodging can range from a rustic campground to the gracious **Ahwahnee Hotel**. It's nearly impossible to get a reservation inside the park on short notice. Plan ahead. Bookings for rooms can be made at all park hotels exactly 366 days in advance. Call Central Reservations (209–252–4848) in the morning, 366 days before your arrival, and have a flexible schedule. You may also mail reservation requests to **Yosemite Reservations**, 5410 East Home Avenue, Fresno, California 93727; (209) 252–4848. For last-minute reservations, try calling thirty, fifteen, or seven days in advance of your arrival, common times when room reservations are cancelled.

Here are the lodging choices.

Right in the center of it all, the **Yosemite Lodge**, a mile west of Yosemite Village, near the base of Yosemite Falls in the heart of the valley, offers cabins, cottages, or lodge rooms plus a pool and restaurant.

The **Ahwahnee Hotel**, set in the woods 1 mile east of Yosemite Village Park Headquarters; (209) 252–4848. The 1927 lodge has a granite-and-concrete-beam facade, stained to look like redwood, and 123 recently redecorated rooms. Public rooms are decorated with hand-woven Indian baskets and Persian rugs. An incredible view includes Glacier Point, Half Dome, and Yosemite Falls. This is the only park lodging offering color TV and room service. A restaurant, pool, tennis, gift shops, and cocktail lounge round out the offerings.

Curry Village is on the eastern edge of Yosemite Valley across the Merced River from park headquarters; (209) 252–4848. It offers eighteen standard rooms, 103 cabins with private bath and eighty without, and 427 tent cabins with central bath. All are within reach of the skating rink, shops, and restaurants of Curry Village. Not fancy, but you'll find the most reasonable rates here. Sometimes, tent cabins may be the only accommodations available on short notice (as little as two weeks in advance); the park suggests booking one, with the chance of upgrading once you arrive.

Hotel accommodations near the Big Trees can be found at the **Wawona Hotel**, 27 miles from Yosemite Valley on Highway 41; (209) 252–4848. About half of the 105 rooms in this Victorian lodging have private baths. Other pluses: a pool, tennis court, stables, adjacent golf course, and dining services from April to November.

The Redwoods, Highway 41, 6 miles inside the south entrance, P.O. Box 2085, Wawona 95381 (209–375–6666), offers everything from rustic cabins to more modern homes with one to five bedrooms.

Tuolumne Meadows Lodge, open in the summer, offers sixty-nine tent cabins, mostly to those heading to the High Sierra Camps or for day hikes in the area. The area has a store, restaurant, stables, and service station.

There are seventeen campgrounds in the park. Some accept campers on a first-come, first-serve basis; most require reservations through **Mistix** (800–365–2267). Space fills quickly, so call early. Reservations are accepted eight weeks prior to arrival. Campground reservation centers managed by Mistix are located in the day use parking area at Curry Village, the Big Oak Flat entrance. A permit for backcountry camping can be obtained from a park permit station; call (209) 372–0310 for information. For additional campground information, call the **Public Information Office** of the National Park Service; (209) 372–0265 or 372–0264.

For accommodations outside the park, call **Yosemite's Gateway**

Reservations at (209) 454–2030. Keep in mind the distance of the gateway cities, via curvy mountain roads: **El Portal**, the closest, is 14 miles from the Valley Visitor Center; **Midpines**, the next closest town, is 36 miles. The most lodging options can be found in Mariposa, 43 miles away. Obtain a free brochure of all lodging in the county from the **Mariposa County Chamber of Commerce**, Box 425, Mariposa 95338; (209) 966–2456. **The Madera County Visitors Guide** contains a lodging guide to the Oakhurst/Bass Lake/Fish Camp/Madera area, including a list of bed and breakfasts (see Day Trips for contact name and phone).

Some good choices for families include the following.

Marriott's Tenaya Lodge, 1122 Highway 41, Fish Camp 93623; (209) 683–6555 or (800) 635–5807 (41 miles from Yosemite Valley, 2 miles from the park's south entrance). The lodge offers ages five to twelve morning, afternoon, and evening programs from Memorial to Labor Day. Clay making, nature walks, pool play, volleyball, and Indian lore storytelling are part of the fun. This luxury resort has some suites, nonsmoking rooms, indoor/outdoor pool, activities, and three dining options.

In Oakhurst, about 15 miles south of Yosemite, you'll find the **Best Western Yosemite Gateway Inn**, 40530 Highway 41, Oakhurst 93644; (209) 683–2378 or (800) 528–1234. The two-bedroom units, many with microwaves and refrigerators, are perfect for families. Indoor/outdoor pools keep the kids happy. Families may cook out at the barbecue area.

The Pines Resort, at Bass Lake, 14 miles from Yosemite's southern entrance, P.O. Box 329, Bass Lake 93604 (800–350–7463), offers chalets with kitchens.

WHERE TO EAT

There are a number of places in the park for snacks and meals. For complete listings, contact the **Yosemite Concessions Services Corporation** (see For More Information).

In Yosemite Village, the **Yosemite Village Store** (209–372–1253) is a year-round operation that sells everything from camping gear to meat, fresh veggies, and granola bars for the trail. **Degnan's Delicatessen**, a stone's throw to the north (209–372–1454), sells sandwiches, salads, candy, and cold drinks. Right next door, **Degnan's Fast Food** (209–372–1437) features fried chicken, frozen yogurt, and pizza.

Restaurants

For the most reasonable prices, try **The Yosemite Lodge Cafeteria**, Yosemite Village (209–372–1265), operating year-round, or the **Curry Village Cafeteria**, Curry Village (209–372–1203), open summers only. **The Four Seasons Restaurant** at Yosemite Lodge (209–372–1269) offers a family setting, children's menu, and dishes such as trout, steaks, enchiladas, and hamburgers. It's open for breakfast and dinner year-round. The dinner line can be long, so sign up early.

The **Tuolumne Meadows Lodge** (209–372–1313), beside the Tuolumne River, is a tent that serves breakfast and dinner during the summer.

The **Curry Village Pizza Patio**, Curry Village (209–372–1415), is open from spring to fall, featuring a nice outdoor area for sunny days.

For a fine dining experience, **The Ahwahnee Hotel Dining Room** (209–372–1489), which some say is the most beautiful restaurant in the country, serves breakfast, Sunday brunch, lunch, afternoon snacks, and dinner. Reservations are required for dinner only, when preferred attire for men is coats and ties, dresses or evening pant suits for women.

DAY TRIPS

If you're en route to or lodging outside the park, you may consider attractions found in communities just south of the park, including Oakhurst, Fish Camp, Bass Lake, and North Fork. Contact the **Southern Yosemite Visitors Bureau**, P.O. Box 1404, Oakhurst 93644 (209–683–INFO), for details on the following.

Fish Camp. Hop aboard **The Logger Steam Train**, a 4-mile, forty-five-minute railroad excursion through Sierra National Forest's most spectacular scenery; or try **Jenny Railcars**, quaint "Model A" powered railcars, offering a thirty-minute narrated trip. The trains are operated by the **Yosemite Mt. Sugar Pine Railroad**, 56001 Highway 41; (209) 683–7273. The station complex houses the **Thornberry Museum** (call the railroad at 209–683–7273), filled with logging company equipment, gift store, picnic area, and sandwich shop, with an inn and restaurant next door. The trains run year-round, weather permitting.

Oakhurst. Take the kids to see Oakhurst's mascot at the corner of Highway 41 and Road 426. The **talking fiberglass bear** tells about the now extinct California Grizzly and about respect for nature. **Fresno Flats Historical Park**, Road 427 (209–683–6570), lets you imagine life here in the late nineteenth and early twentieth centuries when the town (formerly Fresno Flats) was a stopover for travelers on their way to Yosemite. Visit restored buildings, a log barn, two jails, two schoolhouses, and a cabin in which President Theodore Roosevelt is said to have slept. **Oakhurst Community Park**, just off Highway 41, is a pleasant respite for a picnic, and has a playground.

Bass Lake. Bass Lake is a popular vacation spot surrounded by miles of rolling, pine-covered hills, and expansive meadows. Take a narrated tour of the lake aboard *Bass Lake Queen II,* daily during summers and on spring and fall weekends. The bargelike boat docks in front of Ducey's on the Lake on the North Shore; (209) 642–3121.

North Fork. At the **Sierra Mono Museum**, at the intersection of Malum Ridge Road (274) and Mammoth Pool Road (225), between North Fork and South Fork (209–877–2115), see elaborately woven Native American baskets, artifacts, and other crafts. The museum was built and is run by members of the Mono Indian tribe. Early August brings a two-day **Indian Fair and Powwow** at the North Fork Recreation Center. Visit the **Mono Wind Nature Trail and Flower Garden**, Road 209, off Road 233, 2 miles east of North Fork; (209) 877–2710. It has cedar bark houses, a semi-underground sweat lodge, and a granary where acorns were stored for winter use. A self-guided, mile-long trail winds past twenty-three stations identifying plants used by the Monos for healing, utensils, and food. Flower gardens bloom with more than one hundred varieties of perennial and annual plants, and fresh flowers can be cut for a small fee. The Mono Indian family who run this facility give occasional workshops, teaching Indian sewing, food-gathering techniques, and other Mono Indian skills. Grounds are open year-round on weekdays and by prearrangement weekends and holidays.

FOR MORE INFORMATION

The **National Park Service Information Office**, P.O. Box 577, Yosemite National Park, California 95389; (209) 372–0265 or (209) 372–0264—recording with general information. The **Valley Visitor Center**, P.O. Box 577, Yosemite National Park, California 95389; (209) 372–0299. For information on the park's hotels, tours, and eateries, contact **Yosemite Concession Services Corp.**, 5410 East Home Avenue, Fresno, California 93727; (209) 252–4848.

A free list of services and facilities for visitors with disabilities is available at visitors centers.

Emergency Numbers

Ambulance, police, fire, and emergency medical care: 911 from public phones or 9–911 from hotel rooms

Twenty-four-hour medical assistance, including poison control and pharmacy: Contact the **Yosemite Medical Clinic** in Yosemite Village; (209) 372–4637. The clinic and an independent dental office (209–372–4200) are located on The Ahwahnee Hotel road.

ALASKA

35

CRUISING THE INSIDE PASSAGE, MONEY-SAVING TIPS, AND ADVENTURE TOURS

There's an area of land and water beginning from the border of the U.S. and Canada, near Seattle, that winds itself north, past Vancouver, Victoria, Ketchikan, and Sitka, around Admiralty Island to Juneau and the longer inlets of Glacier Bay, Haines, and Skagway. These fingerlike fjords, islands, glaciers, and coves make up what is known as the Inside Passage. Visitors have long delighted in the passage's unique cities, native villages, and historical Alaskan sites, but of special wonder is the abundance of natural beauty and wildlife you see along the way.

GETTING THERE

By Air
   A cruise is the most popular way of visiting Alaska's Inside Passage. Many cruise ships leave from Seattle, San Francisco, or Vancouver. **Anchorage International Airport**, Domestic Terminal Visitor Information Center (907–266–2437), is one of the larger airports. **Alaska Airlines** (800–426–0333) offers convenient flights from most large cities. Other carriers include **Delta** (800–221–1212), **United** (800–241–6522), and **Northwest** (800–225–2525). Always ask for special excursion fares and packages.

By Bus

Alaskah **Express,** 745 West Forth Street, Suite 200, Anchorage 99510 (907–277–5581), serves Haines and Skagway with connections to the Alaska Marine Highway.

By Ferry

Traveling the **Alaska Marine Highway** ferry service is not only a relatively inexpensive way to see the Inside Passage, but it offers a unique opportunity to meet the locals. The ferry departs year-round from Bellingham, Washington, 350 Harris Street, (206) 676-8445, and carries passengers and cars along the Inside Passage with stops at Port Hardy and Prince Rupert in Canada (604–627–1744), Ketchikan, Wrangell, Petersburg, Sitka, and Juneau. Call the central reservations office in Juneau, (800) 642–0066 or (907) 465–3941; in Haines call (907) 766–2111; and in Skagway call (907) 983–2941.

Fares vary with season, distance traveled, and type of accommodations. You can book deck space (bring your own sleeping bags) or a bunk-bed furnished cabin. On-board services are minimal compared to cruise ships, but do include meal service, sometimes movies and storytelling, and on larger ships there may be a children's playroom. For an additional charge you may disembark and reboard a few days later.

Another ferry option is **B.C. Ferries,** 1112 Fort Street, Victoria, BC; (604) 386–3431. It travels year-round from Prince Rupert through the Inside Passage to Port Hardy. This company also offers a fifteen-hour summer day cruise.

By Ship

Decide on a big or small ship. Some small no-frills cruises come with basic accommodations but usually spend more time on the water in narrower channels. Some of these ships aren't appropriate for small children; others might intrigue older teens who want to see more wildlife and have a closer-to-nature experience. With small children, school-age kids, or teens who want nightlife, the larger cruise ships that pack in evening shows, spas, pools, and sometimes kids' programs are good choices.

Large Cruise Ships

Cruise ships sometimes change their itineraries. Always check to be sure that the line, the ship, and the sailing you want features the desired ports and shore tours.

American Family Cruises, World Trade Center, 80 Southwest Eighth Street, Miami, Florida 33130-3097; (800) 322–3130 or (800) AFC–2990. This new cruise line that opened in December 1993 with a KinShip (cruise ship) to the Caribbean may be the answer to the family-cruise-to-Alaska dilemma. American Family Cruises plans to offer full kids' programs on board and on-shore activities for families. Their KinShip *American Pioneer* will begin cruising the Inside Passage in summer of 1995, visiting such sites as Sitka, Endicott Arm/Rainbow Glacier, and Ketchikan.

Cunard, 555 Fifth Avenue, New York, New York 10017; (212) 880–7500 or (800) 5–CUNARD. *Sagafjord,* 750 passengers, offers ten-day cruises with visits to Cook Inlet, Kenai Fjords National Park, Prince William Sound, Yakutat Bay, Hubbard Glacier, Sitka, Skagway, Juneau, Ketchikan, Alert Bay, and Vancouver.

Princess Cruises, 2029 Century Park East, Los Angeles, California 90067; (800) 421–0522 or (213) 553–1770. Several ships to Alaska offer seven-day cruises that depart from Vancouver or Anchorage and cruise the Inside Passage to Ketchikan, Juneau, Skagway, Glacier Bay, and Columbia Glacier.

Holland America, 300 Elliott Avenue West, Seattle, Washington 98119; (206) 281–3535. Land packages can get you to Denali, Anchorage, and other interesting ports. In conjunction with **Alaska Highway Cruises** you can book a seven- or fourteen-day land tour of Alaska that has you driving your own recreational vehicle. (See Adventure Tours later in this chapter.)

Royal Caribbean Cruise Lines, 1050 Caribbean Way, Miami, Florida 33132, (305) 539–6870 or (800) 327–6700, offers seven-night to eleven-night Inside Passage cruises from Vancouver that include stops at Tracy Arm Fjord, Skagway, Haines, Juneau, Ketchikan, and Misty Fjords.

Royal Viking Line, 95 Merrick Way, Coral Gables, Florida 33134, (800) 422–8000, offers eleven-day round-trip cruises from Vancouver that include the Inside Passage, Juneau, Sitka, Glacier Bay, Gulf of Alaska, Seward, Columbia Glacier, Hubbard Glacier, and Victoria. Royal Viking Line also offers thirteen-day Vancouver-to-San Francisco cruises that include the Inside Passage, Ketchikan, Juneau, Skagway, Haines, Glacier Bay, Hubbard Glacier, Sitka, and Seattle.

Smaller Ships

Alaska Sightseeing Tours, Suite 700, Fourth and Battery Building, Seattle, Washington 98121; (800) 426–7702. Several ships, including the *Spirit of Glacier Bay.* Three-day, two-night tours from Juneau to Glacier Bay.

Special Expeditions, 720 Fifth Avenue, New York, New York 10019; (800) 762–0003. Two ships, the **M.V.** *Sea Bird* and the **M.V.** *Sea Lion,* each accommodate seventy passengers. Eleven-day cruises depart from Seattle.

Cunard, 555 Fifth Avenue, N.Y., New York 10017; (800) 221–4770. The *Sea Goddess I,* a luxury liner accommodates 116 people. These seven-day cruises are not really suited for young kids or teens, but families with adult children (yes, parents and their adult children can enjoy traveling together) could find them pampering and pleasing. Departs from Vancouver and visits the Inside Passage, Columbia Glacier, Hubbard Glacier, Ketchikan, Tracy Arm, Juneau, and Skagway.

World Explorer Cruises, 555 Montgomery Street, San Francisco, California 94111; (800) 854–3835. SS *Universe*, 550 passengers, offers fourteen-day cruises from Vancouver with visits to Wrangell, Juneau, Skagway, Glacier Bay, Columbia Glacier, Seward, Sitka, Ketchikan, and Victoria. Alaskan experts sail on every voyage and give lectures on wildlife and other issues concerning Alaska. This cruise appeals to older teens who want to savor the scenery rather than check out the scene.

WHAT TO SEE AND DO

Choosing a Shore Tour

A cruise ship can get you near Alaska's glacial ice fields, pristine lakes, snow-capped mountains, and wildlife. Unless you pick the right shore tour you won't get any closer to Alaska's wilderness than the murky water at the end of the dock. With limited time in port and lots of options, you could easily pick the wrong excursion and end up listening to a boring lecture at a fish hatchery while missing a float trip through streams with riverbanks blooming with bald eagles.

In selecting shore tours, follow these four general rules:

1. **Be wary of any shore excursion that begins with "board your waiting motorcoach."** Because many of these town trips accommodate those with limited mobility, the guide gives guests a point-and-look recitation of local lore as the bus rolls on, usually stopping only at bathrooms and gift shops. Such tours, while providing a service for many less-active passengers, frustrate those who seek a hands-on Alaska experience.

2. **Do in-town tours on your own.** Unless you crave lines or need a group for confidence, don't sign up for visits to local museums, or shops. In Alaska, the towns curl around the harbor, and most city sites are within an easy walk or cab ride of port.

3. **Opt for tours that take you by bush planes, float planes, helicopters, trains, zodiac rafts, kayaks, or any other small conveyance.** You'll want to fly over the ice fields, raft on the rivers, and get into the back country. These sojourns let you commune with Alaska's wilderness. Here's where the pristine Alaska of brochures and imagination pops into view. While expensive, these trips would cost even more if you arranged them yourself, since cruise ships often receive discounts for their volume bookings.

4. **Pack for the weather.** Remember, on any Inside Passage tour, to

pack binoculars for up-close looks at eagles and seals. Dress in layers and don't forget a raincoat for the frequently wet weather. Even in summer Alaska can be chilly. When in doubt about the weather, think fall—crisp, and sometimes wet—but bring a few T-shirts and pairs of shorts just in case.

MONEY-SAVING TIPS

Getting to Alaska can be costly for families, so any money-saving tips are valuable in making this trip affordable for families.

1. **Check the newspapers for airfare bargains.** Airfare from the East can cost more than $700, and from the Midwest more than $500. But as always, check the airline specials, two-for-one packages, and consider using your frequent flyer miles. Try to work around black-out dates, and book frequent flyer seats many months in advance.

2. **Consider the AlaskaPass.** Similar to a Eurail Pass, the AlaskaPass, P.O. Box 351, Vashon Island, Washington 98070–0351 (800–248–7598), entitles a voyager to eight days of unlimited travel on ferries, buses, and trains throughout British Columbia, and the Yukon Territory. There are half-price fares for children.

3. **Try the Alaska Marine Highway**, P.O. Box 25535, Juneau, Alaska 99802; (800) 642–0066. Eight ferries provide year-round travel. The southeast route offers travel from Bellingham, Washington, or Prince Rupert, B.C., to smaller communities. The southwest route provides connections between Whittier, Valdez, Cordova, the Kenai Peninsula, and Kodiak Island. While the comforts are basic, the scenery is as grand as that experienced by the cruisers on pricey luxury ships.

4. **Take a train ride.** Try the state-owned **Alaska Railroad**, Alaska Railroad Corporation, Passenger Services, P.O. Box 107500, Anchorage, Alaska 99510; (800) 544–0552. It features such inexpensive day trips as a rail ride to the Matanuska Valley north of Anchorage, and a combination train and cruise trip along the Kenai Peninsula.

5. **Stay at a family-friendly bed-and-breakfast home for your pre- or post-cruise tour.** From plain to fancy, these lodgings offer hospitality and neighborly advice on what to see, often at costs lower than comparable hotels. Before booking be clear about the ages and needs of your children, and be certain that the bed and breakfast welcomes kids; otherwise, no one will have a good time.

   Among the registries: **Alaska Bed and Breakfast Association**, 369 South Franbler, Suite 200, Juneau 99802 (907–586–2959); **Alaska Private Lodgings**, P.O. Box 20047, Anchorage 99520–0047 (907–258–1717); **Alaska Hospitality Homes**, 326 Fourth Street, Suite 1112, Juneau 99801 (907–463–3995); and **Accommodations**

An exciting train ride through White Pass reveals the rugged beauty of Alaska's mountains. (Courtesy Southeast Alaska Tourism Council)

In Alaska, P.O. Box 110624, Anchorage 99511–0642 (907–345–4761).
6. **Book a state park cabin.** Located along hiking trails, or on the coast, these rustic cabins offer top-dollar scenery at penny-pinching prices. These are popular, so book far in advance, and be sure to inquire about how easy or difficult it is to reach the cabin, and what provisions are a must to bring. Check out the cabins offered in each park, and contact **Alaska State Parks,** Southcentral Region Office, P.O. Box 107005, Anchorage 99510 (907–762–2617); **Alaska State Parks,** Division of Parks and Outdoor Recreation, P.O. Box 107005, Anchorage 99510 (907–762–2261); **U.S. Forest Service,** Public Information, P.O. Box 21628, Juneau 99802 (907–586–8806); **National Park Service,** Alaska Area Office, 2525 Gambell Street, Anchorage 99503 (907–257–2696); and the **Public Lands Information Center,** 605 West Fourth Avenue, Suite 105, Anchorage, 99501 (907–271–2737), or **Alaska Public Lands,** 250 Cushman Street, Fairbanks 99701 (907–451–7352).

7. **Camp in the great outdoors.** Bedding down under the stars in Alaska is a truly wonderful way to rough it. Alaska operates 132 parks with 2,400 campsites, all with nominal fees. Before you set out with your backpack and sleeping bag, please be sure you are an experienced camper with outdoor and wilderness savvy.

8. **Try an adventure.** Alaska offers great opportunities for adventures, not all of which are expensive. If you can't afford an extended Alaska safari, or week-long outfitter tour, try at least a day or overnight adventure.

One possibility: **Bike the backroads.** Besides booking a trip through a bicycle tour outfitter, consider **Alaska Bicycle Tours**, P.O. Box 829, Haines, 99827; (907) 766–2869. They offer day trips from Haines and Skagway, as well as three-day trips through mountain passes.

Try kayaking for a day. This not only gets you close to the water and the wildlife, but these day trips are relatively inexpensive. **Alaska Discovery Tours**, 369 South Franklin Street, Juneau 99801 (907–463–5500), offers guided trips in Juneau and through Glacier Bay.

For more adventures see Adventure Tours in this chapter.

9. **Check out package tours.** Airlines and tour companies often package land and air tours with lodging, airfare, sight-seeing, and some adventure trips for significantly less than it would cost to buy these individual components yourself. Check out the packages offered by major tour operators, travel companies, and commercial airlines. For example, **Alaska Airlines Vacations** (800–468–2248) features build-your-own vacation packages.

10. **Read more about it.** Obtain vacation planners from the **Alaska Division of Tourism**, P.O. Box 110801, Juneau 99811 (907–465–2012), and from each area's Convention and Visitors Bureau (see individual cities). The **Southeast Alaska Tourism Council**, Department 802, P.O. Box 20710, Juneau 99802 (800–423–0568), offers a free and informative brochure on the Inside Passage.

ALWAYS REMEMBER

Always remember this beautiful country is Alaska. Expect lots of rain, with temperatures—even in summer—hovering at *highs* of about 70° F; and the lows, well, these dip much lower, especially at night. Think fall. Bring rain gear, thermal underwear, layers of clothing (including some short-sleeve shirts just in case), and waterproof hiking shoes if you intend to hit the trails. And don't forget the insect repellant. Alaskans have not-so-affectionately dubbed mosquitoes the "state bird."

ADVENTURE TOURS

Alaska, with spectacular glaciers, swift rivers, and rugged mountains is a state made for the adventuresome. In each section we have included outfitters who provide easy access to these wonders for families. Here are some companies that offer exciting statewide journeys.

A new company **Alaska Highway Cruises**, 3805 108th Avenue NE, Suite 204, Bellevue, Washington 98004 (800–323–5757 or 206–828–0989), lets you combine a pampering Inside Passage cruise aboard Holland America Line with a seven- or fourteen-night land "cruise" in your own recreational vehicle. From May through September choose from among six prearranged itineraries, all of which provide guaranteed RV campsites each night. Some routes take you through Denali National Park to Fairbanks; others add Whitehorse and Dawson City, boom towns in the Yukon's gold rush days. Other roads wind through the Canadian Rockies, stopping in Banff, Lake Louise, and Jasper, or hug the Olympic Peninsula cutting through Vancouver, Victoria, and Hood Canal. The scenic byways stretch across rivers, through chasms, past snowcapped glaciers and pristine lakes. Out your window you might see caribou, Dall sheep, moose, or even grizzly bears.

Alaska Highway Cruises acquaints you with your RV and provides a twenty-four-hour toll-free number just in case. While not inexpensive, these tours enable you to obtain a memorable sample of Alaska's wide open spaces by land and by sea. Recreational vehicles, unwieldy but also family friendly, offer room for the road and such conveniences and cost-saving touches as on-the-move meals and sleeping accommodations.

But be careful when assessing these itineraries. Consider how many hours you want to be roaming the highways each day, and remember that RVs lumber along at relatively slow speeds. No matter how glorious the view—and simply looking out your window is a great way to savor Alaska's unique scenery—ponder just how much your kids (you know them best) would want to be inside a vehicle, even a comfortable one. With this in mind, assess the itineraries carefully. Some seem to require long stretches of driving with relatively little time for stepping out into the scenery. Also, ask about the road conditions. Will you need to maneuver sharp curves and steep descents, not the wisest thing for inexperienced RV drivers. A relatively flat route, however, might be much more enjoyable for those with little RV experience.

Alaska Wildland Adventures, P.O. Box 389, Girdwood, Alaska 99587 (800–334–8730 or 907–783–2928), offers an Alaska Family Safari, generally during the first week in August. Geared for active parents and kids ages six to eleven, this trip has you hiking through mountain meadows and forests, picnicking alongside salmon streams, spotting seals on a cruise through the Kenai Fjords National Park, and searching for bears and caribou in Denali National Park. Although it's wilderness and wildlife by day, by night enjoy such creature comforts as heated cabins with hot showers. Usually limited to sixteen guests, the trip emphasizes nature and fun. Besides an experienced naturalist guide, a special assistant helps cater to kids' needs. Babysitting, however, is not provided. This trip emphasizes experiencing Alaska's wilds together. Alaska Wildland Adventures also offers more rigorous camping and cabin trips that would appeal to families with teens.

For more tips, especially when traveling with adventurous teens, check out **The Alaska Alpine School,** P.O. Box 111241, Anchorage 99511; (907) 277–6867. It offers statewide expeditions, from glacier trekking to mountain photography seminars. Trips are custom planned, and college credit can be arranged. Pricey, but pampering, **Alaska's Most Unique Adventure,** P.O. Box 1516, Cordova 99574 (907–424–5552), straps you into a deluxe float plane for a seven-day camping trip complete with hot showers and good food. Only small groups are taken seasonally. For yet another take on the Alaskan wilds, try **Outland Expeditions,** P.O. Box 92401, Anchorage 99509; (907) 522–1670. They devise custom trips to fulfill your Alaskan fancy from dog mushing to skiing, sea kayaking, photographic safaris, and trekking. **Great Alaska Safari,** HCO1, Box 218, Sterling 99672 (800–544–2261 or 907–262–4515), organizes customized small-group safaris.

Alaska Visitor Information Services, P.O. Box 110706, Anchorage 99511 (907–345–0923), promises to save you money on airfare and lodging. The company books a variety of specialized tours from photographic safaris to dog sledding and rafting trips. **Alaska Photographic and Adventure Tours,** Mile 48.2 Sterling Highway, Cooper Landing 99572 (907–595–1422 or 800–595–8687), offers excursions to such top photo spots as Denali Park and Kenai Fjords.

CampAlaska Tours, P.O. Box 872247, Wasilla 99687 (907–376–9438), offers adventure plus the option to either camp or stay at lodges and hotels. Combination trips in summer include options such as bicycling, kayaking, rafting, and canoeing. In winter get into the spirit with ski, snowmobile, and sled-dog journeys.

For more backcountry adventures try **Alaska Discovery,** 234 Gold Street, Juneau 99801; (907) 586–1911. They offer day kayaking in Juneau and Glacier Bay, as well as seven- and fourteen-day wilderness excursions that explore such areas as Glacier Bay National Park and Admiralty Island.

For a sit-in-your-seat tour with a view from your window as big as all outdoors, try **Railway Freedom Train Tours LTD,** 1120 North Walnut Street, #100, Bloomington, Indiana 47404; (800) 457–5717 or (812) 334–4377. This company offers tours from Seattle to Ketchikan, Sitka, Juneau, Whitehorse, Fairbanks, Denali, and Anchorage.

Flight-seeing is a key way to "tour" many of Alaska's natural wonders. These bird's-eye views not only let you cover much ground in a short time, but they get you into places sometimes accessible only by boat or air. When you tour by float plane, you enjoy landing on some pristine lakes. As always when booking small aircraft, find out about the company's safety record, and check them out with the local Chamber of Commerce, the airport, and even the tourist bureau. **Wings of Alaska,** 1873 Shell Simmons Drive, Juneau 99801 (907–789–0790), offers flights across the Inside Passage and claims a good safety record.

GETTING AROUND

Private planes are popular modes of transportation for Alaskans so you won't have a difficult time finding small aircraft companies to fly you to where you want to go. **Alaska Airlines** (800–426–0333) services all major cities in Alaska, as well as sixty bush villages. Some smaller carriers are **MarkAir** (907–266–6802), **Reeve Aleutian Airways** (907–243–4700), **Temsco Airlines** (907–225–9810), **Arctic Circle Air** (907–456–1166), and **Ryan Air Service** (907–561–2090).

The **Alaska Highway** has some sharp curves and scary climbs, but also gorgeous scenery. If you feel up to the challenge—ask specifics about road and route conditions—several companies offer rental cars. **Avis Rent A Car** (800–331–1212) offers one-way rental options and service in several areas. **Payless Car Rental** (907–474–0177 or 907–243–3616 in Anchorage) is located in Fairbanks and Anchorage international airport terminals. Always exercise caution on icy roads (or simply stay put until the weather clears). Carry the milepost map, an emergency first-aid kit, and provisions, including food and water. Restaurants and cafes can be few and far between.

36, 37, and 38
MORE OF THE INSIDE PASSAGE: HAINES, SKAGWAY, AND SITKA

HAINES

Along the Inside Passage on the northern end of the Lynn Canal, Haines is on a narrow peninsula between the Chilkoot and Chilkat inlets. John Muir first visited Haines in 1879, and in 1903 the U.S. Army selected Haines for its first outpost in the Alaskan Territory. The city is known for its scenic setting and for its fall gathering of bald eagles.

Another plus: In fall, winter, and spring, the Northern Lights, the **Aurora Borealis**, are visible from Haines.

The average July temperature hovers around 66° F; the average January temperature is 17° F, but can go as low as -15° F. Dress appropriately. Remember that in fall and winter daylight is limited. While mid-October has about ten hours of daylight, mid-November has about 7½ hours, and by December there are only six hours of daylight with sunrise about 10:00 A.M. and sunset as early as 2:30 P.M.

GETTING THERE

The closest major airport to Haines is 80 miles away in Juneau. **Alaska Airlines** (800–426–0333) offers flights into Juneau. For the thirty-five-minute flight from Juneau to Haines there are three air taxi firms: **Haines Airways** (907–766–2646), **L.A.B. Flying Service** (907–766–2222 or 800–426–0333), and **Wings of Alaska** (907–766–2030 or 800–478–9464 in Alaska only). The airlines provide shuttle service into town.

The **Alaska Marine Highway** has ferries to the Haines area local terminal (907–766–2111) on a seasonal schedule. From Juneau the ferry ride takes about 4½ hours. From Skagway the ferry takes about one hour. During the summer, the ferries run more frequently than in the winter. Contact the Alaska Marine Highway, P.O. Box R, Juneau 99811; (800) 642–0066 in the U.S. and (800) 665–6414 in Canada. **B.C. Ferries**, 1112 Fort Street Victoria, B.C. V8V 4V2 Canada (604–669–1211), offers service to Haines from Port Hardy (north Vancouver Island) and Prince Rupert.

The **Haines-Skagway Water Taxi and Scenic Cruise**, P.O. Box 246, Haines 99827 (907–766–3395), which operates mid-May to mid-September connects these two cities, which are only 15 miles by water, but 360 miles by road. With an early water taxi shuttle service, you could see either town as a day trip from the other.

Haines is also accessible by land. The scenic **Haines Highway** connects with the **Alaskan Highway** at Haines Junction. The 155-mile drive south from Haines Junction to Haines along the Haines Highway takes about 3½ hours, passes through the Chilkat Bald Eagle Preserve, and climbs the summit of Chilkat Pass.

Several bus companies travel to Haines. Contact **Alaska Denali Transit** (907–273–3331), **Alaska Sightseeing Tours** (800–426–7702), and the **Alaskan Express** (800–544–2206).

GETTING AROUND

The Haines **ferry terminal** (907–766–2111) is 4 miles out of town. To get into town, try the **Haines Shuttle and Towers** (907–766–2819) or a taxicab. In town **Sockeye Cycles** (907–766–2869) rents bikes and, in high season, arranges tours. Call ahead to be sure.

Car rentals in town include: **Affordable Cars**, Captain's Choice Hotel, P.O. Box 392, Haines 99827 (907–766–3111); **Avis**, Halsingland Hotel, P.O. Box 1589, Haines 99827 (907–766–2733); **Hertz**, the Thunderbird Motel, P.O. Box 589, Haines 99827 (907–766–2131); and **Independent Car Rental**, the Eagle's Nest Motel, P.O. Box 250, Haines 99827 (907–766–2891).

Be sure to stop at the **Haines Visitor Center**, Second Avenue and Willard Street; (907) 766–2234. They offer a walking tour of town and information about the Eagle Preserve, lodgings, and restaurants.

WHAT TO SEE AND DO

Attractions

Even though the main tourist draw for Haines is its scenic setting and site as gateway to more of Alaska's glorious outdoors and wildlife, the town has a few things worth a brief visit.

Throughout the year, families can learn about Native Americans at the **Sheldon Museum and Cultural Center**, P.O. Box 629; (907) 766–2366. Exhibits focus on the Tlingit Indians and the pioneers who inhabited the upper Lynn Canal. From May to September the museum is open at least from 1:00 to 5:00 P.M., often longer in summer. But in winter the facility is open generally Sundays, Mondays, Wednesdays from 1:00–4:00 P.M., and by appointment.

To keep order in the Haines area during the gold rush era and in times of territorial disputes with Canada, the U.S. Army in 1903 established **Fort William H. Seward**, west side of town at the south end of Haines Highway, named for the U.S. secretary of state who arranged the purchase of Alaska from Russia. Take the self-guided walking tour of the fort, which was decommissioned after World War II. Maps are available from the **Haines Visitor Bureau**, P.O. Box 530, Haines 99827; (907) 766–2234 or (800) 458–3579.

Some buildings are more interesting than others. Outside the **Fort's Headquarters**, #7 on the walking tour, now a private residence, note the cannon, cast in 1861, one of the first breech-loading naval guns designed to use shell casings and to be loaded from the rear. Notice, also, the totem pole, carved by Alaska Indian Artists, featuring representations of the eagle and the bear. The **Post Exchange**, #16 on the walking tour, was a multipurpose recreational center that housed a gymnasium, movie theater, store, and bowling alley. Here the military men kept a pet bear nicknamed "Three Per," short for three percent bear, who legend has it would prefer beer, but if no one was buying him any, he begged for ice cream cones.

On site at the fort now is a replica of a **Chilkat Tribal House**, #8 on the parade grounds, part of the **Chilkat Center For the Arts**; (907) 766–2160. Here local artists can be seen carving totem poles and making jewelry. In summer, the **Chilkat Indian Dancers** perform in their native costumes. Inquire ahead about schedules and performances.

Dalton City, P.O. Box 385, Haines 99827 (907–766–2476), is a recreation of an 1890s gold rush town. In the summertime, the area features sled dog demonstrations, arts and crafts, gold panning, plus restaurants and shops. Dalton City was the set location for the movie *White Fang*.

Nature: The Eagles

In Fall. Each fall from mid-October through January, hundreds of bird watchers from around the world travel to Haines for the world's largest gathering of American bald eagles. Twenty miles outside of town on the Haines Highway between the mile marker 10 and mile marker 28 (when driving into town from Haines Junction you pass this way) is the 48,000-

acre **Alaska Chilkat Bald Eagle Preserve**, Southeast Regional Office, division of Parks and Outdoor Recreation, 400 Willoughby, Juneau 99801. More than 4,000 bald eagles congregate here, with the prime viewing area between mile marker 18 and mile marker 24. This 4-mile stretch along the river flats of the Chilkat River are known as the "Eagle Council Grounds." Thousands of eagles congregate here from early October through February. Some are drawn from their homes hundreds of miles away to this specific area because of the natural phenomena, called the "alluvial fan reservoir," responsible for 5 miles of nonfrozen water on the Chilkat River during freezing months. Because warm water percolates into the flats and keeps the waters from freezing, salmon, who die shortly after spawning, come here. The eagles feast on the abundant salmon carcasses.

When eagle viewing, for safety, be careful to pull off the main road into an eagle-viewing area so as not to block the road or be susceptible to accidents. Also, don't walk on the river flats as this disturbs the eagles, who prefer being viewed from afar. Bring binoculars and, for photography, zoom lenses. Remember that in the heart of winter daylight is only from about 10:00 A.M. to 2:00 P.M., and it rains or snows frequently.

In Spring and Summer. Although many fewer eagles congregate in Haines in spring, April through May, the weather is much kinder, and warmer. April also brings nesting season for the eagles, who begin with courtship rituals, such as diving eagles locking their talons and somersaulting through the air.

In spring you also can view migrating trumpeter swans, sandhill cranes, arctic terns, and shorebirds. You may also get a glimpse of grazing moose, or brown and black bear. A highlight of the first two weeks of May: migration of sea lions, which may be accompanied by humpback and orca (killer) whales.

About 200 resident eagles stay in the preserve in summer. Even though there may be less wildlife, you can still catch sight of eagles diving for fish and perching in treetops.

Alaska Nature Tours (described next) offers guided trips year-round.

Special Tours
For a day tour of the area, bring your camera along on **Alaska Nature Tours**, P.O. Box 491, Haines 99827; (907) 766–2876. Experts on the natural history of Alaska lead a variety of bus tours. Some include guided walks and hikes, and birding treks into the heart of the Valley of the Eagles, the Chilkat Wildlife Preserve. The excursions take place year-round. In summer Alaska Nature Tours offers a three-hour trip, and an all-day tour with a guided hike. Summer is the busy season, so book far in advance. In fall and winter their Complete Chilkat Bald Eagle Preserve package includes a guided tour, meals, and lodging at the Captain's Choice Motel.

Since 1978, Al Gilliam of **Alaska Cross Country Guiding and Rafting**, Box 124, Haines 99827 (907–767–5522), has been operating many personalized trips into the heart of Alaska's pristine wilderness, including the **Chilkat Bald Eagle Preserve** and **Kluane National Park**. Most of his trips are based out of his backcountry cabins—new ones overlook the eagle preserve. Gilliam offers an interesting combination of fly-in, raft-out river trips and day hikes. Your takeout point is 3 miles from the cabin.

On Gilliam's three-day, six-person **Tsirku Valley Glacier Camp Fly In–Raft Out** trip, offered from July 1st through September, enjoy a scenic bush plane flight up the Takhin Valley to the base camp cabin located at the foot of DeBlondeau Glacier. Each night you come back to this cabin where meals are provided. To keep costs down, guests help with the preparation of meals.

Hike around the base of the glacier, and on the last day raft down the swift, yet flat Tsirku River through the Chilkat Bald Eagle Reserve. As you float silently down the river, bald eagles feed, fight, and take flight. Groups range from two to six. There's a slight discount for ages twelve to fourteen; it's not recommended for kids under twelve, but discuss the maturity and swimming ability of your children with Gilliam.

Gilliam also offers raft trips on the wild Alsek River, a class IV whitewater river that cuts through Kluane National Park, Yukon Territory; and another rafting trip on the Tatshenshini River, a class III white-water river. This ten-day trip starts in the Dalton Post, Canadian Yukon, and ends in Glacier Bay National Park.

SPECIAL EVENTS

Festivals
January: **Alcan 200 Road Rally**, a 200-mile snow machine race from the American-Canadian border to Dezadeash Lake on the Haines Highway and back.

August: **Southeast Alaska State Fair**, with lots of entertainment for all ages from horse shows to miniature train rides.

October: **Alaska Day Celebration**, celebrate the purchase of Alaska and pioneer days.

Sportfishing
March and April: **Trout fishing**, from the banks of the Chilkat River.

Mid-September to mid-November: Coho salmon, sportfishing from the banks of the Chilkat River; no boat necessary. Average size coho is ten to twelve pounds.

Mid-December through February: **Dolly Varden Trout Sportfishing**, ice fishing at Mosquito Lake.

WHERE TO STAY

Condominiums are available even in Haines. The **Ft. Seward Condos,** the historic Fort Seward building, P.O. Box 75, Haines 99827 (907–766–2425), offers furnished apartments with cooking facilities. Also in the historic Fort Seward building is the **Ft. Seward Lodge,** P.O. Box 307, Haines 99827; (907) 766–2009. It has ten rooms, some with shared, and some with private baths, and two with kitchenettes.

The **Captain's Choice Motel,** Second and Dalton streets; (907) 766–3111, (800) 247–7153 in continental U.S., (800) 478–2345 in Alaska and Canada. It overlooks Portage Cove and has thirty-nine rooms. The nine-room **Eagle's Nest Motel** is at 1183 Haines Highway, P.O. Box 250, Haines 99827; (907) 766–2891 or (800) 354–6009 in Alaska. Located at the foot of the Chilkat Mountains, it offers basic accommodations and some rooms with kitchenettes. The **Thunderbird Motel,** downtown, P.O. Box 589, Haines 99827 (907–766–2131 or 800–327–2556), has twenty rooms, six of which have kitchenettes.

The **Bear Creek Camp and Hostel,** 2 miles from Haines on Small Tract Road (907–766–2259), offers basic cabins that sleep up to four at an inexpensive price. In addition, bunks are available in the hostel. Upon request, the owners will meet you at the ferry terminal. Several bed-and-breakfast accommodations are available. Ask about the age children the facility welcomes. Bed and breakfasts include **Officer's Inn Bed & Breakfast,** Historic Fort Seward, P.O. Box 1589, Haines 99827; (907) 766–2000, (800) 542–6363 in continental U.S., (800) 478–2525 in Canada.

About 7 miles south of downtown, the **Chilkat State Park** and **Chilkoot Lake,** about 11 miles north of downtown, but 4 miles from the ferry, each have thirty-two sites for tents or recreational vehicles.

WHERE TO EAT

The Haines Visitors Bureau (800–458–3579 in the U.S. and 800–478–2268 in Canada) has a list of restaurants (see For More Information). Here are some choices.

The **Bamboo Room,** Second Avenue near Main Street (907–766–2800), offers seafood, steak, and burgers. The **Chilkat Restaurant and Bakery,** Fifth Avenue (907–766–2920), serves all of the above plus fresh baked breads and pastries. **Howsers Deli,** Main Street adjacent to Howsers Supermarket (907–766–2040), has an inexpensive array of salads, breads, pastries, and sandwiches to go. The **Mountain Market** (907–766–3390), downtown on the corner of Third Street and Haines Highway, features sandwiches, fresh juice, baked goodies, and an espresso bar. **Porcupine Pete's**, Main and Second Avenue (907–766–9999), besides sandwiches, adds sourdough pizza, homemade soup, a soda fountain, and ice cream. At **33 Mile Roadhouse**, Haines Highway, located near the eagle preserve (907–767–5510), hamburgers are the specialty.

For something a bit more upscale try the **Fort Seward Lodge**, in Fort Seward; (907) 766–2009. Offering dinner only, the restaurant specializes in crab, seafood, and steaks.

DAY TRIPS

Among the most exciting day trips are the adventure tours available from Haines (see Special Tours).

The other towns along the Inside Passage, depending on their location, offer attractive day trips such as **Skagway**, by way of the Haines-Skagway Water Taxi and Scenic Cruise (see Getting There). From Haines, plan to spend a few days in the **Glacier Bay** (see Glacier Bay chapter), and **Juneau** (see Juneau chapter).

FOR MORE INFORMATION

Haines Convention and Visitors Bureau, P.O. Box 530, Haines 99827; (907) 766–2202, (800) 458–3579 in the U.S., (800) 478–2268 in Canada.

Emergency Numbers
Ambulance, fire, police: 911
Hospital: The Lynn Canal Medical Clinic, Second and Willard streets (907–766–2521) is open from 9:00 A.M. to 5:00 P.M. and provides pharmaceutical needs. After hours, follow the instructions on their recording for both medical and pharmaceutical services as there is no twenty-four-hour pharmacy.
Poison Control: Call Anchorage (800) 478–3193

SKAGWAY

Skagway, in Tlingit, means "home of the north wind." Skagway, situated at the northern end of the Inside Passage at the head of the Lynn Canal and surrounded by the Coast Mountains, is about 80 air miles northeast of Juneau. Skagway surged as a boom town during the 1897–1898 gold rush days, growing from a handful of residents to about 20,000. Now the town's 750 residents cater to the curious. Skagway can be cool even in summer; in July temperatures range from 55° F to 75° F. In January temperatures range from 15° to 32° F.

GETTING THERE

The **Alaska Marine Highway** ferries travel the one-hour route from Haines to Skagway. You can pick up the ferry in Juneau as well. The Skagway ferry terminal is located at the south end of well-traveled Broadway Street; (907) 983–2941 or (800) 642–0066 for general information. Skagway is the northernmost stop for the Marine Highway ferry system. In addition, many major cruise ships dock in Skagway for the day. Check the itinerary.

The **Haines-Skagway Water Taxi and Scenic Cruise**, P.O. Box 246, Haines 99827 (907–766–3395), operates mid-May to mid-September; it connects these two cities, which are only 15 miles by water, but 360 miles by road. With an early water taxi shuttle service, you could see either town as a day trip from the other.

By car from the Yukon take the **Klondike Highway**, which joins the Alaska Highway at Whitehorse, capital of the Yukon, and connects with Skagway 113 miles away. Tour buses take visitors to Skagway from the Yukon as well as from Alaska's interior. Among the motor coach companies: **Alaska Direct** (907–277–6652), **Alaskon Express** (800–544–2206 or 907–983–2241), and **Sourdough Shuttle and Tours** (800–478–2529 or 907–983–2523).

Airlines that fly into Skagway: **LAB Flying Service** (907–983–2471), **Skagway Air Service** (907–983–2218), and **Wings of Alaska** (907–983–2442).

Skagway offers several **railroad excursions**. The scenic **White Pass and Yukon Railroad** (described later) can take you between Skagway and Whitehorse. There are also day excursions from Juneau to Skagway, and rail/motor coach tours from Skagway to the Yukon and to Alaska's Interior. The train station is located at Second Avenue (907–983–2217 or 800–343–7373).

GETTING AROUND

The downtown area of **Skagway**, only about 6 blocks long, is easily toured by walking. If you must hire a car or cab, call the following. Among the car rental companies in Skagway: **Avis** (907–983–2550 or 800–331–1212), **Sourdough Shuttle Car and Van Rental** (800–478–2529 or 907–983–2523), and **ABC Motorhome Rentals** (800–421–7456 or 907–279–2000).

Skagway has several taxicab companies as well: **Frontier Excursions** (907–983–2512), **Sourdough Shuttle and Tours** (907–983–2523), **Pioneer Taxi and Tours** (907–983–2623), and **Southeast Tours** (907–983–2990).

WHAT TO SEE AND DO

The **Skagway Convention and Visitors Bureau,** between Second and Third avenues and Broadway in the AB Hall (907–983–2854), offers a variety of pamphlets and walking tour brochures.

White Pass and Yukon Railroad

With limited time in Skagway, save town for last, and be sure to head for the hills first, a more interesting tour if you must choose. Sign on for a full- or half-day trip that follows the arduous path of the Klondike fortune seekers up to Lake Bennett in great comfort with a day trip on the **White Pass and Yukon Railroad,** P.O. Box 435, Skagway; (907) 983–2217, (800) 343–7373, or, in Canada, (800) 478–7373. This scenic three-hour ride, offered mid-May to mid-September, is especially good for those with limited stamina for walking such as young tots and some grandparents with limited mobility.

The White Pass and Yukon Railroad, a narrow-gauge train, takes you along one of America's great history trails, climbing almost 3,000 feet in 20 miles. You pass canyons, gorges, waterfalls, rushing streams, mountains laced with clouds, gold rush graveyards, and Dead Horse Gulch, named for the 3,000 animals that died in the struggle over this pass. The narrow footpaths and difficult climb testify to the compulsion of those struck with gold fever.

A trip originating in Canada in Bennett and traveling to Fraser and onto Skagway incorporates time for a short hike before arriving in Skagway at 6:30 P.M.

Klondike Gold Rush National Historical Park

Skagway's business district is the centerpiece of the **Klondike Gold Rush National Historical Park,** visitors center, White Pass and Yukon Route depot building, Second Avenue and Broadway; (907) 983–2921. The wooden facades here look like turn-of-the-century stores. Park brochures relate that in 1976 this park was created to preserve the physical and emotional history of the gold rush. The way to tour this downtown area of the park, which is about 6 blocks long, is to walk. Park rangers offer walking tours and interpretive programs from June through Labor Day.

The visitors center offers some black-and-white photos of prospectors. A thirty-minute film is shown several times a day, May through October.

On your tour of the town, make a stop at the **Arctic Brotherhood Hall**, Broadway Street, whose exterior walls are covered with more than 20,000 pieces of flat driftwood. Once the place of a private fraternal order, it now houses the visitors center. If your kids aren't spooked by cemeteries, you may want to walk a bit out of town to the **Gold Rush Cemetery** to see the graves of such Skagway legends as Soapy Smith and Frank Reid.

Not officially part of the National Park, the small **Corrington Museum of Alaskan History** is at Fifth Avenue and Broadway; (907) 983–2580. With its photos of Klondike legends such as Soapy Smith and his gang, and Dawson Charlie, the museum is worth a visit. It also has a scrimshaw collection, plus a small display of Tlingit totems and masks, and trade beads.

The Skagway Streetcar Company also puts on a show called *The Days of '98*. The musical centers on Skagway's historical past when gold drew them in from all around and when outlaw Soapy Smith created his legend. Kids may like this combination of old-fashioned attire and easy-to-digest history.

Hiking: The Chilkoot and White Pass Trails

This is the real McCoy, the Gold Rush trail that caused many to die. The 33-mile arduous **Chilkoot Trail** is accessible only by foot (unless you want to see part of it from the comfort of your train window aboard the White Pass and Yukon Railroad). The trail, open late May through September, begins near the Dyea town site, 9 miles from Skagway, and travels over the Chilkoot Pass to Lake Bennett. From Skagway, shuttle service and taxis go to the trailhead.

Rangers estimate the hike to take between three and five days one way. Obviously, this trek is suitable for only a few experienced hikers—adults and older teens who are well versed in difficult climbs in changeable weather. Proper equipment includes warm clothes even in summer as temperatures drop near the summit, rain gear, waterproof tent, campstove and fuel as no wood is available, hiking boots, food, and extra rations. Before attempting this hike, talk with the rangers about weather conditions. This is bear country so know what to do about food storage, and take other precautions (wear bear bells).

Most people should not hike this trail simply because of its difficulty. Although arduous, this trail is not a wilderness hike. The park service estimates that in July and August thirty to eighty hikers begin the hike each day. In 1992, more than 2,800 hikers climbed through the Chilkoot Pass. Ask the rangers for reliable, licensed outfitters who offer guided hikes.

The outpost town of Skagway is a great place to visit. (Photo by Clark Mishler/courtesy Alaska Tourism Marketing Council)

Obtain a hiking permit from the visitors center in town, Second Avenue. If you plan to start in Dyea, you must clear **Canada Customs** before leaving Skagway as part of the trail goes through Canadian territory. Call **Fraser Customs** (403–821–4111) or sign the required forms at the Park Service Visitor Center, Skagway.

Most families should not attempt to hike this famous trail. For most, the scenic view from the train window will suffice.

SPECIAL EVENTS

March: Buckwheat Ski Classic; Windfest, a winter celebration.

July: Soapy Smith's Waker, enjoy the local culture and toast the infamous con man Jefferson "Soapy" Smith with complimentary champagne; Fourth of July Celebration.

August: Dyea Dash.

September: Klondike Trail of '98 Road Relay.

December: F.O. Eagles Christmas Party.

WHERE TO STAY

The largest hotel in town is the **Westmark Inn,** Third Avenue and Spring Street, Post Office Box 515, 99840; (907) 983–6000 or (800) 544–0970. It is operated by Holland America Line/Westours, to accommodate the many people who disembark cruise ships and spend the night in Skagway. Other guests are welcome; check for availability.

The **Gold Rush Lodge,** P.O. Box 514 SE, Skagway 99840 (907–983–2831), offers modern rooms. The **Golden North Hotel,** Post Office Box 431, Skagway 99840 (907–983–2451), is among Alaska's oldest hotels, but offers comfortable rooms and a restaurant.

The **Historic Skagway Inn Bed and Breakfast,** P.O. Box 500, Skagway 99840 (907–983–2289 or, in Alaska, 800–478–2290), is open year-round. Once a woman's boardinghouse, it now has twelve rooms with Victorian decor, five of which are family size.

The **Dyea Campground,** operated by the National Park Service, offers twenty-two free sites. For this rustic camping, you must boil, filter, or purify all of your water. Contact the rangers, **Klondike Gold Rush National Historical Park,** P.O. Box 517, Skagway 99840; (907) 983–2921.

WHERE TO EAT

The **Northern Lights Cafe,** Broadway between Fourth and Fifth avenues (907–983–2225), offers a good lunch of burgers and fries. Breakfasts and dinners are also served daily.

While in town, enjoy a night out at the **Prospector's Sourdough Restaurant,** Broadway between Third and Fourth avenues; (907) 983–2865. It has a coffee house decor and a menu of fresh salmon, soups, and salads. The old **Red Onion Saloon,** Second Avenue and Broadway, is considered Skagway's best bar, featuring live music, tasty Alaska amber beer on tap, and great pizza.

For a slightly more upscale meal, try the **Chilkoot Dining Room,** the Westmark Inn (907–983–2291) or the restaurant at the **Golden North Hotel** (907–983–2294).

DAY TRIPS

From Skagway take a day trip to Haines using the water taxi (see Getting There) or fly to Juneau for a day or an extended tour. A popular driving route, called **the Golden Circle Route,** takes you from **Haines Junction,** where you can tour **Kluane National Park,** to **Haines** (see section on Haines), to **Skagway,** to **Whitehorse,** in Canada. For a brochure contact any of the towns' information centers (see For More Information).

FOR MORE INFORMATION

Contact the **Klondike Gold Rush National Historical Park Visitor Center,** White Pass and Yukon Route railroad depot, Second Avenue and Broadway; (907) 983–2921. The **Skagway Convention and Visitors Bureau** is at Seventh and Spring streets, Post Office Box 415, Skagway, Alaska 99840; (907) 983–2854. For the **Skagway Chamber of Commerce,** write to P.O. Box 194, Skagway, Alaska 99840; (907) 983–2297. For Golden Circle Route Information: The **Whitehorse Information Centre,** 302 Steele Street, Whitehorse, Yukon; (403) 667–2915. The **Haines Junction Information Centre** is at **Kluane Park Headquarters,** Haines Junction, Yukon; (403) 634–2345. Contact the **Haines Information Centre** at Second and Willard streets, Haines; (907) 766–2202.

Emergency Numbers
Ambulance, fire: 911. Firehouse located at Fifth and State streets; (907) 983–2300.
Police: 911. The police station is in City Hall, Seventh and Spring streets; (907) 983–2301.
Medical assistance and Poison Control: A medical clinic, Eleventh and Broadway streets, provides services Monday to Friday from 9:00 A.M. to 5:00 P.M.; (907) 983–2255. For after-hours medical emergencies call 911. The **Physician's Assistant** offers after-hours medical referrals; (907) 983–2418.
Poison Control: (800) 478–3193

SITKA

Sitka boasts remnants of native Tlingit Indian culture, as well as traces of its Russian heritage, dating back to the 1799 arrival of fur trader Alexander Baranov. Despite the relatively small size of its downtown area, Sitka, in terms of land mass, is the largest city in North America, with 4,710 square miles.

GETTING THERE

Sitka Airport is served by **Alaska Airlines** (907–966–2266, 907–966–2261, or 800–426–0333), which connects Sitka with Seattle, Ketchikan, Juneau, Anchorage, Fairbanks, and Glacier Bay. The **Alaska Marine Highway** (800–642–0066) ferries stop in Sitka. Several cruise lines visit Sitka as well. Because of Sitka's location on the west coast of

Baranof Island, no roads connect Sitka with other towns, although there are roads within Sitka.

GETTING AROUND

Sitka Ferry Terminal Buses, Prewitt Enterprises, P.O. Box 1001, Sitka 99835 (907–747–8443), meet the ferries in season and transport passengers the 7 miles into town. Prewitt Enterprises also operates **Sitka Airport Service**, P.O. Box 1001, Sitka 99835; (907) 747–8443. These buses meet planes and make regularly scheduled stops at the major downtown hotels. Among the taxicab companies: **Arrowhead Taxi** (907–747–8888) and **Sitka Taxi** (907–747–5001).

A car is not really necessary for visiting Sitka as the downtown area is reasonably compact. Among the car rental companies available: **Avis**, 600 Airport Drive, Sitka 99835 (907–966–2404); and **AAA Auto Rental**, 2033 Halibut Point Road, Sitka 99835 (907–747–8228).

WHAT TO SEE AND DO

Attractions

This is an easy town to visit on your own, so if you're visiting from a cruise ship forget the group tours. Again, as with most Inside Passage towns, the real delights lie just beyond the town's borders in the wilderness areas. Pick up a map at the Centennial Building Visitors Bureau near the dock, and walk to all the attractions. At the bureau, ask about performances of the **New Archangel Russian Dancers**, P.O. Box 1687, Sitka, Alaska 99835; (907) 747–5940. This troupe performs authentic dances in Russian costumes.

Favorite sites include **St. Michael's Russian Cathedral**, Lincoln Street (907–747–8120), with its onion shaped domes. Built in 1844–1848, but burned in 1966, the church was rebuilt by the townspeople who saved its valuable collection of icons.

A highlight of Sitka is the 107-acre **Sitka National Historical Park**, P.O. Box 738, Sitka, Alaska 99835; (907) 747–6281. A half-mile from town, follow the self-guided trail lined with fifteen totem poles to the site of the Tlingit fort, burned by the Russians after their decisive 1804 battle against these Indian warriors. The visitors center displays Indian and Russian artifacts. Bring the kids to the Tlingit arts program, and watch the talent of the Native Indian carvers.

A few other local sites are the **Sheldon Jackson Museum**, 104 College Drive, Sheldon Jackson College, which has Eskimo and Indian sleds, kayaks, masks, and other artifacts; plus the **Isabel Miller Museum**, Centennial Building (907–747–6455), which houses an extensive collection of Sitka's history in photographs, antiques, paintings, and a diorama of Sitka as it was in 1867.

The **Alaska Raptor Rehabilitation Center**, 11015 Sawmill Creek Road, P.O. Box 2984, Sitka 99835, (907) 747–8662, rehabilitates wounded or ill birds of prey and then releases them back into the wild. Kids love seeing these eagles, hawks, and other majestic birds up close. Winter hours are 9:00 A.M. to 5:00 P.M. Monday to Friday and Sundays 2:00 to 4:00 P.M. In summer hours are extended to follow cruise ship schedules.

Special Tours

Enjoy an invigorating journey with **Sitka Sea Kayaking Adventure**, 9085 Glacier Highway, Suite 204, Juneau 99801; (907) 789–0052. On a motorized zodiac, this outfitter leads you to a wilderness base camp where you are taught safe ocean-going kayak techniques. Once you've mastered these, explore the natural beauty of the surrounding protected waters and, with the help of a guide, search for various wildlife. Minimum age is eight. The season runs from May to September. Ask about dates when you may catch sight of migrating whales.

Those who would rather let others do the driving should contact **C-Jo Charters**, 204 Cascade Creek Road, Sitka 99835; (907) 747–8862. They will take you aboard their 43-foot boat to explore secluded beaches and waters. Fishing is available.

Some cruise lines offer marine tours that last almost four hours. Be careful. These are almost always costly, and depending on the outfitter, the weather, luck, and the locale you're visiting, you may or may not see significant amounts of wildlife. Inquire ahead of time. You leave the ocean liner to board a catamaran to travel into the maze of waterways that surround Sitka, then board a zodiac raft for a boat trip along even narrower inlets in search of wildlife. Motoring around the many tiny islands conveys a sense of the intricacy and abundance of the sea, but sometimes the wildlife can be disappointing. One trip revealed only a cluster of starfish—desperately being videotaped by participants— and a lone eagle sitting quietly in the high branches of a spruce.

Alaska Adventures Unlimited, P.O. Box 6244, Sitka 99835 (907–747–5576), offers year-round full- and half-day sportfishing, natural history, and photography tours, and welcomes families.

For a native's view of the area, book a guided day tour with **Sitka Tribe of Alaska**, 465 Katlian Street, Sitka 99835; (907) 747–3207. As you tour the area, guides recount Tlingit history, myths, and legends.

For sportfishing, contact **Alaska Dream Charters**, 713 Katlian Street, Sitka 99835; (907) 747–8612 or, in the U.S., (800) 351–6017. From April to September this outfitter takes you out on the Sitka Sound and lets you try your luck at catching such Alaskan specialties as king salmon, silver salmon, and halibut.

Wolf's Alaska Tours, Inc., 712 Monastery Street, Sitka 99835 (907–747–6769), offers guided hiking and wilderness trips from May to mid-September in the **Tongass National Forest**. These trips are better suited for families with older teens.

SPECIAL EVENTS

January: Russian Christmas and Starring, enjoy Russian food and the lively performances of the New Archangel Dancers.
March: Summer Biathalon.
May: Sitka Salmon Derby.
June: Sitka Summer Music Festival.
October: Alaska Day Festival, join in the celebration on the 18th when Sitka residents wear period costumes and reenact the ceremonies that in 1867 marked the transfer of Russian America to the United States.
December: Christmas Holiday Festival.

WHERE TO STAY

Sitka offers several bed-and-breakfast accommodations that offer a variety of attractions.

Enjoy the peace and tranquility with a view of Sitka Sound and Mt. Edgecumbe at the **Creek's Edge Guest House**, P.O. Box 2941, Sitka 99835; (907) 747–6484. For a cottagelike atmosphere, **Helga's Bed and Breakfast**, P.O. Box 1885, Sitka 99835 (907–747–5497), has beachside accommodations, fresh Alaskan breakfasts, and fishing charters available. The **Anna-hootz Bed and Breakfast**, P.O. Box 2870, Sitka 99835 (907–747–6498), has bedroom suites, with private baths and minikitchens.

The **Westmark Shee Atika**, 330 Seward Street, P.O. Box 78, Sitka 99835 (907–747–6241), offers upscale accommodations for southeast Alaska and is open year-round. Interior walls are decorated with native murals, and rooms have views of the harbor and surrounding mountains.

The **Potlatch Motel**, 713 Katlian Street, P.O. Box 58, Sitka, Alaska 99835 (907–747–8611), is a moderate hotel, open year-round, whose suites offer cooking facilities.

WHERE TO EAT

Channel Club, 2908 Halibut Point Road; (907) 747–9916, offers dinners only and specializes in salmon and king crab. Reserve ahead in high season. For Italian and Mexican cuisine, try the **Marina Restaurant,** 205 Harbor Drive (907–747–8840); or **El Dorado,** 714 Katlian Street (907–747–5070). **Bayview Restaurant,** 407 Lincoln Street (907–747–5440), serves up hamburgers and sandwiches.

FOR MORE INFORMATION

Sitka

Sitka Convention and Visitors Bureau, 330 Harbor Drive, Sitka 99835 (907–747–5940); Greater Sitka Chamber of Commerce, P.O. Box 638, Sitka, Alaska 99835 (907–747–8604).

Alaska

Anchorage Visitor Information Center, Fourth Avenue and F Street, Anchorage 99501; (907) 274–3533. Alaska State Chamber of Commerce, 217 Second Avenue, Juneau 99801; (907) 586–2323. Southeast Alaska Tourism Council, P.O. Box 20710, Juneau 99802; (800) 423–0568 or (907) 586–5758. Alaska Bed and Breakfast Association, 369 South Franklin, Suite 2000, Juneau 99802; (907) 586–2959.

Ferries: Alaska Marine Highway System, P.O. Box 25535, Juneau, Alaska 99802-5535; (907) 465–3959 or (800) 642–0066. Write to the Alaska Division of Tourism, Department 401, P.O. Box 110801, Juneau, Alaska 99811-0801 (907–465–2010), for The Official State Vacation Planner. For disabled visitor services, call Access Alaska (907–248–4777).

Emergency Numbers

Ambulance, fire, and police: 911
Hospital: Sitka Community Hospital, 209 Moller Drive; (907) 747–3241
Twenty-four-hour pharmacy: There is no twenty-four-hour pharmacy.
White's Pharmacy, 705 Halibut Point Road is usually open until 7:00 P.M. For emergencies, call the hospital.
Poison Control: (800) 478–3193

39
GLACIER BAY NATIONAL PARK AND PRESERVE

Encompassing more than 3.2 million acres of mountains, glaciers, and pristine waters, **Glacier Bay National Park and Preserve**, about 90 miles northwest of Juneau, is a highlight of any Inside Passage tour. Established as a national monument in 1925, enlarged and reclassified as a park and preserve in 1980, and declared a World Heritage Site in 1993, Glacier Bay National Park presents the vistas of Alaska you've imagined—fluted glaciers, blue-white sweeps of ice, and dramatic mountain peaks. **Glacier Bay**, the "gem of the Inside Passage," flows within the park, winding for 60 miles at widths varying from 2½ miles to 10 miles.

GETTING THERE

The only access to **Glacier Bay** is by boat or plane, both of which land in the nearby small town of Gustavus, a twenty-minute flight or a three-hour boat ride from Juneau. Even with limited time, try to squeeze in a day trip to Juneau. (See the chapter Juneau). **Alaska Airlines** (800–426–0333) offers flights between Juneau and Gustavus.

GETTING AROUND

In **Glacier Bay National Park and Preserve** getting around is a form of recreation in itself because the primary way to experience this area is by being on the water. Other ways: Fly above the bay or hike the mountains.

To help preserve the spectacular beauty and to protect the wildlife, the park service limits access to this area. If you wish to tour these waters on your own, contact the **Superintendent, Glacier Bay National Park and Preserve,** Gustavus, 99826; (907) 697–2230. For information about which private vessels may enter the bay, and for regulations, call (907) 697–2268.

WHAT TO SEE AND DO

Watch for whales

The best way to see these behemoths of the deep is to be out on the water with them during the summer migration—June through August. But landlubbers can also catch a glimpse of these majestic mammals. A choice spot for observing these giants is from **Point Adolphus,** which is across the Icy Strait from Gustavus. Because the tidal flows from Cross Sound, Icy Strait, and Glacier Bay mingle here, bringing with them large supplies of plankton, shrimp, and small fish, the hungry whales hang out here. There's something magical, almost eternal, about hearing "There she blows," and watching a whale breach the sea, his body slicing cleanly through the waters.

Be dazzled by the glaciers

Thick mountainous ridges of ice—blue, or white, or pink, depending on the light and the hour—rise up from the water, structures so creviced, fluted, massive, and odd that they seem to be from a distant age and an alien world. Quiet pervades the scene, casting an almost primordial spell. Then the glacier "calves," and a huge chunk of ice breaks and tumbles into the sea, throwing up white mists of spray. As the thunderous crash breaks the calm and the deep vibrations bounce off the peaks and echo down the channel, you sense the changing force and face of nature. This is a sight and sound you and your family won't soon forget. Among the most "popular" of Glacier Bay's icy wonders are Muir, Riggs, and Davidson glaciers because they are relatively easy to reach.

One of the nicest things about touring Glacier Bay is the ease with which all ages can share this experience. Whether your family catches these sites from a comfy deck chair of a pampering cruise ship, or snuggled together on a rolling raft, this will be one trip you'll talk about for a long time.

Enjoy the wildlife

What looks like a shadow on a floating chunk of ice could be cream-and-brown-spotted harbor seals and their pups, or sea lions out sunning for the afternoon. Search the horizon for pods of humpback, minke, and orca (killer) whales.

Then there are the birds. More than 200 species hover, nest, and feed on these rocky shores. Be sure to bring your binoculars to see up-close the colonies of such brightly colored birds as the black-feathered oyster-catchers, unmistakable with thin, red bills; the tufted and horned puffins, seeming somewhat comical with white faces, rounded bodies, and thick rouge beaks; and the white-bellied arctic terns crowned with black. In the presence of whales, colossal mounds of ice, fish-catching birds and barking seals, even the most blasé of kids will say, "Wow."

By Water

Some cruise ships have access to **Glacier Bay National Park and Preserve,** and some don't. To protect the park and the wildlife, the National Park Service limits the number of motorized vessels. If this much-heralded attraction is on your must-see list, and you are planning to visit by cruise ship, book a vessel that has the privilege to be here.

Smaller ships have an advantage. They offer more time in Glacier Bay, as much as twenty hours on a small ship compared with the five or six hours on a large cruise ship. Smaller vessels can navigate the narrower inlets in search of pods of whales, and the more abundant wildlife. But smaller ships also have fewer entertainment facilities—no nightclubs, dance floors, video arcade, or children's program. As a result, these are better for adult children, or teens who want to see the most without making the scene. Among the smaller vessels: **Alaska's Glacier Bay Tours and Cruises** (described later) and **World Explorer Cruises,** 555 Montgomery Street, San Francisco, California 94111-2544; (415) 391–9262 or (800) 854–3835. The latter offers fourteen-day cruises with an emphasis on learning about culture and wildlife.

The larger cruise ships, however, still put on a good show. This is a time to be out on deck looking at the icy blue cliffs and listening to the thunderous roar as the glacier calves. (See Cruising the Inside Passage.)

From **Glacier Bay Lodge,** Bartlett Cove, a tour boat departs daily for a nine-hour cruise of Glacier Bay. Inquire at the lodge. During the season, call (800) 451–5952. At other times, contact Glacier Bay Lodge, Inc., 520 Pike Street, Suite 1610, Seattle, Washington 98101; (206) 623–2417 or (800) 451–5952.

By Air

A glide above Glacier Bay presents a unique view of the sweeping expanse of ice and sea. This is a good (if pricey) option if your time is limited. Among the companies offering flight-seeing: **L.A.B. Flying Service, Inc.,** P.O. Box 272, Haines 99827 (907–766–2222), or **Haines Airways Inc.,** P.O. Box 470, Haines 99827 (907–766–2646).

By Land

Only two official trails cut through the park from the headquarters at

Don't miss the breathtaking beauty of Glacier Bay. (Courtesy Southeast Alaska Tourism Council)

Bartlett Cove. Check with the rangers about naturalist-led tours. The **Beach and Nature Trail** may be the easier of the two, with its mile path through the woods to the shore. Some scrambling on rocks may be required. The 1.5-mile **Bartlett River Trail** winds through the woods to the river.

Even though the Glacier allures, like some unknown and enchantingly different country, don't leave the formal trails of Glacier Bay National Park and Preserve unless you and your group are experienced hikers who understand the terrain, as well as the wildlife and the weather. Always consult with the park rangers first. Rain, rising tides, and slippery slopes make backcountry hikes suitable only for aficionados who know this park's topography and potential dangers.

Special Tours

Alaska's Glacier Bay Tours & Cruises, 520 Pike Street, Suite 1610, Seattle, Washington 98101 (800–451–5952 or 206–623–2417), offers both air and small cruise ship packages. See the bay for one to three days with departures from Juneau, Haines, or Skagway. This company also offers seven-day, six-night tours.

Glacier Bay—Your Way!, P.O. Box 5, Gustavus, Alaska 99826 (summer) (907–697–2288) or P.O. Box 2557, St. George, Utah 84771 (winter), creates sportfishing, kayaking, and whale-watching tours for a day or overnight from May through September. What would it feel like to paddle alongside a whale? Find out with **Spirit Walker Expeditions**, P.O. Box 240, Gustavus 99826; (800) KAYAKER or (907) 697–2266.

WHERE TO STAY

In the park

Glacier Bay Lodge provides accommodations from May through mid-September within the park. In season contact the lodge, at Bartlett Cove, P.O. Box 199, Gustavus, 99826; (800) 451–5952. At other times, call or write Glacier Bay Lodge, Inc., 520 Pike Street, Suite 1610, Seattle, Washington 98101; (206) 623–2417 or (800) 451–5952. These park rooms, the only under-roof lodging within the park, frequently come with wonderful vistas, and always have a private bath. (Request a room with a view.) But be sure to book as far in advance as possible.

Camping

Camping is available at Bartlett Cove, and for boaters at Sandy Cove. Camp at the park only if your clan is comprised of seasoned campers, hearty backpackers, and, generally, teens or adult children. As supplies are not available within the park, and only available in limited quantities in Gustavus, you must plan to tote in your gear, and much of your food. Contact the park service (907–697–2232) about sites, weather conditions, permits, and availability.

Condominiums and Bed-and-Breakfast Inns

Even the hamlet of Gustavus has condos. Try the **Whalesong Lodge**, P.O. Box 5, Gustavus 99826; (907) 697–2288 or (801) 673–8480 (October to April). They offer three-bedroom condominiums, or bed-and-breakfast accommodations. Whatever you book, you can add such packages as boat tours, sport fishing, whale watching, and kayaking. Another option, created from an original homesteader farmhouse, is the **Gustavus Inn at Glacier Bay**, P.O. Box 60, Gustavus, Alaska 99826; (907) 697–2254 (September to April) or (913) 649–5220. It overlooks Icy Strait, and welcomes children. Rates can include three meals daily, and locals highly recommend the food, especially the seafood. Guests have access to bicycles and are encouraged to fish in the river. The inn also arranges Glacier Bay boat tours.

A Puffin's Bed and Breakfast, P.O. Box 3, Gustavus, Alaska 99826; (800) 478–2258 in Alaska or (907) 697–2260. From May through September, the inn provides private cottages, bicycles, whale-watching tours, fishing and kayaking outings, and local transportation. Another seasonal choice, open May through September, is the **Glacier Bay Country Inn**, P.O. Box 5, Gustavus, 99826 (in season); (907) 697–2288. At other times write or call P.O. Box 2557, St. George, Utah 84771; (801) 673–8480. This country comfortable inn offers big breakfasts, nature walks, fishing, and whale watching. Ask about the preferred age of children.

Cabins

If your budget is tight, but your spirit willing to explore the wilds, try **Salmon River Rentals**, P.O. Box 13, Gustavus 99826; (907) 697–2245. They offer rustic, stripped down housekeeping cabins—a wood stove, table and chairs, and minimum cooking facilities. But there will be a roof over your sleeping bag (bring your own), and bathrooms in another building.

WHERE TO EAT

Most of the area's lodges have restaurants that accommodate overnight guests and others as well. The **Glacier Bay Lodge**, within the park, serves breakfast, lunch, and dinner from about June through the end of September; (907) 697–2225 (reservations required). The locals recommend the seafood, especially the salmon. For many, the **Gustavus Inn** (see Where to Stay) offers the best food in the area; (907) 697–2254.

DAY TRIPS

Continue your inside passage tour by visiting other classic stops: Juneau, Ketchikan, Sitka, Skagway, Vancouver, and Victoria. (See the appropriate chapters for each of these cities.)

In addition, for more wildlife, continue your journey further west along Alaska's southern coast (not part of the Inside Passage) to **Kenai Fjords National Park**, Headquarters and Visitors Center, P.O. Box 1727, Seward 99664; (907) 224–3175. This national park, comprising 580,000 acres that stretch for 50 miles along part of the southern shores of the Kenai mountains, boasts scores of sea lions, seals, sea otters, and whales as well as porpoises, puffins, and gulls. You can drive to **Exit Glacier**, about 12 miles from Seward. Inquire about summer naturalist programs and ranger-led hikes. A hiking trail allows you close access to this glacier, but be careful of falling ice because pieces break off unpredictably. Hardy teens and good hikers might want to attempt at least part of the 3-mile (one-way) steep hike to the **Harding Icefield**.

Seward, the gateway city for this national park, is reachable via the Alaska Marine Highway System (the state ferry), and in summer via the Alaska Railroad (800–544–0552 or 907–265–2494), which travels from Seward, past Mt. McKinley, and on to Fairbanks. Seward is also reachable by highways.

FOR MORE INFORMATION

Gustavus Visitors Association, P.O. Box 167, Gustavus, Alaska 99826; (907) 697–2358. Glacier Bay Information, Superintendent, Glacier Bay National Park, Gustavus, Alaska 99826; (907) 697–2232. Alaska Airlines Vacations (800–468–2248) offers tour packages.

For information on tour operators, outfitters, and accommodations obtain copies of both *Alaska, the Official State Guide Vacation Planner,* Alaska Division of Tourism, P.O. Box 110801, Juneau 99811 (907–465–2010); and *The Inside Passage Alaska Trip Planning Guide,* P.O. Box 20710, Juneau 99802, available from the Southeast Alaska Tourism Council (907) 586–5758 or (800) 423–0568.

Emergency Numbers
First-aid: For all emergencies, including medical emergencies, contact park headquarters; (907) 697–2230.
Hospital: Juneau—Bartlett Memorial Hospital; (907) 586–2611
Poison Control: (800) 478–3193

40
JUNEAU

In October 1880, Joe Juneau and Richard Harris made a startling find: They discovered gold in Alaska. And so began sixty years of migration and mining in the future Alaskan capital city of Juneau. Today, the boroughs of Juneau stretch far, encompassing several small communities. This gateway city for **Glacier Bay** offers abundant choices for getting up-close to elemental Alaska, with its spectacular ice fields and imposing glaciers.

GETTING THERE

Planes arrive at the **Juneau International Airport** (907–789–7821) from Seattle and Anchorage. **Alaska Airlines** has ticket offices at the Baranof Hotel downtown and the Nugget Mall in the valley, as well as at the airport. Call (800) 426–0333 (for vacation packages) or (800) 468–2248. **Delta Airlines** also flies to Alaska; (800) 221–1212 (for vacation packages) or (800) 872–7786.

    Holland America Line-Westours, Inc., 2815 Second Avenue, #400, Seattle, Washington 98121 (800–835–8907 or 206–728–4202) offers a variety of cruise and land packages. The **Alaska Marine Highway** (ferry) serves Juneau. (See Cruising the Inside Passage.) The ferry terminal (907–789–7453 or 800–642–0066) is 14 miles northwest of downtown Juneau in Auke Bay, so be sure to time your arrival to meet one of the buses, or the **Mendenhall Glacier Transport Ltd.** (MGT) (907–789–5460), a tour van that stops at the town's highlights. Taxi service is available from **Capital Cab, Inc.**, 106 Peoples Wharf, Juneau 99801 (907–586–2772); and **Taku Glacier Cab Company**, 102 North Franklin Street, Juneau 99801 (907–586–2121). Both companies can provide personalized tours—a boon if you only have a short time in town and need to get around quickly.

GETTING AROUND

Juneau has taxicabs and some bus service. Contact MGT (see Getting There) or the **City Bus** (907–789–6901). Negotiate your own taxi tour, or book a city and surrounding area day tour with **Gray Line of Alaska**, 3241 Hospital Drive (summer desk at the Baranof Hotel); (907) 586–3773.

But the best way to see the sights is to combine some sight-seeing on your own with an outdoor adventure, whether a day trip or extended tour. (See Outdoor Adventures.) To go at your own pace, rent a car. Among the rental companies: **Allstar/Practical Rent-A-Car**, P.O.Box 34457, Juneau 99803 (800–722–0741 or 907–790–2414); **Hertz**, 1873 Shell Simmons Drive, Juneau 99801 (800–654–8200 or 907–789–9494); **National Car Rental**, 8602 Teal Street, Juneau 99801 (800–227–7368 or 907–789–9814); and **Rent-A-Wreck**, 9099 Glacier Highway, Juneau 99801 (907–789–4111).

WHAT TO SEE AND DO

In Town

Downtown Juneau features some attractions, but if your visit is limited, start by going on an outdoor adventure, and then tour the city in your remaining time.

For information on city sites, a walking tour brochure is available dockside at the **Marine Park Visitor Information** kiosk, Marine Park, Merchant's Wharf, Admiral and Ferry Way, or from the **Visitor Information Center** (Davis Log Cabin—a replica of the city's first school), 134 Seward Street, Juneau 99801; (907) 586–2201. For a hotline of events, call (907) 586–JUNO.

Start from the Visitor Information Center, Davis Log Cabin, walk a block left along Third Street to Main Street. Turn right up Main Street to see local artist Skip Wallen's life-size bronze bear sculpture, a perfect wildlife specimen for kids to finger and admire.

Continue uphill to the **State Capitol Building**, Main and Fourth streets (free summer tours), constructed in 1930 as the Territorial Federal Building. For more kid-appeal, stop nearby at the **Juneau-Douglas City Museum**, Fourth and Main streets (907–586–3572), with its mining memorabilia and gold rush days lore and legends.

Don't miss the 45-foot totem pole on Seward Street, between Fifth and Sixth streets. There's something special about seeing these tall and strong in the sunlight. For a "token" of another culture, visit **St. Nicholas Russian Orthodox Church**, Fifth and Gold streets. Constructed in 1894 by the Russians, it has a striking onion-shaped golden dome, and inside are beautiful eighteenth-century icons. Nearby, the playground facilities and running space at **Cathedral Park**, Franklin Street between Fifth and Sixth streets, make a good spot for a rest or an impromptu picnic.

Another town attraction: the **Alaska State Museum**, 395 Whittier Street; (907) 465–2901 (free on Saturdays). It offers a good collection of Native American and Aleut artifacts, as well as presentations on the state's Russian heritage. Stop at the **Centennial Hall Forest Service Information Center**, 101 Egan Drive; (907) 586–8751. Besides portraying Alaska's natural history, it offers information about cabin reservations and park conditions. For a splendid view of the Gastineau Channel, the **State Office Building**, Main Street near Third Street, has an observation deck.

Cruise and tour directors tout the **Red Dog Saloon** on South Franklin Street opposite the cruise ship terminal. Don't be fooled by this ersatz, sawdust-on-the-floor, swinging-door replica of what a gold rush era saloon might have been. But the beer is good, and kids like the gift shop's colorful T-shirts and suspenders.

For kids interested in fish, the **Gastineau Salmon Hatchery**, 26197 Channel Drive (907–463–5114), is a big catch, with its saltwater aquarium and tanks. The facility turns more than 160 million salmon eggs into seafood each year.

Outdoor Adventures

Glaciers, Ice Fields, Fjords, and Flight-seeing. From Juneau it's an easy drive, about twenty minutes, to a real Alaskan glacier. To reach the **Mendenhall Glacier**, 13 miles from town, head northwest along Egan Drive, which turns into Route 7, and then turn right on Mendenhall Loop Road. Once you see the **Mendenhall Glacier** (907–789–0097), a 12-mile "river" of white-blue ice, you'll be surprised at how close it comes to the city. Make a quick stop at the visitors center on Mendenhall Glacier Road (907–798–0097 or 586–8800) for the exhibits detailing glacial history.

The Mendenhall Glacier, which had been advancing prior to 1750, now recedes, mostly due to warmer temperatures. Although the glacier moves forward slowly, it wastes away at a slightly faster rate. You might hear the thunderous sound of the glacier "calving" as huge chunks of ice break off and float in Mendenhall Lake.

Often the best time to visit is late in the afternoon when both the crowds and the light are less intense. Bright sun tends to whitewash the glacial colors, but the softer afternoon rays, or a cloudy day, bring out flashing aquamarine hues.

Walk—at least for a little while—on the trails alongside the glacier. **Photo Point Trail**, a .3-mile scenic path adjacent to the visitors center, is handicapped accessible and also good for strollers. Along the .5-mile self-guided **Interpretive Trail**, learn about glaciers. A park service brochure details several other trails. For further information, contact the U.S.D.A. Forest Service, Juneau Ranger District, 8465 Old Dairy Road, Juneau 99801; (907) 586–8800.

When visiting Juneau, you and your family won't want to pass up a trip to the Mendenhall Glacier. (Courtesy Alaska Tourism Marketing Council)

Mendenhall Glacier Transport (MGT), P.O. Box 21594, Juneau 99802 (907–789–5460), offers affordable daily excursions from downtown to the glacier from May to September. To get an aerial view and a "foothold" on this ice wonder, contact **Temsco Helicopters**, 1650 Maplesden Way, Juneau 99801 (907–789–9501). The tour combines flight-seeing with a brief stop on the ice. Other aerial tours swoop over the immense **Juneau Icefield**, a 1,500-square-mile ice cap in the mountains, the source of the Mendenhall Glacier.

Additional **flight-seeing companies** include **Alaska Coastal Airlines, Inc.**, 1873 Shell Simmons Drive, 99801 (907–789–7818); **ERA Aviation**, P.O. Box 21468, Juneau 99802 (907–586–2030); and **Wings of Alaska**, 1873 Shell Simmons Drive, 99801 (907–789–0790).

The **Taku Glacier** is another must-see. Wings of Alaska offers a flight-seeing trip to **Taku Glacier Lodge Salmon Bake**, 8991 Yandukin Drive, Juneau 99801; (907) 586–8258. It combines some of Alaska's best-known wonders: a flight over Juneau's ice fields and a hearty salmon bake at the isolated lodge, decorated with bear rugs and raccoon skins, and beautifully situated across from Taku Glacier. During the half-hour flight to and from the lodge in a five-passenger Cessna, you look down on the 1,500-square-mile ice fields whose soft ridges of white change to deep blue crevices when pierced by sunlight. Book well ahead as cruise ships often reserve many of the tables. Call the lodge (907) 789–0790 or Wings of Alaska.

Fjords. Along **Tracy Arm Fjord**, 50 miles southeast of Juneau, view jagged cliffs rising to 7,000 feet, and see such frequent wildlife as seals and, in season, humpback whales. **Alaska Rainforest Tours**, 369 South Franklin Street (907–463–3466), provides a six-hour catamaran cruise of this region. **Tracy Arm Fjord Glacier Cruises**, 76 Egan Drive (800–451–5952 or 907–463–5570), offers full-day cruises or a half-day cruise and flight-seeing package.

Skiing. **Eaglecrest Ski Area**, 12 miles from downtown Juneau (write: 155 South Seward Street, Juneau 99801); (907) 586–5284. Eaglecrest sports thirty downhill trails and 10K of nordic (cross-country) trails, plus two chair lifts and a ski school. Among the family-friendly features is a Toddler and Parent program that teaches adults how to ski with tots ages three to five. Rental equipment and a cafeteria are on site. In summer come here to use these trails for scenic hikes.

Gold Panning. Find out about Juneau's gold rush roots with the **Gold Panning and Gold History Tour**, 9085 Glacier Highway, Suite 204, Juneau 99801; (907) 789–0052. Elementary-age children especially like panning for these special nuggets.

Shopping

Of all the U.S. Inside Passage ports, Juneau offers the best place to buy your souvenirs. The shops along South Franklin present an interesting array of T-shirts and trinkets. **Taku Smokeries**, 230 South Franklin Street, Juneau 99801 (800–582–5122 or 907–463–3474), is a fine catch for sending something fishy to the folks back home. The smoked sockeye salmon—a Juneau specialty—is very good.

For another strictly Alaskan souvenir, try the gold nugget jewelry at the **Jewel Box**, 248 Front Street (907–586–2604); or browse **Dockside Jewelers**, 145 South Franklin Street (907–586–3910). For Alaskan native arts and crafts, head for the **Mt. Juneau Trading Post**, 151 South Franklin Street (907–586–3246); and **Raven's Journey**, 2 Marine Way, #124 (907–463–4686), which specializes in masks, totems, and jewelry.

SPECIAL EVENTS

February: Alaska Gospel Music Festival, with fine choirs and singers; Winterfest Carnival.

April: Sea-to-Ski Relay, more than 700 athletes gather for the eighteenth annual relay combining skiing, running, and biking; Alaska Folk Festival, a state celebration usually held the second week in April.

May: Juneau Jazz & Classics, renowned jazz musicians celebrate Alaska's Inside Passage Mayfest.
June: Friday Concerts in the Park.
July: Art from the Arctic Festival.
August: Golden North Salmon Derby.
December: Torchlight Parade at nearby Eaglecrest Ski Area, the only developed downhill ski facility in southeast Alaska.

DAY TRIPS

Admiralty Island National Monument, Information Center, 8461 Old Dairy Road, Juneau 99801; (907) 586–8751. You can reach the island, part of the Tongass National Forest, by sea plane from Juneau or Sitka, or by ferry. With beaches, meadows, trees, and an abundance of wild berries, this island supports a large population of brown bears. Also, a significant number of bald eagles nest along the coast. To fish and cruise in the waters surrounding Admiralty Island National Monument, contact **Ocean Ranger Charters,** 6744 Gray Street, Juneau 99801; (800) 233–2033. These outings also take you ashore to natural hot springs and secluded coves. Even though Admiralty Island has a few cabins and campsites, we do not recommend bedding down in the middle of bear country. Contact the U.S. **Forest Service,** 101 Egan Drive, Juneau 99801 (907–586–8751), for conditions and more information.

Alaska Travel Adventures, 9085 Glacier Highway, Suite 204, Juneau, Alaska 99801; (907) 789–0052. They offer a three-hour float trip (calm water, beautiful scenery) down Mendenhall River past icebergs and forests; it includes a smoked salmon snack.

Alaska Discovery Expeditions, 234 Gold Street, P.O. Box 20669, Juneau (907–586–2332), offers kayak day trips, heli-hiking, and a day-long tour of a bear sanctuary on Admiralty Island. A charter plane drops you off, and a guide leads you to Pack Creek for a glimpse of the bears and bald eagles. Be sure to follow the guide's directions. Bears, alas, are not at all like Winnie-the-Pooh; they are wild and dangerous.

Several outfitters get you paddling Juneau's waters in a **kayak.** Besides Alaska Discovery Expeditions, try **Custom Kayak Adventures,** 2215 Meadow Lane, Juneau 99801 (907–789–0326); and **Kayak Express,** 4107 Blackerby Street, Juneau 99801 (907–780–4591).

If your cruise of the Inside Passage does not go to Glacier Bay National Park, or if you are traveling through Alaska on your own, be sure to visit **Glacier Bay National Park,** one of southeast Alaska's most impressive sights. The easiest access to the park is by boat or plane from Juneau. See the chapter on Glacier Bay National Park.

WHERE TO STAY

For comfortable accommodations, try the **Westmark Juneau,** 51 West Egan Drive, Juneau 99801; (800) 544–0970 or (907) 586–6900. It's conveniently located across from the waterfront and close to the convention center. The **Baranof Hotel,** 127 North Franklin Street, Juneau 99801 (800–544–0970 or 907–586–2660), is a historic 194-room property. Some rooms come with kitchenettes. The **Prospector Hotel,** 375 Whittier Street, Juneau 99801 (800–331–2711 or 907–586–3737), is near the State Museum and has some rooms with kitchenettes.

Two bed-and-breakfast homes that welcome families: **Blueberry Lodge Bed and Breakfast,** 9436 North Douglas Highway, Juneau 99801 (907–463–5886), is a handcrafted log lodge overlooking a wildlife refuge and near an eagle's nest. **Jan's View Bed and Breakfast,** P.O. Box 32254, Juneau 99803 (907–463–5897), at the base of Mt. Juneau 1.5 miles from downtown, welcomes well-behaved childen. More temporary home than an actual home stay, **the Cashen Quarters Bed and Breakfast,** 315 Gold Street-J93, Juneau 99801 (907–586–9863), features five apartments equipped with kitchen facilities, television, and telephones. For additional bed-and-breakfast options, contact the **Alaska Bed and Breakfast Association** (907–586–2959) and the other registries listed in the chapter Cruising the Inside Passage.

For those looking for a rough-it-back-to-basics Alaskan retreat, a U.S. Forest Service **cabin** in the Tongass Forest comes with a wood stove and plywood bunks. Contact the Forest Service at Juneau's Centennial Hall (907–586–8751), and reserve in advance.

WHERE TO EAT

What's an Alaskan tour without a salmon bake, many of which are offered in and around Juneau? Some options: The **Gold Creek Salmon Bake,** 1061 Salmon Creek Lane, Juneau 99801 (907–789–0052), has an authentic Alaskan menu of King Salmon. After this meal try your luck at panning for gold in the creek. The **Thane Ore House Halibut Salmon Bake,** 4400 Thane Road, (907–586–3442), serves up salmon and has on site a small mining museum and a fish hatchery. Don't forget about the food and the flight at the **Taku Glacier Lodge Salmon Bake** (described earlier), 8991 Yandukin Drive, Juneau 99801; (907) 586–8258.

After a full day of sight-seeing, take a break in town at the **Heritage Coffee Company,** 174 South Franklin (907–586–1752 or 800–478–JAVA), where the cappuccino's excellent, and at lunchtime, the soups and sandwiches are good. For some evening entertainment with dinner, try **The Fiddlehead Restaurant and Bakery**, the Driftwood Lodge, 429 Willoughby Avenue West; (907) 586–3150. The live jazz and classical piano music is as much a treat as their homemade desserts. For more dining options obtain *Juneau Alaska Attractions and Services* from the Juneau Convention and Visitors Bureau.

FOR MORE INFORMATION

Juneau Convention and Visitors Bureau, 369 South Franklin, #201, Juneau 99801; (907) 586–1737 or Fax (907) 463–4961. The **Juneau Chamber of Commerce**, 124 West Fifth Street, Suite 201, Juneau, Alaska 99801; (907) 586–2323 or Fax (907) 463–5515. **Juneau Visitor Information**, Davis Lodge Cabin, 134 Third Street, Juneau, Alaska 99801; (907) 586–2201, Fax (907) 463–6304, or events hotline at (907) 586–JUNO.

For a **marine forecast** call (907) 586–3997. The **Alaska State Troopers**, 10½ Mile Glacier Highway (907–789–2161), offer information on road conditions. (Don't lose their number in winter.)

Emergency Numbers

Ambulance, fire, police: 911

Bartlett Memorial Hospital, 3260 Hospital Drive, 3½ Mile Glacier Highway; (907) 586–2611. Contact them about twenty-four-hour emergency pharmaceutical needs.

Pharmacies: Juneau Drug Company, Front and Seward streets; (907) 586–1233

Poison Control: (800) 478–3193

41
KETCHIKAN

Ketchikan is Alaska's southernmost major city, and reputedly the wettest spot in Alaska with an average 165 inches of rain each year. Totem poles, salmon, and nearby Misty Fjords National Monument make it famous. Ketchikan, the fourth-largest city in Alaska, is one of the centers of the salmon industry.

GETTING THERE

Ketchikan, situated on the lower tip of Alaska's panhandle on the southwestern shore of Revillagigedo Island, is just ninety minutes by air (660 air miles) from Seattle. Ketchikan's **Alaska Marine Highway** ferry terminal is 1 mile northwest of the town, on the North Tongass Highway; (907) 225–6182 or (800) 642–0066. Ferries travel to Ketchikan from Seattle (a forty-hour trip), from Prince Rupert, B.C. (six hours), and from southeast Alaskan communities. **Alaska Airlines** flies from Seattle, landing on Gravina Island, which is just a five-minute ferry ride across the Tongass Narrows into town.

GETTING AROUND

Ketchikan has limited city bus service, although some buses meet the ferries. Match schedules by consulting with the Alaska Marine Highways office.

WHAT TO SEE AND DO

Start off on the right foot by picking up a map. Sign up for a walking tour with guides from the **Visitor Center**, 131 Front Street (907–225–6166), or, because Ketchikan, like most Alaska towns, is small, browse on your own. On your walking tour, venture over to **Thomas Basin**, one of the three major harbors in Ketchikan, and watch the fishermen pull up their nets after a day's catch.

Stroll by infamous **Creek Street Historic District**, a row of painted wooden houses on stilts, which in gold rush days, as legend has it, housed Dolly's ladies of the night. These shops now sell jewelry, books, and cards. Legend has it that the reason Dolly owned so many frame houses is that the law, such as it was, specified that if you had more than two unmarried women in a home, the property could be labeled a whorehouse and was therefore illegal. To get around this, Dolly bought up a row of houses and put two "working girls" in each. Only the most ardent of gold rush nostalgia buffs will enjoy **Dolly's House Museum**, 24 Creek Street, this madam's former home filled with some of her memorabilia. A better bet might be to use the time perusing the boutiques.

A small museum, but worth a stop, especially in bad weather, is the **Tongass Historical Museum**, Ketchikan Centennial Building, 629 Dock Street; (907) 225–5600. It displays Alaskan Indian artifacts, art, and has research facilities. If you're short on time, skip this and head for the totem poles and objects at the **Totem Heritage Center**, Saxman Totem Park, and Bight State Site.

Some kids love fish hatcheries, while others hate the thought of them, let alone the fishy smell. Depending on your brood, you might also stop at the **Deer Mountain Fish Hatchery**, 1158 Salmon Road (907–225–6760), near the Totem Heritage Center.

For more Indian culture, you may want to stop at the **Shotridge Studios Cultural Center**, 407 Stedman Street; (907) 225–0407 or (800) 770–0407. Not only will you find a museum display and gift shop, but sometimes in summer you can see performances of the Tongrass Tribe Dancers, a Tlingit dance group whose families are descendants of Ketchikan's original people. Also, Monday through Saturday between 9:00 A.M. and 5:00 P.M. watch Isreal Shotridge, a Tlingit Master Carver, at work carving totem poles.

Totem Poles

For nearby totem poles, walk the 6 blocks from the dock, or take an inexpensive cab ride to the **Totem Heritage Center**, 601 Deermount Street; (907) 225–5900. This small museum houses the largest collection of unaltered totem poles in Alaska. The thirty-three poles on display were retrieved from nearby abandoned Tlingit and Haida Indian villages. Up-close, these massive, unpainted, cedar forms convey a powerful presence with their intricate carvings of teeth and combinations of human, whale, and beaver features.

Head south of town for about 3 miles to **Saxman Totem Park** where, displayed in a parklike, outdoor setting, is reputedly the world's largest collection of totem poles. Kids like deciphering the carvings and hiding

The striking features of this mask lend insight into the lives of native Alaskans. (Courtesy Alaska Tourism Marketing Council)

behind these massive structures. Associated with the park is the **Saxman Native Village,** P.O. Box 8558, Ketchikan 99901; (907) 225–5163. It features totem carvers and an opportunity to buy native arts and crafts. Head north of town for about 10 miles along North Tongass Highway to the **Totem Bight State Park,** which features a dozen or so poles and a tribal house.

Nature and Green Spaces

Ketchikan provides easy access to two of Alaska's many wonders: the **Tongass National Forest** and, located within it, the **Misty Fjords National Monument,** Tongass National Forest, 3031 Tongass, Ketchikan 99901 (907–225–2148), a twenty-minute float plane ride from Ketchikan. This 2.3 million–acre wilderness serves up pristine Alaska with cascading waterfalls, emerald rain forests, rivers, fjords, and rugged granite cliffs rising 4,000 feet.

With close to 17 million acres, the **Tongass National Forest** is the largest national forest in the U.S. In this expanse of islands, inlets, greenery, glacier channels, and ice fields, you might catch sight of bald eagles, grizzly bears, and trumpeter swans.

An exciting, easy, but somewhat pricey way to see both a part of the

Tongass National Forest and the Misty Fjords National Monument is to book a **float plane** from Ketchikan. An hour's flight-seeing tour gifts you with an aerial view of this wilderness accessible only by boat or float. As your ten-seater plane heads north, an expanse of water, granite cliffs, spruce tree forests, glacial-carved fjords, and snowcapped mountains appears. Below you stretches a vast, still expanse, which you enter by landing on a blue-gray lake, surrounded by cliffs and forests. Several companies offer day-long guided boat and plane tours.

Ask at the visitors center. Companies include **Alaska Cruises, Inc.**, 215 Main Street, Ketchikan (907–225–6044), which has boat and float plane trips; **Misty Fjords National Monument Cruises**, Dept. 1994, P.O. Box 7814, Ketchikan 99901 (907–225–6044 or 907–225–3498); **Ketchikan Air Service**, 1600 Airport Terminal, Ketchikan 99901 (907–225–6608), which also has access for the disabled; and **Taquan Air,** 1007 Water Street, Ketchikan 99901 (800–770–8800 or 907–225–8800).

The sturdy, the stalwart, and the experienced, can hike more than fifteen trails within the monument from easy .25-mile walks to Hugh Smith Lake, to longer and more demanding treks. (As always, wear your bear bells, bring provisions, and only go if you know what you're doing.)

Special Tours

In addition to flight-seeing, save some time for fishing. Anglers should sign up for half-day fishing expeditions to catch Alaska king or silver salmon. Fees for these half-day expeditions generally include a fishing license (required for all nonresidents sixteen years and older). Teens especially enjoy these excursions. Check with the visitors center for a complete list of outfitters. Among them: **Ketchikan Sportfishing**, P.O. Box 3212, Ketchikan 99901; (800) 488–8254 or (907) 225–7526.

Ketchikan Mountain Lake Canoe Adventure, Dept. 1994, 9085 Glacier Highway, Suite 204, Juneau 99801 (907–789–0052), offers canoe tours through the Tongass National Forest from May to September.

Southeast Exposure, Box 9143, Ketchikan, Alaska 99901 (907–225–8829), offers guided sea kayaking trips April through October through Misty Fjords National Monument. Rentals and instruction are available, as well as handicap access.

For a tour that includes wildlife and Native American culture of Alaska's back country and rain forest by canoe with an experienced guide, call **Alaska Travel Adventures**, 9085 Glacier Highway South, Suite 204, Juneau 99801; (907) 789–0052.

SPECIAL EVENTS

February: Festival of the North, a month-long exhibition of the fine arts.

April: First City Folk Festival, local musicians and guests artists perform free concerts.

Mid-May through mid-July: Little League Salmon Derby, King of Kings Salmon Derby, Killer Whale Halibut Derby. Pick up your fishing rod and join the fun.

July: Independence Day Celebration, fireworks.

December: Christmas Festival of Lights and Holiday Ball, holiday celebration.

WHERE TO STAY

Cedar Lodge, 1471 Tongass Avenue, P.O. Box 8331, Ketchikan, Alaska 99901 (907–225–1900), is a small, comfortable hotel about ¼ of a mile from downtown, near the ferry. Rooms include kitchens, living areas, and jacuzzi baths. Ask the front desk about charter fishing excursions and courtesy car shuttles to town.

The Westmark Cape Fox Lodge, in downtown Ketchikan, is open all year, and offers all the modern conveniences, including private baths, room service, suites, a restaurant, access to a downtown tram, and handicap access. Call (800) 544–0970 in the U.S., (800) 999–2570 in Canada, or (907) 225–8001. The **Ingersoll Hotel** is also in downtown Ketchikan; (800) 478–2124 or (907) 225–2124. Open all year, this is an older property whose moderately priced rooms feature televisions and private baths.

Directly across the street from the ferry, and near the airport, is the **Best Western Landing,** 3434 Tongass Avenue, Ketchikan, Alaska 99901; (800) 428–8304 or (907) 225–5166. They offer reasonable rates and a cafe for convenience. Another moderately priced lodging is **Super 8 Motel,** Ketchikan; (800) 800–8000 or (907) 226–9088.

For a comfortable stay near the Behm Canal, try the **Salmon Falls Resort,** Mile 17 North Tongass Highway, P.O. Box 5700, Ketchikan, Alaska 99901; (907) 225–2752 or (800) 247–9059. This comfortable fishing resort features all-inclusive fishing packages that cover meals. The **Waterfall Resort,** P.O. Box 6440, Ketchikan 99901 (800–544–5125 or 907–225–9461), offers packages from May to September that combine accommodations on a remote island and sportfishing.

Several bed-and-breakfast homes welcome families. **The Great Alaska Cedar Works Bed and Breakfast,** 1527 Pond Reef Road, Ketchikan, 99901 (907–247–8287), is 11 miles from Ketchikan's airport; it offers private cottages with featherbeds and welcomes well-behaved children. For additional bed and breakfast homes, contact the registries listed above.

Within the **Misty Fjords National Monument** and the **Tongass National Forest,** rustic cabins are available for rental. These can be reserved up to 180 days in advance. Contact the supervisor, Misty Fjords National Monument, Tongass National Forest, 3031 Tongass, Ketchikan 99901 (907–225–2148); and the Forest Service Information Center, 101 Egan Drive, Juneau 99801.

For additional listings, see *Alaska's Inside Passage,* the vacation planner available from the **Southeast Alaska Tourism Council,** P.O. Box 20710, Juneau 99802; (800) 423–0568.

WHERE TO EAT

Annabelle's Keg & Chowder House, Gilmore Hotel, 326 Front Street (907–225–6009), in a 1920s style, serves a large variety of entrees for breakfast, lunch, and dinner. On Sundays they feature a champagne brunch. Another popular spot is **Rose's Caboose,** 35 North Tongass Avenue Highway; (907) 225–8377. This renovated caboose features counter service, and has the best milkshakes and burgers in town.

Visitors must try the fresh Alaskan seafood. For the best halibut in Ketchikan, try a favorite of the locals, **Roller Bay Cafe,** 1287 Tongass Avenue; (907) 225–0696. For pizza try **The Pizza Mill,** 808 Water Street; (907) 225–6646. For some ethnic fare try **Chico's,** 435 Dock Street; (907) 225–2833. For pizza as well as Mexican food try **The Diaz Cafe,** 335 Stedman Street (907–225–2257), which serves dishes from the Philippines as well as American fare.

DAY TRIPS

See the Inside Passage Cruising chapter.

FOR MORE INFORMATION

Ketchikan Visitors Bureau, 131 Front Street, Ketchikan, Alaska 99901; (907) 225–6166. For a free visitors guide, call (800) 770–2200.

Emergency Numbers
Ambulance, fire, police: 911
Ketchikan General Hospital, 3100 Tongass Avenue; (907) 225–5171.
    Contact them about twenty-four-hour pharmacy needs.
Poison Control: (800) 478–3193

HAWAII

42
FAMILY TRAVEL ADVICE AND CRUISING TIPS

Every day blossoms as a family adventure in Hawaii. Although Hawaii offers plenty of opportunities to splurge on luxurious hotels and expensive outings, from helicopter rides to boating adventures, Hawaii is affordable as well. You don't need a king's ransom to vacation here: Hawaii's legendary beauty is free. Visit Oahu's north shore, and you watch surfers ride pipelines of sunlit, swirling waves. Drive the road to Hana in Maui, and you wind past hillsides feathered with wild mango, papaya, and bamboo. Hike the Kalalau Trail in Kauai, and you walk along fluted green cliffs ringed by fairy-tale clouds. In Hawaii, for little or no money, explore volcanoes, see canyons that look like moonscapes of brown ash, and swim by reefs where wild fish nibble bread from your fingers.

If you can look for free, you can stay for relatively little, or opt to splurge on some of the United States's most luxurious resorts. Careful planning and comparison shopping net you bargains on airfare, and vacation packages. If you desire, you can forgo the glitzy resorts for inexpensive, but comfortable lodgings. Well-located and well-priced hotels offer nice beaches and big-enough rooms. A condominium stay not only gives you more space for your money, but also enables you to save food dollars by cooking. Camping costs next to nothing, but puts you in the middle of state parks and scenic beaches.

The islands offer great restaurants with cuisine by noted chefs; but you can also eat well, but inexpensively. Cheap eateries line Waikiki's streets and can be found throughout Hawaii. The islands' small towns offer local restaurants whose ambiance, entrées, and prices please both the palate and the budget. With the money you save on lodging and food, you'll even be able to savor the dream option of a helicopter flight to cascading waterfalls, or a raft trip that glides by turtles and dolphins.

Whether you choose a luxurious hotel, a condominium stay, or a camping trip—or combine these—your family vacation to Hawaii comes with the magic of black-sand beaches, grotto-carved swimming holes, gardens filled with butterflies, and hibiscus as big as your heart.

FAMILY-FRIENDLY MONEY-SAVING TIPS

Check out airline packages. Often an airline can package a Hawaiian vacation—with airfare from the mainland, and interisland fare, plus lodging at a condo or a resort—for less than you could if you booked yourself.

Check the tour packagers. These companies also often have prices for lodging, air, and car rental at rates significantly less than you could find by reserving yourself. Mix and match stays at hotels and condos.

Hawaii on a Budget, 1 North First Street, San Jose, California 95113; (800) 221–3949. This subsidiary of Classic Tours specializes in reliable, good value accommodations. **Creative Leisure** packages vacations at condos and hotels, including airfare and rental car; (800) 426–6367. **Runaway Tours** (800–622–0723) offers packages sold only through travel agents to about thirty-five family-friendly resorts, hotels, and condominiums in Hawaii. **Village Resorts,** 3478 Buskirk Avenue, Suite 275, Pleasant Hill, California 94523 (800–542–4253), offers packages at several hotels and condominiums on Maui and Kauai. **Hawaiiana Resorts**, 1270 Ala Moana Boulevard, Honolulu, 96814 (800–367–7040), represents primarily condominiums plus some hotels on Maui, Oahu, and the Big Island.

Consider a condominium. With condominiums plentiful and well located, savvy families book these for the added space, and the family-friendly amenities of pools, kitchens, laundry facilities, and sometimes even kids' programs. (See individual island chapters for specifics about Aston condominiums, and others.)

Other Options

Hideaways International. With this membership vacation home and referral club, you select accommodations from a catalog, and speak directly with the owner. Members receive a 10 percent discount on Aston properties. There is a yearly membership fee, or a trial fee for four months. Hideaways International offers many condo properties. Call (800) 843–4433 or (508) 486–8955 in Massachusetts.

Bed-and-Breakfast stays. These not only put you in neighborhoods, but often give you privacy, lawns, and kitchenettes. **Hawaii's Best Bed and Breakfast,** P.O. Box 563, Kamuela, Hawaii 96743, represents about one hundred accommodations throughout Hawaii, many are cottages on farms, or private estates. For example, Malama Llama, on the Big Island,

even lets your kids get acquainted with the farm's furry and friendly llamas. Puu Manu, Big Island, in Waimea, Parker Ranch Country, is a converted horse barn with pine floors and the original stall doors, plus a full
kitchen, a deck with a view, and two beds. For brochures, call (808)
885–4550; for reservations only, (800) 262–9912.

Bed and Breakfast of Hawaii, P.O. Box 449, Kapaa, Kauai, Hawaii
96746, represents about two hundred places throughout the islands, with
about seventy on Kauai. Ask for their guide *Bed and Breakfast Goes
Hawaiian* (fee); (800) 733–1632.

Island Hopping

Try an island-hopping package. A tour operator can often combine
round-trip airfare and sight-seeing for less than if you booked these yourself. For example, **Akamai Tours** offers a one-day excursion to the Big Island highlights that covers 260 miles from Kona through Volcanoes
National Park, to an orchid nursery to Hilo. Ask about special prices for
children under twelve. Akami offers day tours of Maui and Kauai as well.

Akamai also offers various fly/drive packages that may be booked
with or without overnights at hotels. Call Akamai Tours at (800)
922–6485 from the mainland or (808) 971–3131 in Honolulu. **Polynesian Adventure Tours** offers similar island-hopping packages. Call (808)
833–3000 on Oahu, (808) 877–4242 on Maui, (808) 246–0122 on
Kauai, and (808) 329–8008 on Hawaii.

Aloha Airlines (800–367–5250), and **Aloha Island Air**
(800–323–3345) both offer interisland travel, and a slightly discounted
price for children under twelve. Aloha Island Air lands at airfields that
are too small for jets.

Consider purchasing a **Hawaiian AirPass from Hawaiian Airlines**
(800–367–5320); like a Eurail train pass, this voucher allows *unlimited*
interisland flights for five, seven, ten, or fourteen days. Seniors over sixty
and children under twelve receive a discount. You can buy a voucher for
this pass and book an airline seat through Hawaiian Airlines, or through
your travel agent. If you pick up your pass in Hawaii, you will need to
show the Hawaiian airlines agent your airline ticket to Hawaii as well as
a photo identification card. You can and should still reserve seats even
though you are using a pass. To maximize your free flying time, pick up
your pass on the day of your first interisland flight (not necessarily on
the day you arrive in Hawaii).

FOOD

Ask about kids' (Keiki) menus. Many restaurants offer but don't advertise
these.

Find the early bird specials. These often reduce a full meal to $7.00–$8.00 if you arrive before 6:00 or 6:30 P.M., a convenient family dining time.

Check the free tourist guides. For example, *Spotlight Oahu* and other free island tourist guides, such as *Guide to Maui,* feature discount coupons to restaurants and attractions.

HAWAII MUSTS

Rental Cars

Book your rental car well in advance, and book it from a reliable rental company. Rental cars are a popular, almost necessary item when visiting the islands. At peak times, rental cars can be scarce. Be sure to get a confirmation number when making your reservation. As an added measure of assurance, call the rental agency again a week or so before your trip just to be sure the agency has the car, or van, that you want.

Read Ahead with Your Children

Share the islands' legends and culture with your kids by reading these children's books.

From the University of Hawaii Press (808–956–8697). *Hawaii Is a Rainbow,* Stephanie Feeney. A picture book pairing colors with photographs of Hawaiian people, plants, and animals. For preschoolers.

A Is for Aloha, Stephanie Feeney, offers wonderful photos of Hawaiian life and culture for little kids.

Sand to Sea, Marine Life of Hawaii, Stephanie Feeney and Ann Fielding, is a photographic guide to the islands' beaches, tide pools, reefs, and sea life.

And the Birds Appeared, Julie Stewart Williams. A tale of Maui, Hawaii's mythical boy hero. For preschoolers through second grade.

Maui Goes Fishing, Julie Stewart Williams. Relates how Maui "pulled up" the islands of Hawaii with his fish hook. For preschoolers through second grade.

Hawaiian Legends of Tricksters and Riddlers, Vivian L. Thompson. Retold oral tales based on legends. For ages eight to twelve.

From Island Heritage Books (808–487–7299). These books for preschoolers to second graders come with cassette tapes: *Let's Learn to Count in Hawaiian, Let's Learn the Hawaiian Alphabet,* and *The Story of Aloha Bear.*

From Hawaiian Island Concepts. Peter Panini's Children's Guide to the Hawaiian Islands, Stacey Kaopuiki. Friendly illustrations and brief bits of island information for first and second graders.

From Woodson House Publishing, P.O. Box 16536, Kansas City, Missouri 41335.

Pearl Harbor Child: A Child's View of Pearl Harbor—from Attack to Peace, Dorinda Makanaonalani Nicholson. The author relates her experience as a native island grade-schooler in Honolulu at the time of the Pearl Harbor attack. This kid's eye view of war should interest your grade school children.

From John Muir Publications. Kidding Around The Hawaiian Islands, A Young Person's Guide, Sarah Lovett. Part of a series, this book offers fun facts and tourist information that appeal to ages eight to eleven.

From The Bess Press, Inc. (808–734–7159). *Hawaiian Word Book,* illustrated by Robin Yoko Burningham. Preschoolers to adults will enjoy learning these basic Hawaiian words for food, natural things, numbers, and family relationships.

Peppo's Pidgin to Da Max, Douglas Simonson. Preteens will love the cartoons, as well as the irreverent guide to local lingo.

Fax to DA Max, Everything You Never Knew You Wanted to Know About Hawaii, Jerry Hopkins and others. The lists include the sixteen worst Polynesian song titles, twelve locals who had to leave the island to get famous, the ten worst shark attacks, and lots more, but only through 1985, the date of publication.

Hiking books. These are good guides to the island's outdoor fun.

Hawaiian Hiking Trails, Craig Chisholm, the Fernglen Press. It offers trail suggestions on all of the islands.

Hiking Kauai, Robert Smith. Hawaiian Outdoor Adventures offers detailed information on island trails. *Hiking Maui,* by the same author, does the same for Maui.

From Prima. Paradise Family Guides offers a series of books on the islands, which offer suggestions on sites, restaurants, and more to help you maximize your vacation enjoyment.

CRUISING TIPS:
HOW TO SAVE MONEY ON THE SEAS

Currently, **American Hawaii Cruises,** 550 Kearny Street, San Francisco, California 94108 (800–765–7000), is the only cruise ship that regularly sails the Hawaiian islands, offering stops at fours islands—Oahu, Kauai, the Big Island, and Maui.

This is a great way to sample the islands' diversity without the hassles of packing, unpacking, and schlepping children and luggage to several hotels. The something-for-everyone events from shows, to bridge, to dancing, and children's activities, offer families time to be together and

Everyone has a great time on a cruise aboard the S.S. Independence. (Courtesy American Hawaii Cruises)

apart. To entice families, American Hawaii Cruises frequently lets children under sixteen cruise free on most sailings when accompanied by two full-fare adults who book cabin category "I" and above.

In addition, American Hawaii offers single parents a break. When these parents pay 160 percent of full fare, one child cruises free on most sailings. Also, if bunking with your teens makes you bonkers, then try this solution. In certain categories, you can reserve a second cabin for children sixteen and under at 50 percent of the regular fare.

Both the SS *Constitution* and the SS *Independence* offer children's centers with supervised activities in the summer and at Christmas for kids ages five to twelve, and thirteen to sixteen from 8:00 A.M. to 11:00 A.M., 1:00 P.M. to 5:00 P.M., and 7:00 P.M. to 10:00 P.M.

FAMILY COST-SAVING TIPS

Cruising, contrary to some popular myths, can be a cost-conscious vacation, with an up-front price, few extras (except drinks and shore tours), and good value when adults share bunks with kids.

To get the best deal possible, follow these tips.

1. **Book ahead.** Book six months ahead to grab the ship, the sailing, and the cabin of your choice. Booking early assures you one of the limited number of four-person cabins. The deeply discounted berths for third and fourth passengers let you take along kids and grandparents at a fraction of the individual fares.
   While cruise lines do offer last-minute deals, the best buys come with an early purchase because this allows you to reserve what you want, not just what's available. Early bookings also sometimes come with discounts that range from 5 to 15 percent.

2. **Share a cabin.** The great bargains begin with four in a cabin. Although the first two passengers pay full fare, the third and fourth persons—children or adults—cruise for as much as 70 percent less. But be aware: Some three-quarter rates don't include airfare.

3. **Choose a less expensive cabin.** Inside and lower down means savings. Surprisingly, the higher priced cabins—outside on upper decks—sway the most, while midship cabins are the best for those prone to seasickness.

4. **Sail the value season when rates run 10–15 percent less.** Check the schedules for shoulder season sailings.

5. **Book with a large volume cruise agency.** These cruise-only travel agencies and cruise discounters buy blocks of cabins and then pass savings along. The more expensive and lavish your cabin and cruise, and the longer your trip, the better your savings may be. Some agencies to consider include **South Florida Cruises**, 3561 Northwest Fifty-third Street, Ft. Lauderdale, Florida 33309 (800–327–SHIP or 305–739–SHIP); and **The Cruise Line, Inc.**, 4770 Biscayne Boulevard, Miami, Florida 33137 (800–327–3021 or 800–777–0707 in Florida).

6. **Book bargain airfares or use frequent flier mileage.** Airfare to Hawaii is expensive. By following the airfare specials, you may sometimes be able to find a better air deal than the cruise ships.

7. **Research special promotions and sailings.** Cruise lines sometimes offer special promotions to lure passengers. Ask your travel agent to tell you what special packages and theme trips, from exercise cruises to big band sounds, may be coming up.

8. **Join or create a group.** Check with your alumni, retirement, and professional organizations for discounted cruise bookings. Create your own group, especially easy for large family reunions. With fifteen full-fare bookings (7½ cabins), travel agents commonly book the sixteenth person free. A few agents will work a deal with ten full-fare cruisers. Ask.

9. **Use land packages.** Extend your vacation by taking advantage of the well-priced pre- or postcruise land packages.

10. **Pick your shore tours carefully.** Resist the temptation to rush up the

first day and book organized shore tours. Most of the time, these are nonrefundable. Except for special outings on the water, excursions to volcanoes park, town, or the beach can be more fun and even less expensive for a family of four if you go on your own. As soon as possible book a rental car on each island. You can book these when you buy shore tours. Most of the time, the cars will be waiting for you at the dock. Another tip: Find out what rental company the cruise line uses, call their toll-free number, and book your own car—just to be sure. Then, ask if this can be driven to the dock with all the others. You'll avoid both the long lines on board ship to book and the possibility of not obtaining a vehicle. Because of their popularity, rental cars are in short supply in Hawaii.

11. **Purchase trip cancellation insurance.** Without insurance a cancellation within thirty days may cause you a large penalty, and a two-days-before-sailing flu will cost you the entire vacation. Check to see that the insurance also covers trip interruption, as well as cruise and airline default.

Many cruise lines sell their own insurance. NACOA agents offer Safe Sail Insurance. Travel Guard, another frequently used plan, is available through agents or directly. Call (800) 826–1300. In Wisconsin, call (800) 634–0644.

43
HAWAII:
THE BIG ISLAND

No tour of Hawaii is complete without a visit to the island of Hawaii, known also as the Big Island. This is the largest of Hawaii's islands, with 4,038 square miles. This is the Hawaii of legendary volcanoes and landscapes of lava-striped earth, complete with the active volcano Kilauea, which still shoots red-hot lava, steaming into the Pacific or oozing over a roadside. And on this island you'll also enjoy good snorkeling, lush gardens, and languid waterfalls.

GETTING THERE

Hilo International Airport (808–934–5801), on the eastern side of the island, is the largest airport. Rental cars and taxis are available. The Keahole Airport (808–329–2484) services Kona on the west coast with interisland carriers, and local flights. The Waimea-Kohala Airport, Kamuela (808–885–4520), is a small airport offering service to the Waimea area in the north.

GETTING AROUND

If you want to do much sight-seeing, rent a car. If you want to rent a car in Hilo, and then drop it off in Kona, ask ahead of time about the drop-off charges. Rental car companies available at the Hilo Airport include Avis (808–329–1745), Dollar (808–961–6059), Hertz (808–935–2896), and National Car Rental (808–329–1674). The same companies are represented in Kona: Avis (808–935–1290 or 800–331–1212), Dollar (808–961–6059 or 800–800–4000), Hertz (808–935–2896 or 800–654–3131), and National Car Rental (808–935–0891 or 800–227–7368).

The **Mass Transportation System** (MTS), 25 Aupini Street, Hilo (808–961–6722), operates the **Hele-On Bus.** Taxi service is available in Hilo through **Hilo Harry's** (808–935–7091) and **Bob's Taxi** (808–959–4800). In Kona, call **Paradise Taxi** (808–329–1234) or **Marina Taxi** (808–329–2481).

Bicycles offer a chance to travel at a more leisurely pace, but the roads are rough and sometimes dangerous. Families with teens who are skilled cyclists can rent bikes at **Pacific United Rental,** 1080 Kilauea Avenue, Hilo (808–935–2974); or **Bicycle Warehouse,** 74–5539 Kaiwi Bay 5, Kailua-Kona (808–329–9424).

WHAT TO SEE AND DO

The Eastern Side: Hawaii Volcanoes National Park

If you only have one day on the eastern side of the island (cruise ships dock in Hilo just for the day), head straight to **Hawaii Volcanoes National Park,** about 30 miles (forty-five minutes) southwest of Hilo. (Follow Route 11 south and the signs that say TO VOLCANO.)

At the **Hawaii Volcanoes National Park Visitor Center,** P.O. Box 52 (808–967–7311), watch a twelve-minute volcano film and pick up the *Road Guide To Hawaii Volcanoes National Park,* an indispensable book with clear explanations and mile markers that make a self-driven tour easy and informative. There are two places to eat nearby. If hungry, walk across the street to **Volcano House,** Box 53, Hawaii Volcanoes National Park, perched at the edge of the Kilauea Crater; (808) 967–7321 or (800) 325–3535. A buffet lunch is served from 11:30 to 1:30, and dinner is from 5:30 to 8:00 P.M. Be careful: Tourists arrive by the busload—mostly for lunch—and the place is often crowded. A snack bar also serves a small selection of sandwiches, cookies, and fruit salad.

An alternative is to have breakfast, or lunch on pastas and good burgers, at the **Volcano Golf and Country Club.** Two miles south of the park entrance, take the turnoff near the Kilauea Military Camp; (808) 967–7331.

To explore **Hawaii Volcanoes National Park,** wear good sneakers or hiking boots because you'll want to wander along the numerous trails, many of which are short and easily negotiated by small children. Dress in layers, as the weather is changeable, and bring along some rain gear. In addition to the 150 miles of hiking trails, there are also several scenic driving routes.

Tour **Crater Rim Drive,** which makes an 11-mile circuit around Kilauea caldera, taking you through steaming **sulphur banks,** a rain forest of ohio trees, and roadsides full of ferns, to scenic stops at the **Kilauea Iki Crater,** a crusted lava lake 3,000 feet wide, where steam vents form clouds. Other highlights: **the Thurston Lava Tube and Devastation Trail.** At the lava tube, visitors walk through the .3-mile tunnel of a cooled down lava flow. Along **Devastation Trail,** a .4-mile boardwalk through the swath of 1959 lava destruction that felled an ohio tree forest, the contrast of the white gray limbs against the blackish brown ground gives kids a sense of volcanic force.

At the **Keanakako'i Crater,** a great pit, the fissures in the ground and the black lava fingers that flowed into rifts impart an eerie sense of drama. Steam vents dot the road from here to the **Halemaumau Crater,** where sulfur escapes into the air. (Those with asthma or respiratory problems should roll up their windows and drive by. Don't stop.) Hawaiians say that Halemaumau is the home of Pele, the goddess of volcanoes.

Visit the **Thomas A. Jaggar Museum,** adjacent to the Hawaiian Volcanoes Observatory; (808) 967–7643. Kids love the clever exhibits of seismographs and scientific explanations for volcanic eruptions that are coupled with dioramas of the Hawaiian legends of Pele. This is a true natural history museum, featuring historical documentaries of volcanic eruptions and self-guided tours.

The **Chain of Craters** road takes you 25 miles past more rift zones and crater overlooks. Check with the visitors center or one of the park rangers to see if you may drive right up to some of Kilauea's most recent lava flows.

Hilo

Hilo, the capital, curls around the harbor on the island's east side. The city, with its frequent "liquid sunshine" is a fishing and flower center. Start early by catching the outdoor fish auction with its pungent smells at the **Suisan Fish Market,** Lihiwai Street at the Wailoa River (daily except Sunday).

Gardens and Green Spaces. The frequent rain and sun keeps Hilo lush; it's home to several flower nurseries and gardens. The colorful **Liliuokalani Gardens,** Lihawai Street and Banyan Drive, exhibit Hilo's Japanese influence, with arched bridges and pagodas adorning its thirty acres. With picnic tables and rest rooms, this is a good run-off-some-energy stop. For more flowers stop by **Orchids of Hawaii,** 2801 Kilauea Street (808–959–3581); and **Hilo Tropical Gardens,** 1477 Kalanianaole Avenue (808–935–4957).

For more extensive gardens, tour **Hawaii Tropical Botanical Gardens,** a nature preserve and sanctuary at Onomea Bay, about 7 miles north of Hilo, RR 143–A, Papaikou 96781; (808) 964–5233. Wear pants and long sleeves, carry an umbrella or bring a rain slicker, and use bug spray—but all this is worth it if you like gardens. From Highway 19 north take a right turn where the sign says SCENIC ROUTE 4 MILES LONG. Continue for about 1 mile to the Old Yellow Church, which marks the garden's parking area. Purchase tickets here, grab a trail map for a self-guided tour, and board the van that takes you the a short distance to the gardens. (If you've forgotten your bug spray or your umbrella, these are available for your tour at the small shelter near the van pick-up and drop-off point.)

Go slowly to savor these forty-five acres, which currently include twenty acres of gardens with more than 1,800 species of plants. Allow at least an hour or more. The trail winds you past such niceties as Turtle Point, where the sea spray shoots in the air, and sometimes you see turtles; Lily Lake, filled with koi; Cook Pine Trail, which ends in an amazingly tall tree; and bird aviaries where Hama and Kua, two blue-and-yellow macaws sometimes say "hello" after some coaxing. (Don't feed them.) Other trails take you by bunches of palm trees, a waterfall, orchids, brightly colored ginger plants, cascades of heliconias, and much more. Kids need to walk here as some paths won't accommodate strollers, but most children will enjoy the peaceful, flowering scenery.

Visit **Rainbow Falls**, about 2 miles from Hilo's harbor in Wailuku River Park, for an easy look at this staple of Hawaiian legend. In the morning sun, the splashing waters create a colorful rainbow as it tumbles 125 feet. For another view, try the walkway behind the tumbling water.

Beaches. Locals recommend three beaches most often: **Coconut Island Park**, near the Liliuokalani Gardens, has shade, picnic tables, a view, and a natural shallow area good for kids. **Onekahakaha Beach Park**, off Machida Lane, has a beach, lifeguards, and an area protected by a breakwater. (Swim only within the breakwater; outside of it the waves and undertow are too rough for safety.) While not hard to get to, the directions sound complicated. Ask the locals for the specifics. **Richardson's Ocean Park**, 25 Aupini Street (808–935–3830), offers good snorkeling and swimming.

Mauna Kea

Mauna Kea, sometimes called the "White Mountain" because of its snow-topped summits, reaches a height of 13,796 feet. To get here the hearty take Route 200 northwest from Hilo, which is isolated, and rough in spots, but affords nice views. Route 200 cuts across the Big Island, intersecting Route 190 near Waimea.

Heading up here is advised *only* for those who have four-wheel-drive vehicles and are expert at mountain driving in bad weather. A typical rental car won't make the trek on this extremely rough and steep road with its frequent wind, rain, and even snow near the top. For those few who are confident and meet all the conditions for this journey, including breathing comfortably at 13,000 feet, the reward is the top-ranked **Mauna Kea Observatory Complex**, located at the mountain's peak. (Don't forget to bundle up, as it's cold at the summit.) On selected weekends from May to September, visitors who reserve well in advance can see, and take a peek through, the various world-class telescopes. Exciting as this sounds, remember that the trip up is demanding and not to be undertaken lightly. Always check ahead, and book in advance with the Observatory; call (808) 935–3371.

Hamakua Coast to Waimea and the Waipio Valley

The Hamakua Coast stretches northward for about 50 miles, from Hilo to Waipio. **Akaka Falls State Park**, Akaka Falls Road, Route 220 (808–933–4200), is about 13½ miles north of Hilo on Route 19, then 5 miles west on Akaha Falls Road. It offers hikes, some uphill, to pretty waterfalls. A circular forty-minute path through ferns, bamboo, and other greenery leads you to **Kahuna Falls**, which tumbles and crashes 100 feet below, and to **Akaka Falls**, which plunges even further to more than 400 feet.

Kolekole Beach Park, just a bit north of Honomu, is a popular spot for locals, but *don't* swim here as the ocean is dangerous and rough. Continue along Route 19 until it branches off to Highway 240. (If you continue west on Route 19 you'll reach Waimea.) Highway 240 ends at the **Waipio Valley**, a scenic swath of greenery with taro fields that stretch out below. Locals recommend you *do not* drive the steep road from here that leads to Waipio. Instead go with those who have been doing this for awhile. The **Waipio Valley Shuttle** (808–775–7121) can lead you in their stalwart vehicles through the Waipio Valley, or try a mule-drawn wagon tour with **Waipio Valley Wagon Tours**, P.O. Box 1340, Honokaa 96727; (808) 775–9518. Purchase tickets for these two-hour tours (bring your own food) at the company's ticket office in Kukuihaele.

Waimea (Kamuela)

To reach Waimea, sometimes called Kamuela to distinguish it from Kauai's Waimea, continue northwest from Akaka Falls on Route 19 to where it branches off to Highway 240 (also called 24). Continue west on Route 19 to Waimea. If you are arriving from the Saddle Road, Highway 200 near the Mauna Kea Recreation Area, continue on Highway 200 to Route 190 to Waimea.

In Waimea be sure to visit the **Parker Ranch**, one of the largest privately owned spreads in the U.S. with 225,000 acres. This ranch gives you a view of cowboy life Hawaiian style. First browse the **Parker Ranch Visitor Center and Museum**, Parker Ranch Shopping Center, Routes 19 and 190, Waimea; (808) 885–7655. The **John Palmer Parker Museum** displays photographs and relates the history of the generations of the Parker family who made this land prosper.

At the ranch, you can opt for a guided tour. The ninety-minute **Paniolo Shuttle Tour** takes you by some ranch highlights. But the most fun is to take a horseback ride (most of the time a "walk"). The view of the undulating grasslands atop the windswept volcanic cones is worth the slow pace; doing this conveys a sense of what it must be like to be a *paniolo* (Hawaiian cowboy). Book tours, as well as the horseback ride, through **Parker Ranch** (808) 885–7655.

You can also visit the **Historic Parker Ranch Homes** on Mamalahoa Highway, the site of the Parker family's 1800s ranch house and museum-like home.

Special Tours

Swoop high above Kilauea's lava in a helicopter. Although expensive, a look into the mouth of a steaming volcano may be a once-in-a-lifetime perspective. Try **Papillon Hawaiian Helicopters**, P.O. Box 384043; (808) 329–0551 in Waikoloa, (808) 329–7700 in Kona, or (800) 367–7095. This company offers a variety of flights that leave from Hilo airport, as well as Waikoloa, Waimea, and Kona. You can book them at the Activity Information Center, 76-5828 Alii Drive, Kailua-Kona, near the Kona Hilton. Another flight-seeing company: **Kenai Helicopters—Kona**, P.O. Box 4118, Kailua-Kona; (808) 885–5833 or (800) 622–3144.

The Western Side: The Kailua-Kona Area

In **Kona** there's a small beach in town if your kids must swim and can't wait for a better, and perhaps, cleaner bit of sand and surf. **Kamakahonu Beach** is across from the King Kamehameha Hotel adjacent to the Kailua Pier, where the water doesn't seem the clearest, but there are no waves.

The Kailua-Kona area on the west coast is the home of much impressive Hawaiian history. In Kailua, the **Hulihee Palace**, 75-5718 Alii Drive (808–329–1877), dates back to 1837. The palace features fine koa wood furnishings, Hawaiian quilts, and tapas.

Even more interesting for learning ancient Hawaiian history is **Pu'uhonua o Honaunau**, formerly called the City of Refuge National Historical Park, off Route 160 about 19 miles south of Kailua-Kona. This sanctuary, established in the fifteenth century, gave refuge to defeated warriors, women, and children in wartime, and to breakers of religious taboos seeking purification by priests. Wander among displays of giant carved idols, ruins of a temple, carved wooden images, historic campsites, and displays of koa wood canoes. Try your hand at an ancient game of *konane* (checkers). A simple peace pervades this 180-acre park, a pleasant place to spend an hour or so imagining the Hawaii of ancient kings and priests, and enjoying a picnic lunch.

Green Spaces, Beaches, and Marine Parks. For a respite, stroll the more than fourteen oceanfront acres of gardens at **Kona Surf Resort and Country Club**, 78-128 Ekukai Street; (808) 322–3411. Located about 6½ miles from Kailua-Kona along Alii Drive, the hotel welcomes drop-ins.

Keauhou Bay, about a half-mile further south, is the sailing point of the *Fair Winds*, 78-7128 Kaleiopapa Street; (808) 322–2788. (Purchase tickets at the small *Fair Winds* shop across the street from the harbor.)

During the one-hour sail to the snorkel spot at **Kealakekua Bay**, a Marine Life Conservation District, the guides fit you with snorkel gear and teach you how to snorkel. While child's sizes, including fins, masks, and flotation vests are on board, it's always a good idea to bring your own just to be sure. The snorkeling here during the day can be more relaxed as this area is not as crowded as Molikini off of Maui. The hard corals and the schools of brightly colored fish—including yellow tangs, surgeon fish, rainbow-hued parrot fish, and ornate butterfly fish—charm kids and adults. From the snorkel area you can see a monument to Captain James Cook, who was killed here in 1778 in a dispute with natives.

Hapuna Beach State Park, north of Kailua-Kona off Route 19 (808–882–1111), offers good snorkeling with schools of tropical fish, but *only* for excellent swimmers who can handle the frequent big waves.

Special Tours. The **Atlantis Submarine** plunges into the ocean off Kona. Young passengers should be at least 36 inches tall and unafraid of tight quarters. The reward: a diver's-eye view of coral and schools of fish without the work of diving. Reserve ahead at the Atlantis Submarine's desk at the King Kamehameha Kona Beach Hotel, Alii Drive; (808) 329–6626 or (800) 548–6262.

Papillon Hawaiian Helicopters (See Special Tours Hilo) has flights that depart from Hilo. Call (808) 329–7700 in Kona or (800) 367–7095. You can book them at the Activity Information Center, 76–5828 Alii Drive, Kailua-Kona, near the Kona Hilton. Another flight-seeing company: **Kenai Helicopters—Kona**, P.O. Box 4118, Kailua-Kona; (808) 885–5833 or (800) 622–3144.

More Sports: Bicycling, Snorkeling, Golf. We suggest biking for experienced mountain bikers only—older teens and fit adults. Bike rental shops include **Chris' Bike Adventure** (808–326–4600), **Mauna Kea Mountain Bikes** (808–885–2091), and **Kona Bike Tours**, inside Hawaiian Pedals, on the boardwalk, Kona Inn Shopping Village, 75-5744 Alii Drive (808–329–2294). Ask about tours down the slopes of Mauna Kea (difficult), through a lush forest, or try a leisurely ride to Kona's historic and tourist spots with Kona Bike Tours.

Snorkel Bob's, near the Kona Hilton's parking lot (808–329–0770), offers snorkel gear and boogie boards, including a selection of prescription-lens masks that make it easy for those who normally wear glasses or contact lenses to see the fish clearly. **King Kamehameha Divers**, in the King Kamehameha Hotel (808–329–5662), offers dives for beginners as well as those who are certified, and some snorkel equipment.

Golf in Hawaii most always comes with a view. Among the courses on the Kona side: **Makalei Hawaii Country Club**, 72-3890 Hawaii Belt Road

(Mamalahoa Highway); (808) 325–6625 or (800) 606–9606. Check the free island and rental car guides for discount coupons, sometimes for as much as 30 percent off greens fees. The **Keauhou-Kona Golf Course**, 78-7000 Alii Drive, Kailua-Kona (808–322–2595) is another good bet. Pricier, but with a spectacular view, is the course at **Mauna Kea Beach Golf Course**, One Mauna Kea Beach Drive, Golf Course, P.O. Box 218, Kamuela, 96743; (808) 882–5888 or (800) 882–6060. One hole tests your skill by having you hit over the Pacific. The **Waikoloa Hilton**, Waikoloa Beach Resort, offers good golfing as well; (808) 885–1234 or (800) 233–1234.

SPECIAL EVENTS

January: In Hilo, see the Hilo to Volcano 31-Mile Ultra Marathon, which takes place midmonth. Also, the Senior Skins Golf Tournament features golf legends.

February: Hilo Mardi Gras.

April: The Merrie Monarch Festival in Hilo features Hawaii's renowned hula competition, festivals, and a parade in celebration of Hawaii's last king, David Kalakaua. The Big Island Bounty Festival features Hawaiian cuisine.

May: Don't miss the Kailua-Kona Triathalon in Kona, which tests athletes with cycling, running, and swimming on a "path."

June: In Hilo, Kohala, and Kona, experience the festivals during the King Kamehameha Celebrations. A prime event for golfing fans is the Mauna Kea Beach Hotel's Pro Am Golf Tournament.

July: The International Festival of the Pacific, Hilo, celebrates the diverse ethnic groups inhabiting Hawaii. On the Fourth of July, see real Hawaiian cowboys strut their stuff at the Parker Ranch Rodeo and Horse Races. Also on Independence Day, witness Turtle Independence Day, the Mauna Lani Bay Hotel and Resort, a day that sees turtles raised in captivity released into the ocean.

September: The Queen Liliuokalani World Championship Long Distance Canoe Racing Champs, in Kona, is one of the major canoe races in Hawaii with men's and women's teams from several countries.

September/October: Aloha Week Festivals take place throughout the Big Island, showcasing Hawaii's history with dance and community celebrations.

October: The Ironman World Triathalon Championship, in Kailua-Kona, tests athletes with a 2.4-mile Waikiki Rough Water Swim, a 112-mile Around-Oahu Bike Race, and a 26.2-mile marathon.

November: The Kona Coffee Festival in Kailua and Keauhou has tours of coffee plantations and ethnic foods.

Try your hand at an ancient game of konane *(checkers) at Pu'uhonua o Honaunau.*
(Photo by the author)

December: Hawaii International Film Festival, Hilo, Kona, Volcano, and Waimea.

WHERE TO STAY

Hawaiian **hotels** have a reputation for being accommodating and costly. Not all lodging in Hawaii is expensive, but you may need to reserve up to a year in advance to reserve a place at some of the state parks, or many months in advance for prime weeks at some of the poshest places. Many establishments offer programs especially for children. As these programs differ, check with individual hotels for details.

Best Buys

Best Budget Lodging. At **Hapuna Beach State Park** rustic cabins cost a nominal rate. No baths, but there is a comfort station on property. You must book these more than a year in advance. Call (808) 329-2944. Volcanoes National Park has cabins at the **Namakani Paio Campground**

(808–967–7321), about 3 miles up from Volcano House, that are equipped with beds and towels for four. Cabins share a bathhouse.
Camping. Volcanoes National Park has campgrounds. Obtain a brochure from **Park Headquarters**, Hawaii Volcanoes National Park (808–967–7311); or from the **National Park Service**, 300 Ala Moana Boulevard, Honolulu 96850 (808–541–2693). Remember that the supply of firewood in Hawaii is sparse, and fire building is dangerous; therefore, tote along a small stove.
Condominiums. Condos offer families welcome breathing space, the convenience of kitchens, and often more room for less money than hotels. Condos are a good buy and come with all the civilized amenities (though make sure that the unit you've rented has air conditioning; not all units in a building do). The **Aston Shores at Waikoloa**, on the Kohala Coast, Route 19, 26 miles north of Kailua-Kona (808–885–5001 or 800–92–ASTON), offers one- and two-bedroom condos, and may by the summer of 1994 offer a limited children's program.
Resorts. The **Royal Waikoloan**, P.O. Box 5300 (808–885–6789 or 800–537–9800), with twenty cabanas and more than 500 rooms, is less pricey than its posh neighbors the Mauna Kea and the Hyatt Regency Waikoloa. The Royal Waikoloan, an older property, offers a beautiful wide beach on the Kohala Coast; family-friendly rooms, many with refrigerators, plus a limited program of children's activities, which could turn into a full-scale program by the summer of 1994. Ask about their special packages, often combined with stays at Outrigger Hotels on another island.
The Big Island offers many **Bed-and-Breakfast** homes. Most of the time these are less expensive than a stay at a comparable resort. Even when priced comparably, bed-and-breakfast inns offer families a personal, neighborly sense of Hawaii with accommodations in a community or on an estate. Not all bed and breakfasts welcome families. Check ahead, and be honest about your family's needs. Reservation services include **Bed & Breakfast Hawaii**, P.O. Box 449 Kapaa (808–822–7771 or 800–733–1632), which services all the Hawaiian Islands. For $12.95 you can order their directory, *Bed and Breakfast Goes Hawaiian*, a thick listing of inns on all the Hawaiian islands, plus tips on local restaurants.
Some family-friendly listings include "H-4C," a guest cottage on nine tropical acres, 4 miles south of Hilo's airport, and about thirty minutes to Volcanoes National Park. "H-43" offers two rooms in an eighty-nine-year-old house in Waimea. A two-bedroom apartment, "H-62," about fifteen minutes from Hapuna Beach, has views of Mauna Kea, and comes with a kitchen. "H-38" offers two guest rooms in a large home overlooking Kealakekua Bay.
Hawaii's Best Bed and Breakfast, P.O. Box 563, Kamuela 96746 (808–885–4550 or 800–262–9912), specializes in upscale properties, some of which may be suites for families.

Resorts with Kids' Programs

The **Mauna Kea Beach Hotel,** One Mauna Kea Beach Drive, Kamuela, 96743; (808–882–7222 or 800–882–6060). Located on one of the area's most beautiful beaches, the hotel also has a world-class art collection. Jewel-colored parrots chatter in the lobby, and museum-quality art—from seventh-century Buddhas to Japanese screens—graces garden walkways. The resort offers a comprehensive, free kids' program for six- to twelve-year-olds that runs summer, Christmas, and Easter from 8:30 A.M. to 4:30 P.M. (with lunch), and again from about 6:00 P.M. to 9:00 P.M. for dinner and movies.

Kona Village Resort, 13 miles north of Kailua-Kona on Route 19, P.O. Box 1299, Kailua-Kona 96745; (808) 325–5555 or (800) 367–5290. This resort creates a Hawaiian village feel by having guests stay in thatched (but plush) *hales* (cottages). This resort has a free, year-round children's program for ages six to twelve from approximately 8:00 A.M. to 5:30 P.M. Early dinner for children at 5:30 P.M. is followed by games and movies. Check to see if their summer programs for tots ages three to five, and teens, are operating when you visit. Full American plan.

The posh **Waikoloa Hilton,** 17 miles north of the Kona Airport (808–885–1234 or 800–233–1234), proffers a Hawaiian "fantasy experience" with its great pool (lots of slides) and dolphin education program. A camp operates daily, all year long, for three to twelve year olds, from 9:30 A.M. to 4:00 P.M. and from 6:00 P.M. to 10:00 P.M. (fee). For teens thirteen to seventeen there are intermittent activities when there is enough demand. Check ahead or ask that the hotel provide something for your teens.

Treat yourself to the top-rated **Mauna Lani Bay Hotel and Bungalows,** One Mauna Lani Drive, 25 miles north of Kailua-Kona; (808) 885–6622, (800) 367–2323, or (800) 992–7987 in Hawaii. It offers a complimentary Camp Mauna Lani Bay for ages five to twelve during summer, Christmas, and Easter from about 9:00 A.M. to 3:00 P.M., and 5:00 to 11:00 P.M. Included are Hawaiian arts and crafts, pole fishing, and water sports.

WHERE TO EAT

Family dining can be inexpensive in Hawaii if you choose wisely, and follow the locals.

In the Hilo Area

For pizza, head for the **Cafe Pesto,** on the east coast of the island at South Hata Boulevard, Hilo; (808) 882–1071. The moderately priced **Pescatore Italian Restaurant,** 235 Keawe Street, Hilo (808–969–9090), has a good marinated tuna, as well as other entrées. The **Queen's Court,** in the Hilo Hawaiian Hotel, 71 Banyan Drive (808–923–9361), is noted for its Friday night seafood buffet. For breakfast, try **Ken's Pancake House,** 1730 Kamehameha Avenue (808–935–8711); or **Don's Family Deli,** Akoni Pule Highway (808–889–5822). **Don's Grill,** 485 Hinano Street (808–935–9099), offers ribs, chicken, homemade chili, and fish for reasonable prices.

On the West Side of the Big Island

On the west side of the island, near Kona and Kealakekua, restaurants of choice include **McGurk's Famous Fish and Chips,** Kailua Bay Shopping Plaza, 75–5699 Alii Drive; (808) 329–8956. Their menu features shrimp and chips with macadamia nut coleslaw. Another good option is the **Ocean View Inn,** in the heart of Kailua on Alii Drive (808–329–9998), with a variety of culinary choices.

At the **Kona Ranch House,** Kuakini and Palani highways (808–329–7061), locals especially recommend the breakfasts. Breakfast, lunch, and dinner are served at the inexpensive **Lanai Coffee Shop** in the Kona Hilton Hotel, 75–5852 Alii Drive; (808) 329–3111.

Fine dining is available at many of the luxury resorts, particularly at the **Mauna Lani,** the **Mauna Kea,** and the **Waikoloa Hilton** (see Where to Stay). These resorts also offer poolside snacks, which sometimes are a good deal, and sometimes are too pricey.

Specialty Foods

Be sure to taste some of the Big Island's special treats. Among the best bites: macadamia nuts, mouth-watering papaya, hearty Kona coffee beans, and real sugarcane. Pick up free samples of Kona coffees and macadamia nuts south of Captain Cook at **Kona Plantation Coffee Co.,** Highway 11, Kona Coast; (808) 328–8424.

Downtown Kona—and other places on the island— features **Lappert's Ice Cream,** Alii Drive Kailua Kona; (808) 326–2290. The popular flavors include papaya, lychee, and coconut macadamia nut fudge.

FOR MORE INFORMATION

Hawaii Visitors Bureau: Hilo, 250 Keawe Street, 96720 (808–961–5797); Kona, 75–5719 West Alii Drive, Kailua-Kona 96740 (808–329–7787). Pick up a copy of their *Accommodation and Car Rental Guide.*
Division of State Parks: (808) 933–4200; **National Park Service,** 300 Ala Moana Boulevard, Honolulu 96850; (808) 546–7584; **Volcanic activity hotline:** (808) 967–7977.

Emergency Numbers

Ambulance, fire, police (island-wide): 911
Poison Control: (800) 362–3585

In Hilo

Hospital: Hilo Hospital, 1190 Waianuenuene Street; (808) 964–4111
Pharmacy: Long's Drugs, 555 Kileau Avenue, Hilo; (808) 935–3357

In Kona

Hospital: Kona Hospital, Kealakekua Avenue; (808) 322–9311
Pharmacy: Kona Coast Drugs, Kailua; (808) 329–8886; Long's Drugs,
75-5595 Palani Road, Kailua-Kona; (808) 329–8477

44
KAUAI

More than one year after Hurricane Iniki devastated Kauai, the bougainvillea is back and so are the sugarcane fields, the fragrant hibiscus, and the ferns feathering the roadsides. On Kauai the famed eucalyptus tunnel that signals the turn-off from Highway 50 toward Poipu still impresses. Magically, none of the aged, towering trees were felled by the winds, a sign many locals interpret as confirming the special spirit of Kauai, known as the Garden Isle. This is an island well on its way to recovery.

Back as well are all of Kauai's golf courses, many businesses, and about 30 percent of the accommodations, including several major hotels, with many more scheduled for openings in 1994. The island, more than a year and a half after the big winds, is almost but not quite as green as before, and it offers tourists two big pluses: fewer crowds and frequent discount packages on lodging, golf, and attractions.

Always less developed than Maui, and more lushly green, Kauai currently presents the languid and less populated Hawaii of long ago. On the sands, the fairways, and the hiking trails, you're likely to savor some space.

Kauai also lends itself to camping and to hiking. These budget-minded alternatives put you in close proximity to the island's natural beauty. But plan ahead, as most spaces book a year in advance.

A word of caution: The isolated beaches that look ideal can be dangerous. Rip tides and strong undertows claim many lives in Hawaii. Read the signs, observe the cautions, and when in doubt, look, but don't swim. When camping, always be prepared for sudden inclement weather, register at park headquarters, and keep to the trails.

GETTING THERE

There are two airports in Kauai. **Lihue,** the larger airport, offers flights from Honolulu through **Aloha Airlines** (808–245–3691), **Hawaiian Airlines** (800–882–8811), or **Mahalo Airlines** (800–277–8338). **Princeville**

Airport, on the beautiful north shore, is serviced by **Aloha Island Air** (808–826–7969).

GETTING AROUND

The airport has shuttle buses, taxis, and rental cars. **Robert's Hawaii Tours** (808–245–9101), **Gray Line Kauai** (808–245–3344), and **Kauai Island Tours** (808–245–4777) offer airport-to-hotel transfers. Taxi companies include **Aloha Taxi** (808–245–4609) and **Lorenzo's Taxi** (808–245–6331).

The most convenient place to rent cars (book ahead) is at the airport. (While one spouse or older teen waits for the luggage, have the other spouse get in the rental car line as these can be long.) Companies include **Alamo** (800–327–9633), **Avis** (800–831–8000), **Budget** (800–527–0700 or 808–245–1901), **Dollar** (800–800–4000 or 808–245–3651), **National** (800–227–7368 or 808–245–5636), and **Hertz** (800–654–3131 or 808–245–3356). **Pedal and Paddle** (808–826–9069) rents mopeds, mountain bikes, helmets, and locks, so you and your teens can enjoy a free-wheeling Kauai tour.

WHAT TO SEE AND DO

Because Kauai's roads circle the island, the best way to discuss sites is by grouping them according to region.

The North Shore: Great Drives, Hikes, and Beaches

The 40-mile, seventy-five-minute drive north from Lihue along Route 56 through **Hanalei** to **Haena State Park**, to **Ke'e Beach** (808–241–3444) at the northwestern end of Kuhio Highway, Route 56, is a scenic delight. Subtle shades of green and sunlight dapple the road to Hanalei, and beautiful beaches and valleys mark the landscape. In Kauai even a main road such as Route 56 blooms with vegetation. For the drive wear (or take along) your bathing suits and your hiking shoes as you may want to pause awhile to sun on the sand, or to hike. But don't be tempted to swim at unknown beaches as the surf and tides can be rough. Swim only where you know it to be safe.

Near the town of Kapaia, take a small detour from Route 56 and travel about 3 miles along Route 583 (Maalo Road) to **Wailua Falls** where twin waterfalls cascade 80 feet over the cliffs.

If you need a beach break, push on to just past Kilauea (and before Princeville) to **Kalihiwai Beach**. To get here from Route 56, detour onto Kalihiwai Road, but don't cross the river. Locals recommend this beach for strong swimmers (ask around, and be sure to check conditions). For a calmer beach, continue along Kalihiwai Road to **Anini Beach County Park,** known for its good snorkeling and windsurfing. You can take Route 56 back to **Princeville,** a north shore resort area that offers options for lunch, golf, and good swimming at the Princeville Resort. Nearby the **Hanalei Valley Lookout** conveys a sense of Old Hawaii with its expanse of taro, and sugar fields cut by the Hanalei River. Although not overly disturbed by tourists or trinket shops, Hanalei, a picture-perfect small coast town, harbors a few nice boutiques for T-shirts and sportswear, plus a few informal eateries. On the main street the 1841 Waiol Mission sparkles, a jewel of stained glass and simple lines.

From Hanalei continue west on Route 56 to **Lumaha'i Beach,** site of some backdrops for the movie *South Pacific,* but DON'T SWIM HERE as the undertow can be deadly. Continue a bit further west to **Haena State Park,** Kuhio Highway, Route 56 (808–241–3444), whose three caves intrigue kids. The **Maniniholo Dry Cave** comes at the end of a lava tube. The **Waikapalae** and **Waikanaloa caves,** both created by the goddess Pele according to legend, impart a sense of ancient Hawaiian power with their crashing waves. At **Ke'e Beach,** about 8 miles west of Hanalei, near the beginning of the Kalalau Trail, many locals like to swim and snorkel when the conditions are right, but be careful of the sometimes rough surf and the undertow. Use good judgment; a safe bet would be to check conditions by calling the authorities or enjoy sunning, sand castle building, and tossing a frisbee with new-found Hawaiian friends.

The **Kalalau Trail,** the land route that stretches for 11 miles one way across the Na Pali cliffs, part of the **Na Pali Coast State Park,** can only be reached by hiking or by boat. These cliffs, once home to ancient Hawaiian kings, impress with their fluted green ridges, secluded caves, and dramatic sea views. The sometimes arduous path starts near Ke'e Beach, dips into deserted beaches (don't swim), and passes slivers of cascading waterfalls. For an easy sampling of these scenic vistas without the work, try a helicopter, raft, or kayak trip (see Special Tours). A doable climb for sure-footed grade-schoolers is the first half-mile (yes, it's uphill) to the first lookout point for **Ke'e Beach,** a windswept swath of sand and sea. From the trailhead to this lookout, wild orchid and kukui trees dot the path. Hold young ones hands so they won't slip on the rocks and roots. With older children or teens, continue for another 1½ miles to **Hanakapiai Beach.** (Be sure to bring water and a nutritious snack such as trail mix.) However tempting it is, swimming is not recommended here.

As the trail cuts through the **Na Pali Coast State Park,** it becomes more arduous. Hiking the entire Kalalau Trail gifts you with incredible views, plus a sense of the solitary majesty of these cliffs. Only hearty, healthy, experienced hikers should attempt the entire trek (11 miles each way). We don't recommend it unless you can deal with backpacks, boots, narrow trails, and sudden weather changes, and lots of climbs. And always check with the park rangers first.

The South Shore: Poipu Area, Great Beaches, Green Spaces, and Golf

The drive from Lihue to the popular **Poipu beach** area is about 14 miles (thirty minutes). Take Route 50 West to the turn-off to Route 520 South. (Some road signs label this as Route 52; but don't worry, you're on the right path.) In **Old Koloa Town** on the way to Poipu, many but not all the stores have reopened. Although some of the souvenir and sandwich shops look off-limits, you can still buy your T-shirts from **Crazy Shirts**, grill your own kebabs at the **Koloa Broiler**, and snack on **Lappert's Ice Cream**.

The Poipu beach area, devastated by Iniki, still offers swimming, and great golf packages. For example, The **Kiahuna Golf Club**, 2545 Kiahuna Plantation Drive (808–742–9595), is open and offering discount rates on a less crowded course.

But drive Poipu's Lawai shore road leading to **Spouting Horn**, a public park where black lava blowholes shoot spray ten to twenty feet in the air, and you can easily sense Iniki's force. Scraggly and denuded palms still dot the roadsides, and some houses still lurch off their foundations. But the spirit of rebuilding predominates, and new lumber seems to sprout almost everywhere.

On the way back from Koloa, take a pleasant detour on Route 530 West (again, also called Route 53) to the Hailima Road to the **National Tropical Botanical Garden**, P.O. Box 340, Lawaii 96765; (808) 332–7361. This little-known island wonder is spread on 186 acres of the Limahuli Valley. Be sure to reserve ahead—before you arrive in Hawaii—as the small tour groups fill quickly and to find out about the Garden's status since Hurricane Iniki.

Kids, especially, appreciate the convenience of the van that transports you to various locales for a leisurely, nonstrenuous walk and talk led by a knowledgeable guide. Here thousands of fragrant orchids, towering palm trees, glistening ferns, and flowers line pathways that stretch to the sea on property once home to Queen Emma. This is the place to teach your kids about plumeria, monkeypod trees, orchids, heliconia, banana plants, as well as the myriad types of palms.

The Waimea Canyon and Kokee State Park

Allow at least a half-day to explore one of Kauai's great wonders: **Waimea Canyon State Park**. Dubbed the "Grand Canyon of the Pacific," it's 1 mile wide and 10 miles long. The entrance is about 36 miles (seventy-five minutes) from Lihue. Along the way to the **Waimea Canyon**

Lookout, at 3,400 feet, several easy hikes yield views of the pink-and-gray striated rock formations. For preschoolers, stroll the Iliau Nature Loop, a flat .3 mile, which gives little ones a chance to "hike," hear birds, and view a dreamscape vista of red cliffs shrouded in mist. At the Waimea Lookout the canyon appears as a dramatic sweep of pink-and-gray striations sporadically marked with small ridges of green, and the silvery streams of waterfalls.

Adjacent to the Waimea Canyon is **Kokee State Park,** Division of State Parks, P.O. Box 1671, Lihue, Hawaii 96766; (808) 241–3444. (The entrance is about 8 miles further along the road.) It features camping facilities and sweeping canyon and mountain views. Maps of the hiking trails can be found at the Kokee Museum of the Kokee Lodge, which serves breakfast, lunch, and dinner.

If you've packed a picnic lunch, a good spot several miles away is **Puu Ka Pele.** Waipoo Falls (if there's been enough rain) beckons, and the covered benches have a canyon view. **The Kalalau Valley Lookout,** at 4,000 feet, offers another spectacular view. Arrive early (before 10:00 A.M.) so you have a better chance of a view unobstructed by clouds.

Other Attractions

You are likely to be driving through Lihue, so take some time to visit the small, but interesting **Kauai Museum,** 4428 Rice Street, Lihue; (808) 245–6931. Inside, you'll enjoy the patina of the fine koa wood tables and calabashes, and the kids will like the items of Hawaiian culture such as quilts, bowls, *ipu* (drums made from gourds), and decorated *tapas* (cloth). A bamboo *ohe hano ihui* (nose flute) gets some giggles. The large 1920s canoe and the photographs of old Hawaii evoke the era before tour buses and big hotels. An adjacent building features scenic photographs of the Na Pali Coast and Waimea Canyon. For a sight-seeing pause, bring sandwiches and plan to use the covered courtyard for a picnic. The gift shop offers a nice selection of books about Hawaii for children, as well as the usual assortment of fish magnets and T-shirts.

Although the **Grove Farm Homestead,** P.O. Box 1631, Lihue 96766 (808–245–3202), is difficult to find—the small sign on Nawiliwili Road is easily missed—it may interest older children. The docent-led tours of this former eighty-one-acre sugarcane plantation started by George Wilcox in 1864 may drag on, but you do learn about that era's Hawaiian life-style. Listen for a bit, then ask if you may stroll the grounds by yourself. The barracks built for the workers provide insight into their lives, plus the sense of the rigors and regulations of plantation life.

Convenient to the Lihue airport, the **Kalapaki Beach,** near Route 51 and the Nawiliwili Harbor, at the now closed Westin Kauai, offers a nice, but not overwhelming swath of sand, but lots of calm surf, great for kids. There is also shopping, dining, and tours at the Kauai Lagoons.

Be sure to take in the breathtaking view of Waimea Canyon, the "Grand Canyon of the Pacific." (Photo by the author)

Golf

Golf is a great island draw, especially because the golf courses are open even if the hotels are not. Kauai sports four of the top ten courses in Hawaii, as rated by *Golf Digest,* including the Prince Course on the North Shore, rated number one. Aficionados say that the courses, restored and reopened before the hotels, entice duffers with discounts and uncrowded greens. Locals, in fact, have been swinging in a golf heaven complete with low fees and no waits.

Among the choices: **The Princeville Makai Golf Course**, highly rated (808–826–3580), and the **Prince Golf Course** (808–826–5000). While the Westin Kauai, on the southeast coast not far from the airport, has yet to set a date for its second debut, golfers get to play its noted **Lagoons Course** (808–241–6000) at a preferred rate when staying at a participating hotel. Their signature, the Kiele course, is also open.

Special Tours

Flight-seeing. Besides hiking, enjoy Kauai's coast by air and by sea. A flight-seeing view of the canyon, while costly, is memorable. Soar above the Alakai swamp, through the Waimea Canyon, and along the Na Pali coast. Float over taro and cane fields, across canyon gorges, next to waterfalls, and landscapes made famous by *Jurassic Park,* and beside the cliff burial caves of ancient kings. Surprisingly, this bird's-eye view gives you a sense of Kauai's impressive greenery. The island is lush after all those winds, but not quite as verdant as before. The fluted Na Pali cliffs still loom majestic, but seem a bit browner, and in places the trunks of uprooted trees litter the hillsides like so many dried white bones.

Among the island's best operators are **Papillon Hawaiian Helicopters,** P.O. Box 339, Hanalei (808–826–6591 from Princeville, 808–245–9644 from Lihue, or 800–367–7095); and **South Sea Helicopters,** P.O. Box 1445, Lihue 96766 (808–245–7781 or 800–367–2914). In Lihue both operators depart from the heliport at the airport. In Princeville, Papillon flies from an airport.

Kayaking. Paddle along the snakelike Hanalei River with **Kayak Kauai Outfitters,** P.O. Box 508, Hanalei 96714, on the main street; (808) 826–9844. This easy ride, perfect for small children, glides past banks lined with java plum trees and yellow-flowered hau bushes, and it ends with some snorkel time at a nearby beach.

Rafting. For a water view of the majestic Na Pali coast, book a **Captain Zodiac** (or Na Pali Zodiac), P.O. Box 456, Hanalei 96714 (808–826–9371 or 800–422–7824). Turtles and spinner dolphins often surface on your way to the sea caves. If possible, book the early morning raft trip as often after about noon the ocean gets rough, precluding the exploration of caves, and often proving too bouncy a ride for some tummies. If you or your children are prone to seasickness, be sure to take the appropriate medication before rafting. (Check with your physician.)

Horseback Riding. **Pooku Stables,** P.O. Box 888, Hanalei 96714 (808–826–6777), offers three types of scenic group rides. See the Hanalei valley, enjoy a longer country ride, or (the most fun) take a three-hour picnic ride to a waterfall. Swimming is allowed. The stable encourages you to bring a bathing suit and hiking shoes.

SPECIAL EVENTS

February: The Captain Cook Festival features food, rides, games, parade, and races.

May: All across the island, May Day is Lei Day in Hawaii, with celebrations and lei-making competitions.

July: Each year, Na Hula Ka'Ohikukapulani displays the traditional dances of Hawaii and Polynesia. Koloa Plantation Days remembers the Hawaiian sugar plantations with week-long celebrations.

August: The island's largest rodeo, the Hanalei Stampede, Pooku Stables.

October: At Kalapaki Bay, it's the Kauai Loves You Triathalon, featuring a 10K run, 40K bike race, and a 1.5K swim.

WHERE TO STAY

Poipu

While the Hyatt has reopened, many of the south shore hotels in and near Poipu, which sustained major storm damage, list only indefinite 1994 reopening dates. These properties include the **Sheraton Kauai Garden Hotel** (800–325–3535); the **Sheraton Kauai Beachfront Hotel** (across the street), Koloa, Kauai 96756 (800–325–3535); the **Poipu Beach Hotel** (800–468–3571); and the **Stouffer Waiohai Beach Resort,** Koloa, Kauai 96756 (808–468–3571 or 800–468–3571).

The **Hyatt Regency Kauai**, 1571 Poipu Road, Koloa 96756 (808–742–1234 or 800–233–1234), Poipu, was the first luxury resort to reopen (March 30, 1993) after Iniki. This resort actually gained 30 more feet in the width of its beach after Iniki's waters. As a result, the resort's formerly small swath of sand now seems acceptable. After the winds, this relatively new hotel, which first opened November 15, 1990, required a $30 million renovation that included retiling the roofs, recarpeting, redecorating the lower-level rooms, and landscaping anew. But the tall palms once again sway in the sea breezes, the koi ponds are lively with fish, and the open-air pagodas add grandeur without too much glitz. At **Camp Hyatt Kauai**, children between three and twelve years are entertained from 9:00 A.M. to 4:00 P.M. with Hawaiian stories, crafts, hikes, field trips, and snorkeling. If you request an evening program twenty-four hours in advance, Hyatt will keep your child occupied from 6:00 P.M. to 10:00 P.M. with games, movies, and outdoor activities. When there are enough teens in house (check ahead), the hotel offers **Rock Hyatt**, a series of intermittent outings and activities for ages thirteen to seventeen. Be sure to check with reservations for the frequent packages.

Poipu Kai Resort, RR 1, Koloa, Kauai 96756 (808–742–6464 or 800–367–6046), set on 110 acres, offers one- and two-bedroom units with kitchens as well as several three-bedroom houses.

The **Poipu Bed and Breakfast Inn**, 2720 Hoonani Road, Koloa, Kauai 96756, welcomes well-behaved children. Pick the large Plumeria Room, or the two-bedroom, two-bath suite. The inn also has available a playpen, high chair, and crib on a first-come basis. Call (808) 742–1146 (Hawaii), (408) 688–8800 (mainland), or (800) 552–0095.

North Shore

The **Sheraton Princeville Hotel**, Princeville, on the north shore not far from the famed Na Pali cliffs and coast, reopened October 1993. The noted Makai and Prince golf courses reopened in the spring of 1993. Call the hotel (800–826–4400) or Sheraton Worldwide Reservations (800–325–3535). The hotel plans to operate the Keiki (child) Aloha Sunshine Club, offered free in summer to ages five to twelve. Scheduled activities throughout the day include shell collecting, kite flying, and pole fishing. Evening programs run on certain nights and feature movies, storytelling, and arts and crafts. Call ahead to be sure these programs will be in operation. Scheduled to open in mid-summer, the **Embassy Suites Kauai**, 5380 Honoiki Road, Princeville 96722, (808) 826–6522 or (800) EMBASSY, will have one-, two-, and three-bedroom suites as well as a children's program.

Waimea

Try the rustic cabins at **Kokee Lodge**, P.O. Box 819, Waimea, Kauai, Hawaii 96796; (808) 335–6061. They feature family- friendly amenities at budget prices. Accommodating three to seven people, the cabins come complete with a stove, refrigerator, bathroom, basic dishes, and linens at budget rates. As always with a bargain, book a year in advance, but check for cancellations. Another bonus: cheap eats at the Kokee Lodge restaurant, which serves breakfast and lunch daily. Try the thick Portuguese bean soup called "local soul food" by the natives.

Lihue and Kapa'a

Before Hurricane Iniki the **Westin Kauai**, Kalapaki Beach, Nawiliwili (808–245–5050), featured the island's best pool, one that you and the kids wouldn't have been able to resist. Bustling, filled with ponds, fountains, and lagoons, the Westin Kauai delivered a vacation with lots of choices including nightlife at the Paddling Club disco, plus a special Sunday nonalcoholic night for teens, a fabulous pool, pampering spa, a wildlife boat ride, an award-winning golf course, plus a comprehensive kids' program, **Camp Kalapaki**. We're hopeful that the Westin, one of the island's poshest, but also most family friendly resorts, will reopen as scheduled sometime in 1995.

The **Outrigger Kauai Beach**, 4331 Kauai Beach Drive, Lihue 96766 (800–462–6262), features a swimming pool, and a limited children's program in summer. **Plantation Hale**, 484 Kuhio Highway, Kapaa, operated by Outrigger Hotels, and across the street from Waipouli Beach, features one-bedroom condominiums with kitchenettes; (808) 822–4941 or (800) 462–6262.

The **Aston Kauai Beach Villas**, 4330 Kauai Beach Drive, Lihue 96766, offer oceanfront condominium rentals. This property apparently does not offer a kids' program, although that may change. Call (808) 245–7711 or (800) 922–7866.

Other Accommodations

Camping. **Kokee State Park**, Division of State Parks, P.O. Box 1671, Lihue, Hawaii 96766; (808) 241–3444. Adjacent to the Waimea Canyon, this state park offers camping facilities and views of the Kalalau Valley. To reserve a spot at one of Kauai's state parks, send a letter stating when and where you want to camp, along with a copy of the driver's licenses for each adult in your group. Remember that there is a five-night maximum at Kokee State Park. Some locals suggest avoiding **Polihale State Park** as in years past campers have been robbed.

Kauai also offers **beach camping** at seven parks. Family favorites include **Anini Beach Park** on the north shore and **Salt Pond** on the west, both with broad sands and usually manageable undertow. (Check with officials.) Permits are required per-adult per-night (children under eighteen are free), and they limit you to four days in one park and twelve days total at all the parks. For beach camping applications and information, contact the county office. Write the **Department of Parks and Recreation**, 4193 Hardy Street, Lihue, Hawaii 96766; (808) 245–8821.

More Bed-and-Breakfast Lodging. For additional **Bed-and-Breakfast** lodging, contact **Hawaii's Best Bed and Breakfast**, P.O. Box 563, Kamuela, Hawaii 96743. They represent about one hundred accommodations throughout Hawaii. Many are cottages on farms, or private estates. For brochures, call (808) 885–4550, for reservations only, (800) 262–9912.

Bed and Breakfast of Hawaii, P.O. Box 449, Kapaa, Kauai, Hawaii 96746, represents about two hundred places throughout the islands, with about seventy on Kauai. Ask for their guide *Bed and Breakfast Goes Hawaiian* (fee); call (800) 733–1632. For example, on Kauai's south shore, this registry offers "Kalaheo K29," a one-bedroom apartment complete with kitchen, minutes from Poipu Beach; "K24" in Poipu, which can accommodation twenty people in nine units, several of which have kitchens, and some have two bedrooms; and "K39A," a suite on a three-acre estate (appropriate for children over twelve).

WHERE TO EAT

Grab a skewer and grill yourself some mahi mahi, chicken, or steak at the **Koloa Broiler**, Koloa Road, in Old Koloa Town not far from Poipu; (808) 742–9122. The do-it-yourself approach keeps entrée costs down.

The **Bull Shed**, 796 Kuhio Highway, half-way between Waipole and Wailua, in the Harbor Village, features an extensive salad bar and prime rib; (808) 822–3791. **Chuck's Steakhouse**, at the Princeville Center (808–826–6211), attracts locals as well as tourists. The **Aloha Diner**, 971 F Kuhio Highway, Waupouli (808–822–3851), is another local favorite.

The **House of Seafood**, on Lawai Beach at the Poipu Kai Resort (808–742–6433), features good Hawaiian seafood, but the price is a bit more than the usual family fare. The specials may include fish with macadamia-nut sauce or ginger-baked fish. The **Kapaa Fish and Chowder House**, 4-1639 Kuhio Highway (808–822–7488), offers entrées such as coconut shrimp, seafood fettucini, and sautéed clams.

For island cuisine with an *au naturel* flair, suitable for families, try the **Ilima Terrace**, Hyatt Regency Kauai; (808) 742–1234. Children are sure to find something on the varied menu they like, and if not, the view of Keoneloa Bay and the beach is sure to please.

DAY TRIPS

Take a day excursion by raft, kayak, horseback, or helicopter (see Special Tours). Visit the other islands (see Island Hopping in the introductory chapter.)

FOR MORE INFORMATION

For an up-to-date list of hotel, attractions, restaurants, and activities, take advantage of the **Kauai Updates**. For information from volunteers, phone (800) 262–1400, Monday through Friday from 6:00 A.M. to 6:00 P.M. and 6:00 A.M. to 2:00 P.M. on Saturday and Sunday. Hawaiian Standard Time. For an immediate list of the latest openings, **fax** 800–OK–FAX–ME and request document 6005, or fax your questions to the **Kauai Fax Line** (800–637–5762). Order a Kauai Vacation Planner by calling (800) AH–KAUAI. These services are currently scheduled to be available through June 1994.

Emergency Numbers
The **Chamber of Commerce**, 2970 Kele Street; (808) 245–7363
The **Hawaii Visitors Bureau**, 3016 Umi Street; (808) 245–3971
Ambulance, fire, police: 911
Fire Department: nonemergency, 4223 Rice Street; (808) 245–2222
Police Headquarters: nonemergency, 3060 Umi Street; (808) 245–9711
Wilcox Hospital, 3420 Kuhio Highway; (808) 245–1100
Longs Drug Store, Kukui Grove Center; (808) 245–7771

45
MAUI

Maui, nicknamed the "Valley Isle," offers some of the islands' plushest resorts and best golf courses. It's a popular island, especially for first-timers to Hawaii, and for families with teens as there's plenty to see and do both during the day and at night. Magical Maui moments include bike riding down mountain slopes, snorkeling at a semisubmerged volcanic cone, and driving a scenic highway dotted with waterfalls.

The major resort areas are the Kihei/Wailea region, Kaanapali and north to Kapalua, and the less populated and more-difficult-to-reach Hana, on the island's far eastern tip.

GETTING THERE

Maui has three airports. **Kahului Airport** (808–872–3830), the island's main airport, is the only one that operates at night. **United Airlines** (800–241–6522), **Delta Airlines** (800–221–1212), and **American** fly directly to Maui's Kahului Airport from various mainland gateways. **Aloha Airlines** (800–367–5250) and **Hawaiian Airlines** (800–367–5320) fly to Kahului Airport from Oahu. The small airport at **Hana** (808–248–8208) is limited to propeller planes that take the work out of the long drive to this lovely and less populated spot. The airport at **Kapalua-West Maui** (808–669–0228), convenient to this resort area, accommodates commuter planes and Aloha Airlines planes.

GETTING AROUND

Rental cars make exploring Maui's diversity easy. Book well in advance. You can rent cars at Kahului and Kapalua-West, but not at the Hana airport. For Hana, arrange to have your hotel meet you, or call **Dollar Car Rental** (808–248–8237); they will send a van for you.

Avis (800–331–1212 or 808–871–7575), **Budget** (800–527–0700 or 808–871–8811), **Hertz** (800–654–3131 or 808–877–5167), **National Car**

Rental (800–227–7368), V.I.P./Kamaaina (808–877–5460), and **Rainbow** (808–661–8734) are all regulars, along with about thirty other competing rental agencies.

A & B Moped Rental, 3481 Lower Honoapiilani Highway (808–669–0027), rents mopeds to licensed drivers for about $25 per day. Bicycling about the island is also popular, especially for bicycling down Haleakala (which you should do only under the guidance of a reputable tour operator). Companies include **Cruiser Bob's**, 505 Front Street, Lahaina (808–667–7717); and **MacDougall's Bike and Fitness**, 1913 South Kihei Road (808–874–0068). Both rent mountain bikes.

Maui has no real public transportation system. Those staying in Kaanapali can get a lift with the **Kaanapali Resort Trolley Car**, which stops at major resorts; with the **Lahaina Express** (808–661–8748), a free bus that operates between Lahaina and the Kaanapali resorts from about 9:00 A.M. to 10:00 P.M.; and with the **Kaanapali Shuttle** that transports visitors for free every hour between hotels and condos. Little ones might like a ride on the **Lahaina Kaanapali and Pacific Railroad**, a restored sugarcane train pulled by a steam locomotive; call (808) 661–0089.

Taxis are available. **Red and White Cabs** (808–661–3684) and **Wailea Taxi** (808–879–1059) are two of the island companies.

WHAT TO SEE AND DO

Your kids will never be bored in Maui. Besides miles of beaches for swimming, sunning, and snorkeling, Maui offers good golf, tennis, spas, kids' programs, shopping, and great resorts.

Haleakala National Park

Spend at least one day exploring **Haleakala National Park**, Haleakala National Park Headquarters, Crater Road; (808) 572–9306. You can drive, bike, or hike down this dormant volcano, which dominates the island.

In Hawaiian *Haleakala* means house of the sun, aptly named as this mountain looms formidably at 10,000 feet. If you want to catch the sunrise at the mountain's peak, a spectacular sight, start your drive to the summit early, and dress warmly. It can be cold at the higher elevations. At the top the mountain is a "moonscape" of brown-and-red craters. White wisps of clouds hang suspended against the gray peaks of lava cones, and the earth inside is a trail of black ashen pebbles and thin quietness.

But even if you arrive after dawn (allow about two hours for the drive up), the trip is worth the trouble. The scenery changes from sugar fields, to farms, ranches, eucalyptus groves, koa trees—and near the summit— to an eerie stretch of craters and black earth.

Stop at the **Visitors' Center** for some informative books. From here it's about another 10 miles to the summit. Look for nene geese, Hawaii's state bird, and Silverswords, a plant with spindly shooting tendrils that only grow in the high dry lava beds of volcanic peaks.

On your way up or down, take the kids for breakfast or lunch (11:30–3:00) on Haleakala's slopes at the **Kula Lodge**, Highway 377; (808) 878–2517. The inexpensive entrées include omelettes, bean soup, and burgers.

A popular Haleakala adventure is a **bicycle tour** down this mountain. The trip, from the van ride up, to the bike ride down with a stop for lunch, can take four hours. It's best to go in the morning before the mist obscures some views. Because the mountain features twenty-nine hairpin turns, this exhilarating outing is recommended only for agile parents and children twelve and over who follow directions. The precipice of a mountain is no place for daredevil kids. Some reputable companies include **Maui Downhill**, 199 Dairy Road, Kahului (808–871–2155); and **Cruiser Bob's Downhill**, P.O. Box B, Paia (808–579–8444).

Biking lets you savor the scenery, but a car trip gets you the same views. As you descend, the scenery changes from the earth browns and reds to the greens of koa trees. The wind ripples through the pili grass that covers the hillsides. When you pass the eucalyptus grove, the air is pungent with its aroma. For the last 1,500 feet, you'll see cows grazing in meadows and sugarcane fields.

On Haleakala's slopes be a *paniolo,* a Hawaiian cowboy. Sign up for a horseback ride with **Pony Express**, P.O. Box 535, Kula, Maui; (808) 667–2200. Located at about 4,200 feet, this "up-country" ranch offers two-hour guided rides (minimum age is ten). While the horses keep an easy walking pace, you enjoy the sweeping vistas of sugarcane fields far down the slopes that reach to the blue Pacific. The rustle of the horses' hooves in the calf-high reedy grass creates a tranquil aura. For those who can sit in the saddle for seven hours, Pony Express offers horseback trips into the crater, an exciting venture. **Thompson Ranch**, Thompson Road, Kula (808–878–1910), also offers ranch trail rides as well as trips into Haleakala's crater.

Just a few miles from Pony Express, **Makawao**, a simple town, sports local craft shops and galleries along Baldwin Avenue. For some of the best *saimin,* a native soup of noodles and pork, stop at **Kitada's Kau Kau Korner**, Baldwin Avenue (808–572–7241), a one-room café, where you squeeze in with others at the faded formica tables. For the bargain price of about $2.75, you get a steamy bowl big enough for two. For the ride back to the hotel, grab some pastries from **Komoda's Bakery**, 3674 Baldwin Avenue; (808) 572–7261. This shop is noted for its cream puffs, but most everything looks good.

Also worth a stop on Haleakala's slopes is the **Upcountry Protea**

Farm, Kula (808–878–2544), where exotic flowers are grown. The farm has a half-acre walk-through garden, and a picnic area where you can lunch on sandwiches from the farm store. **Kula Botanical Gardens,** on Highway 377 past the turnoff to Haleakala Crater (808–878–1715), offers more tropical plants. (Admission; open daily 9:00 A.M.–4:00 P.M.)

Great Drives: The Road to Heavenly Hana

The road to Hana is one of America's great drives. From Kahului for 52 miles—about three hours—the route presents a panorama of Hawaii's best: pineapple fields, windsurfers, black-sand beaches, cascading waterfalls, grotto-carved swimming holes, and lush vegetation. Cabbage-sized yellow and red hibiscus, sprays of purple Queen Emma blossoms, African tulip trees, arcing banana stalks, wispy palm trees, delicately fingered ferns, and white-and-yellow ginger blossoms lace the blacktop.

Here are sweeping vistas of coast, cliffs, and clouds; no hotels, billboards, or condos mar the view as you commune with nature. The least expensive and most enjoyable way to experience this scenic but serpentine route (with more than six hundred curves and fifty-six one-lane bridges) is to drive it yourself. Remember to book your rental car well in advance. But like everything in paradise, there's a "price." Don't plan on driving to Hana and back again in one day. The drive is too exhausting, especially for little kids, who may not take to the winding roads. Bring along some anti–motion sickness medicine for your kids just in case.

Ideally, allow at least two days for this drive; stay overnight in Hana (book well in advance). And wear your bathing suit under your clothes, for along this road are wonderful places to pause—sensuous waterfalls and superb beaches are just some of the delights. If you insist on driving the round-trip in one day, be sure to leave Kahului by 8:00 A.M. in order to allow enough time for a rejuvenating swim at Hamoa Beach, as well as a daylight return trip. Be sure to get gas for the car in **Paia** (a small town of T-shirt shops flanked by sugarcane fields and the sea) because the next gasoline awaits in Hana. The **Shell Service Station,** Route 380 **before** Route 36 (which is the Hana Highway), and 1 mile before the airport (808–572–0550), rents a narrated tape describing the scenic points on the road to Hana.

The road surprises at every turn. Hau tree branches canopy the path allowing thin slants of light, but around the next bend the road breaks into bright sun as feathery hillsides of wild eucalyptus, mango, guava, and papaya trees billow toward the sea. The rustle of 30-foot-tall bamboo stands sounds like soft rain, and the rush of waterfalls lures you across the many one-lane bridges.

With frequent ascents, descents, and narrow lanes, the road can be demanding as it winds along Maui's northeastern coastline to Hana, a tiny town well worth a visit for its twin jewels: the **Hotel Hana Maui,** offering good food and comfortably elegant rooms, and nearby **Hamoa Bay Beach,** which James Michener dubbed the most beautiful in Hawaii.

Contrary to what many guidebooks state, the road to Hana is reasonably well maintained, if always narrow and windy. But the 10 miles beyond Hana to **Ohe'o Gulch** (frequently misnamed the **Seven Sacred Pools**) will try your soul. Locals say they like the pothole-and-gravel-packed path to the Kipahulu district, the southeasternmost sector of Haleakala National Park, just as it is to keep the crowds from the pristine serenity of these volcanic-carved pools. But for seekers of lush Hawaii before the tourist floods and glitzy hotels, the Hana drive is heaven.

The first must-see on this adventure comes within 2 miles. Pull over at **Hookipa Beach,** one of Maui's best windsurfing spots. While you can't rent a board here, you can watch as many as twenty-five yellow, white, orange, and red sails of local aficionados glide the perfect wave.

Sixteen miles later, after the pineapple fields have yielded to high ridges of mist-topped hillsides, the **Waianu Fruit Stand,** announced by its HALFWAY TO HANA sign, blooms like an oasis. Let the kids out here for cheap eats—cokes, chips, fruit, shaved iced—and leg stretching.

About 7 miles from the fruit stand, look for cars parked by the roadside (this is a clue to **Puohokamoa Falls**). A short path from the highway leads you to the falls. Cool and clear, these waters deliver a quintessential Hawaiian fantasy: splashing in a waterfall.

Next pull-over: the **Wailua Lookout.** Walk up the stairs almost concealed by a tunnel of hau branches for a picturesque view of this seacoast village complete with the white spires of St. Gabriel's Church.

With waterfalls and bathrooms, **Puaa Kaa State Park,** about 5 miles further along (14 more miles until Hana) draws picnickers, especially those with preschoolers. Tarry here, or try **Waianapanapa State Park,** further along, but just ½ mile beyond the Hana airport, near the town. This is the perfect pastiche of black-sand beach, trails, and underwater caves shallow enough in places for supervised swimming by children. An ancient legend attributes the red cast of the cave waters not to the tiny shrimp but to the memory of a fleeing princess murdered by her jealous husband.

Hana itself, low-key and inviting, curls around the harbor, then stretches for several blocks before fading into grass-covered mountains and fields. Refresh yourself with lunch. For down-home informality, try the ribs and sweet-and-sour chicken buffet at the **Hana Ranch Restaurant** (808–248–8255), or wash up in the park, and head for luncheon at the **Hotel Hana-Maui** (808–248–8211, 800–325–3535, or 800–STAY–ITT), Highway 36, a hideaway of about ninety-six rooms now operated by Sheraton Hotels in the heart of town. The open-air dining room with views of frog ponds, sweeping lawns, and manicured gardens lends the place the feel of an oasis.

Sated, head for **Hamoa Bay Beach**, 1½ miles from Hana. The broad row of kamani trees provides shade, and the sand stretches in a wide arc against the blue sea.

Linger here for awhile—or the entire day and the one after. Rest up because the next 10 miles of road to **Ohe'o Gulch** take at least one hour; bumps and potholes prevail. The reward: the shimmering row of twenty volcanic pools. If limited for time, hike the .2 mile to the lower pools.

The path takes you back to ancient Hawaii. On this wind-blown promontory, white water crashes on the black lava rocks below as you pass the ruins of a thousand-year-old Hawaiian village. Just beyond, the gray lava pools, carved by the Ohe'o stream coming down Mt. Haleakala, offer secluded swimming—though the spot is becoming more and more popular.

Further along this road (ask the locals how to get there) is **Charles Lindbergh's grave**, on the site chosen by the aviator who was buried on August 26, 1974. Read his epitaph, which states in part, "If I take the wings of morning and dwell in the uttermost parts of the sea . . ."

An important warning about the drive to Hana: Many tour groups cart vanloads of tourists along the Hana road, departing from Kahalui about 7:30 A.M. and returning about 6:00 P.M. Some continue to Ohe'o Gulch; others stop at Hamoa Bay Beach. There's no time for swimming, but Hana is a lunch stop. If you are vulnerable to car sickness, be careful. Seven hours in the back of a van may be hard on the stomach, especially for kids. Our advice—avoid these one-day trips; but if you must, operators include **Robert's Hawaii, Inc.** (808–871–6226) and **Ekahi Tours** (808–572–9775).

Special Tours by Sea

Whale watching. More excitement abounds in Maui's seas. From November through April, boats cruise by schools of whales, and the horizon jumps with pods of humpbacks cresting the waters. February and March are the most exciting months as often you can see whales tail slapping, spy hopping, and fin waving. Shoreline sites with great whale-watching views include the beaches at Wailea and Kaanapali, harborside in Lahaina, and Makena Beach.

In season many of the snorkeling and sailing companies offer whale-watching cruises. The **Pacific Whale Foundation**, 101 North Kihei Road, Suite 25, Kihei (808–879–8811), offers whale information and eco-adventures. Often hotels offer whale-watching packages. In January 1994 the **Four Seasons Resort Wailea** (800–334–6284 or 808–242–7075) hosted the Celebration of Whales, a three-day event combining lectures, whale-watching cruises, art, and a Hawaii Humpback Whale workshop for kids five and older.

Snorkeling. Some of the best snorkeling can be found at **Molokini**, a volcanic crater whose conelike crescent breaches the Pacific about an hour's launch from **Maalaea Harbor**. Because Molokini is a preserve, the tame fish eat from your hands. Even the most blasé video tyke will yell "Wow" when tiers of rainbow-colored parrot fish, yellow tangs, and blue-and-green wrasse nibble bread from his fingers. Many boats have some "seeboards" equipped with built-in masks so that little kids and non-swimmers can still get eyeball to eyeball with the fish. These rent quickly, so reserve yours as soon as you get on deck. Most companies include lunch. Four Winds (808–879–8188) is one of the few that offer a hot barbecue lunch of burgers, chicken, or mahi mahi. Another good choice is the *Wailea Kai,* booked by the **Ocean Activities Center,** 1325 Kihei Road, Wailea, Hawaii; (808) 879–4485. En route to Molokini the crew talks about safety, instructing those who need to learn the techniques of snorkeling. A light breakfast is served, and at the site, the crew prepares lunch.

Other snorkeling cruises leave from Lahaina's harbor to Lanai. Ask your concierge; browse the kiosks along Front Street, Lahaina's main drag; and check with the **Ocean Activities Center. Blue Water Rafting,** P.O. Box 10172, Lahaina (808–879–7238), offers a variety of snorkeling expeditions as well as whale-watching excursions. **Kaulana Cruises** (808–667–2518) offers a dinner sail and a cocktail cruise; kids are half price. **Sea Sails,** operated by the **Sea Sport Activities Center** (808–667–2759), offers a dinner cruise as well.

For a diver's view of sealife without having to be certified for SCUBA, try the **Atlantis Submarine;** (800) 548–6262 or (808) 667–2224. In Maui, a boat leaves from the Lahaina harbor for the dive site where you board this recreational submarine outfitted for forty-six passengers. Two each share a porthole for the hour viewing, a wonderful window on the wonders of sea life. (The entire trip lasts about one hour and forty-five minutes.) Kids love seeing schools of fish float by, especially those tots who have not mastered snorkeling. Maui offers the deepest dive of the Atlantis's three locations in Hawaii. Going down to 150 feet it's the only one that shows black coral. While there is no minimum age for a dive, the minimum height for a passenger is 3 feet, so most kids four years and older can experience this. Be aware: If you tend toward claustrophobia, skip this. Atlantis Submarines also dive off Kona, the Big Island, and Waikiki, Oahu.

Flight-seeing

Various companies offer helicopter tours of Maui. While exciting, these flight-seeing forays are pricey. If you want to splurge on one of these, we recommend saving the bird's-eye view for a helicopter ride over Kauai. However, here are some of Maui's helicopter tour operators: **Kenai Helicopter** (808–871–6463), **Papillon Helicopters** (800–669–4994),

Blue Hawaiian Helicopters (800–745–BLUE), and **Hawaii Helicopters** (808–877–3900 or 800–346–2403).

Shopping and Green Spaces: Lahaina

Lahaina is the place for souvenir shopping. For the grandparents back home, pose for a **Bud the Birdman** postcard. You can't miss him with his nine macaws and parrots perched in front of the Pioneer Inn. For about $15, he'll drape six or more of these fine feathered friends on your arms, shoulders, and head. (Ask about Rainbow who likes to pose with sunglasses.) The next day pick up your five postcards with your picture and the ditty "We're on Maui and you're not! Na na na na na."

Lahaina is the place to stock up on **taro chips**, something like a tortilla chip but made from the taro plant, and **Maui chips**, ultra-crispy potato chips.

Fortified, browse for T-shirts in the many shops. Try **The Art Tee Gallery**, Pioneer Inn Arcade, 665 Front Street; (808) 661–6116. It offers some unusual and arty designs with bold graphics, or nostalgic scenes such as "Baseball is Forever." Keep walking along Front Street, and browse the **Lahaina Hat Company**, 705 Front Street, for that perfect sun-hat-in-paradise; nearby **Sergeant Leisure** offers good quality shirts, shorts, and sweats.

Cool off with some of **Lappert's Aloha Ice Cream**, 808 Front Street, at the corner of Front and Marketplace; (808) 661–3310. A great place to pause and enjoy your cone is under the giant banyan tree in the park on Front Street, bordered by Hotel and Canal streets. Kids love this shady, sprawling tree whose limbs and roots seem to take over the entire block. Before leaving here browse the local crafts at the **Banyan Tree Gallery**, Front Street, located in the park; (808) 295–7555.

SPECIAL EVENTS

February/March: The creations of international marine artists are displayed at the Maui Marine Art Expo, at the Kealani Resort, Wailea.

March: Wake up bright and early for the Maui Marathon, which leaves at 5:30 A.M. from the Maui Mall, Kahului to Whalers Village, Kaanapali. The Na Mele O Maui Festival celebrates Hawaii with a children's song contest in the Hawaiian language and a hula festival.

April: Pay homage to the whale during Whale Day at Kalama Park. Admission is free, and there is music and food all day long.

July: Makauoli Fourth of July parade and rodeo. The Maui Onion Festival takes place at Whaler's Village.

August: Watch the long boats skim over the surface of the water at the Hawaiian Canoe Racing Association State Championships at

Hanakaoo Beach. The Haleakala Run to the Sun gets its name because the marathon runners begin the race at sea level and run 36.2 miles to an elevation of 10,000 feet.

WHERE TO STAY

Kihei/Wailea
We like the **Kihei/Wailea** area best. Not as building-to-building dense as Kaanapali, or as isolated as Hana, both Wailea and Kihei (just a holler down the road from Wailea) are near enough to Maalaea harbor for day trips, close to Haleakala for hiking, and near Lahaina for shopping. Kihei, a town, sports a neighborhood feel and is less pricey than the resort-laden Wailea. A nice treat: The drive from Kihei/Wailea to West Maui. After a soft rain shower, make a game of counting the frequent rainbows that arc over the road.

Condominiums. Condominiums are a great buy for families, offering more space for your money and the convenience of cooking in.

In Kihei the **Aston Kamaole Sands**, 2695 South Kihei Road, Kihei, Hawaii 96753 (800–922–7866), is across the street from Kamaole Beach with its lifeguard, sandy shores, and sweeping lawn. Often travelers fifty-five and over receive a 20 percent discount plus a free rental car, and some members of airline frequent flyer clubs get one free night for every three-night stay. In addition, a year-round kids program for ages four to twelve is offered free to guests, Monday to Friday, usually from 9 A.M. to noon, and 1:00 P.M. to 3:30 P.M.

Another good condo pick is **Destination Resorts** (800–367–5246), with six condominium communities in Wailea, an upscale area home to the first-rate resorts of Four Seasons, Stouffer, and Inter-Continental. These condominiums share the same beach as the Wailea resorts. Golf fairways and clever land use convey a sense of greenery and open space. The condominiums **Ekolu** and **Grand Champions**, a short drive to the beach, are the least expensive but the **Ekahi** property offers beachfront convenience for not too much more. Ask about packages.

Another plus: With a Destination Resorts booking, your kids may use Maui Inter-Continental's well-run children's program (808–879–1922), or sign on for a spot at the Stouffer Wailea's children's program.

Resorts: Wailea
The **Grand Wailea Resort and Spa** (800–888–6100 or 808–875–1234), formerly the Grand Hyatt, is a great place for families and among the most elegant (casually elegant, of course) resorts in Hawaii. At Camp Grande choose from six different programs for kids ages three to twelve, which include environmental and wildlife explo-

The surf is always up at Hanoa Bay beach. (Photo by the author)

ration activities, field trips such as a ride on a glass-bottom boat, a trip on the Sugar Cane Train, and educational activities such as a day devoted to learning about whales. Activities are offered daily, year-round, from 8:00 A.M. to 4:30 P.M., with an extra charge for evening and dinner activities from 5:00 P.M. to 10:00 P.M. Rock Grande is a teen program for ages thirteen to nineteen, offering intermittent activities such as sailing trips, shopping excursions, and beach parties, when enough teens are in residence.

The **Four Seasons Resort Wailea**, 3900 Wailea Alanui (800–334–MAUI or 808–874–8000), has 380 rooms and looks out over the ocean. Families with infants are relieved to know that the hotel supplies all kinds of baby equipment, from strollers to bottle warmers. The year-round, complimentary Kids For All Seasons program entertains ages five to twelve from 9:00 A.M. to 5:00 P.M. with Hawaiian songs and legends, hula dancing, and traditional Hawaiian craft making. Day passes, which are relatively costly, are available to guests so that they may enjoy the elaborate pool at the adjacent **The Grand Wailea Resort and Spa**.

The **Stouffer Wailea Beach Resort**, 3550 Wailea Alanui Drive, Wailea (808–879–4900 or 800–HOTELS 1), has two swimming pools, two golf courses, and fourteen tennis courts. All year a kids' program called Camp Wailea runs for ages five to twelve. Counselors keep the young ones active from morning until afternoon, and the fee is $10.00 more for nonguests of the hotel.

The **Maui Intercontinental Resort**, 3700 Wailea Alanui (800–367–2960 or 808–879–1922), spreads out over twenty-two acres of Maui's south shore. The resort's special features include nightly live entertainment, golf courses, grass tennis courts, and the **Keiki's Club Gecko** children's program, which translates to something like "The Kid's Good Luck Lizard Club." The activities include Nintendo games, finger painting, hula lessons, and tide pool discovery sessions. Lunch and a T-shirt are included in the fee, and the program is offered Tuesdays, Thursdays, and Saturdays from 9:00 A.M. to 3:00 P.M.

The **Kea Lani Hotel**, 4100 Wailea Alanui, Wailea 96753 (808–875–4100 or 800–882–4100), is an all-suite and -villa property in Wailea. It offers families extra room and a relatively inexpensive children's program for ages four to eleven, year-round, Monday to Saturday from 9:00 A.M. to 3:00 P.M. The one-time membership fee for the first child costs about $10.00, and the second child costs $8.00. The program seems to have good counselors and creative crafts. Kids paint coconuts, create volcanoes, play beach games, and go swimming. The catch: You must sign up by 6:00 P.M. the night before. Each room features a sitting area with television, stereo and VCR, plus a microwave, refrigerator, and coffeemaker, as well as pull-out couches that can accommodate grade-school kids with no problems. (Teens may feel crowded, so inquire about their villas or larger suites.) For increased privacy, the bathroom opens to both the sitting area and the master bedroom.

The **Aston Kamaole Sands**, 2695 South Kihei Road, Kihei 96753 (808–931–1400 or 800–922–7866), on Maui, operates Kamp Kamaole, a free, year-round children's program for ages four to twelve from 9:00 A.M. to noon, and 1:00 P.M. to 3:00 P.M. Kids go on beach walks, fish, and learn how to make their own leis. Call Aston Hotels and Resorts; (800) 922–7866.

Kaanapali

The **Westin Maui** is off State Route 30, 2365 Kaanapali Highway, Kaanapali 96761; (808) 667–2525 or (800) 228–3000. It features Keiki Camp from June through August, and on major holidays, for ages five to twelve and other kids' programs. Also in Kaanapali, the **Hyatt Regency Maui**, 200 Nohea Kai Drive, Kaanapali Beach (800–233–1234 or 808–661–1234), offers Camp Hyatt year-round for ages three to twelve from 9:00 A.M. to 6:00 P.M. An evening program for a separate fee is available Fridays and Saturdays from 6:00 P.M. to 10:00 P.M. With enough teens in house, the hotel offers Rock Hyatt, intermittent activities and day trips for teens.

The **Whaler at Kaanapali Beach**, 2481 Kaanapali Parkway, Kaanapali

96761 (800–367–7052 or 808–661–4861), offers the complimentary Ohana Summer Activities Program for ages five to twelve from mid-June through Labor Day. Some special outings require a fee. **The Sheraton Maui**, 2605 Kaanapali Parkway (800–325–3535 or 808–661–0031), offers a free Keiki Aloha Sunshine Club from mid-June through August for ages five to twelve. Intermittent activities include arts and crafts and pole fishing; on some evenings, movies and Hawaiian storytelling keep kids occupied so parents can enjoy a romantic dinner. When available, families can book a second room for their kids at a 50 percent discount.

For the most space, try the **Embassy Suites Resort Maui**, 104 Kaanapali Shores Place; (800) GO–2–MAUI or (808) 661–2000. The Embassy Suites offers a complimentary full breakfast, plus a year-round children's program. Hours and activities vary, so check ahead. **The Aston Kaanapali Shores**, 3445 Lower Honoapiilani Highway (808–931–1400 or 800–367–5124), is a condo property that offers a year-round kids' program for ages three to eight from 9:00 A.M. to 2:00 P.M. Monday through Friday. Lunch is extra.

For reservations and information about any of **Aston**'s twenty-nine Hawaii properties, call (800) 922–7866. But shop smart by comparing Aston's prices and packages with those offered by tour wholesalers, and by **Hideaways International** (800–843–4433), companies that also book Aston properties.

Hana

The **Hotel Hana-Maui**, P.O. Box 9, Hana 96713 (808–248–8211 or 800–321–HANA), operated by Sheraton, offers ninety-six units in the heart of Hana, and not on the beach. The free Keiki Aloha Sunshine Club for ages five through twelve operates from the middle of June to the end of August each year. The intermittent activities include arts and crafts, snorkeling, dancing, mini-excursions, a photo contest, boogie boarding, and more. Kids will like the nearby Hamoa Bay Beach most of all. Very active kids or teens may be bored here as this property is laid-back, quiet, and secluded, all of which delights parents and plagues teens.

Aloha Cottages, 73 Keawa Place, P.O. Box 205, Hana, Maui, Hawaii, 96713; (808) 248–8420. This place has about seven units, including two family cottages that can sleep five. The **Hana Bay Vacation Rental**, P.O. Box 318, Hana, Maui, Hawaii 96713 (800–657–7970), offers some condominiums as well as homes. **Hana Plantation Houses**, P.O. Box 489, Hana, Maui 96713, offers twelve rental units near Hamoa Bay Beach; toll-free on Maui (808) 248–7248, toll-free elsewhere (800) 657–7723.

Primitive camping is available near **Ohe'o Gulch** in Haleakala National Park. Rustic cabins are available (book well in advance) at **Waianapanapa State Park**. Contact the Division of State Parks, 54 South High Street, Wailuku, Hawaii 96793, or phone the Maui office at (808) 243–5354.

WHERE TO EAT

On Haleakala's slopes. Near Crater Road, tour **Sunrise Protea Farm's** quarter-acre garden while you picnic on their inexpensive sandwiches. Another good bet for lunch, dinner, or even breakfast is **Kula Lodge Restaurant**, Highway 377 (808–878–2517), where the menu features inexpensive teriyaki burgers, and pasta.

In Paia. Locals swear by **Mama's Fish House**, 799 Poho Place (808–579–8488), which offers fresh fish prepared several ways. A children's menu is available.

In Lahaina. Lahaina offers lots of inexpensive eateries. Try **Take Home Maui**, on Dickenson Street. Even though the store looks like a convenience store and shipping warehouse (which it is), go inside. The deli sandwiches are fresh, and if you're lucky, you'll get a spot at one of the few tables on their porch. The **Hard Rock Cafe**, 900 Front Street (808–667–7400), offers those famous burgers, as well as lime chicken, and ribs. The **Lahaina Broiler**, 889 Front Street (808–661–3111), offers sea breezes with its moderately priced breakfasts, lunch, and dinners. The sandwiches are good at the **Old Lahaina Cafe and Luau**, 505 Front Street; (808) 667–1998.

In Kaanapali. **Leilani's on the Beach**, in Whaler's Village (808–661–4495), has good seafood and steaks. Also in Whaler's Village, the **Rusty Harpoon** (808–661–3123) offers early-bird specials, as well as fresh fish, pasta, and chicken dishes. To treat yourself to some fine dining at upscale prices, try some of the luxury hotels' restaurants, particularly the **Swan Court** at the Hyatt Regency; (808) 661–1234.

In Kihei/Wailea. There are some inexpensive eateries in Kihei, including **La Familia**, 2511 South Kihei Road; (808) 879–8824. The Mexican food here is good. See if your kids will try a crab tostada for a change, but if not, there are plenty of the usual staples. The same shopping center, the Kai Nani Village, also has the **Greek Bistro**, 2511 South Kihei Road; (808) 879–9330. It's a small place with good moussaka, pasta, and lamb gyro sandwiches.

The hotels in Wailea offer some fine dining. For inexpensive lunches, head for the poolside bars for burgers. **Cafe Kula**, The Grand Wailea Resort and Spa, offers healthy food at reasonable (for a hotel) prices. The pastas and salads are wonderful, and save room for the banana split— served with homemade sherbet and fruit. The food here is good-for-you healthy stuff, and it tastes great.

When you want to celebrate by enjoying a pricey meal, the Wailea hotels have lots to offer. Among the finds: **Raffle's Restaurant**, Stouffer Wailea Beach Resort (808) 879–4900. This restaurant is also known for its elaborate Sunday brunch. **Seasons**, the Four Seasons Resort Wailea, offers great food, and half-portions for children; (808) 874–8000.

DAY TRIPS

In addition to the scenic drives, exploration of Haleakala, and snorkeling and whale-watching cruises, try **island hopping**. From Maui, it's easy to visit the other islands, especially **Lanai** and **Molokai**. Lanai's south coast is known for its dive sites. **Hulopoe Bay** offers easy snorkeling and lots of fish.

FOR MORE INFORMATION

Maui Visitors Bureau, P.O. Box 580, Wailuku, Maui, Hawaii 96793 (800–244–3530); the **Chamber of Commerce**, 26 Pourne Avenue (808–871–7711); and **Consumer Complaints** (808–244–7756).

For the **County Department of Parks and Recreation**, Wailuku, call (808) 243–7230, for permits dial (808) 243–7389, and for weather (808) 877–5111.

Emergency Numbers
Ambulance, fire, police: 911
Hospital: Maui Memorial Hospital, Kaahumanu Avenue, Kahului; (808) 244–9056
Pharmacy: There are no twenty-four-hour pharmacies. For extended hours: Call **Long's Drugs** in Kahului, 100 East Kaahumanu Avenue, (808) 877–0041; In Kihei, call **Long's Drugs**, 1215 South Kihei Road, (808) 879–2259.

46
OAHU

Oahu will surprise you. The most populated of Hawaii's islands, with about 840,000 people, Oahu has 594 square miles and is the third largest of the Hawaiian islands. The beat changes from the bustle of the blanket-to-blanket bodies of Waikiki to the sweeping curl of sunlit waves on north shore beaches that made surfing into a world-class sport. As the name suggests, Oahu, the gathering place, pulls together a sampler of Hawaii from the legends of old Polynesia, the lushness of botanical gardens, to the modern skyline of Honolulu.

GETTING THERE

The **Honolulu International Airport**, one of the busiest airports in the country, has an international terminal and an interisland terminal. Among the major carriers that fly into Honolulu are **United** (800–241–6522), **Continental** (800–525–0280), **American Airlines** (800–433–7300), and **Northwest** (800–225–2525). Especially with such long-haul destinations, always check out special, promotional fares, and packages, including airline packages. Often these offer airfare and lodging for much less than if you booked them individually.

GETTING AROUND

Taxis, which are readily available, include **Aloha State Cab** (808–847–3566) and **Charley's** (808–531–1333), both well-known. **The-Bus** (808–848–5555), the city's bus system, can get you around most of the island. When you board ask for transfers and check with the driver (if not beforehand) about the quickest and least expensive way to get to your destination.

Car rentals are popular. Check for the best rates, and book well in advance. Rental companies include **Avis** (808–834–5536 or 800–331–1212), **Budget** (808–922–3600 or 800–527–0700), **Dollar**

(808–831–2330 or 800–800–4000), Hertz (808–831–3500 or 800–654–3131), and National (808–831–3800 or 800–227–7368).

WHAT TO SEE AND DO

Waikiki Area Attractions

Diamond Head State Monument, off Diamond Head Road between Makapuu and Eighteenth avenues (808–587–0300), is probably Oahu's most noted landmark. Allow two hours for the round-trip hike to the 760-foot summit of Diamond Head, a volcanic crater that curves close to Waikiki's shoreline. Bring flashlights (a nice touch for little kids) to assist you through the darker tunnels. The wind in the grass and the quiet let you imagine this landmark as King Kamehameha saw it when he worshipped at a *heiau*, an ancient Hawaiian temple, on Diamond Head's slopes.

Beaches. Waikiki's sands are famous, and very crowded. Some hotels tend to stake out small areas where they offer such helpful beach gear as chairs and umbrellas; some of the less expensive hotels don't offer these items. Vendors sell inexpensive grass mats, which make easily transportable beach "blankets." The mats can also be purchased at local drugstores and sundry shops. If you want the shade, or a choice spot, arrive early. Another option: Tour the town in the morning, and come back to your hotel for some afternoon sun and fun. Check the local conditions, but Waikiki's beaches generally offer safe swimming.

Locals like the Ala Moana Beach at Ala Moana Park, Ala Moana Boulevard, and the Kapiolani Park Beach Center, Kapiolani Park (described next), is also another good bet.

Parks and Zoos. Even in Waikiki authentic Hawaii lives. Especially on Sunday, a *haole* (mainlander) can enjoy a stroll through Kapiolani Park, between Waikiki's beach and Diamond Head, at the end of Kalakaua Avenue. Locals relax here on this 140-acre expanse of lawns and picnic and play areas. Pack a ball and a kite, and soon you and your kids will be sharing a game of catch and a breeze with a local *keiki* (child).

Visit the Waikiki Aquarium, 2777 Kalakaua Avenue; (808) 923–9741. Recently renovated, this is the place to introduce your children, especially those too young for snorkeling, to underwater wonders. Rare monk seals sun and swim here. Kids look wide-eyed at such strangely striped, spotted, and rainbow-hued Hawaiian reef dwellers as lion, butterfly, and squirrel fish, as well as lazy, green sea turtles, and yellow-hued coral that sprouts like wildflowers. The gift shop offers many allowance affordables, including fish magnets, stickers, pencils, and puzzles.

At the Honolulu Zoo, 151 Kapahulu Avenue (808–971–7171), Mari and Vaigai, two Asian pachyderms, steal the show. During Elephant Encounters, these tame behemoths bow, sit, carry handlers in their trunks, and place leis on giggling children. Check the zoo schedule. Admire the giant **banyan tree**, a fantastical conglomeration of limbs just outside the zoo's entrance. *Special Waikiki Tours.* The **Atlantis Submarine** (808–973–9811 or 800–548–6262) offers a diver's-eye view of the deep without the work (and skill) of SCUBA. This recreational submarine, which also hosts tourist "dives" near the Big Island and Maui, has a shuttle vessel that departs from the Hilton Hawaiian Village, Waikiki. To board this sub, which carries forty-eight passengers and three crew members, kids must be at least 3 feet tall. Don't go if you're prone to claustrophobia, but do go if you want to get a new perspective on underwater life. To enhance the reef for the Waikiki dive, the Atlantis Submarine sank a ship, a vintage prop plane, and a man-made reef. From your portholes watch schools of parrot fish, angel fish, and yellow tangs cruise by.

Greater Honolulu Area Attractions

There's more sea life at the **Hawaii Maritime Center**, Pier 7, Ala Moana Boulevard and Bishop Street, Honolulu Harbor; (808) 523–6151. View whaling harpoons, koa wood canoes, and the *Falls of Clyde*, the only four-masted full-rigged ship.

The **Bishop Museum**, 1525 Bernice Street (808–847–3511), details the islands' natural history and cultural heritage. Make a game of searching for treasures amid the somewhat stodgy and static displays, many of which may bore this generation of high-tech video kids. Among the finds: vivid yellow and orange feather capes worn by the royals, Polynesian masks with dramatic swirls, and native carvings. Kids may also enjoy the traveling exhibits, the occasional hula dances performed by area schoolchildren, and the Planetarium shows, which light up the Polynesian skies.

Hanauma Bay State Underwater Park, on the southeastern tip of Oahu, is a good snorkel spot, but often crowded. Tour operators who provide transportation from your hotel and back and rental of snorkel gear include **Paradise Snorkeling Adventures** (808–923–7766).

Other Not-too-Far From Honolulu Attractions

The most famous metropolitan Honolulu must-see is the U.S.S. *Arizona* **Memorial**, Pearl Harbor Naval Base, Pearl City; (808) 422–2771. Arrive before 9:00 A.M. (the visitor center opens around 8:00 A.M.) to be sure to obtain a free ticket to the floating memorial that marks the spot of the sunken *Arizona*, the grave of 1,177 sailors who died in the surprise Japanese attack. Each person must pick up his or her own ticket; this prevents tour groups from totally booking the monument.

While you wait for your timed entrance, browse the small museum, which personalizes the war by presenting some of the "ordinary" heroes and fighters. The gift shop offers a wide selection of books for all age levels. Particularly interesting is *Pearl Harbor, A Child's View of Pearl Harbor from Attack to Peace* (Kansas City, MO: Woodson House Publishers, 1993). Written by Dorinda Makana Onalini Nicholson, who was a child during the attack, this book presents the war from her viewpoint, including trying to escape the bombs and searching for her dog who was left behind in the initial hurry to flee.

Before heading out by boat to the floating memorial, you see a film, which explains the basics of the surprise attack on the U.S. fleet and the devastations the Japanese inflicted. From the memorial itself you can see part of the rusty hull of the ship below. Depending on your child, this may or may not have an impact.

Next to the Arizona Memorial Visitor Center is the USS *Bowfin* Submarine Museum and Park, (808) 423–1341. The highlight is the USS *Bowfin*, a World War II submarine. Kids six and older can squeeze along its narrow passageways for a below-decks look at life alongside big torpedo tubes. At the museum learn about submarine design, and view a Japanese submarine torpedo—manned by one person, bound for glory and suicide.

About a twenty-minute drive from Waikiki, Sea Life Park, Makapuu Point, Waimanalo 96795 (808–259–6476 or 800–767–8046), combines science and showmanship. Watch the sea life in reef tanks, and learn about Humboldt penguins at their Hawaiian Ocean Theater, whales and dolphins at the Whaler's Cove Show, endangered Hawaiian Monk Seals at the Hawaiian Monk Seal Cave Center, and green sea turtles at the Turtle Lagoon. Inquire about workshops that provide an up-close look at sea turtles, dolphins, sharks, and whales; and special Behind-the-Scenes tours, which show how the handlers train sea lions, whales, and dolphins.

Save this one for just before you fly home. For a last bit of island lore, visit the Pacific Aerospace Museum, in the departure terminal of the Honolulu International Airport, near the cafeteria and shops; (808) 531–7747. The modest fee is well worth it because this hands-on museum, while small, is fun, and certainly a welcome break from the bleakness of sitting around the gate. The Great Sky Quest Theatre presents a three-theater multimedia show composed of film, slides, and dioramas that detail the development of trans-Pacific flight.

Learn about the first flights, including one in 1925 in which the pilot ran out of fuel 365 miles from Hawaii's shores, so he stripped the fabric from his plane, created sails, and "blew" into shore. A diorama carefully explains the Pearl Harbor battle, at a level that even early grade-school children can understand.

The main gallery, outside the theater, offers an array of hands-on fun.

You can see authentic hula dances at Waimea Falls Park. (Photo by the author)

Test your flying skills by "landing a plane," design your own aircraft via computer, and plot the best route across the Pacific Rim.

(Be sure to see the Day Trips for the many wonderful attractions on the North Shore.)

SPECIAL EVENTS

January: Professional golfers take part in the PGA Hawaii Open Golf Tournament, and the Hula Bowl hosts college football all-stars each year.

February: Humpback Whale Awareness Month, with a wealth of lectures, and arts on display at the Sea Life Park. View demonstrations and displays of the year's new products at the Family Expo in Honolulu. Oahu hosts the Buffalo's Big Board Surfing Classic, the NFL Pro Bowl, and, just for kids twelve and under, a race of their own—the Keiki Great Aloha Run. Hawaii Mardi Gras is always lots of fun because area restaurants serve Creole and Cajun food, and the parade comes alive with colorfully masked dancers and steel drums.

March: Watch the skies or take part in the Oahu Kite Festival, Queen Kapiolani Park. Oahu celebrates Japanese culture with games, entertainment, and various demonstrations at the Cherry Blossom Festival Culture and Craft Fair. The fifth day of the month is the International Day of the Seal, celebrated at Sea Life Park with prize drawings, games, and crafts for the whole family. Have you ever seen 20,000 yellow rubber ducks race down a canal? Now's your chance, at the Great Hawaiian Rubber Duckie Race, in Honolulu.

April: The Hawaiian Festival of Music takes place all around Oahu, including choir and band concerts. At the Ala Moana Beach State Park, the Tin Man Biathlon features a 2.7-mile run and an 800-meter swim. On Easter, Sea Life Park hosts an Easter Egg Hunt.

May: On Mother's Day kids bring their moms to Waimea Falls Park, and moms enjoy free admission.

June: June 11th is a state holiday, King Kamehameha Day. Events and activities vary yearly, but usually include the King Kamehameha Celebration Floral Parade, and Hawaiian arts and crafts. Fathers enjoy free admission to Sea Life Park and Waimea Falls Park on Father's Day, when accompanied by their children. The King Kamehameha Hula Competition brings contenders to Honolulu from all corners of the world.

August: Witness the qualifying rounds for the Ironman Triathlon, at the Windward Triathlon, consisting of a 10-mile run, 50-mile bike ride, and mile swim.

September: The Outrigger Hotels Hawaiian Oceanfest includes women's professional windsurfing competition, run-and-swim races, paddle boarding, outrigger canoe paddling, and ocean medley relay. Attend the fund-raising Kamokila Hula Festival and Concert, a celebration of the music and dance of Hawaii.

November and December: At the Sunset Beach Park, men and women compete at the Triple Crown of Surfing: Event #3—World Cup of Surfing. Football fans won't want to miss the Aloha Bowl, and on New Year's Eve celebrate with the rest of Honolulu at First Night Honolulu, an alcohol-free evening festival, featuring more than 200 events, including magicians, jugglers, and dancers.

WHERE TO STAY

Although Waikiki long ago turned its palm trees into high rises, this famed strip offers easy access to city attractions as well as inexpensive accommodations. A good lodging bet is the **Outrigger Reef Hotel**, 2169 Kalia Road; (808) 462–6264. Call **Outrigger Hotels**, (800) 462–6264. Unlike many of the twenty other Outrigger hotels in Waikiki, which seem to hunker among the town's noisy blocks, and cater to college kids on the loose, the **Outrigger Reef** sits surfside in a slightly quieter location along Kalia Road. The family-friendly amenities include a pool, rooms with two double beds, plus a pull-out couch, refrigerator, balconies, and no charge for children seventeen and under who share with parents. Ask about the frequent packages that often include free rental cars or deals for staying at the **Royal Waikoloan**, Outrigger's flagship hotel on the Big Island. At Outrigger kids become a part of Moki's Keiki Klub. Members receive a membership card, pencil, stickers, and buttons, but no activities program. Older parents and grandparents should book the 50-plus Program for a 20 percent discount, or receive a 25 percent discount if you're a member of the American Association of Retired Persons.

The **Hyatt Regency Waikiki**, 2424 Kalakaua Avenue (808–923–1234 or 800–233–1234), offers optional packages for families as well as honeymooners. Ask about their often-available package with rental car, welcome gifts, Hawaiian leis, and discounts on local activities. At Camp Hyatt Waikiki, children between the ages of three and twelve enjoy movies, games, arts and crafts, and Hawaiian stories. For the teens, Rock Hyatt, when available, offers occasional night tours of Waikiki, dinner at the Hard Rock Cafe, and nightclub activities. Other options include catamaran sailing trips, pool parties, barbecues, and shopping.

The **Hilton Hawaiian Village**, 2005 Kalia Road (808–949–4321 or 800–445–8667), is a huge complex with twenty acres of gardens, three swimming pools, and a good-sized beach. In addition to the regular hotel rooms, there is also the upscale and quieter (but pricier) Ali'i Tower accommodations. The hotel offers the Rainbow Express Young Explorers Club, a year-round children's activity program for ages four to twelve from 8:30 A.M. to 2:45 P.M. or a half-day program from 12:30 P.M. to 2:45 P.M. Kids enjoy photo safaris, beach expeditions, and field trips.

Four **Sheraton Hotels** in Waikiki offer the Keiki Aloha Sunshine Club, free activities for ages five to twelve from mid-June through August. The toll-free reservations number for all Sheraton properties is (800) 325–3535. Hotels participating in the kids' program in Waikiki are the **Sheraton Waikiki**, 2255 Kalakaua Avenue (808–922–4422); the **Sheraton Moana Surf**, 2365 Kalakaua Avenue (808–922–3111); and the flagship of Sheraton's Oahu hotels, the **Royal Hawaiian Hotel**, 2259 Kalakaua Avenue (808–923–7311). The latter, the "pink palace," once catered to the elite famous when only the wealthy could afford Hawaii. The graciousness is still there, as are the hand-carved wooden doors in the original hotel, whose rooms have been modernized. There's also a newer wing.

All of these Sheratons are beachfront and offer morning child-care sessions (9:00 A.M. to noon), supervised lunch (noon to 1:00 P.M.), afternoon sessions (1:00 P.M. to 5:00 P.M.), and evening sessions (6:30 P.M. to 9:00 P.M.).

The five-star **Halekulani** is beachfront in Waikiki, 2199 Kalia Road 96815; (808) 923–2311 or (800) 367–2343. It features a complimentary children's program (lunch and admission fees to attractions are extra) for ages six to thirteen from 8:30 A.M. to 3:00 P.M. The program operates mid-June through about August 20, and also for two weeks at Christmas. Children visit the Hawaii Maritime Museum, go on catamaran rides, swim in the pool, and try their hand at arts and crafts.

North Shore
The **Turtle Bay Hilton Golf and Tennis Resort**, P.O. Box 187, Kahuku, 96763 (808–293–8811 or 800–HILTONS), offers horseback riding, ocean-viewing pools (the surf can be rough here), and an eighteen-hole golf course. The **Turtle Bay Hilton's Turtle Tots** program offers activities for ages seven to twelve. Check ahead to be sure the program is operating.

WHERE TO EAT

First a word about **luaus**. Most big hotels on every island offer these. Some are more "authentic" than others, but to accommodate tourists many have become less traditional, offering tourists lots of food, little authenticity, and some Hawaiiana. These can also be costly for a family. Check with your hotel concierge or new-found island friends to see which ones are worth the expense. Among the better luaus are the ones at **Royal Hawaiian Hotel** (808–923–7311) and **Paradise Cove** (808–973–5828). Most of the luaus require reservations, and many offer children's prices.

Waikiki Area
Waikiki blooms with inexpensive eateries. Try breakfast at **McDonald's, Denny's**, or at any of the numerous coffee shops. At **Perry's Smorgy Restaurant**, 2380 Kuhio Avenue (808–926–0814), or at the **Outrigger Coral Seas Hotel**, 250 Lewers Street (808–922–8814), the food is just average, but the prices are low for heap-your-plate buffets. With southern fried chicken, mahi mahi, turkey, roast beef, and spaghetti on the unlimited buffet, even the finickiest tot will find something of interest.

The **Waiahole Poi Factory**, Kamehameha Highway and Waiahole Valley Road, open only Friday afternoons, features a lunchtime feast of genuine home-cooked Hawaiian delicacies at a low price. **Monterey Bay Canners**, 2335 Kalakaua Avenue (808–922–5761), features a variety of seafood dishes, a children's menu, and a relaxed environment. They are also located on Ala Moana Boulevard at the Ward Warehouse (808–536–6199) and at the Pearlridge Center (808–487–0048).

When you dine at the **Lewers Street Fish Company**, Lewers Street (808–971–1000), or the **Waikiki Seafood and Pasta Company**

(808–923–5949), you receive half-price coupons for future meals at either restaurant. The **California Pizza Kitchen**, 4211 Waialae Avenue (808–737–9446), is a chain of gourmet pizzerias whose menu also includes salads and pastas. They have several locations throughout Oahu. The **Wailana Coffee House**, 1860 Ala Moana Boulevard (808–955–1764), across from the Hilton Hawaiian Village, is an inexpensive eatery. For a good breakfast buffet, try the **Parc Cafe**, in the Waikiki Parc Hotel, 2233 Helumoa Road; (808) 921–7272. Kids prices are reduced.

While dining out during your visit, ask about kids' prices and use the early bird specials, which can reduce a full meal to $7.00 to $8.00 if you arrive before 6:00 or 6:30 P.M., a convenient family dining time. Also check the free tourist guides, such as *Spotlight Oahu Gold*, for discount coupons to restaurants and attractions.

Ala Moana Center Area

The **Makai Food Court** at the Ala Moana Center, 1450 Ala Moana Boulevard, offers a range of ethnic choices, from Thai to Italian to Hawaiian. The **China House**, 1349 Kapiolani Boulevard (808–949–6622), near the Ala Moana Center, features Oriental cuisine and welcomes families. The **California Pizza Kitchen**, 1910 Ala Moana Boulevard (808–955–5161), offers good pizza and pasta.

At the Ward Warehouse, the **Old Spaghetti Factory** (808–591–2513) specializes in pasta with a variety of sauces.

Other Places Around Oahu

The **California Pizza Kitchen**, 98-1005 Moanalua Space; (808) 486–0373 (see listing under Waikiki Area). At **Stuart Anderson's**, 1050 Ala Moana Boulevard (808–591–9292), adults savor the steaks, while kids usually opt for the barbecued ribs, french fries, and crispy shrimp. For Mexican fare, choose from chimichangas, tacos, and burritos at **Compadres**, 1200 Ala Moana Boulevard; (808) 591–8307. The **Hee Hing Restaurant**, 449 Kapahulu Avenue (808–735–5544), promises fresh fish, delicious noodles, and a large selection of dishes to choose from. **Orson's Chowderette**, 1450 Ala Moana Boulevard (808–946–5548), is known for their clam chowder (some say it's the best in all of Honolulu), grilled mahi sandwiches, and fried calamari.

DAY TRIPS

A must-do day trip takes you across the island to the north shore through sugarcane and pineapple fields bounded by blue sea and green cliffs. Helpful hint: Wear your bathing suit.

Visit **Waimea Falls Park**, 59-864 Kamehameha Highway at Wei Mei; (808) 638–8511 or (808) 923–8448. This 1,800-acre botanical garden about 40 miles from Waikiki features lush vegetation and lessons in island lore. Take the tram, or stroll, through the gardens of red and purple bougainvillea, hibiscus, past trees draped with Spanish moss, and clusters of ginger plants, to the waterfall. Cliff divers, announced by the call of a conch shell, tumble effortlessly from as high as 60 feet. Swim here, then follow the crowd to a performance of a traditional hula, where costumed dancers relate tales of stalwart warriors and stoical princesses. Also visit the ancient temple known as Hale Iwi.

For teens, Waimea Falls Park offers adventure tours, which let you ride through the park's North Valley. To take the three-hour guided ATV (all-terrain vehicle) trek (book only if you know how to handle these sometimes-tricky-to-operate vehicles), you must be sixteen and weigh at least ninety pounds.

The park also offers guided mountain tours, kayak rides along the Waimea River, and a two-and-a-half-hour van tour to less visited areas, which includes a twenty-minute nature hike.

After Waimea Falls Park, continue north for several miles, but pull over when you see the surfboards. Watch the experts catch a wave at such legendary beaches as **Banzai Pipeline** and **Sunset Beach**. Look, but don't swim as the undertow and often 30-foot-high waves make these shores dangerous for even the most accomplished swimmers.

The **Polynesian Cultural Center**, 55-370 Kamehameha Highway, Laie, 96762 (808–293–3333 or 800–367–7060), entertains with lively hands-on history. Allow several hours to explore this forty-two-acre living history park, or even stay for the dinner luau and the elaborate evening review. (Reserve ahead of time.) At the recreated villages of Samoa, New Zealand, Tahiti, Fiji, Old Hawaii, the Marquesas, and Tonga, the costumed interpreters—some sporting elaborate tattoos and dried leaf and feather skirts present facts with quick vaudeville pacing. As you learn how to play the nose flute, twirl poi balls, weave baskets, carve tikis, and blow conch shells, these interpreters crack jokes and deliver deadpan looks. The Samoan villager, for example, was irresistible with his wide-eyed, worried stare as he playfully instructed us in the arduous task of splitting a coconut for its juice and milk.

Don't miss the IMAX film *Polynesian Odyssey* whose montage of canyons, cliffs, and ocean scenes evokes the bravery of the first voyagers who used their starry-eyed wonder and instinctive skills to cross an unknown sea. As always be aware that the larger-than-life IMAX images may scare some younger children.

FOR MORE INFORMATION

For general information contact the **Chamber of Commerce of Hawaii,** 1132 Bishop Street (808–545–4300), and the **Hawaii Visitors Bureau,** 2270 Kalakaua Avenue, Suite 801 (808–923–1811). For **Camping/State Park** information, call (808) 587–0300. For **weather** information, call 833–2849 or 836–0121. **Handicabs of the Pacific,** P.O. Box 22428, Honolulu, Hawaii 96823 (808–524–3866), provides special transportation, tours, and cruises for people with disabilities.

Emergency Numbers
Ambulance, fire, police: 911
Twenty-four-hour emergency care: The Queens Medical Center, 1301 Punchbowl Street; (808) 547–4311. CALL-A-NURSE, (808) 225–6877, is a free health care information referral line, Monday through Saturday 8:00 A.M. to 4:30 P.M. For the hearing-imparied, ASK–2000 (275–2000). **Kunio Pharmacy,** 2330 Kuhio Ave; (808) 923–4466.

CANADA

47
BANFF
Alberta

Banff, Canada's first National Park, is a breathtaking four-season resort in the heart of Alberta's Canadian Rockies. The town of Banff and the tiny village of Lake Louise, forty minutes west, are the park's civilized centers. Banff (the town) is surrounded by a ring of majestic mountains and exudes the atmosphere of a European resort—but don't be surprised to see an elk walking Banff Avenue. Beyond "civilization" is truly spectacular scenery: 2,564 square miles of varied terrain where wildlife roam free among towering peaks, lush forests, alpine valleys, rivers, glaciers, hot springs, and lakes, including Lake Louise, one of the region's most popular destinations. This splendid setting provides countless recreational opportunities for families, from winter skiing to fair weather pursuits: boating, hiking, horseback riding, cycling, and more.

GETTING THERE

The nearest airport is **Calgary International**; (403) 292–8400. You can rent a car here or take a bus to the town of Banff, ninety minutes to the west. Lake Louise is forty minutes further west.

   Via Rail no longer serves Banff. **Rocky Mountaineer Railtours** (800–665–7245) runs two-day east and/or westbound rail tours between Vancouver, Banff, and Calgary from May to early October, with an overnight stay in Kamloops, British Columbia. Add-on hotel and sightseeing packages and car rentals in Banff can also be arranged.

   Bus service is provided by the following companies. **Greyhound of Canada** (800–661–8747—Canada/800–332–1016—Alberta) serves Banff from various points in Canada, including Calgary. **Laidlaw Transporta-**

tion (403–762–9210), on the arrivals level of Calgary Airport, transports passengers anywhere in the park. **Brewster Transportation** (800–661–1152) also offers scheduled bus service from the airport to Banff and Lake Louise.

TransCanada Highway 1 from Calgary leads to Banff and Lake Louise. From Banff, Lake Louise also can be accessed by a slower but more scenic route, the Bow River Parkway, which runs parallel to Highway 1 on the other side of the river and has interpretive signs, scenic viewpoints, and picnic sites.

GETTING AROUND

If you're driving, a map is helpful within the park, since few of the drives connect directly to the TransCanada Highway. The town of Banff is located 10 miles inside the park's entrance. The Banff Information Centre, 224 Banff Avenue, (403) 762–0270, shared by the Tourism Bureau and the Canadian Parks Department, is open daily year-round. A brochure titled "Banff and Vicinity Drives and Walks" lists drives and attractions, with maps indicating their locations.

WHAT TO SEE AND DO

How you spend your days will depend on whether you visit in summer or winter, when the area becomes a skier's dream. Spring and fall (when the foliage is outstanding) offer some of the activities available to winter and summer visitors, at lower prices and with fewer crowds.

Note: Even in the middle of town, you may come within an arm's length of animals. Although some may appear tame, they are not, and the park urges visitors to keep their distance: Never feed them or get too close. Remember: Banff is not a game farm. During mating season, the elk that stroll nearby can become quite territorial and aggressive. Park visitors are asked to report any aggressive animals to the warden's offices (see For More Information).

Here are some sensational sights your family shouldn't miss.

Banff Area

Sulphur Mountain Gondola, open daily from December 26 to mid-November, south on Banff Avenue to Mountain Avenue, then 1½ miles to the gondola's lower terminal; (403) 762–5438. This is an eight-minute journey aboard four-passenger, glass-enclosed gondolas to the mountain top, where observation decks offer spectacular views of Banff and the Bow Valley. For more views, try the short, easy hiking trails along the mountain ridges. The Summit Restaurant has seating in the round, so all diners have a superb panorama. Breakfast and dinner specials are offered seasonally.

Cave and Basin Centennial Centre, 311 Cave Street; (403) 762–1557. The discovery of natural hot springs here in 1883 led to the to the creation of Canada's first National Park two years later to preserve the springs and encourage visitors. You step through a tunnel to see the cave's hot springs and bathhouse, though the sulphur smell (reminiscent of rotten eggs) may be too strong for some kids. The centre shows videos and exhibits year-round that tell the story of the discovery. Take a short, self-guided or guided interpretive walk (free) along the boardwalk on the hillside above the centre.

Another boardwalk follows a marsh trail, which shows how the heated mineral water from the hillside has resulted in lush vegetation. Telescopes and benches are provided along the way along with interpretive signs. Because of funding, the warm outdoor mineral-water swimming pool may not be open.

Up the hill, less than a mile west on Mountain Avenue (next to Sulphur Mountain Gondola), **Upper Hot Springs** offers an outdoor soaking pool of hot water that bubbles up from Sulphur Mountain. Once considered therapeutic, the waters are now appreciated for their relaxing effect. Children ages three and up are allowed, but the temperature (about 104 degrees), the strong sulphur smell, and the twenty-minute-maximum stay may annoy most kids. You can rent bathing suits and towels for a small fee. Massages are also offered by appointment only; call (403) 762–2056 for information. The pool is open all year (though closed periodically for maintenance); skiers find the waters soothing for their sore limbs.

Buffalo Paddock, 0.6 miles west of the Banff interchange, just off the TransCanada Highway, is a free drive-through enclosure open between May and October. Visit in the morning or evening for the best chance to see a small herd of bison.

Lake Louise

This turquoise lake edged by Whitehorn Mountain is truly stunning. Stop by the Lake Louise Information Centre, Samson Mall, (403) 522–3833, for tourist information. The new, architecturally striking building shows a multimedia presentation, *The Building of the Canadian Rockies,* and has exhibits on the area's natural and human history.

The Chateau Lake Louise Resort, the only resort on the lake, hugs the lake's eastern shore. Canoes can be rented at the boathouse on the left side of the resort; call (403) 522–3511. A popular stroll (easy for kids because it's level) starts in front of the chateau and follows the lake's northwest shore for about 1½ miles. You walk below the high cliffs at the far end of the lake, where rock climbers can often be observed. At the muddy delta, just beyond the cliffs, the paved walk ends—and this is where families with young children will want to stop. Hardy, fit families accustomed to hiking may turn this stroll into a day trip by continuing on the somewhat strenuous trail (now called the Plain of the Six Glaciers), which climbs about 2½ half miles over a rocky creek, gravel fields, and, ultimately, to icy glaciers. Mountain goats can often be seen on the slopes of the glaciated peaks surrounding the area. You'll end up at the rustic **Plains of the Six Glaciers** teahouse where beverages, light lunches, and snacks are served during the summer. Prices are a bit steep because food is brought in via helicopter or packhorses.

If all this sounds like too much work, consider taking the **Lake Louise Summer Mountain Lift**, a twenty-minute ride atop Whitehorn Mountain. The lift is located across the valley from the Chateau Lake Louise resort. Although there are open-air chairs, families can take an enclosed gondola car or a covered "bubble" chair. Bring a picnic lunch to eat on the mountain slopes. Call (403) 522–3555 for information; open June to September.

Museums

The following museums, all in the town of Banff, are worth a visit.

Banff Park Museum, 92 Banff Avenue, (403) 762–1558, houses a taxidermy collection of animals, from birds to grizzly bears, indigenous to the park. Built in 1903, this is the oldest natural history museum in Canada, and the building, an unusual type of architecture known as "railroad pagoda," is a Canadian Historic Site. Admission is free; open year-round.

Banff Natural History Museum, Clock Tower Mall; (403) 762–4747. The museum displays the geological evolution of the Rockies via dioramas, models, fossils, and a twenty-minute audiovisual show on the eruption of Mt. St. Helens. It's open year-round.

The Whyte Museum of the Canadian Rockies, 111 Bear Street, (403) 762–2291, recently opened a new wing, almost doubling its size. Everything in the museum portrays the cultural heritage of the Canadian Rockies. The art gallery has changing exhibits that feature historical paintings as well as modern sculpture, and the heritage gallery displays changing artifacts and photos. Summer programs for children and families are frequently offered. It is open daily in the summer, with abbreviated winter hours.

Luxton Museum, 1 Birch Ave; (403) 762–2388. Kids enjoy the exhibits here, honoring the heritage of the Indians of the Northern Plains and Canadian Rockies. Displays include costumes, hunting equipment, and dioramas of native and pioneer life. The building that houses the museum is an old fortlike structure overlooking the Bow River. The museum is operated by the Buffalo Nations Cultural Society, representing Stoney, Blackfoot, Blood, Sarcee, and Peigan tribes. It's open daily year-round.

Interpretive programs, utilizing slides, nature talks and strolls, and dramatizations are offered from late June to early September. Programs are usually held nightly at the theater at the **Banff Visitors Centre**, and on weekends at some of the campgrounds, including Lake Louise, Tunnel Mountain, and Johnson Canyon. Although there are no programs especially for children, topics are chosen to appeal to the widest variety of ages, and, if there are many children in the audience, the program will be aimed at them. Check the posted program schedules at campground kiosks, or at the Canadian Parks Service Visitors Centre, 224 Banff Avenue, (403) 762–1550, and at the Lake Louise Visitor Reception Centre, Samson Mall, (403) 522–3833.

Adventures

Here are some ways for active families to enjoy the best that Banff has to offer.

Boating: Lake Minnewonka, about 15 miles northeast of the town of Banff, off the TransCanada Highway, is the park's largest and the only lake where power boats are allowed. You can rent 16-foot boats with outboard motors from mid-May to Labor Day from Lake Minnewonka Tours (their office is on the dock), (403) 762–3473, or take one of their guided tours to the end of the lake. They also provide fishing licenses, which are required in the park, and fishing equipment rentals. The lake, noted for its trout, splake, and Rocky Mountain whitefish, is the park's most popular fishing spot.

Cycling: The Banff Visitors Centre has a list of rental shops and a trail bike pamphlet. Beware of traffic and wildlife while you ride. Because of the bike's speed and relatively quiet approach (compared with hikers), trail cyclists are vulnerable to sudden bear encounters. So make noise; put bear bells on your pedaling shoes.

Dog Sled Racing: The season runs from about November 1 to April 1. Experienced mushers pick you up at the Banff Springs Hotel; afterwards, you're welcome to take photos and visit with the friendly Siberian Huskies. Two adults fit comfortably in the sleds, plus a child or two, depending on size (babies are welcome). Reserve at least several days in advance from Mountain Mushers Dog Sled Company, P.O. Box 1721, Banff TOL OCO; (403) 762–9423.

Horseback Riding: There are several stables and outfitters in the area. **Warner Guiding and Outfitting Ltd.**, 132 Banff Avenue (office above Trail Rider store), (403) 762–4551, has trail rides that run from one hour to a full day, generally from mid-April to mid-November. While no strict age limits apply, nine years is the recommended age for the backcountry trips that operate from July 1 to the end of September. These range up to six days; but a good ride with children is the 10-mile route along Bow River to Sundance Lodge on Brewster Creek for a two-day stay.

The **Brewster Lake Louise Stables,** located to the right of the Chateau Lake Louise, (403) 762–5454, specializes in guided half-day trail rides around the lake and up to the **Plain of Six Glaciers,** or all-day trips farther afield. There is no strict age limit; a small child may be allowed to ride with a parent. During the winter, horse-drawn sleigh rides follow the lakeside trail.

River Rafting: Rocky Mountain Raft Tours offer float trips along the Bow River (follow Wolf Street to the river). Trips are either one or three hours in length; children's rates are available; no age minimum, but use common sense. Inquire about whether the trip is a float or white-water journey. Call (403) 762–3632.

Skiing: Ski season generally operates from mid-November to late May. There are three resorts within the park, linked with one interchangeable ski/shuttle bus pass, available from **Ski Banff/Lake Louise,** Box 1085, Banff; (403) 762–4561 or (800) 661–1431—western Canada. The company also offers vacation packages and other ski services.

Mystic Ridge & Norquay, (403) 762–4421, ten minutes northwest of downtown Banff, is the closest major ski resort to town. Famous for its beginner and expert terrain, the resort more than doubled the skiing terrain in 1990, adding a number of intermediate runs as well. The new visitor's service complex has a restaurant/lounge, cafeteria, day-care services for ages nineteen months to six years (two-hour minimum; ski lessons available, if desired), ski rentals, and retail shops. Ages six to twelve can take two-hour or all-day lessons (lunch not included).

Lake Louise; (403) 2–LOUISE or (800) 661–4141—Alberta, September to April/(800) 567–6262—western Canada/Pacific Northwest, October to April. This is the largest ski area in Canada, with four distinct mountain faces and a variety of runs that range from gentle novice to challenging expert. **Saturn Play Station** offers day care for infants eighteen days through eighteen months and toddlers nineteen to thirty-five months, either hourly (minimum three hours) or daily. Older kids can attend half- or full-day programs. Ages three to six have supervised indoor and outdoor play with two lessons; ages seven to twelve can take a Kids Ski program, where an instructor teaches while guiding them around the entire mountain.

Sunshine Village; (403) 762–6500. For one thing, it has the only on-mountain accommodations in the Canadian Rockies, the Sunshine Inn (800) 372–9583—Alberta/(800) 372–9583—Canada/(800) 661–1363–U.S. You get here by traveling 4 miles west of Banff town on the TransCanada, then 4 miles south on the access road to the parking lot and gondola station. From there, it's a twenty-minute ride aboard Canada's longest gondola to reach the resort, located on the Continental Divide 7,000 feet above sea level—making it the highest resort in the Rockies. More than half of Sunshine's terrain is for intermediates. Day care is offered for ages nineteen months to six years, with lessons available, if desired. Group lessons for ages six to twelve are also given.

Cross-country skiing: There are thousands of beautiful trails within the park. A map available from the parks department for $1.00 lists the trails and their difficulty.

Theater, Music, and the Arts

The **Banff Centre School For Fine Arts**, St. Julien Road, (403) 762–6100, is the site of year-round cultural events, including ballet, opera, jazz, dance, theater, and free recitals and concerts. It's also head-quarters for the annual **Banff Festival of the Arts**, running from the end of May through the third week of August, with plays, dance, opera, concerts, visual arts exhibitions, and more. For ticket information, call the box office at (403) 762–6300.

Shopping

Cascade Plaza, 317 Banff Avenue and Wolf Street, offers upscale shops (Polo Ralph Lauren, Esprit, Timberland, Godiva Chocolates) as well as those that sell Canadian art and artifacts. There's a food court on the concourse level. The shops along **Banff Avenue** sell Canadian-made goods and souvenirs, British woolens, and Irish linens.

SPECIAL EVENTS

Annual events, fairs, and festivals include the following.

February: Banff/Lake Louise Winter Festival.

June: Banff Television Festival, a conference of TV producers, writers, and actors who meet to sell TV shows, which are shown to the public for free.

July: Banff International Street Performers Festival, with clowns, musicians, jugglers, and fire eaters.

August: Buffalo Nation Days includes parade and native dancing.

September: Melissa's Mini-Marathon is a popular event.

November: Banff Festival of Mountain Films, weekend of screenings, craft fair, and other activities.

WHERE TO STAY

An accommodations guide and a bed-and-breakfast directory are available from the Banff/Lake Louise Tourist Bureau; (403) 762–8421. The bureau can also give you information on the fifteen campgrounds within the park; three have electricity, and four have showers.

The bureau advises summer visitors, particularly those arriving on weekends, to make reservations at least one day in advance. There have been days, particularly in August, when every park lodging was filled by noon; visitors were sent to Calgary and Lake Louise.

Summit Vacations owns and operates the computerized central reservations for hotels in Banff, Lake Louise, and Jasper National Park; (403) 762–5561/(800) 661–1676/(800) 372–9593—Alberta. Despite the splendid winter skiing, summer (early June to early October) is the high season in Banff, with higher prices.

Banff

Families have excellent lodging options in Banff.

Banff Springs, Spray Avenue; (403) 762–2211/(800) 268–9411—Canada/(800) 828–7447—U.S. This majestic, Canadian Pacific hotel is elegant and opulent, a historic landmark styled after the baronial castles of Scotland. Even if you aren't staying here, come to see the sumptuous surroundings. On property are a twenty-seven-hole golf course and a mini-golf course, fifty shops, tennis courts, a bowling alley, indoor and outdoor pools, and fourteen restaurants. An enchanting Festival of Christmas starts in November and runs through January 1, with organized activities such as hayrides, skating parties, scavenger hunts, evening stories by the fire, and a nightly Lighting Ceremony.

Douglass Fir Resort, Tunnel Mountain Road; (403) 762–559/(800) 661–9267. The resort has one- and two-bedroom condos with full kitchens, perfect for families. The convenience store, coin laundry, and barbecues come in handy, too. So does the complex, with two indoor water slides, a children's pool, and a video games room (open to nonguests for a fee and free to guests). Ski packages are available in winter.

Lake Louise

Chateau Lake Louise is 2½ miles southeast off TransCanada Highway 1; (403) 522–3511/(800) 268–9411—Canada/(800) 828–7447—U.S. This lakeside resort was recently renovated with 140 new rooms in the new Glacier Wing and restored public space and guest rooms. A pool, six restaurants, and a shopping arcade are on site. Some suites are available. During ski season, a supervised playroom is open for ages two and up.

WHERE TO EAT

A helpful restaurant guide is available from the Banff/Lake Louise Tourist Bureau. You'll find a wide selection of restaurants in the town of Banff, including the ubiquitous **McDonald's**, 116 Banff Avenue, (403) 762–5232, which also serves pizza. **Joshua's Restaurant**, 204 Caribou

The opulent Banff Springs Hotel is one of many first-class accommodations in this exciting area. (Courtesy Alberta Economic Development and Tourism)

Street, (403) 762–2833, serves a French and continental menu, with pasta, beef, and seafood the specialties. The old-fashioned decor is pleasing, and there's a children's menu. **The Caboose,** CP Rail Station, Elk and Lynx streets, offers beef, seafood, and a self-service salad bar amidst railway memorabilia and a rustic decor. A children's menu is available.

Banff Grizzly House, 207 Banff Avenue, (403) 762–4055, specializes in steak and fondue, though there's also buffalo and rattlesnake on the menu. The kids love the atmosphere, complete with totem poles and Indian crafts. Dine outdoors, if you prefer.

DAY TRIPS

If you have older kids who don't mind a slow, winding car trip, venture out along the **Icefields Parkway** (Highway 93), 78 miles north of Lake Louise to the **Athabasca Glacier.** You see the highest, most rugged mountains in the Canadian Rockies, and you can spot moose, elk, goats, and sheep along the way. Twenty miles north of Lake Louise, stop at **Bow Summit,** the highest point on the parkway. A short access road leads to the **Bow Summit–Peyto Lake viewpoint area.** Peyto Lake, shaped like a grizzly bear, has a distinctive color, ranging from pale green to deep turquoise.

The **Columbia Icefield**, one of the largest accumulations of ice and snow south of the Arctic Circle, is on the boundary of Banff and Jasper National Parks. Continuous snow accumulations feed eight major glaciers, including the **Athabasca**, 4 miles long and located directly across from the **Columbia Icefield Visitors Centre**; (403) 852–7030. The center has maps, brochures, and schedules for interpretive events, such as guided hikes and evening programs, given by park naturalists, as well as a scale model of the entire ice fields and an audiovisual presentation on the area.

Kids like the narrated tour of the icy slopes of the glacier aboard a specially designed Brewster "Snowcoach" bus. (Brewster also has round-trip tours from Banff or Lake Louise.) Passengers are allowed to step out onto the slippery glacier. Contact **Columbia Icefield Snowmobile Tours**, P.O. Box 1140, Banff TOL OCO; (403) 762–6735. Tours are available May 1 to October 10. Children's rates apply for ages six to fifteen; under age six free when sharing a seat with an adult. Reservations aren't required; the busiest time at the ice field is from 11:00 A.M. to 3:00 P.M.

FOR MORE INFORMATION

Banff/Lake Louise Tourism Bureau: 224 Banff Avenue, Banff; (403) 762–0270.
Canadian Parks Service: (403) 762–1500.
Visitor Reception Center: Samson Mall; (403) 522–3833.
Each center is open seven days, year-round.
The park trails and other facilities are constantly being upgraded to be accessible to the physically challenged. Contact the Tourism Bureau for more information.

Emergency Numbers
Ambulance, fire, police: (403) 762–2000
Lake Louise Fire: (403) 522–2000
Police: Royal Canadian Mounted Police; (403) 762–2226
Warden: To report an aggressive animal, call the Banff Wardens Office (403–762–4506) or the Lake Louise Warden Office (closed Wednesday and Thursday) at (403) 522–2000.
Hospitals: Banff's Mineral Springs Hospital, 301 Lynx Street; (403) 762–2222. **Lake Louise Medical Clinic**, 200 Hector; (403) 522–2184.
Pharmacy: Cascade Plaza Drug, Cascade Plaza, Banff Avenue at Wolf; (403) 762–2245. There are no twenty-four-hour pharmacies.

48
CALGARY
Alberta

Set in the lovely rolling foothills of the magnificent Canadian Rockies, Calgary achieved international attention when it hosted the 1988 Winter Olympics. Originally an outpost of the North West Mounted Police, the city became a mecca for "Cattle Kings" who built mansions and sprawling ranches when the transcontinental railway reached town in 1892. Later, Calgary thrived as an oil boomtown. Although still one of Canada's major oil centers with a population nearing 740,000 and a downtown sparkling with shiny skyscrapers, the city has managed to retain a small town feeling. That friendly, Old West atmosphere comes alive during Stampede Week in July when everyone dons western gear for a "rip roarin'" good time.

The feeling also extends to kids. In mid-1993, Calgary proclaimed itself "child friendly" and is encouraging businesses to create places for children to play while parents shop, to provide adequate rest rooms, and, in restaurants, to offer more toddler seating and to provide crayons and paper. An advisory committee of kids ages seven to seventeen meet regularly with city administrators to discuss issues concerning the younger set.

GETTING THERE

Calgary International Airport (403–292–8477) is about 3 miles from the city center. The **Airporter Bus** (403–531–3907) is the most efficient way to get to town. Car rentals and taxi service are available.

VIA Rail no longer serves Calgary. **Greyhound**, 850 Sixteenth Street S.W., (403) 265–9111, provides frequent service throughout Canada.

By car, Calgary is on the TransCanada Highway (Route 1), which runs from coast to coast.

GETTING AROUND

Calgary is divided into quadrants, with Centre Street providing the east-west dividing line, and the Bow River and adjacent Memorial Drive dividing north from south.

Calgary Transit (403–262–1000) operates an excellent public bus and light rail transit (LRT) system. Travel within the downtown core (between City Hall and Tenth Street S.W.) is free. Maps and information are available at the Calgary Transit information centre, 270 Seventh Avenue S.W.

WHAT TO SEE AND DO

Museums

At the **Alberta Science Centre/Centennial Planetarium**, 701 Eleventh Street S.W., (403) 221–3700, see daily star shows in the 360-degree Star Theatre, then have interactive fun in the large Discovery Hall. Activities there usually compliment a current, traveling exhibit; for example, a recent one, Marine Monsters, featured robotic sea creatures. A series of mystery plays (such as Agatha Christie's *Murder in the Vicarage*) are held in the facility's Pleiades Mystery Theatre throughout the year.

The **Calgary Chinese Cultural Centre**, 197 First Street S.W.; (403) 262–5071. This new facility, by the Bow River in the heart of downtown, is quite an eyeful. The impressive six-story Great Cultural Hall was modeled after the Temple of Heaven in Beijing, which took over 100,000 man-hours to build. Twenty-two artists from mainland China contributed the hand-painted, gold-foiled paintings on the dome. Supported by four columns representing the four seasons, the dome boasts 561 dragons and forty phoenix. The museum contains a number of paintings and artifacts from various dynasties, including a full-scale replica of terra cotta soldiers from the First Dynasty, and a pot filled with water that, when rubbed with two hands, gives the illusion that the water is dancing. Special concerts and events are frequently held in the auditorium. In addition to the arts-and-crafts shop with goods from mainland China, there is a restaurant (scheduled to open in the fall), an herb shop, and a snack shop.

Energeum, 640 Fifth Avenue S.W.; (403) 297–4293. Run by the Energy Resources Conservation Board, this free museum devoted to fossil fuel is small but surprisingly interesting. Watch the big-screen video on Alberta's first oil discovery, then try some computer games and interactive displays—including a chance to put your gloved hand into some "black gold." Be sure to see the pink 1958 limited edition Buick in the memorabilia display; it's a beauty.

At **Fort Calgary Historic Park**, 750 Ninth Avenue S.E., (403) 290–1875, experience Calgary's history firsthand. Located at the confluence of the Bow and Elbow rivers, at the site of the 1875 North West Mounted Police post, the forty-acre park is within walking distance of downtown. First stop: the interpretive center to see a fifteen-minute video on the area's history that emphasizes the Mounted Police. Next: the Discovery Room where kids (and adults) can, among other things, try on Mounted Police uniforms and have their picture taken next to a stuffed bison. The permanent exhibit room features life-size recreations of important figures from Calgary's past. Step outdoors to enjoy the beautiful surroundings. A short, paved trail leads to the site of the fort, which is being reconstructed. Currently, the northwest corner has been completed, and in the next few years, the entire fort should be rebuilt. The adjacent 1906 Deane House, 806 Ninth Avenue, S.E., (403) 269–7747, serves as a restaurant, offering lunch, afternoon tea, and Murder Mystery dinner theater. The house was built in 1906 for the Mounties' Commanding Officer, Captain R.B. Deane, and is operated as part of the park. The building beside the Deane House is the oldest (1876) in Calgary that is still on its original site. At press time, this house was being restored and will open to the public.

The largest museum in western Canada, **the Glenbow Museum**, 130 Ninth Avenue S.E., (403) 268–4100, focuses on the area's settlement and its native peoples. There seems to be something for everyone, including lots of colorful "stuff" that should appeal to kids: Eskimo and Inuit art and artifacts, a Blackfoot tepee, a mineral exhibit, modern art and sculpture, military artifacts that include armor, a large gun collection considered one of the country's best, stamps, coins, and a collection of carriages. Some exhibits incorporate interactive displays. Be sure to show the kids the five cases of Olympic pins near the entrance. This museum also hosts major traveling exhibits, so check to see what's currently on display.

Heritage Park Historical Village, 1900 Heritage Drive S.W. at Fourteenth Street; (403) 259–1900. This sixty-six-acre park presents life in western Canada prior to 1914. The original buildings were moved here from various locations throughout Alberta. Hop aboard the old steam train that travels throughout the village. Visit a Hudson Bay Company Fort, a one-room schoolhouse, an oil rig, a bakery, an ice cream parlor, and a working grain mill. Try your luck at the antique midway. The village is on the edge of the Glenmore Reservoir, and for an extra fee you can take a stern-wheeler cruise aboard the S.S. *Moyie*. Inquire about the variety of family programs throughout the year.

Other Attractions

Calaway Park, 6 miles west of Calgary on the TransCanada Highway and Springbank Road; (403) 240–3824. This is western Canada's largest amusement park. Enjoy the rides, a petting farm, mazes, miniature golf, fishing, a driving range, live entertainment, cinema, shopping, and special events. Family passports are available. The park is open daily July and August and on weekends only in May, June, September, and October. There's also an RV park and campground; for reservations call (403) 249–7372.

Calgary Exhibition and Stampede, 1410 Olympic Way S.E.; (403) 261–0101 or (800) 661–1260. This is the big one: Ten days in July of rip roaring fun kicks off with a parade and features rodeo events, chuck wagon races, concerts, shows, an amusement park, agricultural exhibitions, and more. Everybody dresses western style. Plan ahead for a visit: Attendance is over one million.

Calgary Tower, 101 Ninth Avenue S.W.; (403) 266–7171. Take an elevator ride to the top of the 626-foot tower for spectacular views of prairies and the Rockies from the observation deck or revolving restaurant. On special occasions, the Calgary Olympic Flame that tops the tower is lit.

Parks, Gardens, and Zoos

Canada Olympic Park, Highway 1 West, 6 miles west of Calgary; (403) 247–5404. This impressive place is where the bobsled, luge, and ski jumping competitions took place during the 1988 Olympics. School-age and older kids enjoy the guided bus tour open to the public during summer that goes to the top of the 90-metre Ski Jump Tower, the highest point in the city, and along the twisting Bobsleigh/Luge Track. Self-guided tours are also possible. Summer luge rides start from the bottom third of an iced track (for ages ten years and older). At the Olympic Hall of Fame, see displays, films and videos and ride the Ski Jump and Bobsleigh Simulator. From November to April, the park offers downhill skiing and bobsleigh and luge rides.

Calgary Zoo, Botanical Gardens and Prehistoric Park, 1300 Zoo Road N.E., St. George's Island; (403) 232–9300 or (403) 232–9372 for recorded information. Accessible via a river walkway over the Bow River, this world-renowned facility houses some 1,500 animals who live in indoor and outdoor natural habitats. Popular attractions include the underwater viewing area for sea lions and seals, and the children's petting zoo.

The new Aspen Woodlands (opened July 1993) is the first phase of a ten-year Canadian Wilds project to create five unique ecosystems of the Canadian wilds. The Aspen Woodlands, a transitional habitat where the prairie meets mountains, is the most endangered in Canada. The zoo feels that by highlighting habitats close to home, visitors will become aware of the fragility of these areas. Using only plants and animals native to the area, the zoo has created four acres of rolling hills and valleys filled with wildflowers and aspen. White-tail deer, mule deer, and (in the coming months) elk, graze in the meadows. Native birds fly freely in the aviary. Hands-on opportunities include exploring a human-size magpie nest, traveling through a tunnel to view elk from a special blind, and walking through a fox's den to get a peek at these creatures. The colorful graphics by the zoo's director are meant to appeal to kids: More attention is paid to illustration than to text. Docents are available to answer questions. The next phase, the Rocky Mountains, is scheduled to be completed in fall 1994.

Dinosaur fans delight at the twenty-seven life-size models in Prehistoric Park, an eight-acre area with lakes, badlands, and swamps. The Botanical Gardens, with thousands of plant species, provide a fragrant, relaxing refuge.

Devonian Gardens, Toronto Dominion Square, Seventh Avenue between Second and Third streets S.W.; (403) 268–3830. If the weather's bad, this 2.5-acre indoor park provides a welcome oasis with 16,000 tropical plants and 4,000 local plants, plus waterfalls, fountains, ponds, playgrounds, reflecting pool, and occasional lunchtime entertainment. Stores and restaurants, located below the gardens, offer another fun refuge.

Olympic Plaza, corner of Macleod Trail and Seventh Avenue S.W., (403) 268–5203, was created for the medal presentations during the 1988 Winter Olympics. Now this plaza is an outdoor activity center, with skating in the winter and special events year-round. Note: You must bring your own skates; there are no rental facilities here.

Prince's Island Park, Third Street S.W. at the Bow River, is accessible by footbridges from either side of the river. Stop here and enjoy the surroundings, which include a playground, fitness trails, and a snack bar.

Theater, Music, and the Arts

The *Calgary Herald* and the *Calgary Sun* are good sources of information on local entertainment. There are also a number of free publications at newsstands, hotels, and other locations around town that list entertainment, including *Where Calgary, Downtown Calgary, Visitor's Choice, CityScope, Vox* (a publication of the University of Calgary), and *Impact* (a health/fitness/life-style magazine).

Theater is alive and well in Calgary, and chances are you will find a play to appeal to the whole family. The Convention and Visitors Bureau can help arrange tickets, or call Ticket Master Alberta at (403) 270–6700. For the little ones, **StoryBook Theatre**, (403) 291–2247, offers matinees at the Pumphouse Theatre, 2140 Pumphouse Avenue S.W.

Sports

The hottest team in town is the NHL **Calgary Flames** Hockey Club,

(403) 261–0475, skating from October to April at the Olympic Saddle-dome, 1410 Olympic Way S.E. For Flames tickets, call (403) 261–0455. The **Calgary Cannons** Baseball Club, (403) 284–1111, number one minor league affiliate of the American League Seattle Mariners, has seventy-two home games at Foothills Baseball Stadium, 2255 Crowchild Trail N.W., from April to September. For Cannons tickets, call (403) 270–6200. **Calgary Stampeders** Football Club, (403) 289–0205 or (800) 667–FANS—Canada, a member of the professional Canadian Football League, kicks off at McMahon Stadium, 1817 Crowchild Trail, from July to November 30. For tickets, call (403) 289–0258.

Race City Speedway, Sixty-eighth Street and 114 Avenue S.E., (403) 264–6515, hosts stock and sports car, truck, motorcycle, and drag racing on three world-class paved tracks weekends from May to September.

Spruce Meadows, south on Macleod Trail, west on Highway 22X, (403) 254–3200, is a world-famous equestrian facility with three annual jumping tournaments (see Special Events). Visitors are welcome to tour the training facility.

Shopping

The brand new **Eau Claire Market**, Second Avenue and Second Street, S.W., (403) 264–6450, downtown on the Bow River, adjacent to Prince's Island Park. This shopping and entertainment complex combines a fresh food market, specialty retail shops, restaurants, and Calgary's first IMAX Theater (403–263–IMAX) plus a cinema.

The downtown shopping core runs from First Avenue S.W. on the east to Eighth Street S.W. on the west. Shoppers are protected from the elements by an enclosed walkway system of bridges at least fifteen feet above grade level, known as "Plus 15s."

There are several shopping centers downtown; the largest is the **Toronto Dominion Square 1000**, 333 Seventh Avenue S.W., (403) 221–0600 or (403) 221–1368, which includes the Devonian Gardens (described earlier) and two anchor department stores: Eaton's and The Bay, plus about one hundred specialty shops.

SPECIAL EVENTS

Contact the Calgary Convention and Visitors Bureau for more information on the following events.

February: Calgary Winter Festival.

March: Rodeo Royal, Stampede Park.

June: International Children's Festival; Lilac Festival; The National equestrian event, Spruce Meadows.

July: Canada Exhibition and Stampede; Calgary Folk Festival; Shake-

Calgary's Winter Festival draws people from all over the world. (Courtesy Calgary Convention and Visitors Bureau)

speare in the Park (evenings); North American Invitational equestrian event, Spruce Meadows.

August: International Native Arts Festival; Ballet in the Park.

September: The Masters equestrian event, Spruce Meadows; Artwalk at various locations throughout town; Calgary Balloon Festival; Old-Time Fall Fall (CQ), Heritage Park, horse pull competitions, entertainment, and displays.

Mid-November–Mid-December weekends: Twelve Days of Christmas, Heritage Park.

December–January: Lions Club Christmas Lights Display, Confederation Park.

December 31: First Night Festival, various locations throughout Calgary, including finale at Prince's Island Park.

WHERE TO STAY

CCVB offers an accommodations directory and that includes several area guest ranches. If you're coming for the Stampede, reserve well in advance. **Calgary Bed and Breakfast Association,** 3728 Forty-fifth Street

S.W., Calgary T3E 3V4, (403) 274–7281, handles fifty rooms in Calgary and the area, some with kitchenettes.

Several all-suite hotels are located downtown, including: **Prince Royal Inn**, 618 Fifth Avenue S.W.; (403) 263–0520 or (800) 661–1592. This newly renovated hotel has separate, fully equipped kitchens in studios and one- and two-bedroom units, plus offers complimentary continental breakfast and in-room coffee makers. There's a restaurant/lounge and coin laundry, too.

The largest hotel in Calgary is also downtown: the luxurious **Westin Hotel**, 320 Fourth Avenue S.W.; (403) 266–1611 or (800) 228–3000, offers the new Westin Kids Club amenities. These include child-friendly rooms, children's sports bottle or tippy cup upon check-in, as well as a safety kit with a night light, Band-Aids, and emergency phone numbers. Rooms feature bath toys and bath products for kids, and parents can request—at no charge—jogging strollers, potty seats, bicycle seats, and step stools. Restaurants and room service also feature children's menus.

A number of reasonably priced motor inns are located outside downtown. In the Northeast section: **Ambassador Motor Inn**, 802 Sixteenth Avenue N.E.; (403) 276–2271 or (800) 661–1447—Canada. The Ambassador features family suites with kitchenettes, restaurant, and an outdoor pool. In the Northwest section: the **Econo Lodge**, 10117 West Valley Road N.W.; (403) 188–4436 or (800) 424–4777. Here you will find family suites, kids' playground, and an outdoor pool.

WHERE TO EAT

Contact the Calgary Convention and Visitors Bureau (CCVB) for dining information. There's no distinct local cuisine, but plenty of diversity. For steak dinners (jackets required for men), try **Hy's Calgary Steak House**, 316 Fourth Avenue S.W., (403) 263–2222, where kids' meals are served. **Mother Tucker's**, 345 Tenth Avenue S.W., (403) 262–5541, in an informal setting, serves prime rib and features a salad bar, fresh bread, homemade desserts, and a kids' menu. If your children are adventurous eaters, sample the Far Eastern cuisine at **A Touch of Ginger**, 514 Seventeenth Avenue S.W., (403) 228–9884, where the beef satay is one of the specialties, and kids have their own menus.

DAY TRIPS

While it may not be Jurassic Park, the **Royal Tyrrell Museum of Paleontology**, 80 miles northeast via Highway 9 in Drumheller (403–294–1992), should elicit some oohs and aahs as it harbors the world's largest exhibit of complete dinosaur skeletons: thirty-five in all. Watch museum technicians prepare fossils, see a video, and stroll through a prehistoric garden. Something called a "palaeoconservatory" houses more than one hundred species of tropical and subtropical plants that once grew in this area. Computer information terminals plus interactive games add to the fun.

Once in Drumheller, you're not far from **Reptile World**, 1222 Highway 9 South, Drumheller, (403) 823–8623, where among the 150 reptiles are some of the rarest in North America. Hands-on exhibits (do you dare hold a boa?).

The **Head-Smashed-In Buffalo Jump Interpretive Centre**, (403) 553–2731, 11 miles west of Highway 2 on Highway 85, Fort Macleod, ninety minutes south of Calgary, sounds gruesome, but is quite an interesting attraction. Seven levels of displays built into a cliff recreate the hunting techniques used by Native American tribes. For more than 6,000 years, Plains Indians hunted buffalo by driving them over this cliff to their death. Highly valued, the buffalo provided fresh meat, warmth, tools, and shelter. A film simulates the jump and guided tours led by members of the Blackfoot Confederation are available. Browse the displays and Indian artifacts, and walk the trails located above and below the cliff. This site is considedred the best-preserved buffalo jump site anywhere; it's a visit your family won't soon forget.

Banff and **Banff National Park** are 80 miles west of Calgary on Trans-Canada Highway 1. Though it's possible to do in a day, we advise setting aside several days for a visit (see Banff chapter).

FOR MORE INFORMATION

The **Calgary Convention and Visitors Bureau**, 237 Eighth Avenue S.E., Alberta T2G 0K8, (403) 263–8510 or (800) 661–1678, supplies helpful information. Year-round visitors centers are at Calgary Tower, 120 Ninth Avenue S.W. at Centre Street, and at Calgary International Airport, arrivals level. Calgary **Handi-Bus Association** (403–276–1212) provides service to the disabled.

Emergency Numbers
Ambulance, fire, and police: 911
Poison Centre: (403) 670–1414
Hospitals: Alberta Children's Hospital, 1820 Richmond Road, S.W., (403) 229–7211
Twenty-four-hour pharmacy: Shoppers Drug Mart Chinook Centre, 1323 North 6455 Macleod Trail South; (403) 253–2424

49
EDMONTON
Alberta

Alberta's cosmopolitan capital has its share of appealing attractions for vacationing families. For starters, there's the West Edmonton Mall, the world's largest, with everything from a wave pool to a roller coaster. But there's more to Edmonton than mall heaven. In summer, add bountiful festivals that offer days of merriment and culture. All year long enjoy the museums, concerts, cultural and sporting events, and the superb natural beauty that includes 8,500 acres of parkland stretching along the lush North Saskatchewan River valley that curves through the city. Don't forget the clean subway system, friendly people, and a fascinating heritage that started with the fur trade and includes a lively past as a Klondike boomtown.

GETTING THERE

Edmonton is served by two airports. **Edmonton Municipal Airport**, just north of downtown, (403) 496–2836, serving airlines that cover shorter distances, and **Edmonton International Airport**, 18 miles south of the city, (403) 890–8382. For **Grey Goose** shuttle service information, call (403) 462–3456. Car rentals and taxi service are available at both airports.

    Via Rail offers transportation between Edmonton and other major Canadian cities. The station is downtown at 10004 104 Avenue; (403) 422–6032 or (800) 561–8630—Canada.

    Greyhound Bus Lines has service from Edmonton to all points in Canada and the U.S. The station is downtown at 10324 103 Street; (403) 421–4211. **Red Arrow Express**, 10014 104 Street, (403) 424–3339, provides motorcoach service between Edmonton, Red Deer, Calgary, and Fort McMurray.

The two major highways that run through Edmonton are the Yellowhead TransCanada Highway (#16), running east and west, and Highway 2, running north and south.

GETTING AROUND

The city street system is on a grid, with streets running north and south, and avenues running east and west. A series of downtown pedestrian walkways (pedways) offer easy access to shopping, hotels, and cultural facilities. Downtown parking information and maps are available at the Edmonton Visitor Information Centres (403–496–8400).

The city has both bus and light rail transit (LRT). The **Edmonton Transit Downtown Information Centre** is open weekdays at 100 A Street and Jasper Avenue, or call (403) 421–4636 daily for route and schedule information.

WHAT TO SEE AND DO

Museums and Historical Attractions

Alberta Legislature, 97 Avenue and 107 Street, (403) 427–7362, is the seat of the province's government. Older kids may enjoy the free guided tours given every half hour of this grand, ornate building, on which construction began in 1907. (When you get to the fifth floor, listen to what seems to be a torrential downpour: actually, it's the echo of the fountain five stories below.) The beautiful grounds—with flowers, fountains, and pools in summer and a skating rink in winter—make this an extremely pleasant place to linger.

Edmonton Space and Science Centre, 11211 142 Street; (403) 452–9100. From the outside, this facility resembles a sleek, modernistic flying saucer, and inside are fascinating exhibits. Most kids head straight to the Challenger Centre, a simulator composed of a mission control and the space station Alpha 7, where kids transform themselves into astronauts. Call ahead to schedule a visit.

The lower gallery houses hands-on exhibits. The Universe Gallery includes a piece of the moon on loan from NASA and a scale that measures what your weight would be on other planets, such as Pluto. At the ED TEL Theatre to the Future, the audience participates in science demonstrations, and the IMAX theater has a four-story screen. The Margaret Zeidler Theatre boasts the largest planetarium dome in Canada. More than 200 computer-controlled projectors, special effects, and a laser system combine with a powerful audio system to offer visitors unforgettable laser light music concerts, live plays, and planetarium shows. If the weather is clear, stop by the public observatory where attendants show you how their four astronomical telescopes work. For snacks, stop by the Cafe Borealis.

Fort Edmonton Park, Whitemud and Fox drives; (403) 486–8787. Step back in time at this low-key historical theme park located on 158 acres on the south bank of the North Saskatchewan River and home to more than sixty period buildings. The fort is a replica of the 1846 home base of the Hudson's Bay Company fur trading industry. Costumed interpreters grade furs, repair a boat, and bake bread in an outdoor oven. Kid volunteers may get to assist. Three long streets transport visitors to different periods in the city's history. On 1885 Street, a small frontier town, take a horse-drawn wagon ride (small additional charge), browse in quaint shops, visit homesteaders on their farms, and see the blacksmith in action at his forge. On 1905 Street, the city appears as it did in the year it became the provincial capital. On 1920 Street, explore the brickyard and greenhouses, stop by the Ukrainian Bookstore, then have a soda at the old-time soda fountain. Daily special events and programs include visitor participation. A miniature steam engine travels the length of the park (no additional charge). Pony rides are available for an extra fee. This pleasant park, without a lot of glitz, appeals to younger school-age kids. It's especially charming at Christmas when the park can be toured by horse-drawn sleigh or wagon (depending on the snow), and you can feast on a pioneer buffet breakfast at the Jasper House Hotel on 1885 Street.

Combine a visit to Fort Edmonton Park with a stop at the **John Janzen Nature Centre,** at the southwest corner of Quesnell Bridge, adjacent to the park; (403) 496–2939. The place is noted for the displays of the small creatures that inhabit the river valley, such as salamanders, ant colonies, and garter snakes. There are 2.2 miles of marked nature trails. Free admission.

Old Strathcona Model and Toy Museum, 8603 104 Street (Highway 2 south); (403) 433–4512. This free museum is thought to be the only one of its kind—and it certainly is unusual. The more than 400 models on display are made entirely of paper. Included are castles and other historic sites and buildings, boats, planes, trains, space vehicles, dolls, birds, people, and animals. There's also an operating model railroad.

Telephone Historical Information Centre, 10437 Eighty-third Avenue; (403) 441–2077. Kids tend to like this hands-on facility, where they walk through a telephone cable and see an audiovisual show presented by a robot who interacts with the audience.

Provincial Museum of Alberta, 12845 102 Avenue; (403) 453–9100. Devoted to Alberta's human and natural history, this museum focuses on the Ice Age and boasts a gigantic mammoth skeleton. The Bug Room, which has live inhabitants, proved so popular that the temporary exhibit is now a permanent fixture. Preschoolers particularly enjoy the Discovery Room, where they can do lots of hands-on things, such as trying on animal costumes and learning about camouflage.

Parks and Zoos

Muttart Conservatory, 9626 96A Street; (403) 496–8752. The four pyramid-shaped glass pavilions set along the river valley house more than 700 species of flowers, plants, and trees from tropical, arid, and temperate zones. In the show pavilion, displays change frequently. The Conservatory is open year-round—where else would you find bananas growing in January, especially in Canada? For a lovely view of downtown, stand by the reflecting pools at the base of the pyramids.

Valley Zoo, 134 Street and Buena Vista Road; (403) 496–6911. Spend several fun-filled hours at this seventy-acre zoological garden featuring more than 400 animals, including an African veldt and a bird of prey exhibit plus daily elephant and sea lion training demonstrations. The kid's section has a storybook theme. Other attractions include camel, paddleboat, and pony rides; a train; and merry-go-round.

The North Saskatchewan River valley runs through the center of town, providing acres of parkland—the longest stretch of urban parkland in Canada. There are 33 miles of hiking, biking, jogging, and groomed ski trails, plus golf courses, boat launching sites, picnic areas, nature walks, and skating areas located in a series of linked parks. At **Hawrelak Park,** beside Groat Road on the south side of the river, enjoy a lake stocked with trout, pedal boats, a playground, barbecue grills, and lots of room for kids to romp. Call the **Edmonton Parks and Recreation River Valley Outdoor Centre** (403–496–7275) for information on specific facilities and events within the park system. In summer take tots to the wading pools and older kids to the indoor and outdoor pools. Particularly popular: the Wave Pool at **Mill Woods Recreation Centre,** Twenty-eighth Avenue and Seventy-second Street; (403) 496–2929.

Other Attractions

The West Edmonton Mall, 8770 170 Street, (403) 444–5200 or (800) 661–8890, is more than just a mall—it's an attraction in itself, even for those who run from malls. With 5,200,000 square feet—the equivalent of forty-eight city blocks—this is the world's largest mall. There's just about everything for everybody: aviaries with exotic birds; more than thirty aquarium tanks, including shark tanks; a casino; bottle-nose dolphin shows; a Spanish galleon; an ice skating rink covered by a glass dome; Deep Sea Adventure submarine rides; miniature golf; World Waterpark, complete with a giant wave pool; and Canada Fantasyland, (403) 444–5300, the world's largest indoor amusement park, with more than

You can body surf, swim, suntan, or spin down a water slide at the world's largest indoor water park, located at the West Edmonton Mall. (Courtesy Edmonton Tourism)

twenty-five rides and attractions, including the world's largest indoor triple-loop roller coaster and scaled down kiddie rides. And, yes, there are scores and scores of stores as well—more than 800 stores and services, including eleven major department stores; 210 women's fashion shops; thirty-five men's wear stores; fifty-five shoe shops; and many toy, souvenir, sports, book, and record stores.

Check with Edmonton Tourism on the status of **Alberta's World Oil Park,** the $300 million theme park commemorating the discovery of oil in 1947 near Edmonton. Planned for completion sometime in the future, the park will be on a 460-acre site adjacent to Edmonton International Airport. (At press time, however, ground hadn't yet been broken for the park, which was grappling with some financial problems.)

Theater, Music, and the Arts

For information on the arts, check the city's two daily newspapers, the *Edmonton Journal* and *Edmonton Sun,* or the monthly entertainment publications, *See* and *Billy's Guide.* TicketMaster outlets (403–451–8000) located throughout the city handle tickets for most events. There are sixteen professional theater companies in town, including **Chinook Theatre,** Eighty-third and 103 streets, (403) 448–9000, in the heart of historic Old Strathcona, with a variety of story theater, puppetry, music, adapted classics, and modern theater for young people. The **Citadel Theatre**, 9828 101 A Avenue, (403) 426–4811, offers world-class plays from September to May and is host to the Teen Festival of the Arts and International Children's Festival (see Special Events). More family entertainment can be found at **The Stage Polaris**, 85th Avenue and 101 Street, (403) 432–9483, where shows for the very young are performed.

Sporting Events

Edmonton is home to three professional sports teams. The **Edmonton Oilers**, several times Stanley Cup Champions of the National Hockey League, play from October to April in the Northlands Coliseum, 118 Avenue and Seventy-fourth Street; tickets are available from TicketMaster. The **Edmonton Eskimos** are members of the Canadian Football League and play from June to November at Commonwealth Stadium, 111 Avenue and Stadium Road; (403) 448–3757. The **Edmonton Trappers**, members of the Pacific Coast League, play baseball from April to September at John Ducey Park, Ninety-sixth Avenue and 102 Street. Tickets are available at the gate, (403) 429–2934, or through TicketMaster.

Arts

The **Edmonton Opera**, (403) 429–1000, **Edmonton Symphony Orchestra**, (403) 428–1414, and **Alberta Ballet Company**, (403) 428–6839, perform in the Northern Alberta Jubilee Auditorium, on the University of Alberta Campus, Eighty-seventh Avenue and 114 Street; (403) 427–9622.

Shopping

If you find West Edmonton Mall (described earlier) too daunting, there are several more reasonably sized malls downtown (100 to 103 streets). **The Old Strathcona Historic Area**, extending around Eighty-second Avenue (Whyte Avenue) and 104 Street, is a pleasant place to stroll and shop. Restored buildings in the area date back to 1891, the year the Calgary/Edmonton railroad arrived. Browse at the trendy boutiques and year-round farmer's market (403–439–1844) that sells crafts and fresh vegetables.

SPECIAL EVENTS

Contact Edmonton Tourism for more information on the following annual festivals.

February: Local Heroes Film Festival features films and workshops.
March: Northlands Farm and Ranch Show.
May: International Children's Festival, Citadel Theatre, a five-day

event with music, mime, puppetry, dance, and theater from around the world.

June–July: The Works: A Visual Arts Celebration covers the entire spectrum of visual, environmental, wearable, and even edible art; International Jazz City Festival.

July: International Street Performers Festival includes clowns, acrobats, mimes, magicians, and jugglers performing for ten days in more than 900 free shows downtown; Klondike Days, ten days of food, fun, music, costumes, old-time fair, international trade and cultural exhibits, the largest traveling midway; Teen Festival of the Arts, Citadel Theater.

August: Heritage Festival features music, dance, costumes, arts, and food from around the world; The Fringe, a nine-day theatrical event featuring seventeen theaters, three outdoor stages, and over 1,200 performers; Folk Music Festival has over sixty acts, eight stages, workshops, food, handicrafts, and music; Dream Speakers Festival is an international celebration of First Nations art and culture.

December 31: First Night Festival, over seventy-five live performances of music, theater, visual arts, and a rooftop fireworks spectacular.

WHERE TO STAY

A partial lodging listing is available in the *Edmonton Visitors Guide*. For bed-and-breakfast selections, contact AHHA (Affiliated Holiday Home Agencies, Inc.), 10808 Fifty-fourth Avenue, (403) 436–0649, which can arrange stays in cities, towns, villages, farms, ranches, and resort areas. Here are some good hotel choices for families.

Fantasyland Hotel and Resort, West Edmonton Mall, 17700 Eighty-seventh Avenue; (403) 444–3000 or (800) 661–6454. Altogether, there are 355 guest rooms, with 158 theme rooms, including Igloo, Victorian Coach, Hollywood, Polynesian, and Arabian themes. Some, such as the Canadian Rail room, have particular appeal to families: The berths of the train cars are perfect for kids. With the giant mall/recreation center right at your doorstep, this could be a family fantasy come true.

The former Chateau Lacombe, one of the country's finest hotels, has been converted to the Holiday Inn Crowne Plaza, 101 Street at Bellamy Hill, (403) 428–6611 or (800) HOLIDAY, after $12 million in renovations. One of the hotel's restaurants, La Ronde, is the city's only revolving restaurant. The Westin's Hotel Edmonton, 10135 100 Street, Edmonton, Alberta, T5J ON7 Canada, (403) 426–3636 or (800) 228–3000, offers the new Westin Kids Club amenities. These include child-friendly rooms, children's sports bottle or tippy cup upon check-in, as well as a safety kit with a night light, Band-Aids, and emergency phone numbers. Rooms feature bath toys and bath products for kids, and parents can request—at no charge—jogging strollers, potty seats, bicycle seats, and step stools. Restaurants and room service also feature children's menus.

WHERE TO EAT

Edmonton Visitors Guide has a short listing of restaurants, but with more than 2,000 eateries to choose from, it's hard to select a mere handful. Contact Edmonton Tourism; they often have free publications, such as *Billy's Guide*, which lists restaurants. Ethnic food, particularly Italian, is always a good bet with kids. Two to recommend: **The Old Spaghetti Factory**, 10220 103 Street, (403) 422–6088, and **Packrat Louie Kitchen and Bar**, 10335 Eighty-third Avenue, (403) 433–0123, which, in addition to pasta, serves pizza cooked in a wood-burning oven and offers a terrific dessert selection. For moderately priced breakfast, lunch, or dinner, search out a **Smitty's Family Restaurant**, where steaks, chicken, burgers, pancakes, and waffles are among the specialties. There's one at the West Edmonton Mall (403–444–1981) and ten other locations citywide. **Bullwinkle's Family Food and Fun**, 12910 Fort Road, (403) 473–5827, serves burgers, fries, and other standard fare while puppets put on a stage show. There's a game room as well.

DAY TRIPS

Reynolds-Alberta Museum, 4705 Fiftieth Avenue, Wetaskiwin; (403) 352–5855. Located about forty minutes south of Edmonton, this sprawling, sparkling new museum is devoted to transportation, agriculture, and industry, and is also the home of Canada's Aviation Hall of Fame. The museum evolved from the private collection of the Reynolds family, who had started a small local automobile service center in 1910. The exhibits and audiovisual displays of vintage bicycles, cars, aircraft, agricultural and industrial machinery—and their impact on life throughout the province—delight adults and kids alike, especially presented against such nostalgic backdrops as a 1920s grain elevator, a 1940s service station, and a 1950s drive-in theater. This is not a place where stationary artifacts from the past are revered in hushed silence. Instead, you can get behind the wheel of a Model T racer, take a place on a miniature moving assembly line in the car factory, or operate a "Gerber spout," a device that controls the distribution of grain into various bins in a grain elevator. Outdoors on the 156-acre grounds, the vintage machines come to life. Cars and bicycles cruise, farm equipment chugs, and aircraft fly overhead on a regular basis. Other items not to miss: The Aircraft Hall of Fame hangar and the Restoration/Conservation shop, where many of the vintage vehicles have been brought back to perfection. For snacks as well as lunch and dinner, the Galaxy Cafe offers meals and panoramic views. Be sure to ask about special events, live entertainment, and traveling displays.

Elk Island National Park is a nature preserve of unspoiled parkland located 28 miles east of Edmonton, just outside the town of Fort Saskatchewan, on Highway 16; (403) 992–6380. The park was created to save the area's elk from extinction. Today, within the park's fences, herds of elk, moose, and bison live undisturbed (along with hundreds of birds) and can be seen roaming free as you drive through the park. Yes, bison can be dangerous, but they should leave you alone unless provoked. Pick up a copy of "You Are in Bison Country" at the Park Information Centre, just off Highway 16, for safety tips. The center of "people activity" within the park is Lake Asotin, which has hiking trails, picnic areas, a nine-hole golf course, and cross-country skiing in the winter. Check the Asotin Interpretive Center (403–922–5790) for films and a schedule of daily activities.

About a half mile east on Highway 16 is the **Ukrainian Cultural Heritage Village**, Highway 16; (403) 662–3640. It tells the story of the Ukrainian immigrants and the development of their settlement in east central Alberta from 1892–1930. Costumed interpreters recreate a variety of historical characters. Tour farmsteads and the town site, whose historical buildings include a hardware store, and relax with a ride in a horse-drawn wagon.

Very young children love **Alberta Fairytale Grounds**, (403) 963–8161, 15 miles west on Highway 16, just west of the town of Stony Plain. The owner of this private park uses handcrafted puppets and fairytale scenes to delight the younger set as they follow a path through the woods. **Devonian Botanic Garden**, 3 miles north of Devon on Highway 60, (403) 987–3055, is located within 190 acres of rolling sand dunes and large ponds. Nature trails and boardwalks make it possible to explore protected ecological areas and to bird watch. Bring a picnic: Benches are located along the trails. There's also a Japanese garden, fragrant floral displays, and labeled native and introduced plants, as well as a pavilion of live butterflies.

FOR MORE INFORMATION

Edmonton Tourism has a **Visitor Information Centre**, 9797 Jasper Avenue, (403) 422–5505, open daily at Gateway Park (Highway 2), 2404 Calgary Trail Northbound S.W.; (403) 988–5455. During the summer, two smaller offices are open, one on Highway 16 West and one on Highway 16 East. An information center is located at City Hall and at the International Airport arrivals level; (403) 890–8382.

DATS (Disabled Adult Transportation System) gives disabled visitors a temporary registration number. For further information or to register call (403) 496–4570. To book transportation, call (403) 496–4567.

Emergency Numbers
Ambulance, fire, police: 911
Poison Center: (800) 332–1414
Twenty-four-hour emergency room: Royal Alexander Hospital, 10240 Kingsway Avenue; (403) 477–4111
Late-night pharmacy: Mid-Niter Drugs, 11408 Jasper Avenue; (403) 482–1171

50
VANCOUVER
British Columbia

Vancouver, the largest city in western Canada, with more than 1.6 million residents, is surrounded by inlets of the Pacific Ocean on three sides. To the north rise the majestic Coast Mountains; the fertile farmlands of the Fraser Valley nestle in the east. Along with spectacular natural beauty, this cosmopolitan city also offers a temperate climate (the mildest in Canada), a friendly, ethnically diverse populace, and enough activities to ensure a fun family vacation.

GETTING THERE

Vancouver International Airport (604–276–6101), on an island some 9 miles south of downtown, is served by nineteen major airlines. Bus, limousine service, and taxis provide transportation to major downtown hotels.

Greyhound Lines of Canada, 1150 Station Street (604–662–3222), is the largest bus line serving Vancouver from points across Canada and North America. **Quick Shuttle** (604–526–2836 or 800–665–2122—US) has frequent bus service between Vancouver's downtown Sandman Inn, 180 West Georgia, and Seattle, either downtown or to Sea-Tac Airport.

VIA Rail Canada, #215, 1150 Station Street, offers service through the Rockies to Banff; call (604) 640–3741 or (800) 561–8630 in Canada and (800) 561–3949 in the United States. **BC Rail**, 1311 West First Street, North Vancouver has trains to Whistler and the interior of the province; (604) 631–3500.

Vancouver is the major departure point for more than ten major cruise ship lines heading to Alaska.

By car, Vancouver is a three-and-one-half-hour trip from Seattle via I-5, which becomes Highway 99 at the U.S.-Canadian border. Highway 1, the TransCanada Highway, enters Vancouver from the east.

GETTING AROUND

B.C. Transit (604–261–5100) operates city buses, the SkyTrain light rapid transit system, which runs between downtown Vancouver and Surrey, about fifty minutes southeast, and the SeaBus, a 400-passenger commuter ferry between downtown and the foot of Lonsdale in North Vancouver—a scenic, twelve-minute ride across Burrard Inlet. Day passes are available. Transit literature, including a free *Discover Vancouver On Transit* guidebook, are available from Travel Info Centre, public libraries, and BC Transit Lost Property at SkyTrain Stadium Station.

Most of major attractions are located in the city's heart, a peninsula surrounded by English Bay, First Narrows, and Burrard Inlet.

WHAT TO SEE AND DO

Museums and Historical Sites

Science World British Columbia, Quebec Street and Terminal Avenue at the Science World/Main Street Skytrain station; (604) 687–7832. Hands-on fun is the name of the game at this delightful place (formerly the Expo 86 Centre) where all ages find activities that are fun, fascinating—and, yes, educational. Walk inside a camera, or through a distorted room where nothing is exactly as it seems; talk through a tube that echoes back; have a close-up look at an ant farm; play with giant bubbles; compose a tune on an electric piano. The attractions include eveything from eye-boggling "scientific show biz" demonstrations to The Bubble Show. In the Search Gallery, younger visitors explore by crawling through a beaver lodge or walking inside a hollow tree. Check the weekend and holiday special events, as well as the OMNIMAX theater schedule; call (604) 875–OMNI for show schedules. For snacks, try the Bytes Cafeteria.

The Vancouver Museum (604–736–7736) is on the main level at 1100 Chestnut Street (in Vanier Park), a building that also houses the **H.R. MacMillan Planetarium** (604–736–4431 or 736–3656) on the top floor. The planetarium's programs include astronomy shows, laser/rock concerts, and family and children's matinees. At the **Gordon Southam Observatory**, next to the main building, visitors are welcome to gaze through a telescope to view far-off wonders on clear days. Admission is free, but call first to see if it's open: (604) 738–2855.

After the planetarium, head downstairs to the Vancouver Museum, the largest civic museum in Canada, which houses thousands of impressive artifacts from Greater Vancouver and around the world. Kids enjoy the eclectic objects, which run the gamut from a dugout canoe to a collection of vintage police badges to elegant European evening dresses. The museum also houses crafts, carved sculptures, masks, and other ceremonial objects from the First Nations people of the Pacific Northwest Coast.

Ask about the frequent children's programs, which involve creative ways to appreciate the museum's displays; preregistration is often required.

Special temporary exhibits are always on view. Being planned at press time to help celebrate the museum's centennial: an exhibit entitled Teen Age: Inventing Canadian Adolescence. It explores the emergence of adolescence and its changes in the 1890s, 1920s, and 1950s. Furnished rooms contain "stuff" that teens of those eras found impossible to live without. This should be a hit with both aging baby boomers and their kids; it could offer a humorous way to open up some dialogue between teens and parents. Tell your teen your vulnerabilities at his or her age.

Vancouver Maritime Museum, 1905 Ogden Avenue; (604) 737–2211. Just west of the Vancouver Museum, this museum brings to life the maritime heritage of this thriving port city, as well as the history of the British Columbia coast. At the entrance to the museum, the huge Kwakiutl totem pole out front sets the tone. Inside the majority of the exhibits are temporary, frequently incorporating hands-on activities. The model ship displays are particularly intriguing to kids. Admission includes a guided tour of the Royal Canadian Mounted Police Arctic schooner *St. Roch,* one of the first vessels to transit and circumnavigate the Northwest Passage. The harbor behind the museum also includes a floating display of privately owned historical and modern vessels.

Considered Vancouver's most spectacular museum, the **UBC Museum of Anthropology (MOA),** 6393 Northwest Marine Drive, on the campus of the University of British Columbia (604–822–3825—recording), is worth a stop. Some label it one of the finest small museums anywhere. Devoted to collections from cultures around the world, this museum is particularly acclaimed for both its holdings from the First Nations of British Columbia and its setting. Located in an award-winning glass-and-concrete building on the Point Grey Cliffs, the museum is surrounded by Haida houses that overlook the mountains and the ocean. Although this is not a hands-on place, the museum has several "touchables," including the Bear sculpture in the hallway at the base of the ramp and the hanging drums (kentongans) in the Research Collection. Don't miss the contemporary Northwest Coast sculpture, *The Raven and the First Men*; carved from a huge block of laminated yellow cedar, it portrays the moment in a Haida story when a raven discovers the first Haidas emerging from a clamshell. Programs include Sunday afternoon concerts and storytellers for both adults and children.

Later, consider a relaxing stroll in **UBC Botanical Gardens,** 6804 Southwest Marine Drive; (604) 822–0666. This pleasant retreat includes a Physick Garden, with medicinal plants used throughout history; a shaded Arbor Garden, particularly inviting in summer (though its vines thrive year-round); and an Asian Garden, with exotic kiwi fruit vines. The **Vancouver Art Gallery**, City Centre at Hornby Street and Robson Square (604–682–5621—recorded information), is located in the heart of downtown, inside a renovated landmark, nineteenth-century building. Regularly changing exhibits are displayed in an attractive fashion. There's also a permanent display of what's considered the most important collection of works by Emily Carr, one of Canada's greatest artists. Ask about the regularly scheduled family workshops. The Gallery Cafe is open daily.

Special Tours

In Vancouver you must get out on the water. A narrated paddle-wheeler, the M.P.V. *Constitution,* tours Vancouver harbor. Boats depart twice daily from the north end of Denman Street. If you have time, we recommend the boat-train day trip, which features a cruise up the spectacular fjord of Howe South to the logging port of Squamish aboard the motor vessel *Britannia,* followed by a return on the Royal Hudson Steam Train, with 1940s vintage coaches. Bunker C. Bear, the train's mascot, makes frequent appearances to the delight of the kids. Call 1st Tours, a division of Harbour Ferries, for information and reservations; (604) 688–7246 or (800) 663–1500—United States. Or, opt to take the Royal Hudson to and from Squamish. Trains leave Wednesdays through Sundays and holiday Mondays from early June to late September.

Parks, Gardens, and Beaches

Stanley Park, at the northwest end of Georgia Street and within walking distance of the downtown core, is a terrific place for family fun with tennis courts, lawn bowling greens, a jogging oval, three restaurants, snack bars, a miniature golf course, beaches, and more! The thousand-acre park (800 acres of coniferous forest and the rest developed for recreation) sits on a peninsula with a 5½-mile seawall, or pathway, perfect for strolling or bicycling. (Rent bikes from Stanley Park Rentals, 676 Chiko Street, (604) 681–5581, near the park entrance.) Horse-drawn tram tours are available. Northeast of the entrance is the free **Stanley Park Zoo**, populated primarily with small animals, such as seals, penguins, and monkeys (though there are polar bears, too.) More impressive: the **Vancouver Public Aquarium** (604–682–1118), with more than 8,000 deep sea denizens, including beluga whales, sea otters, killer whales, and reef sharks. The aquarium features a walk-through Amazon rain forest, complete with tropical birds, lush vegetation, and piranhas. A five-minute walk northwest of the aquarium leads to the miniature steam train.

Part of Stanley Park, **Prospect Point** is at the northern end of the peninsula, at about the halfway point of the seawall. West is the English Bay side, where several sandy family beaches can be found along **Beach Drive.** **Second Beach,** west of Lost Lagoon, has a large saltwater children's pool with lifeguards, concession stands, and washrooms.

In all, the city has 11 miles of beaches, but the water is generally brisk, so be prepared. **Kitsilano Beach,** not part of Stanley Park, is over the Burrard Bridge, west of the Vancouver Museum/Planetarium. This is the liveliest beach in town, with concession stands, an adjacent park with a playground, and a busy public swimming pool.

Queen Elizabeth Park, Thirty-third Avenue and Cambie, is home to the **Bloedel Floral Conservatory;** (604) 872–5513. Under its huge glass geodesic dome (which offers a sweeping view of the city and its surroundings) bloom some 500 varieties of tropical and subtropical plants from around the world. Tropical birds fly overhead, and Japanese koi swim in pools—a tranquil, delightful place any time of year. Elsewhere in the park, enjoy tennis courts, lawn bowling, pitch and putt golf, and grassy picnic spots.

Other Attractions

Take your kids and walk over the **Capilano Suspension Bridge,** part of the CSB&P Park, 3735 Capilano Road, North Vancouver; (604) 985–7474. This gently swaying suspension bridge—the longest and highest in the world—spans 450 feet across and 230 feet above the Capilano River. On the west side, a nature park provides trails through a lush forest where a waterfall flows to the river below.

CN IMAX Theatre, #201-999 Canada Place, on the waterfront at Canada Place, the cruise ship terminal; (604) 682–2384. Canada's only IMAX 3D Theatre is open daily from noon to 11:00 P.M. Check the schedule of films projected on a giant screen five stories high.

At **Grouse Mountain,** 6400 Nancy Greene Way, North Vancouver (604–984–0661), take a scenic ride up an aerial tramway to 3,700 feet. Besides the scenic vistas, enjoy a multimedia Theatre in the Sky that features hourly shows on how Vancouver evolved from a frontier outpost into a thriving city (admission included with Skyride). Horse-drawn carriage rides are available, and there's a children's adventure playground. From the end November to end of March, Grouse Mountain is a downhill ski area.

Lookout! at Harbour Centre, 555 West Hastings Street (604–689–0421), offers a glass elevator that ascends 550 feet for a sweeping panorama of the city, mountains, and ocean. A twelve-minute multi-image presentation, "Once in a World, Vancouver," displays historical settings and describes the city. A coffee bar serves light snacks. When you come down to earth, browse through the Harbour Mall's specialty shops, or grab a bite at one of its numerous eateries.

Heli-hiking above Howe Sound near Vancouver is an experience like no other. (Courtesy Vancouver Ministry of Tourism)

Maplewood Farm, 405 Seymour River Point, North Vancouver; (604) 929–5610. This municipal park has domestic farm animals to feed; a petting zoo with rabbits, guinea pigs, and ponies; milking demonstrations daily at 1:15 P.M.; and special events, such as a May Sheep Fair. It's open daily year-round, except Monday.

Playland Family Fun Park, Hastings at Cassiar; (604) 255–5161. The park keeps big and little kids happy with more than forty rides and attractions (including the largest wooden roller coaster in Canada), a petting zoo, two live rock 'n' roll revues, and more. It's open spring through Labor Day.

Theater, Music, and the Arts

Check the *Vancouver Sun*'s entertainment section and Thursday "What's On" column for current happenings, or call the Arts Hotline at (604) 684–ARTS.

Ticketmaster (604–280–4444) has tickets to all major events, including those at the **Vancouver Civic Theatres,** 649 Cambie Street. This downtown complex features three major theaters (**Queen Elizabeth, Or-**

pheum, and **Vancouver Playhouse**) where performances include Broadway shows, Ballet British Columbia, Vancouver Opera, and the Vancouver Symphony Orchestra. Every Sunday from September to June, the **Festival Concert Society** (604–736–3737) presents Sunday Coffee Concerts from 11:00 A.M. to noon at the **Vancouver Playhouse**. Performances range from classical music to ballet to modern dance and jazz. Free in-theater babysitting is available for any age child.

From mid-July to mid-August, take your family to the Broadway-style musical at the Malkin Bowl in Stanley Park. Call TicketMaster for information.

Saturday Afternoon Live, a kids' series, is presented at Vancouver East Cultural Center, 1895 Venables Street at Victoria (604–254–9578), from late fall to early spring.

Sports
See **B.C. Lions** football (604–669–2300) at B.C. Place Stadium, 777 Pacific Boulevard, June through November. **Vancouver Canadians**, the top farm team of the Chicago White Sox, go to bat at Nat Bailey Stadium, 4601 Ontario Street; (604) 872–5232. The top-ranked **Vancouver Canucks** NHL hockey team plays at the Pacific Coliseum, 100 North Renfrew Street (604–254–5141), from autumn through spring. **Vancouver 86ers** soccer kicks off from mid-May to September at Swanguard Stadium in Central Park, Kingsway and Boundary, Burnaby. For game information, call (604) 299–0086.

Shopping
Vancouver's underground network of malls makes shopping fun and easy, even when the weather isn't cooperating. **Pacific Centre Mall** (604–688–7236), with some 200 stores, is the largest. The three-level complex spans 3 city blocks connecting two major department stores, Eaton's and The Bay, at opposite corners of Georgia and Granville streets. The city's liveliest thoroughfare, **Robson Street**, which stretches from Burrard to Bute streets, is full of small, trendy shops and cafés.

For something different, head to the **Lonsdale Quay Market**, 123 Carrie Cates Court, North Vancouver (604–985–6261), an indoor, waterfront public market next to the North SeaBus terminal. Fresh fruits and vegetables are sold on the first level. The second level is filled with shops, boutiques, and Kids Alley—several stores catering to kids, featuring clothing, games, and toys. There's an unsupervised "ball room" where kids can play while parents shop. The Lonsdale Quay Hotel (604–986–6111) is on the third level.

Be sure to spend some time browsing **Granville Island**, 1496 Cartwright Street (604–689–8447), located between the Granville and

Burrard bridges. It's a rejuvenated industrial island turned recreation center, with art galleries, bookstores, theaters, a houseboat community, loads of take-out food and restaurants, and **Kids Only Market**—a two-floor complex housing 200 specialty shops, services, and play areas just for families. This large and airy market often features storytellers, musicians, face painters, and crafts workshops. There's a crawl wall for kids and strollers and bike rentals, too, for touring the scenic waterfront. Nearby, at 1328 Cartwright, is a small water park open from June to August (604–689–8447) that offers fun for young ones, with wading pool and sprinklers. The island is accessible by taxi (parking is very limited), bus (about a twenty-minute trip from downtown, involving one transfer), or by Granville Island Ferry (604–684–7781), which is the most fun. The ferry leaves from a dock behind the Vancouver Aquatic Center and makes the short trip across False Creek to the Granville Island Public Market, a mostly enclosed area with everything from summer produce to quick snacks. Kitty corner to the market is an Information Centre, 1592 Johnson Street, (604–666–5784), where you can pick up maps and view a slide show detailing the island's history. If the weather is warm and you have the time, you might want to rent a kayak (children allowed with an experienced adult) from **Ecomarine Ocean Kayak Center**, 1668 Duranleau Street; (604) 689–7575.

SPECIAL EVENTS

For more details on the following, contact the Vancouver Travel InfoCentre; (604) 683–2000.

May: Vancouver International Children's Festival, Vanier Park, with theater, dance, music, and storytelling; Cloverdale Rodeo, Cloverdale (one hour east) one of North America's biggest.

July: Gastown Grand Prix Bicycle Race; Vancouver Sea Festival, English Bay, ten days of festivities featuring a parade, fireworks, salmon barbecues, and boat races.

Late July–early August: Vancouver Chamber Music Festival features six nights of performances by young, internationally acclaimed musicians; Vancouver International Comedy Festival, Granville Island, includes ten days of informal, daytime performances and ticketed evening shows that include everything from standup to mime to puppeteers.

August: International Air Show, Abbotsford Airport.

September: Vancouver Fringe Festival brings some hundred Canadian and international performance troupes for eleven days of drama, comedy, dance music, and clowning in ten theaters.

December: Christmas Carol Ship Parade, Vancouver Harbour.

WHERE TO STAY

Tourism Vancouver has a helpful accommodations directory, which includes maps. Call Discover British Columbia at (800) 663–6000 for bed-and-breakfast, lodging, and travel information. Here are some other "best bets" for families.

On the luxury end, **Westin Bayshore**, 1601 West George Street (604–682–3377 or 800–228–3000), couldn't be at a nicer location for families—right at the entrance to Stanley Park. With the ocean and mountains in the background, it has a resort feel, yet downtown is just a short walk away. No doubt, kids will be thrilled by the circular, outdoor pool. It also offers the new Westin Kids Club amenities. These include child-friendly rooms, children's sports bottle or tippy cup upon check-in, as well as a safety kit with a night light, Band-Aids, and emergency phone numbers. Rooms feature bath toys and bath products for kids, and parents can request—at no charge—jogging strollers, potty seats, bicycle seats, and step stools. Restaurants and room service also feature children's menus. **The Four Seasons,** 791 West Georgia Street, (604) 689–9333 or (800) 332–3442, features large rooms, a heated pool, and free cribs. Ask about their special weekend rates, which makes this first-class hotel much more affordable. Downtown a good choice is the **Hyatt Regency**, 655 Burrard Street (604) 685–1234 or (800) 233–1234. It offers the Hyatt family friendly features of children's menus, including room service. The Regency Club floor rooms, while pricier, include breakfast and snacks that might very well prove time and cost effective for your clan. Ask about their babysitting services.

The more moderately priced **Riviera Motor Inn,** 1431 Robson Street (604–685–1335), is an apartment hotel with forty studio and one-bedroom units, each with fully equipped kitchens and large, cheerful bedrooms. Great location, too—and most of the rooms have views of the North Shore mountains.

Bosman's Motor Hotel, 1060 Howe Street (604–688–1411 or 800–663–1333), offers a convenient location just on the edge of downtown. They have a hundred modern, quiet rooms, a pool, and—a rare commodity in these parts—free parking.

About eight miles south of Vancouver in Richmond the **Delta Pacific Resort and Conference Center,** 10251 St. Edwards Drive, features several pools, a playground, and a supervised children's center. Here for two-hour stretches (no longer at one time, but you can take your child out and then bring him or her back later) children ages 3 through 8 can enjoy crafts and games. The center is open from 9:00 A.M. to 8:00 P.M. This center is convenient if you want a quiet adult dinner, or some pool time by yourself, but this is not a day-long children's program.

WHERE TO EAT

The *Vancouver City Guide* offers a comprehensive listing of restaurants. Try the local seafood: oysters, clams, mussels, crab, and Pacific salmon. If your kids aren't into fish, there are lots of other food that reflects Vancouver's ethnic diversity.

Gastown, the charming, cobblestoned area that surrounds Maple Tree Square—the city's original core—at the end of Water Street, is a fun place to stroll and shop. **The Old Spaghetti Factory**, 53 Water Street (604–684–1288), is crammed with antiques and kid-pleasing decorations. They offer generous portions of pasta, veal, chicken, or steak in the ambiance of a 1910 streetcar.

A block away from Gastown, **Chinatown**—second largest on the continent (only San Francisco's is larger)—has a wide variety of eateries, which serve primarily Cantonese cuisine. Try the **Fish Pond**, 122 Powell Street (604–683–9196), which has vintage Chinatown artifacts and features a fascinating fish pond. Lunch is served Monday through Friday; dinner is served daily.

And for good old burgers, stop by **White Spot** hamburgers, a city tradition since 1928. Their two downtown eateries are at 1012 Robson Street (604–681–4180) and 580 West Georgia Street (604–662–3066).

DAY TRIPS

There are a number of interesting day trips from Vancouver, including Victoria.

Step back in time at **Fort Langley National Historic Park** (604–888–3943), at the corner of Mavis and Royal streets in the historic town of Fort Langley, 25 miles east of Vancouver. Inside the restored fort, established in 1827 as a Hudson Bay Company fur trading post and later a provisioning point for the 1858 gold rush, costumed interpreters practice barrel making and blacksmithing, trade beaver pelts, and present talks. During the summer, daily programs include nineteenth-century cooking and demonstrations by artisans. Across the street, at the **Langley Centennial Museum and National Exhibition Centre** (604–888–3922), exhibits include wood carvings, stone sculptures, and basketry, as well as the Coast Salish Indians' hunting, fishing, and war implements. Other exhibits highlight the life of early settlers and include a homesteader's kitchen, a Victorian parlor, and an early general store. A short ride southeast on Highway 1 leads to the **Vancouver Game Farm**, 5048 264 Street, Aldergrove (604–856–6825), where young ones see some one hundred wildlife species and enjoy a miniature train ride, play park, and picnic area.

Take another historical journey to **Burnaby Village Museum**, 6501 Deer Lake Avenue, Burnaby, twenty minutes east of downtown Vancouver; (604) 293–6500 or 6501. Costumed blacksmiths, pharmacists, and other townsfolk make this village of pioneer life between 1890 and 1925 come alive.

Whistler/Blackcomb, rated the number one ski resort in North America, is 75 miles north of Vancouver via the scenic Sea to Sky Highway. The twin summits offer some 200 trails and the highest lift-serviced verticals in North America. (Be forewarned: Whistler is also acquiring the reputation of being expensive.) Central reservations can tell you about special seasonal hotel and golf packages; (604) 932-4222, 685-3650 in British Columbia, or (800) WHISTLER.

Kids' Camp at Blackcomb includes a Child Minding program for ages eighteen months to three years; a Wee Wizards skiing fundamentals for ages two and three; and various ski programs for ages four to thirteen. Kids Night Out for ages six and older includes dinner and entertainment. Whistler's Ski Scamps ski schools offer fundamentals for ages two to four and five to twelve as well as the more advanced Mountain Scamps classes. Club Free, for skiers or snowboarders ages twelve to sixteen, offers teens challenges and fun with peers.

In summer, when prices are considerably more affordable, there's lots to do, including swimming at one of five nearby lakes and traveling to the top of Whistler Mountain via a fully enclosed express gondola, or to Blackcomb's summit via express chairs. (Both accommodate mountain bikes; rentals are available at various locations, including Whistler Village.) Summer glacier skiing is offered on Blackcomb from mid-June to August.

If there's a tennis hopeful in your bunch, try **The Chateau Whistler Resort**, 4599 Chateau Boulevard; (604) 938–2044, (800) 268–9411—Canada, or (800) 828–7447—U.S. They offer a summer Tennis Tigers program for kids ages five to twelve, ranging from half-day to weekend and week-long camps for ages seven to twelve, with morning tennis and afternoon hiking, in-line skating, and swimming. Two- and three-day Adventure Camps for adults are also open to teens. Twice weekly Kids' Night Out for five years and older includes dinner and entertainment from 5:30 P.M. to 8:00 P.M. The Canadian Pacific resort, at the base of Blackcomb Mountain, also boasts indoor/outdoor pools and hot tubs, golf, and two restaurants.

FOR MORE INFORMATION

The **Vancouver Travel InfoCentre**, Plaza Level, Waterfront Centre, 200 Burrard Street (604–683–2000), provides tourist information and litera-

---

ture. They also operate a kiosk at the corner of Georgia and Granville. Wheelchair travelers can obtain information about services from **Canadian Paraplegic Association**, 780 Southwest Marine Drive, Vancouver; (604) 324–3611.

Emergency numbers
Ambulance, fire, police: 911
Twenty-four-hour emergency care: St. Paul's Hospital, 1081 Burrard Street (604–682–2344), is a major downtown hospital. Also: **Children's Hospital**, 4480 Oak Street; (604) 875–2345.

There are no twenty-four-hour pharmacies in Vancouver. **Shopper's Drug Mart**, 1125 Davie Street, is open until midnight every night except Sunday and holidays when it closes at 9:00 P.M.; (604) 865–5752.

Poison Control: (604) 682–5050 or 682–2344

INDEX

ABOUT THE AUTHOR

(Photo by Matthew Gillis)

Candyce H. Stapen is an expert on family travel. A member of the Society of American Travel Writers as well as the Travel Journalists Guild, she writes several family travel columns on a regular basis including a column for *Vacations* magazine and *The Washington Times*.

Her articles about family travel appear in a variety of newspapers and magazines including *Ladies' Home Journal, Family Circle, Parents, Family-Fun, USA Weekend, Better Homes and Gardens, Rocky Mountain News, The Boston Globe, Family Travel Times, The Miami Herald, Caribbean Travel and Life,* and *Cruises and Tours*.

She lives in Washington, D.C., and travels whenever she can with her husband and two children.

ALSO OF INTEREST FROM
THE GLOBE PEQUOT PRESS